"Dave is compulsive and compulsory rea
You will be entertained, informed and fin
every page."

Chris Bascombe, Daily Telegraph

"A compelling and unmissable account of a season that reestablished
Liverpool as a genuine force and delivered some of the most exciting attacking football that Anfield has seen."

Tony Barrett, The Times

"In recounting the 2013/14 season, Dave Usher has perfectly captured the
highs and lows of what proved to be an incredible period in Liverpool's
recent history and once again proven his credentials as an authoritative and
enrapturing voice on the club."

Sachin Nakrani, The Guardian

"Liverpool's 2013/14 season - the club's finest league campaign since their
last title win - is one worth reliving. And there's no way better to do it than
through the words of Dave Usher, who once again perfectly captures how it
felt to watch the Reds' spellbinding term unfold from the stands."

Ben Thornley, Daily Post

"If you are looking for the thoughts and opinions of a writer who perfectly
captures the mood of Liverpool supporters, Dave Usher certainly provides
that. He sees the game with perspective and superbly details this in his writing. Funny, honest and balanced, you can feel the frustrations and passion in
his words. The phrase 'nail on the head' perfectly describes my thoughts
after reading Dave's descriptions and views on Liverpool games and issues"

Matt Ladson, This is Anfield website

WE GO AGAIN

@theliverpoolway

WE GO AGAIN

THE STORY OF THE
2013-14 SEASON

DAVID E. USHER

First Published 2014 by David E. Usher.

Printed in Great Britain by
Berforts Information Press Ltd

ISBN 978-0-9573498-5-8

As ever, this book is dedicated to my wonderful wife and family, my parents and all of my friends who have helped and supported me over the years. Once again, I'd like to give a special mention to my Dad and my good mate John Gallagher for all the hours they've given up selling the fanzine outside Anfield in hail, wind, rain, snow and the all too infrequent rays of sunshine.

I'd also like to express my gratitude to Paul Natton once more for his help with this book, Jon Salmon for going above and beyond the call of duty keeping the website running and everyone who has supported me by buying my books, the fanzine and contributing to the website.

YNWA

Dave

We Go Again

CONTENTS

We Go Again

PREFACE

I had a great title lined up for this book: *"Back On Our Perch - The Story of the 2013-14 Season"*. I even made up a mock cover for it and had a banner advert ready to go on the website to make it available for pre-orders. I knocked those up in the week of the Chelsea game, the plan being that as soon as the title was clinched (I'd pencilled in the Palace game the following week) I'd whack the advert up on the site and start working on the book. So yeah, I jinxed it and I take full responsibility for it.

Actually, no - I take part responsibility for it. There was someone else who had more than a small hand in that 'slip' against Chelsea. Someone who really ought to have known better and has no doubt been beating himself up ever since that fateful day. No not Stevie (bless him); that was just one of those things that can't be helped. I'm talking about my mate Paul who, for reasons known only to himself, decided not to bother wearing the lucky red undies that had served him (and us) so well during that incredible 11 game winning run. He didn't wear them for Palace either, so blame him for that one too. Him and Glen Johnson, obviously.

Of course none of that played any actual part in what went down in the closing weeks of the season, but still, tempting fate isn't really wise, is it? Maybe if I hadn't gone with *'Back On Our Perch'* before we were actually on that perch or if Paul had worn his lucky red bills then things would have been different. Probably not, but no-one knows for certain do they? That's why so many of us have these stupid superstitions and pre-match rituals. I've got another mate who, as that winning run got longer and longer, ended up with about ten different things he needed to do before games: daft stuff like walking the same route to Anfield and getting there at the same time, etc. I don't go in for that, but the one thing I have always been wary of is unnecessarily tempting fate and I could really kick myself over the 'Back On Our Perch' thing.

Fate is a cruel mistress and I'm not sure I'll ever fully get over just how cruel she was to Gerrard. One minute everyone seems to be saying how they want to see Liverpool win the title because Gerrard deserves it, then the next they're pissing themselves laughing at how he 'cocked it up'. Dickheads.

Back in August though none of us could have even dreamed that at that stage of the season - with just three games to go - the title would have been in our own hands. It was a remarkable journey that got us to that point and it wasn't until probably

Arsenal at home that it became clear just how good this team actually was. We'd hammered Spurs and Everton by that point, but no-one was taking us that seriously; not even our own fan base. Top four had been the aim all season, yet somewhere along the line that went from top priority to the very least we expected. We fell just short in the end, but it was some ride and all the more remarkable considering the disruptive events of the summer, which I'll get to in Chapter One.

If you've read my last two books then you will know the drill: all the match reports and weekly rounds ups are printed as they were written at the time, so there'll be times when I look pretty stupid and, hopefully, some bits that make it look like I know what I'm talking about. Most importantly though, it's how I saw it at the time, which is something I'm sure you'll all be able to relate to as you relive through these pages the highs and lows of what was an absolutely incredible season.

chapter one

Suarez (again)

Another book, another chapter on Luis Suarez. In *'The King's Last Stand'* there was the Evra thing and in *'Like I Say'* there was the bite. This time it's the Arsenal debacle. In some ways this was the worst of the lot because this was entirely his own fault and there was no defending him. Biting Ivanovic was his fault too of course, but he was harshly banned for ten games for that and was hammered by the rest of the country. From the Prime Minister to the 'Loose Women' he was getting battered by everyone. His name was even booed at the PFA awards while the comedian was making jokes at his expense. The press hated him. Other players hated him. Opposing fans hated him. It was open season on him and all he had was the support of his family, his club, his team-mates and the Liverpool fans.

It didn't surprise me that he wanted to leave after how last season ended; I'd have been more shocked if he didn't. Hell, in his shoes I'd have wanted out too. Not out of Liverpool specifically, but out of England. Merseyside was actually the only place he was still loved and appreciated but it was understandable if he felt that was no longer enough. Who'd want their wife and kids having to read about you being a *"racist cannibal"* and living in a country in which the Prime Minister had accused you of setting a bad example for kids? Not me, that's for sure.

Before long reports began trickling out of Real Madrid's interest and we were then subjected to weekly flirtations from Suarez about how it would be *"difficult to turn them down"* and that *"the English press make it difficult for me to stay"*. It was upsetting, naturally. None of us wanted to lose a player we loved and who was as talented as any to have ever played for our great club. But really - who could blame him? For most Iberian and South American footballers the ultimate dream is to one day play for Real Madrid or Barcelona. So if that opportunity presented itself to Suarez he was always going to want to take it. Besides, he'd been demonised in England, so why would he want to stick around? He'd have gone to Spain with no real hard feelings from the majority of Reds' fans.

Where the whole thing turned on its head was when Madrid didn't come in for him and nobody else did either. His performances had been incredible - along with Gareth Bale he was comfortably the Premier League's stand out performer - yet because of the baggage he carried no-one wanted him. Except Arsenal. They wanted him; they just didn't want him enough to pay what he was worth. They came in with a laughable first bid that was rejected out of hand and I wasn't worried about Arsenal. I doubt any of you were either. We'd never sell to them and besides, why the hell would Suarez want to go there when the only reason he wanted out of Merseyside was due to his treatment at the hands of the English press? Most of those who had given him a hard time were based in London, so joining Arsenal would be stupid beyond belief!

The London press wouldn't let it drop though. They were clearly being briefed by Arsenal and suddenly talk of a release clause began to emerge. As well as being tiresome it was now becoming a little troubling. How would Arsenal know if there was any kind of a clause unless the Suarez camp had told them? The most logical explanation was his agent using their interest to try and smoke out Madrid, PSG or maybe Bayern. I mean he couldn't seriously be prepared to join Arsenal as that would make no sense. I wasn't overly concerned at this stage, particularly as everything I was hearing from sources close to the owners suggested they'd not sell to the Gunners under any circumstances at all.

Then came the bombshell: Arsenal bid £40,000,001. John W. Henry told them where they could shove it and Suarez saw his arse. It turns out he did actually want to join Arsenal after all. After the way we all stood by him THIS is how he repays us? I couldn't believe it. What an ungrateful rat. I was furious initially and at that stage I just wanted him gone. Not to Arsenal, or anyone else in England for that matter. I didn't want to see him in the Red shirt again though, not after this betrayal. I mean Arsenal? Fucking hell, Luis! Arsenal fans had been as bad as anyone in giving him abuse too. *"Luis Suarez, you know what you are"* and *"There's only one racist bastard"* were staple chants whenever we played them. And now he was prepared to shit all over us - the ones who stood by him through all his troubles - to go and play for THEM? Most of these footballers really do live in their own little bubble, don't they? They just don't see things the same way we do. How could Suarez even entertain the idea of playing for another English team after the support we'd given him? He didn't even have the excuse of being a money grabber or a glory hunter as we'd pay him more than Arsenal would and there was as much chance of him winning something with us than them. In fact he already had won something with us, whereas the last time Arsenal had lifted any silverware he was still a kid playing in Uruguay!

Champions League football was, apparently, his reason for wanting the move, but again that just didn't stack up. Arsenal may play in the Champions League every year but that's all they do. They take part. Why would you walk out on Liverpool for that? To play in a few group games and then maybe one knock out round? May as well sign for Zenit St Petersburg or Celtic. It was a betrayal, pure and simple. He'd spoken time and again of his love for Liverpool and how settled his family are here. It could all have been lies of course: Fernando Torres made similar noises and look how that turned out. It didn't feel like lies with Suarez though; he did seem genuinely happy and his family definitely love it here. So what changed? It couldn't be the whole *"I need to leave England coz everybody hates me"* thing, as he was prepared to join bloody Arsenal. No doubt he'd have gone to Chelsea or City too if they'd shown any interest (I'll give him the benefit of the doubt and say he wouldn't have jumped ship to United), so it wasn't anything to do with how he was perceived by people in England.

Luis Suarez deserves to be playing Champions League football - we all understood that - but on the day of that infamous Chelsea game an interview was published with him in the Sunday Times in which he said: *"I'm very happy here; so is my family, which for me is very important. I'm at a club any footballer would want to be playing at, who share my goal of playing in the Champions League. If it's not this year then it will be the next. I want to see out my contract — but also in football you never quite know what's ahead. Sometimes the club can decide they don't want you, though you want to stay. Or a player could say he wanted to leave and still end up staying. In football things never turn out the way you plan them. The only thing I have in my head is I'm here and have a contract. I think I'll be here next season, yes."*

A few months earlier he had said: *"I want to say now that, if you want to know what will happen to me if we don't qualify for the Champions League, then I will say this: I have a contract with Liverpool and I am very happy here. I will stay."*

So, I ask again, what changed? He bit some fool and got himself banned for ten games, that's what changed. Liverpool had nothing to do with that, it was all his own doing and the next thing he's telling us he wants to join Arsenal? I couldn't get my head around it then and I still can't even now. Thankfully the club stood firm and both Rodgers and Henry came out of this with their reputations firmly enhanced. Henry's *"What are they smoking over at Emirates"* tweet was fantastic and, between him and Rodgers, they let Suarez know that he wasn't going to be allowed to leave no matter how much he cried about it. When Suarez invited a couple of Spanish speaking English journalists to his house and had a good old whinge about how unfair it all was, Rodgers responded by leaving him out of the squad for the next couple of pre-season games and told him he'd be training with the reserves until further notice.

It wasn't long before he was back with the first team. Apparently Gerrard spoke to Suarez and then asked Rodgers to bring him back. None of us know what state of mind Suarez was in that time and ironically that suspension he was serving probably worked to our advantage as if he did have any lingering resentment it was well out of his system by the time his suspension was up. Arsenal though. Fucking hell, Luis.

Still, if there was one thing most were agreed on it was that when the window closed and Suarez knew he was staying put he'd just get on with it and play. He doesn't seem to be able to play any other way other than flat out. Even if he went onto the field thinking about not giving his all, instinct would just kick in and he simply wouldn't be able to help himself. This is a guy who had a strop when he was rested for an FA Cup game at non-league Mansfield!

I was mad as hell with him when he did that interview slagging off Rodgers and the club for not letting him join Arsenal. I probably took it harder than most because I really loved Suarez; I'd completely bought into all his *"I love the club"* stuff. Some learnt their lesson from the Torres experience and swore they'd never get emotionally involved again. That didn't apply to me as I never really got taken in by Torres - or at least if I did, I quickly snapped out of it when I saw the half arsed performances he was putting in. I loved Suarez though and you just can't switch that off overnight. As pissed off as I was with him at the height of all that crap, I can still remember seeing a clip on Sky Sports News of him driving into Melwood, singing away and tapping his hands on the steering wheel to the music. I saw that and couldn't help but laugh. Who was I kidding? I may have been seriously pissed off with him but I still loved the guy. I obviously wasn't the only one as, despite his antics, he never suffered any kind of fan backlash. His name was chanted more or less from his first game back and everyone seemed to just completely ignore the giant elephant in the room. It was almost as though it never even happened.

Almost.

chapter two

Window of missed opportunity

The uncertainty over Suarez threw the summer transfer plans into chaos. Whilst we were never going to accept any offer from Arsenal, the spectre of Madrid still loomed large. If they'd come in for him towards the end of the window what would have happened then? Did we have two lists of targets, one for if he stayed and one in case he left? Did we even have any plan at all? It looked to me from the outside like the club were just winging it: lurching from one high profile target to another and failing to get any.

I remember Brendan saying something about how the idea is to have lists of players for positions they need to fill and if they can't get the number one target then they just work their way down the list. The key to it, he said, was making sure there wasn't too much of a drop off in the quality of targets on the list. That makes sense, and you'd think with an army of scouts and highly paid stat nerds it shouldn't be too difficult. So how come we're so damn bad at it then?

The Henrikh Mkhitaryan saga ended with him choosing Dortmund over us. They were Champions League finalists and we'd finished 7th. You can't blame the fella really; he probably took less money to go there too. Fair play to the scouts on that one. They identified him and he was clearly a player who would have really improved us. Missing out on him was a blow but we'd just have to just move for the number two option, right? I mean presumably Mkhitaryan had been identified to fill a specific role in the side and there had to be a fall back option, surely? Well apparently not as the next attempted move we made was for…. Diego Costa. A striker. Hmmm.

This was a strange one for several reasons. He's obviously a good player, but why would we be looking to spend that kind of dough (£30m) on another striker when we had more pressing needs and already had Suarez and Sturridge, not to mention the newly signed Iago Aspas and Fabio Borini? The suggestion was that Costa may play in a wider role, but if we're spending £30m on a wide attacker then wouldn't it make sense to get someone who is actually comfortable in that role, instead of shoehorning a striker out there? Mkhitaryan made sense as he filled a position of need and would have improved the first eleven but Costa smacked of opportunism and desperation. Did we even scout the fella or was it his agent touting him to us? From the start it seemed like he was using us to get a new deal out of Atletico and that's exactly what happened. So, having missed out on Mkhitaryan (a midfielder) and Costa (a striker) we then turned our attention to…. Willian. A winger. Hmmm.

That was another bizarre one. Not that there wouldn't have been a role for him; he would have been a more than useful (albeit vastly overpriced) addition to the squad.

Again though, was this just opportunism or was he on the list of targets when the summer began? Perhaps I'm doing the transfer committee a disservice and they'd been tracking him for months, but I suspect it was more a case of him falling into our laps after his club decided to have a fire sale. He snubbed us for Spurs when they offered more money to him and his agent before hilariously jibbing them for Chelsea when they upped the dosh even further. It was all a bit farcical, but the excuse about it not being easy to attract top players without Champions League football does carry some weight. Without Champions League football to offer we had no chance of signing any of those players unless we were prepared to give them a lot more money than, a) they were worth and, b) we could afford. FSG have put a lot of time and energy into getting the wage bill down and they were hardly likely to go down the route of paying well over the odds in a gamble to get back in the top four. No, if we were to get back in the big time it would be on the back of good coaching and picking up a bargain or two in the mould of a Daniel Sturridge or Philippe Coutinho for example.

As the summer progressed, it became increasingly obvious that we'd gotten a bit lucky with those two January transfers and there were not actually anymore where they came from. There'd been an early flurry of transfer activity as soon as the 2012-13 season had ended but, as Rodgers himself said, with the exception of Simon Mignolet that was about adding depth to the squad and now he needed to *"improve the first eleven"*. Unfortunately he never did (through no real fault of his own, I'd say). For me, when you take away the manager's authority to make transfers then you also have to take away the responsibility if the signings don't work out. I'm not absolving him of all blame as he is a part of that transfer committee, but a strong case could be made that the squad that had finished 7th had not been improved. In fact, it could have been argued then - and indeed now - that it had actually been weakened, both in terms of depth and quality.

I felt sorry for Brendan though. He didn't get to pick the players we signed, although obviously he has a say. None of us on the outside know exactly how that transfer committee thing works. We're told that they come up with a list of targets and that nobody is signed without everyone agreeing and that no player is signed who the manager doesn't want. How is that even remotely workable though? For example, everyone knows that Rodgers wanted to sign Ashley Williams and has wanted to do so since he first took the Liverpool job. The rest of the committee simply aren't on board with it though and, regardless of the rights or wrongs of it (I'm not on board with it either but that's irrelevant), that's a bit of a problem, surely? What happens then is Rodgers either becomes resentful and refuses to sanction deals for players recommended by other committee members or he has to be the bigger man and compromise on another player, such as Sakho, for instance, who, despite costing £18m and having a big reputation, was never an automatic choice and generally only got in the side when Agger picked up an injury.

I was hearing from the first week of pre-season that Rodgers didn't fancy Luis Alberto or Iago Aspas. Even before they'd played a pre-season game I was told by a good source that Rodgers felt that they weren't the players he had read about on the scouting reports. It was obvious from the beginning he didn't rate either of them and it's unlikely their stay at Anfield will extend beyond one year. They may not have been signed 'without his approval', but that's not to say he particularly wanted them either.

Hypothetically, let's put ourselves in the shoes of Rodgers for a second. He has this team of scouts, analysts and various other highly paid professionals who have been brought in to identify players who can help the team. However, they keep putting players forward that he doesn't particularly fancy, so he keeps back heeling them. After all, he doesn't want another Nuri Sahin or Oussama Assaidi on his hands (players he didn't sign and who he quickly discarded). Eventually though, there comes a point where you think; *"If I keep saying "no" then I'm not going to get anyone and my working relationship with these people is going to break down completely."* I suspect that's why he agreed to Aspas and Alberto.

I can't imagine him being overly thrilled with using a chunk of his budget on Tiago Ilori either, a player who was going to be fifth choice centre back at best (assuming he proved to be a better option than Martin Kelly or Andre Wisdom). The Portuguese youngster may turn out to be the new Franz Beckenbauer for all I know, but he wasn't what we needed at the time and the cash spent on him, Aspas and Alberto really should have been put to much better use. For me Ilori is the new Sebastian Coates, who was also very highly rated when we signed him (and a lot more experienced than Ilori) but who was too young for us to take a chance on playing him regularly ahead of the more experienced internationals ahead of him. At least Ilori got to go out on loan and wasn't left to rot like poor old Seba, who has essentially wasted the last three years of his career.

I'd love to know who made the call on Aly Cissokho too. One minute we were close to signing the lad from Benfica (Lorenzo Melgarejo) and then all of a sudden we lost all interest in him. Next thing we're signing Cissokho, a player we could have had months earlier if we'd wanted. From what I heard at the time, Rodgers didn't fancy Melgarejo at all and it was him who pulled the plug on that one. He wanted Ryan Bertrand but was over-ruled, so presumably Cissokho was the compromise. Maybe that's not how it all played out; perhaps Rodgers and the committee are all happy little campers who agree on everything and Brendan is fully on board with all the players we signed. Sure seems unlikely though.

As ridiculous as it sounds now looking back, the one signing I actually felt really good about was Victor Moses. I had genuinely high hopes for him. He's a talented player but he barely showed anything for us and he won't be remembered fondly. I'm not sure who gets the blame for that one. Probably Brendan as - unlike the Spanish duo - he certainly knew all about this player. At least we were able to send him back without losing money on him, which makes a refreshing change after the millions we've lost on failed signings over the last decade or two.

Looking at the players brought in and those who were allowed to leave, it was hard to make much of a case that we were stronger than we had been the previous year when we'd finished a lowly 7th. However, that 7th placed finish was a little misleading because the 2012-13 season really needs to be looked at in two halves: 'Before Sturridge and Coutinho', and 'After Sturridge and Coutinho'. Our record after that January window was actually very, very good; second only to Arsenal, if I recall correctly. So, with that in mind, what were we actually expecting when the season kicked off back in August?

I certainly don't recall anybody seriously predicting a title challenge. Most seemed to believe we had a decent shot at fourth spot, possibly even third if everything went our way. By that I mean if Arsenal did their annual choking act (which of course they did) and if Moyes turned out to be as out of his depth as we hoped (which of course he was). The wild card was Spurs who had lost their best player but had spent a fortune on an array of players who made up a football hipster's wet dream. Most of those signings bombed and the combined woes of Spurs, United and, to a lesser extent, Arsenal allowed us to hang around the top four for most of the season until we went on that incredible run and left them all - as well as Chelsea - in our rear view mirror.

The 2013-14 season was a hell of a ride and it's one I'll remember for a long time. Here's the story of it, as told at the time…

chapter three

August

LIVERPOOL 1 STOKE CITY 0

Competition - Premier League
Date - Sat 17 Aug 2013
Venue - Anfield
Scorer(s) – Daniel Sturridge
Star Man – Simon Mignolet

Team: Mignolet; Johnson, Toure, Agger, Enrique; Lucas, Gerrard, Henderson; Sturridge, Aspas (Sterling), Coutinho :

When Stoke were awarded a penalty in the dying minutes of a game we'd completely dominated, there was just a sad sense of inevitability about it all. Typical Liverpool; hammer a team but fail to put them away and end up paying the price. It's been a frequent occurrence over the last few years and the way the final ten minutes of this game had gone you could just see it coming.

You see it happen so often, a team completely pummels an opponent for 80 minutes but only has one goal to show for it and suddenly they get edgy and the opposition start to believe they can get something from the game. Everyone at Anfield knew how vital it was for the Reds to get off to a winning start and when the second goal didn't come, edginess understandably began to creep in and Stoke suddenly found some ambition and belief.

We'd looked vulnerable from set pieces all afternoon so when Sterling gave away a silly foul in his own half, Anfield held it's breath. Our penalty area resembled a scene from Jurassic Park as all these lumbering, pea brained Brontosaurus looking bastards descended upon Mignolet's goal. Charlie Adam whipped in the free-kick, Agger inexplicably handled, the woeful Martin Atkinson made a rare correct decision and pointed to the spot and that was that; another opening day disappointment. But then something completely unexpected happened. Our goalkeeper actually saved a penalty. He also saved the follow up and the roof almost came off the place.

It was as though a sleeping giant had been woken, the noise in the closing stages matched anything we've had since the last big Champions League night at Anfield, it was incredible really. We should have won the game by three or four goals and whilst that would have been a great way to kick things off, in some ways this was even better. It may not have been how we planned it but that penalty save was a truly great moment and the reaction to it from the fans was spine tingling. I don't remember the last time I heard a roar like that from the crowd.

It was also exactly what Mignolet needed. By his own admission he'd had a somewhat nervy start but that penalty save will do wonders for his confidence now. The spectre of Pepe Reina was ready to loom any time the new keeper made a mistake but this will help to alleviate that as he's just deposited a whole heap of credit into the account. The Belgian must have felt ten foot tall as he was mobbed by team-mates and hailed by the crowd, and as far as debuts go this is what goalkeepers dream of. A win, a clean sheet, a great save in front of the Kop and then saving a last minute penalty as well as the follow up. Not a bad way to start a Liverpool career!

Mignolet will deservedly get all the headlines but this was a fine performance all round. The only criticism of the players is that they didn't put the finishing touch to all their excellent approach play. That's what put them in the awkward position they found themselves in late on. You could also point to how suspect they occasionally looked defending set plays but I'm not sure there's too much that they could do about that given the vast difference in sizes between the two line ups and Stoke's well known prowess in this area. Even Lebron James and his Miami Heat would be troubled by Stoke's height. Besides, if the finishing is of a higher standard then the occasional scare from a set-piece is really not that big a deal. It's when the finishing isn't up to scratch that it can be a problem.

Any criticism of us not putting them away has to be tempered with the recognition that you can't win every game 4-0 even when your play warrants it. There are some days when the goals just don't come, either through poor finishing, bad luck or great goalkeeping. This game was a combination of all three, and we had a few of those last season too. At least we managed to find the net once this time, there were times last season when we were unable to do even that.

This team will score a lot of goals, of that I'm certain. They did last season and providing our main men stay fit then hopefully we'll get more this year as Sturridge and Coutinho will have the full season rather than just half of it. Goalscoring is not a problem, and you can almost guarantee that we'll play well in most games now. The players are well organised/coached in what they are doing and the football is really pleasing on the eye. We create as many chances as any team in the league and when it clicks and they go in we can put teams to the sword. If Stoke had somebody else in goal we'd have won this one comfortably, but Begovic was inspired. I lost count of the amount of saves me made, but one in particular stood out when he got the faintest of touches to deflect Henderson's shot onto the post. That was an incredible stop. On another day Henderson could have had a hat-trick.

We started well and had a good tempo to our play, Sturridge had a goal ruled out for offside but the first really clear opportunity of the game fell to Stoke when Mignolet flapped at a cross and Huth crashed a shot against the bar. Next up it was another centre back being denied by the woodwork as Toure came flying in and rose above Shawcross to meet Gerrard's corner with a thumping header. We've seen in pre-season that Kolo will be a threat from set-pieces, he's like a ball magnet and seems to be underneath every corner that comes in. He'll hopefully chip in with three or four goals this season assuming he stays in the side.

Chance after chance went begging and it was beginning to have a whiff of 'one of those days' about it, but then out of nowhere Sturridge drilled a low shot through Huth's legs and into the bottom corner to break the deadlock. I expected that to open the floodgates but Stoke actually responded well and it needed a great flying save from Mignolet to keep out a Walters snapshot at the Kop end. That alehouse blueshite bastard scoring in front of the Kop doesn't even bear thinking about, so top marks for Simon there, it was a superb stop. Of course whenever he makes a save like that it's inevitable that there'll be people saying *"You see, Pepe would never have saved that"* and they may well be right. There's absolutely no way of knowing though so it's really pointless, just as it is to analyse any mistake he makes and say *"Pepe wouldn't have done that"*. Pepe's gone, Simon's here, that's all that matters now.

Mark Hughes' side may have been completely outplayed but they certainly had their chances to score in the first half, which is a little worrying moving forward I suppose. They were not as threatening after the break and spent most of their time on the back foot. We created chance after chance but couldn't get that second goal as an inspired Begovic kept us at bay. The link up between Sturridge and Coutinho was something we saw a lot of in the closing stages of last season and it was evident again in this game. Last year the team was built around Suarez through necessity but now we have the link up between Coutinho and Sturridge, I'd say Suarez needs to fit in around that rather than have others make way for him. If we see Sturridge central and Coutinho playing in behind, that may mean Suarez having to play from the side? Shouldn't be a problem, he's done it Ajax and for Uruguay. I'm sure he was happiest when everything was set up around him last season and he certainly responded by scoring 30 goals, but his conduct this summer means that, to quote Marcellus Wallace, he's *"lost his L.A. privileges"*. Moving others around to suit Suarez shouldn't be a consideration now in my opinion, he needs to fit in with what Sturridge and Coutinho are doing until he makes up for his attempted summer betrayal.

Coutinho was wonderful to watch in this game. He tormented Stoke to distraction, and not even the heavy handed treatment from the sly N'Zonzi and overbearing Huth could slow him down. N'Zonzi certainly has the second most dangerous elbows in the Premier League and is the only genuine threat to Fellaini's crown. Any time someone is in a tussle with him he somehow finds a way to get his elbow in their face and make it look accidental. Coutinho never let the physical approach intimidate him though and one of the things I love about him is his work rate and desire to get back and nick the ball away from people. The main thing I love about him though is obviously just how fucking awesome he is with the ball. He's as good on the ball as anyone in the league, his balance, his touch, his vision… just a wonderful talent. Nailed on for Young Player of the Year, unless Bale stays at Spurs in which case he's got the award sewn up again. He'll still be winning it when he's 30. I don't get how that keeps happening, maybe he's only 19 in chimp years or something?

Anyway, the one thing I'd have to add about Coutinho is that he needs to be a lot more clinical with his finishing. He should have scored when he latched onto a clever dummy by Sturridge and raced clear into the box before shooting inches wide. It would have been a great goal that, it was lovely to see that kind of link up between the pair but Coutinho's finishing is nowhere near the level of the rest of his game. Then again, if it was we'd never have been able to get him I guess.

Loads of chances came and went but as the clock ticked past 80 minutes suddenly we ended up in something of a defensive shell as Stoke realised they had a chance to get something from the game. Adam had a fantastic shot from halfway that Mignolet only just managed to tip over from underneath his crossbar, and the visitors began to force some set pieces that made us look uncomfortable. Rodgers had sent on Sterling for Aspas but the change didn't help us at all.

I was annoyed about the free-kick we conceded that led to the penalty. Yes, Sterling's foot was raised, but all game we'd seen Crouch bringing down passes and juggling the ball with his foot raised at his own head height. That's 6ft 7 inches off the floor, and no free-kicks were ever awarded for those. Little Raheem raises his boot, a Stoke player lowers his head and suddenly it's a free-kick? Irritating that. God knows what Agger was thinking by raising his arm like that though, but as he said afterwards he knows that *"he owes Mignolet a pint"*. Jamie Carragher said recently that Mignolet looks like a monster in the goal, and as he prepared to face down Walters you could certainly see that as he bounced up and down on his line shaking the crossbar with his fists. He'd done his homework on where Walters likes to put his penalties (his second most popular spot is the top tier of the stand behind the goal) and guessed the right way to make the save. Not only that, he leapt to his feet and spread himself big to block the follow up from Jones too. Inspiring stuff, and he was mobbed by team-mates until Toure realised Stoke were taking the corner quickly and frantically tried to get everyone organised and marking up. *"Exactly what Carra would have been doing"* I thought to myself.

The double save got everyone fired up and the noise levels in those closing minutes were just something else. Yes, it was 'only' a 1-0 win over Stoke, but that doesn't tell the full story at all. It was imperative that we got off to a winning start and when it looked like we would fail to do so, a wave of mass despondency was about to envelope Anfield. That save from Mignolet blew that away and the celebrations were relief more than anything else. I think back to the early home games of last year, games where we should have won but ended up either drawing or losing, and it's nice that something has gone in our favour for a change. Perhaps our luck is finally turning?

Final word has to be on Kolo Toure. I swore after Suarez I'd never get emotionally involved again, but Kolo is making me love again. Every time he speaks, every game he plays, he just grows on me more and more. Despite everything he's achieved in the game he's as enthusiastic and energetic as anyone on the pitch, in fact he's like an excited teenager playing his first season. Within a minute he had the fans well and truly in his pocket by soaring like a glorious, ebony salmon to win a header over the top of Peter Crouch. The crowd went mad for that, and that's exactly what I was hoping we were getting when we brought him in. You can tell that rather than seeing his glittering career as winding down, he's desperate to add another glorious chapter to it. Having someone like that around the squad can only be good for everybody else.

There was a moment in the second half that brought back fond memories of Rigobert Song as big Kolo charged forward to support the attack and when he didn't get the ball, he turned around and sprinted full pelt to get back into his defensive position. The crowd love seeing that kind of thing, that kind of enthusiasm is infectious. What a great character to have around the place, Jamie Carragher's retirement left some mighty big shoes to fill, but it would seem that Toure has big feet.

Premier League Round Up (17-19 August 2013)

The big story on the opening day was Arsenal losing at home to Villa. Laugh? I nearly shat. It all started so well for them too, as Giroud took just five minutes to put them ahead with a sharp little finish at the near post. So far so good, but then Villa started to fight back and were soon level as Agbonlahor's brilliant run was halted by Sczieszny. He saved Benteke's pen but the big frontman headed in the rebound.

After that Villa were probably the more dangerous side and deserved the points. Delph hit the post with a fine effort before Koscielny was adjudged to have fouled Agbonlahor in the box. He laughed when he realised a penalty had been given, whilst Mertesacker actually looked like he was crying. Quite apt I thought, as I'm sure Arsenal fans brought up on Adams, Bould, Keown, Campbell etc and who are now having to watch these two bums probably don't know whether to laugh or cry either. Koscielny was booked for that incident and was then sent off for an imaginary foul on Weimann. He didn't even get near the Austrian, but the Villa forward had to jump out of the way of the wild challenge and ended up on the floor. A harsh sending off, but ever mind though, eh.

Left back Antonio Luna, dubbed Tony Moon by Villa fans, wrapped up a great day for Paul Lambert's side late on with a somewhat bizarre goal on the counter attack. Arsenal had a corner and when it was cleared they had no-one back and Luna just ran clear to finish, there were no Arsenal players anywhere near him and it's rare you see a player have so much space to run into unchallenged. Arsenal just looked a complete mess by that point.

This Gunners side just reeks of mediocre. The reason they made the top four last year is because Wenger is a great coach and because they have goals in the side. His teams always play terrific football but he appears to have completely lost his touch in the transfer market in recent years, most notably in developing this weird fetish for short, lightweight, ball playing midfielders. Remember when they had Vieira and Petit and took no shit from anyone? Now they've got Wilshere, Rosicky, Arteta, Ramsay, Cazorla…. and what does Wenger do? Tries to buy Yohan fucking Cabaye, that's what. More on that later.

And any side that has that statuesque Mertesacker in it is completely asking for trouble. Tony Adams ten years retired could do a better job than this goon. In fact Tony Adams back in his heavy drinking days couldn't have been worse. Putting this snail out there against Villa's greyhounds was always going to end in tears for Arsenal and tears of laughter for everyone else, especially Liverpool fans who want to see Gooners fans fall flat on their cocky little faces this season after the smug way they carried on over the Suarez affair. You know where to shove your extra quid now don't you, fucking knobheads.

Everton's season got under way with a 2-2 draw at Carrow Road. The Canaries included new signing Ricky Van Wolfswinkel, or as the always unintentionally hilarious Garth Crookes informed BBC viewers; *"Wolf Van Winkel"*. Haha I love that, so much so that I'm nicking it. From this day forth that shall be his name. Leroy Fer was on the bench for Norwich having almost joined Everton last season. You may remember this joker, he made the headlines for failing the infamous Everton medical and for buying a horse for his girlfriend, who told him to take it back as she lived in a block of flats. Leroy has wound up at Norwich for this season but the name of his brother 'Ifithadnabin' is rarely far from the lips of your typical Evertonian, usually followed by random words such as Heysel, Redshite, Peter Johnson, Clive Thomas, Collina and so on.

Anyway, Steven Whittaker bulldozed his way through to give Norwich the lead after playing a canny one-two with the goalpost to bamboozle Tim Howard. Ross Barkley deservedly equalised for the Blues with a stunning hit from 20 yards. The body shape, technique and power generated put me in mind of the great Patrik Berger, if Paddy had really shit hair obviously. It really was a brilliant, clean hit though, and Barkey isn't even left footed which makes it even more impressive. Barkley looked superb and his parent club Manchester United must be delighted with the on-loan youngster. *"What are you talking about, he's not a Manchester United player"* I hear you all cry. A mere technicality my friends, as rest assured, a few more performances like this and he soon will be. Although perhaps not considering that Moyes continually overlooked him last year. Football genius.

The thing is, Everton and Manchester United share a common goal when it comes to player development; they both aspire to produce players that are good enough to play in Manchester United's first team. Everton managed it with Rooney of course, whilst Rodwell just fell short and ended up at City. Still, at least he made it to Manchester so that's close enough. Baines would be there too except a little thing called loyalty has got in the way of that, whilst Fellaini still has a chance of making the grade if Moyes stops trying to take the piss out of his old club with derisory bids. Bidding £28m for Baines and Fellaini is laughable, I know Evertonians long to have their players and manager one day make it to Old Trafford, but even they have to be pissed off at the bare faced cheek of Moyes over this. Fellaini had a buy out clause set at £22m, a buy out clause set by Moyes as that was his worth to Everton. So if he wanted to buy him he could have done by offering that amount. He didn't, he waited until the clause expired and then bid £6m less. What a snidy, duplicitous twat.

Anyway, I digress, within a couple of minutes of Barkey's equaliser Coleman had given the Blues the lead, but Wolf Van Winkel's spectacular header into the top corner ensured an entertaining game ended honours even. Finally on this one, Roberto Martinez's mouth moves more when he speaks than anybody I've ever seen. Look out for it, he's like one of the Muppets, it's incredible. How has it taken me this long to get onto it? He must be a lip readers wet dream.

Moving swifty on and West Ham got off to a winning start by seeing off new boys Cardiff City with a routine 2-0 home win. Joke Hole put them ahead and Kevin Nolan made it safe in the second half with a typically fine finish. I don't know most of the Cardiff side so I'm assuming they must be a bit shit. I felt the same way about Southampton this time last year though so we'll see. I can't see past the three newly promoted sides when it comes to this year's relegation places, although I probably say that every year and there's usually one or two who turn out much better than most people expected. I don't see any of this year's crop being a Norwich, Swansea or Southampton though.

Speaking of Southampton, they got their season off to a somewhat surprising winning start by edging out West Brom at the Hawthorns. Watching the highlights of this I was pretty shocked to see that Nicolas Anelka is at West Brom. When did that happen, how did I not know about that? He's rocking a pretty crazy looking beard these days too. I've always quite liked Anelka - even when he was at Chelsea - and I do occasionally wonder how things would have turned out if Houllier hadn't gone batshit crazy and sent him packing so he could buy Diouf. Can't see Nico doing anything at West Brom though and I think the Baggies will struggle this year compared to last. Lukaku is a big, big loss for them.

Southampton's winner came in the last minute and capped off quite a week for Rickie Lambert. Scoring the winner on his England debut - against Scotland no less - and then slotting a last minute penalty to get the Saints off to a winning start. Everything is coming up Millhouse for Rickie at the moment. Always good to see someone like him doing well having come up the hard way. He's a much better player than many realise, although him being a massive Red does make me a little biased. He's scored 32 penalties out of 32 for Southampton now according to MOTD. That must be close to Le Tissier's record, he was incredible at pens too. 32 out of 32 is amazing really, fair play. He hasn't faced Mignolet yet though.

Steve Clarke must be proper pissed after this one. The penalty Mulumbu conceded was just plain stupid. Not just that, he was fortunate not to have been red carded just for his hair style. He's just got one little tuft of blonde hair on the side of his head, it looks like a big friggin' caterpillar. It takes ridiculous to a whole new level. Has to be an early contender for worst hair of the season, at least now that Raheem has got rid of the effort he was sporting at the beginning of pre-season.*shudders*

Elsewhere on Saturday, Fulham won at the Stadium of Light with former Liverpool u18 player Pjatim Kasami heading in the only goal of the game from a corner. I see nothing to make me think Sunderland won't be shit again this year. The more they struggle, the funnier Di Canio's antics will be. Can't wait to see the madness that ensues from him this season.

You know what the worst thing about the return of Premier League football is? Having to listen to United's away following singing the same songs on a permanent, nasal, droning loop. It quite literally is the worst sound in the world. Nothing else even comes close to it. Nothing at all. I have no idea what they were even singing, it all just sounds like 'nnnyyaaa nnnnyyyaa nnnyyyaaa', the nasal sounding gobshites. There was some appalling version of 'Come on feel the noise' which I'm assuming is a chant for their new manager. Interesting that, Ferguson was there 27 years and never had his name sung by their fans like this. Give them a few months and they may be singing something entirely different about Moyes, fingers crossed.

He couldn't have got off to a better start than this though, the bog eyed cretin. The performance was nothing special but they're just so damn clinical, especially Van Persie. His superb volley against the run of play gave United the lead and just killed the home side in their tracks. I thought Ashley Williams was a bit of a shithouse on the goal really, if he'd gone for it with his head Van Persie couldn't have volleyed it, or if he had then he'd have volleyed Williams in the head and Swansea would have been awarded a free kick (at least I'm assuming they would now that Ferguson is no longer intimidating officials from the touchline).

More poor defending allowed Emile Welbeck to make it 2-0, meaning he'd already equalled last year's tally for the entire season. Van Persie hit another cracker before substitute Wilfried Bony pulled one back. Swansea never really looked like mounting any kind of comeback and Welbeck chipped in with his second to wrap up a comfortable win for United. I liked him better when he was Danny Welcrap and I didn't like him much even then. I can't stand this version of him, he needs to go back to being shit asap.

I'd been looking forward to getting my first look at Bony, as football hipsters have been going on and on about him for 12 months. Despite never having seen him play I stuck him in my fantasy team, then I saw he had 'Wilfried' on the back of his shirt and I decided on the spot that this would be his first and last game for me. He may have scored but I'm not having those kind of antics in my team so he's history I'm afraid.

Good to see Danny Murphy in the MOTD studio, he speaks well and anything that means less Lawro, Michael Owen and Jason Roberts can only be a good thing. Had to laugh when he put Welbeck's goalscoring down to 'working with Roy Hodgson'. So all those years with Ferguson mean nothing, it's the few weeks he's spent with Hodgson that's turned him into a goalscorer! Kinell Danny, I know Roy's your boy and all that, but come on lad, if he has that kind of midas touch with shit strikers then explain Ngog to me, Danny. Explain Ngog.

Note to Arsenal: You see what Van Persie did in this game whilst you had just been embarrassed at home by Villa? In fact, you see how he fired United to the title last season whilst you scraped into fourth place on the seat of your pants? Well THAT'S why we won't sell Suarez to you, because only an absolute fucking mug sells their best player to a top six rival. Nasri, Toure, Adebayor, Van Persie… no wonder they were so shocked by Liverpool's stance, these divs see absolutely nothing wrong in it. Small time knobs.

Sunday saw two shock results as Crystal Palace and Hull City somehow managed to avoid being completely mauled by Spurs and Chelsea respectively. Palace gave a fairly good account of themselves and were only denied a point by a debatable penalty decision after a ball to hand incident. Next week they might do the same and get away with it. Soldado buried the pen to score on his debut and I'm sick of Spurs already, the player stealing twats. Bale was obviously sold weeks ago, there's absolutely no way am I buying that he's injured, they've just wrapped him in cotton wool until they sign the players we want, I mean they want, and then they'll announce his move to Madrid. If anyone from Spurs is reading this, I've heard Rodgers is looking at Tony Hibbert and Ryan Shotton.

As for Chelsea, they blew Hull away early doors and then just kind of sat back and settled for what they had. If they'd wanted to run up a big score they could have just subbed the hapless Torres for Ba or Lukaku and then wiped the floor with Steve Bruce's side, but they seemed happy enough with 2-0. Oscar grabbed the first and then Lampard smashed in a free-kick from 35 yards that the keeper really should have saved. Lampard had earlier had a penalty saved, that's something that happens about as rarely as him saying 'no thanks' when offered seconds in the club canteen. Hey, I know he's not fat anymore but that's what makes it funny, ok? Besides, this is probably his last season so I've got to get get them in whilst I still can.

Chelsea's announcer had a needless dig at Benitez when introducing Mourinho to the crowd beforehand, whilst Jose was referring to himself in the third person again afterwards. *"Now the fans have to support the team, sing about the players and the club, not José. José knows how much they like me and how happy they are to have me back."* Helmet.

Finally, the Pellegrini era got under way at Manchester City with a routine demolition of Newcastle at Eastlands on Monday night. Dzeko was completely transformed from the lumbering oaf he looked last season, Aguero and Silva appear to have their mojo back and generally they just looked a lot less sterile and dull than they did last year. That doesn't mean Pellegrini is 'the man' just yet, but it backs up what I was writing for two years about Mancini being a fraud. Just by getting rid of him City were guaranteeing themselves an extra 10 points even before buying anyone. They've spent big again, they have a manager who isn't a massive, negative shithouse, and chances are they'll be there or thereabouts at the end of the season.

In fairness to Pardew (and it's not often you'll see me use that expression), Newcastle's preparation for this game was severely disrupted when Arsenal slapped in a £10m bid for Cabaye on the eve of the game. Pardew was understandably furious, as his player was unsettled and he had to leave him out. Cabaye is a French international and Newcastle's best player. Where did Arsenal pluck that £10m valuation from, and more to the point, could the bid not have waited until Tuesday morning? And why Cabaye? Admittedly he's French and he's a bad snide so he fits the Arsenal profile, but how many little ball playing midfielders can one team have? PSG are being linked with a £20m bid for Cabaye now which shows just how insulting Arsenal's opening bid was. But then they did offer us £30m for Suarez I guess, so they've got form for this kind of lowballing shite.

I don't get their thought process at all, but then this is a team that has spent all summer trying to buy forwards when they have deadbeats like Mertesacker, Koscielny and Jenkinson in their back four and a bang average keeper between the sticks. Wenger likes to pontificate about how Arsenal 'always do things the right way', but he's a hypocrite. We're worried about our lack of incoming transfers and missing out on players, but it could be worse, we could be Arsenal. If their summer transfer activity were a penalty kick, it'd be one taken by Jonathon Walters.

ASTON VILLA 0 LIVERPOOL 1

Competition - Premier League
Date - Sat 24 Aug 2013
Venue - Villa Park
Scorer(s) – Daniel Sturridge
Star Man – Kolo Toure

Team: Mignolet; Johnson,
Toure, Agger, Enrique;
Henderson, Lucas, Gerrard,
Coutinho (Allen); Aspas
(Cissokho), Sturridge:

Any win away from home in the Premier League is cause for celebration, no matter who you are. If you do it in style, great, but the important thing is that you come away with the three points as it's so easy to come unstuck if you're not on your game. I mean who'd have thought Man City would lose at newly promoted Cardiff? So I'll take a win at Villa whatever way we can get it.

For 35 minutes this was a top quality performance from the Reds and despite the closing stages of the first half and the entire second period not being anywhere near as impressive, it wasn't exactly 'the alamo' was it? For all their territorial dominance after the break Villa only really seriously threatened an equaliser once. So for me the positives certainly outweigh any negatives, particularly as the biggest positive is another win combined with another clean sheet for Simon Mignolet, who showed his worth once again.

Villa are a bit of a handful these days, their front three are extremely dangerous, especially on the counter attack when they have space to play in. The pace they possess up top is enough to give any defence problems and they've already won at Arsenal and were screwed out of at least a point at Chelsea in midweek. So whilst our second half display was not of the level expected, winning at Villa Park is nothing to be sniffed at.

For 35 minutes we completely bossed this game, it looked incredibly easy and Villa didn't get anywhere near us. The passing and movement was superb, Villa were chasing shadows for most of the half and will have been relieved to only have been one goal behind at that stage. It wasn't so much that we created a deluge of goalscoring opportunities, in fact considering the almost total domination of possession it's probably fair to say we didn't do enough with it. It looked like we had the game completely under control though. The crowd had been taken out of it and it seemed like only a matter of time before the second goal arrived and when it did that would surely be game over for the home side.

The one goal we did score was a work of art. Sturridge began the move out on the left wing when he collected a crossfield ball. He was forced backwards and played the ball back into midfield before just meandering towards the box. Enrique then played the ball into the feet of Coutinho but Sturridge gave him a shout to leave it. The ever alert little Brazilian did just that and Sturridge did the rest, showing great footwork and composure to somehow collect the ball, sidestep a defender, take it round the keeper and then beat the two defenders on the line with a cute finish. It was brilliant, for a second I thought he'd taken one touch too many and the chance had gone, but when you watch it from behind the goal if he'd taken the shot on his right foot and gone low, there were two defenders back to clear it. By waiting the extra second and steadying himself before using his left foot to lift it into the roof of the net, he took the two defenders on the line out of the equation. Such a great finish that. Since he's arrived at Anfield his goals per minute record is incredible. He's not even fully fit at the moment either.

Failing to build on Sturridge's goal has to be a little concerning but in a perverse way it was also encouraging. You can't win every game handsomely, sometimes it gets hairy and you need to dig in and grind out the result. We've done that twice already when it was something we didn't really have in our locker last year at all. If we can make it a habit of turning draws into wins we'll be much better placed when the points are tallied up at the end of the season. Of course it would have been much more preferable if we'd continued to play with the swagger we started with and swept Villa away with a tsunami of flowing football, but if that isn't possible then the next best thing is to just win the damn game and then question what went wrong performance wise afterwards.

The warning signs for what was to come were already present before the second half even got under way as Villa had began to come back into it in the minutes before half time. Benteke had a curling shot saved by Mignolet and Weimann had an effort deflected inches over the bar. Until then, the home side had barely even got near Mignolet. He must have touched the ball about twice in the opening half hour, such was Liverpool's dominance. I was hoping we might see Sterling brought on at half time to allow Coutinho to move central, but Rodgers resisted the temptation to change it and Aspas barely got a kick after the break, as Villa suddenly began to dominate possession and we seemed to be pushed back into our own half. It was the polar opposite of what we saw in the opening period.

Interestingly, Rodgers commented afterwards that it had a been deliberate ploy to sit deep and not press the ball high up the pitch because he didn't want give Villa's forwards any space to run in behind us. In terms of stifling their forward players and closing down the space they wanted to play in it was a roaring success. Where it fell down was that we couldn't keep the ball ourselves and we completely lost control of the midfield after the break. That in itself needn't have been a problem; if we were set up to play on the counter then keeping the ball isn't that important, it's what you do on the break with the opportunities you have that counts; and we did nothing.

Sturridge was isolated and in fact spent as much time defending as attacking, occasionally even dropping in to help Johnson at right back. He's clearly not match fit yet and said himself afterwards that he's fortunate to actually be playing as he wasn't even supposed to be fit this soon after his ankle injury. With all the tracking back he was doing it was understandable perhaps that he wasn't always razor sharp in his attacking play as the game wore on, but he was still responsible for the only two decent attacks we mustered in the second half. Coutinho faded too, in no small measure due to some rough treatment he received from Villa right back Lowton who had a couple of cheap shots at him and was eventually booked for a nasty late lunge at the little wizard's ankle.

With Aspas becoming increasingly invisible Rodgers eventually made a change, but rather than introducing Sterling, he opted to send on Aly Cissokho to play in front of Enrique to shore up that side of the field. Joe Allen was later brought on for a limping

Coutinho, as Rodgers went into full on 'hold what we have' mode. It's rare to see him adopt this approach, he's very much a 'front foot' kind of manager usually, but he obviously felt discretion was the better part of valour on this occasion. It worked, as for all Villa's territorial dominance in the second half they only managed to create one real opening when Agger's weak header was lobbed back into the path of Benteke, who lashed a half volley towards the near post corner of the net. Mignolet flung out a left hand and pushed the ball away for a corner and that was as close as Villa came to getting back into it.

Some of the saves Mignolet has made up to now have been from the kind of shot where if it goes in, you find yourself saying *"it was right in the corner, keeper had no chance"*. Huth's shot last week, the penalty, the follow up, Benteke's two efforts in this game… if any of those had gone in would we have pointed the finger at Mignolet and said he should have saved it? I doubt it, but he saved all of them and we won both games because of it.

Of course it's not just down to Mignolet, Toure has been an absolute colossus too and he dealt with Benteke about as well as you could possibly expect. The big Belgian has been in great form so far this season but Toure was in almost total control of him but for that one turn and shot in the first half (and even then I thought Toure could have been awarded a free-kick as Benteke backed in to him as he went for a header). A year ago we were losing pretty, so if we can now occasionally win ugly then you won't find me complaining, as to be a successful team you have to be able to grind out those 1-0 wins when it may seem like it's not your day.

Premier League Round Up (21-26 August 2013)

Chelsea have slithered their way to the top of the early Premier League table after following up a fortunate victory over Villa last Wednesday with a dour goalless draw at Old Trafford on Monday night. I'll get to the turd sandwich served up by Mourinho and Moyes in due course, but that Villa game was just like old times, as a spawny own goal and a couple of highly questionable calls went in Chelsea's favour to give them three points they didn't deserve.

Better get used to that, it was exactly the same when Mourinho was here last time and with Ferguson no longer around to keep the refs in line you can be sure this absolute helmet will be trying to fill the void left by the unofficial head of refereeing's sudden retirement.

Villa gave it their best shot at Stamford Bridge but what can you do when Ivanovic is allowed to get away with elbowing Benteke in the face and then scores the winner within a minute? The ref saw it and booked him but it's clearly a red card offence, not a yellow. Not just that, but in stoppage time Mongo decides to play volleyball in his own box and no penalty is given. Shocking effort from the match official, Kevin 'nobody's' Friend. Poor Villa got screwed but Mourinho generally gets his way when it comes to referees and this certainly won't be the last time it happens.

Onto the weekend's games and I may as well start at the Pit where the natives had been gearing themselves up for something special to celebrate their new manager's first home game in charge. The 'Martinez March' had been causing something of a storm in Evertonian circles on twitter in the lead up the game, as the organisers revealed that *"A huge banner will be unveiled in Stanley Park at 1.30pm and handed over to supporters so that they can begin the 'Martinez March' to the stadium."* Wow, sounds impressive. Us Reds are no strangers to marches of course, we all remember the thousands who marched in regular protests against Gillett & Hicks and presumably that was the inspiration for the Blues. In my mind's eye I envisioned hordes of them stomping through the Park on their way to Goodison, like the orc army descending on Helm's Deep in Lord of the Rings. And a 'huge banner' eh? Like those massive ones you often see in Serie A, you know the ones, those giant things that are passed around the stadium and take up half of the terrace? Cool. We've even had a few of those things ourselves, usually at cup finals. As it turned out, in typical Evertonian style there was a mass delusion of grandeur about the whole thing. The banner wasn't huge, which is probably for the best given that only about 30 people showed up to carry it, and half of them were kids. I'm trying to decide what's the most shameful aspect of it all. That they had a 'march' for Martinez at all, or that having decided to do it that the turnout was then so damn pitiful. Actually the worst part is that they still took photos of it and tried to pass it off as some kind of success. Said it before but it's worth repeating, if Evertonians didn't exist we'd have to invent them for our own amusement. #evertonarentwe

You have to feel a little sorry for the Blues at the moment though. The way they are being shat on by Moyes from his new, lofty perch is pretty despicable really, especially the way they went way above and beyond the call of duty with the send off they gave him last season. Despite fucking them off before the end of the season to take the United job they not only allowed him to see out the season in charge of Everton, but they cheered him to the wooden rafters on his Goodison farewell. And how does he repay them? By trying to sign their two best players on the cheap and then belittling them when they refuse to just bend over for him. He's a piece of work isn't he? Fellaini had a £22m buy out clause in his contract that Moyes actually put there. That was his worth to Everton and if Moyes wanted to buy him he could have done so at any point up until the end of July by offering that amount. Instead, he waited until the clause had expired and then offered £28m for Baines and Fellaini combined. He'd already had a reported bid of £15m turned down for Baines earlier in the summer, so that valued candy floss head at £13m, which is £9m less than the clause Moyes inserted. Even worse than the derisory offers he's made for them were his condescending comments when Everton refused. *"If I had been Everton manager and Sir Alex Ferguson had come asking for Leighton Baines and Marouane Fellaini I'd have found it very difficult to keep them because I always felt that the right thing was to do what was right for the players."*

Firstly, you aren't 'Sir Alex Ferguson' and no amount of bitching about the fixture list, looking down your nose at other clubs and being a smug twat in interviews will change that. You're David Moyes, you've won fuck all, your biggest achievement is that mural in Taff's Tavern declaring that you proved *'you don't have to win anything to be a winner'*. Secondly, just because you may have dropped your drawers any time Ferguson so much as looked like he was even contemplating unzipping his fly doesn't mean that everyone else has to. And finally, you *'always wanted to do what was right for the player'* did you? Really? I bet Joleon Lescott disagrees… *"We cannot be getting offers a week or two to go before the end of the deadline. And the offers they made shows that we value Joleon Lescott far higher than they do. His head has been twisted and I cannot say the way things have been done is right, it is not how we do things at this club. But maybe their football club is different, I control things here, maybe it is not quite the same there."*

That was Moyes in 2009, bemoaning another club lowballing him with a bid for his best player so late in the window. I guess it's ok to do it now he's no longer the manager of 'little old Everton' and is now with one of the big boys. What an absolute dick. You know how in the movies when a nerdy, plain girl suddenly for whatever reason gets to hang out with the popular hot chicks and acts really mean to her nerdy former friends to try and impress her new so-called pals? That's Moyes that is. He might be hanging with the cheerleaders now but he doesn't fit in as no matter how much he tries to pretend otherwise, deep down he knows he's really an ugly duckling.

I've not even mentioned Everton's game with West Brom and there's a reason for that; it was crap. No goals and not much to talk about. Fellaini hit the post and Jonas Olsson showed once again what a massive twat he is with a sly off the ball elbow on Jelavic, but aside from that it was incredibly dull.

Elsewhere on Saturday, Hull picked up their first three points of the season despite having to play for most of the game a man down against Norwich. The only goal came from the penalty spot when Michael Turner was harshly adjudged to have fouled Yannick Sagbo. Robbie Brady rolled in the spot kick and then Sagbo was sent off shortly after for one of those lame head butts where you stick your head in someone's face and then push it forward a little to try and act hard. Fucking idiot, if you're going to get sent off at least make it for something worthwhile. Finally on this, with each passing year Steve Bruce is looking more and more like something I'd expect to see in "Mrs Brown's Boys" Honestly, put a dress on him and a head scarf (that banner the Blues had for Martinez would do), and you could defo see him trotting off down the bingo with Mrs Brown.

I'm shocked that Hull have three points on the board already, I'll be surprised if they manage 15 points all season to be perfectly honest. I felt the same way about Palace but then they signed my boy Jason Puncheon on loan so they'll be safe now I reckon, as J-Punch almost single handedly kept Southampton up last year. Lambert may have played a small part too but it was mostly my boy Jase. For a while it looked like Palace may collect a surprise win at Stoke after Chamakh's smart finish put them ahead at the Britannia. Unfortunately Hughes' side came back to win with a couple of 'typically Stoke' type goals.

The second was especially bad from a Palace perspective as Chamakh completely bottled a 50-50 with Huth in his own box. I doubt his team-mates will have been too thrilled about such shithousery but as a fellow member of the striker's union I've got Chamakh's back on this. If I'm him, I'm saying to the rest of my team *"Fuck y'all, I scored so I did my job. I'm not here to tackle, that's what you lesser talented oiks who play in defence and midfield are here for"*. Of course given Chamakh's woeful goalscoring record this kind of approach may come back to bite him in the arse every week for the next six months as he repeatedly fails to 'do his job', so maybe a simple *"Sorry boys, my bad"* would be a more sensible course of action.

The big disappointment for me on the Saturday was Arsenal winning at Fulham. Completely typical Arsenal behaviour that though. I've written numerous times about how Wenger always seems to get wins when he needs them the most and he's only gone and done it again. The pressure on him at the start of the week was massive after they lost to Villa having failed to buy anybody this summer. Defeat in that CL qualifier in Turkey could have cranked up that pressure to intolerable levels but they went and spoiled all of our fun by winning that and then seeing off Fulham comfortably as well. Podolski scored twice and Giroud got the other.

They actually had Sagna at centre half in this game. If Wenger doesn't want to buy defenders or a holding midfielder, then Arsenal should use all that money they have to buy some new fans as the ones they have are complete fucking gobshites. Any set of fans that sing *"He scores when he wants"* about a player that doesn't either a) score 30 goals a season or b) score roughly once every five years, really need to have a word with themselves. Arsenal fans were singing that about Podolski, the fucking dolts.

Moving on, West Ham and Newcastle played out a dull goalless draw at St James' Park. The TV highlights package consisted of a few corners and set pieces that didn't really come to anything, a backpass that almost beat the keeper and a goal that was about three yards offside. It looked like a truly woeful game of football which often goes with the territory when Allardyce is involved. It's going to be another long old season for Newcastle by the looks of it, especially as Cabaye has now gone on strike to force a move through. Little rat.

Elsewhere on Saturday, Sunderland were denied a precious away win by a late Southampton equaliser. It was another poor game with both goals coming from set-pieces. Southampton somehow contrived to allow 5ft 5 Giaccherini to score a header from a corner, whilst right at the death the home side levelled when Fonte headed in from a free-kick.

The biggest shock of the season so far - aside from Welbeck scoring twice on the opening day - came in South Wales on Sunday as Cardiff turned over Pellegrini's Man City side. What makes it even more surprising is that 'Citeh' actually scored first and somehow managed to blow it. Dzeko gave them the lead and it looked like they'd run away with it until Fraizer Campbell suddenly went all Van Persie on them, scoring twice and creating a third. Negredo scored a consolation in stoppage time but Cardiff held on for a memorable win. They've got their work cut out to stay up but they may have a chance if they can make their home ground a fortress.

As for City, well the former Champions had loads of possession and on another day would have won comfortably but they have an extremely soft centre at the moment with Kompany and Nastasic out and Joe Hart looking increasingly ropey. They look really weak at centre half and they could definitely use someone with a bit of experience and leadership in there. Someone who can organise those around him and who will stand up to the physical stuff. I don't know, someone like, say, Kolo fucking Toure baby! In your face City.

Also on Sunday, Spurs won 1-0 again, through a dodgy penalty again, converted by Soldado, again. Difficult to complain too much about this one though, it wasn't a penalty but they should have had a blatant one earlier. Both incidents involved Shelvey and Townsend. Jonjo got away with a clumsy foul in the first half and maybe that was on the ref's mind when the pair clashed again in the second half. Townsend simply ran by Shelvey and kicked his ankle on the way past before tumbling. It was either an accidental collision or blatant cheating by Townsend. Neither would surprise me, after all he's had plenty of time to learn the dark arts from Bale in training every day. Well, not quite *every* day it seems. Bale failed to show up for training on Tuesday and appears to now be doing a 'Cabaye'. Hilarious, all summer we've been hearing about how he's doing everything the right way, unlike that wrong 'un Luis Suarez. And yet for all the shit Suarez caused this summer, he never did this. Bale was doing everything the right way when things were going as he wanted but as soon as his dream move hit a snag he threw his toys out of the pram and went on strike.

Swansea have now lost both of their opening games, although the fixture list wasn't kind to them it should be said. I don't think they'll be as good as they've been in the last couple of seasons though, I can see them being rooted in the bottom half all season with the likes of West Brom, Sunderland and Norwich, but we'll see I guess.

Last and most definitely least was the abysmal game at Old Trafford on Monday night. The clash between United and Chelsea had been hyped up all week and was highly anticipated. Even I got suckered in and decided to watch it. That's two hours of my life I'm not getting back. Absolute dogshit this was, so much so that I was sat there contemplating a potential title challenge from us purely on the basis of how shite both of these sides looked. I know, I know, but I bet I wasn't the only one.

Awful crossing, passes straight into touch, aimless hoofs over the top, honestly this was just absolutely fucking brutal stuff. How can two teams with such attacking talent produce such a piss poor game? To find the answer to that you simply have to look in the respective dug outs. Mourinho was happy with a point and Moyes doesn't actually know how to try and win these big games.

Gollum hilariously said beforehand *"I don't know about my record against Jose but someone told me it was pretty good"* His record reads: P8 W0 L5 D3. Who told him it was 'pretty good' then? His fan club at 'Taffs Tavern' perhaps? Kinell. He also said *"It's different preparing a United team to face him (Mourinho) rather than an Everton one. With United, we are out there to win"* And why would Everton not be out there to win then, Davie? Everton were the fourth best team in the country in 2005, yet he didn't feel like they could go out to try and win? The man is just an inherent shithouse isn't he?

Astonishingly the United fans greeted him with a banner proclaiming him as 'the Chosen One'. No really, they did. Seriously, they called him 'the Chosen One'. Look, I'm not making it up, they really did. It's not a joke, there's no punchline, they actually did have a banner calling David Moyes the 'Chosen One'. Ok fine, don't believe me then, see if I care. It happened though, I saw it with my own eyes. That banner actually makes the 'Martinez March' seem almost acceptable in comparison. We got slated for not being more welcoming to Roy Hodgson when he took over, but this is taking it to the completely opposite extreme. The Chosen One!! David Moyes!! Have a word with yourselves, you manc scrotes.

Moyes elected to start Rooney despite all the crap that's been going on with him and Chelsea. When asked about it beforehand he claimed he hadn't even given a second's thought to any of that when he picked his team. Yeah, of course you didn't. Curiously any time Rooney touched the ball his name was chanted by both sets of fans. I'm not sure who I'm more surprised at, United fans for backing some scouse twat who wants to leave, or Chelsea fans for backing some scouse twat they've got no chance of signing.

Do we actually even know why he wants to leave? All summer I've been reading about him wanting out of Old Trafford, but I have no idea why. It can't just be down to Moyes, he wanted out even before they appointed that bum. So what's his beef? It can't be money as I read somewhere he's on 230k a week at United, I was blown away by that as I had no idea he was getting that kind of wedge.

Mourinho was in full on sneak mode afterwards, pretending to be complimentary to United by calling the fans 'special' for 'supporting a player that wants to leave'. He also said the only reason Chelsea have been in for him is because he's been encouraging them. *"The person that started the story has to finish the story. For the good of everyone, it is time to finish the story. If you look at a manager like me, a club like us and the people who work at the club with me, we are not silly enough to try to get a player from a big club that doesn't want to sell. We are not silly enough to try something if somebody didn't start it. If he wants to leave he has to say - or if he has decided now he doesn't want to leave any more then he has to say."*

This whole thing is just bizarre. United have taken the same stance we did with Suarez, and Chelsea are doing an Arsenal in refusing to take 'no' for an answer. Let's face it though, there's no way Rooney is going to leave United. He's a right needy little shit is Wayne. United is Colleen, and Mourinho is some bit on the side he's been stringing along to make himself feel wanted. He's not leaving Colleen though, not unless she dumps a suitcase full of his clothes on the front lawn and changes the locks on the doors. I think Jose is finally starting to see that.

As for the game, nothing happened except for some stray elbows providing various talking points. First, De Bruyne went into the book for using his chin to smash into poor Van Persie's elbow. Shocking from the Chelsea youngster, he could have killed him. Secondly, Lampard's elbow blocked a shot in the area but United's penalty appeals were waved away by Martin Atkinson. A lot easier to say 'no penalty' when it's Moyes patrolling the touchline rather than 'Der Fuhrer'. And thirdly, Patrice Evra is so unpopular that even his own team-mates can't resist an opportunity to take him out, as Vidic nailed him with a pearler of a forearm smash to the throat that left the full back requiring lengthy treatment.

It's rare to see United happy to settle for a point at home and not go throwing on extra forward players to try and win the game. That's the Moyes effect for you right there. Anyone expecting them to completely fall off a cliff after Ferguson left is kidding themselves though. Those United players have been winning for so long and have had that mentality drilled into them by Ferguson for so many years that not even Moyes can fuck that up straight away. It's going to take a bit of time to make his own mark on the team and make them as average as he is.

LIVERPOOL 4 NOTTS COUNTY 2 (aet)

Competition - League Cup
Date - Tue 27 Aug 2013
Venue - Anfield
Scorer(s) – Sterling, Sturridge (2), Henderson
Star Man – Daniel Sturridge

Team: Mignolet; Johnson, Toure, Wisdom, Cissokho (Agger); Allen (Henderson), Gerrard, Alberto (Coutinho); Ibe, Sturridge, Sterling:

Well that didn't exactly go according to plan. When you include so many first choice players for a cup tie against lower league opposition the last thing you want is three injuries and key players having to play for 120 minutes. We got through, yet it's almost unforgivable how difficult we made it for ourselves with a shocking, Billy Big Bollocks 2nd half attitude.

My emotions are all over the place with this one. Happy to be through. Gutted about Kolo. Seriously pissed off with the arrogant, complacent 2nd half attitude that caused the unnecessary situation we found ourselves in but also pleased with the character shown to dig in and come up with the goods when things went really pear shaped. At 2-2 and down to ten men there was a very good chance we could lose this game but the performance from that point on was excellent and the players showed balls to see it through.

It was seriously irritating the way we let them back into it though. The first half went as you'd expect as Sterling gave us the perfect start with a positive run and shot to open the scoring with five minutes gone. He was very bright early on and put a shift in all night. Rodgers had taken the opportunity to rest Agger but that plan went out of the window when Cissokho turned an ankle and had to come off after ten minutes. A nightmare start for the lad but at least it doesn't seem too serious. Agger came on at centre half, Wisdom went to right back and Johnson moved across to the left. Not ideal but not the end of the world either and it didn't affect the flow of the game too much as other chances came and went.

The second goal eventually arrived when Gerrard picked Sturridge out in the box with a superb pass which the striker killed instantly before drilling a shot into the corner. Terrific finish from a man who looks like scoring every time he takes to the field these days. The imperious skipper then hit the post after a surging, overlapping run into the box and everything was going perfectly at that stage.

One more goal before half time would have allowed Rodgers to rest either Gerrard or Sturridge but at 2-0 he understandably couldn't afford to take any unnecessary chances. It would have been nice to put the tie to bed before the break and then give Borini a run out for example, but the lack of a third goal combined with the loss of Cissokho meant Rodgers needed to be careful with his remaining substitutions. Still, an early goal or two after the break would allow him to get his key players off and considering how easy the first half had been there was nothing to suggest that wouldn't happen.

38

Perhaps it was the ease of the first half that caused the horrible complacency that crept in after the break. Chances were still created, but not as many and the general play seemed a lot less intense than it had been. Sturridge disappeared for long periods, Ibe kept running up his own arse and Sterling got little joy out of the defence although he did work tirelessly to win the ball back any time he lost it. He was involved a lot even if it was not always good.

County pulled one back with 25 minutes left when a deep free-kick was headed back across goal by an unmarked player and the big striker got in front of Wisdom to head past a helpless Mignolet. Rodgers was immediately forced into a second substitution when Allen did a hamstring and made way for Henderson, and the boss made his final change not long after when he sent on Coutinho to hopefully try and put the game to bed. The Brazilian came on for Alberto who had done ok without looking anything special. Getting Coutinho on was the right thing to do but unfortunately it took him about 20 minutes to get going.

The Notts County goal appeared to stun the Reds out of their lethargy and Toure was denied by the post at the Kop end. Numerous other good situations were wasted and the longer it stayed at 2-1 the more obvious it became that County were going to get one more opportunity before the end. To their credit when it came they took it extremely well. It was a well worked goal but it didn't make for good viewing for Liverpool fans, especially the role played by Glen Johnson in it. Extra time was the last thing we needed, but I wasn't unduly concerned until suddenly Toure pulled up lame and left the field on a stretcher. Now I was officially worried.

I assumed Henderson would be moved to right back with Wisdom going into the middle alongside Agger and Coutinho dropping back into midfield with Gerrard. I certainly didn't expect to see Sterling moved to right back and I feared it was going to prove costly. Raheem was booked within minutes for a rash tackle and County clearly decided to try and target him and attacked down his side whenever possible. He coped with it extremely well to be fair. It took a few minutes for the players to settle down after the sending off and subsequent reshuffle but eventually the shape came back into the side and the lead was regained when Coutinho sent Sturridge running into the box to claim his second of the game. That's 15 goals in 19 games now.

The win was wrapped up in some style when Ibe did well to hold the ball up and lay it into the path of Henderson who drove through the middle and 'megged the last man before slotting past the keeper. He made a real difference to our play when he came on. The players deserve credit for not letting a drama turn into a crisis but nevertheless it's incredibly frustrating that it came down to this and we now look like having to make do without big Kolo for a while. It was just so damned unnecessary, and Rodgers must be doing his nut.

If you field a weakened side this kind of outcome is a risk you run, but with the team he put out the last thing he'll have expected was to face extra time. When Toure went off I felt sorry for Rodgers. He's done the right thing in taking the competition seriously and fielding a strong side but the players almost blew it by starting to think they are 1970 Brazil or something. The game should never, ever have been allowed to go to extra time and if it hadn't, Toure would not have been injured and it would have been a successful night.

This complacency needs to be stamped out before it becomes a big problem though. We see this team play some fantastic football at times and when on song we look like we could take anyone. It was the same last season though; look good for a few games and they lay an egg because we get too cocky. Maybe this scare will serve as a wake up call. I hope so, because the biggest danger to us may actually be ourselves. We're a good team, just maybe not quite as good as they sometimes think they are.

chapter four

September

LIVERPOOL 1 MANCHESTER UNITED 0

Competition - Premier League
Date - Sun 1 Sep 2013
Venue - Anfield
Scorer(s) – Daniel Sturridge
Star Man – Martin Skrtel

Team: Mignolet; Johnson (Wisdom), Skrtel, Agger, Enrique; Henderson, Lucas, Gerrard, Coutinho (Alberto); Aspas (Sterling), Sturridge:

Wasn't bad that, was it? Beating the Mancs, three new signings sat in the stands watching, going top of the table with a 100% record, still to concede a goal and doing it all without our best player who now only has two games left to serve of his suspension. A far cry from where we were after three games a year ago; fourth from bottom with just one point to our name.

We actually played much, much better in this fixture last season but lost the game. The referee played a huge part in that but hard luck stories were a regular occurrence in the first half of last season. This year we've reversed the trend, winning games despite not being at our fluent best. They say winning is a habit and it's one we now seem to be starting to develop. Rodgers pointed out afterwards that since January we have now amassed more points than United, a stat that I'm sure will surprise a lot of people. Just as significant, we've now beaten them in a head to head encounter too. When it comes to games against Manchester United we often find ourselves on the wrong end of the result despite having played very well. We regularly don't get what we feel we deserve from these games. Playing well is nice and all, but getting the points is nicer and over the years United have found a way to do that at our expense. It's actually quite rare that they impress in games against Liverpool but they generally find a way to win them. Not this time.

This time we beat them at their own game, getting our noses in front and then keeping them at bay. They may have dominated the ball in the second half but did they really do that much with it? I thought we defended superbly as a team and much like last week at Villa the only complaint I'd have is that we didn't do enough with our opportunities to break out and kill them off when the opportunity arose. The return of Suarez will definitely help in that regard though.

Rodgers admitted last week that the second half performance at Villa Park was by design rather than a case of us simply just being forced back by the opposition. Lucas said the same after this game. It's a deliberate tactical ploy to make it difficult for the opposition and whilst I'm not generally in favour of that as it can often backfire, I'm willing to suspend my scepticism of it for the time being as I think it's more a case of Rodgers being pragmatic based on where we are in our development under him as opposed to it be being a long term strategy.

After a bright opening in which we took the lead, we seemed content to hold what we had and didn't attack with the kind of purpose and with the kind of numbers we normally would. I'd also credit United for that though as I thought defensively they were excellent, they let us have the ball in our own half but their pressing of the ball was relentless any time we got past the half way line. We didn't have much time in possession and it was difficult for both sides to create any openings. It was no surprise therefore, that the only goal came from a corner. Agger got free and headed towards goal where Sturridge had got himself into a great position to glance the ball into the net from close range. Agger's face was a picture, initially he looked as if to say *'cheeky bastard stealing my goal'* before realising *'hang on, we've just taken the lead against the mancs!'* and went charging off to join everyone else in mobbing Sturridge. Interesting to see Sturridge fighting everyone off as he wanted to go and celebrate with his manager. His career is thriving now and Rodgers deserves credit for the part he's played in that by giving Sturridge the opportunity to play and putting him in an environment that has allowed him to thrive. Whenever Sturridge talks you can hear the little soundbites that Rodgers must be drilling into him every day. *"Winning as a team", "it's not about individuals" "it's all about working hard for eachother"* etc etc

Sturridge wasn't even fit and hadn't trained since the Notts County game. He reckons he couldn't shoot properly because of the injury but he put in another terrific shift helping out his midfield. He's becoming a real all round striker, scoring all types of goals, creating them too and now he's added work rate to his game as well. And 16 goals in 20 games speaks for itself. Aspas is not really cutting the mustard alongside him yet though, it's going to take some time for him to get up to speed I think. It's not a big deal though as he only needs to hold the fort for two more games and then Suarez is back.

The defence were magnificent all afternoon with Agger and Skrtel completely owning Van Persie and getting right under his skin. The Dutchman was fortunate not to be sent off just before half time after an altercation with Skrtel. He'd already been niggling away at Agger and had been booked for a late lunge on the Dane. No real surprise as it's always a running battle when they face eachother. Agger has spoken in the past about Van Persie and his stray elbows and it's clear there's no love lost between them. Skrtel doesn't seem to like him much either, although he appeared to do nothing to provoke the angry reaction and shove to the chest that could easily have resulted in a second yellow for the frustrated forward. Van Persie tried to justify his actions by claiming he'd been elbowed by Skrtel but I was watching them at the time and Skrtel did nothing other than stand his ground as the cross came in. Van Persie then shoved him in the chest with both hands. The ref missed it but the linesman didn't, and neither did Gerrard nor Agger who both went to confront the Dutchman. Gerrard gave him plenty of verbals, calling him *'a fucking prick'* amongst other things. I love it when Stevie gets in people's faces like that. It doesn't happen that often but it's ace when it does. Agger is always there whenever there's any aggro and you can usually see Lucas chipping in with the odd comment or two as well. Andre Marriner opted to have a word rather than pull out a yellow card, which if I take my red tinted specs off was the right thing to do and sensible refereeing. With my red tinted specs on, however, he should have sent the snidy twat off.

Half time arrived at a good moment for United as their discipline had completely gone. Carrick had been yellow carded, as had the odious Cleverley who went into the book for a scything lunge on Coutinho. Seconds earlier the little Brazilian had backed into Phil Jones as he leapt for a header and the big dopey looking muppet came down awkwardly on an ankle. United wanted us to put the ball out of play and when we didn't Cleverley took the law into his own hands. Because you just know they'd have put the ball out in the same situation, obviously...

Van Persie calmed down at the break and behaved himself in the second half, although Carrick could easily have walked after a late challenge on Aspas. Again, Marriner opted for a warning rather than a second yellow. Chances were few and far between but United's dominance of the ball made for an excruciating 50 minutes for Liverpool fans. I kept thinking it was only matter of time before their made their possession count, but then I looked at the clock and there were only ten minutes left and they'd actually done very little. Lucas and Gerrard broke up numerous attacks before they reached our defence, Agger and Skrtel dealt with anything that came their way whilst the full backs were very solid too. Then there's Henderson, who ran and ran and ran. He probably ran home after the game too, he never stops that boy.

As time ticked away we looked more and more comfortable, despite the loss of Johnson who hurt his ankle in making a courageous block on a rampaging Evra. Andre Wisdom came on and did a good job, even carrying the ball forward to the corner flag to waste some valuable time. Another substitute, Raheem Sterling, went close to killing them off deep into stoppage time when he stung the palms of De Gea and forced a corner that we took an age in taking, much to the frustration of Moyes. When it was eventually taken, Sturridge tried to be too clever and attempted to play the ball off a defender to win another corner, and succeeded only in putting the ball out for a goal kick and straight into the waiting arms of De Gea. Had there been another minute left Sturridge would probably have copped an earful from his team-mates as well as the crowd, but thankfully time was up and Marriner blew the whistle as soon as the ball left the hands of the United keeper.

The expected late onslaught simply never materialised, in fact Stoke probably gave us more problems in the closing stages than United did. Moyes' team had a lot of the ball, far more than he's ever been used to having at Anfield, which probably explains how happy he seemed afterwards. *"Best we've played all season"* he said, before hilariously adding *"I could see why we are Champions today."* The poor bastard seems to have taken that Taff's Tavern mural a bit too literally. *"The boss who proves you don't need trophies to be a winner. But he is a winner"* It would seem you don't need wins to be a winner either based on his comments after this one.

So a huge three points for us going into the international break and whilst no-one is expecting us to stay at the top of the table for any extended period of time, we may just stick around there for longer than many expect as the run of fixtures we have presents a great opportunity to extend this winning run. That's usually when we trip ourselves up though and that's what Rodgers needs to be drumming into his players now. It's all about the next game, don't look too far ahead or set any targets, just win the next game and move on and see where it takes us.

One of the big criticisms last season was that we could never beat anyone that was above us in the table (until we eventually defeated Spurs in March), and it seems that's still the case this season, albeit for a hugely different reason. Well if there's no-one above you, how can you beat them?

And what of Skrtel? This performance has to have put him back in the frame for a first team place. I'm assuming Rodgers was planning for him to leave as why else would you bring in two players in his position at a cost of £25m? He was the best player on the park today though.

We've got a five point cushion over United now, I don't even know when was the last time that was the case. How long before the United fans begin to realise that Moyes is their 'Roy Hodgson'? In between lauding the S*n and calling us murderers the away end repeatedly sang *"So Come on David Moyes, Play Like Fergie's Boys. We'll go wild wild wild!"* Play like Fergie's boys eh? Not that easy when referees appear to have stopped favouring you. 'Der Fuhrer' is no longer there, patrolling the touchline and intimidating officials, and that's two games in a row they've had penalty appeals turned down that Ferguson would have expected to get. Perhaps the most telling moment of the afternoon was when Moyes was told to sit his complaining arse down by the fourth official. A Manchester United manager being put in his place like that? Ferguson will probably be on the phone to Mike Riley today demanding to know what the hell is going on.

A final footnote to this one, as I was selling the fanzine outside, I noticed Kolo Toure drive past the front of the Kop about an hour before kick off. He had Victor Moses in the passenger seat and Mamadou Sakho was following in the car behind. Presumably Ilori was knocking about somewhere too as Kolo was like some kind of bad ass pied piper. Anyway, he stopped, wound the window down and told a steward he was trying to get into the club car park. The steward informed him he'd missed the turning and would have to drive all the way around the ground again to get back in. How embarrassing. For the steward I mean. Kolo Toure does not miss a turning, the car park was simply not where it should have been.

Premier League Round Up (Aug 31- Sep 1 2013)

This has to go down as one of the worst weekends of football the Premier League has ever seen with Saturday's offerings especially appalling. Chelsea had the week-end off as a reward for providing the nation with an unexpected dose of Friday night Comic Relief in the European Super Cup and their absence - combined with the fixture list 'randomly' throwing up two 'Super Sunday' style fixtures in our game with the Mancs and the North London derby - made for a not so 'Super Saturday'.

The early game saw Manchester City taking on the Hull City Bengals or whatever daft name they're currently using. I expected Pellegrini's side to wipe the floor with Fathead's men but to be fair Citeh were largely unimpressive and Steve Bruce's newly promoted side gave a really good account of themselves before losing 2-0. The scoreline didn't tell the story of the game as in the opening stages Hull were rampant and could easily have been a couple of goals ahead. City improved after the break and Negredo eventually headed them in front, or should that be Soldado? No, I was right the first time, it's Negredo. I'm having to second guess myself every time with those two at the moment. I rarely, if ever, watch La Liga and to be honest if you put both of them in front of me now I'd have no idea which one is which, but give me a couple of weeks and I'm sure I'll have it down.

*note to self. Soldado - Spurs, Negredo - Not Spurs

City's second goal came courtesy of another free-kick from Yaya Toure. Impressive, if he keeps this up he may one day go on to be almost as good as his big brother. He's like the Phil to Kolo's Gary. Wait, did I just compare Kolo with Gary Neville? Kinell, that's the worst thing I've done since that 'crop dusting' incident with the Argentina fans I mentioned in one of last year's round ups.

The 3pm games provided virtually nothing in the way of goals or entertainment. Absolute Zlatan they were, especially in South Wales where Cardiff picked up another point by holding Everton to a drab goalless draw. Baines should have had a pen but was instead accused of diving, whilst Fellaini should have won it at the end but hit the post from close range. Everton still without a league win under Martinez, although they have yet to taste defeat yet either.

Newcastle had Cabaye back in their squad for the home game with Fulham. He was greeted by the home fans with a mix of boos and applause when he appeared as a 2nd half sub. It was one of his fellow countrymen who grabbed the headlines though, let's face it, chances are it's gonna be when Newcastle are involved. Hatem Ben Arfa was quality all day and deservedly got the winner four minutes from time with a brilliant individual strike. He's one of the most talented players in the country when fit, the problem is he's not often fit. He's clearly too good for Newcastle in their present state which may explain why Pardew was suspiciously less than complimentary about him afterwards. It smacked of downplaying how good he is in case someone tried to sneak in with a late bid before the window closed. Ben Arfa is ace though, albeit a little greedy.

Watching this got me thinking, remember all that crap about Pappis Cisse and the whole 'great Newcastle number 9s' thing? He was getting all that hype after his first fucking game! Reminds me of when Nigel Clough was crowned the new King after his two goal debut for us against Sheffield Wednesday. I was absolutely convinced we'd win the league after coming out of Anfield that day. Fucking hell.

Elsewhere, Stoke won away at West Ham. I raised my eyebrow a little at that scoreline as the Hammers are relatively strong at home and Stoke are relatively crap wherever they play, but 'Useless' now has two wins under his belt unfortunately. A free-kick from Jermaine Pennant was enough to get them the win and they deserved it too as West Ham were completely toothless. Goals from Pennant are rarer than rocking horse turd, so as bad as they were the Hammers can still consider themselves a little unfortunate as he won't score again this season.

Southampton and Norwich met at Carrow Road and the only thing worse than the game was Motson's commentary on it. At one point he was talking and then suddenly interrupted himself mid sentence to tell himself he was talking shite about a penalty incident. It was bizarre even by his standards. *"One of those situations where the player is so close to the incident that I don't think he could have avoided…OH! it's clearly hit his arms, you're talking shite again you doddering old goat"* I'm paraphrasing, but it's close enough. Nathan Redmond scored the only goal of the game and he was the game's stand out performer. A lot of big clubs looked at him when he was at Birmingham, I think we were one of them actually. Norwich took a chance on him and he's playing well for them.

Moving on to the evening game and I only knew four players in the Palace team that played host to Sunderland. And I can't believe they've still got that Speroni jabroni in goal. Was he not bad enough last time they were in the top flight? And wasn't he crap at Reading too? *quickly checks wiki* No, I'm confusing him with that other loser, Federici. Speroni probably is too unless he's improved massively since the last time Palace were in the top division. Still, at least he didn't wear dirty arl grey tracky bottoms like that other chump they had back then. Sunderland started with Connor Wickham and some Korean lad I've never seen before as a front pair. We'll probably never see him again after this one, he embarrassingly shit out of a free header in front of goal prompting Di Canio to rip him to shreds on TV afterwards, saying *"I can't change the heart of my players"*. He subbed him at half time too. Ouch.

Immediately after the game Palace announced they'd signed a young player by the name of Jack Hunt, which co-incidentally is pretty damn close to what Di Canio was calling Ji after he bottled that header. Whilst I'd say the lad deserves all he gets, footballers generally don't take kindly to being mocked by their manager in public and if Di Canio hasn't lost the dressing room already it's only a matter of time before he does, despite his desperate attempts to fill the squad with his fellow countrymen in the hope they'll have his back. He even signed Andrea Dossena! I know they were desperate for a left back but has he never watched the Doss play? Sunderland look even worse than they did last year and they only just stayed up by the skin of their teeth then. Will Di Canio even make it to Christmas? Can't see it myself. Palace won the game 3-1 and fully deserved it too. Gabbidon scored early doors and my boy J-Punch was inches away from making it two, as was Palace skipper Jedinak who curled just wide after being released by a wonderful ball by Puncheon. That's my boy that is.

Sunderland sub Fletcher headed them level with a typically brilliant finish. He's a great finisher and I do wonder how he'd fare if he was at a top club, as in theory the more chances that are created for him the more goals he'll score, right? How would he do at a Spurs or Arsenal for example? He'll probably never get the opportunity to play for a Champions League side but he's better than a lot of players who have. Like John O'Shea for example. He conceded a pen and got himself sent off in the process, costing Sunderland the game. Gayle converted the spot kick and in stoppage time O'Keefe lashed in a brilliant third after being set up by…. yep, you guessed it, Puncheon. Great bit of business from Holloway that, bringing in my boy. Southampton will live to regret it though, mark my words.

Going back to Chelsea's Super Cup defeat for a second, I know it's 'only' the Super Cup, but still, I loved it. Any time Chelsea suffer any kind of disappointment is cause for celebration and this was fucking hilarious. Remember when Benitez won this trophy with Inter and Mourinho scoffed at him, (correctly) pointing out the only reason Inter were playing in it was because he'd won the Champions League with them the season before? Well the roles were reversed here, it was Mourinho looking to vulture a trophy that Benitez had put him in position to win and I bet Rafa almost pissed his pants when Bayern scored that last gasp equaliser. Along with everyone else who isn't a Chelsea fan of course. The funniest thing was 'the Special One' being a smart arse and sending Mongo on for the last few minutes, either to try and shut up shop or to maybe spare his captain the embarrassment of lifting yet another trophy in full kit and shinnies despite not playing any part in the winning of it. It backfired when Bayern scored with the last kick of the game to force pens and when Lukaku's lame penalty was saved, Terry's attempts at changing into a Bayern kit to try and lift the trophy were foiled when he couldn't get the shirt over his giant forehead. Chelsea have his shirts specially made with a widened neckhole you see.

Onto Sunday, and Arsenal edged out Spurs thanks to another smart little finish from Oliver Giroud. Spurs looked seriously uninspiring again. They've been involved in three 1-0 games now and scoring goals has been an issue for them as the only ones they've managed have been pens. Bale won them an awful lot of points last season before he went on strike and took to walking around the streets of London looking like a giant novelty condom (google 'Gareth Bale pink t shirt'). He was unveiled at Madrid earlier this week amidst the kind of media frenzy he hasn't experienced since 'Escape from the Planet of the Apes' when him and his bird showed up in America in a spaceship.

Also on Sunday, Swansea got their first win on the board with a 2-0 success at the Hawthorns. Left back Ben Davies hit a cracker to open the scoring and then Pablo Hernandez wrapped it up in the 2nd half. West Brom look to be in trouble already, they've got no-one to score goals having lost Lukaku and Odemwingie and bizarrely they then tried to sell Shane Long to Hull only for it to fall through. To make matters worse they went and splashed out £6m on Victor fucking Anichebe!! You can't score goals and that's your answer? Fucking hell!

Tell you what though, it's a good job I've got deadline day to write about or this round up would be almost as dull as Saturday night's MOTD. People complain about Michael Owen and Robbie Savage but to be fair not even the hilarious comedy duo of Jackie Chan and Chris Tucker could have made that entertaining this week. Now 'Transfer Deadline Day' on the other hand, that was a different matter altogether. Mike Ashley must be thanking his lucky stars for Manchester United this week as the bungling antics of Moyes and United's new Chief Exec meant that no-one outside of the North East seemed to notice that Joe Kinnear has actually managed to do even less than everybody expected. I'd have thought he'd have at least managed to sign one or two deadbeats from whatever London backwater he'd been boozing in, but no. They signed no-one. So, what exactly is Kinnear being paid for then? It's looking an even more bizarre appointment now than it did when it happened. And it was VERY bizarre when it happened. Pardew was roped into putting a statement out on the club website stating that they didn't sign anyone because the players that were in their price range were inferior to those already at the club, and because they did most of their business in January. So again, why exactly has Kinnear been hired again? Loony Toon.

The other big losers of this transfer window were unquestionably the Mancs. Who are they missing more, Alex Ferguson or David Gill? Moyes is so out of his depth it's just magnificent, I mean I knew he would be but I thought he'd at least manage to blag his way through for a few months before United fans realised they'd been sold a fugaze, but no, he couldn't even manage that, the small time little shitkicker. I haven't seen anyone drowning so badly in a new job since Mr Burns fired Smithers and gave his job to Homer. Moyes might be even less equipped for his new position than Homer was.

It's not all on him of course, that new chief exec of theirs makes Rick Parry and Christian Purslow look like Peter Robinson. United's attempts at getting deals done this summer have been side splittingly funny. They've been linked with every midfielder on the planet but couldn't get any and in the end Kenwright pulled Moyes' pants down - metaphorically this time - and made him pay £5m more for Fellaini than he'd have needed to had he met the terms of the Belgian's buy out clause before it expired. That deal almost beggars belief. For a start, Fellaini is shit. Yeah, that's right, I said it. Most people have thought it at some point, some still do, but given that we're constantly told by people in the game about how great he is it's only natural that most of us end up thinking *"Well I don't see it, but I suppose he must be good if everyone else keeps saying he is"*. Well guess what, he's not, you're right to think he's crap because that's what he is. When a player's biggest attributes are having good chest control and 'being a nuisance' then he really isn't all that as far as I'm concerned. I mean, what is he? Where would you play him? He's not really a midfielder as all he does is stand in the middle and elbow people. He's not really a striker as all he does is stand in the box and elbow people. In what universe does he improve United's midfield or attack? In Moyes' universe, that's where. The funny thing is though even Moyes didn't really want him THAT much, as if he did he'd have met the buy out clause and then been able to integrate him into his squad over pre-season and have him available for the first three games. He showed what he really thought of him when he offered the Blues a pittance for him not long after the clause expired.

The chief exec can be blamed for all the other deals they fucked up but the Fellaini debacle is all on Gollum. You have to say that Everton played a blinder here though, they held firm until the last minute, eventually forcing Fellaini to hand in a transfer request and forgo any 'loyalty' payments owed to him, and more importantly, waiting until United's desperation reached the point that they paid way over the odds to avoid being left with nobody. And when that happened the Blues then went bang bang bang and brought in three players that will make them a far more effective team than they were with Captain Elbows and Alehouse Vic. I was gutted they got Lukaku. He's a beast and he'll instantly make them a much better side. I don't know whether James McCarthy is worth all the hype he gets; he's one of those players everyone seems to think is boss but who I've never really paid that much attention to. We'll find out now. And finally there's Gareth Barry, the fat arsed crab. I'm made up he's at Everton now as it gives me a better reason to hate him other than the whole 'not being Xabi Alonso' thing.

Going to back to United though, the way they spectacularly ballsed up the deal for the Bilbao lad was just brilliant and they also managed to make a pig's arse out of a deal for Real Madrid's Coentrao too. This kind of shit wouldn't have happened under Gill, but his replacement has had a nightmare summer. The fella is called Edward Woodward, which just adds to the 'LOL' factor. He's hardly 'the Equaliser' is he? I used to love that show when I was a kid and the name Edward Woodward always makes me smile as it reminds me of a boss joke I occasionally used to chat up birds back when I was alive. *"Why are there so many 'D's in Edward Woodward? Because he'd sound pretty stupid if his name was Ewar Woowar"* Hahahaha boss tha! You'd be surprised at how poor a strike rate I had with it though, we're talking Danny Welbeck levels of paucity. I put it down to women and their crap sense of humour....

It wasn't all bad for the Mancs I guess, they did keep hold of Rooney so they'll probably try and market that as being 'like a new signing'. Until January comes and insecure little Wayne gets needy again and Mourinho starts winding them up through the media and it starts all over. Rooney is sidelined at the moment of course with a horrific cut to his head. It's pretty gruesome, it looks like someone has taken a red marker pen to a potato. I could easily make a gag here about Rooney, bad gash, not for the first time etc but where's the sport in that? Like shooting fish in a barrel. Theo Walcott clearly isn't averse to taking the open goal though, describing Rooney's face as *'looking like something from a horror movie'*. I'm assuming he followed it up with *'and it's even worse now with that massive cut'*. According to reports the injury was delivered by the boot of Phil Jones in training. An 'accidental' collision they called it. Yeah right. Allow me to refer you back to something I wrote at the back end of last season...

"Jones is like the big, dumb kid who'd get picked on in school, but you'd have to be careful not to push him too far because if he lost his temper he'd do some real damage. Taunting these kids carried an element of risk, chances are you'd be fine but if he snapped and managed to get hold of you, it could get ugly as they invariably possessed what was referred to back then as 'mong strength'. As you can tell, political correctness wasn't big on school playgrounds back in the 80s. I remember back when I was in 1st year seniors, there was a huge ginger haired kid with glasses who had cruelly been dubbed 'Beaker' after the character on the Muppets. Now this cat was big, he was over six foot tall when he was 12, but he was generally easy going unless his temper snapped, in which case look out. Anyway, one day some lads were winding him up, taking the piss out of him to try and get a 'legger' from him. He may have been big, but wasn't the quickest unless he was in open spaces so generally he couldn't catch any of his tormentors as long as they avoided the playing fields. Except for this one day, when one of them tripped when climbing through a hole in the fence and got a size ten boot to the head for his troubles."

So yeah, I think we all know what happened here. Rooney was getting a 'legger' off Jones and got caught, didn't he? 'Accident' indeed.

For a while there Arsenal were also looking like they'd be massive transfer window losers, but then they made a big splash by signing the brilliant Mesut Ozil. I'm a bit deflated about this as I really like Ozil, he's class. He ain't worth £45m though, and unless he can play in goal or at centre half how is he going to solve Arsenal's problems? He's a luxury signing, pure and simple, but everyone loves a bit of luxury, right? I wish we had him.

Finally, Mourinho actually had the nerve to criticise other clubs for spending too much money. This despite Chelsea spending over £60m in what would be regarded as a very quiet summer by their standards. They only spent £60m this summer because they've spent about £300m in the previous two years. He's got some balls on him, not that anyone will pull him up on it as 'he's good for the game' and 'box office', apparently. They loaned out about 50 players too, which begs the question just how fucking big is their squad? Still, it's good for us I suppose, given that they're basically just our feeder club these days.

Premier League Round Up (September 14-15 2013)

I can't help but feel that this is all a bit beneath me now you know; writing about all of these games involving inferior teams that are just not relevant to us anymore. I almost pity all of these fools, fighting eachother for the scraps that fall from our 'top of the league' table. In years gone by I'd watch these games and reflect on how they may impact us, hoping the likes of Spurs and Everton would drop points so we might have a chance at cracking the top six. Now? Well I may as well be writing about the Championship for all the relevance most of these slapdicks have to us these days.

Still, these inferior teams do provide a source of amusement I suppose. We can point and laugh at them and their losing ways. Take Chelsea for instance. Those bums have lost two games in four days this week having drawn their previous two. That means they haven't won for FOUR GAMES!! I simply can't even imagine how that must feel. As for losing two in a week, well I don't even remember the last time we lost at all, let alone two in a week. How the other half live eh?

'The Special One' isn't doing anything particularly 'special' these days is he, though I suppose you could call loaning out Lukaku whilst keeping Torres is something only a 'special' person would do. Same with his substitutions at Goodison last weekend. Taking Cole off and moving Luiz to left back. Leaving Mikel on and moving Ramires to right back. Putting Torres on…. Genius. In fairness it's a game Chelsea should never have lost as they were vastly superior to the Blues in every area except taking their chances. It was just one of those games, it used to happen to us regularly before we became unbeatable. Everton are unbeaten too actually, but that won't last.

Moving on, and no-one is laughing at Arsenal any more are they? Well, apart from us as we're still above them, but no-one else is. Ozil made his debut at the Stadium of Light whilst they were again boosted by the absence of Mertesacker, who was absent through illness. Probably drank some sour milk, happens to him all the time that as it turns quicker than it takes the poor bastard to drag his lumbering arse off the couch into the kitchen. Sunderland included yet more players I'd never heard of before and Borini was only on the bench. Great that isn't it, he may as well have been sat on our bench as theirs, they'd better start picking him soon or we should bring him back here in January. I mean, it'd be bad enough for the lad to miss out on his title medal, but if he's not even getting a game for them then that would be such a waste.

Arsenal ended up with the points but it wasn't as straightforward as the scoreline suggests and they needed a big helping hand from the ref to do it. Ozil set up Giroud for an early goal but Sunderland almost hit back straight away when Diakite hit the bar. Walcott missed two one on ones that were laid on by the lively Ozil and he also squandered a headed chance that was put on a plate for him by Wilshere, who for once actually completed 90 minutes without getting sick or injured. Gardner equalised from the penalty spot after Koscielny dived in on Adam Johnson. He's crap isn't he? It's not just me, he is genuinley poo, right? Sunderland were doing well and had a few chances but Ramsay volleyed in to make it 2-1 before Sunderland got screwed over big time by Martin Atkinson, who failed to allow an advantage when Altidore was initially held back by Sagna but went through and scored. Atkinson obviously needs to wait and see how that develops before blowing the whistle, and Di Canio predictably went nuts and ended up being sent to the stands. In fairness, who could have predicted that Dozy Jozy would have scored? Ramsay's second of the day wrapped it up for the Gunners, who are staking an early claim to finish as runners up behind Brendan's big red machine.

Spurs looked lively against Norwich. New boy Christian Eriksen set up Sigurdsson for the first and he was very prominent throughout. Sigurdsson scored again just after the break when he converted a cross from Paulinho and Spurs are now sitting pretty alongside Arsenal. In our shadow.

Meanwhile, Moyes finally won at Old Trafford after 11 years of trying. Rooney had recovered from having a nasty gash on his head (insert own punchline) but was wearing some stupid head protection that made him look like a spud with a black rubber band around it. 'Screech' only made the bench, sitting there watching as *sniggers* Anderson was selected ahead of him. Amusingly, loads of United fans were wearing 'Fellaini' wigs. Well, that's what they were being marketed as, but they're basically 'scouser' wigs aren't they? Hilarious that, loads of mancs obliviously sitting round in scouser wigs, the clueless bastards. It's the equivalent of us showing up to games wearing black stone island jackets and doing inappropriate things with our sisters. Ashley Young was booked for diving and was later awarded a penalty for just falling over about two yards outside the box. To rub salt in Ian Holloway's wounds, the Palace defender involved (the lad who's name sounds like a Pokemon character) was also sent off. Absolute joke that. Van Persie scored the pen and Rooney added a free-kick after the break as United predictably ran out relatively comfortable winners.

It was a good day for the Premier League's other United too as Newcastle picked up a surprise three points at Villa Park. Ben Arfa's close range effort early on gave Pardew's side a half time advantage but Benteke headed in an equaliser midway through the 2nd half. Gouffran hit the winner when he tucked in a rebound after Guzan could only parry another effort by the impressive Ben Arfa. Agbonlahor missed an absolute sitter in this game. Perhaps he's been unsettled by the death threats he's been receiving from the 'One Directioners' after he clattered one of their heroes in Petrov's testimonial game last weekend. He deserves all the shit that comes his way after that to be honest. Not that I give a flying feck about the lad he kicked (Niall is my favourite), but because his actions caused some brummy knobheads to make a video about him which might be the worst thing I've ever seen in my entire life. I'm not exaggerating either. Seriously, stop what you're doing right now, go on youtube and search for "One Direction parody of Gabby Agbonlahor"......

See what I mean?? Shocking. Back to Newcastle though, I was thinking about their situation and how come they didn't sign anybody in the transfer window. It makes no sense, they appoint Kinnear to be in charge of bringing in players. If they didn't want to sign anyone why appoint a Director of Football? *"I can pick the phone up to any manager in the world"* he boldly declared. Yet they signed no-one, it was just really bizarre. Then I remembered that infamous radio interview he did, where he was getting all the Newcastle player's names wrong. Amemobi, Ben Afri, Yohan Kebab etc *"That's it"*, I thought, *"that's why they didn't get anyone..."*

ring ring *"Allo Allo?"*
"Awight Arsene, how much for Dick Bender?"
"Who iz zis? Zer is no Dick Bender ere, you av ze wrong number. Au revoir"

ring ring *"Hello, yer through te the chosen one"*
"Wotcha Moyesy son, it's Joe Kinnear. How much do you want for that Dan Woolyback?"
"I've nae got time for this crap Joe, there's still three players on ma list tha' havenae turned me down yet. Feck off"
"Moyesy? Moyesy? Cor, would you adam and eve it, his phone must be brown bread"

ring ring *"Waaaassssuuuppppppp hahaha"*
"Sorry Big Sam, I've dialled the wrong number mate. We'll catch up soon, yeah?"
"Ok Joe, laterz"

ring ring *"Hello?"*
"Brendan me awld china, what's the deal with that striker of yours, Franco Bolloni?"
"Ok Joe, I can assure you that I'll fight for my life to end this phonecall, ok?"

I'm only half joking with all that. I'm obviously not in favour of press phone tapping but imagine the hilarity if someone had bugged Kinnear's phone this summer.

Man City's stuttering start continued as they were held to a draw by Stoke who probably should have won the game and would have if they weren't handicapped by having Jon Walters, who had another 'Jon Walters' of a day in front of goal. Kenwynne Jones also had a bit of a 'Jon Walters' too, wasting three glorious chances to win it for Mark Hughes' men. City were poor again though.

Elsewhere, two of the Premier League new boys met at the KC Stadium as Hull and Cardiff played out a 1-1 draw. Curtis Davies put the home side ahead but Peter Whittingham's composed finish put the Bluebirds level on the hour mark and that's how it finished.

Steve Sidwell gave Fulham the lead against West Brom at Craven Cottage and Martin Jol's side had three goals ruled out for offside before conceding to Gareth McAuley's header deep into stoppage time. West Brom are terrible, Fulham aren't that much better but they have goals in their team, something the Baggies don't have.

Southampton and West Ham played out a goalless draw on Sunday. Not sure how this ended up the only game on the Sunday, Sky really dropped the ball on this one as who the hell wants to watch these two sides? Not me, I'm used to watching a top of the table team, I'm not wasting 90 minutes of my Sunday watching these losers. In fact, I didn't even waste so much as two minutes watching any 'highlights' from it. It finished 0-0, no-one cares, certainly not me.

And that just about wraps this week up. This was actually more fun than I thought it would be. In fact, writing from such a lofty perch whilst crapping on those beneath is fucking ace. It's certainly much more fun than slinging turds upwards at teams that are above us and out of reach, as when those turds don't reach their target they fall back down and tend to land on your own head, as I've found out to my cost at times when writing these things. It's boss being top of the tree and acting all superior though, so don't fuck this up for me Brendan, ok?

SWANSEA 2 LIVERPOOL 2

Competition - Premier League
Date - Mon 16 Sep 2013
Venue - The Liberty Stadium
Scorer(s) – Sturridge, Moses
Star Man – Martin Skrtel

Team: Mignolet; Wisdom (Toure), Skrtel, Sakho, Enrique; Lucas, Gerrard; Henderson, Coutinho (Aspas), Moses (Sterling); Sturridge:

Another game of two halves. Becoming a trend now isn't it? Some may say a worrying one but it seems almost ungrateful to be expressing concern after a ten points from four games start. Results wise we're doing brilliantly but performance wise there's a lot more still to come, so whilst the second half performances clearly need to improve significantly it's nice that we are able to work on that flaw from such a lofty position.

Until tonight I'd put the regressive second half displays mostly down to a tactical shift, with Rodgers opting for a more pragmatic 'have what we hold' approach. This time I just thought we completely got our arses handed to us by a vibrant Swansea and we looked dead on our feet for most of the second half. The lack of energy levels with and without the ball worried me and we could easily have lost this game. I wouldn't say it was a reality check as despite the league position I don't think anyone is getting carried away with what our actual 'reality' is, but if Rodgers was feeling comfortable about these second half performances simply because they'd resulted in maximum points then this game will hopefully force a bit of a rethink, as quite frankly we were fortunate to have escaped with a point from this in the end.

That being said, a point at Swansea isn't a bad result by any means and it did take us back to the top of the table. There are valid reasons as to why we haven't hit full speed yet and why we struggled against Swansea. For one thing we're still having to make do without the best player in the league, but we also had to make two enforced changes to the back four in this game having lost two players who had played key roles in three successive clean sheets. Agger apparently injured himself in the gym whilst trying to prevent a dumbell falling on his foot. My first thought when I heard that was who the hell let Jonjo back into the building, then I realised it was a piece of gym equipment. Agger's absence was a blow (not as much of a blow as Johnson's as the the drop off in replacement quality was far less obvious in the centre than it was on the right) as you don't want to be chopping and changing centre back pairings all the time and this was the fourth pairing we'd fielded in five games in league and cup this season.

A point is an acceptable result, it was more so the manner it was attained that raised concerns. But then this is a team that has finished no higher than 6th for the last four seasons so it's unrealistic to expect them to play well and win every week. If you're expectations are that high then this won't be the last disappointment you have this season.

We got off to the worst possible start when conceding a goal after just a couple of minutes. To make matters worse it was Shelvey who scored it. He tried not to celebrate but it was obviously difficult for him as the goal must have meant a lot. In the end he gave a kind half arsed wave to the Swansea fans but let's face it, anything is better than that lame 'goggles' celebration he does. Not quite as shit as Heskey's 'spinning the decks' one back in the day, but not far off. He wasn't celebrating a minute later when his sloppy backpass presented Sturridge with the equaliser. Whilst it was poor on Shelvey's part, Sturridge's anticipation was fantastic and the finish wasn't bad either.

The goal settled us down and we began to play some much better stuff. Coutinho, Sturridge and Moses started to link up more and Sturridge almost added a second after some brilliant play on the left by Moses, who somehow escaped the attention of two defenders in a confined space and delivered an inch perfect cross that Sturridge headed straight at Vorm. Moses was really starting to look lively now and he capped a fine debut display with an impressive strike after another great assist by Shelvey. Moses had a lot to do when he picked the ball up on halfway, but he was helped out by an unselfish run by Sturridge that opened things up for the on loan winger to cut inside and shoot low into the corner.

Swansea had a few chances themselves but Mignolet made some decent saves and the one time it looked like the keeper was in trouble, Skrtel saved the day with an absolutely fantastic last ditch block to prevent Bony scoring from close range. Brilliant defending, and I thought Skrtel was comfortably our best player on the night. There's a lot of competition for places at the back but if Rodgers picks his team solely based on form then Skrtel deserves to be in it based on what he's doing at present. Fair play to him, hopefully he can keep this up. Alongside him Sakho wasn't having the most comfortable of nights early on. I thought he had a decent enough game but he did have some less than convincing moments. He looked a little bit too eager to impress in the first half and dived into a few challenges when he'd have been better served staying on his feet. He hasn't played since May though, and you always have to make allowances for a new player in a new league, especially one that doesn't yet speak the language.

It was all going swimmingly up until half time. We had the lead, Sturridge and Moses were looking sharp and we looked in control of the game even if Swansea never really looked under that much pressure. Shelvey's head was completely up his arse after the two mistakes and even as the second half started he was still struggling to come to terms with it, continually shaking his head and muttering to himself. To his credit he put it behind him and played well after the break as Swansea dominated the ball (70% possession according to Sky) and Shelvey saw a lot of it. For whatever reason we just never got going. The opening 15 minutes of the half were incredibly scrappy with lots of stoppages and a couple of injuries. There was just no flow to the play and when Coutinho went off we lost any kind of cohesion we had. Basically, it all went to shit when the Brazilian left the field. He was the victim of a really snide, shithouse challenge from Williams, who was acting the twat all night really. He tried to square up to Gerrard in the first half, then had a go at Hendo early in the second and a minute later he clobbered Coutinho and was belatedly yellow carded.

Lucas was booked too after a flare up with Shelvey, who was also yellow carded for his part in it (which in fairness amounted to standing still and being pushed!). Lucas was pissed off that Swansea initially didn't put the ball out to allow Coutinho to receive treatment. Shelvey said something to him and Lucas instantly saw red, marching over and shoving his former team-mate in the chest. I'd love to know what Shelvey said to get Lucas so riled up, although he may just have been on the warpath after what happened to his boy Phil. Lucas is like Coutinho's dad, he's very protective of his boy and he wasn't happy at all seeing Coutinho in pain. Shame he didn't go and stick one on that twat Williams, it would have been worth a red card.

Unfortunately Coutinho couldn't continue and was replaced by Aspas. I had hoped that maybe coming off the bench rather than starting would help him make more of an impression. It didn't. The Spaniard is struggling to impose himself at the moment and without wanting to be too critical of a new player adjusting to a new country, he brought absolutely nothing to this game. He's lightweight, doesn't have the greatest technique in the world and he doesn't look comfortable playing as the withdrawn striker. From what I've seen he doesn't really seem suited to playing deeper. He looked good in pre-season when playing as a 9, but since Sturridge returned and Aspas has dropped deeper he hasn't looked as effective. The higher quality of opposition may also be a factor of course.

With Sturridge and Moses both starting to tire and Aspas struggling to get into the game, Swansea started to take total control of the ball. They equalised when Shelvey made an untracked run into space vacated by Sakho and flicked the ball into the path of Michu who had gotten in front of Wisdom to prod the ball past Mignolet. No more than they deserved and at that stage there was the very real possibility we could lose the game as we were chasing shadows. Mignolet wasn't exactly being peppered with shots but we never looked in control or comfortable.

We were just completely hanging on and offered virtually nothing in attack, save for one nice break by Aspas which came to nothing when he failed to pick out Sturridge in the centre. It was brutal stuff at times and I'd even compare it with watching Hodgson's England whenever they come up against any half decent side. They get into a defensive shell and are then unable to get out and keep inviting pressure by being unable to keep the ball. That's what we did at Swansea, we were hanging on for a point from the moment they equalised. That can't be by design as it goes against everything Rodgers stands for. There's being pragmatic and trying to play counter attack as we have been doing, then there's what we did in this second half. If it is tactical then it needs addressing, but my worry if that it's a fitness issue as that would be more difficult to put right. We have looked out on our feet at times but I'm hoping that's partly due to Sturridge not being fully fit and tiring late on in games. We've been unable to get out of our own half and keep possession of the ball, but that could be due to it not sticking up front as Sturridge's energy levels drop off. That makes it difficult for the entire team as they can't build any attacks and maintain any possession.

That's why I think Suarez coming back is going to make a huge difference to the whole team and it can't come quick enough. Only one more game now until he's back, and when that happens I'm sure we'll see a big improvement in the team's play because having him up there helping Sturridge should make it easier for everybody and give the opposition so much more to worry about. You have to give massive credit to Rodgers and the players for the record they've put together in his absence. He's missed nine games, seven of which have been won and two drawn. That's seriously impressive.

LIVERPOOL 0 SOUTHAMPTON 1

Competition - Premier League
Date - Sat 21 Sep 2013
Venue - Anfield
Scorer(s) -
Star Man - No-one

Team: Mignolet; Toure, Skrtel (Alberto), Agger (Enrique), Sakho; Lucas, Gerrard; Henderson, Aspas (Sterling), Moses; Sturridge:

Back to reality then. I wasn't expecting to remain top of the table indefinitely, but it didn't seem like too much of a stretch to think we might stay there for a few more weeks did it? Following the win over United the upcoming fixture list didn't look too taxing and there was a great opportunity to get a lot of points on the board before the more difficult games arrived. One point from the next six available was not what we were looking for and it's basically nullified that win over the Mancs now. If that result put us ahead of the curve, this loss has put us back behind it.

A draw at Swansea wasn't a bad result as long as it was followed up with three points at home to Southampton. Having lost to Southampton that point at Swansea doesn't look as palatable now. Six from six would have been great, four from six would have been pretty good, but one from six is absolute dogshit. More worrying than the points total is the performance level. If the second half at Swansea was alarming I don't even know what adjective you'd use to describe this. It wasn't surprising though. When I saw the starting line up I even said to my arl fella *"Four centre halves? Knowing us we'll probably concede from a corner."* Sod's law I guess.

On paper this is a game that we really have to be winning yet there was something completely predictable about this defeat. Injuries to key players such as Johnson and Coutinho, the continued absence of Suarez and the general lacklustre performances to this point all hinted at this being a banana skin game, especially as Southampton were the last team to beat us. I just don't get what Rodgers was trying to do at all withat team he started with. It's as though he's gotten carried away with this whole 'winning ugly' thing and set up to play for another 1-0. Winning ugly is not something you do by design, it's just something that good teams can do on the days when they don't play well.

When I think of Rodgers' footballing philosophy, the first thing that comes to mind is possession of the ball. I think about all those buzzwords and expressions we heard when he came in. *'Rest with the ball' 'death by football' 'the longest 90 minutes of the oppositions lives' 'pressing high up the pitch' 'six seconds to win back possession'* etc. Where the hell has that all gone? We aren't actually doing ANY of it now. Last year we were losing games but keeping the ball and generally playing well. You could see what we were trying to do and there was an identity developing. What's this team's identity? This year we've had better results but the possession football has disappeared, the work rate is terrible and the players look shattered after an hour of every game. It's been suggested to me that the 2nd half fatigue is due to a training regime that will see us flying in the second half of the season. I sure hope so. Aside from the finishing of Sturridge we've shown virtually nothing in an attacking sense all season, the hallmarks of what you expect from a Rodgers team have simply not been there so far. It's early in the season and in terms of points we're still in decent shape, but we're getting worse by the week it seems.

The way we ended this game was just horrible. A complete lack of any urgency or energy, it looked like they weren't even trying but I'm sure that's not the case. Southampton just looked fitter, stronger, better organised, more composed and a lot more confident. They did a number on us. Tactically Pocchettino seems to have Rodgers' card marked, although on this occasion Rodgers did as much to beat himself I'd say. Starting with four centre halves across the back line was bizarre, irrespective of whatever injuries may have played a part in it. To then lose to a goal from a set-piece whilst offering zero threat on our own set plays just makes the team selection even harder to stomach. Last season that selection simply would not have happened. If Enrique was unavailable Rodgers used Downing at full back rather than Agger because it allowed the team to continue playing the way he wanted to. Now? Well he's got more centre halves than he knows what to do with and it just looks like he compromised his philosophy to shoehorn them into the side. Toure actually did ok and showed more urgency and desire than anyone else in red. There's a limit to what you're going to get from him offensively though, which is acceptable if a) we have an attacking full back on the other flank, or b) we have someone in front of him who can provide width. We had neither. Sakho started at left back and in an attacking capacity was as much use as an ashtray on a motorbike. Not his fault, I mean what the hell could he be expected to do, he's hardly Roberto Carlos is he?

Moses apart (who kept cutting inside anyway) we had no width in the side so everything came through the centre, which Southampton were ready for. They bottled up the middle of the park and pressed us all over the pitch and we simply couldn't handle it. Southampton saw us coming, they knew exactly what we were going to do and were very clever in how they approached it. Some teams will just push three players right up onto our split centre halves and Lucas, which forces the keeper to kick long. Southampton didn't do that, they sat off just enough to make Mignolet think it was safe to play it short and then they quickly closed it down. It caused all kinds of problems, especially as Mignolet is suffering from what Reina did at the beginning of last season. He knows the manager wants him to avoid long clearances and play out from the back as much as possible and he's taking a few too many unnecessary risks as he adjusts to it. We didn't get punished for it but those kinds of incidents just unsettle everyone. The crowd get edgy and the players are effected by it too.

We never looked settled at any point in the game and the only times Boruc was called into action seemed to be from Gerrard free-kicks. In open play we did virtually nothing aside from one good run and shot from Moses in the first half that Boruc palmed away to safety. We should have had a penalty too when Sturridge was tripped by Lovren. It was a clear foul, even if it was a little soft. Sturridge was tripped and tried to keep his balance, perhaps if he'd just took a swandive he'd have got the decision. The referee's performance was so poor on the day he should have been wearing red as he'd have fit right in with us.

Our first half display wasn't great but it wasn't terrible either. The second half? Shite. And that's being kind. I'm struggling to think of a single positive from that second half. Not one. It was just awful, depressing stuff. Rodgers made a change at half time, hooking the once again completely ineffective Aspas and introducing Sterling in his place. Should have done that from the start, Aspas is not contributing anything. Without wanting to be too harsh on the guy it's like having ten men when he's playing at the moment.

Mignolet had to make a good save from Lallana after we'd fannied around with the ball at the back and eventually Agger's slack pass was intercepted. It was typical of the sloppy, casual approach we showed to the game. The Southampton goal was further evidence of it. Sloppy play from Skrtel led to a completely unnecessary throw in and then Toure immediately conceded a needless corner. From that corner Agger was outmuscled by Lovren, whose header beat Mignolet and also eluded Gerrard on the goal-line (he possibly could have done better). Rodgers then corrected another of his initial errors by putting Enrique on for Agger. I don't care if Enrique has a bit of an injury that 'needs managing', if that's the case then 'manage' it by leaving him out on Wednesday at Old Trafford, a game in which going with a more defensive option like Sakho would be more acceptable than in this one. When Enrique did come on he was absolutely dreadful, but that doesn't alter the fact he should have started.

We huffed and puffed after going behind but never really looked like getting back into it. In fact, Southampton carried more of a threat than we did and Mignolet had to make a brilliant triple save after the impressive Luke Shaw bundled his way into the box and got his shot away. As for us, well Gerrard had a free-kick saved, Sturridge curled a shot over and there were other incidents that could have led to chances but didn't, either due to a bad final ball or good Southampton defending.

The best opportunity came in stoppage time when Sturridge's first time ball over the top sent Sterling clear. The youngster had made a fine run through the centre but completely ruined it with a touch that a baby elephant would have been embarrassed about. Absolutely shocking and not like him at all as his first touch is usually exemplary. It summed up our day though.

You can't get away from it, this was massively deflating and it's difficult to put any kind of positive spin on it. The worry is that teams may now be looking at us and thinking if they can stay in the game for an hour they can then come on strong when we run out of steam. That's what has happened in every game we've played so far.

Injuries are definitely impacting on us right now, we don't have the greatest squad in the world but our first eleven will give anyone a game. At least we now have Suarez coming back, which should help morale as much as anything else. It will give everyone a boost having him back, it's just a pity that having done so well without him we fell at the final hurdle. The defeat doesn't mean we're no longer a top four contender and it doesn't mean the sky is falling in. I can't lie though, that's how it felt coming out of Anfield. There's long way still to go and we need to put together another unbeaten run like the one we've been one. More importantly though, we need to remember how to play 'Rodgeball' again as somewhere along the way we appear to have forgotten.

Premier League Round Up (21-22 September 2013)

I guess I tempted fate a bit too much last week eh? Got a little bit too cocky with our league position and jinxed us. Forget Brendan Rodgers' 'four centre halves' brain-fart or Daniel Agger's slack marking from corners, it was me running my mouth of in last week's round up that cost us that game against Southampton. Rest assured it won't happen again, in fact I'll probably go down the 'reverse jinx' route in future.

Anyway, it was a brutal weekend for us with all of our rivals picking up maximum points. Well almost all of them. Poor old Davey Moyes had an even worse weekend than we did, getting absolutely stuffed by the 'noisy neighbours'. I'd be lying if I said it was any consolation after we lost, but at least they didn't add to our misery by winning. Not even the presence of the great Robbie Fowler could make MOTD a more palatable experience this week though. As soon as the final whistle sounded at Anfield my first thought was *"ah fucking hell, I'm gonna have to watch MOTD and write that frigging round up."* It's taken me until the following Friday to do it, and I'm about as motivated for this as I was with school homework. You know that in five years in senior school I didn't actually do ANY homework at home? Not once. In five years. I'm quite proud of that record, although my parents probably shouldn't be. For five years they swallowed my bullshit about *"we all worked so hard in class today the teacher said we didn't need any homework"* or *"yeah I stayed in at lunch time to do my homework so I could play out when I got home"*. I did some of it by going into school 10 minutes early of a morning and copying from other people's work, and the rest of it I just didn't bother doing. Unsurprisingly the highest GCSE grade I came out of school with was a D, and I only got that due to being a naturally clever bastard. I was probably the laziest kid in that school. Hell, I may have been the laziest kid in ANY school. I was to schoolwork what Christian Ziege was to tracking back. Anyway, it's Friday morning and the next round of games will be upon us in a little over 24 hours, and this is feeling a lot like those mornings when I'd frantically just throw something together at ten to nine to hand in to the teacher just to avoid a lunchtime detention.

May as well get the most depressing one out of the way first I suppose, with the Blues coming from behind to win at West Ham. They're the only unbeaten side in the league now after we shit the bed against the Saints. Of course it's not going to las… wait… I mean, these fuckers are never going to lose a game ever again, are they? Bastards. *reverse jinx*

Ravel Morrison put the Hammers ahead with a deflected shot. He's probably the biggest turd in the Premier League. The whole criminal background and general cuntishness is bad enough, but having 'Ravel' on his shirt tops all of that. Humongous twat that lad is. Leighton Baines then scored twice from free-kicks either side of a Mark Noble penalty before Lukaku won it with a header he knew little about as he was clobbered by O'Brien before the ball had hit the net and was out cold for a few seconds. He's described as the 'new Drogba' and this was further evidence as he clearly shares the same glass jaw as arl Didier. It was the introduction of Lukaku that made all the difference. I was gutted when the Blues landed him and it's going to keep bothering me all season as he's fucking boss. Whilst it's hilarious that Chelsea allowed him to leave and kept the Torres, Eto'o and Ba, it's not so funny that he ended up at the Pit.

Razvan Rat might be the coolest name in the Premier League this season. Allardyce made me laugh afterwards. Noble had been sent off when conceding the free-kick for Baines' second goal and Fat Sam said he *"could see on his laptop that Noble played the ball"*. Ooo la de fucking da, showing off letting everyone know he's got a laptop. Surprised he didn't say 'iPad' actually. He's always buzzed off all that *"look at me, I embrace technology"* bullshit hasn't he? Remember when his power point presentation got him the Newcastle job? Now all it takes to get a high profile job with the Toon is a cockney accent and to buy Mike Ashley a bevvy in his local.

Speaking of the barcodes, Steve Bruce returned to his home town team with his Hull City side last weekend and sprung a bit of an upset. Hull aren't that bad are they? Or are Newcastle just even worse than I thought? Loic Remy put the Geordies in front with a goal on his full debut but Hull came right back into it and created a few chances before Robbie Brady eventually equalised. I'm thinking of ditching Gerrard from my fantasy team to put this lad in, which seems like a great idea right now but probably won't be matched by the reality of it. A bit like 'crumpet bread' I suppose. I saw this in the local bakers last week and was beside myself with excitement (sad I know, but I'm 40 now and don't get out much these days). I love dead thick bread and I love crumpets, so the two of them merged together? How could it not be fucking incredible? I didn't even dare contemplate the enormity of it all, I just wanted to get home and fire up the toaster. What a huge letdown though, turns out it was basically just rubbery bread. Gutted.

Anyway, Newcastle's defending was fucking grim once again, Mathieu Debuchy has the positional sense of a lemming on smack. They're just awful at the back but they can score goals and Remy will do well if he can stay fit. He restored their lead a minute before the break but it all went wrong for them in the second half. Elmohamady headed Hull back onto level terms a couple of minutes after the restart and Aluko's brilliant volley gave them the points. Remy missed an absolute sitter in stoppage time. Still, he said afterwards that he was *"very appy. I'm here to score goals"* Firstly, how come the French are always *"very appy"* and yet they are rarely smiling when they say it? Secondly, the fact he's happy for scoring two even though he missed a sitter and they lost the game says a lot about him I'd say.

Don't get me wrong, in my younger days I didn't always have a team first mentality myself. If I did my job and scored goals I didn't give a shit if my team lost, as it was clearly someone else's fault other than mine and therefore not my problem. I've grown as a person since then and I'm much more team orientated these days, but not even the younger me would have had the balls to declare myself *"very appy"* after a loss if I'd missed a sitter like that at the end. There's no 'I' in team, but there is a 'U' in cunt, and Loic Remy came across as a right self centred cunt in that interview.

So a great day for Hull but poor old Danny Graham though, that lad just can't buy a goal and I don't think he's scored since he left Swansea. He looked a useful player when he was with the Swans too, but now he's turned into Danny Welbeck, the poor bastard. This probably goes against the grain as he's an easy target, what with his bloated head and old woman face, not to mention his Manchester United background and that, but I'll say it: I quite like Steve Bruce, he's one of the good guys. He does say *"wor"* an awful lot though doesn't he? *"we're not kidding worselves" "we've got a really good player on wor hands" "take wor chances"*…. He's the only Geordie I know that actually talks like that.

Things go from bad to worse for his old club though. Sunderland got dicked by West Brom on Saturday and predictably Di Canio found himself sleeping with the fishes on Monday. Metaphorically speaking I mean, he didn't actually get whacked although there would have been no shortage of volunteers in the Mackem dressing room if the board had wanted to go down that road. After the game he walked over to the fans and was gesticulating and trying to communicate with them via sign language whilst many of them hurled abuse his way. Completely bizarre it was, but compulsive viewing all the same. He's a complete head the ball isn't he? Dead funny though, and it's kind of like the Balotelli thing, the best thing about him is that he's someone else's problem. Or at least, he was. The Premier League will be a duller place without him, that's for sure.

I read that Di Canio had a meeting with the squad on Sunday and told them if they wanted him gone they should go to the board and say so, as they'd probably get their wish. Maybe he thought he was being clever and called their bluff, or maybe he'd simply had enough. The players needed no second invitation anyway, they went scuttling off to the board and Di Canio was gone quicker than you can say *"even more unpopular than that knob Mancini"*. The delegation was reportedly led by John O'Shea and Wes Brown. Fucking manc rats, like either those two have made any kind of impression since joining Sunderland. Wes Brown's bean (see what I did there?) stealing a living since he moved there and the only time I remember O'Shea doing anything was when he was scoring own goals or being mullered by Di Canio for conceding a pen and getting himself sent off. I hate the concept of player power and when you hear about some of the antics pulled by players at Sunderland it's hard not to feel some empathy with Di Canio's position, but let's face it the guy's a complete fucking whackjob and you can't really blame the players for wanting him out. Imagine having him as a boss??? Even after a couple of weeks in the job it was obvious this was where it was headed and I don't think anyone thought he'd still be there by Christmas. He's completely nuts, apparently he even demanded regular blood and urine tests from the players, so at least it wasn't just in his TV interviews that he was taking the piss out of them. Sunderland will be better off without him, it's just a shame they could-n't have waited another week before pulling the trigger on him. Typical that, every year we seem to end up having to come up against sides boosted by that whole 'new manager' syndrome.

Elsewhere, Chelsea beat Fulham but didn't pull up any trees in doing so. Mata and Luiz couldn't even make the bench and Mourinho had said some fairly unflattering things about Mata in the build up to the game, comparing him unfavourably with Oscar and insisting that the Brazilian is his starting number 10, not Mata. Maybe it's just me, but I'm not hav-ing Oscar at all. I'm obviously not saying he's shit, but he's defo not what he's cracked up to be and he just looks like a bad dweeb who should be carrying a satchel and thermos rather than playing football. How anyone could pick him over Mata is beyond me, and if it was any other manager doing it Chelsea fans would be frantically scribbling their disap-proval on A4 pieces of paper and holding them up at the game. Actually one of them did, *"JOSE! Mata belongs on the FIELD not the BENCH"* Well that told the Special One didn't it? Jon Obi Mikel actually scored, can you fuckin' believe that shit? Incredible scenes. I really don't know what to say about that other than that this adds him to the list of Chelsea players more likely to score a Premier League goal than Fernando Torres.

Norwich against Villa was always going to be a tight game, there's very little between these sides and it could have gone either way. Snodgrass missed a pen for the home side, which was surprising as surely Wolf Van Winkel should have been taking that? Villa looked to be in trouble when Benteke limped off early on but his replacement Kozak wast-ed no time in making his mark, scoring within seconds of coming on. Norwich had chances to equalise but Guzan was in top form and Villa held on.

Onto Sunday now, and Spurs were heading for a draw at Cardiff which wouldn't have been a terrible result for them coming off the back of a midweek European game. I actually thought it had ended in a draw until watching MOTD2 just now and seeing Paulinho score a late winner. I had to rewrite my intro after that, and it made a bad weekend even worse. I don't even know where we are in the league table, I daren't look. I did read somewhere that we could be as low as 12th by the time we face Sunderland. That can't be true, surely? Spurs caught a huge break in this game when Lloris handled just outside the box but got away with it and Cardiff missed a glorious chance in the last minute when Gunnarsson blazed over the bar. Shite that Gunnarsson, even Arsenal mascot Gunnersaurus would have made a better fist of it than that. Fuckin' Spurs.

Arsenal won again too. A fairly routine victory over Stoke at the Emirates. Oh how we laughed when they lost to Villa. And oh how they've shoved that laughter right back down our throats by winning every game since. Bastards. Ramsay scored his 7th goal in 8 games and then shushed the fans. He's just like Stewart Downing, aside from the 7 goals in 8 thing. Geoff Cameron equalised for Stoke but any hopes of Arsenal dropping points were ended when Mertesacker headed them back in front. There was a real element of good for-tune about the goal, as he was actually making his way forward for a corner they'd won two minutes earlier, it just took the slow twat that long to get into the box that when he did no-one picked him up. Sagna headed Arsenal's third and you'd have got long odds indeed on them beating Stoke with three goals from set-pieces. Tony Pulis will be spinning in his grave about that.

Swansea were coming off a huge win at Valencia in the Europa League and a trip to Palace had 'letdown' written all over it. Credit to them though, they got the job done and their letdown didn't arrive until a few days later when they were hammered by Birmingham in the league cup. Shelvey set up Michu for the opener after just two minutes and Dyer added a second after the break. Getting sick of that Wilfried Bony chump though, I never did get round to kicking him out of my fantasy team for having his first name on his shirt, and the twat has responded to that reprieve by contributing absolutely zilch. No goals, no assists, nothing. If I wasn't such a lazy bastard I'd have ditched him weeks ago. One day Wilfried, one day.

The Manchester derby was the game all eyes were on last weekend and City made a pretty emphatic statement with that performance. United were awful until rallying late on as City eased off. It's been a strange start to the season for all the top sides. City have had games where they've been garbage, and then they produce something like this and look like world beaters. You have to temper it by pointing out it was only David Moyes they beat, but still, this was a real message sent out by City. To think that this time last week we were above them. It will be a long, long time before that's the case again. *reverse jinx*

MANCHESTER UNITED 1 LIVERPOOL 0

Competition - League Cup
Date - Wed 25 Sep 2013
Venue - Old Trafford
Scorer(s) –
Star Man – Kolo Toure

Team: Mignolet; Toure, Skrtel, Sakho; Henderson, Lucas (Kelly), Gerrard, Enrique; Moses (Sterling), Suarez, Sturridge:

I could almost feel my blood pressure rising with each passing minute of this one. It wasn't that we didn't play well - we controlled the game for the most part and never looked under any real pressure - but the complete hopelessness in the final third was making me want to break things. Had I been in my own house rather than my parents I may well have done as I was as pissed off as I've been in a long time.

I was like that throughout most of the game, each poor touch, sloppy pass and bad decision just piled on the anger and frustration and by the final whistle I was seriously struggling to keep my temper in check. The reason for my ire was not so much that we were losing at Old Trafford - let's face it that's what we do - it was that this game should have bucked that trend as it was there for the taking. And we fucking blew it.

We didn't start well but once we got used to the change in formation and everyone settled down we generally bossed the game. On so many occasions we worked our-selves neatly into situations where we could have hurt them but each time it completely fell apart in the final third. We weren't missing chances, it rarely got to that point because every time the opening was there to create a clear goalscoring opportunity someone messed it up with a poor touch, a terrible pass or the wrong decision.

Suarez, Sturridge and Moses were the main culprits. Suarez actually played very well overall all things considered, but in the first half everything he did was just a little off. Well maybe not everything, he hasn't lost anything in terms of his cunning and rule bending ability, as he showed when deceiving Rooney into ducking under a high ball allowing it to land perfectly at his own feet. The reaction of Giggs gave it away, he immediately went complaining to the ref about something (just for a change). Suarez had obviously given Rooney a shout to leave it, the little scoundrel.

So the brain was certainly up to speed, but the feet and body were not quite able to match it. We're talking really small margins; a slightly heavy touch, a fractionally under-hit pass, just being a split second too slow when he was taking people on... All perfectly understandable given the length of time he's been out, and had this been his second or third game back rather than his first I'm sure he'd have made United suffer. I wouldn't be at all surprised to see him and Sturridge destroy Sunderland at the weekend, as with a little more sharpness in this game they could have taken United to the cleaners. You could see in the second half that Suarez was finding his match legs again and he was a real menace. The 3-4-1-2 formation we played suited him well as it meant neither he nor Sturridge had to play wide or deep or with defensive responsibilities. They could both just play as frontmen and I thought they linked up well at times, it just all tended to fall apart when it reached the penalty area. Sturridge was not on his game at all. The ball was getting stuck under his feet too much and he was strangely hesitant at times in the penalty area. Had he been at his sharpest we could have battered United, but we just wasted so many promising situations.

United had some opportunities too, mainly in the opening minutes as our players adjusted to the new system. Sakho had a shocking first couple of minutes, giving the ball away cheaply twice and putting his team under pressure. After that nervy start though I thought he had an excellent game. Toure and Skrtel were both impressive too, and the back three as a whole looked solid barring one or two instances in the second half when United threatened on the break and from Rooney free-kicks. You're not going to keep a team like United completely quiet though, they'll always create some chances, especially at home. Overall defensively we handled them very well, with the exception of the goal of course, which I'll get to shortly.

The first half performance was good aside from the wastefulness of the forward players. Lucas and Gerrard bossed the midfield and some of the football to get us into the final third was as good as we've produced all season. It's just a shame it was not matched by the play when we got there. That will come I'm sure, but it doesn't do us any good right now as we've been knocked out of one of the only two competitions we had any chance of winning. Moses is a wide player but he has played centrally before so it's not a completely foreign role to him. He did ok, but that position is vital in this formation. It's the position Steve McManaman filled when we played this way under Roy Evans and Moses should be thriving in it. Maybe in time he will do (unlikely considering he'll have to hold off Coutinho for the position) but he was just a bit too 'safe' for me in this game. Aside from the diving header after the break, I can't remember anything he did of any note and he seemed very reluctant to try and impose himself on the game and commit people. I'd say he's the one player in the starting line up that probably wasn't helped by the change in formation. 4-3-3 or 4-2-3-1 etc suits him more as he can play wide. Everybody else, however, benefits greatly from the three at the back system we played in this game. It plays to our strengths and nullifies our weaknesses.

There were only two things wrong in this game, the sloppy defending of the set-piece that United scored from and the wastefulness of the frontmen when in promising situations. Neither of those can be attributed to the formation. Midfield is definitely a problem at the moment though. Both Lucas and Gerrard faded after the break once again and to me it looked like the skipper was visibly pacing himself so he could get through the 90 minutes. In the first half the pair were outstanding, pressing the ball and winning back possession quickly, but that dropped off after the break. This change in formation might allow Rodgers to get more energy into the middle in the form of Henderson or possibly even Allen without having to worry too much about being exposed through the centre. It's certainly something he needs to persevere with I think, especially with the wealth of central defenders at his disposal now.

We were comfortably the better side in the second half and did have chances to score, but that ridiculous goal conceded seconds after half time proved decisive. You just can't concede goals that cheaply against good sides, it's unforgivable but we've made a habit of it at Old Trafford. Every year we go there and concede a goal to a set piece. Every fucking year. Without fail. It's been going on for over a decade. Can we not bring Houllier back just to manage games at Old Trafford? Enrique did a lot of things well in this game; his recovery speed and one on one defending got us out of a number of potentially problematic situations and he created a couple of opportunities in attacking areas too. It wasn't that he had a bad game as such, but you simply can't lose your man like that in the box, especially when it's the most clinical finisher on the field.

I didn't think Gerrard covered himself in glory either, he seemed to misjudge the flight of the ball and allowed it to drop over his head, but Enrique simply has to do a better job there. Defending corners continues to be a huge issue for us. There's nothing more galling than defending well and restricting teams to very few opportunities only to let in a soft goal from a corner. We do it all the frigging time, it's utterly demoralising. I knew when that goal went in we weren't coming back. Don't get me wrong, I hoped that we'd get something but I didn't truly believe we would. My confidence in this team has been badly shaken in recent weeks.

The chances were there to get back into it, Henderson missed a sitter, Moses headed straight at De Gea when he should have scored, Toure also missed a great chance and Surarez twice shot wide when he could have done better. Sturridge also failed to take advantage of good situations in the box and all in all it was a completely demoralising, frustrating night. The one crumb of comfort to take from it, and it is just a crumb as this one really hurts, is that the performance was probably the best we've produced since the Stoke game. It was far from perfect, but there were glimpses of something and hopefully when Suarez is fully up to speed (and the second half performance suggests he's more or less there already) and Coutinho and Johnson return to the line up we will start to produce more consistently good performances and continue to pick up points.

It's not all doom and gloom, but it is pretty damn annoying what's happening at the moment, and I'm also extremely pissed off that we allowed Moyes to wriggle off the hook he was on after their indifferent start and weekend humiliation at City. There was a real opportunity for us to pile on the misery for Gollum but we failed to take it and now only have one chance left at lifting a trophy this season.

Final observations: Kolo Toure was immense. I love his enthusiasm and desire to succeed. I also enjoyed Henderson getting up in the grill of Giggs. The old man (wait, he's the same age as me. Am I now officially 'old' too? I guess I am. Fuck!) had spent the entire night trying to referee the game and Henderson eventually snapped, giving him a right mouthful. Probably wasn't the ideal time to do it though, the clock was ticking and all it achieved was to waste precious seconds which were not added on at the end (3 minutes? Are you kidding me?).

Predictably, United's fans disgraced themselves again with their Hillsborough and Heysel chanting, the particular lowlight being when thousands of them sang *"The Sun was right, you're murderers"*. That was in response to *"Fergie's right, your fans are shite"*. Hardly a justified reaction really, was it? Every club has it's knobheads of course, including us. You won't heard thousands on the Kop chanting about Munich though and if you did you can be damn sure there'd be one hell of a media shitstorm about it. Yet these twats are given free reign to chant that in such large numbers without being brought to task by anyone in the national media? Fucking ballbags. You stay classy Manchester.

SUNDERLAND 1 LIVERPOOL 3

Competition - Premier League
Date - Sun 29 Sep 2013
Venue - Stadium of Light
Scorer(s) – Sturridge, Suarez (2)
Star Man – Daniel Sturridge

Team: Mignolet; Toure, Skrtel, Sakho; Henderson, Lucas, Gerrard, Enrique; Moses (Sterling); Suarez, Sturridge:

Back in business then. Last week's loss obviously hurt us but the results this weekend have ensured that it's not as damaging as it could have been. This wasn't the greatest performance you'll ever see, it was patchy at best and the game was in the balance right up until Suarez finished them off on the break late on, but it was good enough and it was an improvement on most of what we've seen so far this season. It's early days but the new formation does look promising and having Suarez back is going to make a huge difference, as we knew it would. That's why he was forced to stay.

Sunderland have been awful this season but with Di Canio now gone they were always going to raise their game. They battled hard and never let their heads drop even when they went 2-0 down and for a spell in the second half they were really pushing for an equaliser. We stood up to it well though and then killed them off on the break, which is exactly what you want your side to be able to do in that situation. We didn't start the game particularly well but we certainly finished it in style and given our 2nd half struggles this season that has to be seen as a positive. We probably played our best football of the game when Sunderland got back to 2-1, which again is a positive as the momentum could have shifted in their favour after that.

This was one of those trap games where we could have come a cropper. With so many results going our way the day before it would have been typical of us to not capitalise on it, so to come away with three points is very pleasing. It's not easy to win away games in the Premier League. Unless you're Arsenal of course, in which case it seems like a piece of piss. What's up with that by the way?

Coming off two successive defeats we needed to win this game and win it we did. The extra quality we had up front proved to be the difference, which will hopefully prove to be the case more often than not from now on. All season we've been saying that having Suarez back would make a big difference and this is exactly why. We've been finding goals hard to come by, Sturridge has been the only one scoring and as a result all of our games have been extremely close. You throw Suarez into the equation and that extra firepower makes things a lot easier for us, but just as significantly, his general play, movement and constant demanding of the ball allows us to keep possession better in the opposing half and that was the main reason for this improved 2nd half showing. You can play the ball up to him and he won't lose it which allows the whole team to play higher up the pitch and not get penned back as we have been doing. Sturridge will be better too just from having Suarez up there with him. The sky is the limit for these two as a pairing, Sturridge is generally regarded as a goalscorer but there's far more to his game than that and he showed it once again in this game by not only getting his now customary goal, but also laying two on a plate for his strike partner with unselfish play.

There's some discussion as to whether his opening goal should have stood as there was a question of handball about it. Technically it did go in off his arm, but his arm was right by his side and it was 'ball to hand' as opposed to 'hand to ball'. If you're a defender and your arm is by your side like that and the ball strikes it, it's not a penalty. So why is this any different? Besides, on first viewing it looked like he either headed it in or it hit his shoulder. It's asking a lot of the officials to spot something like that. I've even heard some idiots asking why Sturridge didn't own up to it. He's not had the witch hunt that Suarez had after Mansfield, obviously, but there are still people questioning whether he should have told the officials it went in off his arm. Fucking hell, the stupidity of some knows no bounds does it?

Up until that point there hadn't been much in the game at all and I'd been quite disappointed with our play. That disappointment was tempered by the acceptance that this was always going to be a tricky fixture, especially early on as they'd need to have the sting taken out of them. The goal should have done that but Sunderland's heads never dropped and Larsson went close to an equaliser with a brilliant free-kick that hit the bar.

Sunderland kept plugging away even after we doubled our lead with a truly brilliant goal. Gerrard's glorious sweeping crossfield ball was killed stone dead by Sturridge, who then surged into the box and skinned his man before rolling a perfect ball across the six yard box to give Suarez a tap in. Stunning football. Under Di Canio perhaps Sunderland would have completely folded, but even at 2-0 down they still posed a threat. Mignolet made a brilliant save with his right boot to deny Gardner and Adam Johnson shot inches over from a after Suarez had given the ball away on the edge of his own penalty area. Thank God Johnson didn't score from that, who knows what Suarez would have done; he was still beating himself up about it anyway as he left the field at half time.

Aside from the Gardner chance, pretty much everything Sunderland had threatened us with had been from distance. Generally that's not a problem but you can't keep giving people open looks from 25 yards and we paid the penalty for that when Lucas didn't do a good enough job of closing off the space in front of Ki and Mignolet could only parry the shot straight to Giaccherini who slotted the rebound. Mignolet probably could have done better with it but in his defence he was partially unsighted as the ball went through the legs of Skrtel and arrived at him quickly. I feared the worst when that went in but we actually dealt with them pretty well after that. Our passing and possession seemed to improve and although they were giving it their all I can only remember Mignolet having to make one real save of note, just about keeping out a cross shot from Gardner.

We were very wasteful again in the final third though. Not as bad as we were against United the other night but it wasn't good. Henderson was especially poor, he got himself into some terrific positions but his crossing was dire. Moses didn't offer enough either. He was ok, nothing special but we need more from that position and he was eventually subbed for Sterling with 15 minutes to go. That was a brave change from Rodgers, I'm sure I wasn't the only one thinking Sterling would just go and play in the role Moses had been in, but instead he went to right wing back and Henderson went central. Moving Hendo inside was sensible - we needed to shore things up and get some extra running power in there - but with a 2-1 lead to protect the obvious move would have been Wisdom to go to wing back. The thing is, Henderson had been getting acres of space out there and was often the spare man any time we attacked. Sterling was more equipped to exploit that than Wisdom, so fair play to Rodgers for that bold move.

Sunderland were lumping it forward to Altidore at every opportunity but Skrtel dealt with him well whilst Sakho and Toure were both outstanding either side of him. Toure was a threat rampaging forward again too and it needed a great save from their keeper to prevent him scoring a spectacular goal after a typically powerful run. He's ace isn't he?

Suarez had a couple of chances that he failed to take but he would eventually make the game safe with a classic counter attacking goal. He led the break and picked out Sturridge on the left. Henderson made a lung bursting sprint almost the whole length of the field into the box which dragged defenders away and allowed Sturridge to roll the ball across to an unmarked Suarez who gleefully tapped in to get us back to winning ways.

Premier League Round Up (28-29 September 2013)

This weekend was only an Arsenal defeat away from being 'the Proclaimers'. It's difficult to get any better than that, obviously, I mean who's better than the Proclaimers? Nobody, that's who. This was still one hell of a weekend though, in fact I'd go as far as to call it the Bon Jovi of weekends.

We won, United lost at home to West brom, City lost away to a Villa side missing it's two best players, Chelsea and Spurs took points off eachother and Torres got sent off. Everton did their best to ruin it by winning on Monday night, but not even that could take the shine of what was one hell of a weekend for Kopites.

May as well start at Old Trafford where mass hilarity ensued as Moyes continued his less than stellar start by losing to the Baggies. The 'Chosen One' might not make it until Christmas at this rate, although Van Persie coming back will probably just about get them enough points to keep him in the job a bit longer. Hopefully anyway, I'd hate to see this ended prematurely before it has a chance to play out to it's full comedic effect. Imagine if 'Only Fools & Horses' had been scrapped after the first series? Doesn't even bear thinking about, and that's how I feel about this Moyes situation. Them losing at home to West Brom and being 12th in the table after six games is hilarious, but we've still got the 'Jolly Boys Outing', 'Blow up dolls' & 'Groovy Gang' episodes plus numerous hilarious Christmas specials to look forward to, assuming the Glazers don't decide to pull the plug on Fergie's little experiment. Slur insisted this week that Moyes was the right appointment, but he would, wouldn't he, given that he made the appointment. Let's hope the Glazers allow him to choose Moyes' eventual replacement too. Maybe all that arse kissing will finally pay off for the Hodge?

United haven't scored a league goal from open play since the opening day of the season. Their goals have all been from set-pieces, usually as a result of some twat taking a dive. Even the goal they scored against West Brom was a complete fluke; Rooney's free-kick from out wide was a cross that sneaked in after no-one got a touch on it and the keeper got caught flat footed. Moyes spent 11 years trying to get Everton above Manchester United in the league, and it looks like he's finally going to succeed this year.

West Brom though, where did that come from? I know it was only United they were playing and everyone is beating them these days, but still. The Baggies looked like relegation candidates early on but this was a good performance and that Amalfitano fella looks handy. His goal was brilliant, evoking memories of Paolo Wanchope's mad goal at Old Trafford all those years ago. The kid who scored the second goal is only on £850 a week apparently. His agent will be adding extra noughts to his contract demands quicker than you can say 'Raheem Sterling'.

Moyes is saying he can handle the pressure as he's been in this situation before with Everton and Preston!! Wow. That's like not being worried about falling into the lion enclosure at the zoo because you had a pet cat when you were a kid. Moyes is very much like Hodgson; a master at lowering expectations. Give him a couple of months and he'll have United fans thinking a top four spot will be a great achievement for them. Considering the position they may be in soon, it probably would be. On the subject of

Hodgson, he won't exactly be Mr Popular at United this week after dropping Ashley Young from the England squad. Well, I say dropped, but Roy sees it differently: *"I don't like to use the word 'dropped'. He just fell outside the 23, I guess ..."* Hahaha love it! No doubt Moyes will be taking notes there, if only he'd thought of that approach last weekend. *"I don't like to use the word 'lost'. We just didn't win. Or draw."*

The natives are definitely restless in the red half of Mancland though. My mate John often likes to have a browse on the forums of other teams to see what their fans are thinking, and he sent me a text with a comment made by a United fan about Fellaini. The pointy elbowed Belgian has been getting caned on there apparently, with one irate fan posting: *"He makes me wish I was being raped by a disease ridden camel just so that I don't have to watch him play for us"* Curious choice of words. If he doesn't want to watch Fellaini playing, he could just, y'know, not watch him play? Or if that's too difficult, then surely he could wish for something a lot less gruesome to prevent him watching? For example, *"He makes me wish that I get stuck in traffic and miss the game just so I don't have to watch him play for us"*. One almost gets the impression that this particular Mancunian WANTS to be raped by a disease ridden camel. They're a strange breed aren't they? Mancs I mean, not disease ridden camels.

There's a lot of pissed off people in that part of the world right now, both City and United fans are giving a whole new meaning to the expression 'Madchester' this week. Who's more pissed off; United after the couple of weeks they've had, or City after losing to Villa and then getting steamrollered by Bayern? I'd say United, as losing to Bayern is no disgrace (even when you've spent as much as City have) and besides, it was only about ten days or so that City were bumming United like... well like a disease ridden camel. Still, them losing at Villa was one hell of a shock given how sensational Pellegrini's men had looked a week earlier. Mind you, they were only playing United I suppose. Nevertheless, losing to a Villa side that was without both Benteke and Agbonlahor is not something I think anybody saw coming, not even Paul Lambert. I was watching the Chelsea - Spurs game with my dad and when the team news from Villa Park flashed up on the screen I said to him *"Villa have got absolutely zero chance of doing anything today. They might lose by six."* Shows what I know. Again.

City went ahead through Toure from a corner just on half time. El Ahmadi levelled but City regained their lead through Dzeko, again from a corner. Then two goals in three minutes turned the game on it's head, as a terrific free-kick by Bacuna was followed by a goal from Weimann, who took advantage of awful defending and hesitant goalkeeping from Hart to win it for the Brummies. I still can't believe Villa managed to beat ANYBODY without Benteke and Agbonlahor, let alone in-form City. Fair play to them. The league has been mad this year, so unpredictable. I mean, you just never know what to expect. United lose at home to West Brom, City beaten by a depleted Villa and Fernando Torres actually looking sharp, aggressive and playing really well. As I said, just a crazy weekend.

Of course Torres' mini renaissance was cut short by a ridiculously harsh red card, but he can't really have any complaints given the shit he'd gotten away with earlier. The scratch was a cowardly, nasty, sly, shithouse thing to do. It was straight out of the South American street footballer's handbook, and I can imagine Luis sat at home nodding his approval as he watched. Torres probably learnt that from Mascherano as that's the kind of sneaky stunt he'd pull (damn, I miss that crazy little fucker). Smile and pat someone on the cheek, make it look nice and cordial and then BAM!! Out come the claws. Classic South American behaviour, and not something usually associated with Torres. This is the same fella remember that was completely punked by Rio Ferdinand last year and did NOTHING about it, just sitting on the floor looking all helpless. Yet the fire was back in his belly in this game, the scratching obviously wasn't good and as much as I don't like him these days, it was good to see he still has a little bit of the old fight still in him. It was even better seeing him red carded later on of course, especially as in the second half of that game he'd actually started to look like the player Chelsea thought they were getting when they threw £50m our way. He was a real menace and had a running battle with Vertonghen, who eventually succeeded in getting him sent off with some awful playacting. You could argue he was justified in doing that after the earlier clawing incident, but he'd no doubt have done what he did regardless of what had gone down earlier. Besides, Torres wasn't blameless either, he also went down holding his face even though there was no contact to either of their heads. They tried to cheat eachother and Torres just got outcheated.

I thought he'd get done by the FA for the scratch though. The officials can't be blamed for not spotting that. It's almost impossible for them to know what happened there and that's why the FA should have stepped in. I'm not even sure why they didn't, some kind of ridiculous technicality but I couldn't even be arsed reading about it. Absolute joke of an organisation. Still, the football Gods decided to intervene and Torres suffered an injury in Chelsea's midweek game in Europe. He'll probably miss around four games now, which was the suspension he would have been looking at. I believe that's called 'karma', bitch. Wait, am I allowed to say that? I'm not sure I am as Robbie Fowler was forced to apologise on BBC after saying Torres and Vertonghen were *"acting like a couple of girls"*. Things are getting out of hand now aren't they? In years gone by, the expression would have been *"acting like a couple of puffs"* which is obviously - and understandably - not allowed now either, but if you can't say *"acting like a couple of girls"* then what actually are you supposed to say to describe such an incident? Seriously what are you meant to say? Not acting very manly also implies that it's acting like a female, which is not cool anymore. Is it ok to say *'wimp'*, or will wimps be offended by it? Does anyone care if wimps are offended, I mean let's face it, what are they gonna do? Go and cry in a corner probably, they are wimps after all. How about *'big girl's blouse'*, is that ok or is that offensive to big girls? What if it's referring to a big blouse on a regular sized girl though? Is that not ok? I hate the expression *'PC gone mad'*, but what happened to Fowler was *'PC gone batshit crazy'*.

Speaking of batshit crazy, what the hell is going on in the not so special one's head? Not content with the insanity of repeatedly overlooking his best player for reasons known only to himself, he then came out with this in relation to what Vertonghen did; *"Some foreign players when they come to England still keep their culture and it's a disgrace you do that to a person from your same job. I think it's a disgrace."* He had a straight face when he said it too, the fucking hypocritical loon.

My boy AVB continues to go up in my estimations though. Not only did he say in the build up to the game that he thinks Mourinho is a bad helmet (possibly not his EXACT words) but look at what he said about the sending off: *"It was difficult for the referee to judge. I don't think Fernando went in as nasty as to deserve a sending off. The referee decided both players went for the ball in an aggressive way, but it was probably an unfair sending off"*. I said when he was at Chelsea that he was too classy for them, but the balance of the universe has well and truly been restored now that gobshite Mourinho is back there.

Moving on, and Hull City won again. Robbie Brady's penalty was enough to see off toothless West Ham. Guess who put Brady in his fantasy team last week? Yep, this guy. When I resort to boring you with talk about fantasy footy that's probably a sign that it's time to move on, so that's what I'll do.

Fulham are a bit of a mess at the moment aren't they? Losing at home to Cardiff should set alarm bells ringing and Martin Jol's arse must be on fire as he's well and truly on the hot seat now. He may only get another game or two to turn this around, which is a shame he's fucking aweshome. Caulker headed Cardiff in front, my boy Bryan Ruiz scored a pearler to get Fulham back into it but some lad I'd never heard of (Jordon Mutch) won it for Cardiff with a brilliant goal in stoppage time. Great result for them. Fulham have now taken one point from their last seven home games, and considering it's their home form that has always kept them up, if they don't improve on that it's going to be a long season for them. It's probably not a co-incidence that their struggles have come since Berbatov stopped scoring. I'm probably his biggest fan but even I've lost faith in him now and this week I ditched him from my fantasy team to put Lukaku in. There I go again, time to move on.

Arsenal won away from home yet again as goals from Gnabri and Ramsay gave them a 2-1 win at Swansea, for whom Davies scored a late consolation. This away run of theirs is getting ridiculous now. They're being tipped as serious title contenders after the start they've made and at this moment in time you'd have to say they look as good as anyone. They always do this though don't they? Every year they have a spell where they look great and put a run of wins together. And then they lose a few and the knives come out for Wenger until he looks like he's one defeat away from being in big trouble, and they start winning again. I see no reason to think that won't happen again.

Elsewhere, Southampton beat Palace 2-0. Osvaldo bagged his first goal for the Saints and Lambert added a brilliant free-kick. Palace didn't offer much other than a silly dive from Chamakh that earned him a booking. His haircut alone is worthy of a red card. I mean, just what the fuck is going on there? We've all have bad hairstyles at some point in our lives, even me (hard to believe I know), but we don't usually keep them for five years like this tool has. Every time I see him I just think back to a tweet I saw years ago saying he always looks like he's just been hit in the face with a water balloon.

Onto Sunday, and Norwich won at Stoke in what has to be seen as something of an upset, even if Stoke are shite. There's a bit of an identity crisis going on at the Britannia. Whilst Hughes may not exactly be trying to get them to play tiki taka footy, he's clearly not totally comfortable with the Pulis alehouse approach either. He's trying to play a bit more football but it's not easy with some of the planks he has at his disposal. He's not helping himself by picking Walters every week though. And just what was the point of us letting them have Assaidi if he's never gonna play? Norwich were good value for the win, Howson's goal giving them a rare away win and a vital three points.

Newcastle were brutal against Everton on Monday night and got absolutely mullered. Lukaku ran riot, scoring one and making two (nice one Jose, you fucking genius), as Pardew's castle was well and truly stormed once again. Whatever plan he had to deal with Everton's 'strongest and fastest warrior' fell flat on it's face, although a late fightback almost nicked them a point. Everton are still unbeaten and that bothers me a lot less than I'd have expected. As long as they're behind us I don't actually mind them doing well, probably because there's very little to dislike about them these days. Kenwright's a knob but he's harmless and a good old egg at heart, Martinez is a nice enough fella too, Fellaini and Neville have gone and so has that bog eyed twat Moyes. So what's to not like? I'll tell you what's to not like, Gareth fucking Barry, the fat arsed crab. Thank God he's there, otherwise I'd be struggling.

chapter five

October

LIVERPOOL 3 CRYSTAL PALACE 1

Competition - Premier League
Date - Sat 5 Oct 2013
Venue - Anfield
Scorer(s) – Suarez, Sturridge,
Gerrard (pen)
Star Man – Jordan Henderson

Team: Mignolet; Toure,
Skrtel, Sakho (Agger);
Sterling, Henderson, Gerrard,
Enrique; Moses (Alberto);
Suarez, Sturridge (Aspas):

Yet another game of two halves but this time the first half was so good that the second was largely irrelevant. Maybe that's why the players went out and performed as though it WAS actually irrelevant? It's easier to forgive when they ease off with a three goal cushion as opposed to just the one though I suppose.

If we ever manage to put a ninety minute performance in then someone's going to get beaten like a redheaded stepson. I really thought it was going to be Palace, I'd gone for a 5-0 win beforehand but I was being conservative with that. I genuinely thought we would get more than five but I didn't want to be the type of knobhead who says *"Yeah, we'll win 8-0 today"*. No-one wants to be that guy. We probably could have gotten somewhere close to eight but we eased off far too much at 3-0. Still, three points, back to the top of the league (albeit temporarily), Sturridge and Suarez ruling…. I'm not complaining. Well, not much.

There was never any danger of us not winning this game, the thought honestly never even crossed my mind. Whereas the Southampton game had danger signs everywhere beforehand this one just screamed out 'walkover' to me. Going into the Southampton game we had no momentum; we'd played terribly in the 2nd half at Swansea, we'd just lost Coutinho, we were still trying to adjust to the absence of Johnson and it was also the last game we'd have to negotiate without Suarez. Southampton were tricky opponents and we were probably due a defeat based on how we'd been playing. I saw that loss coming a mile off. Going into this one? Complete opposite. Everything was in our favour. Palace have a manager who would rather cut off his own head than try and park the bus at Anfield. Ian Holloway actually said in the build up that he would take a 10-0 defeat just to hear the Kop singing YNWA. He was never going to spoil the occasion by coming here and trying and stifle us. They were going to come and give it a go as that's the way Holloway is, and it worked in the past for him when his Blackpool side did the league double over us a few years ago. That positive approach suits us down to the ground though, I wish every side that came here did that. It'd be nice if they all defended as badly as Palace did too.

Then there's our new formation. We're much more settled and balanced than we were when we played Southampton and of course our best player is now back in the fold. Palace really didn't stand a chance with the form Suarez and Sturridge are in. They should probably be happy they got away with only conceding three as other teams won't be so fortunate, especially when Coutinho returns. This was Suarez's first game back at Anfield since his ban and he picked up where he left off by getting himself on the scoresheet early on. Prior to kick off he'd walked onto the pitch showing off his new baby to the fans. His little girl was with him too and both kids were dressed in full Liverpool kit. Seriously, what fucking planet is he on?? Many fans chanted his name during the game (not with the usual gusto it should be said) and it's as though everyone's just pretending that this summer never even happened, especially Suarez himself. There's a huge elephant in the room that some seem to be ignoring, it's fucking weird! Don't get me wrong, it's not as though I'm looking at him and constantly thinking about how much of a dick he was over the Arsenal thing; to be honest I'm too busy enjoying watching him play to even care about any of that now. I can't pretend it isn't there though, and it doesn't sit too well with me seeing him carrying on like none of it happened. If I was sat on the Kop I wouldn't be chanting his name… not yet anyway. Luckily I'm in the Main Stand so I don't have to concern myself with such things.

I don't know if he's just incredibly brazen about it or if he genuinely doesn't think what went on is that big a deal. I'm leaning towards the latter I think, he really does seem oblivious to it all. I can't believe he's dressing his baby in LFC gear though and strolling out onto the pitch with him and little Delfina looking like something out of a Liverworld catalogue. If he'd gotten his way they'd be wearing Arsenal kits and his son's name would probably be some kind of anagram of 'Emirates'. He's completely shameless isn't he? Still, if he and Sturridge keep playing the way they are I don't really care if he has the Liverbird tattooed on his baby's forehead. I'm going to enjoy watching him for as long as he is here but I just can't completely ignore the elephant, even if Luis can.

For all his sins though, it's credit to him that nobody thought for a second his attitude when he came back was going to be anything less than we've come to expect from him. He's performing with the same passion and commitment he always has, and some of the link up between him and Sturridge was fantastic; little dummies here and there, first time passes and anticipating eachothers runs… it was beautiful to watch.

The whole team played some great stuff in the first half. Suarez opened the scoring after a nice combination with Enrique following good work by the lively Moses. It initially looked like the chance had gone when Suarez lost his footing after collecting Enrique's cut back, but he still managed to get his shot away and past Speroni. Sturridge then had a blistering drive from the corner of the 18 yard box parried away by the keeper, but he wouldn't be denied for long as he soon made it 2-0 with a brilliant individual strike. There didn't appear to be any immediate danger when he collected the ball out wide but he ran at the defender and turned him inside out twice before drilling a powerful shot across the keeper into the bottom corner. Great goal that.

Palace almost hit back immediately when Skrtel and Sakho both went for the same ball and Jimmy Kebe went running clear. He shit himself when faced with the Kop and Mignolet and produced a tame effort that was hacked away by the covering Toure. From the follow up a shot struck a Palace player and could have gone anywhere, it actually went straight at Mignolet who parried it out to Puncheon who blasted it over the bar. That's my boy!

As a sidenote, is Kebe the skinniest player in the Premier League? His legs are like twiglets, he's really puny looking. It doesn't help when he's on the same side of the field as Enrique of course, but still, Kebe does look like he should be starring in Mr Muscle TV ads rather than playing Premier League football. I bet Enrique spent the entire game taking the piss out of him whilst 'flexing the guns'. If they were on a beach, Enrique would have been kicking sand in his face and chatting up his missus.

That good little spell Palace were enjoying was brought to an abrupt end when they conceded a penalty. Gerrard buried it for the 99th league goal of his career and that was game over, Palace were not coming back from that and must have been fearful of how many they would go on to concede.

As bright as the first half was, there was always the suspicion that we'd down tools in the second half and sadly that's exactly what happened. It needs to stop, if only to spare me from having to listen to my arl fella warning about it at half time of every frigging game. And then giving it the 'I told you so' at full time. I hate it when he's right.

Hardly anything happened in that second half, it was crap. Palace went close through Dwight Gayle when he latched on to an incredibly sloppy pass from the incredibly sloppy Enrique and fizzed a shot a yard over the bar. Then Palace scored after Sterling conceded a free-kick and our defence allowed Gayle to nip in front of everyone and glance a near post header past Mignolet. It was an up and down day for Sterling. The crowd were on his case, especially in the second half, and I don't think he had a particularly good game at all. Having said that, he did do some good things and some of the criticism he was getting was unfair. He's only a kid and he was play-ing in a position that he'll have hardly ever played in before. It showed, as often he seemed reluctant to carry the ball forward into the wide spaces ahead of him and instead just passed it backwards to Toure. Either he was low on confidence or he was playing it safe because he felt he needed to be more cautious due to the position he was playing. As for the crowd's lack of patience towards him, I think it's unfortunate but entirely understandable. Usually you'd expect an 18 year old kid to be cut a lot of slack and given extra encouragement from the fans; that's how it's always been and it's how it was for Sterling when he first broke through. When your agent starts mak-ing demands of 50k a week and insisting you should be paid like a first team player (and you then sign a 30k a week deal), you lose the right to that kind of leeway I'm afraid. If it was Jordan Ibe in that role, I guarantee he'd be indulged by the crowd a lot more than Sterling. He forfeited the right to leeway when he held the club over a barrel with that contract.

Premier League Round Up (5-6 October 2013)

The Mancs pooped everyone's party this weekend with their second half comeback at Sunderland, but even worse than them winning has been the mass deification and week long media obsession with that Adnan Januzaj twat. I hate this little prick already and I'm sick of hearing his stupid name. He sounds like he should be in Star Wars, not playing in the Premier League.

He scores two goals against the worst side in the country and suddenly he's headline news all frigging week. It's not even like he's playing for one of the top sides either. Two goals against Sunderland, big frigging whoop. Luis Suarez did that a week earlier after not kicking a ball - or a defender - in anger in the Premier League for nearly six months, so I mean, how hard can it be? I was already sick of hearing about Januzaj even before all this 'England eligibility' bollocks flared up. It seems the lad is eligible to play for pretty much anybody, or at least he will be by 2018. England, Belgium, Albania, Turkey, Bosnia, Tatooine, The Mos Eisley Cantina XI... who knows which one he'll end up choosing. And more to the point, who fucking cares? Well Jack Wilshere does it seems, but I'll get to him later.

This Anuzaj lad's contract runs out at the end of the season. City and Juventus both want him apparently, how funny would it be if he walked out on United like Paul Pogba did? Not that Moyes is concerned about it, he said this week *"I'm not too worried about that because every young boy wants to play for Manchester United. If I was a young player, I don't see anywhere better to play, we're a club that promotes young players and I'm a manager who does that."* At least he didn't refer to himself in the third person this time, normally he'd have said *"David Moyes is a manager who does that"*.

This loss meant Sunderland only have one point on the board and are firmly rooted to the bottom of the table. They reacted by finally appointing Gus Poyet as Di Canio's replacement this week. He's got his work cut out there, they've got a real mish mash of players and look to be in a mess.

Next up, the Etihad Stadium. Everton's unbeaten record has gone now after they lost 3-1 to City, but the game was closer than the score suggests. Lukaku - who else - put the Blues ahead but Negredo levelled just seconds later. Lukaku had a great penalty shout waved away and Aguero missed two sitters before making amends just before the break with a superb finish. Milner was lucky not to be red carded right on the stroke of half time for a high, wild challenge on McCarthy. Had it been an Everton player making that challenge I reckon he'd have been off, but this ref - some bum named Jonathon Moss - seemed a bit of a homer. He angered the Blues further by giving City an iffy penalty from which Howard scored an own goal, hilariously tipping the ball onto the post only for it to come back and hit him on the head and go in. Martinez was understandably pissed off afterwards, but still never stopped smiling all the while he was complaining. He may be the happiest chappy in the Premier League, I can see that becoming annoying.

Elsewhere, Newcastle bounced back from their shocking display at Goodison with a surprise win at Cardiff. Remy scored both of their goals and if he stays fit he'll probably be enough to ensure the Geordies are safe as he's a very good player. They've got some good players at Newcastle, they shouldn't be as crap as they are should they? Ben Arfa, Remy, Sissoko, Cabaye.. all very good players. Cardiff improved in the second half and Odemwingie pulled a goal back to give them hope, but they couldn't find an equaliser and this result has cancelled out the win they had at Fulham last week. Gary Medel caught my eye. I like him, he's a proper little badass. He's like the Shelbyville Mascherano.

Moving on to Craven Cottage, where Stoke had two good penalty shouts turned down and also saw Huth have two efforts cleared off the line as they lost to a late Darren Bent goal at Fulham. On the one hand I felt sorry for them, but on the other I just think hahaha-hahaha. My boy Bryan Ruiz also should have had a pen and this ref had a shocker too. I can never remember this fellas name, but he looks like a really shit Howard Webb tribute act.

Referees have been in the news a lot this week after Mark Halsey had a pop at them and then Graham Poll tore a strip off Halsey in response. I'm conflicted here, as I think they're both cunts. Halsey had said *"I reckon currently there is a 'great eight', in no particular order: Mark Clattenburg, Howard Webb, Mike Dean, Andre Marriner, Lee Probert, Martin Atkinson, Phil Dowd and Chris Foy. But as for the other 10 on the elite list, well... some are just not up to it while others need more experience, better nurturing and coaching."*

Some of those he was having a go at include Lee Mason, Kevin Friend and Mike Jones, as well as the blag Howard Webb I was just complaining about and that 'Jonathon Moss' jabroni. So Halsey is right, they are shite, except his 'great eight' aren't much better and Halsey himself isn't in a position to talk after how bad he was at times last season. I say 'bad', but he was probably just following orders to be fair. Ferguson's orders. Poll wasn't happy and hit back at him, saying *"He is 100% betraying what paid him a living he would never have earned as the warehouse manager he was or the taxi driver he was. The refereeing fraternity are absolutely appalled at what he is doing. He hasn't thought it through. Mark has got to take a long, hard look at himself. He won't. I know the guy. I have known him for years. He is that type of character."* Oooh bitchy! He's right though, isn't he? Halsey then came back at Poll, saying: *"I've not let the profession down. If anybody is letting the profession down, some of his comments over the years have been atrocious. I found that 'unfitting' from him what he's come out with. But that's Graham. We don't get on and I don't like the way he's done things over the years."* He's right too isn't he? I think what we can all take from this is that the current crop of referees are crap, Mark Halsey is a hypocrite and a rat, and Poll... well he's not actually done anything wrong here, but he's still a fucking lizard. The problem with all these ex refs is that they are trying to be Jeff Winter. They're failing miserably, because the world is barely big enough to handle even one Jeff Winter.

Moving on, and Hull and Villa played out a goalless draw at the KC Stadium. No sooner had I picked up Robbie Brady for my fantasy team than the knobhead goes and has surgery on a hernia. Isn't that the kind of injury that you're meant to play through and get fixed at the end of the season? The worst thing is I didn't even know about it and I kept him in my team, the shithouse. That meant he picked up no points. If I want a midfielder that's going to get me no points then I'd pick up Joe Allen. Yeah, I know, I'm scraping the barrel talking about fantasy football again, but what else am I going to say about this one? Looking at my notes (yes, I do actually take notes, I take this shit seriously), the only thing I wrote down when watching this was: *"Woah!! Villa have a player called El Ahmadi and Hull have a player called Al Muhammadi. That's weird!"* And I couldn't use that could I? Well yeah, I know I just did, but it was to prove a point.

Moving swiftly onto Sunday now, and aside from Chelsea scoring two late goals to win at Norwich it couldn't have gone much better for us really. Arsenal dropped two points and Spurs got 'hammered' at White Hart Lane. The other game saw Southampton beat Swansea, although the Swans will be wondering exactly how that happened as they played well and had loads of chances. Lallana put Southampton ahead in the first half and then Rodriguez made the game safe late on after Chico committed the cardinal sin for a centre back of letting the ball bounce. In between it was all Swansea. Not a good day for the ref though, Mike Dean made a big mistake awarding Southampton a corner, and obviously he realised it (or was told in his headset?) as he then disallowed a perfectly good Wanyama goal when the corner came in. Definitely trying to make up his initial error. Much more of that and his place in the 'great eight' will be in jeopardy. And why did Michu come dressed as Petr Cech? Do they celebrate Halloween early in Spain or something?

Chelsea winning was a bit of a bummer though, especially as the scores were level with just five minutes to go. Oscar put them ahead after just four minutes and Norwich had to weather a bit of an onslaught but eventually clawed their way back into the game and should have had a penalty when Pilkington was tripped by Ramires. Another poor refereeing decision that. This one was Neil Swarbrick, one of those who didn't make Halsey's 'great eight'. Then Pilkington equalised and the Canaries were pushing for a winner when the arse completely fell out of it all, as from a Norwich corner Chelsea broke downfield and mistakes from Tettey and Ruddy allowed Hazard to score. That bellend Willian then made it 3-1 with a screamer. I fucking hate Chelsea.

That Spurs result though, completely mental that wasn't it? West Ham didn't even have a striker on the pitch yet they've somehow won 3-0. This season has just been nuts so far and this was arguably as big a shock as we've seen. AVB's side were flat all afternoon and the longer it went the more West Ham grew in confidence. Winston Reid put them ahead from a corner, Vaz Te fluked a second and then 'Ravel' added a superb third. Always liked that kid. The downside to this was Fat Sam was in full on smug mode afterwards. He even dusted off his old *"If my name was Allardici they'd say I was a tactical genius"* line. Really Sam? Really? Hopefully normal service is resumed after the international break and they get back to losing. Unless they're playing someone who we need to drop points of course, then it can wait until the week after. The sooner they start losing again the happier I'll be, as moaning Sam makes me slightly less nauseous than smug Sam.

I guess Spurs aren't quite as good as some of us thought though, eh? When we lose a game we're quick to write off our chances and say *"this proves we're just not as good as those above us"*. Yet Arsenal lost at home to Villa, City have already been beaten by Cardiff and Villa, United are shit, Chelsea haven't really got going and now Spurs have shown their vulnerability. It's wide open this year as - relatively speaking - I don't reckon anybody is that good, including us.

You know who I really don't like but couldn't even tell you why? Andros Townsend. I can't shake the feeling that he's a bit shit even though the evidence suggests otherwise, but it's not just that, he really bothers me for some reason. I don't know what it is, there's just something about him that rubs me up the wrong way.

I don't like Jack Wilshere either, if you've been paying attention you'll know that already. Now it seems that a lot of people have woken up to the fact that he's a bit of a tit. I knew that just by looking at him, he's got 'one of those faces'. It's been a mixed week for him, first of all he got caught smoking and tried the old *"I was holding it for someone else"* excuse. Please! I can't say it surprised me, in fact I was more shocked that it was just a normal bifter and didn't contain crack, or at the very least weed. Things picked up for him when he scored the equaliser at the Hawthorns after Yacob's header had given Albion the lead. Arsenal were somewhat fortunate that the referee failed to punish Koscielny's latest madcap challenge in the box in stoppage time, as that was a clear penalty. Another crap refereeing decision to add to the list from this weekend. Just when Wilshere thought the storm over the smoking had blown over, his week then took another turn for the worse when he was asked about his thoughts on whether the likes of Januzaj should be allowed to play for England. I especially loved the *"we're English, we tackle hard, that's what we do"* line. Bet he's got a pet bulldog.

He also ended up pissing off half the England cricket team and half the England u21 squad, as loads of them didn't meet Jack's criteria of being born in England. He might want to have a word with his team mate Jenkinson too, who played for Finland at youth and U21 level before then deciding to play for England. To be fair to the full back, he probably couldn't believe his luck when England approached him as he was fortunate to even be playing for Finland, the shit cunt. Maybe Wilshere's words were taken out of context, it's certainly possible of course, but he's not really someone you're going to want to give the benefit of the doubt too is he? People talk about him like he's some kind of Paul Gascoigne type talent. He's scored three league goals in 80 odd games. THREE!!! Aaron Ramsay only needs around 80 minutes to do that, and he doesn't look like he should be riding a BMX round a council estate selling stolen fireworks, dressed all in black and mugging old ladies. Fucking Wilshere. He's the Danny Welbeck of attacking midfielders.

NEWCASTLE 2 LIVERPOOL 2

Competition - Premier League
Date - Sat 19 Oct 2013
Venue - St James Park
Scorer(s) – Gerrard (pen),
Sturridge
Star Man - Steven Gerrard

Team: Mignolet; Toure, Skrtel, Sakho (Alberto); Johnson (Sterling), Henderson, Gerrard, Cissokho; Moses; Sturridge, Suarez:

I'm really trying to convince myself this wasn't such a bad result, largely based on the fact St James' Park CAN be a difficult place to go depending on which Newcastle side turns up. 'Good Newcastle' showed up for this one, so from that perspective a point isn't the end of the world. You could perhaps compare it to the draw at Swansea; a game from which you'd ideally like to pick up three points but

could just about live with a draw.

Where that 'glass half full' type logic completely falls flat on it's stupid, fat, overly optimistic face though is that for 50 minutes of this game we were up against ten men, so it really shouldn't have mattered which Newcastle showed up, should it? No matter what type of positive spin I try to put on it to try and make myself feel a little less pissed off about it, I just can't get away from the realisation that this was just a completely unacceptable performance. Let's be honest, we were crap and didn't deserve any more than what we got.

There was nothing about this performance or result that was even remotely acceptable. We gave away two bad goals, we didn't do anywhere near enough in attacking areas and we only managed to gain any kind of control of the game when the home side were reduced to ten men. Rodgers' tactics following the sending off also have to be scrutinised. Did we really need to stick with a back three for so long when they had just one, lone, isolated forward?

We were unquestionably second best when they had eleven men on the field and considering the circumstances you could probably argue that we were equally poor if not more so after the sending off. Of course we took control of things then and saw a lot more of the ball - that was always going to happen - but considering that we not only had a man advantage but they had a centre back pairing of Championship quality at best, this was just completely unacceptable from the Reds. One great goal aside, a pairing of Mike Williamson and Paul Dummett kept Suarez and Sturridge quiet for 50 minutes plus stoppage time. That just shouldn't happen, but it's not just down to the front two. I just don't get what is happening with us at the moment. The one thing we're supposed to be looking to do under Rodgers is dominate possession, but this year we can't do it even against average/below average sides like Villa and Newcastle. Last year we regularly did it even against the top teams. Right now we just seem to be disregarding the whole 'keeping the ball' thing and we're just relying on the forwards to do their thing.

Forget what happened after the sending off, Newcastle were better than us for 40 minutes and had Yanga-Mbiwa not been so stupid as to pull back Suarez in the box right under Andre Marriner's nose then who knows how this would have turned out. Cabaye had controlled the midfield up until that point and had deservedly fired Newcastle in front with a wickedly dipping, swerving shot from distance. It was just a great strike, but that's a tightrope we've been walking all season as we seem to allow a lot of shots from outside the box. It was only a matter of time before one went in. I can live with that goal though. It was avoidable, but more often than not we get away with that as goals from that distance are quite rare. I was more annoyed with our offensive play in the first half than the goal we conceded. Far too often we over elaborated in the final third and failed to take advantage of promising situations. The front two were the biggest culprits, continually giving the ball away and not doing what we've come to expect from them. Moses was erratic too. It was incredibly frustrating to watch us toiling so badly against a team we'd put six past last season.

The penalty and red card out of nowhere turned the game on it's head. For some reason Newcastle's players were going mental about the decision. I'm not sure why, it was about as clear a penalty and red card as you'll see. The home crowd booed Suarez, naturally, but again, what was their problem? It's not Suarez's fault that they keep buying defenders who can't defend. All the complaints and commotion caused a significant delay in the taking of the penalty and Krul took advantage of it by strolling out of his goal to talk to Gerrard. Sturridge was straight over there to put a stop to nip that in the bud and Gerrard kept his cool to put the penalty away. He had a bit of a glare at Krul too, as if to say *'don't be trying that shit with me junior, I'm too long in the tooth for your silly mind games'*. That's 100 league goals now for Stevie, what a guy. At that stage things were suddenly looking promising for us. The odds were strongly in favour of a Liverpool win; we'd gotten out of jail with that moment of madness from Yanga-Mbiwa and surely now we'd go on and finish the job?

The second half was going largely as expected. We had taken control, we were completely dominating the ball and Newcastle were on the back foot. Yet I thought our play was too one paced and the tempo was far too slow. It was as though the players just felt it was a matter of time before they went ahead. And then just like that, we found ourselves behind again. It was a horrible goal to give away, absolutely criminal. A routine free-kick was floated into the box, Toure and Skrtel both went for it and neither got it, whilst Sakho and - more specifically - Cissokho completely ignored the run of substitute Dummett who finished well at the far post. Cissokho never even so much as looked at him at any point, it was shocking stuff from him.

Rodgers eventually decided to change it and replaced Sakho with Alberto. It helped, but not that much. Alberto was neat and tidy but I'm not sure exactly where he was supposed to be playing. I think he was on the right of a 442 with Moses switching to the left, but it was difficult to tell. Moses certainly looked happier out wide and he played his part in the equaliser. It was a great goal. Suarez flicked the ball to Moses and then set off into the box. Moses did well to turn back inside and play a perfectly timed ball into his path, and Suarez had a quick look up before putting the ball perfectly onto the head of the inrushing Sturridge who headed in his 20th goal for the club. The fastest ever to that landmark, quite a feat given the great strikers he's beaten to it. Despite the goal (and the pass that led to the penalty) I thought Sturridge had a poor game and being away with England for that double header looked to have blunted his sharpness. Suarez too, he wasn't at his best either having travelled half way around the world this week. Despite both of them being a little off colour, they've combined to create both of our goals and Suarez was only denied a winner by the crossbar and also a late save from Krul, who parried away his free-kick with the last action of the game.

This was one of those all too frequent days when watching Liverpool made me want to break stuff. It'd be easier to take if I knew we were just crap, but there's potentially a really, really good side in the making here but something just isn't working. It's great to have Johnson back but can someone tell him that this whole 'cut inside and shoot with the left foot' thing doesn't work and he needs to knock it off. How many times has it resulted in a goal since he's been here? Two? Three maybe? Yet he does it every game, sometimes two or three times. He's played 116 games so that's a success rate of... hell I don't know, I was never any good at maths, but it's not a high percentage play.

It's difficult to be anything but downhearted about this result. It's so tight up at the top of the league that any slip up is going to be costly. From the moment Gerrard scored that penalty and Newcastle had to resume a man down, we simply had to take maximum points from this game and we failed to do so. I can't shake the feeling that these two points we dropped will haunt us come May.

The conceding of cheap goals is now a huge worry as it's been going on for so long and it happens regardless of the personnel. I don't know why it keeps happening, perhaps the coaches are to blame for not preparing them properly and ensuring everyone does their job, but I'd lean towards it more being the players' fault. Maybe some kind of electric shock treatment would work? Wire them up and practice defending set pieces for an hour a day. If anyone switches off and doesn't pick up their man? ZAP! They'll soon knock that shit off.

Premier League Round Up (19-21 October 2013)

Ronan Keating was right, wasn't he? Ronan Keating is always right. Life IS a roller coaster, at least it is if you're a Liverpool fan. Forrest Gump nailed it too, life is indeed like a box of chocolates' and this weekend was the coffee cream. Yuck.

Being the early game on a Saturday can be ace, providing you win. When you don't it just gives you longer to stew over it, and then there's that horrible feeling of inevitability as everyone else around you goes about their business of picking up points. That's exactly what happened this week. We shit the bed against ten man Newcastle and then had to sit back and watch everyone else win. Arsenal. Chelsea. City. Spurs. Everton. All the teams we're competing with for a top four spot. What's that you say? What about United? Pay attention people, I said all the teams that are competing for a top four spot. I'm just grateful Southampton dropped two points, they'll be kicking themselves for only drawing against a mid table side.

Chelsea had an early scare when they fell behind to a Jordon Mutch goal after David Lolz was guilty of the worst bit of 'defending' of the weekend. Hell, it might be the worst bit of 'defending' of the year, it was just... well it was just David Luiz wasn't it. He's always got something like this in him and it continues to baffle me how anyone would trust him to play centre back. It's one of those things that I've just never been able to figure out and plays on my mind far more than it should. Like if cows need to be milked or they'll die, how did they survive before we figured out this crucial piece of information? And more to the point, who's the dirty bastard that first tried it and what was he/she thinking? I think about stuff like that all the time, it completely wrecks my head. Anyway, Chelsea toiled to get back into it and were far from impressive, but then out of nothing they were handed a controversial equaliser. As far as I'm aware you aren't allowed to do what Eto'o did to the keeper. You probably should be, but that's a different argument and usually that kind of thing always results in a foul.

The ref told Malky Mackay afterwards if he'd bounced the ball it would have been a foul, but that he'd dropped the ball so it wasn't. Clearly that's a huge cock up on the his part as Marshall was bouncing it and had not just 'dropped it on the floor'. But surely the real issue is what the fuck was the keeper doing bouncing the ball anyway, especially when Eto'o was stood beside him? It's not the 1970s pal, you don't need to be doing that shit. What's next, is he gonna rock up for next week's game not wearing any gloves and with huge pork chop sideys? David Marshall, what an absolute melt. Eto'o then made it 2-1 with a nice finish after the break and Oscar added a third, prompting Motson to crack one of his shitty little 'jokes' that only he laughs at. *"This is oss-CAR.. oh HE'S GOT IT!!!"* he yelped, before adding *"well...you're tempted to say that's a goal that would have won a prize..."* followed by a self satisfied, snorting *"haha"* with that irritating Chief Wiggum laugh he does. Twat. Hazard gave the scoreline a flattering exclamation point when he bagged his second with a feeble shot that somehow trickled under the hapless Marshall. The keeper had an absolute Jon Walters of a day. Mourinho was sent to the stands after going mental at the referee over him telling Ivanovic to hurry up taking a throw in. Really? You're going postal over THAT? Attention seeking helmet.

Arsenal also had a big home win and like Chelsea it wasn't quite as comfortable as the scoreline suggested. Wilshere put them ahead with a fine goal but the over the top reaction to it on twitter was ridiculous. No way did he mean the little flick that went to Giroud, he just flicked his boot out at a ball that was behind him and it fortuitously went back to the Frenchman. Spawny little woodbine smoking chav twat. Ozil headed a second from Giroud's fine cross but Howson responded by firing in from 18 yards to make for a potentially uncomfortable finish for the Gunners. Indeed, so desperate did they become that they were reduced to sending on Nicklas Bendtner. In form Ramsay eventually came off the bench to give them breathing space with a fine goal, and unlike Wilshere he didn't need any spawny little ricochet to play himself in either. Ozil wrapped it up with a tap in after more impressive play by Ramsay and Arsenal are looking very good at the moment. How high they finish will depend entirely on what they do in the big games as they've got so much firepower now that they'll continue to beat up on the also rans and I can't see too many repeats of what Villa did to them on the opening day.

Speaking of also rans, how about those Mancs eh? Januzaj signed his new contract this week which including bonuses is reputedly worth close to 80k a week. Jeez. And I thought we got burned by Raheem Sterling. The lad has made a good start but he's done nothing yet and now he's set for life just from one contract. Modern football eh? Van Persie gave them the lead against Southampton and Rooney then hit the bar as United started the game brightly. Van Persie also hit the bar in the second half and then, as so often happens when you don't get the second goal, it got edgy and Southampton grabbed a late equaliser through Lallana. Hilarious stuff, Moyesy's panic stricken little face at full time was a picture.

Fortunately for him, his predecessor has dominated the headlines this week which means fewer people talking about United's awful league position. I don't even know where to start on Ferguson's book, the bits and pieces I've seen people talking about aren't exactly surprising, but it just once again demonstrate what a vile specimen he is. It would be quite poetic if Roy Keane beat him to death with a copy of it. A whole chapter was devoted to Liverpool. That's actually pretty mental when you think about it. Talk about obsessed. He's so obsessed he even deemed it appropriate to discuss Jordan Henderson's gait and awkward looking running style, claiming it will cause him problems in the future. What??? Absolute horseshit, but even if it weren't, how is that worth a mention in the autobiography of a man that has so much more interesting and worthwhile stuff to discuss from such a long, successful and controversial career? If I was Brendan I'd send Hendo over to his his house with instructions to run around on his front lawn in his footy boots for five or six hours until it looked like a ploughed field. Hendo could do that, and then run all the way back to Merseyside without even breaking sweat, awkward gait or not. Steven Gerrard is not a 'top, top player' according to purple nose. Apparently he's not the same calibre as a Keane or Scholes and never got a kick whenever he played against them. You see, this is the problem when you like a bit of a tipple, you talk a lot of shite and often forget about things you've actually said, meaning you're basically just a walking contradiction. Not a top, top player he says, clearly having forgotten about this: *"He has become the most influential player in England, bar none. Not that Vieira lacks anything, but Gerrard does more. To me, Gerrard is Keane. He is where Keane was when Roy came to us in 1993. Everywhere the ball is, he is there. He's got that unbelievable engine, desire, determination. Anyone would take Gerrard."* Unsurprisingly no-one seemed to pull him up on that at any of the numerous promotional events he did to plug this piece of shit book of his. He also admitted that he told Moyes not to sign a new contract with Everton, which if it were any other club would have fans of said club frothing at the mouth. Hardly caused a ripple with Evertonians though. Either because they're still so flattered that United wanted their manager, or because they're counting their lucky stars that they've got rid of the small time gobshite.

The most amusing thing I read about Ferguson this week though had to be his attempts to stick up for Moyes by once again complaining about the fixture list and how he'd have been straight on to the authorities about it if he'd still been in charge. The arrogance of the man knows no bounds but what's all this shite about their tough schedule anyway? Ok, they've played us and City away and played host to Chelsea, but they've dropped five points at home to West Brom and Southampton, so I don't think they are in a position to be complaining about anything fixture related, the fucking bums.

That rat Evra has been in the news this week too, he's got into a row with some pundits on French TV who claimed he wasn't popular with team-mates. Not exactly earth shattering revelations, I mean it's hardly a secret. It's not making too much of a leap to suggest that people who are forced to be around him on a regular basis maybe aren't too keen on him. Evra went nuts about it though, calling them 'tramps' and 'parasites' before referring to himself in the third person, which is always a tell tale sign that a person is a bit of a knob. That's one of the rules Dave Usher lives his life by in fact. *"There are some pundits with whom I will soon settle my differences with them..."* he said. *"They want to sell a lie to the French people that Evra is disliked. But that is not the case at all. I do not know what Lizarazu has against me. Me, I was twice voted best left-back in the world, four times the best left-back in the Premier League. Him I don't even know if he was ever voted best left-back in the world. I'm not arrogant. It's the truth, those people will never have my honours, they have never won anything."* Haha oh my God, how old is he, 12??? *"I was twice voted the best left back in the world"* hahahaha, the absolute weapon. And what's this *'Lizarazu has never won anything'* crap? Hello? Earth calling Evra? World Cup? European Championship? He wasn't done there though. *"I recall my first call-up to the national side, all the others shook my hand apart from him. Thierry Henry said to him 'Oh Liza, here is the opposition'. And Lizarazu looked at me and said 'Why? Someone told you that I was already retired?'"* You know, I've always liked Lizarazu, but after reading that I have to say that my opinion of the man.... just fucking sky rocketed! Talk about a great judge of character, he actually knew Evra was a cunt before any of us had even heard of him. Impressive. Evra continued: *"People have a good impression of me, it won't be these tramps who dirty my image. They must stop lying to the French people"* Hahaha brilliant. The French people have a good opinion of him? I thought he was the one who was largely blamed for them virtually going on strike at the 2010 World Cup? And he's probably the last person that should be throwing around the word 'liar'.

Moving on, and City had a potentially tricky away fixture at West Ham on Saturday. Tactical genius Allardyce again opted to play a 4-6-0 formation with no striker. It worked at Spurs a fortnight ago and it was galling watching Smug Sam after that, as he was really full of himself that day. As flash as a rat with a gold tooth he was, so it was nice to see him brought back down to earth by City, even if I'd have preferred the Hammers to have taken points from one of our rivals. There was something freakish about that result at White Hart Lane though and if Spurs had scored first they'd have probably taken West Ham to the cleaners. City did score first in this one, through Aguero. And they scored second too, little Argentine heading in unmarked from a set-piece. Vaz Te's overhead kick gave the home side some hope but Silva finished them off after being teed up by the excellent Aguero.

Sunderland had a new manager for their trip to Swansea. It made no difference though as they got battered and still only have one point. The odious Phil Bardsley was given a recall and repaid his new manager's faith by missing an absolute sitter and then following it up with an own goal. Good job, dickhead. De Guzman's superb strike doubled the Swans' lead a minute later and not even the introduction of 'Fabio Magnifico' could save the Black Cats. He blazed a great chance over the bar with his more or less his first touch and him being there is not really going to prove to be beneficial to anyone at this rate, I'd rather he was on our bench than Sunderland's.

Bony's penalty made it 3-0 and Chico added a fourth via a deflection. I can't see Sunderland saving themselves, they've just got nothing have they? Can't score, and concede too many. At this stage, them and Palace look certainties for the drop.

Hull would be many people's favourites to join them but they're really winning me over. They were desperately unlucky to lose at Goodison. Mirallas gave the Blues an early lead but the ball looked to have brushed off the heel of an offside Barry which deceived the keeper. The lying twat said afterwards he didn't feel the ball touch him. So why was he spotted celebrating with Barkley and telling him it was his goal? Shithouse. Danny Graham was then stretchered off after an appalling lunge from Barry, the dirty fat arsed fucking crab. No red card, in fact not even a yellow. He then followed it up with another shocker on Aluko which did result in a yellow. Should have been two reds, the dirty bastard. I hate Gareth Barry. I hate him even more than I hate women who put those big daft eyelashes on the headlights of their car, usually a Mini or Volkswagon Beetle. Sagbo equalised as Hull really came on strong, but Pienaar scored with a delightful flick just ten seconds after coming on to win it for Everton.

Assaidi started for Stoke against West Brom. He wasn't a good fit for us and we really shouldn't have bought him, but he's a good little player and I always enjoyed watching him. I can't stand Stoke but I hope he does well there. Somehow Howard Webb failed to give a penalty when Mulumbu got away from Charlie Adam and the clumsy Scot trod on the back of his heel. They hurt like hell those ones, even more so when the blind officials don't see it. Absolutely shocking from Webb. Stoke's best chance fell to Steven Ireland but he put it over the bar. Remember when he was at City as a youngster? I thought he was fantastic in those days. The fact he's now playing for Stoke, and not playing that well, is pretty sad. Still, he's doing better than Michael Johnson at least, so that's something. Adam almost won it with a trademark brilliant shot from the halfway line that Myhill did well to get back and tip over the bar. Stoke are definitely looking to play more football these days. The inclusion of Assaidi, Arnautovic and Ireland shows what Hughes is trying to do, but whilst he's still selecting Jon Walters he's asking for trouble. They can't score goals, but with forwards like Walters and Jones that's hardly surprising.

Just the one game on Sunday as Spurs made the trip to Aston Villa. The Brummies had beaten both Arsenal and Man City so far this season so I had some hope they might be able to take something against AVB's side, but alas, it was not to be. Man of the moment Andros Townsend scored again. It was a fluke as it was just a cross that was missed by everyone and caught out the keeper. I'm sick of hearing about him now though. He's a flash in the pan and a couple of good displays in England friendlies isn't changing my mind. As soon as defenders stop letting him cut inside and shooting with his left foot 30 times a game, we'll see how good he is. Having said that, no-one ever managed to stop Bale doing it. Soldado made it 2-0 with a nice little finish from a great ball by Paulinho as Spurs put the West Ham defeat behind them.

Finally, Monday night. Palace took the lead against Fulham but were left shell-shocked by some incredible goals from Martin Jol's side. I'd read about Kasami's goal on twitter, but unlike Wilshere's this one didn't leave me thinking *'is that it?'* It was stunning, there won't be a better goal all season than that. Sidwell followed it up with a corker of his own to give them the lead at half time before Berbatov and Senderos added goals from corners after the break to give Fulham an easy three points.

Holloway was given a load of stick from the Palace fans apparently. Ungrateful fucks, I've never had any time for them. I used to hate going to Selhurst Park back when I'd do the aways, and Palace fans were right up there with Charlton when it came to being absolute fucking wankers. They shouldn't even be in the Premier League, they're only there because Holloway somehow managed to get them up, yet now he's getting shit from them? Holloway quit a couple of days later, and reading his reasons I'd have to say he's done the right thing and it was refreshing to see him admit that he got it all wrong in the summer and as a result lost the things that had got them promotion in the first place. The team spirit has gone, the players were not listening to him and he knew he couldn't turn it around so he's resigned. Fair play to him, I've got a lot of time for Holloway.

After what happened to Adkins and McDermott last year, and now this, managers in the Championship are probably thinking they're better off where they are and promotion against the odds is really not gonna do them any favours. Chairmen will disagree, as Palace will make an absolute shitload of cash this year regardless of how crap they are, and they are so bad they may set a record for the fewest ever points. We'll probably go there and concede three though.

LIVERPOOL 4 WEST BROM 1

Competition - Premier League
Date - Sat 26 Oct 2013
Venue - Anfield
Scorer(s) – Suarez (3), Sturridge
Star Man – Luis Suarez

Team: Mignolet; Toure, Skrtel, Sakho; Johnson (Kelly), Lucas, Gerrard (Allen), Henderson; Sturridge, Suarez (Alberto):

Every now and then you witness something that makes you think "This is special, we'll still be talking about this in years to come". The performance of the front two in this game had me thinking that. We've had some great double acts down the years and although it's still in it's infancy, this partnership we've got now is another one. What these two are doing at the moment is very, very special.

Older Reds probably felt like that watching Hunt and St John, Keegan and Toshack and of course Dalglish and Rush. I only really caught the tail end of Kenny's career so for me I look back at the Barnes/Beardsley/Aldridge combo, Fowler & McManaman and to a lesser extent the Gerrard & Torres link up. In terms of talent and the excitement they provide, Luis Suarez and Daniel Sturridge don't need to take a back seat to any of those. They don't yet have the longevity to be compared to the greats of course - and may never have it depending on what Suarez decides to do - but I believe we're seeing something very special right now.

Before the game I was actually saying to a mate that I'm not sure that we've ever had a better player than Suarez. Now before you scoff at that and accuse me of blasphemy towards the King etc, hear me out. I'm not crowning Suarez as our greatest ever player; he's only been here five minutes and clearly hasn't done anywhere near enough to earn that honour. In fact he isn't even in the discussion. What I am saying is that I don't think I can categorically say that we've had anyone that is better than him. I know how that sounds, and I hate all that 'in the moment' shit as much as anyone. I just can't in all good conscience say that I've seen anyone who is a better footballer than Luis Suarez. And this was my train of thought BEFORE he went out and did what he did against West Brom. Needless to say nothing that transpired in this game did anything to change my mind! He will never be known as Liverpool's greatest ever player as barring some kind of minor miracle he won't be here long enough to even merit being in the conversation, but he's absolutely world class and would grace any team in any era. He might just even rate as a 'top top player' on the Ferguson scale, that's how phenomenal he is.

I'm not sure those outside of LFC realise it yet though, they're all still wrapped up in all the other shit that comes with him and it clouds their judgement. *"He's a great player but..."* No, there is no 'but', he's just a fucking great player, in fact he's beyond just being 'great', he's easily in the top five players in the world right now but a lot of people don't seem to see it. Even Alan Hansen - who should know better - insisted that the Rooney / Van Persie pairing is the best in the country. It's not, Jocky, it's not even close. In terms of individual players, you can make an argument for who you'd rather have out of Sturridge, Rooney and Van Persie. It'd make for an interesting discussion and there's no clear outstanding choice at the moment. I'd take Sturridge right now, but obviously I'm biased and I wouldn't argue too strongly with anyone who took either of the Manc pair, you can make a strong case for either. But Suarez is way out ahead of all of them, it's not even close.

He's just relentless and what he did to West Brom was almost unfair. I could imagine poor old Steve Clarke sat on the bench bemoaning his misfortune: *"Wait, he's scoring headers now?? Fucks sake"*. The first goal was your classic Suarez strike. In years to come when I'm reminiscing about this brilliant Uruguayan striker we had back in the early 2010s, it will be goals like this one that I think of. Close control, a slalom dribble to the box, a nutmeg and a finish. Vintage Suarez. West Brom are a tough nut to crack and beat us twice last season of course. This game definitely had the potential to go wrong but the early goal was crucial and adding a second so soon after more or less made it safe. What a goal it was too; a bullet header into the top corner from 18 yards. I've seen some discussion as to whether it's the best header people can remember from a Liverpool player. Maybe, but I can recall both Steve McMahon and Steve Nicol also scoring headers from the edge of the box. Hell of a goal though.

Poor old West Brom were just shell shocked. They'd done nothing wrong but found themselves 2-0 down solely due to the brilliance of Suarez. The rest of the team were playing well but Suarez was clearly the difference at this point. The three midfielders were all outstanding and this was the best all around display we've produced all season. Those two facts are not unrelated. The midfield is the key to Rodgers 'pressing and passing' game and the tweak in the system worked very well against West Brom, but you could also argue that it was the performance of the front two that made everything else seem better. Would we still have been saying how well the team played if the front two hadn't delivered as they did? Probably not, but with those two up front the rest of the team don't need to be brilliant, they just need to do their own jobs properly and more often than not we should have enough to get the win.

Hendo must have been the most self conscious man in the stadium, knowing the eyes of the world were on him every time he broke into a sprint just so they could see what all the fuss was about. *"Oh yeah, he does run kinda funny doesn't he?"* etc. He handled the whole thing with a lot of class, as you'd expect from him as he's such a nice kid. Talk about taking the moral high ground, Henderson is so high up Ferguson would need a NASA telescope to see him. If it had been me, I'd have had a t-shirt prepared in case I scored with some sort of unflattering message to Ferguson on it. *"Rather have a bad gait than a purple nose"* or *"at least I've never shit myself on the hard shoulder of a motor-*

way". That sort of thing. Not Hendo though, he's a bigger man than me and a much bigger man than that twat Ferguson.

With a 2-0 lead going into the break the only question I had was whether we'd finally show up for a second half or whether we'd sit on what we had, as we'd done against Palace. Hopefully lessons have been learned as we finally 'won a second half' despite the best efforts of the officials to throw a spanner in the works. All three officials were garbage. Suarez had completed his hat-trick with another fine headed goal, and with Sturridge having suddenly exploded into life after the break too it was looking like we may hit half a dozen. Then out of nothing the linesman awarded a penalty after a challenge by Lucas and West Brom had an undeserved lifeline. There were actually three more clear penalty incidents than that in the game that weren't given. Suarez had his shirt pulled early on, and whilst he went down too easily what's the point in staying on your feet if you are not going to be able to reach the ball because of that tug? You've basically rewarded a defender for cheating. At the other end, Skrtel was twice guilty of shirt pulling himself. The first on Anichebe probably wasn't a pen as the striker lost his footing of his own accord and not because he was pulled down, but the second one on McAuley was extremely risky as Skrtel had hold of his shirt for a good few seconds. That was straight out of the Shawcross/Huth handbook of defending set-pieces. A dangerous game to play, but those offences are rarely punished as often as they should be and Skrtel probably feels the odds are in his favour.

Anyway, Morrison buried the penalty and we had a little wobble for a few minutes after that. Understandable, their tails were up and we needed to regroup as another goal for Albion and things could have gotten very uncomfortable for us in a hurry. Thankfully Sturridge killed the game off with a stunning chip at the Kop end. No more than he'd deserved, he'd been brilliant in the second half but it was looking like it wasn't going to happen for him. He'd fizzed a free-kick just wide, he'd rattled a shot against the bar and he basically looked like he was going to score every time he got the ball. The strength, hold up play, pace and skill from him was a joy to watch. He may have been the supporting act to the Suarez show in this game but he still bagged the goal of the game and kept up his impressive strike rate. If you look at the goals per game ratio of both Suarez and Sturridge from their last 25 games or so, it's remarkable. It's rare to have one striker on such a prolific run, to have two of them doing it is… well like I said, it's something special and if they can keep it up there's no reason why they won't be remembered as being right up there with the other double acts we still talk about years after they've stopped playing.

Premier League Round Up (26-27 October 2013)

Fucking Stoke. Could they not have just hung on in there for another 12 minutes? Useless bastards. Hopefully this result is not some kind of turning point for Moyes, I mean it was only Stoke after all. It may even be a good thing United didn't lose, as Moyes might not have survived that and no-one wants to see him leave before maximum damage has been inflicted. Let him buy another Fellaini or two before he gets the push.

Stoke looked brilliant in the first half and could easily have been 5-0 up inside half an hour as they cut through the United backline at will. Replace Jon Walters with someone who can actually play football and this may have been a different story. For all their dominance they just had one goal from Crouch to show for it and with two minutes to go before the break those spawny manc twats did what they so often do. My arl fella always says the time you've really got to watch them is in the last few minutes of each half, and they do seem to score so many goals in those periods. That was that then, Stoke's bubble was popped. At least, so we thought. A minute later the dopey Phil Jones bundled someone over on the edge of the box and Arnautovic curled in a pearler of a free-kick to put them ahead again. Along with everyone else inside Anfield that afternoon I'd heard the score being read out by George at half time and I obviously had a good laugh about it. I didn't expect Stoke to hold on, but they did for a lot longer than I thought they would. Eventually Rooney headed in from a corner and then Hernandez got the inevitable winner when he headed home Evra's cross.

Walters made Evra look like John Barnes by allowing him to glide past him and whip over a cross. For a striker who's in the side because of his defensive abilities that's pretty unforgivable. Walters is one of those 'honest' 'hard working' frontmen who gets shunted out wide because he's no good up front, an Emile Heskey - Danny Welbeck type if you like. Or a really shite Dirk Kuyt even if you want to be kind. If he's allowing full backs to do that? What's the point of him, seriously? If I was a footballer and people called me 'a good pro' or 'honest' or 'hard working' I'd be fucking gutted, as it's really just a polite way of saying 'shite'. At least it is if you're an attacking player - it's not so bad if you're a defensive midfielder or full back - but forwards are meant to be 'dazzling' 'mercurial' 'explosive' 'clinical' etc. Thankfully, as a striker myself I've never been referred to as 'hard working', but then I'm hardly 'dazzling' or 'explosive' either. I like to think I have a little 'mercurial' in me though.

All this talk reminds me of when I used to do some freelance work for LFC's 'matchday magazine' back around 2000-01 ish. They ran a 'young player of the year' award and because I used to go to a lot of Academy games back then they asked me to do a bit of a write up on the winner. *"Sound, I can do that"* I said. *"Just let me know who wins and I'll get something over to you"*. Only problem was, they allowed the fans to choose the winner and nobody bothered voting. Well, nobody except the friends and family of possibly the worst player in the squad. I think he got 17 votes from what I can recall, all from his mates and family members, some of whom probably voted twice. Don't get me wrong, if the lad ever showed up to play at our weekly footy game on a Thursday night he'd no doubt look like Lionel Messi playing against a bunch of school kids. I mean obviously he could play, you don't get as far as Liverpool's under 18 side without having ability. I'm just saying that judging him against his peers he was arguably the worst kid in the group. So whilst it wasn't on merit, Leon Noel was LFC's Academy Player of the Season and I had to write something positive about him: a striker / winger (see the pattern?) who probably scored about three goals all season and who did very little else of note. The only interesting thing I could come up with is that his surname was actually his first name spelt backwards, but I didn't think that was quite what they were looking for, so I started it off with.... *"Leon is a hard working, honest lad..."* I don't remember the rest, but it's fair to say it wasn't my finest - or most truthful - bit of writing.

I've just googled him and the first result was actually his old Academy profile from TLW back in the day, which read: *"A powerfully built lad, who can be a real handful for opposing defences due to his strength and pace. He's a real workhorse too, and his unselfish running often creates chances for his team-mates. Needs to work on his first touch and finishing, but is as honest as they come."* Wow, a full house, they're all in there! Powerful, unselfish workhorse and the coup de grace, HONEST! Ha! I guess he was the Jonathon Walters of his time.

Getting back on topic, Hughes was pissed off because he thought Hernandez should earlier have been sent off. Much as I hate to side with United over anything, that's rich coming from that snide twat who made a career of doing what Hernandez did. Yellow card all day, never a red, and 'Useless' is clutching at straws, as usual. Amusingly, Nani was booed off by United's fans. It takes some doing to be the worst player on a football field you are sharing with Walters, but Nani managed to do it and the home crowd weren't amused, taking time out from singing about scousers to let the winger know of their disapproval. Nani played like that annoying kid in school who - mistakenly - thinks he's better than everyone else and just wants to take five players on and shoot from anywhere. Basically, he thinks he's Cristiano Ronaldo, the only difference being that Ronaldo can actually do those things as he is in fact better than everyone else. Except Messi. And Suarez. And Puncheon.

It was really disappointing listening to Jocky on MOTD waxing lyrical over United's front two though. Not sure how he can say United will 'definitely finish in the top four' given who they are up against either. Are they really better than any of Chelsea, City, Arsenal, Spurs, ourselves or even Everton? I'm far from convinced, in fact I'll state here and now they definitely won't make the top four. Robbie Savage even agrees with me, which worries me a little. Savage then had to take Jocky to task for referring to Rooney and Van Persie as the best front two in the league. *"Suarez and Sturridge for me"* he said. *"You'd rather play against Van Persie and Rooney than Suarez and Sturridge?"* asked Hansen, almost incredulously. *"Right now yeah I would"* says Savage. Why is this even a conversation? What's Jocky been smoking, this isn't even a fucking contest. I didn't like him throwing the *'how many titles have they won?'* argument in there either. It's Hansen's last year on MOTD before retiring, I don't want to see him going out like this. Up your game Jocky lad.

Moving on, and Arsenal won again. Not really a surprise as they were only playing Palace, but when they were reduced to ten men there was a slight whiff of an upset in the air. The Gunners were 1-0 up at the time courtesy of an Arteta penalty, but the ex-Blueshite's afternoon was ended prematurely when he was adjudged to have committed a professional foul on Chamakh. Shocking decision. There are three reasons why it shouldn't have been a red card. 1) I'm not sure it was even a foul, as Chamakh actually ran into Arteta and even deviated his run away from the ball to do so. How was Arteta meant to get out of the way? 2) It was a long, long way from goal and 3) It was Chamakh, so how that equates to a clear goalscoring opportunity is anyone's guess.

Palace came on strong after that but Giroud wrapped it up on the break after great play by the once again impressive Ramsay.

There was another good win for the Blues this weekend but it could easily have turned out differently as Villa had their chances. Benteke was back for them but the soft get missed a penalty that he'd won himself. He missed another great chance shortly after too, not what you want to be doing when you're going head to head with your main rival for a place in the national team. What made it worse for him was Lukaku then went and scored, having previously twice gone close himself. A composed finish from Osman secured the win for Martinez's side who briefly went third in the table until Chelsea, Spurs and Southampton won and overhauled them. Martinez spoke of getting them into the top four when he took over, and like everyone else I laughed at him. I still don't think he'll do it, but the suggestion of it isn't laughable anymore and they'll be in the shake up as long as Lukaku stays fit as he's a fucking monster.

Like Everton, Southampton may also feel they can at least threaten a top four spot. They've only conceded three goals all season and sit just four points off the top. Chances are they'll fall away, but they've got a great shot at finishing 8th, as outside of the established top seven I don't see anyone better than the Saints at the moment. I like their style; aggressive pressing high up the pitch and they play at a very high tempo. Lambert gave them the lead with a simple header when he found himself unmarked at the back post. Why was he unmarked? Because Berbatov was meant to be marking him, that's why, and Berbatov's defensive awareness is non-existent. That's part of the reason I often compare myself to the languid Bulgarian. The other part is that I don't run much either. This goal was hilarious though, Scott Parker specifically went over to him, pointed at Lambert and told him to stay tight on him. Berbatov nodded, and then stood still as Lambert peeled away to the back post! The lively Rodriguez made it 2-0 when he nodded in from a Lambert header. Do teams not bother doing any homework on the opposition these days? Even I know that Lambert likes to peel off onto the back post, so how come Fulham kept allowing him to do it and never bothered marking him?

Norwich's goalless draw with Cardiff at Carrow Road was memorable only for one incident that almost caused a mass brawl on the field. A Norwich player was injured so Cardiff keeper Marshall threw the ball out of play. What happened next was pretty bizarre, as a Norwich player threw the ball to Leroy Fer who sidefooted it into the net. Technically, the goal should have stood but the ref claims he didn't give them permission to take the throw. The replays tell a different story, it looks like he just didn't want to give it as it was so morally out of order. I'm not going to criticise the ref for that, he may have circumvented the rules slightly but he did the right thing and he prevented a riot. Chris Hughton immediately told the Cardiff bench that if the goal had been given he'd have allowed Cardiff to walk the ball up the field and equalise, but he also thought it had been unintentional on Fer's part and he'd meant to pass to the keeper. Most people assumed that, until the man himself came out and brazenly stated: *"I meant to score, I wanted to win the game"*. Whilst it's a pretty despicable lack of sportsmanship, I can't help but laugh at the total lack of remorse from the lad. He actually seemed to think it was completely acceptable as *'that's what we do in Holland'*. Bollocks! They don't do that in Holland. They don't do that anywhere! What a morally bankrupt, cheating, win at all costs, despicable piece of shit.

Speaking of which, Chelsea had a massively important win on Sunday. Bastards. They've got Joe Hart to thank for it, his mistakes are now getting out of control and this one was just fucking stupid. It'd have been funny if the recipients hadn't been Chelsea, and more specifically Torres. He's playing really well at the moment, and that probably makes Chelsea title winning material. If Torres keeps up this kind of form then they'll take some stopping. That said, this was his FIRST LEAGUE GOAL of 2013. Hopefully it's his last too, but I fear that's just wishful thinking as he looks great at the moment. Twat.

City will be kicking themselves over this, they should never have lost the game and that's three away defeats for them now. Aguero's equaliser was stunning and he's looked back to his best this season. There's just something not quite right with them though, I can't put my finger on what it is but obviously Hart's form isn't helping. Mourinho made a twat of himself again, diving into the crowd after Torres bagged the winner. Helmet. Pellegrini didn't shake his hand afterwards, and when asked about it simply said *"No I didn't shake hands."* Why? *"Because I didn't want to."* Fair enough.

Fucking sick of Chelsea though, wish they'd just fuck off back their pre-Abramovich nothingness. I'd like Chelsea to be where West Ham are, just completely irrelevant and dull. Admittedly, Sam Allardyce is a big reason for that, but West Ham are probably the most negative, pointless team in the league right now, I'd hate to be watching them every week. There's an Andy Carroll shaped hole in their attack, and rather than try and fill it Allardyce has just not even bothered, opting for a 4-6-0 formation yet again as they made the trip to Swansea. That Joke Hole can't even make it into a side with six midfielders says a lot about his fall from grace too. He did come on eventually and could have given away a penalty when he turned his back on a cross and the ball hit his outstretched arm. He got lucky there, the bum. Fat Sam bemoaned the lack of goals afterwards, praising his side's defensive record of five clean sheets from nine games but complaining that they've often been unable to get the solitary goal they needed to win those games. Hey Einstein, here's a thought, perhaps you aren't scoring goals because you don't play any fucking strikers? What a dick.

It was the North East derby on Sunday. Sunderland simply had to win this one, and win it they did. Just. It wasn't pretty, and it needed a late winner from substitute Fabio Magnifico, but they won't care how they won, just that they won. They got off to a great start when Fletcher headed them into the lead. He's a proper striker. His partner Jozy Altidore? Not so much. What can I say about him? Well let's see... Hard working, powerful, a handful, honest, that's what I can say about him. Newcastle were better after the break and equalised through Debuchy. They looked the more likely winners but then Borini came off the bench and unleashed a screamer to win it. Him being sat on the bench watching Altidore is ridiculous really, and hopefully that won't be happening anymore after this.

Finally on Sunday, Spurs picked up another three points but they're really fucking dull aren't they? They've got loads of talent, a really big, strong, deep squad, but they're terrible to watch. I don't know what it is, but I find them to be seriously boring. They say dogs often look like their owners, and football teams are often a mirror image of their manager's personality. Spurs are a case in point, I like AVB as you know, there's something endearing about him, but let's be honest he's a bit of a trainspotter isn't he? He's got the charisma of a baked potato without any butter. He's the Stewart Downing of managers. Spurs may be dull, but they're also jammy. It's as though this season they've replaced 'late Gareth Bale screamer' with 'late iffy penalty'. Getting really sick of them now, the bland bastards. Even the fans are dull, so much so that AVB took the unusual step of telling them to get their shit together because they are hurting the team. That'll go down like a lead balloon when his team is performing like an on pitch representation of one of his interviews.

chapter six

November

ARSENAL 2 LIVERPOOL 0

Competition - Premier League
Date - Sun 2 Nov 2013
Venue - The Emirates
Scorer(s) –
Star Man – Martin Skrtel

Team: Mignolet; Toure, Skrtel, Sakho; Flanagan (Moses), Lucas, Gerrard, Henderson, Cissokho (Coutinho); Suarez, Sturridge:

The more things change the more they stay the same. We probably shouldn't read anything into this defeat, but obviously it still hurts. More often than not we're going to lose away to Arsenal, it may not be Old Trafford levels of stinkage but it's still not a venue where we tend to have much success. We can tell ourselves that this was always likely to end in an Arsenal victory but that doesn't make it any less painful.

Arsenal were strong favourites for the game but I still felt that we had a real chance of coming away with the points. After all, with Suarez and Sturridge in the form they've been in why wouldn't we have a chance? Who knows, if they'd actually shown up, maybe we would have. Ok that's a little unfair on Suarez, he put everything into the game as he always does but it just wasn't his day. Still, at least you knew he was on the pitch. Sturridge was invisible for long spells of this and looked to be in full on sulk mode in the 2nd half. Not surprising, I'd be sulking too if Per fucking Mertesacker marked me out of a game, and I'm 40, fat, slow and not very good. There's simply no excuse for Sturridge being owned the way he was by that big tugboat. That shocked me more than anything else about the game actually. I wasn't surprised that we gave away a couple of bad goals, I wasn't surprised that their attacking midfielders gave us a bit of a runaround at times and I wasn't even surprised that we had one of those days in front of goal when nothing went right. Sturridge doing absolutely nothing and getting no joy whatsoever out of Mertesacker though? I'd never have predicted that in a million years, in fact I was hanging my hat on that mismatch being our best chance of victory. I also liked the match up of Suarez against Koscielny, but that didn't go as expected either as the Frenchman stuck to his task well. I still think he's shite though, and on another day Suarez puts his chances away and everyone is pointing the finger at Arsenal's dodgy backline again. Fine margins.

The lack of quality service was obviously a contributing factor to the front two's lack of impact, but even allowing for that Sturridge was still hugely disappointing. He's set sky high standards now with his play this season (and last) so a game like this stands out like a sore thumb. Liverpool are not going to be able to beat the better teams in this league without the front two doing their thing. It's not as though the front two were the only ones below par either. It's difficult to pick out anyone other than maybe Sakho and Skrtel who performed to the standard you'd expect. Actually add Jon Flanagan to that, under the circumstances he did as well as could be expected and certainly did nothing wrong. The rest? Must do better. And yet despite so many players being off their game, it's not as though we got battered. What does that say about Arsenal? Call it sour grapes if you like, but whilst we were unquestionably poor for long spells in this game, I didn't think Arsenal were that good either and this result was more a case of us performing poorly on the day than of coming up against some irresistible force we could not control. Of course they were better than us - only an idiot would try to suggest otherwise - but they weren't THAT much better and had our finishing been of a more acceptable standard the narrative of this game would have been vastly different.

I think there's a danger we can read too much into Arsenal's domination of the ball and the struggles of our midfield to match them. Arsenal do that to everybody; their whole game is based around it and they do it better than any team in the country. We were never going in there and dominating possession; we wouldn't even be doing that with a midfield of trio of Mascherano, Alonso and a peak of his powers Gerrard, let alone Lucas, Henderson and a Gerrard that is no longer quite the player he was. It's as much down to tactics as anything I think. Look at Arsenal's line up, they had Ramsay and Arteta as the supposed 'holding' players, and then Ozil, Cazorla and Rosicky buzzing around in front of them. None of them played wide, so essentially you have five players in the middle of the park who are all great on the ball, passing it around between themselves and we were chasing shadows. Is our midfield a concern? Absolutely. But those concerns should not be because of this game, as it was five against three a lot of the time. The failure to track runners was an issue but it has been all season. I'm not even bothered about how much of the ball Arsenal had or how easily they passed it around in midfield. They carved us open a few times but it wasn't exactly the Alamo back there. Our biggest problem was what we did when we had the ball. Or rather what we didn't do.

If you take the pragmatic standpoint that when you visit Arsenal they are going to monopolise the ball and you will be playing a lot on the counter attack, then you need to make the most of those opportunities to break on them. We just didn't do it, and that's what was so disappointing about how we played. As shit as we were for most of the game, we still had five very presentable chances and also had a 'goal' disallowed. If we'd actually managed to play anywhere near how we can, there's no reason we couldn't have got something from the game. Of course the flip side to that argument was that we didn't play well because we aren't good enough, and I'm not discounting that yet. Performances like this happen far too often away at the big teams, but the reason I don't think it's an issue of quality is because some of the players that didn't perform on the day are proven top class talent, players with experience who have done it on the big stage. I'm leaning towards 'bad day at the office' but accept that maybe I'm kidding myself.

I'm definitely not buying into the Arsenal hype though, they've got flaws and the better sides will be able to expose that. I suppose that suggests we're not one of the better sides, and perhaps we aren't. It could also just be that we had a bad day. And yet even on that 'bad day' Suarez hit the post and later missed an absolute sitter. Henderson lost his nerve when faced with just the goalkeeper and then blasted another decent opportunity over the bar, whilst Sturridge also missed a good chance when he failed to connect properly with a header. And then there's the disallowed 'goal' when the referee refused to allow Suarez to take a quick free-kick after he'd been cynically fouled. The narrative of this game could have been vastly different, and had we taken a couple of the excellent chances we had then the Match of the Day crew would have been banging on about Arsenal's defensive frailty rather than their pretty football. To win at Arsenal you need to defend well, ride your luck and make the most of the opportunities you will undoubtedly get against what is a defensively vulnerable side. We didn't manage any of that, so predictably we lost.

Hindsight is a wonderful thing of course, but starting with a back three against a lone frontman played into Arsenal's hands. It was entirely understandable why Rodgers went with it, and I'm not having a go at him for it. I'd have picked the same team and even the shock selection of Flanagan made sense to me. Martin Kelly had looked so far off the pace when he came on last week that there's no way I'd have put him in, while using Sterling there against a side as good in attack as Arsenal would have been a huge risk too. So the choice was either move Henderson out of the middle and draft in Joe Allen, or put Flanagan there. Given how well the side played last week - and specifically how well Henderson did in the middle - moving things around too much was not a good idea so a straight swap of Flanagan for the unwell Johnson meant the least disruption to the line up. 'Flano' played well I thought, the only criticism was that his crossing was awful when he got into forward positions, but overall he did a good job.

The same cannot be said for Cissokho on the other flank, who was just wretched and actually looked scared stiff. Hooking him at half time was a kindness. Changing to a back four helped in some ways as we looked more of a threat in the second half and Coutinho gave us a bit of a spark. The problem was we gave away a completely needless goal when we were having a decent spell and that killed the game. Great strike by Ramsay in fairness, but what the hell was Kolo doing? The ball was trapped under Ramsay's feet and he was just waiting for it to sit up perfectly so he could shoot. If Toure closes him down there's nothing he can do, yet he stood off and watched as Ramsay waited and waited for it to sit up, and the next thing you know we're 2-0 down.

If we'd have pulled a goal back quickly then who knows, maybe Arsenal would have bottled it, but it just wouldn't go in for us. The keeper got away with murder when he smashed the ball into Sturridge but was fortunate that it bounced back to him and not into the net, and they then conspired to let Suarez in but he shot disappointingly wide with Sturridge going nuts in the centre because he didn't get a pass. He stood there for ages with his arms outstretched and it did my fucking head in. There's no way he's passing to Suarez if the roles were reversed and the only issue I have with Suarez is that he missed, not that he didn't pass. Any striker worth his salt goes for goal there but when you do you simply have to score. It summed up his - and Liverpool's - day.

Hopefully the next time we face Arsenal the front two will show their true quality and we'll give them much more of a game than we did this time. I really want to beat them next time, I'm still pissed off about the whole Suarez 'extra pound' thing, and the way their players carry on like their shit don't stink. Case in point, Gibbs hurts himself behind the goal, and decides to hobble back onto the pitch before dropping to the floor about a yard from the goal-line. We quite rightly play on and when the ball eventually goes out their players start kicking off because we didn't put the ball out. I can't even tell you how pissed off I was at that, but our team weren't in any kind of position to make them pay for it and I just sat there feeling helpless. It reminded me of Joe Pesci's line in Goodfellas when he's talking about being beaten senseless and says *"Man, I wish I was big just once"*. Quite.

Premier League Round Up (2-3 November 2013)

Could have been worse I suppose. Despite losing at Arsenal we've not dropped out of the top three, so this certainly wasn't the worst weekend in the world despite easy wins for both Manc sides. Chelsea losing was the obvious highlight, but the draw between Everton and Spurs at Goodison was a great result for us too.

United had an easy win on Saturday over hapless Fulham. There's a lot of things I could say about Martin Jol's side but seeing as how we play them this weekend I'm keeping schtum for now as I don't want to tempt fate and end up with egg on my face. They are shit though aren't they?

The punters at Craven Cottage had barely settled into their seats and they were 3-0 down. Valencia, Van Persie and Rooney all scored within 22 minutes and it looked like it could be a massacre. It never turned out like that and Fulham dug in and at least made a game of it in the 2nd half. Former Red Kacaniklic came off the bench to score via a deflection, Bent hit the bar and Richardson missed a sitter. Kasami went close too with a lovely strike from 20 yards. He's really looking a player now. If he keeps this up, he won't be at Fulham for long. He got into it with Fellaini late on, amusingly pulling his hair out of the referee's line of sight. The big Belgian has been a bit of a marked man of late, last week against Stoke he was the victim of an off the ball assault by Walters. Usually I'd frown on that sort of thing, especially from Stoke and definitely from Walters, but in this case I'm happy to make an exception as Fellaini deserves all he gets. Walters was probably just getting some payback for what Fellaini did to Stoke last season. Incredible that he's not been done for it though.

Almost as incredible as Ashley Young still getting penalties for diving. I don't watch much Champions League footy these days as the competition has gone downhill fast since we've not been in it. I haven't watched any of this week's games, I only know what I've read on twitter and that was that Young was diving again and somehow another referee was taken in by it. Obviously that 'word' Moyes had with him had about as much of an impact as those that Ferguson supposedly had last season (or was it the year before? Hard to keep track, it's been going on for so long). Moyes has now adopted an 'if you can't beat them join them' approach it seems, saying *"I've seen it and the boy certainly tugs him in the box. The referee is two yards away from it and decides to give it. All I know is he got a penalty kick from a decision; I don't know about his reputation, but the referee is there and he gave it."* Way to stand up for what you believe in Moyesy, you spineless little toad.

City bounced back from their loss at Chelsea with a 7-0 rout of Norwich at the Etihad. Joe Hart has been benched, unsurprisingly, and if this Pantilimon fella is any good it may take him a while to get back in as I doubt if Pellegrini has much trust in him, and why would he? Hart's been shite since the Chilean boss walked through the door, whatever he'd done before will mean little or nothing to Pellegrini. Toure curled in another terrific free-kick. When did he suddenly become this free-kick maestro? Is that what he spent his entire summer doing, as before this year I barely remember him taking any at all? Fair play to him. Maybe Hart can follow his lead and practice goalkeeping this off season.

As well as City played, Norwich were completely dire from the opening whistle and didn't seem to have any belief they could get anything from the game. They were actually the last away side to win at the Etihad in the Premier League but you'd never have guessed from watching this shambles. They might survive this year but if they do it will be due to the ineptitude of others and you have to say at this stage it's looking like they had a Diouf/Diao/Cheyrou of a summer transfer window.

If those two games went as expected at least there was a shock in the early game on Saturday, as Newcastle were terrific in beating Chelsea. Well, in the second half they were, the first half was pretty dire from both teams. The most likely goalscorer in the first period was Mongo who twice went close to scoring from corners. Chelsea have spent hundreds of millions on attackers yet their best hope of a goal was the gargantuan, bulbous fod of Terry. Clearly something isn't right there. With their team I mean, not with Terry's head, although obviously there's something not right about that too. That goes without saying. Fernando Torres is 'back' though. Someone must have forgotten to tell him, as he was 'back' to being shite and 'back' on the bench after getting hooked midway through the 2nd half, the fucking loser.

Newcastle were ace in the second half to be fair. Even my mackem brother-in-law couldn't help but acknowledge it. In amongst a shitload of angry, disappointed texts about Chelsea's shitness and how they were letting him down he grudgingly admitted *'the scum have played well'*. Praise from Caesar there.

Gouffran got his head on the end of a delicious Cabaye free-kick to put the Geordies ahead and Remy killed Chelsea off late on with a typically crisp finish. Great stuff from Remy and fantasy points for me. He then took off his shirt and got booked, costing me some of those points, the fucking slapdick. I still think Chelsea will win the league as on paper they've got the strongest squad by far, but virtually every time I watch them I think *"you should be way better than this"*. And David Luiz? It's just funny now seeing him highlighted on MOTD every week for his shitness. It wasn't even Jocky this time, it was Shearer. I'm repeating myself I know, but I just don't get it. Why is he not playing in midfield? Or for Barcelona?

I felt sorry for my poor old brother-in-law at the weekend though. Whatever could go wrong for Sunderland, did go wrong. It started with Newcastle beating Chelsea, and ended with them losing to one of their least favourite Geordies - former boss Steve Bruce. In between they scored an own goal, had two players sent off and lost their keeper to injury. Still, if you call yourselves the 'Black Cats' you can't really complain about bad luck. The Doss was one of the players that saw red. Bad challenge, he can have no complaints with that one but it is somewhat out of character. Usually he's too slow to even get close enough to even attempt a tackle, let alone make actual contact with somebody. The other sending off was a far more expected one. Lee Clattermole is a complete tit isn't he? Red card waiting to happen, he'll never, ever learn. On the plus side, the injury to the keeper Westwood opened the door for my favourite Premier League wiseguy, Vito Mannone, to get back on the field. I was wondering what had happened to 'Big Vito' as he just seemed to have disappeared off the face of the earth. I assumed he must have flipped and gone into the witness protection programme, so it was nice to see he's still around and that he ain't no rat. Vito's a stand up guy, a goodfella.

Stoke's 1-1 draw with Southampton was a decent enough result for both sides. Stoke need to start picking up some points whilst a point on their travels keeps Southampton's momentum going. Begovic gave Stoke the lead after 12 seconds with a freak goal. His clearance from his own penalty spot caught on the wind and bounced up over an embarrassed Boruc. Wind or no wind, being able to kick the ball that far never ceases to amaze me. I'd need at least three goes to cover that distance I reckon. Begovic now has more goals this season than Jon Walters. If you leave penalties out of it, it'll probably still be that way until Christmas if not beyond. Jay Rodriguez headed an equaliser for Southampton, and again it looked like a bit of a lucky goal as he headed it into the ground and it bounced over the keeper and in.

Moving on, and West Brom bounced back from their hammering at Anfield last week with a hard fought victory over Palace at the Hawthorns. Berahino put them ahead but Palace wasted several chances before McCauley made it 2-0 with a trademark header from a corner kick.

West Ham v Aston Villa had 0-0 written all over it. There wasn't a surer outcome anywhere at the weekend than this being another snoozefest. West Ham are football's answer to those late night gambling shows on ITV, where losers, pissheads and insomniacs ring up to play roulette and shit. Both are completely pointless, guaranteed to put you to sleep within seconds and have no business being on anybody's TV when there are so many better things that could be shown instead. *"There's only one thing missing from our game, and that's goals"* trumpeted Allardyce afterwards. It was not a criticism, it was said with bravado. He has no idea how ridiculous he sounds. Like a cricket coach saying *"we're doing great, now if we could only score some runs"* or Andy Murray coming out with *"I'm hitting the ball brilliantly, I just need to start getting it over the net and I'll be golden"*. Or a boxer saying *"you wouldn't believe the power I'm getting in my punches, now if I can just start to actually find a way to land them on my opponent I'm in business"*. Lambert felt West Ham should have been reduced to ten men after my old mate 'Ravel' appeared to tug back a Villa player who was through on goal. The question was put to Allardyce by the BBC interviewer afterwards...... *"RUBBISH!!"* Fat Sam scoffed. *"A little lightweight like Ravel Morrison outmuscling one of his players??? RUBBISH"*.

Firstly, Morrison isn't a 'little lightweight', he's average height and build for a footballer. Secondly, it was pint sized Andreas Weimann that he dragged down. Admittedly 'Ravel' may be better known for intimidating little old ladies than other footballers, but the suggestion that he dragged down another footballer half his size is not so ridiculous as to be mocked in the derisory manner Allardyce did. I bet Lambert will have been seething when he saw that interview.

Onto Sunday and the South Wales derby now. Always a highly charged fixture and an especially huge day for Cardiff who have been in Swansea's shadow of late. Perhaps that explained why they seemed to want it far more than Laudrup's side on the day. There wasn't much in the game but Cardiff seemed first to every loose ball and their work rate was tremendous, typified by the performance of Medel who was superb again. Caulker won it for Cardiff by outjumping Chico Flores and planting a header past Vorm. Jonjo should have found himself in hot water afterwards for inciting the home fans by making what's known as the 'swim away' gesture. Apparently Swansea and Cardiff fans had a barney a few years back and the story goes that Cardiff fans ran into the sea to get away. Whilst it's funny and all that, Jonjo really should be facing an FA charge for this but it seems he's gotten away with it. Walters got away with that blatant elbow on Fellaini last week too, despite there being enough video evidence to have him hung, drawn and quartered. What's going on at the FA lately, have the fuckers used the Suarez fine money to go off on holiday or something?

The other game on Sunday went just about as well as we could have expected it to. A win for either Spurs or Everton would have put them above us and Chelsea into second place. Thankfully it ended up as a drab, goalless stalemate. Spurs? In a drab game? I'm shocked, they're usually so fluid and exciting. They should change their kit from white to beige, the bland bastards. They're little more than an upmarket West Ham since Bale left. Soldado was shite again, the only thing of note he did was a sly elbow into the chest of Jagielka. Remember when I kept getting confused between Soldado and Negredo? I'm not confused anymore, I can easily tell them apart as Soldado is the shit one. Both sides had a penalty shout and both incidents involved the same two players. First, Vertonghen took a dive under the attention of Coleman. Never a pen in a million years, the cheating fuck. He's getting a name for himself now, or at least he fucking should be, the diving, playacting gobshite.

Everton's shout was the exact opposite. Coleman was caught by Vertonghen, went down for a second but bounced back up to try and get his shot away. Definitely a pen but he didn't get it through being honest and not staying down after being tripped. There really is no incentive for players for try and stay up when fouled is there? The biggest talking point of the game involved the concussion suffered by Hugo Lloris after he collided with Lukaku. It was pretty irresponsible of Spurs to allow him to go back on, regardless of how much the keeper wanted to. The incident re-ignited the ill feeling between Lukaku and his former boss AVB, whom the striker once said he 'would never forgive' and whom he 'learned absolutely nothing from'. AVB did his best to smooth things over before the game, and then said afterwards: "Lukaku is a fantastic footballer and I don't question his integrity or his human side. We had a warm hug on the pitch before the game so I have maximum respect for him and I think he has for me." All good then. Except.... "But amid all this negative excitement I find it surprising that no time was lost to actually study the incident. I want to believe that Lukaku's leg was not left late to clash into Hugo's head. I find it remarkable as well that nobody has dedicated themselves to find out if the player could have avoided the keeper and I'm disappointed that Lukaku hasn't contacted Hugo."

Ah come on now junior, there's no way that was intentional so why even plant the seed? Perhaps it's because he's getting pilloried for allowing Lloris to go back on so he's trying to draw attention away from that. Hopefully the concussion isn't too bad and there are no long standing ill effects from it, but if Spurs do need to look for a new keeper in January then how about Begovic? They could use all the goalscoring help they can get, as you can't rely on dodgy Soldado penalties every week. Martinez hit back at AVB's jibes by saying: *"We're waiting for Roberto Soldado to apologise to Phil Jagielka and use the same phone call so we don't have to spend two phone calls."* If that were any other club than Everton I'd assume that was a joke, but with their penny pinching history? Remember, this is the club that stopped players from swapping shirts after games because they didn't want to keep replacing them. I still recall the story about the Everton kit man bursting into the LFC dressing room to snatch back a shirt Gregory Vignal had got from Gazza. They probably kept Vignal's shirt and stuck it on ebay though, the cheap blue bastards.

LIVERPOOL 4 FULHAM 1

Competition - Premier League
Date - Sat 9 Nov 2013
Venue - Anfield
Scorer(s) – Amorobieta (OG), Skrtel, Suarez (2)
Star Man – Steven Gerrard

Team: Mignolet; Johnson, Skrtel, Agger, Cissokho (Enrique); Henderson, Lucas, Gerrard (Allen), Coutinho; Suarez, Sturridge (Moses):

We're getting good at this 'beating the shit teams' lark aren't we? And let's face it, they don't get much shitter than this Fulham side. There was a time not so long ago that the Cottagers represented a bit of a challenge, they came to Anfield and got some goalless draws and even a win a couple of years ago. That's two consecutive 4-0 home wins for us over Martin Jol's side though (in between we also hammered them at their place) and this was just embarrassingly easy.

That's not taking anything away from our performance, this is exactly what we need to be doing as whilst there aren't many sides as bad as Fulham are at this moment in time, there's plenty of weaklings knocking around waiting to have a beating inflicted on them. We're becoming quite the bully of late. We got pushed around by one of the bigger kids last week, but we were back to stealing lunch money from one of the dweebs a week later.

In football terms, there's nothing wrong with being flat track bullies, in fact if you want to get into the top four that's the best way to do it. We're second in the league because - Arsenal apart - we're currently doing that better than anybody else. Fulham may be crap but you still have to go out and beat them. We were brilliant in this game, some of the football was dazzling and on several occasions we were one pass or shot away from scoring the kind of goal that gets replayed for years. Fulham were dire but they still needed putting to the sword and we did it.

Rodgers changed his team and his system and was vindicated by a great performance and a clean sheet. With the exception of Cissokho I thought everybody was excellent. The Frenchman wasn't terrible, you could just see he was a level below everybody else. He even managed his now customary 'completely mis-control the ball on the touchline and allow it to go out of play' moment that he seems to throw in every week. Take him out of the equation though and everyone else played well.

The return of Coutinho opens up all manner of possibilities for Rodgers in terms of formations, and even looking at the team sheet didn't provide any real concrete evidence of how the side would line up. Would Coutinho be on the left of a front three with Luis Suarez on the right? Or would we see him in behind the front two with a narrow midfield three behind him? It was neither, as Rodgers went back to the system he'd started the season with. Coutinho on the left of the midfield four, Henderson on the right but both of them moving inside to allow the full backs to provide width. Perhaps this is what we'll see moving forward, but I suspect we have not seen the last of three at the back and Rodgers may well select his system to suit the opposition and the occasion. Certainly this looked good, but Fulham were so hopeless you can't read too much into anything.

Suarez was causing problems from the start but Sturridge took a while to get going. He barely touched the ball in the opening 20 minutes or so but it didn't really matter such was our dominance. It was only a matter of time before the goal came, and when it did Sturridge was involved as it was his clever turn that caused Richardson to hack him down. Gerrard whipped in a great free-kick that looked like it would be met by Agger, but it went in off Amorobieta. Not that DJ George cares, he did what he always does and just gave it to whichever Liverpool player happened to be nearest. *"The goalscorer for Liverpool, number seven Luis Suarez!!"* he declared, as everyone around the ground gave a collective *"eh???"* To be fair, unless you've got the benefit of replays it's difficult to make calls like that. I didn't know who'd scored either until I got home and watched it, I just knew none of our players appeared to celebrate it as if it was their goal. Within no time it was 2-0. Coutinho's shot was brilliantly tipped over by the over worked Steklenberg but from Gerrard's corner Skrtel powered in a great header and whatever meek resistance Fulham were offering was ended there and then. One more arrived before half time, Gerrard nutmegged Berbatov and played a great ball over to Johnson. He rolled it to Henderson, Suarez set off on a run and pointed to where he wanted the ball, Hendo delivered and Suarez did the rest.

The incident summed up Berbatov's day. He couldn't have been any more disinterested, although in fairness to him he didn't start the game that way and early on he looked to at least be trying. Once the game got away from them though he showed little patience for the ineptitude of his team-mates and went completely into 'fuck it' mode. It was funny to watch. In the first half he played one terrific crossfield ball with enough backspin on it to keep the ball in play and allow the wideman to get there. He also plucked a difficult high ball out of the air and killed it stone dead with the kind of technique he's renowned for. That drew gasps then applause from the crowd. Then they went a couple of goals down and he just quit. A similar high ball came at him in the second half and he barely even bothered to lift his leg to try and control it. It wasn't a surprise. When things are good there are few better. When they are bad, there are few worse. Whenever I try and describe my own style of play, the comparison I usually make is that *"I'm like a shit Berbatov"*. Well this was like looking in the mirror.

Fulham were so bad that the danger was that we'd think it was too easy and lose the intensity in our play. We've been in this situation before; 3-0 up against shite at home. We completely eased off against Palace - and in doing so missed the chance to go top on goal difference - but this time we kept going. Only one more goal came, but that was as much down to Steklenberg and our substitutions than any dropping of intensity. We had 32 shots, which apparently is the most by any team all season. The fourth goal was a microcosm of what we did all day. Great pressing by Henderson, lovely pass from Gerrard and a cool finish from Suarez. Great stuff, when we press the ball high up the pitch we look really good. When we don't, we look bang average. So why aren't we doing this all the time?

4-0 was the minimum we should have got from the game and if you wanted to be hyper-critical you could say we should have scored more. You don't get too many days where the opportunity is there to score six, seven, eight. . . A game like that massively boosts your goal difference but in this case I'm ok with it as I don't think we eased off too much, the goals just didn't come.

We've been far from perfect this season and we've certainly had our ropey moments, but despite all that we're second in the table, just two points off the top. We couldn't really have asked to be in a better position when the season kicked off, especially as we were without Suarez for the opening five league games. The biggest thing in our favour at this moment in time though is that all of our rivals for the top four look to have as many flaws and vulnerabilities as we have, if not more. Maybe they'll sort those issues out as the season goes on, but maybe they won't. Either way, we need to make hay while the sun shines and keep racking up the points.

Premier League Round Up (9-10 November 2013)

That couldn't have gone much better really, with Arsenal, City and Spurs all losing and Everton and Chelsea drawing. The Mancs winning wasn't ideal, but given the opposition it's still relatively easy to take positives from that result. I love weekends like this, when we have a big win and can then watch MOTD safe in the knowledge that everyone else has fucked up in some way.

Had Andre Marriner not been a massive shithouse homer then the weekend would have been even better, as by rights Chelsea should have lost to West Brom at the Bridge and it's a bit of a sickener that they didn't. Still, they didn't win and we'd all have taken that before kick off. They were seriously jammy though. To say that Chelsea's opening goal was preventable would be something of an understatement. Liam Ridgewell could have easily made a clearance but the one footed bastard waited and waited as he tried to adjust his body to avoid using his right foot, and Eto'o nipped in to score. Even John Arne Riise would have been shaking his head at this show of incompetance. Why are lefties such one footed twats? Does my head in, there's simply no excuse for it. Righties can be a bit one footed too of course, but not to the extent that lefties are. Steve Clarke should make Ridgewell stay behind after training every day for a month and kick only with his right foot as punishment for this. I'm deadly serious, a footballer being paid tens of thousand pounds a week should at least be semi competent with his 'weaker' foot. I'm not sure how it's even possible to have a 'weak' foot when you've spent hours a day playing footy since you were a little kid.

A great climb by Shane Long made it 1-1 as he hung in the air over Mongo to score from close range. Superb stuff from the Irishman. West Brom then hilariously took the lead when Sessegnon's pea roller somehow beat Cech. Chelsea were complaining about a foul in the build up but they're talking shite. Nothing wrong with it at all, just good pressure by West Brom and Ivanovic tripped over his own knuckles, the neanderthal looking twat. The Baggies could have made the game safe late on but the chance came to nothing because Chris Brunt is a thick, greedy bastard who chose to go on his own when others were better placed. To be fair, when one of the other options was to pass to Anichebe you can perhaps understand him shooting.

The penalty Chelsea got in stoppage time was outrageous but was the kind of thing I've come to expect. When Mourinho was there first time around decisions like this were commonplace, and this won't be the last dodgy one they get. Someone might want to be checking Marriner's bank account over the next few weeks.

Mourinho's post match interview was a shocker even by his standards. You might think that with his former assistant in the opposing dug out he'd be a bit more gracious about things, but no. *"Is difficult to accept for zem as it was last minute penalty, but now zey go home zey see on ze screen and zey change zeir opinion"* he waffled. *"So you believe that was a clear cut penalty?"* he was zen, sorry, then asked. *"I don't BELIEVE… it was penalty. I watch on ze screen two or sree times and is clear penalty. Same way it was free-kick against West Bromwich when zey score ze second goal. So I have ze reason to be very upset with ze referee's work, which I accept, but I have to say clearly is a big mistake. Even ze fourth official talk to me because he was on my side"* He's an absolute wanker. In fact, he's by far the biggest wanker in English football, it's like every time he opens his mouth and says anything you can't but think anything other than 'what a fucking wanker'. Even Abramovich thinks he's a wanker, he just doesn't care because he thinks it's worth tolerating him because he'll bring trophies. If he doesn't bring trophies he'll be out the door quicker than you can say *"bye bye wanker"* though, as you just know Abramovich really doesn't like him much. He was dressed like a hobo too, what's the deal there? Suit jacket, polo shirt, dirty grey t-shirt underneath and he appears to have lost his razor. Special One??? Scruffy One more like, the fucking tramp. Maybe he was in disguise and on the run from Jonas Olsson? He had a bust up in the tunnel afterwards with the big nasty Swede apparently. It seems he was running his mouth in typical Mourinho fashion and Olsson told him to *"Shut up and fuck off"*.

Mourinho responded by calling him a *"Mickey Mouse player"*, which is true in fairness.

If this were anyone else in charge of Chelsea right now their fans would be kicking off big time. Having chanted for years about wanting 'Jose' back though, they're in a difficult spot now and have to be a bit more patient, which must be killing the fickle, impatient bastards. Him having a bit of a pop at the fans isn't going to help though. AVB had a go at the Spurs crowd a few weeks ago and Mourinho has now followed suit by going on about the atmosphere at Stamford Bridge, saying it's due to a 'different profile of fan' attending the game now. No way Jose, I'm not having that. Stamford Bridge is still full of the same 'profile' of fans it has always been. They're commonly known to the rest of the country as 'bad knobheads'. So whilst Chelsea should have lost and it was a bit sickening how they got that late pen, they still unexpectedly dropped two points at home to a team we had hammered a couple of weeks earlier. I'll take that all day, dodgy pen or not.

Everton not winning at Selhurst Park was a pleasant surprise too. Palace are awful and don't even have a manager. I wasn't holding out much hope for them to slow Everton down but they did. They probably should have won as they had the best chances in the game, but again, I can live with a draw. One of their players produced one of the worst headers I've ever seen, trying to head it goalwards and sending it in the complete opposite direction. The most laughable thing I've seen since Walters smashed the ball into his own face when attempting an overhead kick last season. The closest Everton came was a header from Jagielka that hit the bar, but overall they were crap, much to the displeasure of some of the travelling toffees, one of whom got into an unpleasant spat with Sylvain Distin at full time. No idea what that was about, maybe Distin was playing to the galleries and giving it the old 'my bad' routine again like he did at Wembley after his great assist for Suarez's goal, and the fan wasn't impressed? I don't like Palace much and I hate Selhurst Park, but it's ace how they play 'Glad All Over' before the game. Love that, really gets the old foot tapping and it's better than what most other sides do that's for sure. *cough* Z cars *cough*

Southampton looked really good in smashing Hull 4-1. A lot of their success this season has been due to their defending but they were brilliant going forward in this game. Lallana is a player isn't he? Seems to be getting better all the time and he was terrific in this game, scoring the third with a brilliant individual goal, slaloming his way through the Hull defence before rolling the ball into the net. Lovely goal that.

Moving on, and Aston Villa have been finding goals hard to come by lately and they certainly made hard work of it against Cardiff at Villa Park. They'd gone seven and a half hours without scoring until Bacuna eventually curled in a late free-kick from 30 yards. Having waited so long for a goal, in typical fashion another came along within minutes from Kozak and Lambert's men had the win. As for Cardiff, I like their all yellow away strip, we should have something like that.

Elsewhere, Norwich and West Ham met at Carrow Road in the evening kick off. Saturday night TV is traditionally shit and on paper this looked like a worthy companion to the likes of X Factor and Dancing on Ice etc, but it actually turned out to be pretty good in the end. Not that I watched it, I was too busy watching X-Fact... erm, the Spanish footy on Sky. Yeah, that's it, I was watching the Spanish footy. Those who watched this one were probably regretting it at half time, as Norwich stank like a freshly squeezed turd in the first half and West Ham were...well West Ham. The Hammers were just about good value for the lead they had at the break courtesy of Morrison's tap in, but whatever Chris Hughton said to his players at half time worked as Norwich came roaring back. Leroy Fer got the winner, and this time it wasn't disallowed for a heinous lack of sportsmanship. Massive win for Norwich, I'm happy for Hughton who always comes across as one of the good guys and was taking some real stick from the fans in the first half, and of course it's great to see Fat Sam's much vaunted 'mean machine' conceding some goals too.

Onto Sunday now, and Mesut Ozil had said in the build up to the big game at Old Trafford that Arsenal would end United's season. Yeah, couple of slight problems with that son. Firstly, it's Manchester United, you don't say shit like that as it usually comes back to bite you in the arse. I know they've got Moyes now, but still, why tempt fate? Go out and beat them and then run your mouth. Secondly, Arsenal aren't as good as they seem to think they are. When they beat us last week, I called it that they'd probably lose at United as it's been coming. If we hadn't had so many players shit the bed a week ago it would have been us beating them as they were ripe for a defeat.

Arsenal had been given a fitness boost before kick off with the news that Mertesacker had been ruled out after catching some kind of flu bug. Fuck me, how slow must that flu bug have been to get caught by that lumbering bastard? It was probably the same flu bug most of us had this time last year, that slow oaf just finally managed to catch up with it when it had completely ran out of steam. It may even be that Bird Flu that hit parts of the UK in 2011. Wenger had said earlier in the week that Van Persie was 'still an Arsenal man'. Didn't look like it when he was giving it the bifters after heading United in front. Those fuckers win so many of these big games with goals from corners don't they? They've done it to us countless times and it's so fucking annoying. It's not like they've got a team of giants, how do they keep doing it?

Phil Jones was booked after a clash of heads with the keeper. Jonathon Pearce observed *"he came out of that looking groggy"*. I'd observe that *"he went into it looking groggy too"*.

Elsewhere on Sunday, Stoke went 2-0 up at Swansea before getting pegged back and then falling behind with a couple of minutes left. Jon Walters somehow managed to forget that he's Jon Walters long enough to produce a cool finish to open the scoring with his first goal of the season. That was route one stuff, long ball to Crouch, flick on, Walters running off him... Their second goal was anything but though, it was lovely football that ended with Crouch cushioning a ball off to Ireland for a simple finish. I'm not hating on Stoke anywhere near as much these days, I even felt a bit sorry for them when it looked like they were going to lose this one. Swansea had come roaring back to lead through goals from Bony (two) and Dyer, and Stoke looked dead and buried. Then they forced a couple of set-pieces and from one of those the referee spotted a handball that no-one else did, and Adam buried the pen with the last kick of the game.

There was a shock at White Hart Lane as Spurs somehow lost to Newcastle. It's fair to say that the North Londoners are far from convincing at the moment, but it's also fair to say they were seriously unlucky not to win this game as they absolutely fucking hammered the Geordies. Tim Krul was like Superman at times. Newcastle started brightly and deservedly led through another terrific Remy finish, but after that Spurs had chance after chance after chance but it just wouldn't go in. It's easy to laugh at Spurs, and don't get me wrong, I am, but there didn't look to be too much wrong with them based on how they played. Still, just nine goals in eleven games for AVB's side this season is not good and the fans voiced their displeasure at full time. Have to say though, I'm not sure how you can justify booing your team off after they've played like this. AVB's right, his fans are shite. Spurs have had more shots on target than anyone though, so don't be surprised if things turn around pretty quickly on the goalscoring front.

Finally this weekend, City lost away. Again. At Sunderland. Again. This is the fourth season in a row they have lost 1-0 at the Stadium of Light, but much like Spurs, this was a game City should never have lost. It wasn't as freakish as the game at White Hart Lane and Sunderland will argue they defended very well and deserved the points, but City had bags of chances and on another day would have won. Four away defeats already for them now, three of them to shite teams and the fourth to a Chelsea side that is struggling to beat anybody right now.

Notice how Sunderland put my guy Big Vito between the sticks and straight away keep a clean sheet? That's not a co-incidence, Vito had probably warned off the City strikers before the game. *"Hey Aguero, fuckface, you shoota da ball pasta me and I'll busta ya fuckin' face, capiche?"* Keep him in there Gus, he's a good fella. Wes Brown was back too, after nearly two years out injured. No surprise he had a great game against City. If they'd been playing United the useless get would have scored an oggy. Or his buddy O'Shea would have. Pair of losers.

EVERTON 3 LIVERPOOL 3

Competition - Premier League
Date - Sat 23 Nov 2013
Venue - Goodison Park
Scorer(s) – Coutinho, Suarez, Sturridge
Star Man – Jon Flanagan

Team: Mignolet; Johnson, Skrtel, Agger, Flanagan; Henderson, Gerrard, Lucas (Moses), Allen (Sturridge), Coutinho; Suarez:

It was becoming more and more difficult to find things to dislike about Everton these days. Then this game comes along and now we can take our pick. 'Nice guy' Roberto Martinez showed his true colours are now bitter blue by trying to downplay the worst challenge seen in the Premier League since... well since one of his Wigan players (an Evertonian no less!) tried to sever a Newcastle player's leg using only his studs.

And Kevin Miralles, eh? Who knew he was such a cunt? Then there's those crying twats Distin and Jagielka in the referees face complaining about non-existent elbows. It just goes to show that the sight of a red shirt and Liverbird can turn even the most mild mannered of Blues into Attilah the fucking Hun. Shower of bastards they are, thank Christ we didn't lose to them.

We should have won and we didn't because of two key incidents; the failure of the horrifically bad Phil Dowd to send off Mirallas when we led 2-1 and the equally horrific miss by Joe Allen when he could have made it 3-1 and probably finished them off. We also had two glorious chances when both Suarez and Moses failed to score with easy headers, whilst Suarez also had a brilliant left foot shot saved by Howard as we finished the stronger side. And yet Evertonians can also legitimately argue they should have won as for most of the second half they tore through us almost at will and only the inspired Mignolet prevented them scoring a bagful.

This was a great spectacle in terms of incident and excitement but it wasn't a great game in terms of quality, especially to those who appreciate the art of defending. The attacking wasn't great either, as five of the goals came directly from set-pieces and the other came in the second phase of play after a set-piece wasn't fully cleared. I thought we were generally very poor and had too many players well below par. Taking that - and the fact we trailed late on - into account, a point is a decent return from this game as it meant they didn't close the gap on us. Beating them would have increased that gap to six though and whilst we can look at our own poor performance as a reason for that, you also can't get away from the huge impact Dowd had on the result.

I don't know what went on in his head, as he had a clear view of it and having not rushed in with a yellow card straight away there's then no excuse for him to not show a red having taken time to think about it. When no card was forthcoming after 30 seconds I was convinced Mirallas was off. Then when no card was still forthcoming after a minute I knew he wasn't, as you can't leave it that long and then produce a red, there'd have been a riot if he'd done that. He had the fourth official in his earpiece telling him something and maybe that played a part but it really shouldn't have. Dowd saw the tackle and even if there was any doubt in his mind then the two puncture woulds in the knee of Suarez should have removed it. A knee high, full blooded tackle that doesn't get the ball and makes a heavy contact with an opponents knee? That's not only a red card, it's borderline assault. Thank fuck he wasn't seriously hurt. I'll rephrase that actually, as I'm sure he was seriously hurt. He wasn't seriously injured though, and he's extremely lucky.

Suarez is just a fucking warrior though, Everton always try and kick him out of the game but it's easier said than done as he's like the T-1000. Leave him in a heap and he just slowly starts melding himself back together until before you know it he's coming after you again. He's fucking nails is Suarez, and whilst his conduct over the summer may have tarnished him somewhat in the eyes of some fans (me included), it's hard not to love him when you see how committed he always is once he steps onto the field. The balls he showed in this game says everything about his character.

Not having Sturridge alongside him made things difficult and he was too isolated for a lot of the game due to the way we played. Either it was intentional that we sat back or we just ended up doing that because of our inability to keep the ball. I don't know if it was how Rodgers wanted us to play, if Everton are just really good or if we just weren't at it, but we were passive, negative and didn't play anywhere near the amount of football I'd have liked and it was Suarez who suffered the most as he was left to do too much on his own.

We'd gotten off to the perfect start when Coutinho opened the scoring after Everton failed to deal with a Gerrard corner. Aside from his goal though, Coutinho was hardly in the game. On the other flank Hendo put in a shift as always and in the first half he looked quite threatening at times. The way the game went though most of his play in the 2nd half was in his own half helping out the absolutely woeful Glen Johnson. I'll get to him later. It was just a weird game. The first half was crap in terms of quality but brilliant in terms of entertainment. We scored a set-piece, then they scored a set-piece. The pace of the game was a million miles an hour, it was like a throwback to some of the derbies of old where little football is played in the opening half hour as there just wasn't any time to do it. With Rodgers and Martinez in the manager's seats many expected this to be something of a game for the purist, but I guess the occasion takes over as this was no different to many games we've seen over the years. In fact, the only real difference was Everton playing to win rather than not to lose.

They were dirty bastards though. Even the foul that led to our second goal was proper snidey as Barry deliberately stood on Suarez's foot. Having that fat arsed crab put all of his not inconsiderable weight on your foot has got to hurt. I had a feeling that Suarez was going to make them pay for that though; his free-kicks have really become lethal over the last year or so and this was a beauty. Blame Tim Howard or the wall all you like, but I didn't see too much they could have done about it. The ball curled at least a yard in the air and flew right into the bottom corner. How are you meant to stop that?

Suarez was being kicked all over the place - even many of the fair challenges were ones where they made sure they hammered him after they'd won the ball - and before long he was hobbling around seemingly bothered by his right knee. No-one is going to convince me that this didn't influence what Miralles did. He's not making that challenge on any other player on the pitch, but he knew Suarez was struggling and he wanted to put him out of the game, the massive fucking shithouse twat. And Dowd saw it all, that's the worst part.

In typical Everton style, they then began screaming for fouls and yellow cards any time one of our players made any kind of challenge. Gerrard went up for a header with Barry, the pair of them had their arms up and they collided in mid air. Barry didn't have an issue with the challenge yet all of sudden here come Jagielka and Distin demanding Dowd send Gerrard off for an elbow. Twats. Worse than that was Martinez complaining about it afterwards, despite acknowledging that the elbow didn't even make contact. Didn't take him long to be indoctrinated into the ways of the Blues did it? Gerrard's arm was raised in a natural manner for that kind of challenge, he didn't make any contact with Barry and trying to make any kind of issue about it says a lot about Martinez, especially given that Miralles later led with his arm way above his head and smashed it into the face of Henderson, splitting open his eye. The punishment for that? Nothing. It's fucking bullshit.

I hate derby games, especially the Goodison ones. They're just too stressful and this was one of the worst ever due to the open nature of the game and with both sides defending like school kids. One thing that Martinez will bring to this fixture is that he won't go out there and play for a draw like Moyes always did, so there won't be any shortage of drama in future encounters. Everton went all out to win the game and for a long spell in the 2nd half they did absolutely batter us. We've seen it several times already this season where we have a lead and just stop playing. The problem is, we aren't good enough defensively to just shut up shop, we need to have the ball because when we haven't got it we can be vulnerable.

Lukaku ran riot after the break but I don't just blame the two centre backs for that. They generally dealt with him as best they could but when their midfielders are running uncontested at our defence and he has clear space to run into, how are Agger and Skrtel supposed to deal with that? Perhaps Sakho would have been better equipped to deal with it but the main problem for me was how easily they just kept running through the middle of the park, especially galling given we played with three central midfielders. That worries me as it just shouldn't happen, should it? Our midfield is generally fine against 70% of the league, but against the decent sides we are struggling in there. Gerrard wasn't at his best, probably due to his unnecessary England exploits, and you could have grabbed someone out of the away end and put him in Lucas' position and he'd have done a better job. No really, you actually could have done, as French international Yann M'Vila was sat in with the Liverpool fans and I'd take him all day over this post-injury Lucas.

And you could have found 3,000 fans that would have done a better job with that chance than Joe Allen did. Fucking hell, that was shocking and Allen will need to be a strong character to come back from that. I hope he does as I still think he's a quality player. The uncertainty over what is our best formation isn't going to help him though, he was bought to play a defined role in a 4-3-3, but we don't play that anymore so where will that leave him?

As underwhelming as the midfield was, however, it was nothing in comparison to the pitiful performance of Johnson. I've always been one of his biggest supporters, but I'm not oblivious to his flaws and I've often pointed out that you'll get four or five absolute stinkers from Johnson every season. When he's good he's class, when he's bad he's seriously fucking awful, like in this game. Looking at him and Flanagan you'd never have guessed who was the £18m England international with the big fat contract, and who was the 20 year old kid with a handful of games under his belt.

Firstly, Flanagan was having to play out of position and secondly, he didn't have the diligent Henderson in front of him working back to help him out, he had Coutinho there and as a result was often left alone on an island having to deal one on one with Mirallas and Deufeleu. Despite being beaten once or twice - understandable given how Everton targeted him and how many times he was left in tricky situations - overall he did everything you could have asked of him. So much so that I'd even ask the question as to why it's Flanagan that should have to play on the left? Johnson should be the one to move, he has the experience and has shown on numerous times he is effective at left back. In fact, he's arguably better in that role because he has to think about what he's doing and doesn't get in the comfort zone we sometimes see from him at right back. Like in this game for instance. I was screaming for him to be substituted after 55 minutes, after 65 I was screaming for him to be sold and after 85 I was screaming for him to taken round the back of the Park End and shot. I've calmed down somewhat since and I'm no longer advocating selling him (or shooting him), but there's absolutely no way I'd be giving him a new contract on the terms he's currently getting. As talented as he is, he's one dozy, lackadaisical bastard sometimes. On those bad days, he plays like he's half asleep and needs a rocket up his arse. He gave the ball away cheaply on so many occasions, the worst being when he casually lobbed the ball straight to Barkley when under no pressure. Lucas - as he often tends to do - then committed a foul and that was the free-kick from which Everton's equaliser eventually came.

It was no more than they deserved on the balance of play - but more than they deserved on the balance of them having a player on the field who shouldn't have been there - and the only surprise was that it had taken them so long to score. For that we have Mignolet to thank, he made some brilliant stops in one against one situations, especially against Lukaku and Deulefeu.

The goal woke us up though and it became a pulsating end to end game. Rodgers had been bold in his substitutions once Everton drew level, sending on Sturridge and Moses for Allen and Lucas. Whilst you can argue that left us wide open in the middle of the park, I'd argue that we were already wide open, so what the hell. At least now Suarez wasn't left up there all on his lonesome. He should have put us ahead again but headed straight at Howard when a yard either side of him was a certain goal. That chance came from a sensational first time Gerrard cross, no other player on the pitch could have put the ball in like that as the layoff to him hadn't been great and it came at an awkward height. It was a stunning delivery and Suarez will be kicking himself he didn't put it away.

Neither side appeared to be bothered about defending now and neither had a clue how to deal with set-pieces, as witnessed with both of the goals that would follow. Everton's third was an absolute gift and Johnson's half arsed attempt at marking Lukaku summed up the full back's day, but the bigger issue for me would be why we had Johnson marking him anyway? Surely one of the centre backs should have been doing that job?

My anger had completely boiled over now, I'd completely lost it and although I was aware that the family members in the room were probably a little bit uncomfortable I couldn't help it, I was ready to explode. I thought we were done and I was about as pissed off as it's possible to be regarding a football match. It wasn't just Mirallas or Dowd that was the focus of it now, it was our team, who had been shite for most of the game but particularly in the second half until Everton had eventually scored the goal they'd been threatening since half time. Mignolet was terrific, Suarez heroic and I can't speak highly enough of Flanagan's display, but aside from them I thought everyone else simply had to do better. And lo and behold, when we found ourselves behind, that's exactly what they did.

From going 3-2 down we were superb and should really have won the game. Sturridge had earlier had a chance when he moved the ball onto his left foot but then inexplicably failed to shoot, tried to check back and lost it. In his defence he'd only just come at that point so you can understand him not being up to the pace of the game. The next chance he had he made no mistake with, Gerrard whipped in yet another great set-piece (even if his general play wasn't great his delivery into the box all afternoon was imperious) and Sturridge connected perfectly to glance the ball into the far top corner. Great header, and he celebrated by running off and doing the wriggly arms whilst facing the Everton fans. You can bet your life he'd been getting dog's abuse whilst warming up so this was his way of giving some back.

That Everton crowd really is something to behold isn't it? The contorted, hate filled faces any time one of our players is in the vicinity never ceases to amaze me. Players will get stick at away grounds all the time, Suarez especially, but you rarely see the kind of out of control pure hatred that you see on Evertonian faces on derby day. You don't even get that when we go to Old Trafford. One sewer rat was captured on TV trying to spit on Suarez (presumably he'll be banned? The fan I mean, not Suarez, although you never know), whilst I also saw a couple of kids of around 11 or 12 running down to the front with their ugly little Evertonian faces all scrunched up spewing out bile at Suarez. Skrtel got into it with them too after one of them lashed the ball at him. It's just a pity there was no camera on them when Sturridge was dancing in front of them, that would have really been something to see, I can imagine it being like a scene from the Walking Dead or something, with all the mutants desperately wanting to get to him but being penned back and instead having to stand there slobbering and hissing.

I'd have to say that Sturridge not only got his team out of jail with that goal, but himself too. Playing 90 minutes for England whilst injured, with a massive derby game just four days later was irresponsible to say the least. The same goes for Gerrard, but at least in his case he was always going to make himself available to start this game. Hodgson is partly responsible, but Sturridge is a big boy and can make his own mind up. He chose to play for England knowing it would put at risk his place at Goodison. I have some sympathy with him to be fair, as unlike Gerrard his World Cup place is not guaranteed. He'll be in the squad of course, but his place in the team isn't secure. It should also be pointed out that he pulled out of a squad earlier in the season to be fit for the Swansea game and got absolutely hammered for it, so he was stuck between a rock and a hard place. I'm not holding this against him, but only because he came on and scored!

We should have won it in the end as we certainly had the chances. Moses headed over from a great Suarez cross, and then Suarez forced Howard into a save with a spectacular half volley with his left foot. It wasn't to be though, and both sides will be both pleased and disappointed with a draw. Overall, it's a much better point for us than them given they had the lead late on and were at home. It's quite remarkable how rarely they manage to beat us and whilst it's disappointing not to win you'd have to say it must be seriously galling for them to once again fail to put one over on us. That's two years in a row now though they've been bailed out by a referee in this fixture. Not that they'll ever acknowledge that of course, some things never change regardless of who their manager is.

Premier League Round Up (23-25 November 2013)

A mixed bag for us, with wins for Arsenal, City and Chelsea but Spurs losing and Everton and United both only picking up a point. Arsenal had a potentially tricky home fixture against Southampton on Saturday, I had hoped that the Saints might nick a point there but sadly it wasn't to be. For that they can thank the clown they have in goal.

I don't even know what to say about what Artur Boruc did. They all make mistakes of course but I can't ever remember seeing one trying to do a Cruyff turn in his own box, not once but twice! It actually looked as though he wanted to get caught out, it was absolutely staggering. What a dickhead. Southampton might have got something from the game with a bit more luck and lot less Boruc. They had chances through Lallana and Rodriguez but when your keeper is pulling shit like that it's difficult to get results anywhere, let alone at Arsenal.

There's trouble brewing in the Arsenal camp though, as Flamini has been defying the kitman and chopping the sleeves off his shirt. What's the big deal? Well apparently - and I'm not sure how I've never heard about this insanity before - but Arsenal have a policy whereby the captain decides whether the team wears long or short sleeves, and everyone has to go along with whatever he says. Wenger said he was not happy at all with Flamini's actions, whilst Flamini was like *"I want to wear short sleeves, so fuck y'all"*. Is Wenger really one to be laying down the law on fashion though? Captain fucking caterpillar over there on the touchline.

Staying in London, and West Ham shot themselves in the foot against Chelsea by conceding a needless early goal. Demel's horrible touch put them in trouble and the tramp in goal made it worse by bringing down Hazard for a penalty which Lampard emphatically converted against his former club. Oscar made it 2-0 and it was panic stations on the West Ham touchline as Fat Sam made a double change before half time. Joe Cole was one of those replaced, and the fans let Allardyce know of their disapproval by chanting *"You don't know what you're doing"*. He probably thought he was back at St James' Park for a second there, until the smell of jellied eels brought him back to his current nightmare. Guess what Hammers fans, it's not 2004 anymore and if you honestly thought Joe Cole was going to do anything at 2-0 down against a side like Chelsea then it's Allardyce who should be mocking you, not the other way round. And I say that as someone that loves nothing better than seeing Fat Sam mocked. To be fair to Allardyce whatever changes he makes to his attacking players is akin to re-arranging the deckchairs on the Titanic. Maiga missed an absolute sitter at 0-2, and they really have absolutely nothing up front do they? Lampard made it 3-0 and kissed the Chelsea badge. Makes me laugh that, the only reason he 'loves' Chelsea is because Abramovic came in, spent shitloads of dough and they've won plenty of trophies.

Mourinho had gotten on my tits again in the build up to the game when he discovered that Mike Riley had phoned West Brom to apologise for the penalty given against them at Stamford Bridge a fortnight ago. He started kicking off about it and shamelessly demanded an apology of his as *"it was free-kick in build up to West Brom second goal"*.

Helmet. Any normal person would know that coming out with that kind of shit is just plain embarrassing and will have people laughing at you, but he is completely without shame. I don't think Mourinho could ever be embarrassed about anything, there are some people who just don't give a fuck what people think of them and literally have no shame. My arl fella is a bit like that, it's almost impossible to embarrass him as I don't think he even knows what the emotions of shame or embarrassment even feel like. I remember one time when I was about 21 or so and we were sat around watching 'Jerry Springer', as everyone did back then before the main man Jeremy Kyle came along and stole his thunder. Anyway, these folks had brought their parents on to the show to try and get Jerry to have a word with their 'pop' to stop him embarrassing them by dressing up in their moms clothes and then walking around town. My mum says to me, *"You see how lucky you are, imagine if your dad did that, what would you do?"* I looked across the room at him and said *"If he ever pulled any of that crap I'd kick him out onto the street"*. He sat there, kind of scoffed at me and said nothing. Later on he goes upstairs for a bath, and then casually comes back down and strolls into the living room wearing one of my mum's dresses. He was calling my bluff, so I frogmarched him to the front door and kicked him out of the house. Now at this point, I'm thinking *"that'll teach him, he'll be mortified now and won't be thinking he's funny anymore"*. I was expecting him to start hammering on the door to be let back in, but I looked out the window and there he was, ambling down the path to close the gates, and casually saying *"hello"* to one of the neighbours that was walking by. He may have no shame but me and my mum do, and this little stunt of mine had kind of backfired and was now becoming embarrassing to us rather than him. Still, I didn't want to back down so easily and was prepared to leave him out there for a bit longer, but my mum caved and opened the door for him before any more of the neighbours saw her husband walking around with one of her frocks on. I have no idea why I just told that story or what relevance it had to what I was saying. How did I get so off topic? Oh yeah, the 'Special One' and his complete lack of shame. Complete tit.

Moving on, and Palace appointed Tony Pulis as their new boss. In terms of football philosophy, going from Ian Holloway to Tony Pulis is like trading in your Ferrero Rochet for a Yorkie. Holloway is a purist, Pulis is a.... I don't know actually, what's the opposite of purist? Is there even a word for it? If not, then it should just be called 'pulis'. Tell you what though, Chamakh's days there are numbered as I can't see Pulis indulging him at all. He's absolutely woeful and he's also a bit of a fanny. He actually left the pitch in tears after being physically dominated all day by Paul McShane. PAUL McSHANE!!! He picked up a couple of bangs to the head and as he left the field he rubbed his head, saw some blood and then began crying!!! Most Irish lads I know reckon McShane is the worst player they've ever seen, so what does that say about Chamakh? And crying???? Kinell, who does he think he is, Nani?

Despite being a man down away from home, and despite being an absolutely terrible side, Palace somehow came away with the three points when Bannan sidefooted home after good work by Jerome. Terrible result for Hull though, they'll have had this one down as a home banker so it's a bit of a setback to say the least.

Up in the North East Loic Remy gave Newcastle an early lead against Norwich and

Gouffran added a second after yet more poor goalkeeping by John Ruddy. If Ruddy is one of the top three English keepers then it just shows how the mighty have fallen. Fer headed one back for the Canaries but Pardew's men were good value for the points. Three wins on the bounce for them now.

Onto the Britannia now and Adam sidefooted Stoke ahead against Sunderland after being teed up by NZonzi. Two Stoke midfield players in the box and not from a set piece? When was the last time that happened. Then came the Wes Brown sending off. It's difficult to think of a worse sending off than that one, it was ludicrous. Kevin Friend didn't even blow the whistle initially, he let play go on, then saw Adam in pain and blew up. A second later he pulled out a red card. Just a horrible decision that. Poyet went ape on the touchline. Literally, he went ape, as that's exactly what he looked like. I'm talking Gareth Bale levels of chimpage here. His post match interview was hilarious too, he was proper pissed off as you'd expect. It was some good rage from Gus, but I couldn't help wondering what would have happened if mad Paolo had still been in charge.

NZonzi completed the Mackems misery when he ran onto a lovely ball from Crouch to slot the ball home. Is he actually any good? I know he's a bit of a dirty bastard, but can he play? I only ask as I've heard some people say he's a really good footballer, but until this season how would anyone have known that as he kicked more opponents than footballs? Adam said it wasn't a red card, whilst Mark Hughes tried his best to suggest it was without actually coming out and saying it was. Gobshite. Referees are getting worse and worse though, and if I had to pick the lowest of the low it would be that twat Friend. At least he's consistent I guess, he sent Jay Spearing off for something similar at Fulham. Final note on this one. I spotted Jon Walters clearing his lines with an overhead kick. Nice to see there's no lasting mental scars from when he smashed one into his own face last season. Way to get back on the horse, son.

Fulham's woes continued as they lost at home to Swansea. An unfortunate own goal from Aaron Hughes gave the Swans the lead against the run of play but Fulham hit back when Parker equalised with a curler that found the top corner. Martin Jol's side pushed for a winner but cruelly ended up getting sucker punched when Shelvey won it for Swansea with an absolute corker. I can't say I'm particularly bothered that we sold him, but I can't help wondering what the point of it was when we replaced him with Luis Alberto.

There was a cracking game on Monday night, apparently, as Villa came from 2-0 down to get a draw at the Hawthorns. I didn't watch it so don't have much to say other than I heard Shane Long was very impressive and scored twice. He's one of those players that if he'd been around 25 years ago would be playing for a title chasing side. The influx of top foreign talent means that people like him, Rickie Lambert, Steven Fletcher, Adam Johnson etc are now having to play for mid/lower table strugglers. Look at the Forest side that finished second to us in the late 80s. Chock full of jabronis like Chettle, Rice, Crosby, Woan, Wilson, Charles etc So yeah, Shane Long would have been a star if he'd been born 30 years earlier.

The real drama this weekend was on Sunday of course. City absolutely bummed Spurs senseless at the Etihad but it wasn't such a good afternoon for their neighbours

United who conceded a stoppage time equaliser at Cardiff. I'll get to that shortly, but first City. They were brilliant going forward and could have even had more than six as Spurs were embarrassing. Remember when people thought AVB was the new Mourinho? If anyone still thought that might be the case then all doubt was removed when said afterwards that: *"we have to be ashamed of ourselves"*. Ashamed? Clearly he's nothing like Mourinho. Or like my Dad for that matter.

Robbie Savage was analysing this one for MOTD2 and after me praising him the other week he let me down big time. When asked about Negredo and Aguero he replied *"they must be the best partnership in the world"*. You fickle, fickle bastard, Savage!! Three or four weeks ago you were saying that about our two! Speaking of the dynamic duo, apparently both Suarez and Sturridge have scored the same amount of league goals this season as Spurs have. That's pretty shocking from a Tottenham perspective, especially given the shitload of dough they spent on attacking players like Soldado, Lamela and Eriksen.

Onto United now, and how funny was that!! Cardiff deserved that point in fairness, they gave it a good go and United looked bang average again. Fellaini is just shit isn't he? If you look up 'Manchester United player' in the dictionary, there's a picture of this goon and it says *"not this guy"*. Ok, that's not true, but it should be. Rooney once again carried his team by scoring one and making another, but he shouldn't have been on the field to be allowed to do it after he petulantly kicked out at Jordon Mutch. The ref saw it too, but completely shit out and gave him a yellow, a decision which, unsurprisingly, Moyes agreed with, saying: *"I thought Mutch runs across his path and runs down the line of the ball and I think Wayne's half in motion. I don't think it is anymore than a booking that's for sure"* Eh? He's half in motion? What the hell does that even mean!!! He's turning into Roy Hodgson.

Cardiff's ire at that decision only got worse when Shrek put United ahead with a shot that the keeper had covered until it was deflected over him. Spawny manc twats. Cardiff hit back as Fraizer Campbell equalised with a good finish following two great passes that split United wide open. Lovely goal that was, and Campbell would later be denied by the crossbar with a clever chip. United regained the lead when they scored from a corner yet again. Rooney's deliveries are quality but teams really need to put a stop to this 'letting Evra win headers in their box' thing. It's like being beaten in a sprint by Rick Waller, it just shouldn't ever happen. And how come Hernandez is always crap when he starts but he's lethal as a sub? He's the Mexican Solskjaer. It's a nice luxury to have that kind of option on the bench, I wish we had one like that. Mind you, Iago Aspas should be back soon. Can't wait for that...

It was looking like another typical 'play crap and win' kind of day for United when they gave away a silly free-kick in stoppage time and then failed to deal with it, Kim heading past De Gea to send the home crowd wild and to make the rest of the country piss their collective pants laughing. United should have won it at the death though when a glorious ball from Giggs played Rooney in, but he ballsed it up when trying to lay it off to Welbeck. Firstly, you simply have to take that on yourself in that situation. Secondly, it was Danny fucking Welbeck, why would you be trying to lay it off to him? Welcrap had earlier missed a great chance when he failed to even hit the target.

Remember when he scored twice on opening day and some people were talking about how he'd matched (or was it eclipsed?) his tally from last season and that he was ready to take off? Turns out he'd just got his season's total in early this year, that's all.

There was some talk as to whether Gary Medel should have been sent off for slapping Fellaini. I'd agree with that statement, providing you replace *"sent off"* with *"heartily congratulated"*. The candy floss headed oaf had elbowed Medel in the face and the Chilean was just reacting to that. In fairness, that's probably the closest Fellaini will ever get to getting his hands on a 'medel'. What? Come on, that's not bad that.

You wouldn't mess with Medel though, he's like a little fucking bulldog isn't he? The fact he's called 'Gary' never fails to make me laugh. I always think of that episode of Only Fools & Horses when Del & Rodney find an illegal immigrant in Denzel's lorry and take him home. He was an Arabic lad who didn't speak English, so they named him 'Gary'. Every time they called him 'Gary' he'd just repeat "Garrrry". Every time I think of Medel I imagine him at the training ground, his team-mates saying *"Morning Gary"* and him just replying *"Garrry"*. It probably doesn't happen like that but until someone proves otherwise that's how it will play out in my head.

Evra was pretty scathing of his team's efforts after the game, saying that they didn't do enough and that Manchester United should be better than this. The MOTD2 host then described this as *"refreshingly honest there from Patrice Evra"*. Well there's a first time for everything I guess. Moyes is great though isn't he, he said after this one that *"it's a tough place to come after international duty and I would have taken the result before the game."* Hahaha brilliant, he just doesn't get it does he? You're not in Kansas anymore, Dorothy!!!

chapter seven

December

HULL CITY 3 LIVERPOOL 1

Competition - Premier League
Date - Sun 1 Dec 2013
Venue - The KC Stadium
Scorer(s) – Steven Gerrard
Star Man – Jon Flanagan

Team: Mignolet; Johnson,
Toure, Skrtel, Flanagan;
Lucas, Gerrard; Moses
(Coutinho), Henderson,
Sterling (Alberto); Suarez:

If this is what life without Daniel Sturridge is going to be like then I might just find myself a nice little cave and hibernate for the winter, Yogi Bear style. This was just brutal; an utterly abject, listless, shameful, unforgivable performance. Rodgers tried to be upbeat and pointed to the Norwich game in midweek as an opportunity to put this one behind us, but I'm sorry, you can't 'put this one behind us' as it's going to haunt us all year. They all need their complacent, arrogant fucking arses kicking for this.

Hopefully we'll win our next two home games but even if we do it cannot make up for this. Every time we look at the table it's going to be impossible to escape from the thought *"If only we'd beaten Hull"*. Irrespective of what happens over the coming weeks, these are three points we should have had that are not coming back. There are some fixtures where it's almost acceptable to drop points; Arsenal away, Everton away, maybe even Swansea away. Losing at Hull though, fucking hell, you just can't be doing that, and least of all to do it in the unforgivable manner we did. Having said that, had it been 'one of those days' where we played well, ran into an inspired keeper and just generally had no luck, then although it's still frustrating, you can just shrug it off and move on. Shit happens as they say. When you see the team stink it up as badly as this, it's hard to just forget it. I've been saying all season that I really want to believe in this team but I just don't trust them. This is exactly why. Even if we win our next six games (which we won't) I still won't trust them as they always have a performance like this in them.

We're obviously going to miss Sturridge, but we shouldn't have missed him in this game. Away at City or Chelsea you can bemoan the absence of Sturridge as major handicap. At Hull City??? Come on. It's embarrassing to talk about a lack of depth' when you're being shamed by a side stocked with Championship calibre players. Hull were beaten by ten man Crystal Palace last weekend, who had Marouane Chamakh up front for fucks sake!! If Victor Moses and Raheem Sterling aren't good enough to do anything against Hull then they can't be trusted to do it against anyone unfortunately. It's easy to hammer Rodgers for his team selection, but aside from bringing in Toure for Agger (if Agger was to be rested/dropped, then why would £17m Sakho not be out there? I'll get to that later), I'm not sure he had much choice in any other selection he made. No-one wants to see Sterling starting games at the moment but what was the alternative if Coutinho wasn't up to starting the game? Even a fully fit Aspas wouldn't have been a safer bet, but he's only had a couple of days training so wasn't even an option. Who else is there? Alberto? Hahaha yeah, good one.

Sterling SHOULD have been able to come in and do a job against Hull, as SHOULD Moses. If they can't do a job against this level of opposition then they have no business being here and the fact they were both abysmal says everything. No fucking wonder they haven't been getting a game. Who else is there though? Prior to this I'd have said no-one, but having endured this horror show I'd have to say that it's highly unlikely that Jordan Ibe or even Ryan McLaughlin could possibly contribute less than Sterling did today. He doesn't do anything anymore. Doesn't beat anyone, doesn't cross, doesn't shoot, does absolutely fuck all and has been like that ever since signing that fat contract. Still, at least he can say he's only 18, Moses has no such excuse. For someone who was complaining about not getting much playing time he gave a pretty good impression of someone who doesn't actually even want to play. He didn't look arsed most of the time, in fact that seems to a feature of his game. I don't think I've ever seen a player who shows less emotion than Moses. He's just got a vacant expression on his face most of the time, whether things are going good or bad. Completely passionless and looks like he doesn't give a fuck. That may not be the case but it's how it looks.

I mean, look at what he did for their first goal. I can live with a player giving the ball away with a pass that is intercepted, or being tackled trying to take somebody on, but to hand possession to the opposition as casually and as arrogantly as that is just not acceptable. It was showboating and he's not good enough to showboat. Seriously, who beats a man in their own half by chipping the ball over their head and then running onto it? It never happens as it's almost impossible to do it, it's a reckless, stupid, irresponsible thing to try and it cost us a goal. Yes, we were unlucky with the deflection but that goal is all on Moses for me. A case can be made for simply not picking him anymore, as he's not our player and he's shown nothing to suggest we should be looking to make the deal permanent.

Without Sturridge, it looks like it's going to be all on the shoulders of Suarez now as no-one else appears likely to step up. Coutinho provides some hope - assuming his ankle injury isn't too big a problem - but his best moments have come linking up with Sturridge rather than Suarez. Now they have a chance to strike up some kind of partnership and let's hope they do because they're pretty much all we have.

It's probably unfair to single out Sterling and Moses from this debacle as they were no worse than some of their team-mates. It's just that they had a rare opportunity to show they should be playing more often and they blew it. Sterling has gone backwards at an alarming rate, does anyone actually have any faith in him to do anything anymore? He appears to be everything that is wrong with young modern day footballers wrapped up in one silly haired little package. What happened to that brilliant, hungry, fearless 17 year old? I miss him.

And what the fuck has happened to Glen Johnson? He was borderline disgraceful last week in the derby and he was more or less invisible in this one. I've been one of his biggest supporters but I'm done with him. £18m and £120k a week for THIS?? When he's on his game there are few better. When he's off his game there are few worse. Then there's Lucas, who's contributing very little and looks like he's got lead boots these days, and Henderson who ran around a lot but in terms of cutting edge provided none today. Gerrard still has quality but the lack of class around him is negating that and exposing the weaknesses in his game. None of them can hold their head up after this.

At the back Toure looked unconvincing at times and whilst I thought Skrtel was mostly fine, his part in the second and third goals cannot be overlooked. It doesn't help that they were both going for the same ball half the time and played like a couple of strangers. The pertinent question here is why were they paired together when there were other options? Skrtel has been playing really well as the right sided centre back, yet he was moved over to the left to bring Toure in. If Agger needed resting (although from what I hear he was dropped because of his derby display) then why not just play Sakho, y'know, the guy we were told was our 'marquee' summer signing? It's bizarre really, you'd think having splashed out £17m on him that Rodgers would want to get him some games. He will have been flying after what he did for France in midweek, yet he comes back here and can't get a game as the manager prefers to include a 32 year old free transfer ahead of him. It's just baffling, unless of course Rodgers is making some kind of point about how he is not in charge of signing players. He wanted Toure but the committee signed Sakho? That kind of thing. I hope we're not starting out down that road but Rodgers has previous for it with Sahin and Assaidi. The manager complaining about the depth of the squad doesn't sit well with me. He's right of course, but it still doesn't sit well as they should have had more than enough to beat Hull.

Let's be honest here, Suarez and Sturridge have been papering over some pretty big cracks. What makes it so puzzling is that last season I could see how well coached the team was and how everyone had a clearly defined role. There was a pattern to the play and it was mostly good to watch, regardless of results. The lack of quality up front held us back until the January window but Rodgers was doing a good job. I'm not seeing that anymore, it's as though he has completely abandoned everything he was trying to do. I look at Southampton and I see a well coached side, I look at us and I see a disorganised mess who have been getting by because of the quality of certain individuals. Chopping and changing the back four all the time is not doing us any favours either. It's the strongest area of the squad on paper yet we're shipping goals all over the shop now, especially away from home. Those three consecutive clean sheets we started the season with were not the evidence of some new found resilience after all, they were an aberration and we're now leaking like a sieve.

The lack of depth should also raise questions about those in charge of transfers, whether that is Rodgers or (more likely) the much vaunted 'committee'. Did anyone really think Luis Alberto was riding to the rescue? The £8m spent on him added to the £8m on the completely pointless Ilori could have bought us someone that might actually be of some use, especially if you add the £8m squandered on Aspas to the pot as well.

We may well beat Norwich and West Ham and this will look like a complete over-reaction, but it isn't an over-reaction as regardless of what happens over the next few weeks, this was just completely disgraceful. For a team that has no European football and therefore no midweek commitments, how the hell can they have a week of training geared towards one game, and then go out and play like boiled shite in a bag? HOW??? They had all fucking week to get ready for this game, just what the hell must they have been doing in training? Imagine how shit we'd be if we also had to contend with Champions League games? Not that we'll have to worry about unless there's a major attitude adjustment from players and manager. We can no longer talk about a good start, as it's nothing of the sort now. We're level on points with Everton while City and Chelsea have both gone above us despite having 'bad starts'. And for all the piss taking we've done of Moyes, United are only two points back now Hell, we're only three points ahead of 9th place, and with those away fixtures on the immediate horizon who knows where we'll be come January. That's why this result and performance was so unforgivable and could cost us big time when the points are tallied up in May.

And not that it has any bearing on the result, but playing in an away strip when there is no colour clash pisses me off big time. It's bad mojo, there's just no need for it other than to try and sell more kits, but when the kit looks as God awful as this one then people won't be buying it no matter how many times a season the team wears it, especially when they play like this.

LIVERPOOL 5 NORWICH CITY 1

Competition - Premier League
Date - Wed 4 Dec 2013
Venue - Anfield
Scorer(s) – Suarez (4), Sterling
Star Man – Luis Suarez

Team: Mignolet; Johnson, Skrtel, Agger, Flanagan; Allen, Gerrard; Henderson (Alberto), Coutinho, Sterling; Suarez (Aspas):

Poor old Norwich, they must be sick to death of being picked on by Luis Suarez. It's not just that he always scores against them, it's not even that he always scores hat-tricks against them. It's the stupendous quality of most of the goals; they have to be wondering just what the hell they did to continually be on the receiving end of our superstar number seven's best work.

The sight of those yellow and green shirts in front of him seems to turn Suarez into Roy of the Rovers, so this time Norwich showed up in their white away kit in a bid to confuse him. Maybe next year they should remove the badge too, as this clearly didn't fool Suarez, he was like, yeah nice try, but this time I'm gonna add one extra for trying to be smart arses.

It was vitally important we didn't slip up in this one and I'm sure people will say that the players bounced back from the shocker they had at Hull. I'm not sure I buy that entirely though. Luis Suarez bounced back, that's for sure. He bounced back in just about the most emphatic manner possible, he was just incredible. The rest? Mostly a bit 'meh' I thought. Some were good, others were indifferent. No-one was bad though, so that's a step in the right direction after last weekend. The game did little or nothing for me to dispel the theory that we've not got too much going for us other than a dynamic front two. It's actually only a dynamic front one right now until Sturridge comes back, but when that 'one' is as phenomenal as Suarez he can cover up for a multitude of sins.

The game wasn't going especially well until he opened the scoring out of absolutely nothing. At that point passes were going astray all over the place, it was very disjointed and possibly heading in a direction none of us wanted to see. Then a ball bounces to Suarez 45 yards out and he just launches it goalwards, over Ruddy's head and turns the game completely on it's head. Suddenly the crowd woke up, the players seemed more relaxed and Suarez just took over. He quickly added a second with a quality finish after Gerrard had flicked on a Coutinho corner. It was actually a really good finish but it will be largely overlooked as it pales in comparison with the other strikes.

Once that second goal went in it was obvious to everybody he was headed for his third hat-trick against Norwich in as many seasons. They knew it, we knew it, he knew it. The only surprise was that his third goal might just have eclipsed all of all the other goals he's put past them, and that's some feat considering the incredible strikes he's had against poor old Ruddy in the last few years. It was a stunning goal, as he controlled the ball on his chest, carried it forward, lobbed it over a defender's head and then blasted it into the corner with as sweet a half volley as you'll see anywhere. A technically perfect goal, one that even seemed to take Suarez by surprise judging by his reaction to it as he celebrated. If his face were a text message it would have read: *"OMFG! did I really just do that? LOLZ"* There are just no superlatives to adequately describe him anymore, he's just transcended to a level I've never seen before. I wrote after West Brom that I don't think we've ever had anyone better than him. I'm saying now that I KNOW we haven't, he's just sublime. He's out on his own, an incredible talent combined with an incredible work ethic.

I remember at the start of last season I was bemoaning that as great as Suarez is, he was more of a 'Beardsley' and it was unfair that he didn't have a Barnes and an Aldridge alongside him. His goal record at that time backed up that point of view, but it turns out I was only half right, he still doesn't have a Barnes, although Sturridge has come in and is adequately replicating the Aldridge 'goal quota', but Suarez is actually Beardsley and Barnes rolled into one, with a smidgen of Aldo thrown in for good measure (the strike rate merits comparison with Aldo, even if the type of goals are vastly different). He's simply incredible, if we could only add more quality to the side we could really go places whilst we have him because he is just that special.

Sadly, much as it hurts to say, he's way too good for us at the moment. He's a top three player in the world playing in a top six/seven team in the Premier League. If we don't make the top four this year with Suarez playing like this, then we won't deserve to keep him as let's face it, he'd have done all he could. It's almost unfair on him that if he has a day where he isn't at his best - such as Hull last weekend - we aren't capable of winning (especially if Sturridge is not there to pick up the slack). He should be allowed to have the occasional game where things don't go his way without worrying about whether the rest of the team can compensate for it. He virtually won this game on his own and whatsmore, he'd won it by half time. For good measure he added a fourth in the second half with a brilliant free-kick. I knew he was going to score as soon as he shaped up to take it. His free-kicks now are just top drawer and I expect him to score every time, he's striking the ball so well. We had one a little earlier and for some reason he left it to Coutinho. Predictably, the result was a pea roller that barely made it to the goal.

Coutinho is a terrific little player, but (and I may have written this before) but can we have a clause inserted into his contract to prevent him from EVER shooting from outside the 18 yard box? He was a joy to watch again, but his end product was largely non-existent and he seems to suffer from Sturridge's absence as much as anybody. He was playing in the number 10 role with Henderson and Sterling flanking him, but really Luis had to do most of it on his own all night - at least in terms of providing the cutting edge. Coutinho's play around the box wasn't great but what he does well is link the play and help us keep the ball. With both him and Allen in the side, the ball retention is much better and it keeps us ticking over nicely. The ball appears glued to his foot at times, he truly is 'a wonderful technician' as Rodgers would say.

With a 3-0 lead at half time I did wonder what kind of approach we'd see after the break as too often we've just eased off with the game in the bag. The scoreline would suggest we did that again but we were probably better as a team in the 2nd half. The main difference was Suarez only scored one after the break.

Norwich pulled one back with a fine header by Johnson after he'd gotten the better of Agger. I wouldn't be ultra critical of Agger as I was watching it unfold and Johnson was just hanging about outside the box but suddenly made a good run from behind the Dane and arrived just at the same time as the ball. Agger probably should have been more aware of the runner in behind him but it's not as though Johnson was just standing around unmarked. Good cross, good header, but a goal we could really have done without conceding as we're letting too many in these days.

Gerrard then almost scored a goal that even Suarez would have been proud of when he acrobatically stuck out a leg and diverted a Coutinho pass goalwards only to see it hit the inside of the post. Desperately unlucky from the skipper who was impressive all night and could easily have had a hat-trick himself on another night. Gerrard has played very well in these kind of home games this season, it's away from home where he hasn't made his presence felt as much. I'm not sure Joe Allen is the answer alongside him, certainly not in a midfield two anyway, but I'd rather him be given an opportunity to show what he can do now,as we know what Lucas can - and more importantly can't - do. Allen played well I thought, and only a magnificent flying save from Ruddy kept him off the scoresheet.

As for the rest, I wouldn't say Sterling was particularly good but he did very little wrong and grew into the game as it went on. He was neat and tidy without penetrating much but it was nice to see him get a goal as that can't do any harm can it? It was a good finish too, made by... well I don't even need to say do I? Sterling has put himself in pole position now to get the starts until Sturridge returns, so let's hope the goal gives him a lift and he starts to play with the spring in his step he had a year ago. Johnson was improved on his last two outings, but it would have been difficult not to be. He's still in my doghouse and it will probably be some time until he gets out, if ever. Flanagan continues to impress though, he was quietly efficient and can once again be pleased with his night's work. Aspas was really up for the 30 seconds he got at the end, you could see how eager he was to do something (bless him) and it would be nice to see him get some minutes against West Ham to try and get him going. With Sturridge out and still a month before the window opens, we could really use some kind of contribution from Aspas and it was a little disappointing he did not get 15 minutes or so in this one, as it would have been an ideal chance to maybe get him a goal. What? Stranger things have happened. Like that time when... or what about when... Yeah you got me there.

Premier League Round Up (November 30 - December 4 2013)

A real bittersweet week for me this one. Obviously the footy was pretty distressing over the weekend and naturally I was in foul form after our loss to Hull, but then I experienced something fairly monumental in my homelife. No, not the birth of a kid or anything, I'm talking something much bigger than that.

I was in Iceland - the foodstore not the country - and I discovered Hula Hoops and McCoys in... get this... in chip form!!! Yes, you read that correctly, you can now get Hula Hoop shaped chips. I know, mad eh? That's not all though, there's more. Just like the crisps, they come in different flavours! Ready Salted, Barbecue Beef and even Cheese & Onion. Un-believable. Those of you who don't know me on a personal level will probably be wondering what the big deal is here, but if you had as limited a diet as I have, and if potato products were as big a part of your life as they are mine, you'd understand. Without potato products I'd be left with just bread, chocolate, cornflakes and pretty much nothing else to eat. I don't eat meat or fish, and I don't eat vegatables either, aside from potatoes obviously. Actually that's not quite true as I eat peas as well, but only as an accompaniment to chips or roasties, it's not as though I'd eat peas without them. So this was huge for me, it was the biggest food related discovery I've made since goose fat roast potatoes (and what a day that was!!) Anyway, I stocked up on as much potato related comfort food as I could fit in my freezer and for a brief time the football was not exactly forgotten, but the anger subsided at least a little until Suarez put the smile back on my face with his demolition of Norwich.

That Hull defeat really hurt us though as everyone else picked up at least one point last weekend and most collected three. Arsenal won comfortably at Cardiff as Aaron Ramsay went back to his former club and stole the show. All season I've been waiting for this purple patch of his to come to an end, but it's not happening is it? This is who he is now, and he's fucking ace. It's quite remarkable really, I haven't seen such a transformation in a player from 'decent' to 'unbelievable' since... well since Gareth Bale actually. Is it a Welsh thing? If so I can't wait to see Joe Allen tearing shit up next year. Cardiff fans applauded Ramsay after both goals, probably due to him not celebrating either of them. He's very difficult to dislike is Ramsay, seems like a decent lad. Ozil notched up two more assists, he even set one up for Flamini in this one, and that takes some doing. I bet he couldn't get Lucas on the scoresheet though, he's not THAT good. How are Arsenal conceding so few goals when their defenders are all shite though? Is it just because they're so good going the other way teams aren't committing people forward as much? Has to be, as I'm not having it that they're any good at the back.

Moving on, and the Blues absolutely demolished Stoke at Goodison. As some wag put on twitter, *"Everton are borrowing goals for fun these days"*. I had expected Stoke to put up some stiff resistance to be honest, but they just got completely dicked. In my defence, I hadn't expected them to throw in some Spanish kid I'd never heard of at centre half. Where was Huth?? And whatever happened to Jonathon Woodgate, is he still alive? It was Everton's own Spanish kid that made the headlines with a superb display, capped by a fine opening goal on the stroke of half time. You have to wonder how our scouts can spend time watching Barcelona B and then report back to Rodgers and tell him that we should pay £8m for Luis Alberto rather than take Deulofeu on loan. Good job you guys, way to earn your massive salaries.

Coleman sliced in a flukey second a couple of minutes after the break and Oviedo added a third. It would prove to be quite the week for the Costa Rican understudy to Leighton Baines, who also created the fourth for Lukaku and then got the winner at Old Trafford a few days later. I'll get to that in due course though. The Blues were running riot against Stoke and the goals were raining down. Then they brought on Jelavic, who has strangely turned into the Croatian Stuart Barlow. He couldn't hit Yakubu's arse with a cricket bat.

Martin Jol had been on the brink for some time and Fat Sam pushed him over the edge of the precipice as West Ham thumped Fulham 3-0. Allowing West Ham to score three is arguably a sackable offence on it's own, but when two of the goalscorers are Joe and Carlton Cole, then you have to expect your P45 to be forthcoming really. And if you're down at the bottom is there a player you'd want in your team less than that fucking show pony Adel Taraabt? Sorry to see Jol go though, he's cool as fuck.

Newcastle put themselves right on the coat tails of the top four with a victory over West Brom. There's quite a few players in that squad that can really play. None of them are defenders though and that's what will be Newcastle's undoing.

Gerry Francis was in the crowd at Carrow Road as Norwich beat Palace. He's still got the same fucking haircut he had in the 70s!!! Does this man not have a family? Does he not have mirrors in his house? Does he have the worst haircut of anyone associated with football? I can't think of any worse. It really is one of the most incredible things I've seen. You look at it and just think is that real or am I seeing things. It's like when my mum was dancing to the Prodigy at my wedding. True story that, I look across the room and there she was, the only person on the dancefloor, casually dancing away to "Firestarter". She was sober too. *shudders*

Tell you what's weird, I watched Pulis talking after the game and wasn't yelling *"fuck off knobhead"*. I don't have much hostility in me for Stoke these days either. I think perhaps it was the combination of Pulis and Stoke that I hated rather than them as individual entities, and once they parted ways I discovered I'm not arsed about either. I guess it's like when Robbie Williams left Take That. I ended up quite liking both of them for a while, but then Take That sold out and eventually took that arsehole back which has rekindled my disdain for all of them. There's a lesson for Stoke there.

Prince William was at Villa Park to witness his Aston Villa side play out a goalless draw with Sunderland. I'm not a fan of most of the royals, but him and his half brother seem like good lads. The fact William follows Villa as opposed to being a glory hunting twat with Arsenal or the Mancs gets him plenty of man points in my book. Thankfully the Monarchy don't have the kind of sway they used to and if he ever becomes King he's not likely to be making the kind of decisions that rulers had to back in the day. I mean come on, this lad CHOSE to support Aston Villa, so that instantly throws a red flag up over his judgement for me. Villa should have lost this one really as Giaccherini put one over an empty net from four yards out. When that happens to a side down at the bottom you usually know it's not going to end well, but Sunderland held out for a point and could even have won it when Fabio Magnifico's header crashed against the bar.

Onto Sunday now, and what an absolutely stinking day that was. Our loss at Hull allowed both City and Chelsea to leapfrog us in the table. Realistically we were never really competing with either of those sides this season but it would have been nice to stay above them for a little longer. At least until we have to go and play them and inevitably get turned over. Spurs and United drawing was good for us though I guess, wouldn't have wanted either of them picking up three points so this was the best we could hope for. Spurs dropped Kaboul after his horrendous display at City but I don't even know who that fella they brought in was. Chiriches or something? Who he? Bet he cost at least £10m though didn't he?

Walker's free-kick gave Spurs an early lead and Soldado then blasted one high over the bar from close range. I keep hearing about how he's a penalty box player and Spurs aren't playing to his strengths. Well this was in the penalty box so what's his excuse for that? Spurs were swarming all over United and could easily have been 3-0 up but if you don't take your chances against those feckers you usually pay for it. And they did pay. Walker's howler put one on a plate for Rooney and despite all Tottenham's dominance suddenly it was 1-1. Sandro's screamer gave Spurs the lead once again but an outrageous dive from Welbeck conned Mike Dean into giving a pen and Rooney buried it. I'm sure Moyes will let Welbeck know of his disapproval though. AVB nailed it afterwards, saying Welbeck left his leg there to con the ref and it's not the first time it's happened to him against United. Go ed lad, you tell em.

Elsewhere, City had another comfortable home win as Swansea proved to be no match for Pellegrini's side who ran out comfortable 3-0 winners. What the fuck is going on with Motson and his pronunciations? Neg-reddo was puzzling, De Mishelliss was irritating but when he came out with Jolly-ann Lescott I was convinced he had to be taking the piss. Senile old goat.

Moving swiftly along, Chelsea had a tricky looking fixture at home to Southampton. It was looking a whole lot trickier when the Saints scored within 14 seconds as Rodriguez latched onto a shite backpass from Essien and rolled it past Cech. Essien was booked soon after for what might be the worst dive of the season, the Southampton player was nowhere near him. Embarrassing stuff, especially as his manager is such a hard line, outspoken anti-diving campaigner. Remember when Essien used to be awesome? He's nothing these days is he? Imagine going from being one of the top three midfielders in the world to Jon-Obi Mikel's back up. That has to be difficult for a man to live with.

Southampton held onto their lead until half time before blowing it after the break by failing to defend set-pieces properly. Cahill equalised and then Mongo put them ahead seven minutes later. Substitute Ba made it 3-1 in stoppage time. Mourinho didn't need to run into the crowd to celebrate this time as he's now put his kid in a seat behind the bench. For the record, his kid looks like a twat as well.

Monday night saw Pulis pick up his first win as Palace boss, Chamakh's goal proving to be enough to see off a wretched West Ham side who were so bad that Fat Sam refused to do the post match press conference as he was 'so angry with his players and the officials'. Ah, he's learnt so well from his master, that's right out the Ferguson handbook that. Well, apart from the being mad at his own players bit of course. He did speak to the BBC, so I guess he didn't learn THAT much from him. Ravel Morrison should have been red carded after the game for throwing his hands into the face of a Palace player after an argument, but Fat Sam said he's ok with it *"as long as he doesn't get in trouble"* and that he was right to be angry, because *"I'm angry too"*. Fergie would indeed be proud.

Speaking of old bacon face, he will be turning in his grave at what's happening at United these days. Well, he would be if he were dead, instead he's turning up at United games and heaping further pressure on the 'chosen one'. What happened at Old Trafford when Moyes faced Everton was entirely predictable. I keep seeing it described as a 'shock' result but I'd have been more shocked if United won. Everton are above them in the table, in better form and Moyes is a proven big game bottler. This had Everton win written all over it. The longer it went, the more likely Everton looked like winning it and with a few minutes left Oviedo nipped in at the back post for second goal of the week.

Moyes never managed to win away at a top four side and people are crediting Martinez with doing it after just a few months. Yeah, just one problem with that, United don't look like being a top four team. The other thing I kept hearing was how Moyes had been trying for eleven years to get an Everton win at Old Trafford and it took Martinez just three months. I can't in all good conscience gloat about that stat as you have to be fair to Moyes here. Yes, he did have over a decade to try and win at Old Trafford as Everton boss, but unlike Martinez he never got the opportunity to go up against a David Moyes coached team did he? Fairs fair now.

There was a bit of a storm on twitter the next day as some blue reckoned he was in a bar with the 'Chosen One' after the game and that Moyes was slating Everton fans. The lad posted a picture of himself with Moyes, so there was at least some truth to his claims. He reckoned Moyes was drowning his sorrows and was absolutely furious at the stick he got from the travelling blues. What the fuck does he expect though? Maybe he thought because they were so stupid to give him that totally undeserved send off last seson that he can say and do whatever he likes. Sorry, but not even Evertonians are that blind and stupid. The alleged comments were hilarious though. *"after 11 years it's a disgrace how the fans treated me tonight. From how I found them to how I left them.....a fucking disgrace"* hahaha brilliant! He screwed them over by talking to United behind their back and allowing his contract to run down so they got no compensation. No matter, the dopes still gave him a rousing send off he didn't deserve. How did he repay them? By repeatedly trying to shit on them from a great height ever since. Offering derisory sums for their best players and unsettling those players in the process was bad enough, but he's coming out with a stream of shite too, including one crack about how the team he left is so good they could do what they've been doing even without a manager. Bitter bastard, doesn't like that the fans have taken to Martinez and that they're playing better football than he ever did.

The line that really tickled me though was this, as it's something I could well imagine him coming out with: *"if that's how they want to play it they'll regret it"* Hahahaha what are you gonna do tough guy? What can he possibly do to get back at Everton fans? He thinks he's Fergie junior doesn't he, the absolute dolt. You've been warned Everton fans, he'll make you regret it!!

Staying with the mancs for a second, what the hell is this about Adnan Januzaj being nominated for the BBC's Young Sports Personality of the Year or some crap? He's only played a handful of games, and if that little gobshite is up for it then why isn't Jon Flanagan? What's the difference, other than Flanagan actually being British and therefore more eligible for something like that? I hate that Januzaj gobshite already, the overhyped little shithouse.

Also on Wednesday night, Chelsea were involved in a 4-3 thriller with Sunderland. The MOTD commentator said before the game that Torres has scored more goals against Sunderland than any other Premier League side. Six goals he's put past them apparently. Big fucking whoop. How many years has he been playing in England? Six goals is about 110 minutes work for Suarez against Norwich. For the record, Torres didn't add to his six goals, he never looked like doing so and he was subbed in the second half. The bum. Hell, even Jozy Altidore managed to get on the scoresheet. His first goal for Sunderland that, and didn't he only score one or two when he was at Hull? This fella makes Jon Walters look like Ian Rush. The Yanks love him though, he's actually a big star over there and carries most of their world cup hopes on his broad shoulders. Imagine HIM being your star player. Jesus.

Hazard set up the equaliser for Lampard then scored one himself before O'Shea levelled following a corner. Hazard's stunning second put Chelsea in front again and then Bardsley scored one of the most inexplicable own goals you'll see. It looked like he deliberately slotted it at the back post. Mental. Bizarrely he then went up the other end and pulled a goal back. Didn't he do something like this a few weeks ago too? For such a nondescript, bang average player he's always involved in some kind of shit isn't he? Hazard took his shirt off after scoring and got booked. Knobhead, any player who does that should have his fucking head kicked in by the manager. The only exception is if it's someone who never scores and suddenly slots one, you can almost forgive it in those circumstances. I mean, if Torres were to score this weekend for example, you could turn a blind eye to him taking his shirt off. Hell, you could even forgive him for stripping bollock naked. One Premier League goal in 2013. ONE!!!

Elsewhere, Villa sprung a surprise at Southampton as a classic counter attacking performance saw them run out 3-2 winners at St Mary's. Agbonlahor scored a brilliant opener, top quality stuff that was. When he's on his game he's one of the best players in the league for me, but unfortunately for Villa he's only on his game maybe four or five times a season. Rodriguez equalised but Kozac headed Villa in front once more. He was playing instead of Benteke who was benched after going seven without scoring. Is something going on there? Will he be available in January perhaps? Would you take him? More to the point, would Brendan? I'm going with no, no and no.

Osvaldo pegged Villa back again and just as it was looking like Southampton would push for a late equaliser, they got caught on the break once more as Delph ran half the length of the field before almost bursting the net from 25 yards. The results have dried up for the Saints of late but I like watching them and there's a lot to admire about that side. They've had some tough games lately and this was one they'd expect to win, especially as they had 77% possession!! Is that some kind of record for a losing side? Seems like an incredible stat to me that.

City look to have put their away problems behind them now, it's not easy to win at West Brom but they dominated and were 3-0 up before almost blowing it late on as the Baggies gave them a scare with two goals at the death. Anichebe got one of them, using the only move he has to get away from the dreadful Demichelis and score. You know the move I'm talking about, it's literally the only thing he can do, and curiously enough I've noticed that it's the one thing Altidore can do too. They let the ball roll across them and use their body strength to roll the centre back. It's their signature move, like the Mark Walters stepover, the Jon Walters overhead kick into his own face and the Ashley Young triple pike with twist.

Moving along, and Arsenal are just taking the piss now aren't they? They're getting seriously cocky, as shown by them resting Giroud and starting Nicklas frigging Bendtner. Whatsmore, he scored inside two minutes, much to everyone's surprise. Fucking spoilsport, making it difficult for the fans to boo him. Everything is going their way at the moment. Of course, they were only playing Hul... oh. Ozil added a second as Arsenal just cruised through the game. Best defensive record in the league? How does that happen? I cant get my head around it. It's the equivalent of West Ham having the best attacking record, it just defies all known logic.

Spurs got a lucky win at Fulham in midweek to ease the pressure on the Portuguese Arnold J Rimmer. Apparently Berbatov wants to quit Fulham. I'd take him. I know there are loads of reasons why that's a terrible idea and why there is zero chance of it happening, but it's the closest I'll ever get to seeing myself in the red shirt so I'm all for it. Imagine him and Suarez? More to the point, imagine how Suarez would react to Berbatov just not doing any running? His new found self control would be tested to it's limits by the languid Bulgarian, but it would be fun while it lasted.

Stoke v Cardiff was dire. 0-0 and the only thing worth mentioning is how the hell was Adam not sent off? He'd already been booked and then shoved Campbell to the floor as they lined up in a wall. Michael Oliver booked Crouch instead, which to be fair is easily done given how similar they look. Adam then went on to lead with his elbow on Mutch and it appeared he was actually doing his level best to get sent off. Did he have something better to do next weekend? Had he promised the wife he'd take her Christmas shopping? He must have been deliberately trying to get sent off, as no-one is THAT stupid to do what he was doing. Interesting that Mark Hughes dropped Walters for this one, ending a run of something like 120 consecutive starts. You might not be aware of this as I'm not sure I've mentioned it before, but I really don't like Walters. Still, Mark Hughes is a fucking arlarse for dropping him when he's on a run like that.

Newcastle were a bit unlucky to lose 3-0 at Swansea. There was some talk afterwards that Shelvey would be charged for making a 'head butt gesture' at Debuchy. He escaped any punishment as apparently it's not an offence to feign to do something and not actually make contact. It throws up an interesting argument though, as does that mean it's ok to pretend to throw a punch but stop just short of connecting? I bet Suarez is already mulling over that possibility.

LIVERPOOL 4 WEST HAM 1

Competition - Premier League
Date - Sat 7 Dec 2013
Venue - Anfield
Scorer(s) – Demel O.G., Sakho,
Suarez (2)
Star Man – Luis Suarez

Team: Mignolet; Johnson, Skrtel, Sakho, Flanagan; Allen, Gerrard (Lucas); Sterling (Moses), Coutinho, Henderson; Suarez:

Since being turned over by Southampton we've won our last five home games and scored 20 goals whilst conceding just four. It's difficult to believe that a side who has no trouble whatsoever seeing off anyone outside of the top six or seven sides at Anfield can fail to win at ten man Newcastle and then lose at Hull, but that's the problem facing Brendan at the moment. Why can't his side reproduce their home form on the road?

He needs to find the answer to that quickly as three of the next four are away from home and whatsmore, they are against some of the best sides in the country. Still, all three of those sides have been equally as inconsistent as we have, hence all three being below us in the table right now. As galling and infuriating as it is to go to places like Hull and lose, at least it's fun going to Anfield again. For several years that hasn't been the case, but in 2013 more often than not we've been very good at home and have scored a lorry load full of goals. The main reason for that of course is a certain world class number seven. Suarez was just absolutely fantastic again today. He didn't have the goals to show for it like he did against Norwich in midweek, but damn, he was good. Some of his little touches and first time layoffs were ridiculously good, whilst he continues to amaze with his ability to wriggle past defenders when it looks like there is no way through. And of course, he was still going flat out deep into stoppage time, as that's what he does. He's fucking relentless.

This was a strange game. For 80 minutes we were utterly dominant but when the Hammers pulled a goal back out of the blue, I'm sure it wasn't just me that thought we were about to blow it. Thankfully that never happened, but it was close and if Maiga was anything even resembling a competent striker we'd have been screwed. He missed a glorious chance at 2-1 before we regrouped and Suarez eased the tension with a goal and a half late on. That ten minute wobble aside, it was a good performance though and 4-1 was the very least we deserved from it. We played well in the first half but it was difficult as West Ham often had eleven behind the ball and there wasn't much space. What we did well, however, was counter attacked whenever West Ham did venture out of their own half and that was good to see as we'll need to be able to do that over the next few weeks.

The reason we were so dangerous on the break was because Sterling suddenly remembered that pace is his biggest asset and started using it again. He ran West Ham ragged in the first half but he had nothing to show for it because, unfortunately, his finishing was woeful. Still, it was good to see him looking direct and positive again. He had two great chances himself and he did really well to create another two that Suarez and Henderson squandered with wild finishes high over the bar. The common denominator in all of those opportunities was his pace and eagerness to run in behind the Hammers defence. The catalyst for his sudden revival appeared to be early in the first half when he made a good challenge near the corner flag in his own half and showed good strength to come away with the ball. The crowd responded to it and Sterling immediately seemed to grow in confidence. All of a sudden he began sprinting in behind the Hammers backline and displaying the kind of searing pace that defenders hate. Where has that pace been? It's been a long time since we saw it, but clearly confidence is a big factor.

Sterling's direct running off the ball helped to bring out the best in Philippe Coutinho too. One of the Brazilian's biggest attributes is the ability to thread the ball into gaps for team-mates to run onto; that's why he struck up such a good rapport with Daniel Sturridge. If people make runs in behind, he'll pick them out. Sterling missed two good opportunities due to him having no left foot (similar to Owen at the same age), and he also put two chances on a plate for Suarez and Henderson who both failed to take them. His best moment for me came when he burst through onto a lovely chest layoff by Suarez, lobbed the ball over a defender and unselfishly headed the ball through to Suarez who sadly leathered the ball high into the Anny Road. Great to see Sterling so positive and bright though, it's been a long time since we saw that.

The goal breakthrough eventually came just before half time and arrived in somewhat fortuitous circumstances as Suarez struck a shot that was parried by the keeper onto Demel, who could only look on helplessly as the ball rebounded off him into the net. No more than we deserved, but it was a bit spawny. It made for a much less stressful half time interval though, that's for sure.

Stewart Downing didn't come out for the second half and was replaced by Joe Cole. Honestly, I never even noticed that until Cole launched into a reckless challenge on Allen and was booked. I don't think DJ George noticed either, he certainly didn't announce the change. Turns out that Downing had a bad injury that he sustained very early in the game. At the time I didn't think the tackle by Flanagan was too bad, but having seen the replays it was certainly a painful one.

Sakho made it 2-0 when he met Gerrard's free-kick at the far post and the ball looped up over everybody and beat Collins' attempts to clear it from under his own crossbar. It was all going perfectly until Gerrard pulled up injured. As soon as it happened he sig-nalled to the bench that he had to come off and that's never a good thing. The news that it's a hamstring and he'll be out 4-6 weeks is the last thing we needed, it looks as though he'll be sidelined until roughly the same time as Sturridge. Not even the loss of Gerrard hampered our play though. At least, not initially. We had a brilliant spell of pressure lead-ing up to West Ham's goal, some of the football was superb and should have led to a third goal. Sterling wasted another glorious chance when terrific play from Suarez and Coutinho created an opening for Henderson, who unselfishly squared for Sterling eight yards out with the goal gaping. Somehow, he struck the ball against his own foot and it flew up into the air and well wide. Almost immediately he had another chance when Allen's beautifully disguised ball picked him in almost the same spot, this time he struck it cleanly but the keeper got down to make a great save. We were really playing some great stuff at this stage, high tempo, quick passing and great pressing to stop West Ham getting out of their own half. It was superb stuff, but all of a sudden we conceded a daft goal and ended up living on our nerves for ten minutes or so.

I don't blame Skrtel for the own goal, he had to try and cut out the cross as there was a player behind him waiting for a tap in. He was at full stretch though and could only divert it past Mignolet for his second own goal in a week. The goal gave West Ham some belief and they almost grabbed a completely undeserved equaliser when Maiga should have done better at the back post after a scramble in our box. That was a huge let off and it was a worrying period until Suarez came to the rescue with a great header from a sump-tuous Johnson cross. That killed off West Ham's resistance and it got even easier when Kevin Nolan's frustration got the better off him and he raked his studs down the back of Hendo's calf to get a straight red card. Strange that, Nolan isn't normally that kind of play-er and if you were going to do that to anyone, Henderson would surely be low on anyone's list. How can anyone have a beef with Hendo? He's the most inoffensive lad in the world.

Fat Sam accepted the decision but pointed out that if Nolan's was a red card then so was Flanagan's. Now I'll agree there is a similarity between the two incidents in that both players caught the opponent on the back of the leg with their studs, but there is also a big difference in that Flanagan was going for the ball and the contact made with Downing was completely accidental. Was it a little clumsy? Absolutely. Was it deliberate, like Nolan's? Not a chance. Not like Allardyce to talk through his hoop is it?

Suarez wrapped up the win when he turned Tomkins inside out on the edge of the box, and then outside in just for good measure before unleashing a shot that found the net via a massive deflection. He should have followed it up with another goal not long after when Coutinho sent him through with just the keeper to beat, but he tried to be too clever and attempted to walk it in and ran out of pitch. Classic case of a man who thought he could do no wrong after the week he's had.

Joe Allen was superb all game. His use of the ball was excellent and not just in an eco-nomical sense. People often say he just passes sideways and backwards, but I think that's harsh as when the forward pass is on he's not scared to look for it and some of his passing in and around the box was quality. He's got balls has Joe, you have to give him that. He's bounced back well from his derby miss and it's nice to see there's no lingering effect on his confidence.

Premier League Round Up (7-9 December 2013)

All the games this weekend started with a minutes applause for Nelson Mandela. Obviously Mandela's death upset some more than others, but surprisingly John Terry took it particularly hard. Poor old Mongo was panic stricken, blabbering on about *"What's gonna happen to poor old Del Boy and Rodney now the fella who owns the block of flats where they live has died?"*

It was a hell of a game at the Britannia and fair play to Stoke for bouncing back from being spanked at Goodison a week earlier. Putting three past Mourinho's Chelsea is almost unheard of. At least, it used to be. They're shipping goals for fun these days. Schurrle put Mourinho's men ahead inside ten minutes with a cracker but it was cancelled out by Crouch after more suspect keeping from Cech. Becoming a weekly occurrence that. Stephen Ireland then put Stoke in front with a well placed curler after the break. Amusingly, there was a clear foul by Walters in the build up to that. Usually I'd be hammering the big dopey blueshite bastard for that, but it's Chelsea so… well in lad, I guess. Schurrle bagged another corker to make it 2-2 and then hit the bar with yet another fine strike. It was looking like Chelsea would be left frustrated with just a point from a game they will feel they should be winning, but then Assaidi hilariously won it for Stoke in the last minute with a screamer.

That's karma that is, as Mourinho had been bragging last week about how clever he was having one of his players scoring goals against all of Chelsea's rivals. *"I'm happy that he's scoring goals against our direct rivals, and he doesn't score against us because he can't"* he said of Romelu Lukaku, completely overlooking the fact that none of his own strikers that he preferred to Lukaku are scoring against anybody. *"It's phenomenal you have a player that, even when he is not playing for you, is scoring against your opponents."* Isn't it just! Soft twat obviously didn't realise that we had our secret weapon lining up against him for Stoke. In fairness, nobody else realised either. Great though wasn't it? Have some of that, shithead. Speaking of shitheads, Torres was crap and got subbed again. I see that Assaidi took his shirt off after he scored. You know my thoughts on that kind of narcissistic behaviour, but when it's a stoppage time winner against Chelsea all bets are off. He could have stripped down to just his socks and you'd hear no criticism from me.

That result capped a great day. We hammered the Hammers whilst the early game had produced another home defeat for the Mancs. I fancied Newcastle to go there and get a draw, but them winning was beyond even my expectations. Van Persie was back but Rooney was missing and it showed. He's been carrying them for most of the season and without him they looked completely devoid of inspiration. Hernandez started but once again did nothing. Actually that's not true, he did do something. He produced an embarrassing dive which thankfully the ref didn't fall for. Januzaj then followed suit and hit the deck after feeling Sissoko breath on him, and later took a tumble under no challenge from Ben Arfa. Cheating little rat, and what makes it worse is the commentator saw the replays and didn't call him on it. How come? What the fuck is it about the national media's obsession with this little gobshite? I really hate this kid.

135

Poor old Moyesy will have been livid at all of thesediving shenanigans as we know how much he frowns on the sort of thing. Baffling how these United players keep defying their manager's instructions though, isn't it? I mean, he can't be turning a blind to it, as that would make him a massive, bog eyed hypocrite. It's telling how the constant stream of dubious decisions they used to get have started to dry up too. It seems that Ferguson goes and suddenly refs are no longer intimidated. Who'd have thunk it, eh?

Newcastle played well and won it through Cabaye's accurate finish after Sissoko got the better of Evra. Van Persie thought he'd equalised but it was ruled out for off-side. Eagle eyed Sian Massey right again with the big decision there. Unlike many of her colleagues she'd have given that regardless of who the manager was, but 'the Chosen One' must still be wondering how come he's not getting the same kind of perks his predecessor did. United were booed off by those that stayed til the end, which wasn't many. Half the stadium had left by then, which is almost unheard of as United have always been known for scoring late goals so their fans have generally stayed to the end in these situations. They didn't miss much, Newcastle spent most of injury time playing keepball by the United corner flag and saw this one out pretty comfortably.

Their fans taunted the Mancs by singing *"You're going down with the Mackems"*. Of course, they aren't going down, but it's still amusing that we're in December and opposing fans are in a position to take the piss in such a way. And what's all this about Van Persie putting in a transfer request? Moyes says it's bollocks, and it probably is, but something obviously isn't right there. After growing up under Wenger and then winning the title last year with Ferguson, Van Persie is probably wondering how he's ended up playing for this dickhead. Bet the fickle twat is looking at Arsenal at the top of the league and fancying a move back there now.

There'll be no living with Pards after this though. He was Mr Magnanimous after-wards, patronisingly saying how great Moyes is and how he's *"proved that he'll be great for Manchester United"*. Eh? How's he done that then? Ah hang on, I get it now. I'm surprised Pardew could even speak given how firmly wedged his tongue must have been in his cheek when he said all that. I think Moyes is the best thing to happen to United since Massimo Taibi, I reckon Pardew is looking at it from that perspective too?

Wasn't a great day for Manchester, as City didn't win either, but at least they didn't lose. Aguero scored yet again, but the Saints hit back with a brilliant goal from Dani Osvaldo and were good value for the draw. It's difficult for me to root against City too much, I mean, obviously I want to stay ahead of them and as long as that's the case then I'll want them to drop points, but if and when we start to fall away then City are my 'Plan B' if you like. Far better for them to win it than any of the others.

Southampton though, you can't help but really admire what they are doing. I like watching them, they play good stuff and are brilliantly organised. They've spent a few quid but they are also complementing that with their own home grown players. They had five or six of their Academy products in the team, including two 18 year old full backs. Good luck to them, I'd love them to get into a European spot this year.

Moving on, and Spurs had another close away victory, the jammy twats. This one could have gone either way but Sunderland aren't having any luck this season, typified when clueless Lee Mason missed one of the most blatant handballs of the season by Sandro. Adam Johnson had opened the scoring but Spurs hit back through Paulinho just before the break. O'Shea put through his own five minutes into the 2nd half and that proved to be the decisive goal. Is it me, or do O'Shea, Brown or Bardsley seem to score own goals every other week? Someone has to fill the gaping void left by big Titus I suppose. Borini wasted a great chance to equalise when he shot straight at Lloris. If he'd been playing for us and missed that I'd have wanted to kill him. He's not playing for us, so I just wanted to slap him. Soft get, he's meant to be scoring against our rivals, Lukaku style. He's no Assaidi is he?

West Brom surprisingly lost at home to Norwich. They're a funny side the Baggies. After a few games I thought they might well go down this season, then they turned it around and looked like they'd be a top half team again this season. Now they're losing at home to Norwich. Like most of the rest of the league this year, they're just really inconsistent. I heard on the radio that Steve Clarke is apparently under a bit of pressure now. Seriously? Where do West Brom think they should be finishing? At worst you can say Clarke is shooting level par, in reality he's probably a couple under but he's definitely not firing bogeys so why there's talk of his job being on the line I have no idea. If they get rid of him, perhaps we can bring him back to sort our defence out, as that's clearly not Brendan's area of expertise.

Palace had their second win under Tony Pulis, deservedly so as well as they outplayed Cardiff at Selhurst. Jerome headed them in front early doors after some lovely play by my boy Jason Puncheon. Chamakh added a second after the break and by all accounts played very well. It'll never last, but if it does then Pulis should be nailed on for manager of the year.

Sunday now, and much as I hate to say it, Everton were really good against Arsenal. Deulefeu scored a cracker, but he's still no Luis Alberto. Tell you what's pissing me off though, this sudden arrogance from their fans. They're now singing a song about Moyes 'playing football the negative way' which is pretty funny, but still, they've got a fucking cheek haven't they? We've been saying that about Moyes for years, about how he was a bad shithouse who was scared to try and win big games and instead tried to not lose, and they went fucking ballistic any time we said it! A few months of the thin Spanish waiter and suddenly they think they're Kenny's boys of '88 and Moyes is Mike Walker. That's some serious 'Saul on the road to Damascus' shit from our neighbours that is. They're acting like they just invented the fucking wheel and are turning into proper little football snobs. It's basically what happened to Arsenal fans after they ditched George Graham's alehouse footy and went all fancy dan under Wenger. Actually wasn't there someone in between those two? Someone really shit? *checks wikipedia* Bruce Rioch!!! Fucking hell, whatever happened to him?

Anyway, Arsenal fans have become the worst kind of football snob, looking down their noses at everyone else because of this 'superior' style of theirs. Yelling "HOOF!!!" any time an opponent passes a ball more than ten yards. I'm telling you, the blueshite will be doing that before long, you just wait and see. Knobs.

Also on Sunday, Fulham finally got a win as Berbatov turned on the style against Villa. Lambert's men are generally pretty useful away but a change of manager can often transform a team and Fulham actually have a fair bit of quality in their ranks. It's not like Reading last year; they sacked McDermott but not even the re-incarnation of Bob Paisley could have turned that group into a Premier League standard side. Fulham though? They shouldn't be as bad as they have been and the new manager has clearly got them at it now, none more so than Berbatov who I heard several pundits saying even actually 'ran about a bit'.

Finally, onto Monday night. I watched Swansea v Hull for about an hour and then switched it off. Hull did what they do; worked hard, defended for their lives and nicked a goal when a chance came along. It was inevitable that Danny Graham would score, he was on an 11 month drought and was returning to a former club so it was nailed on that he'd get one. He didn't celebrate it and when he was subbed in the 2nd half the Swansea fans gave him a warm reception. He was decent when he played for Swansea but he's been Welbeck-like since he left though.

From what I saw of this, Swansea were dogshit. Everything was in front of Hull who dealt with it with relative ease. Swansea had no-one running in behind as Michu always wants to come deep and had his back to goal every time he got the ball. They just looked completely toothless. I was watching this and found myself thinking: *"Swansea are fucking terrible yet they battered us when we went there. Hull are making them look very ordinary. Fucking Hull!!!"* Then I remembered that Hull beat us 3-1 and I was that pissed off I just switched it off and missed Chico's equaliser.

TOTTENHAM 0 LIVERPOOL 5

Competition - Premier League
Date - Sun 15 Dec 2013
Venue - White Hart Lane
Scorer(s) - Suarez (2),
Henderson, Flanagan, Sterling
Star Man - Luis Suarez

Team: Mignolet: Johnson,
Skrtel, Sakho, Flanagan; Lucas
(Alberto), Allen, Henderson;
Sterling, Suarez, Coutinho
(Moses):

Where the hell did this performance come from? I couldn't believe what I was watching, I mean two weeks ago we lost at Hull and looked completely hopeless, yet here we were absolutely slaughtering one of our main rivals for the top four and a side that had beaten us five years in a row in this fixture.

I can't remember the last time Liverpool produced a more complete away performance than this, it was truly stunning. Spurs got off lightly with just the 5-0, as we hit the woodwork twice and the once again stupendous Suarez even missed three one on ones. It could easily have been much, much worse for the Londoners. Granted, Spurs were truly pathetic and offered very little resistance on the day, but this is a side packed with talent and who were just three points behind us going into this game. Most of us would probably have taken a point if it had been offered prior to kick off, and even those that wouldn't could never have dreamt of this outcome. Hell, look at the Spurs bench and compare it to ours!!

This is our most significant away performance since the 4-1 at Old Trafford, it was just complete and utter dominance for almost the entire 90 minutes. Spurs had no idea what had hit them. We started the game very positively and I was thinking after 20 minutes that this is as well as we've played away from Anfield in some time and it just got better and better from there. We looked bright in attack, strong at the back but most impressive for me was the high intensity pressing game that really knocked Spurs out of their stride. Before the game I was very worried about how we'd cope in midfield. Spurs are just so big and powerful in that area of the park; Sandro, Dembele and Paulinho are big, physical specimens and my fear was that they might just overpower us in there. Incredibly, the exact opposite happened.

Joe Allen set the tone for it all, his pressing and constant harassment of the Spurs midfield just knocked them out of their stride and they simply had no answer to it. Allen was the catalyst for that pressing game as it's something he does brilliantly, but others followed his lead and both Coutinho and Sterling were just as impressive in that aspect of the game. It was fantastic seeing these little lads just completely mithering the life out of the Tottenham players. So many times we won the ball back just through snapping at people's heels and hunting in packs and it happened so often that it just got into the Tottenham players' heads. Often they ended up knocking the ball into touch even when they weren't under any pressure.

Tottenham were as bad as it's possible for a good side to be. How much of that was down to us though? I'd say that some of their defensive issues were completely of their own making, but their attacking game never got going and for that I'd give total credit to our players for simply not giving them a second on the ball. It's been a long time coming, but this was finally the kind of performance we've been waiting for. 'Rodgeball' at it's finest. It's probably not a co-incidence that the pressing and energy in the middle of the park was so impressive without the captain. Gerrard simply can't do what Allen and Henderson did without the ball but he still has a lot offer with the ball and for me there is most definitely still a place for him in the side when he returns to fitness.

We'd already missed chances before we eventually went ahead through Suarez. Sterling was running riot early on and poor old Kyle Naughton was made to look what he is; a really poor Kyle Walker tribute act. Not that Walker was faring much better on the other flank. Coutinho was giving him more than he could handle defensively and any time the Spurs man ventured forward he had to deal with the immovable Flanagan. Walker even picked up a first half booking when Flanagan got the better of him and he got frustrated and tugged the young scouser back by his shirt. Dawson was booked too after a cynical foul on Henderson who was bursting through the middle. Hendo really enjoyed himself in this one, he produced close to the complete midfield performance as he was doing it all. It's great seeing him playing with such confidence but he must wish he could play against these type of tactics every week. Spurs defended with such a high line that this reminded me of the Newcastle game last season, they were just so wide open.

It's just football suicide if you play with a high line and don't pressure the ball. If teams are daft enough to play like that against us Hendo will just run by them all day as he loves nothing better than to just gallop around into wide open spaces behind defences. In that kind of scenario he's fucking awesome, especially when the opposition can't be bothered to try and run with him, and none of those Spurs players fancied trying to keep up with the tireless Henderson. The first goal only happened because Henderson made a run in behind. Suarez didn't quite find him with the initial pass but Hendo was so alert to the situation that he got back to nick the ball off the toe of Dawson and knock it into the path of Suarez who did the rest. When you watch it again, you see exactly why Suarez gets himself into these kind of situations so often. The man simply never stands still, he's always on the move and he had anticipated what was going to happen before anybody else on the pitch. Four Tottenham players were stood still, watching as Dawson intercepted the initial pass. Suarez had already started moving and was pointing to Henderson to show him where to knock the ball. Brilliant stuff.

The second goal was a corker too and once again it was Henderson running through the middle that created it. Had he scored with his first attempt then this is a goal that we'd be watching over and over as it was just beautiful football. Sterling played a wonderful crossfield pass to Coutinho who just cushioned the ball first time into the path of the charging Henderson. The Brazilian's touch was just incredible and with no Spurs player tracking the run Hendo was through on goal. His shot was saved by Lloris who then did brilliantly to also save the follow up from Suarez. It was symptomatic of the entire day though that Liverpool were first to react to the loose ball, as Henderson did well to volley into the bottom corner. *"Is there any finer sight in football than a Hendo goal celebration"* I was thinking. Turns out there is, but I'll get to that shortly.

At 2-0 we were well in command but it's a sign of how little trust I have in this team that I was still half expecting us to blow it in the second half. As magnificently as we'd played in that first half (as well as the two goals, Suarez missed two great chances, Coutinho hit the bar and had also missed an early sitter) a goal for Spurs after the break and suddenly everything would change, we'd lose momentum and end up hanging on for dear life. I should have been relaxed and comfortable at half time as Spurs had not threatened at all other than a poor shot from Holtby and a disallowed goal from the petulant Soldado (for a blatant shoulder barge into the back of Mignolet) but I wasn't at all relaxed or comfortable. There was a nervous excitement, a certain giddiness even at how well we'd played, but confidence that we'd go on to see the job through was still in short supply. I imagine others felt the same way, as this team is too unpredictable away from home for me to have any real faith in them and it's going to take a lot more good results on our travels to change that lack of faith. This is a good start though to be fair.

Everyone knew there would be a reaction from Spurs after the break. They had been so, so bad in the first half that they were always going to come and have a good go at the start of the second half so it was vitally important we held firm in that spell. We did, there was only one real scare when Soldado ran through and shot over the bar. Aside from that we defended very well, with Sakho especially catching the eye. It was definitely a more even contest at the start of the second half and Spurs were having their only decent spell of the game. Then Paulinho kicked Suarez in the chest and that was that, game over.

As soon as that happened, my worries disappeared. There was no way we weren't going to see this one out now; it was just a matter of how many we'd score. We continued to create chances and should have scored more than the three we did add to our tally. It was one way traffic, utterly dominant stuff. I asked earlier if there was a finer sight in football than a Hendo goal celebration, and I got my answer when another fine move ended with Suarez picking out Flanagan at the back post and the young full back lashed in a superb half volley off the underside of the bar. I'm sure I wasn't the only whose reaction to it was to cheer and then just start laughing uncontrollably. Well I know I wasn't, as the camera panned to 'the King' in the stands and he was doing exactly the same. Apparently Rodgers went charging off down the touchline in celebration and everyone was just elated about it. None more than Flanno himself, he'll remember that for the rest of his life, it was just a great moment for a young Kopite living the dream.

What I loved about it was how happy all of the players were for him. Suarez, for example, was completely ecstatic and led the charge after his young team-mate before eventually diving on him in front of the travelling Kop. The rest soon followed and there was a massive piley on. You could tell after the game in his post match interview too just how delighted Suarez was for Flanagan and I'm sure that goal probably gave Suarez more enjoyment than the ones he bagged himself. Flanagan seems like an incredibly popular lad with everyone in the squad, which you have to put down to how he must be in training every day. His team-mates are all rooting for him to do well because no-one deserves it more.

Staying with Suarez for a second though, one of the many great things about him is how happy he is when other people score. He seems to love Sterling for example. Look at how he always reacts any time Sterling scores, he's like a proud big brother, he's genuinely delighted for him. He was absolutely buzzing for Flanno too and despite him being one of the world's greatest players there doesn't seem to be any ego about him when you see how he interacts with his team-mates. With Torres for example, you could see he loved Gerrard because he saw him as an equal. He never had the same kind of relationship with some of the 'lesser players' that you can see Suarez has though. I'm sure that was a big part of why Rodgers gave him the armband in the absence of Gerrard and Agger. There were a lot of valid reasons why he should not have been made captain, but just as many as to why it was a no brainer to give him it. I was as pissed off with him as anybody last summer (mainly because it was Arsenal that he was trying to force a move to) but from Rodgers' perspective it's completely different. There are other factors for him to consider, the main one being how the players in the dressing room feel about Suarez and it's blatantly obvious they all love him and respect him.

It's the effect he has on those team-mates that made giving him the armband the right decision for me. He's one of the greatest players in the world but he doesn't act like he is. There's no air of superiority about him on the field or when he's around his team-mates; he's just one of the lads and no-one works harder than him. Of course, demanding a move because the team weren't in the Champions League was a bit 'superior' but leaving that aside you have to say he's a great team-mate. Another factor to consider is that anything that strengthens his bond with the club and his team-mates has to be a good thing in terms of trying to keep him, and keeping him is absolutely vital for our immediate and future prospects. You only have to look at Spurs to see that, there's no way we'd be keeping them so quiet if they still had Bale in their side. Losing Bale seems to have completely taken all of the wind out of their sails.

But I digress. At 3-0 everyone could relax and enjoy themselves. Everyone except Tottenham of course, who were now just praying for the final whistle. It's a sign of how high the standards of Suarez are these days that I was feeling a little disappointed he'd only scored one and made two. Shit that isn't it? Not good enough Luis. With plenty of time left though I was desperately hoping for more goals from him to keep this remarkable scoring record going. As ever, he didn't disappoint, running onto a pass from substitute Luis Alberto and coolly lobbing the ball over the advancing Lloris. He wasn't done there either as he then turned provider to set one up for Sterling, who thoroughly deserved his goal after producing what for me is the best performance of his career so far. He was positive, direct, he worked his bollocks off and showed the kind of fight and deceptive strength that we saw when he first broke into the side. That was one of the most impressive things when he initially broke through, he may be small and slight but he wasn't often knocked off the ball and when he was he'd fight to win it back immediately. That disappeared for a while and he began to look really lightweight and was getting pushed around, but it's amazing what a bit of confidence can do and he more than held his own physically against Spurs.

This win sets us up nicely for the Christmas period and whilst nothing can bring back the three points lost at Hull, this certainly lessens the blow. I'd liken it to a round of golf. The loss at Hull was like a double bogey but we've responded with two pars and then an eagle at Spurs. Nine points from those four fixtures is probably level par, it's just that we went about getting them the hard way. I was furious for days after that loss at Hull, and to be honest the anger is still there even now. Having said that, I'm probably as excited by the Spurs performance as I was disgusted by what happened at Hull.

Premier League Round Up (14-15 December 2013)

So poor old AVB is a gonner then eh? Not really a shock, but is it the right decision? I don't know and don't really care, it's not my problem. Clearly things weren't right there, and without taking anything away from our performance it has to be said that Spurs were way, way beyond shite. All that money spent and what do they have to show for it? A strong looking subs bench but that's about it.

AVB seems like a good guy though and I take no pleasure in his demise. I misjudged him badly when he was at Chelsea and he's actually a fairly good egg. Even after his team had been snotted by us he kept his dignity, didn't make excuses or blame anyone else and was very complimentary about us. So yeah, nice fella, but this football management thing isn't working out too well for him is it? Maybe it just isn't meant to be? It would seem that it's not just his looks that draw comparisons with Arnold J Rimmer. Remember how Rimmer kept taking the science officer's exam and repeatedly failing it? He just wasn't cut out for anything above the rank of 2nd technician, and it's the same with AVB, who it appears may be just a glorified scout. Smegheads.

Tim Sherwood has now taken temporary charge of Spurs. Man, I can't fucking stand Tim Sherwood you know. It's one of those irrational hatreds but I can't bear even looking at him. He was the Dean Holdsworth of midfielders. I hated Holdsworth too. Sherwood was shit as a player, he was shit as a pundit on sky, no doubt he's been shit in whatever role he's been filling for Daniel Levy and he'll be shit at this too. Poor mans David Batty. The first thing he did was bring Adebayor back into the fold for the league cup game against West Ham. Yes, the same Adebayor who within minutes of us humiliating his team was pictured on twitter with his boy Assou-Ekotto gloating over it. He scored against the Hammers, got a standing ovation off the fans (what the fuck??) and then watched from the bench as West Ham scored twice in the last ten minutes to dump them out. I bet AVB almost shit a lung laughing at that. It will have been one of the greatest days of his life, he's probably been walking around with a permanent smile on his face ever since, like when Rimmer found out Lister was going to be giving birth to twin boys.

So who's going to get the job then? The hilarious thing is most Spurs fans I've heard on the radio want Glen Hoddle. When it's pointed out to them that AVB has the highest win percentage of ANY Spurs manager and a far superior record to Hoddle, the response is usually "Yeah but he don't play Spurs football, we'd rarver lose 6-5 than win 1-0 wouldn't we? We're Spurs, we wanna be entertained, guv'nor" Why not go and get Ossie Ardilles back then, knobheads. At least he's not a complete mentalist who thinks disabled people were all paedos in a former life.

Staying with Spurs, remember when they let in six at Man City and Arsenal's keeper was taking the piss on twitter? Well that came back to bite him on the arse didn't it? You reap what you sew. I didn't watch it live and when I saw the score I assumed it was another example of City just blowing away one of their rivals. From watching the highlights though that wasn't the case. Arsenal gave as good as they got, the main difference was finishing. City took most of their chances, Arsenal missed most of theirs. As Wenger said afterwards, City could easily have let in six themselves. Arsenal should have had a pen when they were only one behind and Bendtner had one wrongly disallowed for offside. It could easily have been 6-6 and it was a fantastic game of football, absolutely breathtaking stuff.

I'm pleased to see Arsenal's defence shown up for what they really are though. That record of theirs has been pissing me right off as I'm not having it that their back four is anything other than dogshit. Collectively and individually they're all shite, except Sagna who has developed into a very good player in the last year or two. The rest? I'm not having them at all. City's attacking play is scary though, they're coming at you from all angles but injuries to Aguero and Zabaleta should hopefully slow them down a little for when we play them next week. Those two are such a massive part of what they do, they have good players to bring in but they'll definitely be weaker as a result of losing them.

Arsenal understandably didn't take it well. Mertesacker let rip at Ozil for not going to applaud the fans whilst Wilshere is in hot water after giving the finger to the City crowd. He's been given a two game ban for that, which is a little odd given Suarez only got one for committing the same offence at Fulham. Considering the usual disparity in FA punishments for Suarez as opposed to everybody else, Wilshere was probably expecting a basket of fruit delivered to his door and a one game ban for the Man City crowd. Don't despair Jack, just turn up to your appeal hearing in your England kit and it'll probably still happen. They'll probably just hand the ban to Suarez instead.

It's just mad though isn't it, this season. I honestly can't remember anything like it. City have demolished United, Spurs and Arsenal but lost to Sunderland, Cardiff and Villa. We twatted Spurs at White Hart Lane but got humiliated by Hull. Arsenal have lost at home to Villa and conceded six against City. United have been awful, ditto Spurs. The most consistent side has actually been Everton, who've only lost once.

You can't predict anything with any degree of certainty. Except Villa shitting the bed against the Mancs of course, that's one thing you can ALWAYS hang your hat on. Villa are so inept in this fixture that not only did they lose to a United side managed by David Moyes, they allowed Welbeck and Cleverley to get the goals. Fuck me, they deserve to be relegated just for that. Bunch of losers. Puts things in perspective though doesn't it? I mean, this week my recently turned seven year old daughter has been absolutely destroying me on various iPhone games. I'd given up trying to beat her on Temple Run, but at least I had Fruit Ninja. Until she started beating me at that too. Still, she was never going to beat my top score of 164. Or so I thought, until she went and put up a whopping 442. How can that happen? She's seven!! It's not like I'm some technophobe either, like my arl fella. He only used a cash machine for the first time in his life a couple of months ago. He'd steadfastly refused to even entertain the idea of it as *"I don't trust them, what if it charged me but didn't give me my money?"* So anytime he wanted to take money out, he'd have to go inside the bank, which meant he could never draw any money out at weekends or after 5pm. I'm not sure what changed to make him suddenly trust this *'new fangled technology'*, but now he's using cash machines. The next step is to get him to buy diesel at Asda using his bank card, as at the moment he'd rather pay 7p a gallon more at the BP because he can pay by cash. You probably think that's funny, endearing even. But that's my inheritance he's whittling away there due to this daft technophobia of his.

Anyway, the point is that unlike my Dad I know my way around technology. Hell, I've been playing computer games and stuff my whole life, yet now I can't even beat a seven year old girl at Fruit Ninja?? Of course I'm proud of her accomplishments, I mean how many seven year olds can beat their Dad at anything? That pride is tempered by the humiliation I'm feeling personally though. And when I say 'tempered', I mean 'completely overshadowed'. Nevertheless, this weekend has taught me that it could be worse. I might be getting my arse handed to me by a seven year old girl, but at least I'm not shipping three goals to Danny Welbeck and Tom Cleverley. Shame on you Aston Villa, shame on you.

Elsewhere this weekend, Chelsea were a little fortunate to beat Palace as they were crap once again. Torres scored a tap in, Ramires added a cracker but Chamakh found the net for the third game in succession (more league goals in three games than that bum

Torres has in the whole 2013) and Chelsea could easily have ended up drawing as Palace had chances. It seems that most Chelsea games are on a knife edge these days, they don't seem to be doing anything very convincingly and were hilariously knocked out of the league cup in midweek by Sunderland. Poor old Jose, if he had even an ounce of humility he'd be regretting upsetting the football Gods with that kissing of his own arse over Lukaku scoring against Chelsea's rivals. Last week it was Assaidi punishing him on our behalf, this week it was Fabio Magnifico dumping his pompous, preening arse out of the cup with a last minute equaliser in normal time followed by a last minute assist in extra time. Fuck you Jose, how d'ya like them apples.

Moving on, and the other Blueshite briefly threatened to drop points at home to Fulham after getting pegged back to 1-1. I got a little excited as Fulham were on top at that stage, then they suddenly remembered they are Fulham and caved in to lose 4-1.

Over at Upton Park West Ham and Sunderland played out a dire 0-0, whilst Stoke and Hull also ended goalless. Sky actually chose that one for their live Saturday evening game. Who the hell made that decision? Was it done to win a bet?

The funniest moment of the weekend came as a player knocked a referee on his arse by accidentally smacking him on the nose during Newcastle's 1-1 draw with Southampton at St James Park. In addition to that, the coaches of both sides got into a bit of a scuffle and both goalkeeper coaches were sent to the stands. Pardew called it 'pathetic' and compared it to 'panto season' whilst Pochettino said 'it did not set a good example'. Panto season eh? Yeah, I could definitely see Pardew as a pantomime dame. He certainly looks the type. As for 'not setting a good example', well far worse than anything that happened on the touchline was the conduct of referee Mike Jones, who hit the deck like he'd been picked off by a sniper on the roof. Fair enough, he did get a bit of a bang on the nose from Sissoko, but there was no need for that over the top reaction.

The funniest part of it was the complete lack of remorse from Sissoko though. It was accidental, obviously, but you'd think he'd have shit himself at bloodying a referees nose, no matter how inadvertent it was, but he genuinely didn't care and was more interested in continuing his disagreement with the Southampton keeper. If I'd have been Jones I'd have sent him off, not for bopping me on the nose, but for not even having the courtesy to see if I was ok, the cheeky disrespectful fucker.

Norwich drew 1-1 with Swansea, a result that will probably satisfy both teams, whilst Cardiff beat West Brom 1-0 and Steve Clarke immediately got the sack. I must be missing something here, as although West Brom haven't been pulling up any trees in 2013 it looks to me like Clarke is suffering from having such a great first six months at the Hawthorns. West Brom aren't a top eight side, but that's where Clarke had them after his first season. Now they're back punching at around their own weight and he's been given the bullet. Where do the Baggies actually think they should be in the table? Strange one to me, but then I wondered what the hell Southampton were doing last year and that's worked out well for them.

As for Cardiff, it looks like Malky Mackay could go any day too, not because he isn't doing a good job but because that owner of theirs is a complete fucking whackjob. It looks to me like he's trying to 'out-mental' the crank at Hull. Hopefully if Mackay is going then we'll give him the same kind of send off we gave Rimmer last weekend.

LIVERPOOL 3 CARDIFF 1

Competition - Premier League
Date - Sat 21 Dec 2013
Venue - Anfield
Scorer(s) – Suarez (2), Sterling
Star Man – Luis Suarez

Team: Mignolet; Johnson,
Skrtel, Sakho, Flanagan (Kelly);
Lucas, Allen, Henderson;
Coutinho (Agger), Suarez,
Sterling:

Winning at Spurs last week was a statement that we can go to difficult venues and win well but with the opportunity to go to the top of the table this game presented a challenge of a different kind. It may have 'only' been Cardiff - the kind of side we've been hammering at home for most of 2013 - but this was different simply because of what was at stake. It was a test of nerve, and thankfully we passed.

If we'd failed to perform in this one it could only have been because of a lack of bottle and not being able to handle the pressure. The fact we went out and got the job done by half time is encouraging and hopefully bodes well for the rest of the season. Having battered Spurs last week and with a trip to Man City coming up on Boxing Day, it would have been just like modern day Liverpool (and by modern day I'm talking twenty years or so rather than just under Rodgers) to overlook Cardiff and shit the bed. It could easily have been one of those let down games, but I never had the feeling it would be, especially after the lift everyone was given the day before when Suarez penned his new contract.

Cardiff didn't make it easy though, they were defending well early on and also tried to get forward whenever possible. They got down our left a few times as Flanagan had something of an uncomfortable opening to the game. Liverpool fan Craig Noone got past him a couple of times and looked lively early doors before disappearing without trace the longer it went on. He stung Mignolet's palms with a good strike from 20 yards after they hit us with a quick break after Sterling had lost possession and Cardiff always looked like they had a goal in them. Nevertheless, we were well on top and playing some lovely stuff again. We'd had chances to score before Suarez eventually broke the deadlock with yet another terrific strike. The finish itself was quality but what I liked most about the goal was the subtle change of direction from him that started the move. He'd initially looked like he had lost the ball but it broke back to him and anyone else would have gone to their left with the ball as that's the way he was facing and the way his body was moving. Suarez isn't like anyone else though, and instead just twisted back inside and wriggled away to his right, completely catching the defender unaware before laying it off and then setting off towards the danger area. Coutinho then rolled it to Henderson who lobbed it first time to Suarez to volley it home. Champagne football.

I loved the second goal too, albeit for different reasons. There was so much to admire about it and I always think there's something really satisfying about scoring from another team's corner kick. It's like a pick six in the NFL or an alley oop fast break dunk in basketball, it's a real momentum shifter and is completely demoralising to the opposition.

146

The speed of the counter attack was just a joy to behold. Henderson's pass with the outside of his foot to release Suarez was class but I loved the unselfishness of Suarez to roll it to Sterling for a tap in. How many strikers would do that when in the kind of form Suarez has been in? Ok, that's a daft question as there are only two players in the world who even know what it's like to be in the form Suarez is in. One of those would pass in that situation, the other would rather cut off his own cock. I'll leave you to work out who I'm talking about. The point is, Suarez is breaking all kinds of records at the moment and had a glorious chance to add another goal to his haul, yet he passed that opportunity up because he wanted his young team-mate to get a goal even more. That speaks volumes about Suarez, he knows how important it is for us to have people like Sterling contributing and he's now set up three goals in four games for the 19 year old, who is now absolutely flying himself and is full of confidence. It's an incredible turnaround for him, he was a little boy lost just a few weeks ago and now he's terrorising defenders and scoring goals.

Credit to Sterling for how he's playing but how much of it is down to Suarez and the effect he's had on him and the rest of the side? He's making everybody better, the likes of Sterling, Henderson and Coutinho are all thriving playing alongside Suarez. Hell, even Flanagan is benefitting from it and he's playing left back. Flanno was a whisker away from another goal as he stole in on the back post and did ever so well to divert Johnson's cross goalwards. It hit the inside of the post and was then hacked off the line by a defender. Desperately unlucky from the youngster, who may not be as easy on the eye with his attacking as some other full backs, but he's certainly proving to be effective and is getting himself into some great positions.

He wasn't the only one left cursing the goalpost as Coutinho was also denied by the woodwork after a fantastic little turn in the box followed by a shot from a tight angle. Would have been a special goal that one. He did some great things in the game but also lost the ball quite a bit. There were shades of Luis Garcia about Coutinho as he was very hit and miss.

Suarez quickly made it 3-0 with another wonderful finish, curling the ball into the far corner from 20 yards after collecting a backheel from Henderson. When that went in I just think everyone in the stadium was in absolute awe of what they were seeing. Not that the goal itself was THAT special, it's more just the sheer ridiculousness of what Suarez is now doing each and every game. 19 goals in 12 games. 14 goals in six games at Anfield. Read that again. 14 goals in six games at Anfield!!! We're witnessing history here, we're privileged to be watching the most talented player we've ever had. Hell, he may well be the most talented player to ever play on these shores. The lad who sits in front of me said at home time he'd pay double his season ticket price just to watch Suarez run around on his own. I know what he means, but I wouldn't want to be giving FSG any ideas!

Even in the second half when we dropped our performance level significantly, Suarez was still a huge threat and was only denied a hat-trick by the post. He also curled one just wide after yet another superb move. We certainly had our chances in the second half but for a 15 minute spell after they scored things were a bit uncomfortable and had they managed to get another then it could have got extremely nervy. We brought that pressure on ourselves through once again failing to deal with a routine set-piece. You can kind of accept conceding from corners or free-kicks in dangerous areas but we've let in quite a few from free-kicks that were nowhere near our goal. A long punt into the box has resulted in goals against Newcastle, Hull and Cardiff now. There may well be others that have slipped my mind too. This one was appalling and completely unnecessary, as somehow Sakho was left to mark two players at the back post and he was unable to win the header as one of them blocked him off whilst the other - Jordon Mutch - stole in behind to head past Mignolet. That just can't happen but there wasn't much Sakho could do in that situation other than perhaps do a better job in yelling at his team-mates to ensure he wasn't left alone on an island like that. Rodgers had just made a defensive change prior to that goal - taking off Flanagan and introducing Kelly - and I wonder if that played a part in the goal? I didn't really see what the point of it was, presumably it was to get Kelly some minutes but it seemed a bit unnecessary to me and it arguably cost us a goal because there was a definite breakdown in our organisation on that set-piece.

Skrtel got away with a couple of shirt pulls on set-pieces, one of them was absolutely blatant and could easily have been called and given the media attention given to it I'd suggest he lies low for a few weeks and doesn't take any chances as refs will be looking for that in the next couple of games. With City and Chelsea up next, that's the last thing we need.

At 3-1 the crowd were getting a little edgy and frustrated at how the game was going, and eventually Rodgers opted to send on Agger for Coutinho and go to three at the back. No-one likes to see that kind of substitution but it was the smart play and as soon as he did it, Cardiff ceased to be any kind of a threat and we regained our grip on the game.

Lack of clean sheets aside, something special is happening at the moment. We have our faults and there are still a number of things that concern me (not least the lack of faith I've got in those in charge of transfers), but we're playing great football and Suarez is simply that special that his presence alone makes us a threat to anybody. We did well without him when he was suspended, but look at what we've done since he came back! I look at what we've done in the last four games, scoring 17 goals and conceding three, and wonder how the fuck did we lose at Hull???

Too often this season we've slacked off in the second half of games but if ever there was a time when it was forgivable to do so then this was surely it. The game was more or less won by half time and if the players were trying to conserve some energy in the second half with the City game in mind, I've got no issue with that on this occasion. We'll need to play with such a high intensity to get anything from that game, and if we'd gone flat out against Cardiff we may not have been able to do that as we'll more than likely be fielding an unchanged line up and don't have the luxury of making four or five changes to keep people fresh. Plus we then have Chelsea three days later of course.

It's nice to be top of the table at this stage of the season, we were there earlier in the season and once we'd been knocked off I didn't think we'd be back there again, yet here we are. It doesn't really mean anything but it is good for confidence and obviously we'd all rather be top than 5th or 6th, regardless of whether it only lasts for two days or not. If we're still in or around this spot come Easter, then we're in a title race. Right now, we're just making a good fist of breaking back into the top four. It's fun to watch though, that's for sure.

Cardiff's fans spent most of the game chanting against Vincent Tan and in support of Malky Mackay. Liverpool fans applauded Mackay, but to be honest I couldn't give a shit about it all. Obviously Tan is a knobhead, but Mackay can fuck off too as far as I'm concerned. The crying twat got Sterling booked for a perfectly good tackle near the touchline in front of the Cardiff bench. His furious reaction to it was pathetic and so over the top that it probably made the referee think it must have been worse than it was. So no, I don't give a shit if he does get the sack, and I couldn't care less about Cardiff fans either with their 'feed the scousers' crap. Season of goodwill to all men? Humbug. I hope Tan changes their kit to pink and appoints Christian Gross as manager.

Premier League Round Up (21-23 December 2013)

I'll kick this one off at Craven Cottage where Man City faced a struggling Fulham side who were without the injured Berbatov. Joe Hart was back for City whilst they had Clichy at right back. You never see left footed right backs do you? I know left footed players are a lot rarer than right footed ones, but even so, if a club (or indeed a national side) has two top left backs they never move one of them over, they'd prefer to use an average right footer instead.

Case in point, Baines couldn't get a game for England before Ashley Cole went over the hill. Hodgson would have picked his sixth choice right back rather than play either Cole or Baines on the opposite flank. It's not just Hodgson either, all managers are the same it seems, yet they think nothing of using a right footed full back on the left. Anyway, I'm sounding like a 'Boring James Milner' tweet there so I'll press on before I lose you all. City went ahead with a superb free-kick by Toure, Kompany then made it 2-0 from a set-piece but Taraabt set up Richardson just after the break to make a game of it. Fulham were transformed after that and Sidwell headed wide before Kompany scored the own goal of the season when he comically sliced the ball up in the air and over Hart into the far corner. It's just a pity it didn't cost them points, but there's just no accounting for the awfulness of Fulham this year.

Nevertheless, for a spell after that City were woeful and were really on the ropes. With just 12 minutes left it was looking like an upset could perhaps be on the cards but then Navas ran clear to beat Steckelenberg (who should have done better) and Milner added a fourth. City are rolling now, even without Aguero. The more I see of Negredo, the more I think he's fucking brilliant. To think at the start of the season I kept getting him mixed up with the bang average Soldado. Given how the season has progressed, that now looks like akin to not being able to tell David Ngog and Thierry Henry apart. Speaking of the Gog, what the hell has happened to him these days? Has he retired? Obviously I don't follow Bolton closely, but if he'd even been scoring the occasional goal I'm sure I'd have heard something about it, either on the radio or Soccer Saturday or something. As it is, I don't remember the last time I heard his name mentioned. *wiki tells me he's scored one goal in 14 games this season. I'm surprised he's got one to be honest.*

Whilst Negredo is unquestionably ace, at the other end of the scale you have Demichelis. He's awful isn't he? I think it's safe to say that if you're a defender and you have a pony tail, chances are you're a bit poo. I don't know why they bothered signing him really, he's their Soto Kyrgiakos I guess.

Finally on this one, what in the blue hell has John Arne Riise done to his head? Ridiculous state of affairs. It looks like he's got a dead animal on his bonce, or he's wearing one of those Davey Crocket hats. He's far too old now to be experimenting like that. That's all well and good when you're in your early twenties, but come on lad, just accept your fate. You're ginger, embrace it, don't run from it. It's nearly 2014, being a fanta pants isn't anything like the handicap it used to be.

Elsewhere on Saturday, whilst his boss Fergie may have gone it seems that Fat Sam is still bending over at Old Trafford. Old habits die hard I guess. United won't have a more comfortable home win all season. The Hammers were pitiful and I really hope they get relegated now, the shit boring bastards. It was Ravel Morrison's big homecoming and predictably he was invisible. Typical that, ex United players never do anything against their old side, unless it's scoring own goals. West Ham have a new keeper now, some fella called Adrian. Never heard of him, but if he's putting that scruffy, Kop ignoring twat Jaaskelainen out of a job then he'll do for me. He made a couple of good saves but could also have done better on a couple of goals.

Emile Welbeck scored again, that's how shit West Ham were. Januzaj added a second and then Ashley Young came on and scored the third. Remember when we bought Downing and the Mancs bought Young and everyone said we bought the wrong player? Well I'm putting it out there, Young has been an even bigger flop than Stewy was, especially considering he's been playing in a side competing for (and occasionally winning) titles. If they sell him they'll get less than West Ham gave us for Downing, he's worth about £3m these days I reckon. He's more known for his diving than his football now. I'd take Downing over Young all day, although I'd obviously prefer to take neither. And have I mentioned before that I fucking hate that Januzaj kid? Diving little shithouse bastard. He did it so often in this game even the commentator couldn't continue to ignore it, especially when Mike Jones booked him for it. Horrible little baby faced twat. Januzaj that is, not Mike Jones.

I hate that Cleverley knobhead as well. It's his face I can't stand, he's just too damn manc-like. Look up 'manc' in the dictionary and it will say *'nasal sounding, scouse hating tribe from the North West of England. Usually found wearing black Stone Island clobber, dripping in hair gel and with one or both ears pierced'*. And there'll be a picture of Tom fucking 'Cleverleh' next to it. He's another cheating twat too, he blocked a shot with his hand and walked away holding his chest. Fucking scumbag. When he was at Everton Moyes always used to try and be Mr Morals didn't he, waging his little one man crusade against the dark arts of the game. Now he's turning a blind eye to all sorts, the hypocritical little bog eyed turd. Of course he said he'll *'have a word'* with Januzaj, but no-one is buying that now are they? His players are acting the twat on a weekly basis and he does nothing to stop it because now he's not at little old Everton anymore and the stakes are so much higher, it's win at all costs.

Anyway, moving on before I give myself an aneurism, Newcastle are in great form at the moment - helped by being in the middle of a relatively easy run of fixtures it should be said - and they continued their winning ways as Pardew stormed his former Palace. I bet the Selhurst Park staff are still finding knickers and suzzies and shit in the drawers and filing cabinets of what used to be his office, the old horn dog. Cabaye put them ahead with a deflected shot and Gabiddon then put through his own net shortly after to make it 2-0. Cabaye went close to a second with a stinging free-kick that was just about kept out by Speroni. The Palace keeper has the strangest face in the Premier League. I wouldn't go as far as to call him ugly, but his face definitely looks like it's been made up of parts he's salvaged from other people. For example, his mouth looks like it was stolen from an eight year old boy; that thing is frigging tiny. Anyway, Ben Arfa eventually made it 3-0 from the penalty spot as the Geordies enjoyed a comfortable afternoon in South London. As for Palace, I've now decided that I hope they stay up, simply on the basis of how ace *"Glad All Over"* is. I can even put up with Tony Pulis and their knobhead fans if it means hearing them play that great tune before games.

Moving on, and Stoke took on Villa in a game no-one will have wanted to see, not even the long suffering fans of both teams. I had this nailed on as a 0-0 as Villa were without Benteke and Agbonlahor and Stoke were... well they're Stoke aren't they? Plus they recalled Jon Walters to the side, which reduces the likelihood of a goal by around 39%. I don't have any stats to back that up, but it's probably true. I was wrong though, incredibly there were goals in this one. Three of them. I guess crap defending trumped crap attacking on the day, or should that be the other way round? It's easy to forget that Stoke have four ex Reds in their squad. Well, three plus Assaidi, who surely won't be coming back to Anfield. They've a long way to go to reach Chelsea or West Ham levels of charity though, as the likes of Pennant and Crouch didn't go there straight from Anfield. Stoke did take Salif Diao off us though and deserve some gratitude for that I guess.

Speaking of Crouchy though, his missus won that dancing competition on BBC and he was asked about it afterwards. *"I'd like to say that I've helped but I've only got the robot in my locker, that's it"*. Ah the robot, brings back some good memories that. I loved Crouchy when he was a Red, and the 'Robo Crouch' was ace. Remember the scissor kick he scored in Europe? And the hat-trick against Arsenal? Good times. For a couple of years he was quality. And now he's at Stoke, a fate most certainly not befitting a man of his standing.

Managerless West Brom took on Hull at the Hawthorns. The visitors took the lead with a great counter attack, Livermore making a lung bursting run to get up in support of Graham and finish well. He booted a camera as he ran off to celebrate, and then ended up having to pay for it to be replaced. Six grand it cost him. SIX GRAND!!!! For a fucking camera!!! I reckon the cameraman saw him coming there. *"Oy soft lad! You've broke me fuckin' camera yer dickhead" "Sorry mate, I got lost in the moment, I'll pay for a new one of course. How much do I owe you?" "Errrrr, let's call it an even six grand"*. To Livermore's credit he's also donating an extra six grand to a cancer research charity, apparently.

Just as Hull were in sight of the finish line and a welcome three points, some fella called Vydra equalised for the Baggies very late on. Never heard of him, where's he been all season? Steve Bruce was funny afterwards, talking about how Hull need to follow the lead of West Brom and establish themselves as a Premier League club, before hastily adding *"not by sacking the manager mind"*. I know I've said this before, but I quite like Bruce, he's a decent sort of chap and you'd never believe he used to play for THEM. You know who's actually a really good player? Tom Hundredstone, that's who. He's not top four or five club good, but Hull have done well to get him as he can definitely play, even if he can't run.

Sunderland's home game with Norwich was a great opportunity for them to put some much needed points on the board as a gap was beginning to open between them and the rest of the strugglers. They couldn't do it though, and you have to wonder now if they are going to save themselves. I'd say there are several teams worse than them on paper, and Poyet seems to have them playing quite well, but if you can't win at home against Norwich? Uh-oh. They had my favourite footballing wiseguy Vito Mannone to thank for even getting a point. He made a couple of great saves and it's nice to see him getting regular footy. He's a good keeper and a stand up guy. Sunderland's misery was compounded when Wes Brown got sent off again and this time he had no cause for complaint, the reckless bastard. Anymore of this and he'll have to change his name to Wes Red, the dirty manc twat. Is it just me thinking he wanted Christmas off? Finally on this, I'm nominating Jozy Altidore as the worst player in the Premier League. Who's with me?

Onto Sunday now, and Tim Sherwood took charge of his first Premier League game as Spurs made the trip to Southampton. He picked a ridiculously attacking midfield four with Dembele as a holding player alongside Eriksen, Lamela and Sigurdsson. Playing to the galleries that, you know how Spurs fans are about their 'attacking football' and 'playing with style'. AVB got the push in no small part because he was seen as being too cautious, so Sherwood comes in and immediately it's good old 4-4-2 with a typically lightweight, typically Tottenham midfield. I remember when I was a kid and they had Hoddle, Ardilles, Villa, Micky Hazard and Gary Brook in there. All nice footballers, all soft as shite. Great to watch, but they never won anything other than an FA Cup any time the year ended in a one or some shit like that. The likes of Souness used to have them for breakfast.

Lallana put the Saints ahead and Rodriguez wasted a great chance to double their lead before Adebayor volleyed in a Soldado cross to level things up. Great finish but we know he can do that, ability has never been an issue with Adebayor. When he's on his game he's brilliant, but how many managers have bombed him out? There has to be a reason for that. Carragher called him 'a disgrace' on Monday Night Football, and I'm inclined to agree. Hooiveld put through his own net to give Spurs the lead but Lambert equalised after great vision by Lallana presented him with an open goal. Great play by Lallana, he's class that lad. Adebayor then won it for Spurs with another good finish and followed it up with a typically shit dance. Sadly this time Ryan Babel wasn't around to win a penalty seconds later to make him look like the tit that he is.

Amazingly, the result was enough to get Sherwood the job on a full time basis. Great stuff, I was worried they may actually appoint someone capable but instead they gave it to a fella with no qualifications, no experience, and no clue. Daniel Levy is meant to be a shrewd operator, but this is just daft. It'd be like us sacking Rodgers and appointing Don Hutchison.

Elsewhere on Sunday, and I really wish Everton would just fuck off now. I didn't anticipate them winning at Swansea and to be frank, I've had more than enough of them being good now. The novelty has worn off and the sooner they remember who they are the better, as I can't lie, I'm getting worried. Seamus Coleman put them ahead with a fine strike that the keeper should have done better with. Must be nice to have a right back who can score and create goals. Even nicer when he isn't on 120k a week. Hell, it didn't even cost that much to buy him. Dwight Tiendali equalised more or less straight away, immediately jumping to number two on my 'favourite Dwights' list in the process. Number one is obviously Dwight Schultz, who played Howling Mad Murdoch on the A-Team. To be honest I only know two other Dwights and they are both egotistical twats (Yorke and Howard), but for what it's worth, Tiendali is number two. Barkley was brilliant and he won it with a superb free-kick. I was sick when that went in as the fixtures they have coming up compared with those we have to play meant that there was every chance they could be above us at the start of 2014. Fucking scabs, borrowing their way to the top of the league. The sooner the big clubs call in those loans the better.

The biggest game of 'week 17' was on Monday night as Chelsea made the trip to the Emirates. It was dire, negative shite and I found myself thinking *"we're miles better than both of these"*. The highlight of the entire ninety minutes was my arl fella commenting on what he thought was a Chelsea counter attack and saying *"Look at this, three against one again"* and me gleefully pointing out *"Yeah, that's a replay, Dad."*

Mikel could have been sent off after catching Arteta with a studs up challenge. That prompted a heated debate in the Sky studio between Carra and Gary Neville, and to my eternal shame I found myself siding with ratboy over Carra. The fact that the battle in the studio was more entertaining than that on the pitch said it all though. Mourinho is such a shithouse isn't he? All that talent available and he plays like that? He's Tony Pulis with better players. Ramires could have gone too, also for a nasty lunge on the unfortunate Arteta. Now that one I would have given a red card for, and not just because I'd prefer Ramires to be suspended for our game at the weekend than Mikel. There are a few observations I could make on this about certain Chelsea players, but as we play them in a few days and I don't want to tempt fate, I'm keeping my own counsel for now.

Arsenal had the better of the second half and Giroud went close twice, but neither side deserved to win. That Ivanovic is a twat isn't he? First he almost decapitated Ozil with a high boot to the face then he's rolling around like he'd been shot after barely being touched by Rosicky. No wonder Luis bit the fucker. Neanderthal looking goon. He's the next one up from Martin Keown on the evolutionary scale I believe. Arsenal fans were chanting *'boring boring Chelsea'* at the end. Fair point but what about their own side? They were shite too and weren't exactly gung ho. Typical Arsenal fans mentality though, acting like their shit don't stink. I was almost offended at having to watch this. I dunno, maybe I'm just spoiled from watching all this 'Rodgeball'.

Mourinho was typically antagonistic towards Arsenal afterwards. *"You know, they like to cry. That's tradition. But I prefer to say, and I was telling it to the fourth official, that English people – Frank Lampard, for example – would never provoke a situation like that. Players from other countries, especially some countries, have that in their blood. So, if there is contact or an opponent is aggressive, they don't keep going. But this is English football. Foreign players are bringing lots of good things. They come here because they are talented. But I prefer English blood in football. English blood in this situation is: 'Come on, let's go.' Mikel's tackle is hard and aggressive but football is for men or for women with fantastic attitude. It's true."* Provoking a situation??? Is he talking about Arteta? How did he provoke anything other than lying in pain with a broken shinpad? And is he seriously suggesting that Chelsea players don't react to challenges? Honestly, he's just an absolute gobshite. I can't get my head around how the media think he's the fucking Fonz or something; a proper cool, suave bastard. He's not, he's actually a bad, bad biff. He's even more of a biff than poor old AVB, but he's managed to fool people into thinking otherwise. I'm onto him though, the fucking biff. He should be laughed at and mocked, not revered and respected. He's a complete gimp, I'm embarrassed for him whenever he speaks these days. Absolute helmet.

I mean have a read of this: *"There are other sports without contact, fantastic sports which demand a lot from the players, and I respect those sports full of big champions. But [there is] no contact. Football is a game of contact. English football, winter, water on the pitch, sliding tackles at fantastic speed ... Be proud. Play with pride. If you are hurt, OK, you are hurt. If you have pain ... well, I have pain every day and I work every day."* He has pain? Listen to him, the knobhead. Ok, I'll concede that having to look at John Terry's stupid fucking gargantuan head every day, trying to teach David Luiz how to defend or witnessing Mikel trying to play a forward pass probably isn't fun, but it hardly qualifies as pain does it? Like I said, he's an absolute gobshite. I mean, what other manager would continually not pick Juan Mata?

chapter eight

Christmas & New Year

MANCHESTER CITY 2 LIVERPOOL 1

Competition - Premier League
Date - Thu 26 Dec 2013
Venue - The Etihad Stadium
Scorer(s) – Philippe Coutinho
Star Man – Martin Skrtel

Team: Mignolet; Johnson, Skrtel, Sakho, Cissokho; Lucas (Aspas), Allen, Henderson; Sterling, Suarez, Coutinho (Moses):

There's no such thing as a good defeat but I suppose this is as close to one as you'll find. We were the better side, we did not deserve to lose and we gave City the biggest scare they've had all season on home soil. In fact, we probably played better against them than the four sides to beat them did. Pellegrini's men are most people's favourites for the title but they've just been given the hardest game of their season so far. Would you bet against us beating them at Anfield? I wouldn't.

Sadly we don't get any style points and that meant we slipped from top spot to fourth. It would have been fifth had the Blues not shit the bed at home to Sunderland, that's how tight things are at the top of the table. That's why being top didn't mean we were going to win the league and why being fourth now doesn't mean we won't win it. I mean, we probably won't win it, but we're only three points off the top halfway through the season so from that perspective you'd have to say we've got as good a chance as any. Especially as we've probably got the easiest second half of the season compared to the rest of the top six or seven.

There are a lot more twists and turns to come over the next five months, and I like where we are right now. I'd like it a lot better if we beat Chelsea this weekend of course, but there's no doubt we'd all have taken this position back in August. No loss is easy to take and this one obviously hurts, but there's no cause to be disheartened about it either. Quite the opposite in fact. The game was on a knife edge throughout and when you break it down to it's bare bones, the only real difference between success and failure was Joe Hart making a save at one end and Simon Mignolet failing to do the same at the other a few minutes later. That's not to put the loss on the shoulders of the Belgian, it's merely highlighting the fine margins that these games are often decided by. So often in these big games it's the side that makes the least mistakes that wins. Last season individual errors cost us twice against City and the same thing happened again as Mignolet failed to keep out a poor effort from Negredo that he saves 99 times out of 100. Sadly for us, this game was the '100'.

Of course it's easy to pick holes in the performance and point to mistakes here and there; be it Mignolet not saving Negredo's shot, Coutinho or Sterling not converting glorious chances, the defence not dealing with the counter attack better or conceding yet another goal from a set-piece. Any one of those moments could have turned the game on it's head and we also had a goal farcically ruled out for a phantom offside and two clear penalty shouts. So yes, things could so easily have been different but the fact is we lost and have to take it on the chin. It's frustrating to come away with no points, but if anything the game should do more for the players' confidence than some of the recent big home wins will have done. I felt like we played well in this game from start to finish. We didn't dominate the game for 90 minutes, obviously, as nobody will go to the Etihad and do that, but we stood toe to toe with them, traded punches and it was a hell of a game. City were always dangerous and hit the post early on through Navas, but we carried a real threat of our own and Sterling's running in behind them was causing havoc in the first half.

We were working it very well, Suarez would drop deep and Sterling would sprint into the space behind him. It almost led to the opening goal when Suarez did brilliantly to turn away from Kompany and play a great ball in behind to the sprinting Sterling, but as he slowed up to steady himself to shoot on his left foot Kolorov got back to make a block. The same two players combined again soon after and this time there was no catching Sterling as he advanced on Hart's goal. He went round the keeper but the linesman had ludicrously flagged him offside and although Sterling put the ball in the net the whistle had long gone. Sometimes you need to see a replay to know if the player was offside or not, but on this one I knew even watching it at normal speed that it was a terrible call. The replay merely confirmed it was even worse than I initially thought. How is it even possible to get it so wrong? Kolorov was actually the nearest player to the linesman, it's not as though he was on the far side of the pitch which can make those decisions difficult. A Christmas hangover perhaps? That was really hard to take, but it would have been even worse had City got the first goal. Thankfully we put that disappointment behind us and Sterling and Suarez were both involved again as we went ahead through Coutinho. Lovely football once again, and it was Sterling's willingness to come off the flank and run in behind the centre backs that created the chance once more. Coutinho's finish was a simple one in the end.

Having worked so hard to get in front it was pretty galling to then concede so soon afterwards from a fucking corner. When you play a side like City you know how hard it's going to be to keep all their attacking players quiet, so to let one in from a bread and butter corner kick is really hard to take as it just feels like they didn't have to earn it. Had they scored from one of their flowing attacking moves, you can just shrug that off as a good team doing what a good team does. When they score a goal that any league two side could have scored, it just feels cheap.

I suppose you can point the finger at Skrtel as Kompany was his man, but he literally could not have been any tighter to him as he had a firm grip of his shirt (as he did on every set-piece all day) and his head was touching Kompany's as the City man met the ball. You could legitimately argue that instead of being so close to the man he should be concentrating on winning the ball, but I find it difficult to be too critical of Skrtel. Kompany is a big powerful fella and it's inevitable that he'll win the battle occasionally, you just have to hope that when he does it doesn't result in a goal. Unfortunately for us it did. If he'd been unmarked and allowed a free header, that would have been completely unacceptable. This was more a case of 'shit happens' I'd say, although I can see why others disagree. As for Skrtel's constant shirt pulling, well we've been pointing that out for years and he's yet to be penalised for it, so perhaps the fella knows what he's doing? It's an offence that's rarely called, he's playing the percentages and in fairness Kompany was giving as good as he got and often had a forearm in Skrtel's face/neck. Neither man complained, they just got on with it and it was a good contest between them. Skrtel had a brilliant game, the problem is that the shirt pulling is now getting so much media attention it's inevitable he's going to get called on it. I wouldn't be surprised if Mourinho was already on the blower to whoever is reffing our game on Sunday, telling him to watch out for it. I've got no problem with Skrtel doing it, but he defo needs to pack it in until the heat dies down as it's getting far too much airtime at the moment.

The equaliser could have knocked the stuffing out of us but it didn't. We continued to take the game to them and almost regained the lead with some breathtaking football. Once again, it was Sterling, Suarez and Coutinho involved and when a brilliant touch from Suarez teed up Coutinho the little Brazilian should have had his second of the game but shot too close to Hart. A real shame; it would have been a stunning goal as we sliced City's defence to ribbons and it was great to watch.

City's second goal was a real hammer blow though, not just because it was avoidable from Mignolet's point of view, but because it came from our own bloody corner. I wrote in the Cardiff report about what a great feeling it is when you score from the opposing side's corner with a swift counter attack, but it's a HUGE kick in the balls when it happens to you. Doubly so when it comes right on the stroke of half time. At that point I must admit I was ready to throw in the towel. I believed we could score again but feared that we'd get taken to the cleaners at the other end as we pushed forward. To the players' credit that never looked likely as we were generally in control of most of the second half. City always looked menacing but we had the better chances after the break and also seemed to have more of the ball. A draw was the least we deserved really, Henderson curled one just over, Johnson wasted a chance when an awful touch let him down, Suarez had an effort hit Henderson almost on the line (it may have been going wide anyway) and Sterling blazed over from close range. It was an admirable effort from the team but they fell just short. Most of the side performed very well, with Skrtel and Suarez the two stand out performers for me. It's rare that Suarez doesn't score these days, and he didn't threaten too much in this one. His all round play though… fucking hell. I thought he was brilliant; he led the line, he chased everything, he twisted defenders in knots and he created several chances for team-mates. Ok, at one point he tried a shot from an almost impossible angle when he had four players waiting in the centre, but aside from that he was fantastic.

I'm not going to comment on Glen Johnson, other than to say you won't be shocked that he's still in my doghouse. I was disappointed with Coutinho too, especially after the break. He wasn't bad by any means, but with his talent I keep expecting him to produce one of those games where we are all just blown away by him, yet it just isn't happening. Maybe I'm expecting too much, he's still a kid and he's still making a good contribution. I just think he's capable of so much more. We may not see it until Sturridge returns though.

Sterling on the other hand, I'm absolutely made up with him. Yes, he missed that sitter in the second half, but he was terrific again and he's a big threat to teams at the moment. He's bounced back brilliantly from his dip in form and is now playing with great confidence again. Right now he'd be one of the first names on my teamsheet, and if you'd told me that a few weeks ago I'd have laughed in your face.

Brendan had a right go at the officials afterwards. I don't think that was wise to be honest, especially when you bring up that Mason is from the Greater Manchester area. That implies he was biased, when he absolutely was not. He was shite, not biased. Where he is from is irrelevant in terms of his performance, but it is a valid point considering Mike Dean (who's from the Wirral) is never allowed to referee Liverpool games, so how can a manc be in charge of City against a scouse team? That said, if Ferguson had made the implication Rodgers did I'd have been all over him, and Brendan will be very lucky if he isn't charged over it. It wasn't down to Lee Mason that we lost this game, he may have been shite but it wasn't his job to pick up Kompany on corners, and it wasn't him that flapped at Negredo's weak shot. He didn't shoot straight at Joe Hart or balloon one over the bar from a Suarez cross either, or…. well you get the point. In fact, had he wanted to, Mason could have awarded a penalty against Skrtel on pretty much any City corner. He didn't though, which makes it easier to swallow that he didn't penalise Lescott for the blatant shirt pull on Suarez late on either. Skrtel was actually going nuts appealing for that, believe it or not! If Rodgers had a problem with Mason's appointment he should have voiced those concerns before the game, not afterwards, as that just makes it look like sour grapes.

CHELSEA 2 LIVERPOOL 1

Competition - Premier League
Date - Sun 29 Dec 2013
Venue - Stamford Bridge
Scorer(s) – Martin Skrtel
Star Man – Raheem Sterling

Team: Mignolet; Johnson, Skrtel, Sakho (Toure), Agger; Lucas, Allen (Smith), Henderson; Sterling, Suarez, Coutinho (Aspas):

For fuck's sake. This was just like the City game. Same scoreline, conceding twice before half time after taking the lead, keeper not doing enough on the winning goal, controlling the second half but not being able to find an equaliser, being pissed off at the officials…. yet this one hurt way, way, way more. We played better at City but there was more of a sense of injustice about this one. Rodgers thought he had cause

for complaint about Lee Mason, but Howard Webb showed him exactly what a dodgy referee can really do.

As I said, I didn't agree with Rodgers' attack on Mason. For me he needs to pick his battles better as he didn't have enough just cause to go after Mason in the way he did. And his chickens came home to roost at Stamford Bridge when he genuinely was screwed over by the referee but couldn't say anything about it because he's in trouble after his attack on Mason. Instead we had to listen to him describing Webb's performance as 'excellent'. He was being sarcastic, but it wasn't reported that way. It was clear how our day was going to go right from the first minute when Webb failed to produce a card after Eto'o had lunged at Henderson's knee. A knee high, studs up challenge that doesn't get the ball but makes contact with the opponent is supposed to be a red card isn't it? There are some exceptions of course (such as if it's on Luis Suarez in which case it's obviously acceptable), and when it's a bouncing ball and you miss it by a split second sometimes you can understand leniency being shown. This one was bizarre though. The ball was rolling along the floor so why was Eto'o going in with his foot raised so high? It's inexplicable really. Plus it was so late that the ball was nowhere near either player when contact was made. Taking all that into account, you can only assume it was deliberate as no-one can miss a tackle as spectacularly badly as that unless they are not going for the ball. It's a red card all day, Henderson was left in a heap and was clearly troubled by the injury for the remainder of the game. Incredibly, Webb didn't even produce a yellow.

I've heard it suggested that he was lenient because it was the first minute of the game. Ok, so explain Oscar not being sent off for a disgraceful lunge at Lucas in stoppage time then? That was such a bad tackle that Lucas lost his rag and went after his international colleague. Lucas actually lost his temper! If that doesn't tell you what a bad challenge it was then nothing does. I don't think I've ever seen Lucas physically confront an opponent like that. Shocking challenge, yet only a booking. So first minute or last, it doesn't matter to Webb. At least he gave the free-kick for the Henderson one I suppose, we should be grateful for small mercies. He was no doubt regretting it when we scored from it though, as Suarez nipped in front of his man to cause confusion and Skrtel finished it off. A great start, but even at this early stage I was concerned because of Webb, he'd nailed his colours to the mast in the first minute. I'm just sick of getting shafted by officials, it's been happening to us in big games for years now. Too often to be a co-incidence?

In fairness to Chelsea, they did react well to going behind and they were comfortably better than us in the first half (but would that have been the case had Eto'o been sent off?). They played well, but that doesn't make it any easier to take, especially given the huge amount of playacting and gamesmanship from them. I lost count of the amount of times their players simply stopped running and just waited for our lads to run into their back before hitting the deck to win cheap free-kicks. That was bad enough but some took it to another extreme by going out of their way to deliberately initiate contact with our players and then hurl themselves to the floor to get free kicks. They were actually moving away from the ball to draw contact and then take a dive, and Webb gave a free-kick for it every damn time. It was Hazard and Oscar who the main culprits, serial offenders if you like, but I saw Azpila.. whatever the fuck his name is do it a couple of times too. The one time Webb didn't buy it was when Hazard went looking for a pen against Lucas, but then he takes a completely viewpoint on incidents inside the box than he does to those outside. Hazard was on his way down before the challenge even came in and he embellished it further by kicking out his right leg towards Lucas to initiate contact. Webb wasn't interested, and some are using this as evidence that he wasn't just looking to screw us over. Maybe. Why would you not book Hazard though? It's either a penalty or a booking, there's no in between in that scenario. Yet Webb - once again - found one. Classic Webb behaviour.

Hazard was giving us loads of trouble in the first half and the Chelsea dangermen (as ever, the three behind whatever poor sap they have doing the donkey work up top) were finding far too much space between our midfield and defence. Lucas was struggling to cope with the onslaught and his lack of pace meant he was late to everything, whilst Allen and Henderson were decent enough with the ball but didn't seem to have the zip in their pressing that we've seen in recent weeks. Understandable, it would have been tough to maintain those energy levels even if fully fit, but with Allen needing an injection to play and Hendo also going into the game injured (and then being nobbled by Eto'o in the first minute) this was a real slog for the players.

Chelsea have been shite for most of the season and it's just our luck we ran into them when they produced their best 45 minutes of the year. Even so, both goals had a large slice of luck about them and came out following fortuitous deflections that fell nicely to their players. It was one of those days for us. Again. Having said that, the second goal should have been prevented by either Skrtel (who was more interested in trying to grapple with Eto'o instead of watching the ball) or Mignolet who got a good hand to the shot but failed to keep it out.

I was relieved when the half time whistle went and we were only down by one, but I lost the plot when I saw Sakho swapping shirts with Eto'o as they left the field at the break. This twat tried to do Hendo and he'd then scored the goal that had put them ahead, and Sakho is wanting to get his shirt at half fucking time??? Honestly, I wanted him subbed there and then, I was livid. At the very least I hoped that when he got back to the dressing room and asked for a new shirt, Rodgers would have told him to go into the Chelsea dressing room and get his shirt back, or he could watch the second half from the bench. You can say it's not that big a deal, but to me it is. It sends out all the wrong sort of messages. You're playing for fucking Liverpool lad, not some Micky Mouse team that is in awe of the opposition. I heard that Coutinho may have done it too, if so then he needs a bollocking too. Judging from the reaction of Rodgers afterwards when he found out about it, both players will be told in no uncertain terms that shit is just unacceptable. If it was Real Madrid or Barcelona, you could 'almost' turn a blind eye to it, but fucking Chelsea???

Whilst I'm venting, I didn't like seeing Mourinho and Suarez sharing a joke at half time either. Not because I felt like Luis was being too pally with him, it just bothered me that he didn't appear to realise what a cunt Mourinho is. Our players shouldn't give that twat the time of day, let alone share a joke with him. He'd said some mildly supportive things about Suarez in the build up to the game over the Ivanovic thing, but you can't take him at face value as he's the most self centred, egotistic, patronising cunt in football. If Suarez wasn't aware of that at half time, he sure as hell should be now after the snide accused him of diving. Suarez should just respond to it by calling him a gobshite. Nothing else, just get a friendly reporter to ask *"what did you think of Jose Mourinho saying you should have been booked for diving?"* and then reply *"He's a gobshite"*. That in itself would be worth 200k a week to me.

Same goes for Rodgers too. I know him and Mourinho go back a bit and he's grateful for the opportunity he was given and all that, but if Brendan thinks this guy is his friend then he's seriously fucking naive. Mourinho doesn't have friends, just people who are useful to him. He doesn't give a fuck about Rodgers and if and when the time comes that he sees us as a major threat, you'll see just what little regard he has for his former protegé. The patronising way he spoke afterwards should tell Brendan all he needs to know. Stay in your place little man and you'll be fine, start to have some success and watch how quickly your 'friend' turns on you.

Credit to our players for how they came out for the second half and took it to Chelsea. We had a lot of the ball and were the better side after the break, but I'd say a fair bit of that was down to Mourinho being such a negative, overly cautious, boring, shithouse, catenaccio cunt. When Chelsea have a lead, this is what they do, they sit on it and try and play on the break. They hadn't done that in the first half, they'd pressed us and put us under pressure when we had the ball, but after the break they dropped off and that meant we were able to get our foot on the ball a lot more.

We generally dealt with their counter attacks well but we found it difficult to create any really clear openings of our own. The closest we came was a fine header by Sakho that hit the bar, whilst we also had one decent penalty shout and of course one stonewaller. The decent shout was when Mongo clumsily leaned all over Suarez before hooking the ball clear. Outside the box that was 100% going to be given by Webb. Inside? No chance. I wasn't especially angry about that, it was one of those that you'd expect to get at home against a Fulham or West Brom, but not away from home to one of the big boys, and definitely not with Webb in charge. So I could live with that one, it wasn't that clear cut and Webb could legitimately not award that one without getting too much flak for it.

The second one though.... fucking hell. Inexcusable. He's just a fucking scumbag and a complete coward. Only he knows why he didn't give the penalty when he saw Eto'o hack down Suarez right in front of him. The other decisions that went against us - and there were loads, some more serious than others - can be put down to various other theories. From him just being a bad homer, to him being a shithouse who lacks the balls to make major decisions to him being a South Yorkshire copper. The Eto'o foul though, I honestly don't know what the reason was for him not giving that, only Webb himself knows. I know one thing though, he saw it and it's impossible to see that and view it as anything other than a foul. There's no room for debate, no grey area, he knew it was a foul but he chose not to give it. Perhaps he was teaching Brendan a lesson after having a go at Mason the other day? That's as plausible a reason as any I suppose.

In some ways though the club only have themselves to blame for this. As soon as the findings of the Hillsborough enquiry were released, Liverpool should have immediately insisted that Webb not be allowed to officiate any of our games again due to the huge conflict of interest involved. For his sake as much as ours. I remember writing about it last year, it just seemed like common sense to me and I'm surprised it's been allowed to continue. How can an ex South Yorkshire Policeman (who still has mates on the force) be refereeing Liverpool games? Think about it, it's fucking ludicrous. Even if he was the most honest, impartial referee on the planet (don't laugh), the element of doubt would always be there any time he made a decision that went against Liverpool. His mates at SYP are facing legal action and criminal charges for their actions at Hillsborough, and even if he is completely on the side of the families (he may be for all I know) he should not be put in this position as people are always going to be sceptical.

I'm not closed to the possibility that he shafted us because of his links to SYP, or that he was doing it because of Brendan questioning the integrity of Mason. Both could be true, we'll never know though. I'd lean more towards the theory of Graham Poll that Webb deliberately doesn't make decisions because it's a calculated ploy to get himself to the World Cup. I thought this was an interesting insight into how refs think, as Poll said: *"It could be that World Cup selection is affecting him and he is perhaps trying to avoid controversy in the build-up to Brazil 2014 - the list of referees for the tournament will be announced in May. Referees believe that you are remembered for decisions you make and not those you 'miss'"* Interesting. Poll said ages ago that Webb tries to avoid making big decisions on that basis, and I've watched him a few times since hearing that and it's definitely true. It may have been personal towards Liverpool, or it could just be Howard Webb doing what Howard Webb does. Incredibly, he's yet to award a single penalty or send anyone off this season. That makes me think Poll's theory is probably spot on, but given Webb's 'previous' with us I can certainly see why others think differently.

It's really infuriating though isn't it? It's hard enough getting results at the likes of Man City and Chelsea even when you have a full team. To get a win you really need to play well and to also have a fair bit of luck. But if a refereeing performance goes against you it's nigh on impossible to win these kind of games no matter how you play. Call it an excuse if you like, but it's a fact. Had Webb done his job properly we would not have lost against Chelsea. Hell, we may even have won as they'd have been playing with ten men instead of twelve. I'd say that Chelsea were far too streetwise for us, they've been well coached by Mourinho in the dark arts and with Webb an all too willing accomplice it must have been an incredibly frustrating day for our lads. They did well not to completely lose their composure, as had I been in their shoes I'd have unquestionably sparked someone. Probably Hazard ('that weird whiskered little freak' as my mum calls him) as he's a short arse and I reckon I could take him. Maybe Oscar though, I hate his stupid fucking face, the chinless little dweeb. Lucas should have sparked him, I mean it's not like Webb would have done anything about it. He'd probably have given a yellow, which of course means the FA can't do shit about it.

I'm rambling here, I feel like this report is heading off in all different directions as there's just so much I need to get off my chest. The City game I was ok with, but I fucking hate Chelsea, more than any other team, even United. I just hate everything about them, they're just fucking vile from top to bottom. No wonder Juan Mata can't get a game, far too decent a chap to fit into Mourinho's set up. Doesn't dive enough I expect. And for all their expensive attacking talent, they're dull as fuck and I can't wait to get them back at

Anfield. Fucking twats.

I'm not even going to get started on Mourinho and his lame cheerleading or the complete horseshit he came out with after the game (lapped up by the London press as usual), I'd be here all day if I opened up that particular can of worms. All we can hope is that one day he gets what's coming to him again, and if there's any justice it will be us that gives it to him. Again. Where's Luis Garcia when we need him?

These hard luck stories in big games are becoming a trend under Rodgers and that's the next step we need to take. He's got us scoring tons of goals and beating everyone outside the top seven or eight, but we let in too many goals and seem to be perennially unlucky against our main rivals. I definitely get the feeling that we're getting there, but we need more depth to the squad as seemingly every other week the opposition has a stronger looking bench than us. Manchester City and Chelsea are better than us. I wish they weren't, but they are. With a first choice eleven there's not a great deal in it and we've shown we can give them a game even with players missing, but in terms of squad depth the difference is night and day. It would have been difficult enough taking on Chelsea a full week after playing at the Etihad, but doing so just four days later, with so many players missing and others playing through injury because there was nobody else to come in and take their place? Factor in the presence of Webb and it was close to being an impossible task. I'm really pleased with the players that they managed to make such a close game of it and that merely adds to the utter contempt I have for Webb. Having battled so hard to stay in the game and then managed to take control of the second half, those players deserved more than to have Webb spit in their faces the way he did.

Premier League Round Up (26-29 December 2013)

I love Christmas footy but maybe it's time for a winter break? Anything to avoid having to listen to those manc losers and their shitty Cantona Christmas song. There literally is nothing worse in the world than having to listen to that. I hear it's even used as a method of torture in some countries. I have to admit I'd sing like a bird within seconds if I was subjected to that ear aids. It's lucky I don't know anything of any real importance really.

The footy over Christmas was nightmarish from our perspective. Virtually every result went against us as we lost both our games and everyone around us took maximum points. Well, almost everyone, thankfully the Blues provided us with some much needed festive mirth by losing to bottom club Sunderland. Goodison is Sunderland's bogey ground too so no-one saw this coming. The decisive moment of the game was when Howard and Osman got into a muddle and the keeper ended up bringing down Ki after he went round him. Obvious red card, but Howard still argued against it, the dick.

Even with ten men they battered Sunderland but they couldn't find a way past Big Vito. And the one time they did? There was Fabio Magnifico to clear off the line. Good lad. Mannone has mastered the art of making a save and then going postal at his defenders. I usually don't condone that crap, but it's Vito so whaddayaggonado? The funniest example of it was when he saved a free-kick from Barkley and then started randomly abusing all of his defenders. What the fuck were they meant to do about that, Vito? It was a free kick that was curled over the wall, what the hell was he shouting at them about, the crazy bastard?

So that one went our way at least, and West Ham briefly threatened to do us a favour too by going ahead against Arsenal at Upton Park through a Carlton Cole tap in. Sadly, O'Brien and Cole wasted great chances and eventually the Hammers bowed to the inevitable. Following those two huge let offs, Arsenal got their act together and absolutely destroyed them.

The Mancs had another spawny win to continue their recent 'revival'. I'm not having it though, they're fucking shite and just because they're in a nice friendly little run of fixtures doesn't change that. Same thing happened earlier in the season when they put a nice little run together and knobheads like Stan Collymore were giving it the *"you can never write Manchester United off"*. That doesn't apply any more. This isn't the Manchester United we're used to, it's not Ferguson's United, when will people realise that. This is 'the Chosen One's' Manchester United, and they're bang average. They should have lost at Hull and I'm telling you the next time they meet anyone half decent they will lose. Hull went 2-0 up inside 13 minutes through Chester and Meyler, but lo and behold, another United goal from a set-piece as Rooney whipped in a free-kick (won by the latest dive from that little jamrag Januzaj) and Smalling headed in. Rooney then hit a screamer to draw them level and all this had happened in the first 26 minutes of the game. Crazy stuff.

Rooney got away with an absolutely outrageous dive after already having been booked. United are pulling this kind of shit even more since Moyes took over, and they were bad enough before he got there. The likes of Rooney, Welbeck, Young and that Januzaj prick are doing this every week, it's completely shameless now. Alex Bruce was denied by the bar before Chester headed into his own net in ridiculous circumstances. Seriously, what the fuck? Is there a clause in the contracts of players who leave United that they must score an own goal whenever they face their old club? O'Shea, Bardsley, Brown, this Chester loser, and I bet there's loads more too. To make it even worse he then missed a sitter to equalise at the end, the fucking bum. As bad as that was, the worst thing I saw in this game was Danny Graham stepping aside and letting Bruce take a shot right at the end. You're a centre forward, he's a defender, you don't defer to him you fucking coward. Bruce scuffed his shot wide but that was all on Graham for me. No wonder he never scores, the massive shithouse.

Stoke went in front at Newcastle through our boy Assaidi but Martin Atkinson then took over and things went south in a hurry for Mark Hughes' side. Whelan was sent off in contentious circumstances (his first booking was outrageous), and then Wilson joined him after tugging back Gouffran in the box. Just for good measure, 'Useless' himself was sent to the stands for protesting about it. It got worse for them when a brilliant counter attack led by Assaidi was brought to a halt by a clear handball which Atkinson didn't give and the Geordies broke up the field and scored through Remy to make it 1-1. And if that wasn't enough? Newcastle then went in front through

Gouffran but the ball appeared to have gone out before Ben Arfa crossed it. Remy and Cabaye added to Newcastle's lead before Atkinson awarded them another penalty (blatant this one), which Remy generously allowed Cisse to take. He buried it for his first goal in like three years or something. This is not something you'll hear me say very often, but I felt really sorry for Stoke as I'm sick of these shite officials influencing games more than they should. Assaidi is doing well though, good for him. I'd rather he was still here instead of Moses and Aspas.

Malky Mackay went into the festive fixtures fresh on the back of assurances from Vincent Tan that his job was safe 'for the foreseeable future'. I guess that foreseeable future was basically 'until you lose again', as Cardiff got stuffed by Southampton. Mackay was sacked after the game, and whilst it seems like the whole of football is in an outrage and mourning his dismissal, allow me to be the first one to say 'fuck him'. That's payback for that yellow card he got Sterling last week, the crying cunt. Also, it's no more than Cardiff fans deserve for turning *"Achy breaky heart"* into a terrace chant. I mean fucking hell, really?

Chelsea had another dull, close win, this time over Swansea at Stamford Bridge. If you take Hazard out of the equation there's not much left to get excited about really. He seems to be the only one not being stifled by the negative, shithouse football played by the 'Special One'. Swansea have slipped under the radar this year a bit. By that, I mean they seem to be avoiding a lot of criticism considering how badly they are doing. Maybe it's the Europa League commitments having an effect on them, but they've been really disappointing so far. Laudrup seems untouchable, no-one wants to say anything negative about him because he's such a nice fella and was a legendary player. Look how close they are to the bottom three though.

Elsewhere, Spurs were held to a draw at home by West Brom and Berbatov failed a fitness test before Fulham's 2-1 win at Norwich. I have a question. How would anyone know if he passed or failed the test? I've never had one, but I'm assuming it involves telling a player to do some various sprints and running exercises and judging how he looks. I can't imagine anyone being able to get Berbatov to run on command, he doesn't even do it when there's a ball to chase after. Man after my own heart that is. Both these teams will be in the relegation shake up though, and this year may be even more exciting than last year's battle at the bottom. There's about eight or nine teams who could be involved.

Including Villa, who lost at home to Palace. At least they had more than 26% possession in this one, which is progress I suppose. Dwight Gayle got the winner with a belter in stoppage time. Credit to Pulis, whatever we all think of him you have to say what he's done since going to Palace is pretty remarkable. For me that was the worst group of players in the Premier League, yet somehow he's got them winning games. And they haven't even gone full alehouse yet. That Palace result meant that the bottom three all won away on Boxing Day.

Onto the weekend's games now, and Palace continued their impressive renaissance under Pulis and gave City a real game at the Etihad, keeping it goalless until well into the second half when Dzeko eventually broke the deadlock. They ended up losing 1-0, but they were well worth a point and Joe Hart had to make several good saves to earn City the points. Not gonna lie, I'm a little pissed off that Palace went there and did so well as it took a lot of the shine off how we'd played two days earlier.

Having won away on Boxing Day Fulham went to Hull in good spirits. They didn't leave that way though, having been spanked 6-0. All of the goals came in the second half and Fulham didn't have anybody sent off. Six goals in one half when you have a full compliment of players? How can that can even happen? Fulham should be ashamed of themselves. What's with their manager's weird accent too? He's Dutch apparently, but sounds like a mixture of various English regional accents. Apologies for not knowing his name, I've not bothered learning how to spell it as I figure he won't be there long enough to make it worth the time and effort. I miss Martin Jol.

Fair play to Hull and Steve Bruce though, they've been far better than anyone expected. Huddlestone was brilliant on the day and even got himself a rare goal (his first in three years). His set piece delivery was ridiculously good and his all round game was impressive too. He's a quality player, like the midfield Berbatov, but Bruce went a bit far in saying *"If there's anybody better than him then I've yet to see him"*. As Raheem Sterling would say, *"Steady"*. When pressed on whether Huddlestone should be in the England squad, Bruce replied *"I mean, who am I to tell Roy who to pick..."* Hahahaha come on Brucey lad, it's Roy Hodgson you're talking about here, not Rinus Michels. I agree with the calls that he should be going to the World Cup mind, I mean if Tom fucking Cleverley is in the England set up then why not big Tom Hundredstone? Apparently the goal means that he can now get his hair cut. In fact, he started it on the pitch when he ran over to the physio, who had scissors prepared and snipped off a lock of his barnet. Very good that, made me laugh. They often say a haircut can make a person look a good few pounds lighter. I hope not though, as Tom Ninetyninestone just doesn't have the same ring to it.

Staying on the hair theme for a second, and George Boyd's locks are far too nice for a Scotsman. Actually is he even Scottish? I assume he is as the only way that name could be any more Scottish would be if there was a 'Mc' in front of it. Wherever he's from, he's got South American hair, that's for sure. South American hair!!! That's just reminded me of an uncomfortable experience I had last weekend. It was a friend's 40th and we stayed over at the hotel where the party was, it was just outside Wigan and I believe it is owned by Dave Whelan. I'm assuming that's the case as all the hotel staff had been instructed to greet guests by saying *"Hi, welcome to Wrightington Hall Country Club & Hotel. Did you know that Dave Whelan once broke his leg in an FA Cup final?"* Ok, I made that bit up, but the rest of this story is all true I swear.

So anyway, whilst I was there I figured I'd take advantage of the facilities, such as the pool and steam room. I get back to the changies and there was the entire Wigan squad hanging around my locker, preparing to go for a swim. There was no escape, I had to squeeze through them all to reach my locker, it was a really enclosed space and fairly claustrophobic, and here's me, with my gut and moobs jiggling about, having to get changed right in amongst all these superfit footy players with their six packs and shit. It's fair to say I was feeling pretty self conscious and more than a little inadequate, especially when Marc Antoine Fortune strolled past, with his wash-board abs and chiselled physique. Honestly, that was a sight to behold. Still, I had better hair than all of them at least. Or so I thought, until Roger Espinoza came float-ing through the locker room looking like something off a shampoo ad. It was as though everything turned to slow motion as he walked past. Some seriously beautiful hair that. The very definition of 'South American hair' in fact. It took every ounce of restraint I had not to just reach out and stroke it, or worse, sniff it, as he breezed by.

It was a really uncomfortable situation to be in though, so I was generally trying to avoid making any eye contact with them and just wanted to get changed and get out of there as quickly as I could. Because I was just keeping my head down I only recognised a few faces so I'm not entirely sure who was there and who wasn't. I recognised Ali Al Habsy, James McArthur and Callum McManaman, all of whom have taken some flak in these round ups in recent years, but I've no idea who else was there. It's funny though, as I'm looking at their squad list on wiki now and I've taken the piss out of so many of them in the last couple of years it's a damn good job they had no clue who I was or what I'd written. There was Gary Caldwell (I absolute-ly ripped him to shreds after one of their games last year), Ryan Shotton (I've mocked him unmercifully for his crapness), Leon Barnett (I called him all the shit-houses under the sun after his assault on Suarez last season), James McLean (I slaughtered him all last season), James Perch (slated him after he got Pepe sent off) and Grant Holt who I was poking fun at for being fat! Fair to say I wouldn't have been calling him fat as I unsuccessfully tried to hold in my gut as I got dressed. I did think about saying to McCarthur *"Hey I know you, you're James McCarthy, right?"* just for a laugh, but I didn't have the balls.

Anyway, back to the footy, and there were more comical scenes at Cardiff. The fans were understandably pissed off at Mackay's sacking and let Vincent Tan know about it. They went 2-0 up and everyone was happy, but Sunderland staged a late fightback and equalised deep into stoppage time. The fans booed at full time, and Tan joined in!! He was actually stood there booing! I don't know what or who he was booing, but he was there in the director's box booing!! I shouldn't laugh, as we know all too well what it's like having unfit owners at your football club, but I'm finding Tan's antics hilarious and can't wait to see what he does next. The black leather gloves, the replica shirt over his suit, his funny little face…. he's batshit crazy that guy.

Other notes from this one, Borini was taken to hospital after feeling unwell. It seems he's ok thankfully. He played well and had two good efforts in the first half. Playing with Jozy Altidore is enough to make anyone feel a bit 'tom dick' though. I wrote last week that the big American is the worst player in the Premier League, and as if to prove my prove he goes and misses from a yard out in the very next game. Honestly if there's one thing I know - apart from great hair - it's how to identify a shite player when I see one. Last year Ryan Shotton was unquestionably the worst in the league, this year it's Altidore.

West Ham's woes continued as they failed to beat managerless West Brom at home. Joe Cole gave them a perfect start by firing them in front after just four minutes but a five minute brace from Anelka just before half time wiped that out. Maiga equalised and a minute later Nolan poked them ahead. As they were still celebrating Berahino conjured up a brilliant equaliser to leave Fat Sam on the brink of the push.

Elsewhere, another win for United against yet another shit team. Wes Hoolahan missed an absolute sitter when it was 0-0, made all the more unforgivable because the manc gobshites were in the middle of that shitty Cantona song at the time and it would have been ace to see them silenced. Boring, nasal, droning twats. Moyes is definitely feeling the pressure though, his touchline antics are becoming more and more erratic, his eyes are darting around from side to side nervously and he just looks permanently on edge. He's even muttering to himself now, there's definitely shades of Gollum / Smeagol going on there. Not surprised he's nervous, they're fucking awful.

Norwich had been all over them but couldn't score and then they get a poxy ricochet that ends with Welbeck running through to score. Jammy twats. Moyes was celebrating it like a cup final winner. At least, I'm assuming that's how he'd celebrate a cup final winner, he's never won a cup final so obviously I'm just guessing. The biggest scandal of the season is that these chumps got within two points of us after this result. That's pretty outrageous when you think how much better we've played. Stan Collymore was loving it, thinking he'd been proved right for 'never writing them off'. He's even taken to calling them *"Manchester - THEY'RE BEHIND YOU - United"* now, the big fucking dope. That's right Stan, they are behind a lot of teams and they'll stay there, as they're fucking shite. I say again, the next decent side they face will beat them, you mark my words.

Moving on, and Gaby Agbonlahor might be the biggest under achiever in the league. He put Villa ahead against Swansea with only his second goal in 16 games. He's better than that, or at least he should be. Swansea were all over them though and Lamah headed them level ten minutes before half time. That's how it stayed, and Swansea had something like 75% possession. Must be pretty grim being a Villa fan right now, their home record is absolutely disgusting and they spend most of the game chasing the ball like dogs in a park. I've mocked Agbonlahor in the past for coming across as a bit dim, the kind of lad who we all remember from school, you know the type, the one who eats flowers and shoves crayons up his nose. He did a 30 second interview after this game and managed to fit 'you know' in there seven times. Deary me.

Everton bounced back from the loss to Sunderland by beating Southampton at Goodison. Coleman put them ahead with a stunning goal (take note again Glen Johnson) but Ramirez equalised with a scorcher that Everton's back up keeper should have saved. Bizarrely, Ramirez took off his shirt and ran to the Everton fans before giving it to a little kid who celebrated as though Everton had scored. Weird.

I was listening to this on the car radio and had my hopes up at this point, but Everton quickly regained the lead through Lukaku and collected the three points to cap a shitty day for us. The novelty has long worn off and I just want them to be shit again.

Stoke were once again left cursing the referee after they got dicked at Spurs. With the game goalless Jon Walters was shoved over when he was clean through on goal. Stoke wanted a red card, but I don't think they have much of a case as it has to be a clear goalscoring opportunity, and as it was only Jon Walters that's pushing it quite a bit. It was definitely a free-kick though. They had a penalty shout turned down too when Assaidi beat a couple of players and appeared to be tripped by Dawson. Not much has been going their way of late has it? Tottenham made the most of their good fortune and went in front from the penalty spot when Shawcross used his hands to block Adebayor's scissor kick. Big brave Ryan Shawcross scared of taking a ball in the face? What next, Lionheart John Terry crying? Oh...

Soldado scored the pen, which begs the question, has he scored any goals from open play this season? It sure doesn't feel like it. Dembele added a second, which begs the question, how can a player as lavishly gifted as him score so few goals? He should be doing that every week, he's that good. Lennon added a third, and I've said the same thing about him, he should score way more goals than he does. I've come to the conclusion that he's just a bit poo though, he flatters to deceive and just because he runs fast he looks better than he is.

I had high hopes that Arsenal might drop some points up at unpredictable Newcastle. They almost did, but once again came away with the win, the bastards. Newcastle had their chances to go in front but they didn't take them and Arsenal went ahead with a scrappy goal from a set-piece. The closest Newcastle came to an equaliser was when Remy blocked a clearance from the keeper with his face and the ball rolled inches wide. He was flat out on the floor and had no idea where it had gone.

Seeing that brought back painful memories for me of being a kid playing in my Sunday league side. We were awful, I don't think we won a game all season and I was top scorer with just four goals. One of those came when the keeper and defender went for the same ball, and the defender hoofed it into my face from about a yard away. My nose got busted open and my tooth went through my lip, but the ball went into the net and my team-mates all mobbed me. Fucking knobheads, my face was a mess, I was crying my eyes out and we were still losing about 5-1 anyway, what the hell did I care that I'd just scored? My parents were watching from the sidelines, and I think my dad almost had a heart attack from laughing that much. He reckons it's the best goal I ever scored.

I don't have many happy memories of that team, the only other stand out memory I have was of going on a mazy run through the middle, beating a few players and then the last man getting a foot on the ball but only diverting it up into my bollocks. It broke kindly for me and suddenly I found myself clean through on goal, but as anyone who has been hit in the nutsack knows, the pain isn't immediate, there's a brief delay before it hits home. In that little delay I'm thinking *"That hit me in the nuts, did I get away with it or is that horrendous, sickening pain suddenly gonna kick in?"* Now I'm running towards goal thinking *"I may have got away with this"* and then WHOOMP THERE IT IS!!! I crumpled to a heap on the floor in agony and the chance was gone. On the plus side, at least my dad wasn't there to see that one, he may have quite literally died laughing from that.

LIVERPOOL 2 HULL CITY 0

Competition - Premier League
Date - 1 Jan 2014
Venue - Anfield
Scorer(s) – Skrtel, Suarez
Star Man – Raheem Sterling

Team: Mignolet; Johnson (Toure), Skrtel, Agger, Cissokho; Lucas, Henderson; Sterling (Moses), Coutinho, Aspas (Gerrard); Suarez:

I'd have taken any win at all from this game. I wouldn't have cared if we'd been battered for 90 minutes and won with a freak own goal, I'd have been happy and wouldn't have complained about anything. That may seem a strange thing to say about a home against Hull City, but I was worried about this one. Very worried.

Losing two games on the bounce put pressure on the players to get a result. It doesn't even matter that both of the games they lost were ones you'd expect to lose and it didn't matter that they'd performed admirably in defeat. You can afford to lose away at Chelsea and City but only if you win the games that you should be winning, such as at home to Hull. Had we gone into this game having had a week off, I wouldn't have been worried at all, we should have enough to be beating Hull even with a few players out injured, and we've been hammering everyone outside of the top seven or eight at Anfield.

We hadn't had a week off though, we were playing our third game in seven days, we had several players missing and some of those we did have available were carrying injuries that would normally see them left out. We weren't in a position to leave anyone out though, if they were able to play then they'd just have to get out there and deal with the pain because we had nobody else to bring in. And even those who weren't carrying injuries had to be feeling the strain of those two huge games we had over Christmas. Throw in the fact that our opposition had battered us a few weeks earlier, were coming off a 6-0 win in their last game and were managed by Steve Bruce (a man who seems to have our number), and this one had 'letdown' written all over it. So yeah, any win would have done me, so I was delighted with what we got from the players. Not just a win, but a comfortable win and a good performance. Hull didn't even manage a shot on target and we should have scored more than the two we did manage. Brendan described it afterwards as our best performance of the season. I don't necessarily agree but it's easy to see why he feels that way. It was certainly our most important win to date.

For all the kudos we'd earned from the performances over Christmas, the bottom line was that we'd slipped from first to fifth and were now six points off the leaders. Perhaps more significantly, we'd gone from having an eight point cushion over Spurs and the mancs to being just two ahead. Anything other than a win against Hull and things would suddenly be looking pretty gloomy, and everything was pointing towards this being a tough old day. In the end this was a great win and gets us back on track again. Halfway through the season and we're fourth, within touching distance of those ahead of us and we still have to face almost all of our rivals at Anfield. We'll take that won't we?

This was a good performance but it wasn't as good as most of our previous home wins. That's understandable as it's unrealistic to expect us to be able to press Hull in the same manner we'd done to the likes of Cardiff, Norwich, West Ham etc. The players didn't have enough in the tank to do that as unlike some of our rivals we can't make five or six changes to keep the team fresh. What we did do very well against Hull was pass the ball around and conserve energy that way. It felt like Skrtel and Agger touched the ball as much as anyone on the field, we often passed the ball backwards to go sideways and then forwards again, which was a sensible approach as if we have it then we're not having to chase it.

Hull seemed content to keep as many men back behind the ball as possible and for a while we found it difficult to create anything. The closest we'd come was a disallowed header from Suarez from a Coutinho free-kick. The linesman just about got it right but it's typical of our luck at the moment though that any close calls are going against us and even ones that aren't close are still going against us. Generally we had a lot of the ball but were finding it difficult to break down a physical Hull side who were taking no prisoners. I didn't think they were exceptionally dirty but they were physical and quickly realised that the official was letting a lot of things go, so they continued with the rough stuff. The ref looked as out of his depth at this level as poor old Iago Aspas. I had hoped that open season on Suarez was a thing of the past, it was getting out of hand for a while but then things seemed to calm down a bit. The last couple of games though, Luis has been on the end of some rough tackles and awful decisions. I don't blame Hull for trying to get physical with him as he's far too good to just stand off him and let him play. Opposing defenders are going to try and do all they can to stop him, it's up to referees to ensure it doesn't go too far and this arsewipe completely failed to do that.

Suarez felt he should have had a free-kick following a heavy looking challenge near the halfway line. The ball flew off behind the goal and the referee gave a corner rather than a free-kick, much to the annoyance of Luis and the crowd. Fortunately Agger head-ed in from Coutinho's corner kick so there was no real harm done, but Suarez had gone into the game with a bad foot injury and challenges such as that were hardly going to help. Alex Bruce had already been booked when he kicked Suarez in the chest yet aston-ishingly he got away with it. Mind you, if Howard Webb is help up as the beacon of good refereeing by the authorities is it any wonder that these young refs adopt the same approach?

We should have been out of sight by half time as we'd started to play some really good stuff, perhaps due to Hull having to come out of their shell a little. Henderson should have scored when he ran onto a flick by Aspas but dragged his shot wide while Coutinho also failed to hit the target after collecting a great ball by Hendo, killing it with a beautiful first touch and then dragging a shot wide. Coutinho's shooting is absolutely brutal; it's hard to understand how a player that can be so accurate with his passing is so wild with his shooting. It has to be down to composure, and if he can sort that out then we'll have ourselves one hell of a talent. Suarez made the game safe just five minutes after the restart when won a free kick 25 yards out and promptly dispatched it into the top corner at the Kop end. He tried one later on from ten yards further out but it went miles over the bar, much to his embarrassment. The chant of *"what the fucking hell was that?"* from the Kop brought a smile to his face though.

The second half was very comfortable. We didn't particularly look like adding to our lead but we never looked like conceding either. Even when Hull had a spell of pressure and forced some set pieces with around 15 minutes to go we dealt with it all easily enough. Johnson went off midway through the second half, presumably due to an injury he picked up very early on in the game. Kolo Toure slotted in at right back and made some marauding runs down that side that went down well with the fans, especially when it was followed up by the customary mad dash to get back into position. Rodgers also brought Gerrard on for the hapless Aspas and Moses later replaced Sterling. Coutinho looked the most likely to add to our lead but a mixture of bad luck, bad shooting and good goalkeeping kept him off the scoresheet. The stoppage time run that saw him glide past three defenders really deserved a goal but credit to the keeper for spreading himself and keeping it out.

The Brazilian dazzled and frustrated, but eventually he's surely going to sort out that finishing as he's still only a kid. There are shades of Steve McManaman about him at times and whilst Macca never really became a good finisher he certainly got better with experience. Perhaps Coutinho and Henderson should arrange for special after training 'finishing sessions', as both are outstanding until it comes to putting the ball in the net. Imagine how scary we'd be if those two added goals to their game.

Premier League Round Up (1 January 2014)

How fantastic has 2014 been so far? We've won all our games and United have lost all of theirs. They've been knocked out of one cup and are halfway to being dumped out of another while their fans are tearing eachother apart on their message boards. They're experiencing a phenomenon that experts (and by experts I mean us) commonly refer to as 'The Roy Hodgson effect'. I'll save all the United fun and games til last though I think and just get everything else out of the way first.

Cardiff went to the Emirates with new boss Ole Gunnar Solskjaer in the stands next to Vincent Tan. It says a lot about that goblin faced little manc fuck that he'd take that job when no-one else would touch it with a shitty stick. Why would anyone worth their salt go and work for that loon under those working conditions? I don't get it, it's pretty bizarre really. I can only assume Tan must be paying him a shitload. Like everyone I else, I expected Cardiff to get spanked but they made a real game of it and I went and got my hopes up didn't I? I was constantly checking livescore while I was watching us cruising against Hull and as the minutes ticked away it was genuinely looking like it would finish 0-0. That would have been an nice unexpected New Year bonus for us, but then with a minute left, Nicklas fucking Bendtner scored and then in stoppage time Walcott added another. Arsenal are doing my fucking head in now, but at least both their goalscorers are now injured I suppose. Feel a bit bad for Walcott who has been ruled out of the World Cup, but on the plus side, fuck off Hodgson, have some of that.

Man City won at Swansea in a game that could have gone either way. Fernandinho put them ahead but Bony levelled in first half stoppage time. Swansea played well in that first half and deserved to be at least level. Toure's deflected effort put City back in front after the break and I was shocked to discover that was his 12th of the season. I can only assume a load of them have been in Europe as I don't watch that Champions League thing these days, as I said it's gone right down the pan since we stopped playing in it. Can't believe Toure has 12 goals though, I thought he had about four and that they were all free-kicks. Kolorov added a third but Swansea had chances to get back in the game, most notably when Ashley Williams missed an open goal from four yards out. Knob. That miss proved decisive as Bony pulled one back in stoppage time but the Swans fell just short. Nice one Williams, you fucking bum. Bony has really hit form recently though hasn't he? I wonder if Michu being out injured has anything to do with that. He certainly seems to have thrived being the main man. Hey, I wonder if he's still in my fantasy team? Obviously I totally forgot about it after a few weeks of the season, that's always the way though isn't it? You have to be a pretty bad virgin to keep on top of a fantasy footy team.

Elsewhere, Chelsea had a good win at Southampton. They weren't anything special and Southampton had some great chances to go ahead but Chelsea's defenders made some fantastic blocks when the game was still in the balance and they ran away with it in the second half. Torres scored a tap in after the ball came back off the post right into his path, and hilariously he then gave it the big 'un celebration in front of the Chelsea fans. You know the one, the preening, pouting, nodding *"look at me, aren't I fucking ace"* celebration that the likes of Ronaldo has perfected. Just how lacking in self aware-ness is this tool? That was his first league goal away from home in over a year. I think he only scored one league goal in the whole of 2013, yet here he is acting like Billy Big Bollocks.

Willian and Oscar wrapped it up for Chelsea, but Oscar will be in Mourinho's bad books after his ludicrous dive put the Chelsea boss in an awkward spot in his post match interview. You have to laugh at the irony, he launches a ludicrous attack on Suarez and the very next game one of his players is booked for diving. He must have been livid. The worst part was that if Oscar had stayed on his feet he had a tap in. It was a certain goal yet he opted to dive instead, no doubt to try and get the keeper sent off. Fucking Pob faced scumbag, I might even hate him more than Hazard you know. In fact yeah, I do.

Of course Mourinho had to condemn him, what else could he do? Not even he is that much of a helmet that he could try and defend that, although I bet it crossed his mind, the fucking helmet. And then guess what? The game after that, Ramires was booked for an even more outrageous dive. All Mourinho could say again was that the referee was right, as unlike the West Brom dive that won them a penalty there wasn't any contact with this one and there was at least a foot of daylight between Ramires and the would be tackler. Mourinho is such a cock though, he still had to try and get his little digs in by saying that there are no divers at Chelsea and that *"the referee was right, I just hope it's the same for all teams."* Get to fuck, in the last 15 years there are two teams that stand head and shoulders above the rest when it comes to diving. Chelsea and the mancs. And Chelsea have been at their worst under this gobshite. I just wish some of the interviewers had the balls to pull him on it instead of just allowing him to talk shite without being checked.

Moving on, and how shit are West Ham? Shit enough to lose to Fulham, who'd been beaten 6-0 by Hull the previous game, that's how shit West Ham are. It started well for them though as Diame's early strike put them ahead and Nolan almost added a second with a header. Motson actually sounded like he'd been stabbed as he painfully yelped 'NOLAN!!'. If only eh? Nolan was then sent off for a bit of afters with a Fulham player who had blocked his run off the ball. I thought it looked harsh, yes he had a little kick at the player but it was nothing really and the Fulham lad was writhing around like he had a broken leg. Stupid from Nolan though. Berbatov's tap in won it for Fulham and plunged West Ham into even deeper shit than they were in before. Fat Sam was understandably pissed off with his skipper who has suddenly developed a snide streak that has never been there before. Allardyce didn't help his own cause by then sending his under 21 side out to get bummed by Forest in the cup. Hammers' fans were absolutely livid at that, understandably so too. Might wanna prepare one of those famous power-point presentations, Sam. I get the feeling you may be attending several job interview in the near future.

Newcastle's recent good run came to a shuddering halt at the Hawthorns. Lee Mason actually got a decision right for once as he sent off Debuchy for a two footed tackle. He got another one right when he awarded the Baggies a late penalty that Berahino converted to give the home side a much needed three points.

What would Sunderland give for three points right now? The win at Everton was something of a freak result that hinged entirely on Howard's sending off, but aside from that they are really finding wins hard to come by and even managed to lose at home to Villa. Poyet likes his teams to play football but there's an element of Martinez at Wigan about it all for me in that he's got players trying to play football when they aren't really footballers. Cattermole is a dog, you can't have him playing like Andrea Pirlo. That's just asking for trouble. Horrendous result for them and after this they must have been wondering where their next win was coming from. Fortunately for them the Moyes train rolled into town a few days later for a cup game to get them back on track.

Agent Assaidi continues to do good work. Having scored the winner against Chelsea it looked like he'd repeated the feat against the Blueshite until the bastards got a stoppage time penalty and equalised. The foul was by Jermaine Pennant, who'd not long come on for Walters. Comes to something when a team would be better served by keeping Walters on the field. Kinell. Pennant initially had a nibble at Osman and was lucky a pen wasn't given for that, probably due to Osman's honesty in immediately getting back to his feet and playing on. So what does Pennant then do? Goes flying in and makes sure that this time there's no room for doubt. That football spread betting investigation might wanna have a word with him as that was about as dubious an act as you'll see. It's hard to fathom how any player would be that stupid, but then it is Jermaine Pennant and everyone knows he's got the brains of a rocking horse. Thankfully Match of the Day never bothered interviewing Martinez afterwards, so at least we were spared having to hear about his fucking kid again. Seriously, is he the only fella in football who's wife has ever had a baby? She dropped that sprog months ago yet he gets asked about it all the time, I'm sick of it. *"Getting much sleep Roberto?"* Fuck off, who cares.

Norwich took the lead against Palace at Selhurst through Bradley Johnson and were more than a little aggrieved that Chamakh wasn't then sent off for choke-slamming Wes Hoolahan. Mike Dean somehow missed it and then angered Norwich further by awarding a penalty to Palace (converted by my boy Jason Puncheon) and then sent off Leroy Fer for good measure. Decent point for both teams though.

And finally, how about them mancs eh? I did say in the last couple of round ups that I wasn't buying into this 'United revival' garbage and that they were just benefitting from an easy run of fixtures. Well I'm not the kind of guy to say I tol.. actually yeah I am that type of guy, and I told you so didn't I? I told you all that the next half decent side they came up against would beat them and I was right. In fact, the next two half decent sides they came up against beat them, so I was doubly right. And then just for good measure, Sunderland beat them too, which not even I saw coming.

The Spurs game was hilarious as United felt they were denied two penalties by their old mate Howard Webb. They clearly missed the memo, Webb doesn't give penalties anymore, not even to United. Neither of them were pens anyway, Welbeck's was a dive and the one with Ashley Young wasn't as blatant a pen as it was made out to be either.

Adebayor continued his revival under Sherwood and headed Spurs in front shortly before the break and Eriksen doubled their lead from close range. United pulled one back almost immediately through Welcrap, but Spurs held on for the points and Moyes blamed Webb for the loss. Welcome to our world, you fucking melt.

The United comedy festival continued as they lost yet another game at Old Trafford when Bony's bullet header in stoppage time sent the nation into mass waves of side splitting laughter as Swansea dumped them out of the FA Cup. Everyone is loving what's happening to United, not even the Blues have United's back anymore and they're enjoying Moyes' struggles as much as anyone. The funniest element of any bad United result these days is how immediately at full time the camera cuts to Moyes and his panic stricken little face on the touchline and then immediately to that 'Chosen One' banner in the stands. There's then the obligatory shot of Ferguson in the director's box. Cracks me up every time, all that's missing is the 'Laughing Policeman' song playing in the background. Chosen One!!! Hahaha you just know whoever made that banner is desperate to take it down but they don't want to give us all the satisfaction so they're leaving it there, hoping, desperately, that he manages to turn things around.

They say cheats never prosper but Chelsea are living proof that that is absolute bollocks. United's cheating isn't getting them anywhere though is it? That Januzaj gobshite is now the second most booked player for simulation in Premier League history. Up until three months ago I'd never heard of the little scrote, and now he's been booked for diving more than anyone other than Gareth Bale. He's only played 14 games!!!!! Little fucking rat, have I mentioned before that I hate him? I'm sure I must have. I've seen at least four or five dives that he didn't get booked for too, so Bale's record won't last for long at this rate. Can't really blame him though when he's been brought up in that kind of environment. Rooney's as bad as anyone in the league on the sly, of course there's Young and Welbeck, and before them you had Ronaldo, who co-incidentally cut right back on all that crap after jibbing United. Scholes loved a dive as well, and I even remember as far back as the 80s seeing Mark Hughes fling himself to the floor holding his face when replays showed he'd been nudged in the stomach as he tried to disrupt a wall at a free-kick. That's actually the first piece of blatant playacting I think I ever saw. It was in a cup winners cup game against some French team I think. So yeah, they've always been snide, cheating bastards.

Moyes' touchline antics continue to greatly amuse, he's so twitchy and stressed looking and he's aged about ten years in six months too it seems. Taking the job at Mordor is having the same effect on his features as the Ring did. He's completely losing the plot now, I thought it was funny earlier in the season when we beat them and he reacted by saying *"I could see why we were champions today"*, but that was nothing compared to the bizarre ramblings after the Sunderland loss in the League Cup: *"We're having to play the opposition & officials at this moment..maybe I've got to understand that's what happens at Utd"* Fucking hell, I always said he was too smalltime for United but I never thought he was THIS smalltime. Does he actually know where he is? Once again, the phrase *"You're not in Kansas anymore Dorothy"* springs to mind. He loved nothing better than to play the 'little old Everton don't get de decisions dat de redshite get' card, but trying to apply the same logic to United? Really?

And isn't it funny how some of the pundits are defending him by saying it wasn't a great side he inherited? They won the fucking league last season!!! I know they looked shite for most of the season, but they still won it (by 11 bloody points!) so they couldn't have been THAT bad could they? I wonder where they predicted United would finish this season? I don't remember hardly anybody saying they'd be outside the top four, even with that 'awful squad'.

The same argument was used by some to defend Hodgson, but at least in that situation Hodgson had taken over a team that had finished 7th, not 1st. If Moyes was an overseas coach he'd be getting absolutely caned by all and sundry right now. Poor old AVB got ripped to pieces and he's actually won stuff in his short career. Moyes has been a manager for nearly 20 years and his biggest achievement is still that mural in Taff's Tavern. I bet he looks in the mirror every night and reads out that Taff's Tavern mantra to himself. And then probably says *"You're a tiger. Grrrrrr"*. Fucking loser. Being British sure is getting him a hell of a lot of leeway in football pundit circles. Gordon Strachan (who I've normally got a lot of time for) even claimed that people should be supporting him because *'he's British'* and because *'we want British managers to get top four jobs'*. Yeah, couple of problems with that, Gordon. One is that most of us don't really care if a manager is British or not, just that he's good. The only people that seem bothered about it are British managers complaining that fellow British managers don't get the big jobs. Players and fans couldn't give a shit. Secondly, they aren't a top four club anymore, they relinquished that when they appointed this particular British manager.

Neil Warnock was another who had Moyesy's back, as he hilariously ranted *"you tell me another manager who could have that group of players doing better than they are"*. Well.... hmmm, let's see. Off the top of my head I can think of one fella. Elderly chap, purple nose, once shit his kecks on a motorway hard shoulder. Actually won the league with *'that group of players'* funnily enough. And speaking of the devil, isn't it hilarious how he's following Moyes around like the fucking Grim Reaper? Every United loss, there he is up there in the stands, like some old buzzard. He's really not helping and the decent thing would be to just stay away for a while until they get backon track. He's never been one for the 'decent thing though has he. This isn't a sentence that is used very often by anybody, but I think Joey Barton summed it up best on twitter: *"What was the point of him retiring. He's at every game. Go on holiday. Play golf. Spend time with your family. Or friends Busy c*nt #fergie"*

Finally, I'll end on this note. Britain gets hit by severe floods in the same week that every football fan in the nation is collectively pissing themselves at David Moyes. A coincidence? I think not.

chapter nine

January

LIVERPOOL 2 OLDHAM 0

Competition - FA Cup 3rd Rd
Date - Sun 5 Jan 2014
Venue - Anfield
Scorer(s) – Aspas, Tarkowski O.G.
Star Man – Raheem Sterling

Team: Jones; Kelly, Toure, Agger, Cissokho; Gerrard (Suarez), Henderson, Alberto (Lucas); Sterling, Aspas, Moses (Coutinho):

Fairly routine in the end. The first half wasn't great but we never looked in any kind of danger and the second half was much better as we upped the tempo and created several good chances, two of which were taken. A goal for Aspas, a clean sheet, another encouraging display from Sterling and the Mancs being knocked out at home to an injury time winner... We've had worse days, that's for sure.

Ideally Suarez would have been able to keep his feet up for the entire game but at least he was only needed for 15 minutes and should therefore be nicely rested for next week's trip to Stoke. Coutinho and Lucas unfortunately had to play for 45 minutes because Moses and - to a lesser extent - Alberto were so ineffective. The fact both were hooked at half time says a lot about what Rodgers thought of their performances. His explanation was that we needed to play at a quicker tempo and that certainly happened after the break, probably due to the changes as much as anything else.

We had a lot of the ball in the first half but our play was pretty laboured and our attacks took a long time to reach their box, by which time they usually had all their players back behind the ball. That's probably what Rodgers meant by needing to play at a quicker tempo. Alberto was ok, he did some nice things but he plays at such a slow pace and the lad can't run. It didn't help that Moses was running down blind alleys and Sterling kept hitting wayward shots into the Anny Road stand. The Oldham fans were on Sterling's case from the start, booing him every time he got he ball. Apparently he injured one of their players in that game last season and he hasn't played since. Can't say I remember that. We dominated possession and the midfield three all saw plenty of the ball, but the front lads just weren't getting it done. Sterling didn't have his best half, Aspas didn't do much wrong but really wasn't involved much and Moses just got worse and worse as the half went on. His confidence looks shot to pieces right now and you have to wonder if there's any real point in playing him anymore. It's a pity as he really should be much better than we've seen so far, but it would only take one game to turn it around and he may still be needed before the end of the season. Sterling is a shining example to anybody that is lacking in confidence, as the turnaround in that lad of late has been remarkable.

Such is his confidence right now that even a below par first half didn't phase him and he came out after the break and simply tore Oldham a new one. Their poor left back just couldn't cope with him. Raheem made the first goal by skinning his man and standing a good ball into the box that was well finished by Aspas. Massive relief for him, and it's nice that we won't have to see a Liverpool number nine go through and entire season without scoring. That 'honour' is still owned by just El Hadji Diouf thankfully. Aspas didn't deserve to be lumped in with that twat, and everybody in the stadium seemed really pleased for him, not least his team-mates. The pair combined again soon after as Sterling once more jinked his way down the line and sent over a cross that was met by the Spaniard. This time it was a header, a damn good one too in fact, but it hit the post and Coutinho's follow up was saved by the legs of the keeper.

We were creating plenty of chances but Oldham were giving it a good go as well and had a couple of decent efforts of their own. It was turning into a proper cup tie, which isn't what we wanted as ideally we would have gone a few goals up relatively early and then just given some of the younger players a run out. Having to bring on Suarez was not part of the plan and had the finishing been better then we wouldn't have had to. The worst miss of the game was unquestionably Coutinho's. Once again Sterling created it by beating his man and cutting the ball back into the danger area. The Brazilian ran onto it but showed a total lack of composure and hammered the ball miles over the bar into the Kop. His poor finishing is definitely a mental thing; it seems like he always tries to leather the ball as hard as his little legs will let him, instead of just picking his spot the way he would when threading a pass through. The difference in his ball striking when shooting as opposed to passing is night and day, he ALWAYS goes for power when shooting and often as a result he scuffs his shot because of it. If Rodgers could somehow convince him to pretend one of his team-mates is stood in the corner of the goal calling for a pass, Coutinho would be a 30 goal a season man.

Aspas then shot wide after he'd produced a stunning first touch to pluck a long pass out of the air and then ran at a defender. That showed what a boost his confidence had been given by finally getting a goal, as all game he'd been looking to the lay the ball off and now suddenly he was willing to commit defenders and go for goal. Whilst that was good to see, he pissed me off big time when he failed to play in Suarez and instead tried to go on his own and was easily tackled. Yeah, you've got your goal and we're all happy for you, but don't go getting all cocky kid. Suarez wasn't amused and rightly so, it was still 1-0 and that could have proved costly especially as we ended up having to play the final stages of the game with just ten men after Agger hobbled off. It didn't prove costly, thankfully, as Sterling's wayward shot hit a defender on the shin and went in.

Brendan's son came on and looked a tidy little footballer, passing the ball around well and looking busy. Must have been a proud moment for the boss seeing his son playing at Anfield, but no doubt he'll have given him specific instructions not to tackle anybody, especially Suarez.

Final word has to be on Sterling who was brilliant at both ends in that second half. Going forward he was really direct and positive, but when we ended up a man down and he was moved to right back, he was brilliant there too. They kept trying to to get at him and each time they did he got his body in the way and won back possession before starting us on the attack again. I can't speak highly enough of him at the moment. If I'm being honest, I'd have happily sent him packing after that loss at Hull and I had all but written him off, but he's come back strong and is playing well every week now.

STOKE CITY 3 LIVERPOOL 5

Competition - Premier League
Date - Sun 12 Jan 2014   **Team: Mignolet; Johnson,**
Venue - The Britannia Stadium   **Skrtel, Toure, Cissokho;**
Scorer(s) – Shawcross O.G.,   **Gerrard, Lucas, Henderson;**
Suarez (2), Gerrard (pen),   **Sterling, Suarez, Coutinho**
Sturridge   **(Sturridge):**
Star Man – Raheem Sterling

I was watching the Hull v Chelsea game on Saturday and was struck by how completely bored I was with it. It was third time I've watched Chelsea away from home this season and each time it's been like watching paint dry. They won by a two goal margin and rarely looked in any trouble, but it was awful, negative, safety first bilge. Mourinho football.

For all the millions spent on attacking players, it seems that only Eden Hazard is capable of escaping the shackles placed on him by the 'Especially Dull One'. In contrast, we also won by two goals away from home, but that's where any similarity with Chelsea ended.

Did Brendan Rodgers really serve his apprenticeship under that negative shithouse? It's difficult to believe, as the pair are chalk and cheese when it comes to footballing philosophy. That makes us great to watch but it isn't necessarily a good thing for the blood pressure of the fans. This was hard to sit through at times as it was completely nerve shredding stuff, but if the alternative is to go 'the Chelsea way' then bollocks to that, I'll ride the rollercoaster that is 'Rodgeball' thanks.

While we're always going to give up chances based on how attack minded our approach is, I still maintain that our biggest issue when it comes to conceding goals is as much individual mistakes as it is tactical approach. We're never going to be George Graham's Arsenal, we commit too many men in attack to ever be impregnable in defence, but if we cut out the stupid mistakes we won't concede anywhere near as many goals. Look at the three we let in against Stoke. Two of them (the second and third) were directly a result of our mistakes and even the other could have been prevented too for that matter. The winning goals we conceded at City and Chelsea too were a result of errors by Mignolet, and if we cut out those mistakes then we can win even with this gung-ho approach, because more often than not we're brilliant going forward.

Having Suarez and Sturridge back in tandem for the final half hour of this game provided a glimpse of what is possible. When they've played together before Sterling was out of form and usually not in the side. Now the teenager is flying as well and it's going to be interesting to see how the trio play together. That's without even mentioning Coutinho, who if the penny ever drops with his finishing is going to be something very special indeed. Perhaps in time he'll end up playing deeper, in the way Luka Modric did for example?

Stoke has been a notoriously tough ground for us in recent seasons, we've done ok in cup competitions there but in the league it's been horrific. Nobody likes playing at Stoke but we've fared worse than most. This season, however, they've been a lot less 'robust' and have been playing far more football than we've been used to seeing. Yet the Britannia has still been a fortress and both City and Everton failed to win there whilst Chelsea were beaten. Only Norwich had won there and Stoke had conceded only seven goals at home all season, so this was never going to be easy. Taking all that into account this was a great win and not even conceding three goals is going to put a dampener on it for me. We've scored five at the Britannia and got three absolutely massive points.

The late kick off on the Sunday meant that everyone else in the top seven (other than Arsenal who play on Monday night) had played and won. We'd slipped to sixth before kick off, eight points behind leaders Man City. Whilst a loss at Stoke wouldn't have killed any top four hopes we have, it would have been a big psychological blow. All things considered, the players showed great character to get the win. They shouldn't have needed to show character though, at 2-0 the game should have been over, especially as Coutinho had also wasted two glorious opportunities that would have seen the game ended by half time. We'd opened the scoring early on in fortuitous circumstances, as Cissokho's awful shot was miles off target until it his Shawcross and went in. That was unlucky on the part of the Stoke defender but the second goal was just down to his own crapness. A long punt upfield was chased by Suarez and whilst Wilson's header back was short, Shawcross still should have dealt with it but an awful touch allowed Luis to nip in and slot in his 21st of the season. Stoke's fans had been giving him stick just before that, so he celebrated with a hilarious 'flex' in front of them, that had our substitutes pissing themselves laughing as they looked on.

Stoke were offering nothing at that point and we couldn't have been any more comfortable. In fact, we were so comfortable we began to look like we had the pipe and slippers out and before we knew it, it was 2-2. I don't think we conceded those two goals due to being 'too open', I mean the first goal came out of nothing but we had plenty of men back and it was preventable. Suarez had tracked back to cover Arnautovic and he and Johnson appeared to have it under control. Once the winger cut inside it was as though they both felt that was 'job done' and they didn't close him down and allowed him time and space to put the ball in the box. That was mistake number one. Mistake number two was that the defence were a little too deep and Crouch was able to head the ball around the penalty spot rather than on the edge of the box, where he should have been.

That being said, sometimes there's not THAT much you can do. Toure was marking Crouch tightly but the cross was behind the striker who had to come back for it. That created a bit of separation between him and Kolo but what is the defender supposed to do there? Crouch is 6ft 7, if a ball is directed to his head then quite often all you can do is hope he doesn't direct it well enough. The second goal was worse, but on another day Adam's shot goes into orbit and nothing is said about it. Unfortunately this time it flew into the corner so fingers are pointed as to how it could be allowed to happen.

At 2-2 I really thought we'd blown it. Then out of nothing we were back in front. We definitely got lucky as had either the handball or the penalty decision gone in Stoke's favour we couldn't have complained much. The handball wasn't an easy one to spot. On first viewing I was convinced it had smashed Sterling straight in the chest - it was only after a few different replays that it became clear the ball bounced off his chest onto his arm - but you could argue that it was completely unintentional and that he couldn't get out of the way. You can't give what you can't see though and neither ref nor linesman could have been sure on that. The penalty itself was a strange one. Outside the box it's a free-kick all day long. Inside? Generally you're not going to get that call, even though the defender did impede Sterling and there was no question of it being a dive.

Rodgers went for the jugular by bringing on Sturridge for Coutinho. Initially it looked like Suarez would go to the left of the front three but it soon became apparent that we were going with more of a 4-4-2. It paid off nicely as Sturridge collected the ball and ran at the Stoke defence before playing a wonderfully disguised little ball to his striker partner who despatched it into the bottom corner. 4-2 now, game over surely? No, once again we found ourselves pegged back and this one was by far the worst goal we conceded. Gerrard and Lucas went for the same ball and Stoke picked up possession. Arnautovic played a great ball into Walters and had the striker finished well into the corner with an unstoppable shot then it wouldn't have been THAT bad a goal from our perspective. This is Jon Walters we're talking about though, he'd scored only once all season, the chump. The finish was typically shit, yet Mignolet somehow allowed it to go through him. Completely unacceptable that, and worryingly his form has started to become an issue of late. That's three goals he should have done better with in his last three away games. It can be a slippery slope with goalkeepers, one mistake often leads to another, and another, and before you know it you have a Jerzy Dudek situation on your hands. Mignolet needs a few clean sheets to get this out of his system.

Now it was backs to the wall, Stoke had come from two goals back once and now sensed they could do it again. They had chances too - Mignolet needed to save well to keep out a Walters header almost immediately - but we always looked dangerous on the break with the quality we had at the top end of the pitch. The killer goal came when Sterling made a run down the left wing to latch onto a long ball. He did well to hold it up and then roll it inside to Suarez, who looked up and then played an inch perfect ball to Sturridge on the back post. I thought his first effort had gone in and was already celebrating. Next thing I see him juggling it on his chest and then head and I'm wondering what the hell happened. He lashed in at the second attempt and at that point I didn't care what had happened. Loved the celebration between him and Suarez too, they clicked immediately as soon as Sturridge got back on the field and it's going to be a lot of fun watching them play together over the next few months. If they both stay fit then we've got a chance of doing something special this year, even with our leaky back-line.

Premier League Round Up (12-16 January 2014)

The weekend's action kicked off at Hull where Chelsea were the visitors. Typical boring Mourinho football, as Chelsea's tactics once again were to just keep the game tight and wait for Hazard to do something at the other end. The Belgian is just about the only thing worth watching when it comes to Chelsea these days. He's the spark for them every week, the rest of them are like watching an Alan Shearer / Michael Owen episode of Match of the Day.

Predictably, he delivered once again, his superb goal putting Chelsea ahead and after that they just shut up shop until Torres added a second late on with a complete mis-kick that went in at the near post when he was trying to go across goal. Fucking loser. I see that Chelsea fans have stolen our Torres song lock stock and barrel, from the *'we're gonna bounce in a minute'* to the *'Fernando Torres Chelsea's number nine'*. Sad, shameless, embarrassing twats. In fairness, considering they paid £50m for the bum the least we can do is throw in the song. That reminds me, remember when they ripped off our 'El Nino' banner too, complete with Shankly Gates! Losers.

Hazard was named man of the match after this game, but it wasn't enough for his knob-head manager; *"He deserves more than man of the match, probably player of the month. Not many are doing what he is doing"* Player of the month eh? No way Jose, Suarez was the player of the month and you know why he was? Because he scored ten fucking goals in one month, that's why. Honestly, I know I keep saying it, but what an absolute helmet. Ian Darke said during commentary, *"On comes Jon Obi Mikel, who had been hoping to be named African Footballer of the Year but missed out to Yaya Toure."* Yeah, I know how he feels, I was hoping to be named in the lead role in 'Drive' but missed out to Ryan Gosling. And I'm putting it out there, Oscar is the most over-rated player in the country. What exactly does he do? He cost a similar amount to Hazard but there's simply no comparison between the two. The only thing they have in common is the diving and general cuntishness. Oscar is such a twat that even Lucas doesn't seem to like him, and Lucas is the nicest man on the planet so what does that say about Oscar? I hate his face and his 'sensible haircut', the chinless wonder. Proper gormless looking he is. If Phil Jones is the King of Gorm then this dweeb is the crown prince. Fuck him and fuck Chelsea. My Chelsea hatred is bordering on 2005-06 levels at the moment. Final footnote to this one. Huddlestone was absolutely crap, I blame the haircut. Some serious Samson shit going on there.

Moving on, and Fulham's woes continued as they were battered at home by Sunderland. Taraabt went close to putting Fulham ahead but was denied by a point blank stop by Big Vito. The commentator said *"Taraabt had Wes Brown on toast there"*. Baked bean on toast then, sounds about right. Adam Johnson's superb free-kick gave the visitors the lead and Ki doubled their advantage just before the break. Sidwell pulled one back when he headed in from a corner but Johnson grabbed his second after a swift counter attack in which Altidore actually did something good. He wasn't finished there either, diving for a penalty short afterwards to allow Johnson to claim his hat-trick from the spot. I say dive, that's a bit harsh, it was more of a flop but Senderos did stick his leg out and was asking for trouble. How shit is Riise these days though? Sad to say it, but he's really awful now. And sort that head out lad, 'kinell.

West Ham signed Roger Johnson last week. If that's not a sign they're preparing for life in the Championship then I don't know what is. They were boosted with the news that the big fella was back on the bench for them though, he was sporting an impressive beard as they made the trip to Cardiff. George McCartney was back in the Hammers side too. Isn't he about due for a move back to Sunderland soon? His entire career seems to have been spent bouncing from West Ham to Sunderland and back again. Carlton Cole put the Hammers ahead and that's how it stayed until he was replaced by Carroll in the second half. Tomkins was sent off for a second yellow card after almost beheading Frazier Campblell, but the ten men wrapped up the points when Carroll teed up Noble to make it 2-0 in stoppage time. Have that Solksjaer, you fucking manc goblin.

I see the mancs were at it again with the cheating, this time it was Rafael hurling himself to the floor clutching his face to try and get Shelvey sent off. Replays showed Jonjo never touched him. Twat. Valencia broke the deadlock early in the second half but he was a mile offside. Welcrap then deflected in an effort from Evra to keep his good recent run of goalscoring going. Ferguson stays away and United win. Co-incidence? Well yeah, of course it is, but still it's pretty funny that the old goat only ever seems to see them lose these days.

The Blues had a comfortable home win against Norwich. Gareth Barry dragged his fat arse up the field and opened the scoring with a screamer. Norwich should have equalised but Wolf Van Winkel blazed a shot over the bar. Mirallas doubled Everton's lead with a free-kick but Norwich still had their chances to get back into it. Snodgrass hit the bar and Van Winkel wasted another glorious opportunity as the Blues ran out winners despite not playing well.

There were fun and games during and after Palace's game at White Hart Lane. The talking point was the horrific penalty by my boy Jason Puncheon. It's hard to believe anyone could miss a penalty by such a margin, let alone a professional footballer. He was mortified, the poor lad. He's still my boy though. Some lad called Bentaleb almost scored the goal of the weekend with a brilliant curling shot from distance that hit the inside of the post. Never heard of him, was he one of the sixty five players Spurs signed last summer to replace Bale? One man who was definitely one of those sixty five is Christian Eriksen, and he drew first blood with a smart finish after latching on to an Adebayor flick. Sherwood sent on Defoe for what was supposed to be his last appearance before moving to Toronto and the striker responded with a goal. Funny player him, seems to score a shit-load of goals but has never really been first choice. Now there's talk he'll stay at Spurs until the end of February. Can't believe someone who is still close to being in his prime is choosing to go and play over in the MLS. No doubt he'll say he's going 'for the challenge'. Yeah, the challenge of counting all that money.

After the game all the talk was of Puncheon's penalty, and Neil Warnock (one of his former managers) made some less than complimentary remarks about him on the radio, which tipped Puncheon completely over the edge, as he took to twitter to launch an assault of his own: *"What I won't accept is an opinion from a man who's crooked and ruining the game. NEIL WARNOCK the man who signs players, gives them extra wages and appearance bonuses to make sure they pay him to get in the team or on the bench. The fact he could even talk about training is shocking, he was never there...."* Fucking hell!! I've got three words to sum all that up. Thats. My. Boy.

West Brom finally have a new manager. I'd never heard of him until they announced his appointment. Seems a weird one, but then so did Southampton's appointment of Pochettino. Ironically the Saints were Pepe Mel's first opponent. Lallana bagged the only goal of the game and revealed a 'Happy Birthday Mum' message under his shirt. Ah bless him, nice touch that. Good to see that the England call up hasn't gone to his head so much that he'd forget about his dear old mum, eh Clattenburg? I can't believe I forgot to mention all that nonsense in last week's round up. If you missed it, Southampton got their knickers in a knot because Clattenburg apparently said to Lallana: *"You're very different now since you played for England. You never used to be like this."* Lallana was kicking off over not getting a penalty, and as much as I don't like Clattenburg I have to say that Southampton have some balls on them don't they? We've all seen on TV the abuse players hurl at officials every week. Some of the things Rooney has been caught on camera yelling would make a docker blush, and yet a club reports a ref over this??? The ref's governing body said there was no case to answer, but Southampton issued a statement saying: *"An official insulting any player, no matter his intentions, is clearly not acceptable behaviour."* Oh, but it's ok for players to insult officials as much as they like? Can't believe I'm defending refs as I've got a lower opinion of them than most, but this is a joke. Fuck off Southampton, you over sensitive fannies. And what's all this talk about Pochettino leaving? The chairman who sacked Adkins and brought him in has quit because the owners want to cash in on their best players, and now Pochettino is ready to walk too. Apparently some bird whose family owns the club has now appointed herself as chairman and wants to sell Shaw, Lallana, Lambert & co and the whole club is on the verge of meltdown. Modern football eh?

Onto Sunday and a fiery encounter at St James Park. The Geordies got completely screwed by the officials. Trailing to Dzeko's early strike, the Toon thought they'd equalised when Tiote's screamer flew into the top corner. The linesman had other ideas, telling the ref it shouldn't stand because Gouffran was in an offside position. He was offside but he wasn't in Hart's line of sight and it was a woeful decision. Fair enough if that's going to be called across the board in every game in every situation, but it's not is it? Newcastle got shafted, plain and simple. What made it worse was the flag didn't even go up at the time. Tiote had ran off celebrating, so had his team-mates and Pardew was just about to sit back down again after his own celebration when he got wind that something was up. A few City players had appealed for offside so the ref - Mike Jones - went to talk to the lino and between them they they decided to rule it out. When Pardew first realised what was going on, he didn't seem worried, you could clearly see him saying *"nah they can't rule that out"*. They did though, and it was only at that point that the flag eventually went up. Newcastle were furious and who can blame them? Jones has been demoted for next weekend, but that doesn't do Newcastle any good does it? Or those challenging at the top for that matter; these points that City undeservedly picked up today could be decisive. The last time Jones had reffed a Newcastle game he was 'accidentally' smacked on the nose by an unapologetic Moussa Sissoko. I'm just saying like…

Pardew had a blazing row on the touchline with Pellegrini, in which he yelled at the City boss *"shut your noise you fucking old cunt"*. Brilliant! Pards is only eight years Pellegrini's junior. In his head he's still 21 though, the smooth bastard. He had to apologise afterwards when he realised it had all been caught on camera. Yanga-Mbiwa should have been sent off for a wild kick at Nasri, who was stretchered off. Perhaps Jones let that go because he knew he'd gotten the Tiote decision so badly wrong? Or maybe he just thought, *'ah fuck it, it's only Nasri'*. Either way it was understandable. Negredo finally killed plucky Newcastle off deep into stoppage time with a bit of a poxy goal that he finished at the second attempt. Really harsh on the Geordies. I wouldn't have wanted to be a horse on Tyneside on Sunday night, that's for damn sure. And Pellegrini's take on the disallowed goal? *"It was a valid decision. The player was clearly offside."* Ah shut your noise, you fucking old cunt.

One more game to cover. Arsenal won at Villa on Monday night. They went 2-0 up but Benteke pulled one back and Villa threw everything at them to try and get an equaliser but just fell short. I'm saying nothing about Villa as we play them next. They are seriously shit though aren't they?

LIVERPOOL 2 ASTON VILLA 2

Competition - Premier League
Date - Sat 18 Jan 2014
Venue - Anfield
Scorer(s) – Sturridge, Gerrard (pen)
Star Man – Daniel Sturridge

Team: Mignolet; Johnson, Skrtel, Toure, Cissokho; Sterling, Gerrard, Henderson, Coutinho (Lucas, Allen); Sturridge, Suarez:

Well that was a bit of a shock to the system to say the least. In the end we should probably be grateful for a point as Villa could have had this game wrapped up by half time. There was a sense of total disbelief around the ground at what we were witnessing in that first half, it was almost surreal. Were we playing Aston Villa or Barcelona? We'd probably have made a better fist of facing Barcelona. We certainly wouldn't have gone in with no midfield, that's for damn sure.

I can only assume that Rodgers was taken by surprise with how Villa lined up, as their midfield diamond completely dominated us in that first half, whilst our ever more suspect defence simply couldn't cope with Benteke and Agbonlahor. We just looked absolutely shellshocked, especially Gerrard who had a torrid first half before bouncing back well in the second. When was the last time we were taken to the cleaners in the manner Villa did to us in the opening 45 minutes? They actually went 3-0 up against us last season but didn't play anywhere near as well as this. We were playing ok that day until we got sucker punched and it started to go downhill fast. This time? Well Villa should have scored in the first minute, they had numerous others chances and were well worth the 2-0 lead they established before we grabbed a lifeline with a goal just before half time. Basically Paul Lambert took Rodgers to school in this one, it's as simple as that.

The initial team selection was the start of our problems on the day. It smacked of arrogance and a lack of respect for Villa. I can say that with some degree of confidence because I would have picked the same team and I was predicting a 6-0 win! I was definitely arrogant about it and I had zero respect for Villa; I thought we'd just steamroller them. I was wrong, but that doesn't matter because I'm not the manager and I can afford to be wrong. Brendan does not have that luxury. He under-estimated Villa and he over-estimated his own players. The first half was completely embarrassing as Villa came at us from all angles and we just did not have the numbers to deal with them. I said I was happy with the starting line up, but I'd have to add the proviso that I wasn't expecting the 4-4-2 we saw. Playing with Coutinho and Sterling wide and with two up front left us horribly exposed in the middle. Even the Gerrard of ten years ago would have struggled to cope in this scenario. In terms of his new role as a deep lying midfielder, I wouldn't read too much into this game though. He simply didn't stand a chance as our tactical set up left him horribly exposed. Play him there with Allen and Henderson in front of him and then let's judge it.

That said, the skipper was seriously rattled and endured an absolute nightmare first half. Defensively our midfield were all at sea, but just as damaging was the inability to get on the ball and maintain any kind of possession. It was just very naive football we were playing, desperation stuff that you'd expect to see at the end of a match when you throw on extra attackers to chase the game. You don't normally see it from the opening kick off! It was all too hurried, too frantic, too un-Liverpool like. We couldn't build from the back because we didn't have the bodies in midfield to play the ball in to. Having more forwards on the pitch doesn't always mean better forward play or more goals, in fact it can be just as detrimental as not having enough of them. There needs to be a balance, and it seems like any time Rodgers has tried to go too attacking it hasn't worked and we've been top heavy. The one really glaring example I can think of was Oldham away in the cup last season. Because of the poor result and defensive shambles of that day, it's easy to forget that Rodgers actually started that game with Suarez, Sturridge, Borini and Sterling all on the pitch, no doubt think they'd just blow away an inferior side. The same thing happened, we tried to score as soon as we got the ball and ended up frequently giving the ball away within seconds of getting it.

I think to play the way we want to we need to have three in the middle of the park all the time now, whether it's a two and a one, a one and a two, a reverse pivot, an inverted triangle or whatever the hell you want to call it, it needs to be anything other than two in the centre. If Aston Villa (and Oldham!) can dismantle us when we play that way, then you'd have to say there's probably not too many sides against whom we could get away with it.

It's easy to blame the players for what happened - and obviously they have to take a share of the responsibility - but I felt that what was happening in the first half was almost completely tactical and so easily avoidable. We couldn't keep the ball or play it out from the back the way we normally do and Villa were just sat back there waiting to pick us off and spring their counter attacks. They were outstanding, but we played right into their hands and took too long to change. It was obvious how it was going and Brendan should have switched it much earlier than he did. Even if he didn't want to make a substitution so early on he should have at least moved Coutinho into centre midfield alongside Henderson (in front of Gerrard) to allow us to gain some control of the game and slow things down a bit. It was like watching a basketball game at times, it was just end to end and that was always going to suit Villa as they have so much pace on the break.

That change may have made Coutinho play with a bit more composure too, as it was he was just constantly looking to play the killer pass and more often than not failing miserably. The lack of possession meant it was difficult for Henderson to get forward much as every time he made a run we'd lose the ball and Gerrard was left all on his lonesome as the Villa cavalry charged up the field. It was just horrible, schoolboy like football and for that I lay the blame squarely at the door of Brendan. He's got us playing great attacking football anyway, he doesn't need to go THIS gung-ho because this is what happens. Villa's first goal was a classic counter attack. We lost the ball on the edge of their box and two passes later Agbonlahor was streaking past Toure down the left and into the box. I could almost hear the 'meep meep' as he flew past him like the fucking road runner. He got to the box, held it up whilst support arrived and then squared for Weimann who nipped in front of Gerrard for a tap in. He was fractionally offside and the goal shouldn't have stood, but it was no more than Villa deserved.

Rodgers eventually made a tactical switch and went to a back three, moving Coutinho central and deploying Johnson as one of the three centre backs with Sterling at right wing back. It helped a little but not before Villa bagged a second. This one wasn't system related, it was caused by the latest howler by Mignolet, who came for a cross that Johnson was about to comfortably head clear under no pressure. The keeper missed it completely and in the process he put Johnson off and the ball dropped over his head and fell perfectly for Benteke who could hardly believe his luck. I'm officially worried about Mignolet now as that's four goals in the last five games that he's been culpable for. We've seen in the past how easy it is for a keeper to completely lose the plot after a run of mistakes and the Belgian is going to have to show his mettle to not let these affect his confidence. I can live with him making the odd howler on crosses because his shot stopping is normally so good, but given that he's let three tame shots beat him recently it's a lot more difficult to forgive him flapping at crosses too.

The crowd were completely stunned by what they were witnessing and had

Sturridge not pulled one back just before half time then it would have been interesting to hear the reaction to the half time whistle. That goal changed everything though, and what a goal it was. The flick from Henderson to put Sturridge in was absolutely brilliant and shows the confidence he's playing with this season. Great awareness and superb technique too. Sturridge did what Sturridge does and that must have been a huge blow for Villa. To only be one goal ahead after the way they'd played had to be pretty demoralising for them. From our point of view, we'd got out of jail somewhat and the stage was set for us to turn it around attacking the Kop end in the second half.

The flow of the game turned on two substitutions; us bringing on Lucas and Villa having to take off Agbonlahor. The Villa striker had ran our defence ragged and created two goals. Their gameplan was largely based around speed on the counter and having to replace him with Grant Holt severely handicapped what they were trying to do. Imagine the Jamaican relay team suddenly having to switch Usain Bolt for Geoff Capes mid race. That's the kind of impact the change had on Villa, who no longer offered anywhere near the same threat they had previously. The arrival of Lucas also helped to turn the ship around as the extra body and calming presence provided by the Brazilian meant that the visitors were longer running through the centre unopposed, and just as crucially, we were now able to maintain possession and a control of the game that we never had in the first half.

It wasn't long before we were level as Gerrard's sublime pass sent Suarez in and although I thought his first touch was a little heavy he still got there before Guzan who brought him down. Could he have stayed on his feet? Maybe, I don't know. Should he have? Of course not, there's no reward for being honest in football, referees never give penalties when you try to stay on your feet and when everyone else is doing it then you're severely handicapping yourself by not doing the same. Guzan recklessly committed himself to the challenge, he didn't get the ball and he caught Suarez. Everything else is just white noise really, but it won't stop another Suarez witch hunt in some quarters.

Gerrard showed his bottle once again by dispatching the penalty and with almost 40 minutes still remaining we should have gone on to win the game. That we didn't win it from there is more on the shoulders on the players than the manager. Rodgers can be blamed for the first half horror show, but having corrected his error at half time and seen the players get back on level terms, there's not much he could then do other than trust the players to get the job done. He had his best available players on the field, they were in a system that they were familiar with and they had momentum. They should have won it but they didn't do enough. That was almost as disappointing for me as the first half performance as we've come to expect much better from the players at Anfield. In that respect they're a victim of their own success; we've been spoiled at home this season and now expect to win every game. When we don't, it's a big disappointment. It wasn't so long ago that wasn't the case, so I give Brendan credit for that.

He definitely dropped the ball in this one though, despite his claims to the contrary. *"For me the system is irrelevant,"* Rodgers said. *"But we never got control of that midfield and we couldn't really build the game from behind."* We had two midfielders against Villa's four so I'd say it's pretty damn relevant! And one of the two was bombing forward, so there were times when Gerrard had three players running at him. And if the system is irrelevant, why bring Lucas on and change it? Because the system we started with got it's arse handed to it, that's why. Brendan got it wrong, his team selection cost us points and it's the second time it's happened at Anfield this season. The line up he picked for the Southampton game was the biggest contributing factor to the result that day, just as it was against Villa in this one. His decisions hamstrung us on both occasions, but it's easy to forget sometimes that he's still a young manager learning on the job. Overall he's getting a lot more right than wrong and as long as he learns from mistakes then he'll do for me. And he certainly does learn from his mistakes, I doubt we'll see anything like this again this season.

Premier League Round Up (19-23 January 2014)

It was shaping up to be one shitty week.... then along came Moyesy! From our perspective it's not been a great few days due to one thing and another, but you'd have to be one seriously depressed individual to not be able to crack a smile or two at the plight of 'the Chosen One'. United's League Cup semi final exit to Sunderland after a penalty shoot out was just side splittingly funny. Even when they win they lose.

You've got to hand it to Davey Moyes, he's quite the achiever isn't he? Not content with proving you can be a winner without actually winning anything, he's now proved that you can be a loser even without losing. I don't even know where to start with it, it was just complete comedy gold. They were seconds away from going through to an all Manchester final but conceded a goal right at the end of extra time. Whatsmore, it was scored by a former United player, Phil Bardsley. That was hilarious enough and had that turned out to be the winner it would have been cause for much merriment and piss taking at United's expense, but for them to immediately equalise and get Moyesy's little hopes up only to then shit the bed on penalties just made it even sweeter. Throw in the fact that Hernandez injured himself celebrating that goal and therefore couldn't take a pen in the shoot out... well you just can't make that shit up. To top it all off Phil Jones blasted his pen into orbit and it actually twatted a United fan behind the goal full in the face. Brilliant!

Sunderland's pens were actually crap, they only scored two but incredibly that was enough. United somehow managed to miss four out of five penalties, the massive bottlers. Ironic that Darren Fletcher was the only one not to shit himself. The trademark gurning grid of Jones as he saw his kick flying over the bar was an absolute picture, but not even that could top the various haunted facial expressions of the tormented Moyes as it all unfolded in front of his bog eyes. How much funnier can this whole Moyes at United possibly get? I don't know but I'm looking forward to finding out.

I'm happy for the Mackems too, my brother in law and nephew will be going to Wembley and hopefully Sunderland can spring another upset, it'd be nice to see them win something as they've got a great fanbase and have been very supportive of the Justice Campaign. They've beaten Chelsea and United so why not City? Stranger things have happened, I mean Moyes managed to beat Arsenal not so long ago so anything is possible.

The hero for Sunderland was 'Big Vito', who's proving to be quite the hit up in the North East. He should get 'made' after that, and bumped up to 'Capo'. He's no longer just a 'friend of mine', he's a 'friend of ours'. Definitely deserves to 'get his button' after this. That United loss was the only thing that went our way this week though. We'd just about been hanging onto the coat-tails of the top three, but failing to beat Villa has opened up a bit of a gap and with our midfield now looking thinner than an Iago Aspas arm, it looks like we're in a four way battle for that Champions League spot with Spurs, the Blueshite and United. Newcastle United I mean, obviously.

City continue to look invincible at home, comfortably seeing off Cardiff 4-2. City have now scored 103 goals this season (they made it 106 with a comfortable cup win at West ham in midweek), and I'd say that more than vindicates what I've been writing for a couple years about Mancini being a complete fraud. Pellegrini is doing well, but he's not exactly punching above his weight. He's doing what he should be doing, and it highlights just how fucking shit and negative Mancini was.

Cardiff actually gave a decent account of themselves in fairness, especially Noone. It'd be ace if one day he developed into a really top player and ended up at Anfield. As a lifelong Kopite at least we wouldn't have to worry about him and his agent using us to get a better deal from fucking Chelsea like that Salah jabroni. And signing Noone would make a welcome change from signing no-one.

But I digress. Arsenal were making hard work of beating Fulham at the Emirates but got the job done thanks to Cazorla's five minute double strike early in the second half. They're still hanging around at the top and if it hadn't been for all the Suarez crap over the summer I'd probably be rooting for them to win it as it becomes clearer by the week that we're probably going to fall by the wayside. At least they'd be doing it the right way and not off the back of some billionaire owner bankrolling it. Thing is, Arsenal fans are unbearably smug even when they have nothing to be smug about, I don't think I could live with them being Champions so I'm reluctantly hitching my wagon to City again as the lesser of three evils.

Moving swiftly on, and 'Slimer' took Newcastle back to the home of one of his former clubs as the Toon travelled to the East End to face Fat Sam's Hammers. Trying to choose someone to root for between Pardew and Allardyce is like being asked if you want to eat dogshit or catshit. Either way it's going to leave a foul taste in your mouth. West Ham's complete hopelessness meant it was a fairly routine win for 'Pards' in the end.

Elsewhere, Southampton put their recent off the field troubles behind them and raced into a 2-0 lead at Sunderland. They were superb in the first half and the Mackems had no answer to it until 'Fabio Magnifico' fired them back into it. He's really growing on me now, I'd definitely be looking at bringing him back into the squad next season as our third striker. Unless someone wants to give us back what we paid for him of course, I'd probably take that if it was offered but if not then get him back here. I wish he was here now in fact.

Sunderland are a much improved side under Poyet and in-form Adam Johnson earned them a point with a good strike that Boruc really ought to have kept out. Ramirez was stretchered off after a heavy challenge by Wes Brown. He got the ball first but his follow through looked like it snapped the Uruguayan's ankle in two. Not nice to see that, and Brown was lucky to not pick up yet another red card.

My boy Jason Puncheon got the only goal of the game as Palace beat Stoke, taking advantage of a mistake by Assaidi to fire a low shot into the bottom corner. He had a slow start to the season but he's flying now. He could have made it 2-0 in stoppage time but was denied by Butland, who had a great game for Stoke. If Palace stay up - and I'm starting to think they will - Tony Pulis should be manager of the year. No, I can't believe I just wrote that either, but fair dues to the scruff, he's done a hell of a job and they aren't even playing alehouse football either. But then when you have such a special talent like J-Punch you play to his strengths I suppose.

Jelavic almost marked his Hull debut at Carrow Road with a goal with his very first touch but saw his left foot shot come back off the post. I still think he's decent, I know things turned to shit with him at Everton but for a while there he looked lethal and you don't lose that overnight, unless you're Fernando Torres. Ryan Bennett's late, late header won it for the Canaries and Hull's misery was compounded when Huddlestone was sent off after picking up two extremely soft yellow cards. Said it last week, it's Samson Syndrome that, should never have cut his hair off. Name me one player who went on to better things after chopping off an impressive set of locks. Just one. You can't, because there aren't any.

Interesting little footnote to this. Last week it was confirmed that Howard Webb will be the English representative at the World Cup. He hadn't sent anyone off or awarded a penalty all season, which as I wrote after our loss at Chelsea prompted Graham Poll to claim that this was a deliberate ploy by Webb to get to the World Cup. Poll insists that some referees believe you are graded far more harshly for decisions you make that are wrong than for ones you don't make that you should. He said that's why Webb hadn't sent anyone off or given any pens. So, Webb gets the World Cup gig and the very next game he's flashing a red card for two completely innocuous fouls. The cynical, scheming, calculating baldy twat. Bet he gives a pen next week too. I really hate that scumbag.

Onto Sunday now and the big game of the weekend at Stamford Bridge. Had we beaten Villa I'd have been rooting for United to win this, and not just because of the state of the league table either. My current hatred for Chelsea far outweighs that which I have for the Mancs. It's partly because Chelsea are better than them, but mostly because of Mourinho. I can't bring myself to hate David Moyes. How can anyone hate Davie Moyes right now? Unless you're a United fan obviously. It'd be different if Ferguson was still around, but he isn't, and as a result I've got more disdain for Chelsea right now.

And what the fuck are the BBC doing wheeling out that little fucking gnome Pat

Nevin on MOTD? Is it because Mourinho was bitching about there not being enough 'Chelsea pundits'? They even ran a stupid, cringeworthy little feature on 'Jose's rules of punditry' where he came out with this bollocks: *"First rule; Chelsea always deserved to win. [The second rule is] Chelsea always the best team on the pitch. [The third rule is] every referee decision was against Chelsea. [And the fourth rule is] the man of the match is a Chelsea player. This is not the same role as Chelsea manager but sounds the same as pundits who support other teams! But when your heart is red, or blue or stripes, black and white, you cannot hide it - and they do not hide it, they do not hide their heart colour. I just think a couple of Chelsea pundits would be good!"* It was supposedly tongue in cheek and a bit of a joke, except we all know that this is exactly how that whopper thinks it should be.

So yeah, had we beaten Villa I'd have had no qualms about wanting a United win, but once we'd failed to win there was no choice but to hope that United got no points as we need to keep them at arms length. Not that they had a chance of getting other than an arse whupping of course, they're so average right now without Rooney and Van Persie. I almost referred to him just 'Persie' then, that's coz of my dad that is, for some reason he's completely dropped the 'Van' whenever he talks about him now and it's rubbing off on me. File that one away with 'Coataneenio' (Coutinho), Dimitar 'Burgerchov' 'Cesc Fibreglass' and my personal favourite, 'Ponytail' (Andriy Voronin).

Eto'o bagged a ht-trick before Hernandez poached a late consolation, but any feint hope of a United comeback ended when Vidic was harshly sent off. Never a red card in a million years, if you want to see a red card then look at the one Rafael got away with shortly after. Not Phil Dowd's finest hour.

United understandably appealed Vidic's red card.... and lost! Their chickens are well and truly coming home to roost now aren't they? There's not a snowball's chance in hell that Vidic would have been sent off had Ferguson still been ruling the coop, and even less chance that they'd have then lost an appeal over it. I'm almost starting to feel sorry for Moyes. Almost. It's impossible to feel anything when your sides are splitting with laughter. Mourinho's United arse kissing still knows no bounds though. *"2-0 at half time was hard for them, and only a team like them with their pride and their tradition would fight back. Normally another team would give up."* Fuck. Off. We went in trailing to them and gave them all they could handle in the second half, and only the fact they had Webb helping them out we'd have got something. Hull were 2-0 down at half time on the opening day and came out slugging in the second half and kept it 2-0. West Brom were behind at the break and actually came back to lead before Ramires dived to win a stoppage time pen and scrape a draw for them, and I bet there's other examples too if I could be arsed checking. Mourinho in talking absolute horseshit shocker. He also backed United to make the top four too. Pass me the fucking sick bag. He's defo still hedging his bets there, he'd love that job one day when Abramovich gets bored with his antics again, the fucking sewer rat. He's even selling them Mata to keep them sweet and to try and help make the top four at the expense of us. Same reason he wouldn't let us have Bertrand but then loaned him to Villa just before they played at Anfield. Knob.

Wenger made an interesting point about it being unfair that Chelsea are selling Mata to United knowing that they don't have to face him this season, whereas Chelsea's title rivals do. He's right, it does stink and it is unfair, it's like the Lukaku thing I suppose. Wenger's comments might have carried more weight if they had come from someone other than the fucking sap who sold United the title last season though.

Eto'o and Mongo's post match interview was one of the most excrutiatingly uncomfortable things I've ever seen. For some reason Eto'o decided to answer all the questions in French, completely catching Sky off guard as they - correctly - assumed he could speak English. Mongo acted as a makeshift interpreter, except he doesn't speak French and was reduced to lame gags such as *"He says JT is his best mate"*. Hah fucking hah, you oversized foreheaded goon. If Eto'o needed a translator he should have just asked his fucking gobshite manager. He's no stranger to that role, just ask Barcelona.

Also on Sunday, Spurs had a comfortable win in South Wales over struggling Swansea. They're in free-fall at the moment and I'm starting to wonder if Laudrup is maybe not all he's been cracked up to be, especially as he's even trying to sign David Ngog!!! Honestly, I had to check to see if there was another David Ngog out there because I can't get my head around why anyone would want to buy the one who played for us and who has done fuck all at Championship level for Bolton. Reports claim that Bolton are happy to let him go on the cheap to 'get his 32k a week salary off the books'. David Ngog is on 32k a week????? Fucking hell. Presumably that must have been roughly what we were paying him too as Bolton are hardly likely to be giving him a wage rise. Modern football *shakes head*.

Most people would say that we're having a good season and Spurs are having a bit of a bad time of it, yet here we are both on the same points now. Funny old game eh? Tim Sherwood must fucking love Adebayor right now, he's completely turned Spurs around with his goals. The in-form striker's interview afterwards was pretty funny too, he was asked about the way he kicked off after Dembele didn't pass to him and instead shot wide. *"The most important thing is we won the game. If he did that and we lost the game that would end up in a fight"*. Pretty sure he was being serious too, there was no hint of a smile when he said it.

The final game of this weekly round of fixtures was at the Hawthorns on Monday night where Everton had the chance to leapfrog us and go into the top four. Thankfully they blew it, but it was touch and go there for a while. I couldn't bring myself to watch it, I was still sulking after the Villa game and didn't want to put myself through an Everton victory. Mirallas gave them the lead but thankfully Suarez's buddy Diego Lugano equalised and we're still above them for now. The only thing I've seen from that game was a gif of the shocking dive by Leighton Baines. That was hilarious considering the amount of hand wringing and gnashing of teeth from the Blues after the so-called 'dive' from Suarez against Villa. Strangely quiet after Bilbo's theatrics though. #evertonarentwe

BOURNEMOUTH 0 LIVERPOOL 2

Competition - FA Cup 4th Rd
Date - Sun 25 Jan 2014
Venue - Goldsands Stadium
Scorer(s) – Moses, Sturridge
Star Man – Martin Skrtel

Team: Jones; Kelly (Flanagan),
Skrtel, Toure, Cissokho;
Gerrard, Henderson;
Sturridge, Coutinho (Alberto),
Moses (Sterling); Suarez:

It wasn't always comfortable, but by the end it was fairly routine and that'll do for me. Bournemouth gave it a good go and had their moments but we generally kept them at arm's length and our greater quality in the final third proved decisive.

Bournemouth huffed and puffed but never threatened to blow our house down. They played well up until they reached our penalty area but I don't remember Brad Jones having to make a save of any note. The closest they came to forcing him into one was a shot that Kolo Toure flung himself in front of and deflected over the crossbar. Aside from that, there was the occasional dicey moment from crosses and set-pieces, but defensively we did quite well, especially Skrtel who I thought was excellent.

Still, we were somewhat fortunate to go in at half time with a lead. It was a well taken goal by Moses but we'd been second best for much of the half. It took a while for me to even work out what system we were playing as we looked all over the place at times. Coutinho was definitely playing central, Moses was left, but the right side wasn't as clear cut as it seemed like Sturridge and Suarez both took turns filling that shift and both spent more time than they would have liked chasing back after the Bournemouth left back.

That perfectly illustrates the continuing problem facing Rodgers. He has two world class strikers who play superbly together, but setting up the team to allow them to both play up top is proving to be increasingly difficult, not least because of the injuries to the midfield and full back positions. 4-4-2 is just not a realistic option with the personnel available, 3-4-1-2 wasn't really possible either due to injuries to Sakho and Agger as well as having no natural wing backs to call on, so Rodgers had little option but to go with the system he did, which meant his two star men having to take turns on wing duty. It highlights the need for re-enforcements as we surely cannot sustain a top four challenge with the limited number of bodies we have available. It's all well and good saying we have players to come back from injury, but who's to say others won't be struck down in the meantime?

These games are rarely easy for us for some reason, look at Mansfield and Oldham last year for example. Ok, the first half was disappointing and Rodgers claimed afterwards that we didn't work hard enough. Surely it's understandable? The players have been hearing for weeks about how stretched the squad is, how we only have 15 bodies available and can't really freshen things up because we don't have anyone else to bring in. So, if they go into a game against a Championship side (four days ahead of a Merseyside derby) and aren't at full throttle is that not kind of to be expected? I think the players wanted to just get in, do the job and get through to the next round whilst expending as little energy as possible. And I'd say they did just that.

Bournemouth were denied a clear penalty when Kelly dragged back Francis by his shirt right under the refs nose. It was an obvious foul and should have been a penalty, but there seems to be an unwritten rule that these kind of offences don't get punished anymore. I heard Mark Halsey talking on the radio a couple of weeks back and he was asked about all the high profile incidents involving Skrtel recently. He said he gave a pen in a game last season for a blatant shirt pull that all the pundits agreed was the right call. He was marked down for it by the referees assessor though and told that it wasn't a clear enough foul to award a pen. Given that it was just about as obvious a shirt pull as you'll see, he said it made him think he couldn't give anything like that again, as if that wasn't a clear enough foul then what is? He also made the point that being marked down hits refs in the pocket, so that's why officials won't give pens for holding in the box. So yeah, Kelly blatantly pulled the guy back by the shirt and was fortunate to get away with it, but most officials don't want to give penalties for things like that because they are told not to.

That won't make it any easier for Bournemouth to take, especially as seconds later Suarez released Sturridge to make it 2-0. But for some slack finishing we'd have added a couple more. The finishing often didn't match the approach play but the front two combined extremely well in the second half and I thought Sturridge was brilliant. Everything he did just oozed quality and he's scored in every game since his return; he's even outscoring Luis at the moment. The travelling Kop bestowed a new chant on him, or rather a reworking of an old classic, as the 'Patrik Berger la la la la la la la' is now 'Daniel Sturridge la la la la la la la'. I'm not thrilled about it, that's Paddy's song that is, but Sturridge deserves his own song and if it's to be this one then so be it, it's better than nothing.

We're having a good season to date but there's the very real threat that it could turn to shit in a hurry due to the lack of depth in the squad. None of our top four rivals fielded as strong a side as we did this weekend because they all had players they could bring in to allow some of their regulars to put their feet up. We don't have that luxury, largely due to the poor spending last summer (in addition to NO SPENDING this January *grinds teeth*) that has left Rodgers fighting this battle with one hand tied behind his back. Imagine where we might be if we'd bought the right players last summer? Imagine where we could be if we got the right players this window? I'm trying not to imagine where we may end up because we failed to do so.

LIVERPOOL 4 EVERTON 0

Competition - Premier League
Date - Tue 28 Jan 2014
Venue - Anfield
Scorer(s) – Gerrard, Sturridge (2), Suarez
Star Man – Philippe Coutinho

Team: Mignolet; Flanagan (Kelly), Skrtel, Toure, Cissokho; Gerrard, Henderson; Sterling, Coutinho (Alberto), Sturridge (Moses); Suarez:

There's nothing like a thumping derby win to raise the spirits is there? There had been a bit of a dark cloud looming over Anfield these last couple of weeks between one thing and another, but the Red two thirds of Merseyside are buzzing now after handing Everton their arses in a one sided encounter in front of the Kop.

The win gives us some much needed breathing space in the race for 4th spot, extending our lead over the Blues to four points. It preserves the six point gap between us and the Mancs and perhaps significantly, it saw us claw two points back on Arsenal, who we play in a fortnight. Sign a player or two in the next couple of days and I might just become optimistic again!

Brendan deserves a lot of credit for how he's responded to our injury problems and the lesson he was given by Paul Lambert a couple of weeks ago. Whilst he's well known for being a possession obsessed manager who ideally wants his teams to dominate the ball and pass the opposition to death, he realised that he doesn't have the personnel to play that way right now and adjusted his approach accordingly. What he did against Everton was actually similar in some ways to what Villa did to us. *'Control the spaces and counter attack'* is how he described it. It couldn't have worked any better, Martinez and his players fell right into the trap and whilst Brendan will say it's all about the players, I'd say this win was as much down to him as anything. The dropped points against Southampton and Villa were mostly on him, so it's only right he's given his due for how he masterminded this victory.

Tactically Rodgers played this one perfectly, soaking up pressure and drawing them onto us before…. BANG!! Hitting them with lightning fast counter attacks. It was exhilerating to watch and their defence looked completely shellshocked as our front three stretched them all over the place. The work rate from our players was superb too, closing down space, winning the ball high up the pitch and turning defence into attack.

And how about that Steven Gerrard, eh? Guess he's not quite the liability some have been portraying him as after all. I honestly don't get it, I think he's having a pretty good season overall. He's not carrying the team like he used to, but he's not some kind of weak link or passenger either. It's as though some think he's on his last legs when he quite clearly isn't. The set up has to be right though and him and Lucas go together about as well as David Moyes and silverware, but Gerrard would still get in most if not all Premier League teams. I don't really understand the viewpoint that he can't play as the defensive midfielder either. I made the point in the Villa report that although he had a torrid first half it wasn't any sort of indication as to whether he could play that role or not. He may or may not prove to be the answer in that role and Rodgers might still have to look elsewhere for the solution, but the sample size is too small to make any kind of judgement on it yet and the Villa game was no indication either way as to whether it can work because our tactical approach left him completely isolated and exposed that day.

Against Everton that wasn't the case at all, he had Henderson in alongside him for the entire game and Coutinho was also in there as a third midfielder. We may see Allen back in there again in the coming weeks too, and Gerrard sitting with Henderson and Allen in front (when we are looking to dominate possession), or Gerrard and Hendo sitting with Coutinho in front (when we're playing counter attack such as in this game). All I'm saying is we haven't seen enough of either combination to know yet, and Gerrard has been prematurely written off by a lot of people. I seem to remember the same thing was happening a couple of years ago too and then he went and hit a derby hat-trick to silence his critics. There's nothing like an Anfield derby to get Gerrard firing on all cylinders, he loves it doesn't he?

Unlike the Villa game, Hendo didn't venture forward much and the result of that was we had a solid base in front of the back four from which to win back the ball and spring counter-attacks. It worked like a dream, and as a result Gerrard was fucking brilliant. He was majestic, winning tackles, spraying the ball around to turn defence into attack and hurling himself in front of shots to make some crucial blocks. And of course he scored the all important opening goal. That goal shows the folly of having him taking most of our corners over the past decade. Whilst his set-pieces have been brilliant this year, he's still the best player we have at attacking crosses and in his younger days he scored several headed goals from attacking the front post. Not even Steven Gerrard can get on the end of his own corners though. At least I don't think he can. Not at 33 years of age anyway, maybe a few years back…

The point is, having him attacking corners makes sense and I'd like to see more of it. The beauty of this goal was that Suarez had been getting all kinds of shit from the Blues as he prepared to take the corner. They threw coins at him, they hurled abuse at him, and he just shrugged it off and planted the ball on his skipper's head to give us the lead. There are few things more satisfying than a Gerrard goal against the Blues, especially when it's right in front of their fans. He looked like a maniac as he ran towards Suarez to celebrate. And as if the goal wasn't enough of a boost for us, in the process of Gerrard scoring the Blues also lost their best player to injury after Gareth Barry's gigantic arse landed on Lukaku's ankle and put him out of this game and possibly several others. Haha! I don't remember Xabi ever doing that kind of clumsy shit. Fucking Gareth Barry *shakes head*.

Any hope Everton had of getting back into the game left on that stretcher with Lukaku. With Steven Naismith as their lone striker they just didn't have the firepower to compete with us. The only thing Naismith is the answer to is the question *"who's currently the least skilled attacking player on Merseyside"*. Is he even in the Scotland team? I'm not sure he is, which tells it's own story. If you're Scottish and playing in the Premier League, it takes some doing to not be first choice for Scotland.

The goal had been coming as we'd looked very dangerous early on. The movement up front was very fluid and aside from a blistering drive from Barkley Everton had not threatened at all. That changed at 1-0 and the Blues were enjoying a decent spell of pressure prior to us doubling our lead. Mirallas was inches away from an equaliser when he eluded the attention of Gerrard and fizzed a low shot just past the far post. The Blues were pushing men forward and clearly fancied their chances of an equaliser, but little did they know they were being suckered in.

Every time Everton attacked I felt like we could score from it. As soon as we nicked the ball we'd counter through the lively Coutinho linking the midfield and attack. Clearly it was something we'd worked on as every time we won the ball back Sterling just took off and ran in behind their defence. There were three or four times I saw him do it where he would have been in if we could have got the ball to him first time, but it didn't break kindly for us and his runs often came to nothing. The threat was always there though and the youngster had another fine game. Our front four were tearing the Blues apart, with Suarez and Sturridge taking turns again to play wide, Coutinho pulling the strings in the middle and Sterling running Baines ragged we looked rampant. Dazzling stuff and so exciting to watch.

The second goal was quality. Sterling did well to win the ball on the right and quickly shifted it to Coutinho in space. The Brazilian cleverly delayed his pass and waited for the perfect moment to release Sturridge through on goal and the outcome was never in doubt. Sturridge is usually lethal in those situations and proved it again with a confident finish. Great counter attacking goal that. It got even better for us a couple of minutes later when Toure's ball over the top found Sturridge running clear again. It was a difficult ball to deal with and with Howard right on him there was only one thing for Sturridge to do, and he did it beautifully; controlling the lob to perfection as the ball went high into the air before coming down into the net. Anfield went mental, but Sturridge was Mr Cool. He didn't break out the wriggly arm dance, instead he just stood there eyeballing the blues behind the goal. They'll hate him as much as they hate Gerrard and Suarez at this rate.

At 3-0 and with no Lukaku to worry about, it was now just a case of how many we'd score and also whether we could also register a rare clean sheet. We safely negotiated our way to half time and I found myself wondering what Rodgers would be saying to the players. I hoped it would be *"You can score six here, go out and be ruthless."* Given the way we were playing the opportunity was definitely there for us to do something very special, but we didn't start the second half well. Everton were on the front foot and we had a couple of anxious moments as Sterling twice got caught out defensively in the space of a few seconds. Both errors were down to a lack of concentration, and my worry was that the team may relax and allow Everton to get a foothold in the game again. That worry didn't last long, however, as literally seconds after that double mistake from Sterling, Suarez was streaking away towards the Kop having picked Jagielka's pocket, and all of a sudden it was 4-0. Amazing stuff.

When Suarez robbed Jagielka he was still in his own half and had to outrun two Everton defenders to score. Now Luis is many things, but lightning quick isn't one of them and I didn't think he'd be able to outrun two centre backs in a footrace whilst taking the ball with him. I was wrong, he did it with ease, cleverly running across Jagielka's path so the defender had to be wary of clipping him and got sent off. He just kept going and going until he reached the box and slotted the ball past Howard. He's just incredible and it's a privilege to see him do his thing week in week out for however long it lasts.

There was plenty of time left to increase our lead and we looked like scoring every time we went forward. Everton probably should have just taken the 4-0 at that point and stopped committing men forward, but they didn't. They kept making the same mistakes over and over, and we caught them with yet another counter when Skrtel won it in his own box and then just took off downfield. Suarez collected a pass from him and found Coutinho who played Sterling through with just Howard to beat. He got to the ball first and was brought down by the reckless keeper, and that should have been 5-0 and another goal for Gerrard against the old enemy. It was a great chance to make derby history, as if we got to 5-0 with still over half an hour to go, who knows what kind of tally we could have racked up as their heads were starting to go completely.

I'm not being wise after the event here, as soon as I saw Gerrard hand the ball to Sturridge I didn't like it at all. Had there been five or ten minutes left I'd have been fine with it, but with so long still to play I wasn't on board with that decision at all. Gerrard should have just buried the penalty himself as Sturridge still had more than enough time to complete his hat-trick, and who knows, maybe Stevie would have got one too? I don't blame Sturridge so much for taking - or missing - the pen, and whilst I commend Gerrard for his unselfishness in wanting his team-mate to experience a derby hat-trick, I just felt that because it was a derby it was the wrong thing to do. And so it proved, as we failed to add to the four goals and Everton got off lightly in the end. We had our foot on their throat and we took it off and allowed them to breathe. I'd have preferred us to have just stamped on their windpipe and sent out a message to them and the rest of the league.

What made it even worse was that for some reason Sturridge's head went completely after he missed the pen. He looked like he was going to burst into tears and he took it extremely hard, which is ridiculous when you think about it. We were 4-0 up and he was going to be the hero regardless of missing a penalty, but he was crestfallen and his head wasn't fully in the game after that, as we saw with the horrible botched job he made of his next opportunity. There's no excuse for that really. When Coutinho played him in he should have taken the shot but hesitated and once he did that the chance for HIM to score had gone, but he had Coutinho with him and only needed to roll the ball back to him for a great shooting opportunity. Instead he turned towards goal and tried to score himself, failing miserably. It was a three against two attack and Sturridge turned it into a one against two because of his temporary selfishness. Suarez went completely mental, Coutinho wasn't pleased, neither were the fans and clearly nor was Rodgers, who subbed him almost immediately.

I think a bit much has been of the reaction of Sturridge as he came off, but there was a little bit of a disconnect there between him and Rodgers for a second. It looked to me that after the awkward hand shake between the pair (the striker didn't exactly brush his manager off but he didn't embrace it either), Sturridge instantly thought *"uh-oh, I was a bit of an arse there"* and he immediately turned back towards Rodgers to make sure there wasn't a problem. As for the incident itself, I'd bet that the second Sturridge spurned the pass to Coutinho and turned the other way, he regretted it but it was too late then and he had to go for goal.

He's an emotional lad and does have a bit of a selfish streak that can rear it's ugly head occasionally, but he's mostly been a model citizen since he's been at the club and although he didn't cover himself in glory in the minutes between the penalty miss and his substitution, I knew before I even managed to get on the internet to read about it that he'd have apologised straight away. He'll have meant it too. He's a genuinely nice lad is Sturridge, but his emotions can get the better of him and he does seem to get upset at times when he's missing chances.

Rodgers is great when it comes to dealing with players though and I'm sure he'll be drumming it into him that he needs to not be so hard on himself and it's about the team as a whole, not just him. Sturridge knows that, he says it in pretty much every interview, almost as though he's having to convince himself as he does have to battle that little selfish streak of his. Suarez tearing him a new arsehole will help too, but Luis himself was pulling that kind of shit a couple of years ago and it's something that will hopefully disappear as Sturridge matures. It's a minor quibble for me anyway as Sturridge has been fucking incredible for us. His goals per game record is remarkable, only the fact that Suarez and Aguero are doing even better is stopping people from talking about Sturridge as much as they should.

Finding the best way to accommodate our dynamic duo whilst ensuring the rest of the team does not get exposed is the perennial problem for Rodgers, but perhaps in some of the more difficult games this is the way to go now? Counter attacking football clearly suits us, but it will only work against sides who are willing to come at us and commit men forward. Not every team will play the way Everton did unfortunately. That's a worry for another day though, right now we should be just basking in the glow of a convincing derby win in which all of our players performed well.

There were no weak links, not even the much maligned Cissokho. He did ok; he didn't contribute anything going forward but he didn't need to as this was a performance based largely on the counter attack. His job was to defend and give the ball to those who can actually play, and I thought he did very well. There was one occasion when he overhit a pass to Suarez and Luis completely bollocked him for his shitness. I kinda felt sorry for him as he can't really help it. Overall he was steady, defended well and did about as much as he is capable of doing. I can't ask any more of him than that to be fair, he just needs to hold the fort as best he can until Enrique comes back. It's great having Flanagan back though, with Enrique out he's the best full back we have (and I include Johnson in that based on his form in the last few months). He stepped back in after his injury and looked like he'd never been away.

How good was Coutinho though? Everton couldn't get near him. This was his best display of the season by a mile, many of our counter attacks went through him but even aside from what he did with the ball, his work without it was terrific too. He got his foot in on plenty of occasions, and when he couldn't do that he still made enough of a nuisance of himself to make it difficult for Everton. He was perhaps the pick of an outstanding bunch as the Redmen laid down a marker as Merseyside's top dogs.

It's funny really, a lot of Evertonians had convinced themselves that this was the year they would finally win at Anfield. They actually believe they're better than us and now that they've rid themselves of the 'negative Moyes' (funny how they didn't feel that way until after he left) they'd come here and give us a chasing. No wonder there was hardly a peep out of them, this must have been quite the reality check. I've seen us hammer Everton before, but I've never heard their fans as quiet as they were this time. They were in a state of shock, the delusional fuckers. It's almost as though they forgot for a little while that they're Everton and we're Liverpool. They'd convinced themselves that Martinez was going to bring them here with their sexy new passing style and beat us on our own patch at our own game. Well this is Anfield, knobheads, do you really think you're coming here and out-footballing us in a derby game? Really? Not on Steven Gerrard's watch. Now go get your fucking shinebox.

Premier League Round Up (January 29 - February 3 2014)

It's been quite a week to be a Red. A thumping derby win, points dropped by most of our rivals and Mourinho finally put back in his box by a Premier League manager happy to expose him for what he is rather than wanting to cosy up and be pals with the self proclaimed 'Special One'.

I'll kick things off at St Mary's where Southampton threw in another youth product for the game against Arsenal. 18 year old Sam Gallagher started up front as the Saints were without the injured Lambert and the mental Osvaldo, suspended for two weeks for nutting Jose Fonte in training. Osvaldo's kirkby kiss on the defender seemed to have the desired effect as Fonte opened the scoring with his first goal since August to put the home side in front. Gallagher then missed an absolute sitter as Southampton dominated the first half, but the Gunners came out firing after the break and were level within two minutes as Giroud flicked in from a Sagna cross. Five minutes later Cazorla found the bottom corner from 18 yards to put them ahead. Their lead only lasted a minute though as Rodriguez picked out Lallana to square it up. Flamini was then sent off for a two footed tackle on the impressive Sneiderlin but Arsenal just about held on for a point.

Shock horror! Wenger wasn't happy about the sending off, which is rich coming from a man who is constantly bleating about his players not getting protection from dangerous tackles. Flamini got the ball first but you can't tackle like that and he could easily have hurt the Southampton player. If the roles were reversed, Wenger would have gone apeshit. Imagine if that had been a Stoke player making that tackle on one of his little fancy dan attacking midfielders? Sacre bleu! A draw at St Mary's isn't the worst result in the world but with the run of fixtures coming up for Arsenal they could really have done with maximum points. They've relinquished top top spot to City, and with the games they have on the horizon they may not even be in the top four soon if they aren't careful. I just hope we stick it to them in a couple of weeks with a Suarez hat-trick. We were shite at their place, especially Sturridge, so we owe them one.

Moving on, and Van Persie was back for United as Juan Mata made his debut. The Dutchman scored within six minutes as the Mancs recorded a largely unimpressive 2-

0 victory against bottom of the table Cardiff. The worst part about Van Persie being back isn't the goals he'll inevitably score, it's that we have to listen to that lame White Stripes 'Seven Nation Army' song they have for him. That song was ace when we used it for Mascherano because it fitted perfectly. If you have to put 'oh' in front of a players name to make it fit, then that means that 1) it doesn't fucking work and 2) you're a bunch of unoriginal twats.

United play Stoke at the weekend and they'll probably win that too, as Stoke can't buy a win at the moment. When it happens I can't wait to read about how 'they're back' and how Mata has inspired a revival. Yawn. Let's not forget they won five in a row not so long ago and people were talking them up, but all of those teams were in the bottom eight and in most of those games United looked shite, just as they did against Solskjaer's cellar dwellers. Staying with United for a second though, did you hear that crap about Januzaj and his date with some little wannabe gold digger? Apparently he met her online and arranged to go on a date with her. His mum dropped him off on the corner (ah bless) and this girl then picked him up in her car. It seems she didn't take kindly to being taken to Nando's by a Premier League footballer who's on a reported 75k a week and she was also offended by having to pay for the car park and that he showed up wearing tracky bottoms and trainers.

Now as much as I can't stand the diving little shithouse, I'm gonna have to stick up for him here a bit as the little scrubber went running to the S*n to badmouth him after the date. That tells you all you need to know about her. I read about it on the Metro site and they were quoting a piece from the rag. Metro actually described Nando's as a *'discount chicken joint'*. You fucking what? I've only been in there once, and it was £4.50 for a plate of chips!!! They might be the most expensive chips I've ever had, there was nothing 'discounted' about the place. It's not exactly KFC.

She said: *'I expected him to come to me in a flashy car, but I ended up driving him about in my old blue Fiesta and I was left to pay and display. Then he said he was taking me to Nando's – my face fell. I usually go there for a quick bite to eat with my mates. I didn't expect to be going there on a date with a Man United footballer, especially in my dress and heels.'* Hahahahaha serves you right, you silly cow. Januzaj is an 18 year footballer, and most 18 year old footballers basically live in Nando's, so who the fuck is she to be going to the S*n to slate him for it? As for the car park ticket, maybe he didn't have any loose change on him? Footballers who earn thousands a week tend to not bother carrying slummy around with them. It doesn't make him a mingebag, especially as it seems he paid for the meal. Ungrateful bitch.

Anyway, moving on. . . Fulham lost again as Swansea recorded a much needed victory. Jonjo got their first with the aid of a double deflection having earlier been denied by the crossbar. Chico headed the second and that was also heavily deflected. Not much is going right for Fulham of late, they're in real trouble now, especially with other sides at the bottom like Palace and Sunderland now picking up wins. They've lost Berbatov now as well so they're going to be even less enjoyable to watch. Still, on the bright side they've also managed to get shut of Adel Taarabt, to AC Fucking Milan of all people! I know Milan are having a bad time of it at the moment and aren't the force they were, but this just seems completely mental? It makes Ngog to Swansea look almost above board in fact. Come on, I'm not the only one thinking this has to involve dodgy agents and backhanders surely? *"I feel very happy and I'm so proud to be here"* Taraabt said upon his arrival at the San Siro. A more appropriate response would have been *"No, I haven't got a fucking clue how this happened either, I must have the best agent in the known universe!"* Milan fans are in for a treat watching him, Balotelli and Robinho not passing to eachother. Mad Mario is gonna really hate Taraabt isn't he?

Palace had yet another 1-0 win, this time at home over Hull City. Shane Long may have changed clubs but he's not changed his ways, trying to win penalties by running into defenders and then hurling himself to the floor. Surprised he ended up at Hull though, he's better than that isn't he? Anyway, the Palace revival under Pulis continued as my boy Jason Puncheon lashed in the only goal of the game. No-one's laughing at him now are they? Never doubt J-Punch. Hull keeper McGregor was sent off in stoppage time for a little kick out at O'Keefe after the Palace player had caught him late. Technically the ref was justified in sending him off, but that was about as soft a red card as you can get.

That said, there were a couple in the Norwich-Newcastle game that gave McGregor a run for his money as Remy and Johnson both got their marching orders after a spot of cringeworthy handbags. Both shoved the other in the chest but that wasn't why they saw red, the ref only took action when Remy put his head into Johnson's face and the Norwich player made a five course meal of it. Actually it was more of a three course meal in fairness, he pulled away as though he was about to hurl himself to the floor but thought better of it and stayed on his feet, albeit it staggering about like a punch drunk boxer. Embarrassing. The ref had to send Remy off by the letter of the law, but I think he sent Johnson off just for being a twat and because he felt a bit bad for the Frenchman. The Geordies were without Cabaye who was finalising his move to PSG, but despite that they played well and should have won. Remy hit the woodwork twice and Ben Arfa was robbed of a clear cut penalty when he was blatantly tripped. Awful decision that, but interestingly I heard a stat the other day that penalties are down by more than 50% or something compared to this time last year, it's almost as though refs have been told not give them. Either that or they've all adopted the Howard Webb 'don't give anything' stance in a vain attempt to get to the world cup. 'If you can't beat him join him' type of thing.

Onto Wednesday night now and Spurs got their arses handed to them by City again. At least they only let in five this time. Fucking losers. I can't even begin to explain how much it upsets me that Spurs were level on points with us before these midweek games, as frankly they're not even in the same stratosphere as us this season. Our goal difference is actually better than theirs by thirty!!! Fucking thirty!!! We're miles better than Spurs and we even battered them 5-0 on their own turf, yet somehow only goal difference separated us from them going into the derby game. A goal difference of plus thirty, but still.

City murdered them and could have been 5-0 up inside 20 minutes it was that one sided. Aguero was running riot, he'd scored once and been denied by the post as well as by a fabulous save by Lloris, but then he pulled up with a bad hammy and had to go off to be replaced by Jovetic. I saw a report this week that the Blues were trying to take Jovetic on loan, the bad fucking scruffs. Isn't there a rule against loaning half a fucking team? Aguero's injury probably puts paid to that anyway, but still, I'm pissed off at the sheer nerve of them. How about buying some players, you scrounging cunts.

Spurs will say the game turned on two decisions by the linesman. The first when he disallowed a goal from Dawson just before half time (he got that right but it was probably more down to luck than anything as I doubt that he saw the touch from Adebayor), and the second when he wrongly flagged for a foul by Rose that resulted in a penalty and a red card for the young left back. It's immaterial for me, they were getting hammered by City and would have lost the game regardless of those decisions. Yes they were hard done to by that liner, but boo fucking hoo, join the club. How often this season have City been helped out by dodgy decisions by linesmen? Too often, that's how often. Aside from Toure, Negredo and Aguero, I'd say 'dodgy linesman' has probably been City's most important player this season. Not that they need it most of the time, they're just steamrolling teams now and may not actually lose another game all season at this rate. As for Spurs, they can get to fuck, the player stealing twats.

Elsewhere on Wednesday there was a cracking Midlands derby at Villa Park where the home side edged out West Brom in a seven goal thriller. It was 3-3 at half time and the deciding goal came via a contentious penalty won and converted by Benteke after the break. Lugano was wrestling with him but generally you'll get away with that more often than not. The Uruguayan was livid and then tried to go and win one at the other end immediately after, taking a tumble after Clark had a little grab at his shoulder. He went charging at Clattenburg with those crazy, maniacal eyes of his bulging out of their sockets. Fair play to the official, he's a much braver man than me as if Lugano came running towards me like that I'd give him whatever he wanted. And I mean, WHATEVER he wanted. One crazy looking hombre that.

You know what the worst thing about Benteke being back among the goals is? That lame "Oh Christian Benteke" White Stripes chant. Hang your heads in shame Villa fans, you're as bad as the fucking mancs. Is it just me or is Delph starting to look like a really good player of late? I thought he was excellent at Anfield the other week and this goal was simply brilliant. Worth keeping an eye on him I think, he could be a late bloomer.

It's been another eventful transfer window for Peter Odemwingie. Unlike last year he did get his move this time, but the stigma of embarrassment has stayed with him as signing for Stoke is at least as shameful as what he did last year with the QPR car park fiasco. He made his debut for the Potters in a narrow loss at Sunderland as in-form Adam Johnson got the only goal of the game, tapping in after the once again lively Borini's shot was only parried by Begovic. Nzonzi was sent off for two bookable offences, the second of which was for the faintest of touches on Altidore who hurled himself to the floor. So as well as being utterly hopeless, he's a diver as well. No surprise that he missed the customary one on one chance that he gets every game too, the shit bastard.

Regrettably, you can add Sunderland fans to the 'White Stripes' roll of shame too,

"Oh Vito Mannone" they sang. Getthefuckouttahere! A goodfella like Vito deserves better than a generic shite chant like that. *"Ho! Vito Mannone"* would be acceptable though I guess. Sunderland fans should have some of the kids from the neighbourhood carry his mother's groceries all the way home from the store. You know why? Outta respect. Instead they're breakin' his balls with that shit chant. Wassamatterwityou Mackems?

West Ham holding Chelsea to a draw was an unexpected bonus wasn't it? I was anticipating a typical Chelsea 'do enough to win and bore the shit out of everyone in the process' style performance and result, but the Hammers defended well, rode their luck when they needed to and could have even won but for a horrific miss by Carroll after being well set up by Downing. I'm livid about that, imagine the piss taking opportunities we'd have had there if the big fella hadn't fucked it up?

Chelsea should have won, they certainly had enough chances but the West Ham keeper had one of those nights and they just couldn't beat him. Mourinho took the result in typical spoilt twat fashion, bemoaning West Ham's defensive approach without any sense of irony whatsoever. *"It's very difficult to play a football match where only one team wants to play. It's very difficult."* That's true, just ask Wenger and Moyes who have both had to endure 90 minutes of "Mourinhoball" this season. And who could forget Inter Milan's bus parking at Camp Nou a few years back? What's worse, a West Ham side fighting relegation going to high flying Chelsea and playing defensively, or the Champions of Italy going to the Champions of Spain and playing the same way?

"A football match is about two teams playing and this match was only one team playing and another team not playing. I told Big Sam and I repeat my words: they need points and, because they need points, to come here and play the way they did, is it acceptable? Maybe, yes. I cannot be too critical, because if I was in his position I don't know if I would do the same. Maybe." You're doing it now and you're in a title race, you fucking bad, bad helmet! Who was it who went to Old Trafford and played without a centre forward? You, that's who, you boring, negative fucking shithouse. *"At the same time I told him also this is not Premier League, this is not the best league in the world, this is football from the 19th century. The only (other) thing I could bring was a Black and Decker (tool) to destroy the wall."* That's one option I suppose, another would be to hook Lampard up to a crane and use him as a wrecking ball.

Mourinho's touchline bleating to Fat Sam didn't phase the Hammers boss in the least though. *"He was laughing,"* Mourinho said. *"His objective was won: come here and take a point. It was not to come here and play good football or to try to win or to feel part of the quality of the Premier League. He takes the point. After that he's a happy man and I'm a sad guy."* Have to admit, I find the idea of Fat Sam just laughing at Mourinho as he complained about his defensive style extremely funny, and it makes me hate Allardyce a little bit less. His post match quotes were even better. His first interview was with the BBC and at that point he hadn't heard any of Mourinho's complaints. Still, he knew it was coming…. *"Jose will probably say 'how can they come here and play like that' but we're in a relegation battle. What does he want us to do, come here and be wide open like Manchester United and lose 3-0? I'm not that fool-*

ish". Hahaha love it! Digs at Mourinho and Moyes in the same breath, kudos Big Sam! It got even better when he went into his press conference and was told what Mourinho had said. *"He just can't take it! He just can't take it! I knew he would say that! He can't take it because we've out-tacticed him, out-witted him. He just can't cope. It's brilliant when you get a result against him! I love Chelsea moaning."* Out-tacticed? Hahaha that's fantastic! When asked if he was bothered by the criticism he just laughed and snorted *"I couldn't give a shite!"* As much as I hate that man, you've got to love that quote. Pity Brendan didn't adopt a similar approach the other week.

I'm going to say something now that you probably won't have heard anybody say in the history of ever. *"I wish more managers were like Sam Allardyce".* Why? Because he's just about the only one with the balls to pull Mourinho up on his shite, the rest all seem to want to be his fucking mate, it does my head in so, *gulp* well in Big Sam.

chapter ten

February

WEST BROM 1 LIVERPOOL 1

Competition - Premier League
Date - Mon 2 Feb 2014
Venue - The Hawthorns
Scorer(s) – Daniel Sturridge
Star Man – Raheem Sterling

Team: Mignolet; Flanagan (Kelly), Skrtel, Toure, Cissokho; Gerrard, Henderson, Coutinho (Allen); Sterling, Sturridge, Suarez:

And it was all going so well wasn't it? A thumping derby win followed by the Mancs and Spurs dropping points and a 1-0 lead at half time here at the Hawthorns. Good times. Then, sadly, the second half started. Kolo Toure's howler may have been the key moment that caused two points to be dropped, but that error was symptomatic of a sloppy, casual, tired looking second 45 minutes from the team.

The first half wasn't great either but - defensively at least - it was about as comfortable as you can get. West Brom were woeful in the opening 45 minutes, they offered no threat whatsoever and had we stepped it up at the other end even a little bit and got to 2-0 before the break there's no way the Baggies were capable of getting back into it. At 1-0 though they always had a chance, regardless of how poor they were.

Rodgers unsurprisingly went with the side that had demolished the Blues last week and seemingly went with the same tactics too, with counter attacking the obvious plan. It was a lot more disjointed than it had been in the derby though. Gerrard was incredibly deep, almost operating as a third centre back at times, whilst Coutinho seemed to be a little too far forward which left Henderson in no mans land and unable to get into the game. The plan was presumably to do what we did against Everton, but that's not easy to do when the opposition aren't leaving the huge gaps that the Blues did and when the players don't hit the same heights.

Take Coutinho for instance. He was brilliant in the derby but he was just frustrating against the Baggies. We were caught between two stools I thought. We couldn't play a possession game and dominate the ball because the midfield was set up to counter attack, but we couldn't play on the break that well either due to a lack of execution and a much more streetwise opponent that was happy to just commit a foul any time it looked like we were going to break away. The net result was a dull first half in which

208

we scored from just about the only decent chance either side created. It was a fine goal, the impressive Sterling broke into the box, fed Suarez who delayed and delayed before conjuring what looked like an impossible ball to pick out Sturridge at the back post for a tap in. It was a rare moment of quality that did not fit in with the rest of the game.

Still, we had the lead at the break and with our forward line you always fancy us to do something; we just needed that second goal and the points would surely be in the bag. There didn't appear to be anything to worry about from West Brom who had been completely lacking in any threat up front. But no matter how shite the opposition are a one goal lead is easily wiped out and we needed to come out and kill them off quickly after the break.

Instead we did the opposite. We were flat, complacent and careless, and whilst it's also true that West Brom raised their game, that was always going to be the case and we should have been ready for that. It looked as though we thought we could protect what we had and the second goal would automatically come because.. well y'know... Suarez and Sturridge like. We weren't exactly under the cosh but Albion certainly had more belief about them and we gave them plenty of encouragement by continually giving them free-kicks and corners. I don't care who you're up against, if you give them enough set-plays they're going to get some chances and Mignolet had to make two excellent stops to deny McCauley and Brunt. The save from McCauley was brilliant, absolutely superb reflexes from the Belgian. The one from Brunt was smart handling as that could easily have squirmed out. At least his recent wobbles don't seem to be affecting his confidence.

He had no chance with the goal, although I've heard it argued that he shouldn't have passed the ball to Toure in the first place. I can't go along with that; he's playing the way he's instructed to. If the pass to a defender is on he's supposed to take it. If the defender then fucks up in the kind of catastrophic fashion Toure did, that's not on Mignolet. It's not as though Toure was under any real pressure, and how the hell did he not see Victor Anichebe? We're not talking some little short arse here, and he's as wide as he is tall. It's galling that 'Alehouse Vic' got the goal, the useless Blueshite twat. He'll probably not score again all season but we always seem to do this. If you're a crap striker who never scores goals, a game against us is like Christmas morning. Thinking about it, it's pretty incredible that Torres hasn't scored against us since he left.

Anichebe? Fucking hell Kolo. I can't say I was that shocked though, I'd even sent a text to a mate at half time ripping into Toure saying he was making me nervous. In the first half he caused panic a few times with his tendency to run forward with the ball, carry it into trouble and then give it away. West Brom's ineptitude meant he wasn't punished for it, but not even Anichebe was going to pass up an opportunity like that.

Rodgers eventually reacted by making a double change, bringing on Kelly for Flanagan and Allen for Coutinho. Allen should have been on much sooner as we had no control of the midfield at all. It wasn't so much that West Brom had control of it either, but we needed to start keeping the ball to build a platform for our attacks instead of rushing everything, and Allen is the best player we have at doing that. We improved when he came on, but not enough to make it count.

The game ended in a fairly tame stalemate. Neither side looked like winning it and aside from one effort from Suarez that was brilliantly saved by Foster we never came remotely close to a winning goal. It's incredibly frustrating, not just because we missed out on an opportunity to really put ourselves in pole position for that fourth spot, but we could have gone within a point of third placed Chelsea who have to play Man City on Monday night. I was thinking before this game that catching Chelsea (and maybe Arsenal who we play next week) is a realistic goal for us, but every time I start thinking along those lines we seem to piss down our own leg.

The squad size is definitely an issue, for example we're relying on Sterling and Coutinho to produce the goods every week but they're young lads and that means there'll be some dips in form. Sterling is flying right now but Coutinho has become a bit erratic. It looked like the derby game had signalled a return to his best form but he took a step back again at the Hawthorns.

The biggest problem we have though is this habit of conceding stupid goals due to our own mistakes. There was a stat flying around twitter that we've made more defensive errors leading to goals than anyone else in the league. That includes Fulham who've actually conceded 53 goals to our 29. How is that even possible? And how do we fix it? It's not as though it's just one or two players making the mistakes either, it's scattered around a load of them so what can be done about it? Brendan's head must be done in by it. Take away just three or four of those stupid, costly mistakes and we may even be top. You can't emphasise enough just how much these fuck ups are costing us, whether it's Mignolet flapping at Negredo's weak chip, Agger and Johnson losing people on corners or Toure passing the ball straight to the opposition, all these things have cost us and will continue to do so as there's only so many cracks Sturridge and Suarez can paper over. Sterling was brilliant again though. West Brom's answer to the youngster was to just foul him as much as possible. On a day when most of his team-mates were below par, he stood out like a beacon I thought. Some turnaround isn't it?

As disappointing as this draw was, it's not the end of the world as we're still in a good position and at least we didn't lose. This wasn't good, but it wasn't a "Hull away" type display either. With Arsenal coming to town next week though we could really have done with the three points here as under Rodgers we've not matched up well against the Gunners and that's going to be tough.

Premier League Round Up (January 29 - February 3 2014)

Saturday was shaping up to be a hell of an afternoon for us at one point. United were losing, Everton were losing and Spurs were losing. Then Aston Villa remembered that they are Aston Villa and succumbed to an Everton fightback, whilst Spurs grabbed an equaliser at Hull. Of course we added to our own disappointment at the Hawthorns on Sunday, but the weekend wasn't a total write off as at least Moyesy delivered for us again; we can always rely on him.

I assumed they'd scrape a win at Stoke but they were deservedly beaten on the day. This was Stoke's first win over United in the Premier League era and it was 30 years since they last beat the Mancs in any competition. Good old Davey has been busting records like that all season though. Swansea claimed their first ever win at Old Trafford, Newcastle and West Brom won there for the first time since the 70s and he even managed to lose at home to his old Everton side at the first attempt after having failed to win there in 11 years as the Blues boss. I'm gonna be seriously pissed off if we don't go there and win at least 8-0.

Phil Jones was stretchered off in the first half after smashing his face into the big fat head of Jon Walters. An really ugly clash that; if there's one person's head you wouldn't want to bump into it's that big goon. Poor old Jones' floppy little face just went SPLAT, it was like throwing a turd at a wall. Jones was down for a good five minutes and eventually went off with a concussion. It probably took that long for the physio to realise that the confused, dazed, stupid look on his face was actually a result of the bang on the head and not just the usual confused, dazed, stupid look that he has even when he hasn't just rammed his gurning grid into a human bowling ball.

Stoke drew first blood in fortunate circumstances when Adam's wickedly deflected free-kick left De Gea as powerless as Ian Ayre in a transfer window, but Persie equalised after Mata had seized on a woeful clearance by Marc Wilson to play him in. Wilson would surely make most people's 'Worst Premier League XI' as he's a horrific excuse for a footballer. Speaking of which, what's happened to Andy Wilkinson these days? Did 'Useless' bomb him out or is he injured? Ryan Shotton is back there last I heard, but I don't think he's seen any playing time yet, not even Mark Hughes is that much of a tit. Wilson is only a slight step up from those two deadbeats though.

A screamer from Adam (who was continually abused and called 'Murderer' by United fans courtesy of the one, largely forgettable season he spent at Anfield) put Stoke in front again and after that I thought they looked far more likely to get a third than United did to find an equaliser. No matter how shit the opposition though if you're only one goal up when you get to stoppage time then things are going to get a bit edgy. Rooney hit the post with a free-kick and Cleverley hilariously blasted the rebound over the bar, but aside from that United offered very little.

"I don't know what we have to do to win" Moyes stated afterwards. No shit Sherlock, tell us something we don't know. Of course he didn't mean it like that, the poor deluded twat genuinely thinks they're doing enough to win games and it's just a case of their luck being out. *"I thought we played well"* he repeatedly said. They didn't. I watched the whole game in the pub and they were shite, even with Mata, Rooney and Van Persie on the field together. They had nothing other than the occasional bit of quality from those three. They remind me of us under Hodgson; enough individual talent to still get wins against a lot of teams but no team structure or style and they have no footballing identity.

Not that Moyes sees it that way, obviously. *"We must have got to the byline 8 or 9 times"* he boasted. So that's an indicator of playing well now then? Interesting, maybe we should just bin goal difference off and go with how many times a team reaches the byline? In fact, fuck it, let's scrap goals altogether and decide games on how many times a team gets to the byline, a bit like rugby I guess. United would soon be sweeping the board again if we did that, especially with the likes of Welbeck, Cleverley and Jones spooning the ball over the upright for conversions.

Moyes is rapidly becoming the funniest man on British TV since Del Boy hung up his sheepskin coat. Each post match interview seems funnier than the last, they should start showing them on Paramount instead of Sky Sports. I know why he thinks they played well though, it's because he's still judging things by 'little old Everton' standards. He has no comprehension that he's in the big time now and that expectations are vastly different to what he's been used to. I'll say it again, *"Hey Dorothy, you're not in Kansas anymore."*

Elsewhere on Saturday things went from bad to worse for poor old Newcastle as they got dicked at home once again by Sunderland. It capped a miserable week for them in which they lost their best player and replaced him with... nobody. Still, at least Kinnear fell on his sword. Pity he didn't do it sooner, they may have been able to buy some players. We thought we had a bad window, but spare a thought for the Geordies. They insisted Cabaye wasn't for sale, then they sold him and Cabaye revealed that after the Arsenal move didn't happen last summer he came to an agreement with the club that he could leave in January. So basically they were bullshitting their fans, just like they did when they said they'd sign a replacement.

What makes this so difficult to understand is that they had Joe Kinnear on board, he was hired for his vast array of contacts and ability to spot players and because he can *"pick up the phone to any manager in the world"*. I mean, who could have predicted that he wouldn't have been able to deliver on his extravagant boasts? Well Mike Ashley, possibly Kinnear himself and just about nobody else, as we all knew it was the worst appointment made by a football club in the history of ever. Kinnear was there for two transfer windows and he failed to sign a single player on a permanent deal. His most significant contribution was selling 'Yohan Kebab' for £5m less than Ashley wanted. Hilariously, reports are coming out of Newcastle that he kept losing his phone and when it was found there'd be loads of missed calls from agents, and he also had a habit of running his mouth in bars to Newcastle fans about which players he was going to sign, including Gareth Bale before he went to Madrid for £87m!! It's incredible that something like this can actually happen. When Kinnear was appointed it seemed like there were only two people in the entire country who thought it was a good idea; Mike Ashley and Kinnear himself. It's rare that you get an appointment that's so unanimously objected to, as it's in the nature of many fans to convince themselves it could work and to try and look at things positively. Hell, some of us even gave Hodgson a fair crack of the whip until he showed himself up for the dope that he is, whilst there are still United fans out there who are trying to convince people that Moyes can turn it around. Kinnear though? Everyone knew that was just fucking lunacy, and two failed transfer windows later Ashley eventually cottoned on. First Dennis Wise and now this? For such a successful businessman he's a bit... well what's a nice way of putting this? Thick as pigshit. He'll probably hire Vinny Jones next.

Things are looking up for the Mackems though. A cup final to look forward to, climbing the table fast after being rooted to the bottom a few weeks back, and now they've bummed their biggest rivals again. Our boy Borini played his part once more, converting an early penalty after Bardsley had been brought down. When did Bardsley stop being shite? When Gus Poyet arrived in town it seems as he's been superb recently. Borini's pen was class and he then jumped over the hoardings to celebrate in front of the Sunderland fans. Unfortunately they were up in the top tier so it ended up looking like he was taunting the home fans, who weren't happy about it. Tough shit Newcastle fans, if you're gonna stick the away fans up in the rafters with the pigeons then you've got no grounds for complaint when this kind of thing goes down. Johnson tapped in a second after good work by Colback. The hapless Altidore missed his customary one v one with the keeper but when you've got Fabio Magnifico he can cover for a multitude of sins, even the shitness of Altidore. One minute he's heading one off his own line, the next he's leading a counter attack and laying on the third goal for Colback. The Mackems fucking love Fabio, scoring in consecutive derby wins will do that though.

Cardiff moved off the bottom by coming from behind to beat Norwich. Snodgrass scored inside five minutes but Bellamy scuffed an equaliser and then appeared to give the bird to his own fans. He gave it the 'Shhhhhh' and then followed it up with a few F-bombs, and explained afterwards that it was because the fans had turned on the team and were targeting individual players and he didn't like that. Love that guy, he's fucking ace. A minute later new signing Kenwynne Jones scored a fortunate winner but it needed three stunning saves from Marshall and a goal-line clearance from Bellamy to secure the points. Norwich will wonder how they didn't get something from a game in which they were comfortably the better side. Perhaps they didn't get to the byline enough times? And how come Johnson was playing after being sent off last week but Remy got banned for three games? The fuck's that about then? I assume Norwich successfully appealed his dismissal on the grounds that 'acting the twat' isn't a legitimate reason for a red card. A pity, as if it were we'd never have to see Jonas Olsson on a football field again.

Moving on, and how much do Aston Villa miss Agbonlahor? Against us they looked devastating on the counter attack but at Goodison they could barely get out of their own half. Understandable perhaps when you replace a speedboat like Agbonlahor with a milkfloat like Grant Holt. Villa went ahead through Bacuna after a great tackle by Delph on Barkley had set them away, but after that they just set up camp on the edge of their own box and eventually the Blues wore them down in the final fifteen minutes with goals from Naismith and a Mirallas free-kick. Pretty sure I heard a *"Oh Kevin Mirallas"* White Stripes chant too, the fucking blueshite losers.

Speaking of losers, seriously, how bad are Fulham? They got spanked 3-0 at home by Southampton at the weekend, with Lallana, Lambert and Rodriguez (an absolute corker) the scorers. They then went and got beat in the FA Cup at home by struggling League One side Sheffield United. I still haven't bothered learning their manager's name and that's looking like a good call as it's only a matter of time before he's binned off for Alan Curbishley.

Or perhaps Fulham will go for Michael Laudrup who this week joined the unemployment line after Swansea decided they'd had enough of passing the ball around prettily and losing every week. Remember how everyone was up Laudrup's arse last season, especially when Brendan was having a difficult start to life at Anfield? It reached fever pitch when he led them to a trophy, but he's been found out this year when he started to shape his own team with a load of unknown Spaniards rather than working with the good squad Rodgers left him. Of course losing star man Michu hasn't helped, the goals from the Spaniard last season were the main reason they looked better than they did under Rodgers, but take him away and they've started to fall like a stone. They're actually in a relegation battle now after losing at West Ham, and the suspicion that Laudrup was a bit of a fraud was beginning to creep in. If you ask me, the final straw was probably buying 'the Gog'.

The counter argument to that of course is that Swansea were mid table when he took over, they're midtable when he left and in between they won a trophy and they're still in the Europa League. What were Swansea expecting him to do? It smacks a bit of West Brom sacking Steve Clarke to me, but will Swansea appoint some Spanish fella no-one has heard of to coach the Spanish players they have that no-one has heard of? Pepe Mel would have been a better fit for Swansea than the Baggies.

Carroll and Nolan were back in tandem for the Hammers and the scouser plundered two goals after knock downs from his big geordie buddy. Carroll was unplayable but his day ended on a sour note with a red card for a stray arm that grazed the top of Chico's bun. He milked it for all it was worth, as he tends to do. He's a horrible twat him and he's got previous with West Ham and Allardyce. You've probably all seen that gif of him playacting and Fat Sam laughing in his face, but Chico had the last laugh as Carroll bizarrely lost his appeal and will now miss three games. For the second week in a row I find myself siding with Allardyce. What the hell is happening to me?

Here's the really interesting thing here though. Howard Webb was the referee that decided that it was worth a red card. The same Howard Webb who wouldn't make a fucking decision all season (no penalties, no red cards) until he got the World Cup gig, and now he's sent off two players in the space of two weeks for bugger all. It fucking stinks, how come the press and pundits aren't all over this shit?

Moving on before my blood pressure increases further, and Long grabbed his first goal for new club Hull to give them an early lead against Spurs. Paulinho equalised after the break but Spurs were largely second best and were lucky to escape with a draw..

Arsenal had a routine 2-0 win over Palace on Sunday. Oxlade-Chamberlain was brought into the side to replace the suspended Flamini and scored twice. It does my head in you know, everyone talks about them needing steel in midfield but it just seems like they can play any five of their fancy dan attacking midfielders in there and not lose a step. Have to hand it to them I guess, I just don't like handing anything to them as their fans are just such arrogant gobshites.

Which brings me nicely onto Monday night, and the king of arrogant gobshites. Arab Oil against Russian Oil as it was dubbed by some. The two clubs who've done more than anyone else to ruin football with their blatant disregard for Financial Fair Play. Still, at least one of them has the self awareness to stay quiet about it rather then hurl accusations at the other. No surprise that it was Mourinho shooting his mouth off about City's 'dodgy' financial practices, without any hint of self awareness whatsoever. Care to explain to us Jose, how a club whose average attendance is under 40,000 and has a comparatively minuscule worldwide fanbase can spend around £800m on players over a ten year period and sustain a monthly wage bill that could feed a third world country for a decade? I only ask because none of the journos present when he was spouting his crap bothered to. But then he's 'good copy' isn't he, don't want to upset him by pointing out he's completely full of shit. The knobheads actually gave him some kind of special achievement award a couple of weeks back. Unbelievable.

Give the devil his due though, he knows how to get a result when he needs it. He didn't even park the bus at City either, he didn't need to as City played right into his hands. Pellegrini really isn't all that is he? Most weeks City's superior talent will just steamroller the opposition, but games like this are often won and lost by the managers and Mourinho just did a number on him. That Demichelis is just a yard dog, how has he ended up at City? And more to the point, how has he ended up playing centre mid? And for that matter, how bad must Jack Rodwell be? Ivanovic got the only goal of the game but Eto'o, Matic and Cahill all hit the woodwork. It didn't help City that the erratic Dzeko had one of those games when he looked like a drunken Lee Chapman either.

Mourinho was in gobshite mode all night, bouncing up and down on the touchline waving imaginary cards wanting people sent off. For someone always harping on about the fair play of the English and how foreigners have brought a lot of shithouse ways to the game, I'd have to say that's not very sporting is it, Jose? Snide, hypocritical twat. He dismissed Chelsea's title chances though, on the grounds that... well I'm not really sure. This is what he said: *"Two horses and a little horse that still needs milk and to learn how to jump. A horse that next season can race"* Referring to Chelsea as *"A little horse"*? Yeah, a little horse who two years ago were European Champions and who since then have spent £200m on improving that squad. Do I even need to say it? Probably not, but I will anyway. Fucking helmet.

LIVERPOOL 5 ARSENAL 1

Competition - Premier League
Date - Sat 8 Feb 2014
Venue - Anfield
Scorer(s) – Skrtel (2), Sterling (2), Sturridge
Star Man – Raheem Sterling

Team: Mignolet; Flanagan, Skrtel, Toure, Cissokho; Gerrard (Ibe), Henderson, Coutinho; Suarez (Aspas), Sturridge (Allen), Sterling:

And now you're gonna believe us? Well not quite. It was telling that the Kop never broke into a chorus of *'We're gonna win the win the league'* even though the possibility of it must have crossed everyone's minds after this, even if only for a split second. The thing is, any time we've allowed ourselves to start pondering on 'what if?' this season, we've threw up on ourselves the next game.

If we beat Fulham this week and then see off Swansea at home then maybe we can dare to dream, but right now I think we're all just enjoying this for what it was; a stunning exhibition of high tempo, fast flowing, attacking football the likes of which I personally can't remember seeing for a long, long time, if at all. That opening 20 minutes... wow... that was like nothing I've seen before. Four goals was the very least we deserved from it, it could so easily have been six or seven. It was incredible stuff. I don't usually do a blow by blow minute account type match report, but that opening 19 minutes needs breaking down bit by bit I think....

It all started inside a few seconds with a long throw down the line from Cissokho towards Sturridge. It went over his head, but the ever alert Suarez had already set off from his spot in the centre in anticipation of Mertesacker allowing the ball to run instead of clearing it upfield. The ponderous German had no idea Suarez was there, he turned back towards his own goal and had his pocket picked. He could do nothing other than tug Suarez back by the shoulder to concede a free-kick. The big men went forward and Gerrard whipped in a glorious ball that Skrtel diverted past Szczesny with his knee. A goal up in the first minute of such an important game, but that was just the start.

Arsenal almost hit back straight away when our attack broke down on the edge of their box and they launched a lightning quick counter. It needed a great challenge from Skrtel to prevent Giroud going through after great play by Cazorla. Sturridge then went close after four minutes when he cut in from the right and stung the palms of Szczesny from 18 yards. Three minutes later a minor scare at the Kop end as Mignolet inexplicably decided to punch a routine through ball instead of holding onto it. The ball bounced off Flanagan but luckily Skrtel was on hand to clear the danger.

Seconds later, a great Liverpool move. Hendo to Sturridge, Flanaldo on the overlap, a great first touch to take it in stride but the keeper was on him in a flash to make a save. Relief for Arsenal, but not for long. Gerrard swings in the corner and there's an incredible looping header from Skrtel to make it 2-0. As the ball was met by Skrtel, Colin Pascoe did one of those imaginary flick headers on the bench. Love it! Anfield is completely rocking now and Arsenal are under siege, except Steven Seagal isn't coming to save them. Liverpool's players are swarming all over the Gunners and win possession back immediately from their kick off. Coutinho picks out Suarez on the right, he volleys an exquisite first time layoff into path of Sturridge who is clean through with the keeper bearing down on him. Unusually for Sturridge, he shoots wide. Breathtaking football though.

A let off for Arsenal, but it's only temporary as seconds later they're on the back foot again. Sturridge releases Sterling in behind, he advances into box but his cut back gets a slight nick of Koscielny, taking it off the toe of Suarez who would have had a tap in. From the corner, Gerrard fires it to the edge of the box to Suarez. The ball is a little wayward and Suarez finds himself running away from goal. He controls, it looks like the danger is gone but then he twists his body and unleashes a ferocious shot against the post that took everybody by surprise, including Toure who couldn't convert the rebound when faced with an empty net. Incredible stuff, what a hit. What a player.

With 15 minutes gone the third goal arrives. Henderson harassed the shit out of Ozil on the halfway line, chasing, snapping, harrying the German until he eventually tried a drag back and fell flat on his arse, appealing in vain for a free-kick. I believe Hendo also took the German's lunch money before scurrying away with the ball. With Ozil still on his backside waving his arms around, Hendo was on the charge towards goal. Sterling was in acres of space to his left but the midfielder opted to roll the ball to his right to Suarez. One perfectly weighted ball across the box later and Sterling was tapping in to make it 3-0. If he hadn't got there Sturridge would have, they were lining up at the back post.

This was dreamland now, but incredibly within a couple of minutes we'd scored again. This goal summed up the performance in a nutshell for me. It showed the relentlessness and desire of the team to let nothing stand in their way and to simply crush Arsenal. Sturridge was fouled near the halfway line but Michael Oliver waved play on and Arsenal were on the attack. No problem, if you're not going to call the free-kick we'll just win it back and score anyway. Coutinho nipped in to rob Arteta, carried it forward a few paces to give Sturridge time to make his run, and then delivered perhaps the most inch perfect pass of the season to allow the striker to get between both centre halves and have a clear run on goal. The outcome was never in doubt, he'd missed once he was not going to miss again. This was like last season revisited, with Coutinho threading the needle for the pacy Sturridge.

Sturridge broke out the wriggly arms dance again, which will have just rubbed salt in the Arsenal wounds really. Good. Fuck them. This has been a long time coming. 4-0 with just 19 minutes on the clock. Absolutely incredible. The crowd didn't really know what to do anymore and when things eventually settled down at 4-0 there was a bit of a stunned silence around Anfield as we all just tried to digest what we'd witnessed. Tell you what was funny though, Arsenal fans singing about the lack of atmosphere. Are you fucking kidding me Arsenal fans? We never heard a peep from them for about 35 minutes as even if they had been singing (they hadn't) the noise from our fans was so loud no-one would have heard them anyway. The lull only came when everyone just caught their breath at 4-0 and realised, *"this one's over, let's sit back and just enjoy the show"*.

We'd done our bit by then, just as the team had done theirs. If Arsenal fans want to suck their own dicks by acting like some lower league side on a big day out to Anfield, cheering corner kicks and asking where our famous atmosphere is, have at it boys. After all, their team was made to look like some league two daytrippers so why not get into the spirit of things. Good for you Arsenal fans (those that didn't head for the exits when the fourth goal went in that is), you sang a few songs whilst your team was getting their arse completely handed to them. Well done. *pats on the head in a condescending manner* Now, go get your fucking shinebox. We should put that slogan on the 'This is Anfield' sign above the tunnel actually. *"This is Anfield.... now go get your fucking shinebox"* Seems appropriate for how Brendan has us playing at home these days.

Arsenal went the same way as so many others and it's just a pity we can't play Chelsea and Manchester City any time soon. Barring the very occasional blip we're looking devastating at home and had we beaten Villa we'd have the same home record as City now. We're only six goals worse off than them now too, and the prospect of finishing as the country's leading scorers is definitely a realistic one at this stage. More realistic than the title anyway.

Scoring five past Arsenal seemed unlikely before kick off, but scoring five and

Suarez not getting any of them seemed impossible. Yet that's what happened. Even Sturridge only got one, it was another SaS that did the damage, as Sterling added to Skrtel's first half double by grabbing his second of the game to make it 5-0 early in the second half. At that stage Arsenal must have been wondering just how humiliating it was going to get, and although we didn't add any more to our tally it wasn't for the lack of trying. There was no deliberate easing off, although there was a natural dropping of the intensity in our game as it's physically impossible to do what we did in that opening half an hour for an entire game. Still, at no point did Rodgers 'settle' for what he had and Gerrard revealed afterwards that the manager's half time team talk was not to protect what they had and conserve energy, it was to go out and try to kill Arsenal all over again. I love that attitude, it's just so refreshing.

When it clicks, there's a vibrancy about our play that is unmatched by any of our rivals. Only Man City in full flow can play the kind of devastating attacking football that we've seen from Liverpool this season, the rest can only dream of it, even Arsenal. What we need to do is learn to win the scrappy ones, to get the result on the days when it doesn't click. Newcastle away against ten men, Swansea away with a 2-0 lead, Villa at home, West Brom last weekend... those kind of games. It's still so early in the Rodgers era to be complaining about that though, Rome wasn't built in a day and it's understandable that we're not witnessing a perfect product. We're seeing something pretty special though and Rodgers is clearly on the right track. He's got us playing far better than most of us dreamed we would, and we're demolishing some very good sides by playing simply stunning football.

It's no longer just about Suarez and Sturridge either. Sterling ran Arsenal ragged all day and if he could finish better then he'd be scary. That will come in time I think, but what he's doing at the moment is fantastic. The fifth goal summed him up I thought. Toure did very well to find him with a ball over the top into space. Sterling's run to beat the offside trap was fantastic and his first touch was exquisite, but I had no confidence that he'd finish it. His first effort just looked completely lacking in any composure as he hit it straight at the keeper. Fortunately the rebound fell kindly to him and he tucked that away nicely. He's not a terrible finisher by any means, but - as with Coutinho and Henderson - it's without doubt the area he needs to work on the most as if he can get that right then the sky is the limit. He nearly had a deserved hat-trick a few minutes later after another teasing Gerrard free-kick was flicked on by Sturridge but he just couldn't convert at the far post.

Overall Sterling was phenomenal. His work rate and tracking back is beyond reproach, but he's got a real intelligence when he's back there too, often using his body to win free-kicks and to hold off bigger players. He's been brilliant for the last few months, and his presence has really helped the shape of the team too, regardless of which flank he's asked to play on. He was used on the left against Arsenal to nullify the attacking threat of Sagna, which he most certainly did. The Arsenal full back barely got out of his own half and Sterling ran riot against him. Great to see. The tactical flexibility shown by the front three has given us a real boost of late. Sturridge and Suarez have been sharing duties on the opposite flank to Sterling, but against Arsenal it was Suarez who was used almost exclusively on the right until the substitution of Sturridge midway through the second half.

The genius of Suarez is unrivalled, you can play him anywhere across the front line and he'll wreak absolute havoc. Look at what he did with free-kicks from identical positions in the 2nd half. The first he curled onto the head of Sturridge, only for the striker to misjudge the flight and let it hit him on the shoulder. The second, in exactly the same kind of area, with everyone expecting the same kind of delivery, he pinged towards the top corner and forced a great save from Szczesny. That ball was inch perfectly placed into the top corner from about 35 yards, the accuracy was incredible. Suarez is incredible. He didn't score and you could argue it was one of his quieter games, and yet I still thought he was absolutely fucking brilliant.

Arsenal will take some comfort from 'drawing the second half', and may even say that after that opening 20 minutes it was an even contest. They're kidding themselves if they really believe that though. They had more of the ball because we let them. They did get a consolation goal courtesy of an Arteta penalty (needlessly conceded by Gerrard) and the ex Everton man briefly threatened a second with a free-kick that was superbly saved by Mignolet, but by and large the players did a great job of filling the spaces that Arsenal like to play in, in and around the edge of the box, and there was a real intelligence to their pressing too. It wasn't incessant, energy sapping chasing after the ball, it was measured, intelligent, let's pick our moment to do it kind of pressure. When one went, they all did. Henderson would harry someone, they'd lay it off but there was Sterling in someone's face, he'd try and pick a pass but suddenly there was Coutinho nipping in to steal it. It was like that throughout the game, even in stoppage time at the end Henderson was charging off up the field putting pressure on and winning the ball back near the Arsenal box.

It's a pity we didn't score more than five as our play certainly warranted it. We had several chances to score more but proved to be somewhat wasteful. The most disappointing miss saw Henderson lob wide after some incredible play from Coutinho. That may have been the best moment of the game actually (the Suarez shot notwithstanding), the way the Brazilian won the ball on the edge of his box and then completely skinned three Arsenal players before delivering as good a pass as you'll see anywhere into the path of Hendo. He went for the chip, which was the right choice, but his execution was off and the ball drifted wide. Coutinho's set up play was so spectacular that when Henderson collected the ball he must have been thinking *"Don't fuck this up, that pass from Phil deserves a goal and people will hate me if I don't finish it off!"*. Bet he felt dead guilty afterwards.

We ended the game with Gerrard, Suarez and Sturridge all with their feet up on the bench. It's not often you can do that against a side that was top of the table. It was great to see Ibe get some playing time in a big game too, I felt he should have got on in some of our previous fixtures, particularly Bournemouth when Sterling was brought on instead late on. He's a real talent, and when young players see what the likes of Sterling and Flanagan are doing it gives them an extra spring in their step too.

I look around the team and there were just top performances everywhere. Coutinho's skill on the ball and eye for a pass are no secret, but what about the tigerish tackling and pressing, forcing Arsenal backwards time and again, occasionally even as far as the keeper? He never stopped. In terms of the role he was asked to do, he was close to perfection. If that 2nd half shot had found the corner of the net instead of the arms of the keeper it probably would have been the perfect performance from him. He even got into some verbals with that rat Wilshere too, which was good to see.

Behind him, Gerrard was simply imperious in front of the two centre backs. Being inside the stadium you could get a real feel for the determination, power and sheer bloody mindedness of the captain in this game. It was etched on his face with every challenge he made. He was right up for this one and led by example. I've since watched a recording of the game and I loved the bit when Wilshere followed through on Gerrard just before half time and Michael Owen completely nailed what would happen next. Owen grew up playing with Gerrard of course and he knew exactly what was coming, saying something like. *"He had a little look to see who it was, look out for that in the second half as he'll probably want to give a little bit back to Wilshere"* And sure enough, as Cissokho and Wilshere tussled for the ball Gerrard arrived on the scene and flattened Wilshere with his shoulder. No apology or anything either, just stood there looking non-plussed as Wilshere writhed around on the floor. Have some of that, junior. Stevie fucking Gerrard. Love it. He's making that 'controlling role' his own now and it's great to see. The penalty he gave away was probably borne out of complacency more than anything as he'd won pretty much every challenge he'd made prior to that and must have felt like Superman.

Elsewhere, Skrtel had a great game at both ends of the pitch. Collossal performance from him, although he needs to reign in the knee slide celebration I think as he almost ended up in the Paddock and that could have been nasty. Alongside him, Toure bounced back well from what happened last week, whilst even Cissokho came out of this with a lot of credit too. In fairness, he has been gradually getting better each week and he's quietly become a solid defender. It's gone under the radar a little but he's been ok for a while now. I thought he had his best game for the club at West Brom last week but he definitely topped it in this one. Remember when part of a full back's remit was to 'put the winger in the stands'? Cissokho literally did that, his thunderous challenge on Oxlade-Chamberlain in the first half ended with the young Arsenal man in the front row of the Kop. He no longer looks completely overawed by 'the weight of the shirt' and one of my favourite moments in the game was him getting in the face of Wilshere after he'd fouled Sterling. That tells me he's feeling more of a part of things and good on him for how he's settled down after his woeful early season form. My mum's a really big fan of his, *"Awwww I like him.... oh I really want him to do well... he tries so hard that lad.... look at his little face you can see how hard he's trying..."*. She really loves Enrique too though, maybe it's a left back thing? I must ask her what she thought of Konchesky...

On the other flank, Flanagan was quality again. He was unlucky not to score in the first half but after that he didn't get forward much, he didn't need to as we were 4-0 up in no time of course. He was solid defensively and his use of the ball is excellent. There were a couple of passes he picked out after Arsenal had cleared corners in the second half that were just stunning. He continues to cement his place in the side and although Johnson is now back in training, there's no way he's ousting Flanagan from the side, is there?

Henderson was absolutely phenomenal too, he was everywhere and the quality he shows on the ball is often overlooked. All the hype is about Wilshere, but Henderson completely overshadowed him in every facet of the game and whatsmore, he did it without acting like a twat, something the snidey Wilshere is completely incapable of.

When we play like this no-one can live with us, and whilst it's unrealistic to expect us to be able to play this well every week, it should not be too much to ask for us to not suffer the kind of letdown we did at the Hawthorns following the Everton game. We have a real opportunity to do something special this season, just how special remains to be seen. 4th spot is still the goal, but if we can win our next couple of games and hopefully increase the gap on those behind us, we can then start to target those in the places above us. To do that we need to learn to win ugly, as it looks like we've mastered the art of winning spectacularly. Just ask Arsenal, Everton and Spurs.

Premier League Round Up (8-12 February 2014)

I'm bored rigid now with all these horse puns about Chelsea after that arsehat's quote last week. If Chelsea are a horse, then why the fuck can't they be Shergar? I'm sick to death of Mourinho already and he hasn't even been back on these shores for a full season yet.

Chelsea have been a one man team for months now, Hazard has been carrying them as the rest of their attackers seem to be stifled by Jose's anti-football and the Belgian bailed them out again with a hat-trick against Newcastle this weekend. The Geordies started the game well but Hazard swept the Rent Boys in front after 17 minutes. Sissoko should have equalised but his elephant like first touch allowed Cech to save and Hazard immediately made them pay with a stunning goal on the counter attack. Much as I hate Chelsea, that was a fantastic goal. And guess what happened then? Howard Webb finally gave a penalty. I called that one, although admittedly I was a week late. It wasn't even a clear pen either and there's no way he was giving that decision a few weeks ago. Webb seems to have a little thing for Eto'o though doesn't he? Something to keep an eye on there. So to recap for those who haven't been paying attention these last few weeks, Webb gave no red cards and no penalties in 16 games prior to getting the World Cup gig. He gets that, and in the next four games there's two soft red cards and an iffy penalty. Hmmm.

Elsewhere, City followed up their loss at home to Chelsea with a goalless draw at Norwich. They were fortunate to get away with a point really and in the last few minutes they got pummelled by Norwich. I'll say it again; Demichelis is crap. Pony tailed footballers in general seem to be shite. Is Baggio the exception that proves the rule? There must be others, but I can't think of any (don't bother suggesting that Zlatan jabroni, you're wasting your breath on me). Yaya Toure was investigated by the FA over a kick at Wolf Van Winkel that was missed by the ref. Not surprising the ref missed it, there was barely anything in it. Still, Toure was stupid for doing it and other players wouldn't have been so lucky as the FA let him off. As soon as he heard about the incident Mourinho immediately demanded Toure was banned, the fucking grass. What's it got to do with him anyway? He says Chelsea aren't in the title race, so why's he crying about wanting Man City's best player to be banned for a nothing little half kick? Helmet.

He's been trying to lure Pellegrini into a war of words for weeks too, and eventually the City boss fell for it, responding to questions about the 'little horse' nonsense by pointing to the money Chelsea have spent. Seriously fella, it's not worth it as you're just allowing him to continue with his bullshit. And of course he did... *"I think he's a fantastic coach, and I respect that a lot, and on top of that, outside his football career, he's an engineer by academic qualifications. So I don't think an engineer needs a calculator to add the £37million we got for Juan Mata and the £18m for Kevin De Bruyne. That's £55m. Nemanja Matic cost £21m and Mohamed Salah £11m. That's £32m and £55m minus £32m is £23m. So Chelsea, in this transfer window, generated £23m. It's easy to understand that this is working with Financial Fair Play, with ''fair'' Financial Fair Play. There are no arguments against that. This is what we're doing. Others aren't doing the same."*

One fucking window!!!! Chelsea follow the rules for one window and he's running his mouth about how they're complying with FFP!! If they were following the rules properly they'd have less spending power than Newcastle!! *"We are building a team for the next decade, if possible. They have a team to win now because they don't have a team for 10 years. They have a team for now, for the next three or four. So they have experience, potential, power and are not worried about FFP because, in the summer, they just spend."* Ok, he's kind of right about City, but still, fuck him and the 'little horse' he rode in on.

Anyway, moving on, and the South Wales derby went the way of the home side as Swansea ran out 3-0 winners. They have appointed Steve the Pirate from Dodgeball to replace Laudrup and this was obviously a dream start for him. I don't know what's going on behind the scenes there but it all seems a bit mental. And what the hell is Marvin Emnes doing playing for Swansea? Did Laudrup buy him? He must have I guess. So he bought Emnes and Ngog in one window? No wonder he was sacked. Fucking hell. The scoreline flattered Swansea a little but Cardiff are looking really shite now and it's difficult seeing them getting out of this. Good. Tan and Solskjaer can fuck right off.

Later in the week Bellamy was charged by the FA after an off the ball swipe at De Guzman. He did leave a little bit on the Swansea man with his arm, but considering Toure escaped punishment Bellamy can feel a little bit aggrieved. Actually I think Bellers was born feeling a little aggrieved and has remained that way ever since, except for the times when 'a little aggrieved' morphs into being 'seriously fucking pissed off' and the nine iron comes out. I love Bellamy though.

Palace won again, seeing off West Brom comfortably at Selhurst. Tom Ince scored on his debut and then set up the second from a corner for another debutant, Joe Ledley. The Baggies pulled one back through a debutant of their own, some cat called Thievy who I'd never heard of before and who has a simply horrific haircut. Chris

Foy's awful decision to award Chamakh a penalty killed West Brom off, the Moroccan picking himself up to calmly stroke home the spot kick. He's a lot less shit these days isn't he? His hair continues to alarm, disturb and offend me in equal measures though. Never seen anything like it, at least not on anyone who hasn't just had some kind of radiation therapy or suffers from alopecia. It actually dawned on me when watching this game that Chamakh could be Cristiano Ronaldo's ugly twin. Or the Shelbyville Ronaldo if you like.

Hang on, Andriy Voronin!!! I knew there must have been another top player with a pony tail, how could I have overlooked 'the Wolf'? Shame on me.

Villa lost at home to West Ham. Their record at Villa Park is absolutely disgusting, I'd feel sorry for their long suffering fans if they weren't such bad knobheads. Villa are the kind of fans who come to Anfield and sing the same shit as every other set of fans, except they think they're the first ones to do it and you can see them laughing and congratulating themselves on their wit and originality. Knobs. Where the hell was Andy Carroll? Suspended they said, but I thought West Ham were fighting that in the courts? Must have shit out in the end. Shame, I was really looking forward to seeing the FA dragged through the courts. Nolan's clever flick put West Ham in front after Downing had turned Bertrand inside out to set him up. A couple of minutes later Delph lost the ball on the edge of his own box and Nolan made it 2-0. Guess I jinxed Delph last week when I said he was worth keeping an eye on. Albrighton hit the post with a screamer and then Benteke hit the bar after a brilliant run and cross from Albrighton. He was ace about three years ago and then he just seemed to vanish. He's got the brummiest looking face I've ever seen that lad. Apart from Agbonlahor, obviously.

Southampton drew 2-2 with Stoke at St Mary's. Lambert's brilliant free-kick from a difficult angle put the Saints ahead, Odemwingie equalised with his first goal for Stoke, Steven Davis fluked one to restore Southampton's lead (his cross caught on the wind and deceived Begovic) but Crouch quickly made it 2-2. All the goals were in the first half and then pretty much nothing happened after that.

Sunderland lost at home to Hull as 'Wes Red' struck again, getting sent off for the 15th time this season (haven't checked that but it'll be close enough) after scything down Long as he went clean through. Poyet responded to that by subbing Borini, which is a little odd considering his comments this week about how our on loan Italian would *get into any starting eleven*. Whilst you clearly need to make a tactical switch when one of your centre backs is sent off after a couple of minutes, taking off Borini and leaving on Dozy Altidore???? Really Gus?

Hull dominated the game after that and the front two of Long and Jelavic both got on the scoresheet. Long was brilliant, and you have to wonder what West Brom were thinking? The Baggies aren't exactly well off for strikers, but selling their best one to a side who they are in a relegation scrap with? That's up there with subbing Borini and leaving Altidore on that is. Steve Bruce didn't celebrate the goals, he kept a low profile and showed a lot of class against his former club. Thing is, he got so much abuse from the fans when he was there (*"you're just a fat geordie bastard"*) he could have been forgiven for giving it the Mourinho knee slide down the touchline, or the

Di Canio fist pump in the centre circle, but he didn't. He's one of the good guys is beach ball head.

Onto Sunday and the latest fun filled episode at the Comedy Store, formerly known as Old Trafford. Where do I start? 81 crosses is as good a place as any I suppose. It's been fairly obvious for most of the season what Moyes' tactical masterplan is. It amounts to little more than get the ball wide and cross it into the box. Nothing new, as he correctly said afterwards when quizzed about it, *"crossing the ball is in United's DNA"*. So was winning, but you soon put a stop to that. He's right though, crossing was a staple tactic under Ferguson; get it wide, whip it in and flood the box. However, it wasn't the ONLY tactic they used, they mixed it up a bit and could come at you from anywhere. They'd counter attack, they'd score from set-pieces, they'd play their way through the middle, and if all that failed they'd play the 'dodgy penalty' card. Now? All they do is fucking cross the ball, it's hilarious. That big beanpole kid from Fulham who has replaced Hangeland in the side said he hasn't had to head the ball so much since he played in the conference. A damning inditement of Moyesball if ever there was one.

He spent £37m on Juan Mata - one of the great 'number tens' in world football - and he's playing him on the wing in a 442. Genius. United signing Mata is like me buying my arl fella an iphone. He'd use it to make calls but all of it's other uses would be completely wasted on him, he simply wouldn't have a clue how to make any of the fancy apps work but it wouldn't matter as he's a man with simple needs and extremely limited techy skills. He needs a phone to make calls, nothing else, so why spend £400 on getting him one when a £10 Nokia brick will meet his requirements? United spent £37m on Mata when they could have got Jermaine Pennant for next to nothing? Still, with all these crosses coming in at least when that big dope Fellaini comes back he might actually be of some use to them now.

I have to admit though, as much as it was hilarious seeing this unfold, United weren't actually THAT bad and if they replayed this game another 100 times with both teams using the same tactics I reckon United would win all of them. It was a freak result, but that doesn't make it any less funny obviously. There was one stage in the first half when the possession stats came up and Fulham had just 2% possession in United's final third. I don't think I've ever seen that before, and yet they were 1-0 up (nice goal by Sidwell) and had also wasted the best chance of the half when Richardson blasted over. Ex-United man in shitting the bed against old club shocker.

Somehow, Fulham held on to their lead until a little over ten minutes to go when the equaliser finally came through Van Persie and a minute later they were behind courtesy of Carrick's deflected shot. Ah well, nice whilst it lasted I guess... The reaction of Moyes to going 2-1 up was side splittingly funny. Seeing his happy little face just made what was to follow even more special. Mancini didn't even react like that when Aguero won City the title with the last kick of the season. Rooney was giving it the beans too, dropping to his knees and fist pumping his arse off on the penalty spot. Worth pointing out I think that this was the defending league champions taking the lead at home to the league's bottom club. How the mighty have fallen eh? How far will they fall though, that's the question? It's difficult to imagine it getting much worse than when Darren Bent headed that stoppage time equaliser. That's about as big a kick in the balls as you can get. This kind of thing simply doesn't happen to Man United, at least it didn't until Moyes arrived. I keep asking the question, just how funny is this going to get until a halt is eventually put to it? I think there's still some mileage left in this yet, but we'll see.

Elsewhere on Sunday 5th met 6th as the Blues went to White Hart Lane. Spurs were shite and were incredibly lucky to win. The Blues got screwed by Clattenberg late on when Coleman was clearly fouled inside the box but the ref waved play on. Poor decision that. Adebayor has given Spurs a huge shot in the arm with his goals though, the sooner he reverts back to 'not arsed' mode the better. His winner in this game was class.

Wasn't a great week for Everton as Lukaku said he's ready to return to Chelsea, and to make matters worse for Martinez, Arsenal are rumoured to fancy Gareth Barry. I'd shit a lung if that happened, let's see how they'd cope without them next season. Then again, they'll probably just scrounge a few more squad players from the financial doping twats at the Etihad and Stamford Bridge. *"Let's buy a shitload of players to stop others getting them, and then loan them out to someone who doesn't pose a threat, like Everton or West Brom and hope they can take points off our rivals".* (yes, it's not just Brendan Rodgers that can completely overlook Victor Moses)

In other transfer rumours Van Persie was linked with Arsenal again this week. Wenger refused to comment on it, adding further fuel to the fire. If there's anything in that at all then what a glory hunting twat Van Persie is! Mind you, at least back at Arsenal he wouldn't have to worry about Rooney not passing to him. Remember when Jocky was arguing with Robbie Savage about who the best strike partnership was, as Jocky said it was the Manc pair? Hahaha! The only time those two egotistical knobs pass to eachother is when they're restarting after United have conceded.

Staying with Arsenal, and Giroud went public to say that Spurs' keeper Hugo Lloris wants to join the Gunners. *"We talk about life and sometimes the French team a bit and our wish to have a great experience together at the World Cup. Have I asked him (Lloris) to join Arsenal? Yes, I have with 'Lolo' (Laurent Koscielny). He would have liked to, he would quite like to. You will have to ask him the question."* Talk about dropping your mate in it. Assuming Giroud is not lying, he's put Lloris in a bit of a spot there with the Spurs fans. And I bet Szczesny is just thrilled at two of his team-mates tapping up his replacement, he'll be especially happy to know that 'Lolo' (fucking hell, wonder what Mertesacker's nickname is? PeePee?) wants him replaced. Great to see that kind of loyalty from your team-mates. Arsenal players always seem to be dicks though don't they?

In yet more transfer news Ravel Morrison signed for QPR on loan. Hang on, I thought he was the next big thing who would be going to the World Cup? You mean he's actually not really that good, and certainly not worth indulging considering he's such a massive twat? Who'd have thunk it eh? Oh yeah, ME, that's who. Something iffy has clearly gone down there though. There were rumours that he went on strike after West Ham turned down a bid from Fulham in the January window. Fat Sam was asked why he wasn't playing, and basically accused Morrison of downing tools and using injury as an excuse. *"Listening to our medical staff, there is no problem that he can carry on – not at all. He says he feels it occasionally. Instead of gritting your teeth and getting on with it, he's not the type. Lots of players throughout the country will be playing with a similar type of injury that the medical team say you can carry on, it's not a problem".* Yep, that screams out *"saw his arse because we didn't let him leave".*

Allardyce also said: *"Some come, rise to the occasion and don't realise how far they have risen then, all of a sudden, when they start realising where they have gone, that can be a bit of a problem."* Yep, that screams out *"Ravel is a big time charlie who thinks he's the dogs bollocks after scoring one good goal against Spurs".* When pressed further, Fat Sam flipped his lid. *"Stop talking about Ravel. He's not fit. He's not here. He's not in the squad so shut up talking about it."* A few days later 'Ravel' joined QPR and when 'Arry was asked if he'd go straight in the side? *"Yeah he's fit so he'll play".* Says it all. Who the hell would go on strike because they were denied a move to Fulham though? West Ham might not be Real Madrid, but Fulham is a definite step down, surely?

Speaking of Fulham, they sacked their manager again this week. Just as I finally learned the bum's name too. I knew I shouldn't have bothered. That's one fucked up club that is though, they're defo going down. Bunch of clowns.

Getting back to on the field matters, and the midweek fixtures were hit by the weather and there were a few postponements. Thankfully Chelsea's game at the Hawthorns went ahead though, as our mate Victor Anichebe shocked Mourinho's men with a late equaliser after someone other than Hazard (Ivanovic) had scored. Always liked Alehouse Vic me.

Elsewhere, Stoke drew with Swansea. Crouch got on the scoresheet again but Chico equalised. Crouch thought he should have had a pen when one of his trademark 'mazy ones' was halted by a sneaky little trip from behind. A clear foul, except it was soft arse Odemwingie who tripped his own team-mate.

Hull lost at home to Southampton as Jose Fonte hit the only goal of the game. Cardiff and Villa played out a goalless draw at…. actually what is Cardiff's ground called? * checks wiki * Cardiff City Stadium. A lot of thought obviously went into that one. How long before Vincent Tan decides to call it the *"The Malky Mackay can suck my balls Arena"*?

West Ham beat Norwich thanks to late goals by James Collins and Mo Diame while Spurs absolutely demolished Newcastle 4-0 at St James Park. Pardew said afterwards his players had not put in an honest performance. They're prone to that aren't they? When they're good they're a match for anyone, but when they're not at it they're a joke. The Geordies have drawn a blank in seven of their last eight games now. Incredible lack of punch there, they're the Audley Harrison of the Premier League.

As the week drew to a close, big mouth Mourinho ensured that most of the weekend's headlines would be about him. Again. Having been unable to get any further rise out of Pellegrini, he went back to the tried and trusted tactic of abusing his old foe Wenger. To be fair, Wenger brought it on himself a little due to his complete inability to say to the press *"I've got nothing to say about that"*. He's such an old woman isn't he? He's got an opinion on everything and he just can't help but tell the world about it. They could literally ask him anything, and he'd give them an answer instead of a 'no comment'. *"Hey Arsene, what do you make of what's been happenin' darn the Queen Vic then me awld China?"*... *"Well I fink dat Peggy Mitchell is doing a good job but dat her sons are not really 'elping much."* Ok, so it's about 15 years since I saw an episode of Eastenders, but come on, who watches that shit these days? It's the David Platt of soaps, it was shit even when it was good.

Anyway, Wenger was asked why Liverpool and Chelsea were reluctant to admit they were in the title race. Instead of saying *"No idea, why don't you ask Brendan and Jose?"* he took the bait and said *"Fear of failure. You cannot lose a race dat you are not in"*. And that was all it took, word travelled quickly across London to the Chelsea press conference, soft shite got wind of it and immediately went on the offensive *"He's a failure specialist. Eight years of failure. If zat is true what he says, zat I fear to fail, it is because I do not fail many times"*. *sigh* And just like that, the weekend's headlines were written, the talking point on sports radio was set in stone and we'll no doubt now have a week or two of daft puns about failure.

Whilst it's fun to mock Arsenal and Wenger for their lack of trophies, Mourinho has got a fucking cheek. How many trophies would he have won in that time with the same lack of spending power that Wenger has had? What Mourinho did at Porto was a long, long time ago, and ever since he's made sure that wherever he's gone the deck has been stacked well and truly in his favour. You just know he's the type of shithouse who'd go into the editor on Footy Manager before starting a game.

All this 'mind games' bollocks and managers throwing barbed comments at eachother, it's boring now. And pointless. I'd love to see Wenger just lay Mourinho spark out when Arsenal next play Chelsea. Wenger defo sees himself as a bit of a badass, I still remember him fronting Big Martin Jol, that was ace. Imagine if he just walked up to Jose and planted one square on his jaw, and then went all 'Goodfellas' on him as he lay on the floor. *"You fuckin' mutt"* and then said to the groundsman *"I'm sorry, I got blood on your pitch."* If he did that, I'd probably be willing to give up the title and let Arsenal win it this season. Probably.

They'll need to get their shit together for that to happen though, I mean they couldn't even beat the Mancs this week. United probably should have won it, and Moyesy - bless him - was delighted with the result and performance. The fact it's the kind of result United would generally have been a bit disappointed with in the past was completely lost on him, the poor deluded fuckwit. Hilarity had ensued in his pre-match press conference when he was asked about United being 21 points worse off than they were this time last season. *"I'm not 21 points off, I was at Everton last season"* he replied. Hahahaha he's great isn't he? He just doesn't get it. For the record, he's actually on the same points he was on at Everton this time last season, so go ed Davey son, don't let the bastards get you down.

Had to laugh at this from him though: *"They've all got medals and when you've won you want to win more. When you've won you want to win more so I think they're all still hungry and determined to be successful."* Erm, how the fuck would you know, you've never won anything. Ever.

FULHAM 2 LIVERPOOL 3

Competition - Premier League
Date - Wed 12 Feb 2014
Venue - Craven Cottage
Scorer(s) – Sturridge, Coutinho, Gerrard (pen)
Star Man – Steven Gerrard

Team: Mignolet; Flanagan, Skrtel, Toure, Cissokho; Gerrard, Henderson, Coutinho (Agger); Sterling (Teixera), Sturridge, Suarez:

So come on then, who's thinking we're gonna win this damn thing now? I know it's overstating things, but honestly, when Gerrard was shaping to take that penalty I was genuinely thinking that our title chances were on the line. If he'd missed, it would have been a huge setback, one from which we probably wouldn't have recovered from. All that would have been left is the fight for fourth and - hopefully - an FA Cup run.

He didn't miss though, he buried it, the massive fucking hero. It doesn't mean we're winning the league but we're closer to it than we were before the game. We're chipping away at the gap between ourselves and the three teams above us and we've got momentum on our side now. Perhaps most significantly, I got the impression that the players are starting to believe they can do it. Some of them have probably felt that way all season, Suarez for example said months ago that we could win it, others have perhaps been slower to come around to that way of thinking but you could see the longer this game went on that there was an urgency to force a winning goal that hasn't always been there in some of our other close away games.

The players were absolutely desperate to win this game and I don't believe the fight for fourth spot was uppermost in their thoughts as they poured forward trying to find a winner. That they needed to show such desperation to win a game which they had dominated shows the biggest weakness we have, and the flaw that is most likely to undermine any run at the title. Basically, we hand goals to the opposition. Teams don't have to do much to score against us.

Fulham's two goals were pitiful from our point of view. The first was a personal nightmare for under fire Kolo Toure. Richardson got in behind our defence far too easily but his cross was little more than a bloody pea roller. Toure pointed to the pitch after haplessly slicing the ball past Mignolet, but there was no bobble and the pitch was not to blame. He put that in his own net because he was falling on his arse before the ball even got to him and was completely off balance when he tried to clear. Sorry Kolo, your fault, just like at West Brom. I feel bad for the guy though, sometimes shit happens when you're a defender but unfortunately for him, his mistakes have come in consecutive away games and have cost us two goals. He actually played well after that, but who's going to care about that really? The mistake is all anyone's going to remember. The only saving grace was it came eight minutes into the game rather than with eight minutes left. I wasn't even particularly worried about it as I just figured we'd have enough to come back, and going behind might make us play with more of a sense of urgency.

The problem was that Fulham were defending very deep and getting lots of men behind the ball, and for some reason we decided the way to break that down was to try intricate through balls all the time. It was as though we decided to just do the exact opposite to what the Mancs did at the weekend. They peppered Fulham with crosses, we tried to go through the middle with through balls. Neither worked particularly well, but sometimes it's incredibly difficult breaking down a packed defence, especially one that was so deep. Fulham were clever in how they did it, usually when the likes of Sterling and Sturridge are trying to make runs in behind, defenders will hold their line or even push up for off-side. What Fulham did was to just drop off towards their own goal any time we tried to run through them, there was just no space in behind them and it was extremely frustrating to watch attack after attack come to nothing.

Ironically, our equaliser came from the exact kind of pass Coutinho had been unsuc-cessfully attempting all through the first half. The reason it worked this time was because Fulham had been on the attack and suddenly lost the ball on halfway. Gerrard was onto it in a flash and before Fulham's defenders could drop off towards their own goal he fired a gorgeous ball in behind them with the outside of his boot into the path of Sturridge and suddenly we were level going in at half time.

Having recovered from the self inflicted wound we would surely apply enough pres-sure to Fulham in the second half to get the win? It was certainly looking that way when the second period got under way; we were camped in the Fulham half and they weren't even attempting to counter attack, they were just sat back trying to keep us out. We looked more dangerous than we had in the first half and Fulham looked to be feeling the pace a little. Then we went and shot ourselves in the foot yet again. Skrtel is being blamed by most for the goal and it's true that he should have dealt with it better than he did. I'd argue that he shouldn't have been having to deal with it all. Mignolet simply has to come and claim that ball but he was rooted to his line all night and didn't want any part of it. Skrtel then had to try and clear it and he made a pigs arse of it, presenting the odious Richardson with a tap in. I can't stand Richardson, even going back to his days in United's Academy he was a horrible, mouthy twat. He'd always end up involved in a war of words with the families of our youth team lads, he was a proper gobshite. I used to stand with the dads of a few of the lads, and I got on especially well with Dave Raven's arl fella. "Big Ravo" I used to call him, he was a great fella, drove a flashy car, wore a brown leather jacket and looked like a bit of a gangster (he wasn't, in case you're won-dering). Anyway, Richardson is acting the dick as usual, and he gets a bit of heckling from some of us on the touchline. He looks at Raven's arl fella and tells him to fuck off. Cool as you like, Big Ravo stares him down and says *"I'll let you have that, but you only get one of those."* He was like a scouse Tony Soprano, it was fucking ace.

Anyway, when Richardson scored it took me back to those days at the Academy, and it pissed me off. Of all the Fulham players it had to be that little skidmark that scored. Mignolet really needs to start being more assertive, there was an incident just before half time that was even worse, when the ball bounced in the six yard box and he left Skrtel to try and deal with it from a standing jump against Bent. It came to nothing, but it was risky an unnecessary. It's as though he's got it into his head that he's not going to come for anything now after he flapped at that one against Villa.

That Richardson goal was just a massive kick in the balls and at that point I was thinking a draw was the best we'd do. It was one of those nights, chances were not going in and Suarez had hit the post and saw another shot flash just wide. Then our luck changed, Coutinho cut across the box and hit a shot with his left foot that took at least one deflection on it's way past Steckelenberg. The keeper's night got even worse soon after when he bravely dived at the feet of Suarez and got a kick in the face for his troubles. No blame can be attatched to Suarez for it but I couldn't help thinking if this incident had happened a year ago what would the referee have done? Actually speaking of the ref, how could I have forgotten what happened in the first half when Toure just ran him over like a runaway freight train. Kolo never even stopped to see if Dowd was ok, he just flattened him and carried on running. Dead funny it was, but I'd have laughed even more had he not long just put through his own fucking net.

Having drew level the winning goal just didn't look like it would come and it was so frustrating seeing the points slipping away from us. Brendan made a bold change, taking off the well shackled Sterling and sending on Joao Carlos Teixera for his debut. Moses and Aspas were probably sat on the bench wondering what the hell the point t is of them being here. Join the club boys, many of us have been wondering that exact same thing too. I love that about Brendan though; he's not scared to throw a youngster in if he feels he can bring something to the game and it doesn't matter if it's a high pressure situation either. Brad Smith at Chelsea, now Teixera in this one. Ideally you'd want to send him on with a nice lead and no pressure, such as with Ibe against Arsenal last weekend, but this was a difficult situation for Teixera to come into and he did well. If his shooting had been better he may have even had a couple of goals but he looked confident and assured and he definitely brought something to our play. It was from his pass that Sturridge accelerated away from Riethe and won the penalty. Awful play from the full back but credit to Sturridge for luring him in and drawing the foul.

The initial joy of realising we had a penalty was soon replaced by the fear that we'd miss. I could barely bring myself to watch it, all I could think of was how if Stevie missed then we could nip these title dreams in the bud before they'd even really gotten started. Facing a substitute keeper did little for my confidence either, I don't like that kind of thing as it always feels like it's all set up for the sub keeper to make the headlines and be the hero. Thankfully Gerrard hadn't read the script, he was only interested in the script where he once again flies in to our rescue like the superhero he is. Seriously, how big are the cajones on that guy? I've lost count of the amount of high pressure pens he's converted for us. The way he celebrated it tells me everything I need to know about where his head is at. It's not in the hunt for fourth spot, that's for damn sure. That celebration was all about a title challenge. How amazing would it be if Stevie finally won one? I'm not going to get too far ahead of myself here as there's a long way to go and we still have three teams to catch. It's not as though we need just one of them to slip up. We need three teams to drop points and we need to continue to rack up wins ourselves. It's going to be tough but I'm genuinely starting to think it can be done.

Fulham went full on alehouse for the five or six minutes of stoppage time played, but we dealt with it extremely well. Fit again Daniel Agger was sent on immediately after we scored to help man the barricades and he did it superbly by winning his first three headers. We probably should have added another goal on the counter but weren't clinical enough. It didn't matter in the end as we held on for what could be a huge win come May.

The defence remains a worry but we do have players coming back from injury to give Brendan more options there, and who knows what kind of confidence and belief the players will take from winning a game in this manner. We came from behind twice and we won it in stoppage time. Is that not what Champions do?

We've won our last two games without Suarez scoring too, which is a great sign as it's only a matter of time before he's banging them in again. If we can win when he's having a lean spell, we shouldn't have too much trouble when he's back amongst them. In the meantime of course, Sturridge continues to score at a record breaking level. He's now scored in his last eight games, which I read somewhere ties a club record. Hopefully he can add to it on Sunday against Arsenal in the cup. I'd have preferred another league game to keep the momentum going but I'm not complaining about still being in the FA Cup. After all, if we're going to win the title we may as well make it a double and add the FA Cup as well. What's wrong? Did I go too far?

ARSENAL 2 LIVERPOOL 1

Competition - FA Cup 5th Round
Date - Sun 16 Feb 2014
Venue - The Emirates
Scorer(s) – Steven Gerrard (pen)
Star Man – Luis Suarez

Team: Jones; Flanagan, Skrtel, Agger, Cissokho (Henderson); Gerrard, Allen, Coutinho; Sterling, Sturridge, Suarez:

Hands up if you feared the worst when you saw that Howard Webb was refereeing this one? Wow, that's a lot of hands. He hasn't screwed us over every time he's been in charge of one of our games, but he's done it on more than enough occasions for it to be seen as a trend. We've won just eight of the last 22 games in which the chrome domed copper has been the whistle blower. I'd love to see how that compares with every other Premier League official. Still, we've brought it on ourselves though really, had the club kicked up enough of a fuss about him years ago when they should have we wouldn't still be having to deal with this crap now.

It says a lot for the man's complete ineptitude that he was being jeered by both sets of fans at the end of this one, although it also says a lot for the idiocy of Arsenal fans that they somehow felt hard done to when they'd escaped punishment for the most blatant non-award of a penalty since... well since Webb allowed Eto'o to take Suarez out at Stamford Bridge a few weeks ago. It wasn't even just the non-penalty decision that riled me, I was cursing him in the first half too; not for being biased, for being crap. Arsenal were also on the end of plenty of Webb mistakes, it's just none of those compared to the outrageous failure to award the most blatant of penalties.

Some players were booked for relatively minor offences whilst more serious incidents drew insufficient or no punishment (Podolski on Flanagan, Monreal's snide stamp on Allen and Arteta getting away with murder all afternoon). Then there was the ridiculous incident with Sterling that summed Webb's personality up to a tee. Firstly, there was a clear foul on the Reds' winger by Jenkinson. Secondly, if you aren't giving the foul and are playing advantage, fair enough then it's a corner as the defender clearly put the ball out. What did Webb give? A fucking goal-kick. And when Sterling got a little too close to him and made the slightest contact as he protested the decision, the look of complete disdain Webb gave him had 'jobsworth copper' written all over it. Everyone knows you aren't supposed to touch the referee but it's all about context and players touch referees all the time and vice versa. What Sterling did wasn't aggressive and shouldn't have even drawn any kind of response from the official, yet Webb looked like Raheem had slapped him in the face. The look of incredulity said it all, *"How dare you touch me!!"*

All that said, we should have won this game comfortably and Webb's incompetence should have been a trivial, irrelevant footnote on another fantastic Liverpool win. Unfortunately things just didn't go our way and a combination of slack finishing and sloppy defending on our part (along with great goalkeeping from Fabianksi) meant that it was yet another 'big away day hard luck story' under Brendan. They're racking up now aren't they?

We started on the front foot and had Sturridge taken one of the two great early chances he had then who knows what would have happened. I suspect Arsenal would have fallen apart but we'll never know as Sturridge missed them both. I'm not too upset about them though, shit happens. He's been a revelation for us but you can't expect him to bury every chance he gets, especially on his right foot. Suarez had a great effort well saved too as we dominated the early part of the game. When chances like that go begging though you always fear the worst and gradually Arsenal began to settle and enjoy some good possession. They weren't threatening much though until they scored a fortuitous opening goal. Flanagan conceded a silly free-kick when he fouled Monreal (he's crap, there's no need to foul him as he'd have probably put his cross into the stands) and although the initial set-piece was cleared, the ball fell to Sanogo who's shot was superbly blocked by Gerrard. Unfortunately the rebound fell perfectly to Oxlade-Chamberlain who buried it.

We came out flying after the break and almost equalised through Suarez seconds after the restart. A minute later we conceded a bad goal on the counter. Oxlade-Chamberlain completely ruined Agger for pace and as soon as he went by him you could see Podolski in too much space in the box and when the cross found him he finished past Jones. I've seen some criticism of Agger for the goal but short of suddenly developing an extra three yards of pace what was he supposed to do? Maybe he should have fouled him and taken a yellow card? Other than that, he was powerless to do anything.

At 0-2 we were in big trouble now, and it crossed my mind that in chasing the game we may leave ourselves so open at the back that Arsenal could get four or five and get proper payback for last week's humiliation. We responded really well though and for a spell we completely battered them. Unfortunately Fabianksi was having one of those days when nothing was going to get past him.

Rodgers made a bold move in sending on Henderson for Cissokho, meaning Flanagan switched flanks and Sterling went to right back. Sterling was having a lively game and switching to right back didn't change that. I love him at right back you know, his tenacity is fantastic and opponents rarely get the better of him. Whenever he's been asked to play there he's been brilliant. He's a fierce little competitor.

I was surprised when we got the penalty, not because I didn't think it was a foul, but because it was Webb and given what happened at Stamford Bridge, short of Podolski pulling out a Luger pistol and shooting Luis in the back I didn't think he'd give us anything. Webb thought about it longer than he should have but he got it right in the end. Gerrard did the business once again and it was game on.

Arsenal were shitting themselves now as we were at full steam and throwing everything at them. That probably explains the panic shown by the Ox when he clattered Suarez. It was stupid as Luis wasn't really going anywhere dangerous, but it's as obvious a pen as you'll see and Webb had a perfect view of it. Suarez over-egged the pudding on this one a bit but he did get barged into by an opponent who ran into him at full speed and got nowhere near the ball. That's a penalty in the eyes of everyone except Webb and the odious Wenger, who said it's *"difficult to tell when it's Suarez"*. Twat. Didn't stop you trying to buy him though did it?

Once again there'll be all manner of theories as to why Webb didn't give it. Once again, I'm personally putting it down to him being a bad shithouse who doesn't like to give decisions. Giving a pen at 2-0 is going to bring him less heat than giving it at 2-1. He didn't want to give it because he'd already given one a few minutes earlier and so he completely bottled it. If he'd have set out to simply screw us over he could easily have sent off Gerrard for a second yellow (not that he should, not every foul is a yellow card and worse tackles had gone unpunished earlier) and if he wanted to be a complete twat he could have red carded Sterling for daring to make contact with him. Like I say, I just think he's a shithouse. Coward Webb.

After that shocking decision we lost a bit of momentum and it was a bit more comfortable for Arsenal. Jones made a brilliant save to deny Ozil but aside from that they didn't threaten much either. That Sanogo is fucking garbage isn't he? As much as Andy Gray and whoever that co-commentator was on BT Sport tried to big him up, it was obvious that he was terrible. He did nothing other than run around a lot and fling his arm into Agger's face every time he went up for a header. Not that Webb did anything about that either like.

I thought we'd equalised late on when Agger got on the end of Gerrard's free-kick. From the camera angle it seemed certain that the ball was going to nestle in the net but it drifted agonisingly wide. I couldn't believe it, it looked a goal all the way and I knew as it sailed wide we were out; that was our big chance and we didn't take it. Still, you've got to love how a keeper is allowed to come flying out and smack an opponent with both fists in the head and not be penalised for it. I'm not even blaming Webb for this one as there's not a ref in the world who would give a pen for that, but seriously, how is that allowed to go unpunished? Fabianksi came out, missed the ball and punched Agger in the head with two hands. It happens all the time and it's never given as a foul.

There's no point getting too down about this one as on another day we'd have twatted

Arsenal just like we did a week earlier. I'm excited at some of the football we played but I'm livid about Webb shafting us again, and I'm livid that once again we're being the good soldier about it and saying fuck all instead of calling him out by highlighting all the times he's pulled this kind of shit and demanding he's never allowed near a Liverpool game ever again.

Arsenal can fuck off too, their players carrying on like they'd won the final and their fans just being typically 'Goonerish' acting like their shit don't stink. Fuck Arsenal, the fan fleecing twats.

I wanted to win this one badly but I'd rather lose in the cup than lose in the league. We have 12 games left this season and if we were to win them all we'd probably be Champions. Unrealistic? Yeah of course it is, but we've got to target that and see how close to it we can get. What I take from this game is that we're better than Arsenal and we should finish above them. Our players now know they're better than Arsenal and despite this result I daresay their players are aware of it too after the last eight days.

We obviously need to tighten up at the back though and we need Suarez to start scoring again. It's something of an anomaly really; it's not like he's doing anything wrong but incredibly he's only got one goal in his last six games or something. Yet every game it has looked like he could get a hat-trick but for the woodwork and great goalkeeping. It's only a matter of time before he's back in the goals and hopefully he and Sturridge can take Swansea to the cleaners next week.

The players will be hurting, and Sturridge in particular seems to be taking it very hard. That's good, they should embrace the pain of this and then come back stronger and absolutely destroy Swansea next weekend. We've got a shot at doing something very special between now and May. It's an outside shot admittedly, but it's a shot nonetheless. We're playing well - arguably better than anybody right now - but we simply need to start being more secure at the back as you can't expect to score three goals every game, even when you have the firepower that we have.

LIVERPOOL 4 SWANSEA CITY 3

Competition - Premier League
Date - Sun 23 Feb 2014
Venue - Anfield
Scorer(s) – Henderson (2), Sturridge (2)
Star Man – Jordan Henderson

Team: Mignolet; Flanagan, Skrtel, Agger (Toure), Flanagan; Gerrard, Henderson, Coutinho; Sturridge (Moses), Suarez, Sterling (Allen);

If we are to somehow upset the odds and win the title this year, we're not going to do it the easy way that's for sure. We've got eleven games left and each one of them looks like it could be an epic. We score more goals than anyone else but just can't keep them out at the other end.

This game just made me think back to the Roy Evans era and those two Newcastle epics. It wasn't as dramatic as those two classics but the similarity between the Evans team and this one was there for all to see. That team could score goals for fun with the likes of Fowler, McManaman and Collymore, but they couldn't defend to save their lives and would often shoot themselves in the foot against sides they should be beating with ease. One major difference is that this current team looks to have more bottle (not to mention far more discipline off the field, but that's another story) and this is two games in a row now where they've pulled a win out of the fire when it looked like points could be slipping away.

Realistically, we might have to win every game to win the title. Perhaps there can be one or at most two slip ups along the way, but you don't want one of those to come at bottom club Fulham or at home to struggling Swansea, so from that point of view these were two huge wins for us. Tougher tests await and we may well come unstuck in one or two, so it was vitally important to get three points from this one. It turned out to be a lot tougher than many of us expected, in part due to our defensive uncertainty but also due to the quality of opposition. Swansea played really well and this was a difficult afternoon for us. This looked like two Brendan Rodgers' sides going head to head, Swansea in many ways were a mirror image of ourselves, which is unsurprising given the influence Rodgers has had over many of their players as well as their newly appointed manager.

The main difference was at both ends of the pitch. We were more potent in attack, they were less accident prone at the back. In the end, our attacking prowess just about came through for us, but the way the game started few would have predicted that we'd be struggling to find a winner late in the second half. In fact, after 20 minutes it seemed like business as usual. It took just three minutes for us to go in front and it's the exact kind of goal that we've become accustomed to in recent weeks; winning the ball back high up the pitch and then striking with lightning pace. Simply devastating football. Rangel ran into trouble and tried to buy a free-kick as he lost his balance near halfway, but Coutinho hadn't touched him and the referee correctly waved play on and Sterling was onto it in a flash. Sturridge knows just what he's supposed to do in this situation and immediately set off on a run in behind the defence. Sterling delivered a stunning pass with the outside of his boot into the path of the in form striker who didn't have to break stride as he rounded the keeper and gleefully put the ball into the empty net. For me Sterling's pass was perhaps as good as the Gerrard one at Fulham or the Coutinho one against Arsenal. Top drawer.

The second goal was class too. Suarez was a fraction away from releasing Sturridge with a wonderful ball but put just too much on it and sent his strike partner wide on the right. No matter, Sturridge did well to cut inside and pick out Henderson on the edge of the box and he curled a shot past Vorm and with just 20 minutes on the clock we looked to be on the way to another routine home win.

Swansea had other ideas though and had pulled one back within three minutes through the lively Shelvey. I don't like all this 'not celebrating' stuff. It's all very admirable and respectful and that, but it also seems a little bit forced and clichéd, and every bugger is doing now. That's not a knock on Jonjo at all; clearly his sentiments were genuine and he's always been very respectful towards the club since he left. It just looked like he didn't know what to do. He started to run off and celebrate, then shit himself and ended up apologetically holding his hands up to all sides of the ground. Just celebrate lad, no-one is going to think any less of you providing you're not giving it the beans in front of the Kop. Shelvey earned warm applause from pretty much the entire crowd, in part due to the gesture but also because of the quality of the strike. I'd have been clapping him regardless of whether he celebrated or not, it was a hell of a goal and it was no more than Swansea had deserved really. It was like Davie Thommo's goal for Coventry back in the day, only without the pointing and yelling of *"FUCK OFF!!"* at the Liverpool manager!

We've gone up early against a lot of teams this season at home and more often than not it has been due to a bombardment that the opposition simply couldn't live with. That wasn't the case this time. Swansea had played well and could count themselves a little unfortunate to be trailing by one goal, let alone two. It's easy to point to Liverpool's goals against column and complain about the defence, but there are times when you are going to concede and there's not a great deal you can do about it. This was one of those occasions for me. You can nitpick and say Shelvey had too much space and perhaps he did, but he took the shot first time before anyone could close him down. I can live with that goal as more often than not Jonjo puts that into the back row of the Kop.

The second goal was a different story. I wasn't sure who to blame the most at the time, the referee, Skrtel for putting himself in unnecessary trouble or our terrible marking from the free-kick. It looked to me like Skrtel clearly won the ball in his challenge with Shelvey and the crowd were livid with that decision. I've seen several replays of it since and I'm struggling to even see why it was a free-kick. He won the ball and he then made some incidental (and relatively minor) contact with his studs on the back of Shelvey's calf. It didn't look deliberate to me, but only Skrtel will know if there was any intent. The free-kick was harsh but we've got to do a better job of defending it. Who was picking up Bony? You can't let the opposition's centre forward - not to mention most accomplished header of a ball - have an unchallenged header in your own box. That's just negligence that is, but it happens too often.

Having been pegged back to 2-2, suddenly what was looking like a typical walk in the park at home now had the potential to be one of those massive letdowns we have been prone to from time to time. We were facing a real test of our mettle but responded well and regained the lead after some lovely football. I lost count of how many passes were in the build up before Suarez chipped an inch perfect ball onto the head of Sturridge who nodded past Vorm with some aplomb. Heading isn't his strong point by any means but he took this chance well and it's no surprise to see him bounce back from the disappointing day he had at the Emirates last week. It's been massive for us that he's gone on this run just as the goals have dried up for Suarez, and the two of them now sit first and second in the Premier league goalscorers chart. Suarez is joint top of the assists table too (with Gerrard).

Usually in this situation I'd be fairly relaxed at half time. After all, we'd gotten over the setback of surrendering a two goal lead and were in front again, so panic over. We'd scored three goals already, we were attacking the Kop in the second half so things were looking good, right? Well no, not really. There was just something about the performance that didn't seem right and everyone seemed to have picked up on it. There was a definite edginess there, the players looked unsettled, the crowd were nervy and Swansea were giving us all we could handle.

The second half began in the worst possible fashion as within minutes Swansea were level after another controversial decision; Mike Jones awarding a penalty when Skrtel and Bony had a coming together in the box. Yes there was contact, yes Skrtel had a bit of a grapple with him, but Bony threw himself to the floor and the ref bought it. This was 100% a case of a referee having marked a player's card before the game. For months Skrtel has been highlighted by pundits on TV for the holding he does on set pieces. It's human nature therefore for any referee to see this on telly and think *"Hmm, I'll have to keep my eye on this cat"*. However, as I've said before, refs won't give those from set-pieces as they get marked down by their assessors for it. You very rarely see those decisions given from set-pieces regardless of how blatant the hold is and if Skrtel had done what he did to Bony from a corner he'd have gotten away with it. He did it in open play though and gave the referee the opportunity to act on the seed that had been planted in his head going into the game. When you consider all that Skrtel has gotten away with over the years, for him to finally get pulled up for such a trivial one as this… well my mate Julian summed it up best I think, it's like Al Capone getting done for tax evasion.

Bony's penalty was firmly struck and right in the bottom corner. It needed to be as Mignolet made a terrific attempt to stop it and went really close. At 3-3 there was a real sense of panic around the ground, the main reason surely being that we all know what's at stake in these remaining games. A lot of people aren't taking us seriously as title contenders (including many in our own fan base) but the cold hard facts are that with eleven games left we're just four points off the top and two of the sides ahead of us have to come to Anfield. We can win this, but for it to happen we need to avoid any slip ups and when Bony's penalty drew Swansea level it looked like we were about to completely blow it.

For a spell after that we were really shaken. Rodgers eventually decided he'd seen enough of Swansea's midfield control and sent on Allen for Sterling. I was a little surprised it wasn't Coutinho that got hooked but it had been apparent since the first half that we needed Allen in there. We were too open and Gerrard was left exposed time and again. Coutinho and Henderson would go pressing the ball but it's not easy to do that against Swansea as they are possibly the league's best passing team and they don't panic under pressure. Any time they worked the ball out beyond our midfield two then Gerrard was left facing both Shelvey and De Guzman and it made for some hairy looking situations (insert your own Jonjo gag here).

I'm sure I wasn't the only one thinking *"Flip the damn triangle, Brendan!!"* We've seen how well this midfield trio can work in recent weeks, but the difference between this game and others was the intensity they played with. Against Everton and Arsenal they were flat out, 100mph, chasing anything that moved and tackling anything with a pulse. Against Swansea it was a lot more passive, and the spaces were appearing all over the place. When Allen came on those spaces mostly disappeared. He won the ball high up the pitch, he carried it into dangerous areas and he passed it sensibly. We looked a lot more structurally sound with Allen in there, and I'd also say that the introduction of Toure for Agger probably helped too, simply because Bony stopped being as much of a threat as he had been.

I assumed Agger must have been injured, but it turns out he wasn't, he just got the hook. Toure started warming up immediately after the penalty so I figured it was Skrtel who would be pulled. Not only was he having a 'mare, but he was probably one more foul away from a red card too. It looked like he might have gotten a second for the penalty incident until the official either realised it would mean a sending off, or Gerrard talked him out of it. He definitely looked like he was contemplating going for his pocket for a second or two.

What this decision says about the manager's feelings towards Agger I'm not sure, but if I was in the Dane's shoes today I'd be feeling pretty aggrieved to be the one to make way when my defensive partner had lost possession cheaply before conceding a free-kick that led to the second goal (a goal that he also deflected into his own net), followed it up by conceding a penalty and was one more foul away from an early bath.

The game was in the balance at 3-3 as neither side were on top and there was a feeling of next goal the winner about it all. Swansea had a spell where they looked the more assured side, then we had a spell (after the introduction of Allen) where we were apply-ing pressure. It was during this spell that the referee made his third contentious call of the day when he turned down a penalty claim by Suarez. Having given the penalty for Bony's tumble, for me he really can't justify not giving this one to Suarez. It was prob-ably 60-40 against being a pen, much the same as the one given against us for that mat-ter.

I'll tell you what I think happened on this one. The incident came directly as a result of us not giving Swansea the ball back after they'd put it out so Chico Flores could get treatment (I'll get to this in a moment). Whilst the rest of our team were expecting the ball to be given back to Swansea, Luis was having none of it and played on. Whatsmore, he cajoled Johnson into playing on too (he was looking pretty sheepish and hesitant about it initially). So, when Suarez then went into the box and took a tumble after going past Canos, I believe the referee either thought *"I don't want to give a pen here, it'll cause murder with the Swansea players"* or he thought *"fuck you Suarez, I'm giving you nothing after what you just did, you unsporting little bastard"*. Take your pick as to which one, but I'm sure it was one or the other.

I was disappointed at what Rodgers said about this incident too, *"It wasn't a penalty because we should have given the ball back. I don't know why we did that and I'll be having words about it."* Would he be saying that if Swansea weren't the opposition and if his mate wasn't now their manager? And would he be saying it if we hadn't gone on to win the game? We did win, so it wasn't a definitive moment in the game, but if I'm Suarez and Brendan tells me I should have given them the ball back then I'm telling him to give his head a wobble.

Everyone inside Anfield knew that Chico was taking the piss and that he was fine. Outside of Adnan Januzaj he might be the biggest cheat in the Premier League, appar-ently he even play acts and dives in training! Rangel only put the ball out as he was being put under pressure from Suarez and decided to take the easy way out. Chico was complaining about his knee for a couple of minutes and Swansea had three chances to put the ball out but didn't. Furthmore, Chico had plenty of opportunities to go down and ensure they did. In fact, as Chico eventually did go down Vorm had the ball in his hands and could have put the ball out, but instead rolled it to Rangel who did not put the out immediately either! It was only when Suarez put the full back under pressure that he decided to put the ball out. THAT'S why Suarez played on.

It's always funny when something like this happens though as the side that feels they have been 'wronged' always lose the plot and charge around just wanting to kick some-one. It's like they feel they've got a free pass to just go and boot someone up in the air and then they'll say to the ref *what do you expect, look what they did, the bastards!"* On this occasion it was Nathan Dyer who lost it and wanted to take out anyone in red. Our players knew it was coming though and you'd see them lay it off and then just jump out of his way. All very amusing.

We kept plugging away and eventually got our reward when Henderson fired in at the second attempt after Vorm made a superb save to keep out his initial effort. The move started with a raking ball from Gerrard to pick out Suarez, and although his shot was weak, Williams could only divert his clearance straight at Henderson who did the rest. Very few things lift the soul as much as a Hendo celebration, on this occasion he didn't go running off on a mad one, he just stood there yelling at the top of his lungs. Works just as well for me, doesn't hurt to mix things up a bit. He's a great lad and he's having a hell of a season. Goals are the only thing that's been missing but Rodgers spoke afterwards about how Henderson's finishing in training is 'sublime' and that he's been challenging his midfielders to try and get not just into the penalty area, but also the six yard box. Hopefully there are more where this came from. Imagine how good he'd be if he was banging in 15-20 a season? He had a chance for a hat-trick soon after after a bewitching run from Suarez saw him beat two defenders and cut the ball back to the edge of the box but Hendo's shot was straight at Vorm.

In an obvious act of desperation Swansea sent on David Ngog for Dyer. I was filled with dread at this point, not because he's any good, but because we make a habit of allowing the worst strikers around to find the net against us. If Ngog had come on and got the equaliser I think I would have just had to end it all. As it was, Swansea never really looked like scoring but given how brittle we'd looked at the back it was impos-sible to feel safe. Gerrard almost wrapped it up when his deflected shot struck the post following some brilliant interplay between Allen and Coutinho on the left wing, and the skipper then had another effort parried by Vorm as we continued to attack rather than try and protect our lead.

It's not good for the blood pressure watching the Reds at the moment that's for sure, but then I imagine it was pretty stressful for Chelsea fans this weekend as well. Their games are often on a knife edge too but for vastly different reasons. Whereas they're happy to just keep it tight and hope to sneak a goal we are the exact opposite. I know who I'd rather be watching though, that's for damn sure. Far better to be stressed and entertained then stressed and bored shitless.

The general consensus seems to be that you can't carry on winning games when you have to score three or four times to ensure victory. Another way of looking at it is that if you can score three or four as often as we do then you'll win a lot of games, even with a leaky defence. We're not going to concede two or three in every game we have left - at least I hope we're not - so therefore in theory we shouldn't have to score three or four to win every game. More often than not our attack will score more than our defence lets in, the problem is it only needs one or two games where the opposite is true and we can kiss goodbye to any hopes of winning the title. Those hopes are still slim, but if we can just keep winning - no matter how we do it - then let's see where that takes us.

Premier League Round Up (23-25 February 2014)

Olivier Giroud continued his good 'scoring form' with a couple of first half goals against Sunderland at the Emirates. Not like him to be doing it at home though, he's had far more fun playing away it seems. He kissed his wedding ring after scoring the opening goal and he's clearly got some serious making up to do after some bird he was knocking off sold her story to the S*n and dropped him right in it.

He didn't handle it particularly well, in fact he fell apart to such an extent that Arsene Wenger actually decided that the God awful Yaya Sanogo was a better option than him for the games against us and Bayern. What kind of state must Giroud have been in to be deemed worse than that big lump? What an absolute fanny though. He took to twitter to say *"I apologise to my wife, family and friends and my manager, team-mates and Arsenal fans. I now have to fight for my family and for my club and obtain their forgiveness."* He should be sorry for what he's done to his wife and family, but is twitter the place to be saying it? And what the fuck has it got to do with Wenger, his team-mates or the fans? Arsenal fans wouldn't care if he was shagging Nicklas Bendtner as long as he was still finding the back of the net. Putting that on twitter was just cringeworthy, it reminded me of that horrific televised apology Tiger Woods had to do to appease his sponsors.

Anyway, Giroud needed just three minutes to open the scoring against the Mackems as Arsenal completely dismantled Gus Poyet's men in a rampant first half display. Poyet was without the suspended Wes Brown once again, which you'd think would be an advantage given his exploits this season, but his replacement (some lad called Bargini) had an absolute 'mare. How many of these random players are Sunderland going to wheel out though? There's a new one every week and they're usually Italian. I think Di Canio must have signed about thirty of them and there's probably some we still haven't seen yet. Poyet may have brought a load in too, they seem to have a never ending supply. Sunderland played like a team with their mind on a cup final. I remember last year we hammered Swansea 5-0 the week before they played in the League Cup Final, so Sunderland not being at the races wasn't exactly a surprise.

My brother-in-law has been texting me all week, either to tell me how he's been sniffing Fabio or to let me know 'how many sleeps he has left' before Wembley. But mostly it was to rant about Steve Bruce. He's a much happier camper lately than he was a few months ago when he was resigned to relegation. Now he's going to Wembley and it looks like they'll stay up, but the mere mention of Bruce is enough to turn him into an even angrier version of Roy Keane. He loves Fabio though, a little bit too much maybe. Last week I got a text off him saying *"talking to Borini at the Academy today. He smelt gorgeous"*. Naturally I forwarded that to Fabio on twitter, which may ensure some slight unease for both parties next time they run into eachother. He sent me one later that night too when he was watching the Champions League on telly. He's got a massive downer on Adrian Chiles, he hates him like I hate Jon Walters. Anyway, he sends me a text saying *"Look at that ugly fucker Chiles. Bet he smells of Brut, not like sexy Fabio"*. I briefly contemplated sending that one on to Borini on twitter too, but felt that might be a step too far. Slight unease is one thing, restraining orders are another.

After the League Cup final this weekend they play Hull in the FA Cup next week, and he's obsessing about that one already, such is his hatred of Bruce. He's totally convinced that beachball head has the media in his pocket and the depth of his hatred he has for him is something to behold. Here's a selection of messages I got from him this week:

"See the Steve Bruce media are praying the Geordie cunt gets to Wembley, fucking dickheads. We hadn't won in 16 games, that's why he got the sack. Wankers"

"I hope we crush the fuckers next week. Parsnip nosed cunt with nans hair"

He even managed to find a way to slate him after Bruce had generously given his two cup final tickets to Sunderland and told them to give them to a couple of fans instead...

"See parsnip nose sent his final tickets to Sunderland and said to give them to fans. He should have went, coz he's not fucking going there with Hull"

He then somehow managed to shoehorn Bruce into a rant about Andy Townsend when he was watching the United game on Tuesday night...

"Townsend is talking utter fucking bollocks. He's best mates with parsnip nose nans hair. Pair of cunts"

If Hull manage to knock Sunderland out of the FA Cup I'm not sure he'll be able to cope, he may have some kind of breakdown. 'Parsnip nose nans hair' is some insult though, wish I'd thought of it.

With there being no round up last week due to the lack of Premier League games, I didn't get the chance to follow up on the latest spat between Wenger and Mourinho. The Arsenal boss didn't rise to the bait after Mourinho's 'specialist in failure' jibe, simply saying that *"it's more embarrassing for Chelsea than for me"*. A decent enough riposte I guess, the one flaw in his logic being that Chelsea and especially Mourinho don't have enough class to feel embarrassed about anything. That being said, I reckon even Jose was left a little red faced this week when 'off the record' comments were put well and truly 'on the record' by a French TV crew.

He was preparing to do an interview with a French TV station and was chatting with some Swiss businessman at a sponsor's do before filming the interview. During the course of conversation with this complete stranger, he decided he'd put down some of his players, y'know, just for a cheap laugh or two as you do, and was filmed saying *"The problem with Chelsea is I lack a striker. I have Eto'o but he is 32 years old, maybe 35, who knows?"* Not content with slagging off his own players, he then moved on to insult Monaco. *"I need a striker, Falcao needs a club. A player like him cannot play in front of 3,000 people. Monaco is a club to end (your career with)."*

The French aired the footage and Mourinho was left looking like even more of a cock than usual. When he faced the press the next day, he said: *"I think you should be embarrassed as a media professionals because by the ethical point of view I don't think you are happy your colleague is happy to be able to record a private conversation and to make it public. I think you should all be embarrassed because it is against your ethic. Is it a not happy comment, absolutely."* Hahaha what does any of that even mean!! He talks like a five year old at times. *"Is it a not happy comment, absolutely?"* Kinell. *"I am not defending what I am saying, I am attacking something that is from your professional area. It was a funny conversation between me and someone not in the football world. It is a disgrace someone is taping a private conversation."*

It wasn't a funny conversation, I've seen the video, he's not laughing and joking when he says it, he's reeking of sneering arrogance and he knew exactly what he was saying. Admittedly my French isn't what it should be, we were forced to do it in school for a couple of years but I was kicked out of the class in my very first lesson and it kind of went downhill from there.*

The point is, you didn't need to know what Mourinho was saying to be able to tell how he was saying it. It wasn't a throwaway line, made in a light hearted way. It was a cheap shot at Eto'o pure and simple. As for it being 'private', well he knew the camera was rolling so more fool him. If I were Eto'o I'd have chinned him.

On the field the spawny bastard beat Everton with a last gasp winner. Never have I been so upset about an Everton loss as this. For so long it looked like Chelsea were going to drop two points and had that happened, it would have been in our own hands to finish above them. Then Tim Howard rode to their rescue by making a pigs arse of a Lampard free-kick under pressure from Mongo.

Chelsea are shite (in relative terms) and they're awful to watch. Unfortunately they keep managing to churn out narrow wins. How can you spend so much money on so many attacking players, and be so fucking sterile? Mourinho, thats why. He keeps trotting out this narrative of Chelsea being unable to kill teams off. So nothing to do with him being a shithouse and sitting back on one goal leads then? No, apparently it's the players fault for missing so many chances. Chances that they aren't actually creating due to his negative approach, but if you say something enough times it becomes fact.

Hearing him whine about 'not having a striker' and nobody pulling him up on it is infuriating. I mean, for one thing he loaned out Lukaku so if he has no striker who's fault is that? What I take issue with the most though is this suggestion that he's working without any strikers. As much as we love to mock Torres for not being what he was when in his Anfield pomp, he'd still get in most sides in this league, as would

Eto'o and Demba Ba, who was fucking lethal at Newcastle. Chelsea might not have a Suarez or a Sturridge (not anymore anyway, the daft twats), but the three strikers they have are all good players who would improve most Premier League teams. Yet we're expected to believe that all three of them can't score because they're shite, and it has nothing to do with the manager? Bullshit. None of them are scoring because of the Special One's 'not so special' style of football. Anyone would think he's having to select between Altidore, Holt and Graham up front. Laughable. Anyway, that's enough on Chelsea, I'm moving on before I upset myself further.

Struggling Cardiff faced Hull and got absolutely spanked all over the place. They started well enough, Zaha and Jones both went close but Huddlestone's deflected shot put the visitors ahead and after that they ran riot. Cardiff look completely fucked now, they've got nothing. Things can turn around so quickly though that you never really know.

I mean look at West Ham, they were bottom not so long ago having suffered 5-0 and 6-0 losses in successive games. The heat was on Fat Sam, but now look at them, they've had a few wins and have flown up the table. They came from behind to beat Southampton at home as goals from Jarvis, Carlton Cole and Nolan cancelled out Yoshida's early header. I guess Hammers fans don't hate Nolan anymore? Staying with West Ham, was I wrong about Ravel Morrison in my last round up? There certainly seems to be more to the story after claims he was being pressured by Allardyce to sign with a certain agent. Morrison reckons Fat Sam and Nolan were on at him every day, trying to get him to sign with their agent. He reckons that's why he had to leave. I can't see Allardyce being involved in something like that, Big Sam's as honest as the day is... hahahahaha I can't even finish that sentence.

Elsewhere on Saturday, City just about edged past Stoke at the Etihad. They huffed and puffed but didn't do much until Toure popped up with the winner midway through the second half. Dzeko missed an absolute sitter, this was as bad as anything I've seen in ages. The best part of it was him completely losing his rag and running over and booting the post. I do that pretty much every week when I'm playing. Of course I do shit things far more frequently than Dzeko, but seeing him kick out that that that was just like looking in a mirror. One of those fairground mirrors that make average height, middle aged fat blokes look young, tall and athletic, obviously. And is it me or is that Jovetic a bit average? His mouth is way too small for his face too, and he has no lips. It kind of freaks me out.

It was a rare good weekend for Moyes as United won at Selhurst Park. They didn't play very well but they won, which must have been a huge relief to the Chosen One. Rooney celebrated his new 300k a week deal (hahahaha just how desperate must they have been to agree to that?) with a goal. As shit as they've been domestically, incredibly they were unbeaten in the Champions League this season until they went to Greece this week and shit the bed against Olympiakos. My God they were terrible weren't they? I'm not gloating yet as I still think they've got more than enough firepower to go through, but they were laughably bad. The first time they've ever lost to a Greek side apparently, as Moyesy continues to break records.

Van Persie had a bit of moan about his team-mates to the Dutch media afterwards.

Not a shock, he's always given off an air of *"my shit don't stink"*. I guess that sitter he missed was down to team-mates *'being in the areas he wants to play in'* too. You can tell when you watch them play that Rooney thinks Van Persie is a knob, it's blatantly obvious. Van Persie downed tools in the summer when Moyes came in, he's had a face like a slapped arse ever since and he'll be gone in the summer unless they give him 'Rooney money'. They probably will too, they're so desperate right now.

Elsewhere, West Brom took on Fulham in a game no-one wanted to see. Fuck knows what's going on at Fulham, and West Brom are just a completely weird team who take points off the big boys but seem to lose to everybody else. They almost lost to Fulham, that's how bad West Brom are.

Onto Sunday now, and I just knew Norwich would get something out of their game with Spurs. I wasn't convinced they'd win - that was an added bonus - but I knew Spurs would drop points as they always seem to be shite after Europa League games. All the hype around Sherwood has been a bit silly. Because he's young, English and a former Spurs player he's been getting bigged up far more than he's merited. A lot of people WANT him to be good so they're convincing themselves he IS good. His record since taking over is pretty decent in fairness, but look at who they've been playing. And look at HOW they've been playing. Has anyone watched Spurs and seriously thought *"hey these look really good"*? No, because they're bang average and it's only the little purple patch Adebayor has been in that's kept them on our coat tails.

Norwich were good value for the win, they should have won by more than one in fact and probably would have if Wolf Van Winkel wasn't so damn terrible. If Mourinho thinks he's got striker problems he should spare a thought for poor old Chris Hughton. He thought he was getting a highly rated international class frontman and he ended up with the Dutch David Ngog. The Norwich chief exec had piled the pressure on Hughton in the build up to the game, so I was pleased to see them get the win and not just because it meant Spurs losing. There are a lot of arrogant, obnoxious gobshite managers in football but Chris Hughton is not one of them, he's probably one of the most inoffensive people in the game actually. Good luck to him.

Sherwood and his stupid sleeveless body warmer can fuck off though. Hopefully he does just well enough to earn himself another season and ensure Spurs don't go out and actually get someone who might make them a threat again.

* In case you're wondering about my indiscretion in French class. It was first year seniors (so I was 11), most of the class were still getting to know eachother having come from various different junior schools and obviously you want to impress the kids you don't know, especially the girls. We were learning the basics, left and right etc, playing this role play game where one kid had to be a tourist asking for directions to the train station and another had to be a local telling them how to get there. I was the local. We were told that it was 'tourner à gauche' for turn left, and - intriguingly - 'tourner à droite' for turn right. I saw my opening and went for it. *"ou est la gare s il vous plait"* said some kid I didn't know. *"Ternay a twat"* I immediately responded in my broadest scouse. The class was in uproar, I was sent to go and see the year head but a strong marker had been laid down for the position of class clown.

chapter eleven

March

SOUTHAMPTON 0 LIVERPOOL 3

Competition - Premier League
Date - Sat 1 Mar 2014
Venue - St Mary's Stadium
Scorer(s) – Luis Suarez, Raheem
Sterling, Steven Gerrard (pen)
Star Man – Luis Suarez

Team: Mignolet; Flanagan,
Skrtel, Agger, Johnson;
Gerrard, Henderson, Allen,
Coutinho (Sterling); Suarez,
Sturridge:

Ok this is getting serious now isn't it? We really have a shot at this. Every time an obstacle is put in front of us, every time the opportunity to blow it rears up, we find a way to get it done and keep on rolling. If we were going to just fall away, surely it would have happened by now? Instead we're emerging victorious from situations where in the past we'd have been found wanting.

It looked like we'd blown it at Fulham but we found a way to win. We then let in three at home to Swansea, normally if that happens you're not winning the game. We did though. And now? We've just won at our bogey ground, weathering a real storm in the process before coming through to win very comfortably in the end. We're not going away and Chelsea and City will know they can't afford too many slip ups as we're chasing them down like the T-1000 in Terminator 2. That's not to say we'll win the whole damn thing of course (it didn't work out too well for the T-1000). It wasn't a flawless performance at St Mary's by any means, but given the difficulties we've had in this fixture - combined with the success Pochettino has had over Rodgers - then this was a great win and it's now becoming more and more difficult not to dream. As Gerrard said afterwards; *"Why not us?"*

Of all the fixtures we had left, this was one I was perhaps the most worried about; the one where it could have all come unstuck for us, where the dream could die. Had we lost this then seven points to make up on both City and Chelsea would surely be too much. Like every game we have left, it was 'must win' but unlike many of those remaining fixtures, history didn't favour us in this one. Southampton away has always been a shitty fixture for us, but this Saints team had also beaten us at Fortress Anfield. The key to Southampton's success over us recently has been their high tempo pressing game. They get right in your faces and they do it high up the pitch. Some teams wait until you get in their half before they press, some will do it around halfway, but Southampton push right up onto the defenders which is a problem for teams like us who want to play out from the back.

Rodgers has shown he's a quick learner and that he's tactically flexible. He was always going to come up with something to counter how Southampton play and Gerrard revealed afterwards that the plan was to use the midfield diamond to give us extra midfield bodies and to also get the ball to the frontmen quicker to exploit the space left by their full backs. He also said *"If you want to go two v two against those two (Suarez and Sturridge)... all the best"* Love that.

I've wanted to see us try this system for a while, it's one of the few ways of playing two up top without weakening the midfield, but you do sacrifice width and given how well Sterling has been playing that's not ideal either. He was extremely unlucky to be left out but it was an understandable call given how Rodgers wanted to set the team up. Coutinho is a more natural fit for that role at the point of the diamond but seemingly he can only do it at Anfield. Away from home of late he's generally resembled Luis Garcia on a bad day.

I thought we started this game really well , we were on the front foot in the opening 15 minutes and looked quite good. Sturridge got away early on down the right with a move that Rodgers probably drew up on the tactics board earlier in the week. Sturridge had gone out to the right wing into the space vacated by Shaw. As soon as Southampton's attack had broken down the ball was immediately played into space down the line by Gerrard and Sturridge flew past Lovren and headed for the box. He could have gone on his own but chose the better option and was a fraction away from putting one on a plate for Luis. Good to see that, just a pity it didn't quite come off.

Southampton were obviously not expecting us to play this system and in the early stages I thought we controlled the game. Suarez put us ahead with a clinical finish after a lucky ricochet and it was all going swimmingly. After five games without a goal it was a relief to see him back on the scoresheet and hopefully normal service will now be resumed, starting at Old Trafford where I'm looking for at least a hat-trick from him.

As bright as we'd looked early on, the one concern I had was Coutinho who was contributing nothing. He's probably the key to making that whole diamond system work, it's a perfect role for him yet he couldn't get in the game at all and was very wasteful in possession. The longer the half went on, the worse he got and the less grip we had on the game. It wasn't just down to Coutinho that the game began to get away from us (Allen and Henderson were little better) but he didn't help the situation much either.

Southampton really got the bit between their teeth and there was a spell of 15 or 20 minutes where they hammered us. We couldn't keep the ball, which in itself wouldn't have been a major problem if made more of the chances we had to counter attack, but we repeatedly cocked that up too and couldn't seem to release Sturridge or Suarez despite having plenty of opportunities to do so. Shaw was marauding forward from left back and Lallana was pulling the strings as the Saints got right on top of us and built up a head of steam. Lallana hit the post after a great chested lay off by Lambert, and Mignolet then had to make a brilliant save to keep out Rodriguez after Lambert cleverly dummied a cross from Shaw.

The Lallana chance came about because Skrtel inexplicably tried to cut out the cross with his foot instead of sticking his head on it. Overall Skrtel had a brilliant game but had Lallana put that chance away Skrtel would be getting hammered for not dealing with that cross. It's nice to finally get away with one of those for a change though isn't it? The save from Mignolet though, that was fucking ace. He came off his line to punch a couple of dangerous crosses away too and overall looked more assured than he often has of late. And that save was right out the top drawer, great agility that, I don't think too many keepers would have stopped that.

We were on the ropes at this stage and half time couldn't come quickly enough for us. I thought Rodgers might even change it at the break as the diamond hadn't really worked either offensively or defensively. Allen and Henderson were being dragged wide to cover their rampaging full backs which meant Gerrard was over ran in the middle and the superb Lallana was causing all kinds of problems. Rodgers left things as they were though, at least to an untrained eye like mine. I don't know what little tactical adjustments he made within the framework of the diamond, but he must have done something as the second half was vastly different and I can barely remember them giving us any trouble. Lallana all but disappeared too.

Even when Sterling did eventually come on the system stayed the same. It worked a charm too. We were great in the second half and really should have ended up winning four or five nil given the chances we created. You have to credit Rodgers for that change as most of us would have been expecting Raheem to play wide rather than just come on as a like for like replacement for Coutinho. He scored with his first touch a little over a minute after coming on. Rodgers' celebration seemed to have a little extra 'oomph' in it, as it would do when a change you've made has had such a spectacular impact. If Sterling had been playing out wide he wouldn't have been there, so well done to the gaffer, that worked like a charm.

The second goal killed the game really and it's surprising it took so long to add a third. After numerous missed chances Gerrard eventually wrapped it up from the penalty spot in stoppage time after Suarez had turned Fonte inside out and been sent tumbling. One goal and two assists means he now leads the league in both categories. Incredible, especially as he gave everyone else a five game start.

Unlike our previous two victories this one was relatively stress free - at least once we got to half time with our noses in front anyway. The second half was very good, we completely stifled Southampton and it was a highly efficient display. Dare I say it, the kind of display you see from Champions. How many times have you watched the Mancs in a difficult away game where they've been put under a lot of pressure only for them to ride out the storm and then go and win the game at a canter? That's what successful sides do. Over recent years when we've found ourselves in that kind of situation we've wilted, conceded a goal and then dropped points.

There's a belief starting to grow among the players now though, you can absolutely see it in Gerrard, he definitely fancies this and thinks we can do it. So does Suarez, and when your two biggest stars have that belief then it's infectious. Plus there's Rodgers, he's just so calm and in control of everything. He doesn't look like he's feeling any kind of pressure at all, he's so relaxed you'd think it was still pre-season, although we'll see if that continues if we stay in the hunt. So far so good though. With each win the belief grows that little bit more and it's becoming extremely difficult to try and keep a lid on it. If we win at Old Trafford then I'll probably go from *"we could do this"* to *"we will do this"*. Even if we win all of our remaining games though we'd still need both Chelsea and City to slip up in one of their remaining fixtures. My big fear is that one - or both - of them will do what United did in 2009 and just match us result for result and preserve that four point gap.

Whatever happens over these last ten games though, what we've done so far has been quite remarkable. We're the joint second top goalscorers in Europe right now (Barca edged one in front us this weekend, whilst we're level with Real Madrid), who would have predicted that at the start of the season? We're four points off the top and we're the form team in the country going into the home straight. Again, who have thought that, especially after a crap summer window and a non-existant January one? A top four spot was the goal going into the season, it was still the goal at Christmas and even until the last couple of weeks it was still the main target for most of us. Now though? If we finished fourth, I can't lie, I'd be disappointed as we deserve more given how we've played. That's not really fair I know, fourth was the target and it looks like I'm now moving the goalposts, except it's not me who's moved the goalposts, it's Rodgers and the players. They're much better than anyone expected them to be, and as a result expectations have changed.

With greater hope comes the greater risk of disappointment but having been without any kind of hope for several years it feels good to have it again doesn't it? I'm starting to get that 2005 vibe. You know the feeling, like when we knocked out Juve in the quarter finals. There was still a long way to go, we were not favourites but it just felt like something special might be happening. It could all go up in smoke at Old Trafford next week of course, but it feels great that we're going there with more to play for than they do. In recent years it's been us trying to stop their title charge, or hoping to get three points to stay on the coat tails of Everton. It's great to see the roles being reversed.

Premier League Round Up (1-2 March 2014)

With 'the Chosen One' having the weekend off due to cup final commitments (not his, obviously, I'm on about their 'noisy neighbours' who they were due to face), I was a little worried as to where the comedy element was going to come from this weekend. I needn't have been, as Alan Pardew stepped up to the plate to make Saturday night's MOTD essential viewing.

He's great isn't he? Of course I mean 'great' in the loosest possible sense of the word, as in monumental gobshite 'great'. Still, he is great in his own, ridiculously embarrassing, colossal dickhead type way. I think I've made my feelings on 'Slimer' pretty clear (the guy's lawyer threatened me for God's sake so I've got no love for him whatsoever) but even I thought the reaction to what he did went way overboard. I mean come on, was it really THAT bad? Most people seem to think it was, I just thought it was dead funny. Not as funny as his run in with Pellegrini the other week or the time he shoved a linesman, and definitely not as funny as the time he tried to fight an irate Arsene Wenger, but it was funny nonetheless.

And let's not paint David Meyler as some innocent victim here either, he started the whole thing by shoving Pardew. What happened after that wasn't great but it's not as though Pardew went running on to the field and got involved in something that didn't concern him; he was pushed by a player and he reacted excessively. They were 3-1 up and cruising at the time, so I dread to think what he'd have done if they'd been losing. Machete perhaps? I especially loved his explanation of it and how all of these incidents have happened because he's *"standing on the touchline"*, and not because he's a complete fucking head the ball who can't control himself. *"I'll be sitting down from now on"* he assured everyone. Brilliant.

Just watching it back again now and his reaction when everyone comes steaming in to sort it out is perhaps even funnier than the actual headbutt. Meyler is pointing at him and shouting insults whilst being held back by team-mates, 'parsnip nose nan's hair' comes over with a couple of his backroom team and Pardew has his arms outstretched in a *"what the fuck did I do?"* pose. He's defo got some South American in him has Pards. He should get a fairly lengthy ban as it's not his first touchline indiscretion, but all this talk of sacking him? Behave. Even if Newcastle wanted to it's fairly obvious they can't, he's defo got something on Ashley, hence the unprecedented eight year contract he got. Give him a touchline ban for the rest of the season, I'm fine with that, but hopefully he'll be back patrolling the technical area in time for next season, as I'm living in hope that one day he'll slap the living piss out of Mourinho in front of the watching world. Do that, Pards, and all is forgiven mate. I'll even let the lawyer thing slide.

His antics took the shine off what was an impressive 4-1 win at the KC Stadium for the Geordies. They're such a Jeckyll and Hyde team aren't they? They can give anyone a game when they're up for it, but when they're bad they're awful. The Glen Johnson of football teams if you like.

The best thing about what Pardew did was he took the headlines away from that other attention craving arse candle, Mourinho. Chelsea were dire in the first half against Fulham, which for some reason seemed to surprise people. I'm not sure why, they're dire any time I watch the boring bastards. Anyway, they improved in the 2nd half and ran out comfortable winners, but soft arse had to try and grab the headlines when answering a question about what he said to his players at half time. *"I told nossink. Nossink. Not a word, I walk in I walk out. I told zem nossink. Do you believe me?"* That will be hailed by all his media cronies as a typical Mourinho masterstroke. Horseshit. He's a sulky, preening fucking dickhead and Chelsea won this one despite him, not because of him. Helmet.

I've decided that Schurrle looks like a bit of a tit too. I'm basing that on his goal celebration and ear-rings (and the fact he plays for Chelsea), but I bet I'm right. It's no co-incidence that Fulham fell to pieces after Hangeland went off through injury and was replaced by the lumbering Dan Burn. The young defender is fine when it comes to facing the Mancs and heading away 150 crosses a game, but he clearly struggles when he's up against better footballing players like Hazard, Schurrle and Tor... er yeah, like Hazard and Schurrle. Finally on this one, Fulham's new manager seems lost without Dangermouse (one for the 80s kids amongst you there).

Maybe I'm going soft as I get older, but I'm beginning to quite like Stoke these days. Obviously them beating Arsenal, Chelsea and United has helped (as has taking points off City and Everton too), but I've seen them a few times this season and surprisingly I've quite enjoyed watching them. They play some decent stuff these days and they were good value for their win over the Gunners last weekend. Whilst Fulham were never going to get a result against Chelsea, there was always a chance Arsenal could come unstuck at the Britannia and that's exactly what happened. Arsenal were shite, they barely even managed a shot and they were lucky to only lose 1-0, although they were perhaps unlucky with the penalty that beat them. More often than not that wouldn't have been given, so Arsenal caught a bad break there. Still, never mind eh.

Jon Walters buried the penalty (always liked that guy) and this result combined with our win at Southampton saw us leapfrog Arsenal in the table. I'm desperate to finish above Arsenal, the Suarez thing is part of it but it's their fans more than anything. Since I started writing for ESPN I've had more shit off Arsenal fans than any other team. It's weird, they're completely fucking obsessed. Even when the piece doesn't even mention them within minutes of it going up there they are on twitter or on the comments section, mouthing off. I don't think I've had anything from Evertonians or even United fans, it's 95% Arsenal and the other 5% Chelsea. There was one absolute whopper who called himself "Blue and Red Army" and claimed to support both (@chelseagooner if you want to look him up!). He's in America I think, where some states still have the death penalty, presumably for offences such as that. Those Gooners seem to have a real chip on their shoulder where LFC is concerned though, so us finishing above them would be pretty damn sweet.

That penalty was Walters' 24th career Premier League goal for Stoke (and probably his 20th penalty), and according to the BBC that's a club record!! Wait, Stoke haven't had a single player score 25 Premier League goals for them? Fucking hell, they're almost as bad as Chelsea when it comes to killing their strikers. I thought Crouch must have been close to 50 goals for them but apparently not. Suarez has more this season than Crouchy has managed in all the time he's been at Stoke. And what about Kenwyne Jones, it felt like he was there for about ten years, how many goals did he score? * checks wiki * 13!!! Hahahaha!

Meanwhile, Adam has been charged by the FA for a stamp on Giroud. I call bullshit on this one. There is no way on this earth anybody but Charlie knows whether that stamp was intentional or not. He was jumping over the Arsenal player and was looking up field at the ball as he landed on him. We see far worse than this go unpunished every week, yet the FA decide they're going to do something about THIS? Bunch of incompetent bums.

West Ham got screwed over by referee Jon Moss at Goodison as Nolan was clean through and was brought down by that fucking crab Barry. Clear red card but the ref waved it away. The game was a bit of a shitfest, neither side deserved to win but the Blues nicked it late on through substitute Lukaku. That was only his second goal in eleven games. You can take the striker out of Chelsea, but you can't take Chelsea out of the striker. Unless it's Sturridge, obviously.

Onto Sunday now, and Villa were given a scare at home to Norwich when Hoolahan fired the Canaries ahead after three minutes. Villa had tried and failed to sign Hoolahan in January, and the winger refused to celebrate the goal, presumably as he didn't want to piss off the Villa fans in case it eventually goes through this summer. Not sure how I'd feel about that if I were a Norwich fan. His effort on the day wasn't in question so it's hardly crime of the century I guess. Still doesn't sit right though does it? Villa's fans had a banner on the Holte End declaring themselves the '12th Man'. They were booing the shit out of their team early on though as Norwich dominated, but four goals in 15 minutes had them singing from the rooftops, the fickle bastards. The first was an absolute worldy from Benteke, bringing the ball down on his chest and firing in an overhead kick whilst being punched in the face by Joseph Yobo. Can't believe Yobo is still playing in the Premier League, he must be in his forties now, surely? That's not an 'African age' gag either, I'll leave those to Davie Moyes and Helmet Mourinho, Yobo must actually be pushing 40 now, he was playing for the Blues in the 90's wasn't he? He's like the Nigerian Thomas Rosicky. Benteke referred to himself in the third person afterwards. Disappointing. That's Zlatan behaviour that is.

Spurs had enjoyed a thrilling win in the Europa League in midweek, coming from 2-0 down on aggregate to win 3-2 with a rousing second half comeback. Tim Sherwood reckoned he knew after their first goal they'd go on to win it, saying *"I just thought 'this is it', another one of those nights at the Lane"*. Yeah, another one of those nights, it reminded me of that incredible win against.... Um... or that famous night when they... no sorry, I got nothin'. They just about overcame Cardiff but looked crap in doing so. All season they've been completely mediocre, AVB got the push for not playing enough 'Spurs football' but they're the same under Sherwood even though he's picking as many attacking players as he can shoehorn in there. Completely uninspiring. I imagine this is what Chelsea would be like without Eden Hazard. Soldado won it with his first goal in nine league games, he'd fit right in at the Bridge too.

Elsewhere, my boy Jason Puncheon was fined 15 grand by the FA this week for his comments on Neil Warnock on twitter. Seems a bit low that considering the seriousness of his allegations. Warnock was apparently 'considering legal action', but I bet we hear no more about it, which tells it's own story. Puncheon was absent as Palace drew with Swansea at Selhurst. Two Palace players (Thomas and Chamakh) were guilty of diving and Pulis hammered them afterwards, saying it's a 'disease' and that he'll be fining them both. He was always banging that drum at Stoke too, he was ok with players smashing elbows into opponents and breaking people's legs, but he wouldn't tolerate diving, no sir. To be fair to him at least he practices what he preaches and isn't a complete hypocrite about it, like Moyes.

Gerry Francis was in the stands watching as he's on the staff at Palace these days apparently. That haircut of his bothers me far more than it probably should. It's highly offensive, I mean what the actual fuck, does he not know how utterly ridiculous he looks? How can he not know, I really need to know the answer to this as any time I see him on TV it plays on my mind for the rest of the day, and occasionally even into the day after. I was at my parents house a couple of weeks ago and Francis appeared on SSN. I immediately launched into a familiar tirade about how he mustn't have any mirrors in his house and probably has no friends or family (pretty sure I had the same rant earlier in this book, but I'm not going back to check), as surely they wouldn't let him go out of his front door looking like that, let alone appear on TV. What did my arl fella say? I'll tell you what he said. He said *"that'll be you in a few years that"*. Cheeky bastard.

Premier League Round Up (8 March 2014)

To think I was actually harbouring some hope that Spurs might do us a favour and give Chelsea a bit of a game. Don't I look stupid now. Honestly, I don't know what I was thinking. Spurs are little more than an expensive Aston Villa. Neither Spurs or Villa ever win when it counts or when you need them too, losing is sewn deep into the fabric of their collective DNA and this shouldn't have been a shock as it's what Spurs do. It's who they are.

I don't know if I'm more mad at Spurs for what they did in that second half at Stamford Bridge or myself for not seeing it coming a mile off. Tottenham Hotspur are fucking losers, they have been for more or less my entire lifetime. They've got a long history of choking in big games and their record against Chelsea is horrific, especially at the Bridge where they haven't won since 1990 (which scarily is actually 24 years ago now. 24!!). They were never going to win, I knew that, but that was ok as we didn't need them to win. A dull 0-0 draw would have done us just fine and at half time that's how it was shaping up.

Spurs had to overcome a big blow just before kick off when Torres injured himself in the warm up and was replaced in Chelsea's starting line up by Eto'o, but they recovered well from that setback and probably shaded an uneventful the first half. It was a typical Chelsea game; dull as fuck. Then Spurs must have suddenly remembered who they are and also where they were playing. Normal order was quickly restored as Vertonghen inexplicably fell over and then whilst lying on the floor played a stupid back pass that was never going to get there. Eto'o gleefully collected and put Chelsea ahead. I'm still livid at Vertonghen, the stupid fuck. A week ago he's doing Zidane turns in the centre circle and skinning two opponents, but when it actually counts he's falling down like a pensioner on an icy pavement, the big clumsy fucking dope.

As if that wasn't bad enough, a minute later Kaboul concedes a penalty and gets himself sent off for a needless shove on Eto'o (who milked it for all it was worth and then some). Hazard stroked in the pen as Lloris dived out of the way (any chance of a keeper actually standing up and making Hazard put one in the corner for once?) and suddenly Spurs were 2-0 down and playing with ten men. For the third goal Sandro just fell over his own stupid feet and presented Ba with a tap in, and the fourth was even worse as Walker headed the ball straight to Ba from the halfway line. Not only did this result mean Chelsea went seven points clear of us, but they clawed back four goals on us too. Cheers Spurs, you absolute fucking cowardly, bottling shithouse twats.

People are buzzing off the Eto'o 'old man' celebration. Fuck him, the cheating mercenary prick. Fuck his manager too, the rancid little skid mark. The continual stream of shite coming from him shows no sign of drying up, he gets worse every week: *"City have everything in their hands. They have three matches in hand, so if they win all the three matches they are top of the league. I would like to be in their position, because if they win the matches they are top of the league. If we win the next nine matches, we may not be champions."* He then went on to state that if City win all their games they'll be Champions, but here's a novel idea, why not try and improve your goal difference by actually playing some football for a change instead of parking the bus and waiting for the opposition to make a mistake. They've won this game 4-0 without even having to create anything as all four goals were gift wrapped by Spurs players. Maybe if he didn't base his tactical approach on Howard fucking Wilkinson they could outscore City and not have to even worry about goal difference?

Sherwood has been getting a bit of stick for throwing his players under the bus afterwards, but seriously, look at the goals they conceded!! You can't blame him for those goals, every one of them was down to one of his players having some form of Jon Walters moment. I'm not Sherwood's biggest fan by a long way, but he had every right to lay into those fucking losers after this. Preferably with a baseball bat. That's been set on fire. And has nails in it. Nails that have been dipped in dog shit. Fuckin' Spurs.

Elsewhere on Saturday Fulham took another huge step towards the Championship by losing at Cardiff. Fulham gave a debut to some kid who's been on loan in the lower leagues. Cauley Woodrow strutted around in bright orange boots with his fucking name embroidered on them! So much for that new manager of theirs being some kind of strict disciplinarian. Magath said afterwards they don't have enough fight as they have too many players who are not used to being in that position. It also doesn't help that they're on their third manager of the season. Or is it fourth? I've honestly lost track. I guess Martin Jol wasn't the problem though eh? Cardiff are still in big trouble despite this result, but Vincent Tan was stood there in his replica shirt, doing 'the Ayatollah' afterwards. What a fucking crank. I kinda like him though. And Craig Noone is ace.

The mancs had a fairly routine win at the Hawthorns. Not really a surprise, West Brom have done really well against the good sides but they've lost to everyone else so this was par for the course. Pepe Mel hasn't won a game yet, what an inspired appointment he's been. So yeah, maybe Steve Clarke wasn't so bad, eh Baggies? Van Persie was lucky not be sent off when he lunged at Reid when already on a yellow card. He got a tiny bit of the ball but I don't think the ref knew that, especially as he gave a free-kick. Moyes subbed him soon after anyway, but that doesn't do us any good as he should have been suspended for next weekend, the dirty twat.

Norwich and Stoke drew 1-1 at Carrow Road. Far better result for Stoke considering the fixtures Norwich have left. They need to get points on the board now as they're not going to be getting many in the closing weeks. Mixed day for my mate Walters though. He scored, from the penalty spot, obviously but was then sent off for a clumsy lunge on Tettey. Not the worst foul in the world and certainly not as bad as the one Eto'o got away with on Henderson, but it looked a painful one. He's more clumsy that dirty though.

I think I may have written last season that I wouldn't be able to pick Wes Hoolahan out of a line up, and I still wouldn't. He's a good little player but he must have the most forgettable face in football as I don't remember ever seeing it, but I obviously must have. Come on, be honest, do any of you (non-Irish) know what he looks like? It's not just that he plays for Norwich, as I think I could identify everyone else in their side but I've got no idea at all what Wes Hoolahan looks like.

Finally, Palace lost at home to Southampton in a close game that the Saints just shaded. Rodriguez won it with a fine goal after he seized on a poor header by my boy Jason Puncheon and then bravely won a 50-50 with the keeper before rolling in a shot as he lay on the floor. There's a lot of things to like about Southampton, but their haircuts certainly aren't one of them. What the fuck is going on there? Half their team look like they should be smuggling booze for Nucky Thompson in Boardwalk Empire, the 1920s looking bastards.

MANCHESTER UNITED 0 LIVERPOOL 3

Competition - Premier League
Date - Sun 16 Mar 2014
Venue - Old Trafford
Scorer(s) – Gerrard (2 pens),
Suarez
Star Man – Steven Gerrard

Team: Mignolet; Johnson, Skrtel, Agger, Flanagan; Gerrard (Lucas), Henderson, Allen, Sterling (Coutinho); Suarez, Sturridge (Aspas):

It's the season that keeps on giving. Go back to pre-season and try to imagine your reaction if someone had told you that not only would we be right in the thick of a title race with nine games to go, but that we'd be the leading scorers in the league and we'd have spanked Spurs 5-0 at White Hart Lane, completely destroyed Everton and Arsenal at Anfield and humiliated the Mancs at Old Trafford, having been awarded THREE penalties in the process. None of us would have believed it, and yet here we are. Football, eh? Bloody hell.

All that's left is to give Chelsea and City the 'Anfield treatment' and then clinch what would surely be the most unlikely title success of any team in recent memory. It won't be easy of course, but with each week it seems to become more of a possibility and this weekend has seen a massive shift in the balance of power. Prior to this weekend's fixtures I couldn't really see past Chelsea. Their fixture list was the kindest, they had a seven point lead over us, they're jammy bastards and this weekend they were playing Aston fucking Villa.

Our away record at United is grim, we all know that, and even though this isn't the Manchester United we're used to it still had the potential to go tits up for us. So when Chelsea shit the bed at Villa Park I could hardly contain myself, it was almost too good to be true. It didn't even matter that ten man City had won at Hull, there'll be plenty of time to worry about City over the coming weeks, but beat United and we would no longer be relying on Chelsea to slip up to be able to catch them, it would be in our own hands.

Could we beat United though? In theory it shouldn't be that difficult, after all it feels like everyone has been winning at Old Trafford this season, except for United themselves obviously. But we've been in United's position so many times down the years with nothing to play for other than trying to stop our most hated rivals from winning the title. So many times they've come to Anfield and we've been playing only for pride and to put a dent in their title hopes. Now the shoe was on the other foot, we were going there trying to make a run at the title and they were in the 'party poopers' role. I guess they aren't as good at it as we've been, but in fairness we've had a lot more practice. We won this one so, so easily, it wasn't even a contest. United had one shot on target in the entire 90 minutes. ONE SHOT!!! Moyes has completely destroyed that team, I knew he would but I didn't think it could happen THIS quickly. We didn't even play that well, at least the forwards didn't. We were much better at Spurs and in the home games against Everton and Arsenal. In fact, we were better in the FA Cup defeat at the Emirates a few weeks ago.

Neither Suarez nor Sturridge were at their absolute best, whilst Sterling was disciplined and sensible as opposed to the rampaging, free running menace he has been in other fixtures. Despite all that, we won by three goals and all bias aside, it should have been at least double. Imagine what would have happened if we'd actually been at our best. This was incredible. We actually got three penalties in one game at Old Trafford. I don't think they've had three penalties given against them at home in the last five years. We could easily have had five truth be told.

There were only a few minutes gone when we should have had the first one. Flanagan mugged Mata inside the United half and fed Suarez who set off into the box. The oafish Fellaini clipped his heels but Luis fought to stay on his feet, went past Jones and was then eventually bundled over from behind by Fellaini. We should have had two penalties for that, but Clattenburg took the easy way out and gave a corner. Don't expect Suarez to get credit for staying on his feet, and don't expect it to be mentioned the next time he wins a contentious penalty either. What this shows once again is there is no reward for staying on your feet. This is exactly why players generally go down when they're clipped in the box.

We'd started confidently though and had all kinds of room in midfield to pass the ball around. Brendan had once again gone with the midfield diamond, meaning we essentially had four players in the middle of the park when we had the ball. 'Captain Tactics' Moyes had gone with a basic 442 with Fellaini and Carrick in the middle, meaning United had all the mobility of a couple of traffic cones in there. I doubt if the likes of Allen and Sterling have had an easier game all year. I can't remember any of our lads even being tackled in the middle of the pitch. Football has evolved so much in recent years, there are so many young, forward thinking coaches of which Rodgers is at the forefront. Moyes is a fucking dinosaur, he's completely overmatched and Rodgers took him to school in a big way. United are playing prehistoric football this season.

Gerrard would collect the ball, take a look up and see Allen, Sterling and Henderson in pockets of space every time. It was just too easy for us to play, and we completely controlled the game from start to finish. Of course United still have individual talent in their side so they will pose a threat, but that threat does not come through teamwork or organised play, just off the cuff play from talented footballers. That's a lot easier for a defence to cope with and by and large we restricted them to next to nothing. United started with Mata on the right (Captain Tactics strikes again) but it didn't stay that way for long as Flanagan was bullying the Spaniard off the ball at every turn. Januzaj was switched over to that side and he presented a different set of problems to Flanno, but he didn't do much either.

Rafael was booked for a late challenge on Gerrard and almost immediately after he conceded a penalty and should have been sent off. It was hilarious, Suarez could have played on as the ball landed at his feet but instead he just ran off screaming for a handball and put Clattenburg in a position where he was under real pressure to give it. This time he pointed to the spot but he was unmoved by the demands of Suarez and Henderson for a second yellow card for the Brazilian.

Something that I think has been overlooked due to the controversy over whether Rafael should have walked or not, is that the touch from Suarez was simply incredible. Any other player in the league is bringing that ball down and then trying to take the full back on. Not Suarez, why take two or three touches when one will do? That's how he forced the handball, because he completely caught Rafael off guard with that incredible touch. Other players wouldn't have even thought of that, let alone had the ability to carry it out.

Gerrard expertly placed the penalty a couple of inches inside the post and tellingly didn't celebrate. He was all business, he knew there was still a job to do. Everyone else went mental though, as you do. Gerrard was then booked after a clash with Fellaini. It was a joke that, Clattenburg didn't even give a free-kick and only stopped the game because both Fellaini and Sterling were down with head injuries. He blew the whistle for them to get treatment, and only then when he saw Fellaini bleeding like a 1970s bush at a certain time of the month did he decide to book Gerrard. The United physio eventually stopped the bleeding, presumably by shoving a tampon up one of his nostrils, and that was just about the last time I even saw Fellaini until he was subbed in the second half. Flanagan also went into the book after a foul on Rooney. He did obstruct him but Rooney went down incredibly easily for a fat lad.

I was a little annoyed we were only one up at half time, we'd been so superior in every way up until the last few minutes of the half when United had a little spell that led to a Rooney shot that was parried comfortably by Mignolet (the impressive Skrtel made a fantastic block on the follow up too). We'd let them off the hook a little though. Sturridge had failed to make the most of two good situations when he got in behind the United defence. The first time he decided not to score but instead took the option of leathering the ball into the face of a manc behind the goal. Fair enough, it was early in the game and there was plenty of time to get a few goals, but having the opportunity to drill the ball at one of those mutants from close range is a temptation few of us would be able to resist. The second one he cut back onto his left side but then scuffed his shot when he really should have done better. We hadn't created as much as we possibly could have based on the control of the game we had, but you could see there was a gulf in class between the sides. I just hoped we could make it count in the second half. We did, and it didn't take long either. Seconds after the restart Allen was bundled over by Calamity Jones and Gerrard rolled in his second penalty of the game. This time he celebrated, and even re-enacted his 'kissing the camera' routine from 2009. Love that.

United tried to rally and had a bit of a go but I never felt they were building any kind of momentum, in fact it just seemed like we were trying to lure them in so we could hit them on the break. We were still in control, and had we been more efficient on the counter we'd have murdered them. Instead, Sturridge and Suarez kept falling over or making the wrong decision, and it was getting a little bit frustrating as we just couldn't kill them off. As much as we were on top, I kept thinking that if we gave away a daft goal we'd find ourselves under pressure as they pushed for an equaliser. They never looked like scoring but unless a third goal or a United red card arrived I was not going to be able to relax. I thought we were getting both when Vidic lunged in on Sturridge and Clattenburg pointed to the spot for a third time and also gave Vidic his walking papers. Incredible scenes, THREE penalties at Old Trafford? What kind of alternate reality is this?

Credit to Clattenburg, he called the incidents on their own merits and didn't do a Howard Webb and allow the circumstances to dictate his decisions. Webb didn't give the Suarez pen at Arsenal because he'd not long given us an earlier spot-kick and didn't want to have to give us another. I'm sure Clattenburg wasn't entirely comfortable giving three pens to one team either (hence him ignoring a blatant fourth not long after), but he refereed the incident and not the situation. The irony is, the third one wasn't actually a pen, it was a dive by Sturridge. Vidic went mental at him, understandably so but he should also be looking at himself as if you go flying in like that and don't win the ball you're asking for trouble. Sturridge made it look so convincing that no blame can be attached to the referee for that call. It's an almost impossible job making those decisions without the benefit of replays.

Still, having been on the end of so many bad penalty calls on this ground down the years I'm not apologising for this one. I'm not going to have a go at Sturridge either as if you give me a choice of him doing what he did or staying on his feet and us not getting the pen or red card, then I'm taking the cheating option all day. There's a league title at stake here, and everyone else is doing this kind of shit so bollocks to it. Well in Studge lad.

I was desperate for Stevie to score the pen, not because I felt we needed the third goal now (Vidic going off ended any fear I had of an unlikely Manc comeback), but because I just wanted it for him. The first game he ever went to was the Coventry game when Molby scored a hat-trick of pens, it would have been pretty cool for him to do it at Old Trafford. As he said afterwards though, Molby is a better penalty taker than he is.

After that we just toyed with them, we could have scored another three or four easily but had to settle for just the one when Sturridge's dreadful shot landed at the feet of Suarez who finished in style. He'd earlier been denied what would have been a stunning goal when he completely destroyed Jones only to be denied by a magnificent save from De Gea. Other opportunities came and went and Sturridge was denied a stonewall pen when he was tripped by Carrick. He probably didn't get it because Clattenburg maybe realised he'd been duped on the other one (fourth official may have told him?), but the reaction of Carrick was disgraceful. Sturridge will get criticised for diving (not too much, after all he's the England centre forward now so he'll be shielded from a lot of flak), but what Carrick did is just as dishonest in it's own way. He knew he'd caught Sturridge, knew it was a pen but he made a big deal of accusing Sturridge of diving and wanted the referee to book him. That's cheating too you know!

The closing stages of this game were just glorious as we completely took the piss out of them by passing the ball around in their half. I'm not sure what made me laugh the most, Moyes bringing on Ferdinand to try and keep the 0-3, or Rodgers sending on Aspas as the ultimate 'fuck you'. If it was me I'd have sent Cissokho on at centre forward just for a laugh, with instructions to 'do what Dossena did'.

What of their fans though, how fascinating was it watching (and listening to) them? The Hillsborough stuff came across loud and clear, and they can't play the Munich card either as they were responding to *"Fergie's right, your fans are shite"*, which hardly calls for them to stoop to those levels. Tens of thousands of them were singing *"the S*n was right, you're murderers"*. We're not talking a few hundred dickheads, it's half the crowd doing it. Something should be done about it, I know it's been brought up with Ian Ayre in the past so hopefully this will give the club the ammunition they need to make something of this and bring it to the attention of the authorities.

Leaving that aside though, I found the conduct of the United fans to be hilarious. As it became clear their team were out of their depth and it was simply a case of damage limitation, the defiance of the United fans grew and they cranked the volume up. That surprised me. In the build up to this game when I'd played out the various scenarios in my head the one in which we were giving them a chasing usually ended with their fans losing their shit and turning on Moyes. Turns out I gave them way too much credit, they're much more stupid than I thought. Whilst they are no doubt this morning sucking their own dicks about what great supporters they are, the massively deluded Moyes will be consoling himself in the knowledge that *'the fans are still with us'*. Hell, he's probably penning them another heartfelt letter of thanks right now. Honestly, I hope they do this every week. It might even convince the Glazers to stick with him for next season. *"Twenty times twenty times Man United"* they belted out for the closing 15 minutes of the game. If I could give them all a massive condescending pat on the top of the head I would. I'd also ask them if they take requests, as I really miss that *"Come on Davey Moyes, play like Fergie's boys"* ditty. Whatever happened to that? Did they tire of going *"wild wild wild"*? Still, at least that 'Chosen One' banner is still up in the Stretford End. Not sure for how much longer, much like Moyes being their manager we should just enjoy that for as long as it lasts.

As for us, onwards and upwards. Gerrard has been believing we can do this for weeks now and slowly but surely the fans are starting to come around to his way of thinking. I was in the *'we can win it'* rather than the *'we will win it'* camp, but when Chelsea lost at Villa I got this overwhelming feeling that if we could win at Old Trafford we would go on and win the damn thing. And win at Old Trafford we did. Easily. We might actually do this you know. Kinell.

Premier League Round Up (15-16 March 2014)

Quite a weekend for us. Winning at Old Trafford was cause for celebration in itself but Chelsea unexpectedly dropping points too just capped a great couple of days and who knows, this might be the weekend we look back on as being crucial when the season ends. I'll get to the Chelsea shenanigans in due course, but may as well get all the irrelevant, non-entities out of the way first.

So where better to start than at Goodison where the Blues needed a spawny, sliced stoppage time goal from Coleman to see off second from bottom club Cardiff (their first goal was a poxy deflection too, the jammy blue bastards). Remember the days when they used to finish above us? Kinell. It's funny listening to them absolutely destroying Moyes at every opportunity now they've got 'the thin Spanish waiter'. Good luck finishing above Liverpool three times Roberto, especially when Bill tells you there's no money to buy those players you've borrowed.

Nothing can wipe the smile off Solskjaer's face though can it? Is there a happier little chappy anywhere in football than the goblin faced former Manc super sub? Do you reckon he's ever shouted at one of his players or lost his temper about anything? I just can't see it, he's the world's cheeriest man. His scouse accent is ace too, probably perfected that during all those years he was a paid up member of LFC's Norwegian fan club. He was still paying his subs for that even when he was at United, until Soccer AM got wind of it and put him in a spot with the manc fans and he had to cancel.

Elsewhere, Pepe Mel got his first win as West Brom boss as the Baggies came from behind to win at Swansea. The Baggies continued their recent habit of getting better in the 2nd half. Mel's half time team talks must be incredible, like Al Pacino in 'Any Given Sunday' or some shit. Maybe he should give his half time speech BEFORE the game instead. Just a thought. Incredibly there had been talk that Mel would be sacked if they didn't win this game. What the fuck is wrong with football clubs these days? Look, for all I know Mel might actually be the shittest manager in the history of world football (barring Mike Walker obviously), but West Brom sacked Steve Clarke and hired this guy, so if he is bad enough to be sacked after a couple of months then what does that say about the people who hired him?

Norwich are in deep shit now after losing at Southampton. Their run in is brutal and they need to be picking up points now. As difficult as St Mary's is to go this was a game Norwich really could have done with taking something from. They almost did but it would have owed more to the Saints shooting themselves in the foot than anything Norwich did themselves. The Saints went 3-0 up and were coasting but then Norwich threatened a shock comeback with two late goals to spark a grandstand finale. Both Norwich goals came from Southampton players passing the ball straight to Johan Elmander. Bizarre stuff really, I know he's shite but you can't just give him the ball and let him have a free run at your keeper. He's bad but he's not Jozy Altidore bad. As Norwich threw everything forward looking for the equaliser they got caught on the break and young Gallagher made it 4-2. I suspect Norwich are probably doomed now (along with Fulham and Cardiff if you're wondering).

Two beanpole ex Liverpool strikers were on the mark as Stoke edged out West Ham at the Britannia. Carroll headed West Ham in front, Crouch headed Stoke level, although Odemwingie might get credit for it as it hit his goal hanging arse on the line on it's way in. Arnautovic made it 2-1 to the home side and then West Ham were the victims of a shocking decision from the ref Craig Pawson (who?). A Stoke defender punched the ball away from Carroll but when the big fella appealed Pawson started yelling in his face *"that was never handball in a million years. No way"*. Awful decision, but hilarious reaction. Odemwingie then finished off a quick counter attack with a stunning drive to make the game safe for Stoke, who continue to play some decent stuff and aren't anywhere near as dislikable as they used to be.

Speaking of dislikable, Alan Pardew served the first of his three game stadium ban as Newcastle went to Craven Cottage. His place on the bench was taken by his assistant John Carver, who's arguably even more of a hothead than Pardew. *"Hey it's ok folks, we've removed the Great White from the aquarium.... we've put a Hammerhead in there instead"* Dejagah got the only goal of a game that ended in controversy when Newcastle were denied a stoppage time penalty as Heitinga blatantly handled to stop a shot from Newcastle keeper Krul who'd come up for a corner. In that situation you need a strong ref who isn't afraid of making a decision at a crucial stage of the game. Unfortunately for the Geordies they got Howard fucking Webb.

Sunderland have somehow landed themselves back in the shit. How'd that happen? A few weeks ago they were looking ok, they'd moved out of the relegation zone and were going great guns in both cups. Now? They lost in the League Cup final, they were dumped out of the FA Cup by a manager they sacked (a manager with a parsnip nose and nan's hair no less) and they're back in the bottom three and being booed off by the fans after a goalless draw with Palace. Fabio played well again though; he hit the bar with a great effort and also went close with an overhead kick. He's looking sharp. Still smelling great too I bet.

That's all the also rans out of the way, so on to the games that matter. The only three games that were of any concern to us were those involving our title rivals Man City, Chelsea and Arsenal. One was the early kick off, one was the late game and the other was on Sunday. First up were City, and that game got off to an unexpected start when a furious Kompany was sent off after just ten minutes for pulling back Jelavic. Must have been a tough call for Lee Mason though, what with him being from Manchester and all, eh Brendan?

We know as well as anyone how dangerous Hull can be, so the news that City were a man down so early got my hopes up good and proper. Even when Silva put City in front not long after I wasn't overly upset as that's a long, long time to have to play with only ten men and we didn't even need Hull to win, a draw would have been fine. Surely they could find one goal, couldn't they? No they couldn't, the chumps. They didn't even really make much of a fight of it. I'm not sure how a central defensive pairing of Demichelis and Javi Garcia kept a clean sheet, especially as Long and Jelavic have been on a good run recently, but somehow they did. Demichelis was even beaten one v one by Jelavic who used a stepover to get round him. Jelavic doing stepovers? What next, Jon Walters doing a rabona? Fucking hell. If that doesn't tell you how crap this Demichelis fella is then nothing will.

City did have to survive two penalty shouts, both involving Boyd. The first was an outrageous dive but the second was a clumsy shove on him by Fernandinho and it could easily have been given. Joe Hart completely lost his shit over the dive and should have been sent off for shoving his head right into Boyd's face as the pair screamed at each other. Replays showed that Boyd had spat in Hart's face but the keeper probably didn't even notice as he'd proper flipped his lid by that point anyway. It wasn't the worst spitting incident you'll ever see, but it was still a shithouse thing to do. Looks like Boyd's impressive hair isn't the only South American trait he has. He's facing an FA charge and rightly so. Dzeko wrapped it up in the last minute and this could prove to be a huge win for City who've been wobbling big time recently.

I was expecting both City and Chelsea to win at the weekend, but of the two games the one I held out the least hope for was obviously Chelsea's at Villa Park. I've learnt to never rely on Villa for anything, they're just too... well they're Aston Villa aren't they? Yet bizarrely, Jose Mourinho has never won at Villa Park. I wasn't aware of that prior to kick off, but even if I had been it would have just made me think 'well that's about to come to an end right here'. What happened over the course of that ninety minutes was bordering on being too good to be true. I'm still not sure it actually happened. Villa actually doing something worthwhile? Kinell.

They had a little helping hand from referee Chris Foy and his assistants though. Matic had a goal disallowed for handball in the first half. It was the correct call but it wasn't massively obvious and it wouldn't have been a surprise if it had been given. Thankfully the liner spotted it. He learned his trade in the Maghull & Lydiate league, apparently. Maybe he's a red? He might even be a blue, in which case he's now number two on my favourite Evertonians list. Chris Foy is number one (yes, he's a blue, apparently). Torres got hooked having done fuck all again, and Willian was supposed to go with him but the 'Special' one changed his mind and subbed Oscar instead. Seconds later, Willian got himself a second booking and was off. Hahahaha good one Jose, you fucking genius. The sending off was seriously harsh though, that was never a yellow card in a million years but... well never mind, eh?

At this stage I'm listening on the radio thinking *"that'll do, hopefully Villa should be able to hold out for a point against ten men"* and then something wonderful happened. The outstanding Delph back heeled Villa ahead with eight minutes to go. He was then denied by a combination of Cech and the crossbar too as Villa looked to kill the game off. As for Chelsea, they had nothing. They're fine when defending a lead but ask them to chase the game and they haven't got a clue. They handled adversity with a typical lack of class, Ramires being red carded for a despicable lunge at a Villa player and Mourinho then being sent to the stands for coming on the pitch to try and argue the decision. Helmet. I dunno what the hell was going on with Lambert and Mourinho all game though, they were constantly in discussion, sometimes laughing and joking and other times it looked a little bit hostile even though they'd have their arms on each others shoulders. It was bizarre stuff, and more than a little uncomfortable to watch. Not as uncomfortable as Maureen's post match interview though, what a train wreck that was.

BBC Lackey: *What did you think of the result Jose?*
Helmet*: The result? One zero to Aston Villa*
BBC Lackey: *Did you think your performance deserved more than that?*
Helmet*: My performance deserved more than that.*
BBC Lackey: *What about your team's performance?*

Ah fucking hell, really? We actually pay our TV licence to have to put up with this shit? How great would it have been if the interviewer had said after his second answer: *"You know what, if you're going to act like an arse we'll just leave it and go and speak to Paul Lambert instead"*. Instead it carried on with him being a dick, repeatedly saying *"I prefer not to speak" "I prefer not to comment" "If I speak I am accused of bringing the game into disrepute"* and then hilariously.... *"It's difficult to close my mouth"* No shit, Sherlock. Then, despite 'preferring not to speak' he went on for five minutes slagging off the ref. He kept going on about how he *"wanted five seconds"* to speak with him but Foy was having none of it. *"Mizter Foy, can I have five seconds" "No!"* Haha go ed there Chris Foy!

A few days later Mourinho was still banging on about how Foy should not be allowed to referee Chelsea anymore. Ho! The fuckin' balls on this guy. If we have to deal with Howard fucking Webb than you can put up with Foy and shut your damn piehole. It's hilarious listening to him going on and on and on about the ref though. Remember what happened to Villa at Stamford Bridge earlier in the season? You probably don't, but here's what I wrote in the round up after that game:

"Villa gave it their best shot at Stamford Bridge, but what can you do when Ivanovic is allowed to get away with elbowing Benteke in the face and then scores the winner within a minute? The ref actually saw it and booked him, but it's clearly a red card offence, not a yellow. Not just that, but in stoppage time 'Mongo' decides to play volleyball in his own box yet no penalty is given. Shocking effort from the match official, Kevin 'nobody's' Friend. Poor Villa got screwed, but Mourinho generally gets his way when it comes to referees and this certainly won't be the last time it happens."

And it wasn't the last time it happened either, look at Webb's performance against us for example, and that farcical pen they got against West Brom. It seems Mourinho has forgotten about the favours he got from Kevin 'Jose's special' Friend back in August in his quest to play the victim and absolve his shithouse players of any blame for their lacklustre display and shameful conduct at Villa Park. *"I don't think this result makes any difference to the title race because we are not in the title race. All we are trying to do is win every match. Sometimes we do, sometimes we don't, but that's our race."* Top of the league with nine games to go, and they're not in a title race? Honestly, if it were anyone else coming out with this crap he'd be getting ridiculed by all and sundry, yet this clown seems to have a free pass, and it's put down to 'mind games'. He defo plays by a different set of rules this twat, and it will only get worse if he actually manages to win something. The worst thing he did though was to blame Foy for what Ramires did, basically saying that Foy's performance caused Ramires to lose his temper and that's why he committed that shocking challenge. He made that ludicrous statement a couple of days after the fact, he can't even use 'heat of the moment' as an excuse, the complete cock. If that's not worth a disrepute charge then I don't know what is. And how has nobody lamped him yet?

They're still in the Champions League after seeing off a woeful Galatasaray side for whom Drogba stunk the place out. He put one free-kick so high over the bar it hit a banner in the top tier with his own fucking name on it, the colossal shithead.

Speaking of colossal shitheads, Mancini and Mourinho's long running feud continued. They didn't shake hands before the game (don't know if they did after as I'd long since switched the TV off) and even though Mancini had extended an olive branch by offering to buy him dinner, Mourinho refused, saying *"No, I have no interest. The only thing we have in common is the fact we're both football managers"* Not true that though is it? They have something else in common, they're both massive dickheads with an ego the size of a small solar system. They say 'opposites attract', so that'll be why these two can't get on as they're so similar. Ok, admittedly Mancini is nowhere near as much of a thundercunt as Mourinho, but then who is?

Not Tim Sherwood that's for sure. I think I misjudged him you know. Ok, 'misjudged' is probably the wrong choice of word actually as I judged him pretty well. I said he'd be shit and I also said he was a massive twat and without wanting to blow my own trumpet too much I was right on both counts. Yet I can't deny there's something endearing about him. I don't hate Sherwood anymore; I think he's ace and hope he gets a new contract. I love his no nonsense style of management and complete disregard for tactics. The body warmer is class too, it just feels like Spurs have just hired some fella off a fruit and veg stall or a pub landlord and sent him out there to put a rocket up the arses of some under-performing prima-donnas. He's throwing fits on the sidelines when his players are making mistakes and he's generally just acting like some angry fan. *"Fackin ell boys, what the fack do you fink you're playin' at??"* *"Oy, Vertonghen you fackin slaaaaag, what the fackin ell was that?"* *"Eriksen, where the fack do you fink you're s'posed to be playin' son? I said four four fackin two, you silly Danish cant"*

Spurs meekly lost the North London derby on Sunday which wasn't great news for us as we could have really done with Arsenal dropping a point or two before their games with Chelsea and City (which ideally we need them to win). Spurs are now in a three way fight with the Mancs and Blueshite for 5th spot, and to me they look like the worst of three, yes, even worse than United.

Poor old Moyesy though, it seems like the world is out to get him right now. I'm sure he expected most of the flak that has come his way, but he's probably a little bewildered at the hostility coming his way from Evertonians. It's bad enough listening to their fans going on about how over-rated he is and bemoaning his negative football, but as we were wiping the floor with his Manc side even the Everton staff he left behind started to pile on. Everton youth coach Kevin Sheedy, who worked with Moyes for 7 years, laid into him on twitter during the game. *"Punt the ball up to*

Fellaini. Great viewing." Wait, what? He actually wrote that? I didn't hear any blueshite complaining when Everton did that for years. If anything I'd say that United did anything but punt the ball up to Fellaini. I'd be the first one to rip them if they did, but it's almost as though Moyes is scared to do that as he knows he'll get hammered for it. More to the point though, why has Sheedy suddenly got sand in his vagina? He must have beef with Moyes, perhaps because he's one of the few staff Gollum didn't take with him to Mordor? Whatever his reason he's obviously decided that now is the time to stick the knife in whilst Moyes is at such a low ebb. *"All of you out there, Moyes was never interested in our youth team or youth players"* he then added, before then telling an Everton fan that they now have a manager *"who wants to win games"*. Whilst Sheedy has a point, it can't just be me thinking he's a bit of a rat for doing that, especially given the moment he chose to do it?

I was genuinely concerned for Moyes, it was looking as though he might not even get to see out the week and that would be bad news for everyone. Well, everyone except United's players and fans, but they deserve all they get. Thankfully United managed to pull one out of the fire against Olympiakos and that will have earned Moyes a little longer to show what he isn't capable of. Ideally they'll get Bayern, Barca or Madrid in the next round and be completely humiliated. Or perhaps they'll get Chelsea, giving Mourinho's side easy passage to the semis where they themselves can then get Bayern, Barca or Madrid and be completely humiliated. Either is good for me.

CARDIFF CITY 3 LIVERPOOL 6

Competition - Premier League
Date - Sat 22 Mar 2014
Venue - Cardiff City Stadium
Scorer(s) – Suarez (3),
Skrtel (2), Sturridge
Star Man – Luis Suarez

Team: Mignolet; Johnson, Skrtel, Agger, Flanagan (Cissokho); Gerrard, Henderson, Allen, Coutinho (Sterling); Sturridge (Sakho), Suarez:

Another one down, eight more to go. That's six wins on the spin now and, dare I say it, we're beginning to look pretty damned near unstoppable. Not even the defensive errors are slowing us down anymore as our attacking play has scaled never before seen heights. Suarez continues to score at an astonishing rate and Sturridge is almost matching him. When was the last time two players from the same club finished at the top of the scoring charts? Hell, even Skrtel is getting in on the act, he's got more Premier League goals this season than Fernando Torres now. Not sure who that says more about though really.

At long last I'm finally starting to trust this team. I'm no longer expecting them to throw in a stinker every five or six games and when they do suffer a setback I expect them to overcome it. Twice they fell behind in this one but my over-riding feeling each time was of annoyance rather than panic. I knew we'd come back to win because as an attacking force we have no equal in English football; past or present. Yes, I'm putting it out there, this is the best attacking side I've seen in my lifetime. My eyes tell me that and the numbers back it up. Not even the Barnes/Beardsley/Aldo team was this devastating.

It's a wild, wild ride we're on at the moment. We've had one sided victories, we've had dramatic, narrow victories and we've had roller coaster games like this one. When was the last dull game we were involved in? West Brom away probably, and before that I don't even remember. We haven't been involved in a 0-0 all season, no wonder almost all of our games on TV these days. This one wasn't, and no doubt both Sky and BT are kicking themselves over it. Cardiff gave it a good go and caused us some problems, especially early on, but in the end it was a lot like the Stoke game; no matter how many problems they gave us they simply couldn't deal with our firepower at the other end and eventually we just overpowered them.

Rodgers stuck with the midfield diamond but recalled Coutinho at the expense of Sterling, but we didn't start too well and quickly fell behind when Allen's sloppy pass sold Flanagan short and Mutch finished with a crisp low drive. Gerrard then went into the book very early on for a clumsy trip and he's now got to get through the next few games without another booking or he'll be hit with a two game ban, and that's the last thing we need given how he's playing. And besides, what will we do if we get a pen? Is there anyone else in the side you'd trust with an important spot kick? Hopefully we won't have to find out.

Perhaps Cardiff's three at the back system caught us a little off guard (apparently Solskjaer had them lined up in a four during warm ups and then sprung the five on us once the game started, the sneaky goblin looking little fuck), but once we eventually adapted to what they were doing we began to settle and take control of the game. Initially we kept trying to attack through the middle but there was just no space or gaps to exploit as they packed that area of the field. When the penny dropped that this wouldn't work and that Johnson was the spare man whenever we attacked, we suddenly looked a lot better. We did a good job of working the ball down that side as Henderson and either Coutinho or one of the strikers would drift over there and ensure Cardiff were overloaded, leaving Johnson free to charge forward. The equaliser came from a perfectly weighted ball by Hendo into the path of the overlapping Johnson whose cross was finished off by Suarez from close range.

He'd been standing miles offside right up until the point Johnson cut the ball back by which time he was behind the play. There was nothing wrong with the goal under the current laws, but something doesn't sit right with me when the centre forward can hang around by the goalkeeper and not even try to get back onside, and instead just wait for the wide player to advance and then cut the ball back to him. It's not right, but thems the rules and Suarez has done nothing wrong. In theory, a striker can now just stand next to the keeper all game, just waiting for a team-mate to get to the byline and cut it back to him for a tap in. If we'd had those rules when I was a kid I might have made it.

That should have seen us take control of the game but defensive vulnerability cost us again and Cardiff hit back to regain the lead through Fraizer Campbell. This was a horrible goal from our point of view. It was seriously amateurish defending from Agger. Look at his position in the build up, he's stood about two yards away from Skrtel as they're both marking the same Cardiff player. That left a huge gap between Agger and Flanagan and Campbell just drifted into it, collected the ball and then beat Agger far too easily to fire in a low shot past Mignolet. Hard to believe that two experienced, international centre backs could get themselves into that situation. That goal really annoyed me, but that's all it was; an irritation. With Suarez and Sturridge on the field it was only ever a matter of time before we scored again, yet surprisingly it was Skrtel who bagged our next two goals.

So we went in at half time level and Cardiff's chance had gone now. We were always going to be better in the 2nd half because Rodgers would make whatever tactical adjustments he needed to (he said we were too deep and corrected that after the break) and Cardiff would tire as the game wore on. The third goal - the decisive one according to the bitter Solskjaer - owed everything to the genius of Suarez. Lining up a free-kick from outside the box, instead of going for goal Suarez took out Mutch by hammering the shot straight into his nut sack, he then collected the rebound and took out Theophile-Catherine by blasting it into the side of his face, leaving him in a crumpled heap. With the two Cardiff players off the field receiving treatment, we took advantage of it when Skrtel headed in Coutinho's corner. Is there nothing Suarez can't do?

Solskjaer had a good old moan about it afterwards, not blaming the officials but pointing out the unfairness of the rule itself that states injured players must leave the field before being allowed back on. I'd maybe have some sympathy with that view if it wasn't coming from a snide little twat who benefitted from the exact same rule when his awful challenge on Sami Hyypia forced the big Finn off the field to have stitches in a leg wound and he then scored whilst we were a man down. Weren't bitching then, were you Ole, you little fucking rat.

That goal was just what we needed, we were well on top in the second half and once we got in front Cardiff had to come out of their defensive shell and that plays right into our hands. Our fourth goal was brilliant as Sturridge back heeled the ball perfectly into the path of the incoming Suarez who gleefully side footed in his second of the game. We've scored some great goals this season but this is one of my favourites, I loved it. Suarez then returned the favour for his strike partner when he collected a raking 60 yard left footed pass from the outstanding Johnson (best game of the season from him I'd say), advanced down the left and then rolled the ball perfectly across the box for Sturridge to tap in. The run from Sturridge to get there was terrific though, he just wanted it more than the Cardiff defence. Made up for him, I was desperate for him to score as it really bothers me now any time either he or Suarez don't get their name on the scoresheet. It's ridiculous when you think about it, but for me it kind of takes the shine off our wins if they don't both score!

You know, Sturridge is far, far better than he's being given credit for I think. Maybe it's because Suarez is that good that Sturridge is almost getting overlooked a little, but he's absolutely fucking brilliant. Some of the things he does just blow me away, and

I'm not even talking about his goals; I mean his general play and ability on the ball. Most partnerships seem to have either a big man little man combo, or a pacey goalscorer playing ahead of a skilful playmaker. You can't pigeon hole either Sturridge or Suarez as any of those as the pair of them are just brilliantly creative footballers as well as being lethal goalscorers. They can play wide, they can play central, they can drop off, basically both of them can do it all and how do you come up with a plan to stop that?

Suarez is a level above as his involvement in the game is almost constant whereas occasionally Sturridge can be quiet for spells, but aside from Luis, is there a better forward in the Premier League than Sturridge? Aguero is the only one who's even in the conversation (unless you're as clueless as Solskjaer and would take Rooney and Van Persie over our pair), but even Aguero might not be better given how Sturridge is performing. Aguero is top drawer but I wouldn't swap Sturridge for him. He scores goals, he makes goals, he links play, he drifts out wide, he holds the ball up, and yet he's not really seen as being in that 'superstar' bracket yet. If we go on to win the title this year then these two can take their place alongside any great pairing of the past, be it Hunt-St John, Toshack-Keegan or, whisper it, even Dalglish and Rush.

It's still a big IF of course, there's a long way still to go but with each week and each win our chances increase a little more. We gave away another bad goal against Cardiff to make it 5-3, but even then, as they sensed the faint whiff of hope, we still looked more likely to score than they did and duly wrapped it up deep into stoppage time when Suarez outmuscled the last defender, advanced on goal and then completed his hat-trick. He owes a big debt of thanks to substitute Sterling for that goal though, the lung bursting run of the teenager from the inside his own half to get up in support meant that Cardiff keeper David Marshall couldn't commit fully to trying to stop Suarez; he had to respect the pass too as Sterling would have had a tap in. Under normal circumstances Suarez probably should have passed (and he apologised to his young team-mate afterwards) but the game was won and you can't blame him for wanting his hat-trick. Sterling did a similar thing against Arsenal when he was on a hat-trick I seem to remember. Raheem's despairing 'hands to his head' gesture when Suarez went himself was pretty funny. If I'd sprinted that far to get into the box and he'd ignored me, I'd have done a lot more than show a little bit of frustration, that's for sure. I'd have needed oxygen treatment first like, but once I'd gotten my breath back an hour or two later I'd have been all over Suarez for that.

I'm well past caring about our defensive issues now, it is what it is. Besides, I'd rather win 6-3 than 3-0, although 6-0 would obviously be far better for the heart. That may have to wait until next year though, one step at a time and all that. I just think that there's no point getting into a lather about the goals we're conceding when by and large it's not costing us any points. We're constantly being told that you can't win anything without a solid defence, but the more I see this team I think why the hell not? This team is rewriting the book on how you can and can't win games and what they're doing is simply ridiculous. I fucking love this team you know, they're boss aren't they?

LIVERPOOL 2 SUNDERLAND 1

Competition - Premier League
Date - Wed 26 Mar 2014
Venue - Anfield
Scorer(s) – Steven Gerrard,
Daniel Sturridge
Star Man – Philippe Coutinho

Team: Mignolet; Johnson,
Skrtel, Agger, Flanagan;
Gerrard, Henderson, Allen,
Coutinho; Suarez, Sturridge
(Sterling):

However this thing eventually plays out, the one thing that's clear now is that we're not going away without a fight. This made it an impressive seven wins on the spin, but it looks like we'll need to make it 14 if we're to have a chance of winning the damned thing. To win all of our remaining games would be an incredible feat, and the closeness of this one shows just how tough a task that will be.

We know that this team is capable of blowing opponents away, but just as crucially they're also finding a way to win when things aren't going especially smoothly. The result of this should never have been in doubt really, but the final ten minutes were tense and it was a huge relief to hear the final whistle. We weren't exactly under the cosh but one slip was all it was going to take to put a huge dent in our title hopes, so understandably the players and crowd were edgy. It reminded me of the Stoke game on opening day, another game in which we ended up hanging on despite being clearly the better side. We needed a penalty save from Mignolet to see us through that day, and whilst this one wasn't quite as hairy as that we did have to ride our luck late on. When Johnson conceded a soft free-kick on the right flank as the 90 minute mark approached, my arse went and I just had an impending feeling of doom. I could see it coming, they were going to equalise and this brave charge at the title we've been making was going come to a shuddering halt. All the hard work we've put in and we were going to blow it at home to the second worst team in the league. Adam Johnson whipped a great ball in, an unmarked John O'Shea rose to meet it and then… it didn't go in. I can't believe it didn't go in. How didn't it go in? It was a real Eidur Gudjohnsen moment.

Sunderland didn't deserve a draw and had that O'Shea header gone in it would have been incredibly cruel on the Reds. Having said that, we brought it on ourselves to a degree by failing to kill the game when we had the Mackems where we wanted them at 2-0. Still, any criticism should be tempered as overall I'd say the perform- ance was fine. We're not going to score four, five, six in every game… just most of them. This was a difficult game early on, the opening goal was always going to be crucial as it would then open the game up. It took a while to come because Sunderland went with three at the back and had eight men behind the ball at almost all times. They defended well, and also deep, which made it difficult to get in behind them and most of our play was in front of them and resulted either in a shot from distance or us running into a yellow wall in the middle of the pitch. They packed the centre of the pitch to prevent Suarez and Sturridge finding any space and to nullify our diamond formation. That meant Johnson was often the spare man as he was against Cardiff last weekend (who also played this system). This time Johnson's end product failed to match the high standards he set last Saturday. He was quite wasteful, especially in the first half. If we persist in playing this way, I'd expect other sides to follow suit and perhaps a switch back to the approach that hammered Everton and Arsenal may be on the cards soon?

For all our possession Sunderland had actually gone closest to scoring when Wickham's deflected shot forced a fine stop from Mignolet. The loose ball fell to Cattermole and the danger hadn't passed as they had men running into the box in support, but remarkably Cattermole just allowed it to run out of play for a corner. Any self respecting footballer would have kept that in and backed themselves to do something, I couldn't believe Cattermole preferred to just play for the corner. Shows that even he knows he's crap.

Vito Mannone had very little to do in the first half but such is the firepower that we have now that it's a tall order for any side to keep us out for long. Even when they defend well it only takes one split second for us to score and Sunderland found that out to their cost shortly before half time when we finally made the breakthrough. Suarez wriggled free between O'Shea and and Vergini was clumsily brought down by the South American. He was the last man and it was a clear red card, Wes Brown may have been in the vicinity but no way was he getting back goal side of Luis and it's a sending off all day that is. Kevin Friend, as he often tends to, had other ideas and produced only a yellow.

The crowd were furious but still, we had a free-kick on the edge of the box and we've been pretty clinical from these situations all season, so all was not lost. Suarez hadn't made the most of his last few free-kicks, however, and although it looked as though he was shaping up to take this one, Gerrard suddenly stepped up and emphatically leathered it past Mannone and into the top corner. Hell of a hit from the captain and his celebration was brilliant too, especially when he playfully points at Luis, tells him *"ey, no more free-kicks for you!"* and then grabs him around the neck. One of the great moments of the season that, and there's been plenty of them.

The goal made the referee's decision to not send off Vergini a little easier to take but when the Argentine then hauled down Suarez again and escaped a yellow card, that was just plain ridiculous. Friend should be sacked. Not demoted to League Two or whatever, just sack the useless turd as he's as bad now as he was when he first came on the scene. I don't know why he refereed this game the way he did, but he clearly saw things yet for whatever reason didn't act on them. I call this 'Howard Webb syndrome'. Maybe he felt sorry for Sunderland and wanted to give them a chance, to keep the game interesting or whatever because it was on telly? Maybe he's a Chelsea fan? Maybe he just doesn't like Liverpool? I don't know. What I do know is that for whatever reason when faced with making a big decision, each time he came down in favour of the visitors.

On another day it may well have cost us. Had Vergini been sent off on either of the occasions that merited it there's no way Sunderland would made a game of this. Not a chance in hell, we may even have hit double figures. If he'd given the penalty he should have given after the break when Coutinho was tripped, again, it would have been game over. They weren't even the worst decisions he made though, the most incredible 'non-call' he made was when Suarez had his heel clipped by Cattermole as he shaped to shoot on the edge of the box. It was the clearest foul of the game yet both Friend and his assistant ignored it. Henderson was still abusing the linesman about 15 minutes later.

We were 2-0 up at that point thanks to Sturridge's 20th league goal of the season. He seemed strangely subdued in his celebration, Henderson on the other hand was well fired up. Talking to a mate before the game and the subject of Hendo came up, would he celebrate if he scored against his old team? *"He won't celebrate if he scores, but if someone else does he'll go nuts like he always does"* I correctly predicted.

For a spell after that some of the football we played was absolutely magical. Coutinho was dazzling in the 2nd half, the ball seemed to be glued to his foot and the quick changes of direction he makes are incredible at times. He can be running at full speed and then immediately come to a complete stop before heading off in the opposite direction, all the while keeping the ball on the end of his bootlaces. The problem was that it became so easy for us we were looking to score the perfect goal. Suarez was really hit and miss. By his own standards this was one of his poorer games and yet some of the things he did were still bordering on incredible. One touch out on the left wing that took him clear of O'Shea and led to him flashing a shot wide was ridiculous. For a fifteen minute period after we got the second goal it was bordering on exhibition stuff, with Suarez and Coutinho especially linking up to great effect. At least they were up until it came to the final shot. There were shades of Arsenal about us, trying to walk the ball in.

Not that it looked like it would cost us, we were in total command of the game and a third goal was surely only a matter of time? There are a couple of reasons the game changed. One, we began to get a little sloppy, and two, Gus Poyet made a double substitution that transformed his team. Ki Sung Yeung and Adam Johnson came on and gave the Mackems new life. Both were excellent, especially Ki who was busy and inventive and caused us all kinds of problems. They were also encouraged by our insistence on passing the ball around at the back and involving Mignolet in it. He's just not comfortable having to play football but we kept putting him in difficult positions by passing it back to him. Instead of just clearing his lines and relieving the pressure he's trying to pass it out (as he's no doubt instructed to do) and it repeatedly caused us to lose possession in our own half. That gave Sunderland hope and added to the edginess in the crowd. Out of nowhere Cattermole hit the bar with a thunderous shot. We then hit the bar ourselves through a terrific curling effort by Sturridge, who was also denied by Suarez when he got in the way of a goal bound shot.

The game was end to end now as Sunderland sensed they might be able to give us a problem or two. The excellent Ki looked to have a clear shot at goal but Agger made a good block to deflect the ball behind for a corner. He didn't deal with the corner anywhere near as well though, not getting a clean head on the ball at the near post and allowing it to roll across the six yard box where Ki headed in at the back post.

The goal was greeted with complete silence inside the stadium. Even the Sunderland fans didn't seem to celebrate, in fact they were quiet all night, it's as though they've completely given up. I was shitting myself now and didn't like how this was going at all. It feels as though any points we drop now will more or less end our challenge (not necessarily the case, but that's how it feels) and there are going to be some hairy moments between now and May. The O'Shea miss was crucial, when that didn't go in I knew we'd be ok and after that we just kept the ball in their half and played out time.

It's not the ideal way to win a game and we'd all have been happier with a routine win by four or five goals but we deserved the win and had that bit of luck that you need, our 'Gudjohnsen moment' if you like. One step closer.

Premier League Round Up (22-26 March 2014)

"Galatasaray are pants" tweeted Lee Dixon during Chelsea's routine 2-0 win over the Turks last week. Three days later Dixon's Arsenal are letting in six at the same venue. D'oh! A week earlier Szciezny was tweeting out pictures of himself celebrating on the pitch after a win over Tottenham. As Chelsea's sixth went in, Spurs winger Andros Townsend couldn't help himself: *"Who thinks we'll see another selfie of him after today's game?"* Ouch!

Arsenal players are just such fucking dicks though aren't they? That 'selfie' taken by Szciesny with his team-mates photo bombing it in the background just summed Arsenal up perfectly. It's like the invisible trophy celebrations in the dressing room after they clinched fourth spot last season, the embarrassing fucking goons. Somewhere along the way, Arsenal have gone from being 'the Invincibles' to being total fucking losers with no balls and no stomach for a fight. To let in six at City, five at Anfield and six at Chelsea almost defies belief for a top four side. Think about that for a second; the fourth best team in the land let in six, six and five in the three away games to the sides immediately above them. And the five they let in at Anfield should have been more too, only we went easy on their sorry arses in the second half. They're a fucking disgrace. A rule should be brought in that allows the Premier League to expel them from the top four as they aren't worthy of it, the mentally weak shysters. Everton are more deserving of a top four spot than Arsenal as at least they've got some fight in them and haven't been letting in fives and sixes. The way things are going they might just get it too.

Arsenal though, kinell, what they did at Stamford Bridge was bordering on criminal negligence. You'd think after what happened to them at Anfield the other week they'd have been a little bit more streetwise at Chelsea. Instead they made the exact same mistakes in what was Arsene Wenger's 1000th game. It's his own fault though. He's never beaten Mourinho and it's no wonder. Could he not have just been a little bit pragmatic and told his team to keep it tight, defend a bit deeper and hey, here's a thought, maybe pick Mathieu Flamini! No, Wenger sent them out to do what they always do; defend high up the field, fanny about in midfield and don't bother tracking runners. This was just like what happened at Anfield, except Chelsea did it with a lot less style, swagger and panache than us, obviously. There's no 'Rodgeball' with these dullards. And how come Mourinho looked like he's been sleeping on a park bench? Scruffy twat. He skulked off before full time so he didn't have to shake Wenger's hand too, the classless piece of filth.

Andre Marriner got slaughtered afterwards for sending off Gibbs and rightly so. It's not the mistaken identity that's the issue here, that can happen to anyone to be fair. But when all the players are telling him he's got the wrong man and Oxlade-Chamberlain is even owning up to it, he has to know he's dropped the ball. So then he has to have a rethink and ask his assistants and the 4th official for some help. That's his crime here, not the original error which was understandable as the two players were stood in close proximity, and you'd automatically expect Gibbs to be the one defending the far post as he's the full back. Tell you what bothered me more than anything, that the Ox didn't get a ban because the shot wasn't on target. Fuck off with that shit. Nobody knew it wasn't on target until they'd seen the replays. The player didn't know or he wouldn't have handled it. Put it this way, if Marriner hadn't got the wrong man, would the red card have been overturned? Would it fuck. Typical FA bullshit, they make it up as they go along.

Anyway, moving on, and the other game that was of interest to us last weekend was at the Etihad where City battered Fulham. No surprise there, Fulham are about mid-table Championship standard at the moment and 'Penfold' isn't going to turn that around any time soon. Toure bagged a hat-trick, two of them penalties and the third a brilliant curler from distance. Take away Suarez and Sturridge and Yaya might be the player of the year, he's been class. If you remove the LFC contingent from it, then he'd get my vote over Eden Hazard on account of him not being a twat with stupid Amish looking facial hair and because of how much it would piss Mourinho off. I wasn't even bothered about City winning as there was never even the remotest possibly they wouldn't. I'll be bothered if they win this weekend though, because as shit as Arsenal are I'm still expecting a reaction from them when they entertain City.

Hopefully they'll make a better fist of it than United did in midweek anyway. Call me stupid, but I was actually expecting them to get at least a point from the Manc derby, but that expectation last about 40 seconds before City scored. Fuckin' Moyes. Serves me right though I guess, I should have known better. United had actually gone into it on a bit of a roll, well... a roll by their recent shitty standards anyway. Two successive wins, two clean sheets and five goals scored. Incredible achievement that, I bet Taff's Tavern was buzzing. They beat West Ham 2-0 on Saturday thanks to Rooney's brace, but it can't just be me who thinks people are going way, way, way overboard on Rooney's first goal surely? It was good and all, but people are talking about it as goal of the season and even more laughably, better than Beckham's. What am I missing here? Even Shearer and Carragher have said it was better than Beckhams.

Here's how I judge this. If you gave me 20 attempts at doing what Rooney did, I reckon I could do it, or at least come pretty damn close. Hitting a bouncing ball is a piece of piss, you automatically get the power, distance and dip you need to lob the keeper and it's really not that difficult. Hitting one off the deck like Beckham did though? I couldn't do that if I had a million goes at it. It's no contest, it wasn't better than Beckham's, it wasn't goal of the season and it wasn't even the best goal of the day (Tettey's volley was better for me). And just what was the keeper doing? Turning his back, losing his bearings and then falling over, that's what he was doing, the chump.

Anyway, having won a couple of games United should have been a bit more confident facing City, yet they were truly pitiful. They were even worse than they had been against us, I could barely believe some of things I saw. Some of those players are performing like they're trying to get Moyes sacked. I'm not mentioning any names, so let's just say Fio Rerdinand. And how shit is Fellaini? There were cheers when he was eventually subbed in the 2nd half, but he was lucky to last that long after the ludicrous elbow on Zabaleta. The ref saw that clearly but only gave a yellow. I think I know why, it's because it was so blatant that he thought *"What the fuck??? No, that didn't just happen, I must have seen that wrong, as no-one makes it that obvious."*

Makes me laugh how everyone is up in arms over it though, like it's something shocking. He does it every fucking game!! No-one cared when he was playing for little old Everton but now that he's on a big stage people are seeing him for what he is. I'm also amazed at people being surprised at how bad he's been. The thing about Fellaini is he has a lot of attributes and isn't a bad player as such, but what is he? He's not a midfielder, certainly not in a passing side anyway. He's not a number ten, not unless you want to do what Moyes did with him at Everton and launch long balls at his chest and then play off him. And he's not a forward as he can't run. You know what his position is? He doesn't have one, he's created a new one in fact. I call it 'Nuisance'. You've got all your fancy new hipster terms for different positions; trequartista, reverse libero, midfield pivot, false nine etc and then you have Fellaini blazing his own trail as a 'nuisance'. He wins headers, he puts himself about a bit, he uses his elbows a lot and he's a bit of a pest. £27m for someone to play the 'Nuisance' role. David Moyes - Football Genius.

Not been a great week of PR for United players, as Chris Smalling made the headlines for the wrong reasons too after he was spotted singing *"We're Man United we'll do what we want"* as he left a bar in Mancland at 3am. Yeah they'll do what they want alright, except win at Old Trafford, the fucking has beens. United's players and fans are revolting, and they're in revolt too (never gets old!). There have been various reports about senior players having a problem with Moyesy's coaching and training, whilst those fans who just a few weeks ago were smugly chanting *"every single one of us stands by David Moyes"* have now done a complete about face. It's hilarious really. That superior attitude they've had all season about how they're so much better than the rest of us because they back their manager no matter how shit he is? Yeah, that's gone now, all it took was home defeats to their two main rivals and that went right out the window that Phil Jones has been licking.

The City loss was the straw that broke the camel's back, and no I don't mean Rio Ferdinand, the camel faced twat. The bastards even tried to take 'the Chosen One' banner down and stewards had to intervene. How dare they, I love that fucking banner. The group who designed it are now having a vote to see if it should stay or not. We should probably try and hijack that vote really. Someone even had a go at Ferguson afterwards, trying to get in the directors box to give him shit for 'choosing' the 'chosen one'. It gets better too, the losers are actually hiring a plane to fly over Old Trafford with a "The Wrong One…Moyes Out" banner. Moyes is obviously on borrowed time but there's still plenty of 'lolz' left in this one yet I think.

Moving on, and Sunderland's problems continued as they lost at Norwich. Snodgrass got the first and Tettey then thundered in a brilliant second. Hell of a goal that was, Chris Hughton's celebration was hilarious, bless him. Wolf Van Winkel's problems continue though, he makes Jozy Altidore look like… like.. I dunno, Jon Walters maybe? Altidore though, fucking hell. I saw a stat the other day saying that Stoke right back Geoff Cameron has 2 goals in 65 Premier League games, whilst Altidore, a centre forward, has two goals in 54 Premier League games. How is that even possible? A centre forward averaging a goal every 27 games, that's Torres-esque that is. We got a close up look at Altidore at Anfield on Wednesday night. I just don't see the point of him at all, I don't know what he does other than take up space with his huge frame. They could just stick a fridge freezer up there, it would have the same impact and would save them a shitload of cash. It'd probably score more than 2 in 54 as well, just from deflections alone.

It was no surprise to see Long running wild all over his old team as Hull beat West Brom at the KC Stadium. Why did they sell him again? Oh yeah, because they've got Victor Anichebe and… erm… actually who else have they got? There's that bloke they signed on loan with the wild haircut and there's the Czech lad who seems a bit shit, but Long is better than all their other frontmen put together. He 'won' the penalty that led to the first goal (very dubious but the Baggies have some nerve complaining about it considering the number of dodgy pens and free-kicks he 'won' for them while he was there), scored the second himself and he also hit the bar with a great strike from distance. As for West Brom's forwards… they barely managed a shot. In terms of transfer decisions, the sale of Long to Hull in the middle of a season is one of the most stupid ones of recent times. Batshit crazy in fact.

Newcastle had a dramatic stoppage time win over Palace on Saturday as Pappis Cisse finally found the net. His record of late has been bordering on 'Altidorish', but it's still better than his on loan strike partner Luke De Jong who hasn't scored for either Newcastle or his parent club Borrusia Moenchengladbach all season. What is it with all these strikers who never score? I know we're spoiled with our two like, but still, it's difficult to comprehend how you can play regularly up front and never score.

The Blues are flying at the moment. They beat Swansea at the weekend and then had a great 3-0 win at Newcastle in midweek. They're right on the tail of Arsenal now for fourth place, which is good for us as they both have to play City. Arsenal can't afford to lose to them and Everton may need something when they play them too. Ideally we need them to be in contention for 4th place when they face City, otherwise they'll just lube themselves up if there's any chance of us winning the title. Imagine if the Blues beating City got them 4th place but handed us the title! I literally don't know what I'd do if that happened. Or what they'd do for that matter. Would they even celebrate? We'd probably witness the kind of scenes usually reserved for relegated sides, with jabronis still sat in their seats crying into their scarfs half an hour after the game has ended.

Swansea might be one of those sides this year, it's unlikely but they certainly aren't safe yet. Gary Monk seems to be losing the plot a bit now after a promising start. He said afterwards that it was about *"Doing the right decisions, making the right things"* Hmmm. Still, he's come along way from his 'Dodgeball' days when all you'd get out of him was the odd *"Gaarrrrrrr"*. They've been having a rough time recently but got the train back on the track at the Emirates on Tuesday night by holding Arsenal to a hilarious draw. Swansea were the better side and led early on through Bony. Arsenal toiled away without success until suddenly two goals in a minute looked to have ensured they would bounce back from their bumming at Stamford Bridge. Then in stoppage time Flamini put through his own net. Hahaha!

Jumping back to the weekend again though, and how about that Stokealona eh? They went 1-0 down early on at Villa on Sunday but came roaring back to win 4-1. They were brilliant, there wasn't a set-piece goal in sight as they just tore through Villa with incisive football and crisp passing. Now that they're playing football Crouchy is starting to shine again as he can play to his actual strengths rather than his perceived ones.

Also on Sunday, Spurs edged out Southampton in an exciting game at the Lane. Rodriguez put the visitors ahead with a composed finish after a howler by Naughton. Another clanger by the hapless full-back allowed Lallana to make it 2-0 and Spurs were staring down the barrel of a humiliating defeat. Saints' right back Cline then pulled a 'Naughton' and allowed Eriksen to get one back before the break and give Spurs a much needed lifeline. Cline was hooked at half time but it didn't do any good as Spurs scored within seconds of the restart through Eriksen again and Gilfi Sigurdsson won it in stoppage time. I'd have obviously preferred a Tottenham defeat but it was worth it just to hear Kevin Phillips trying to pronounce Sigurdsson's name on Sky afterwards. *"Silef Gudjersson"* haha boss that! It's not quite Garth Crooks *"Wolf Van Winkel"* standard, but it's up there. *"What did Tim Sherwood say to you at half time"* they asked Eriksen afterwards. *"Errrr... he was a bit angry..."* the Dane replied. Hahaha no shit! Bet it went something like: *"Fackin' pull your fackin' fingers owwt you fackin' slaaaaags"*

Finally, West Ham beat ten man Hull on Wednesday night but were booed off by their unhappy fans. Apparently Fat Sam cupped his ear like a wrestling bad guy when he heard the booing! Brilliant. If the Premier League were the WWE then Allardyce would make a fantastic heel. He'd probably wear one of those black leotards with the single shoulder strap, like Andre the Giant or the Big Show. I'd imagine he has a big hairy back too. Steve Bruce would obviously have to wear some kind of mask, whilst Alan Pardew on the other hand would be surely model himself on 'Nature Boy' Ric Flair. He'd wear a stunning, sequinned robe and shout *'wooooooooooooo'* a lot, whilst repeatedly bragging about his sexual prowess. *"Kiss stealin', limousine ridin', jet flyin', wheelin' and dealin' son of a gun. Wooooooo!!"* Him and Big Sam would form a dastardly tag team, until the day when one of them, without warning, suddenly turns on the other and repeatedly beats him over the head with a steel chair. You just know that would be Pardew, the slime ball. Poor Big Sam.

LIVERPOOL 4 TOTTENHAM 0

Competition - Premier League
Date - Sun 30 Mar 2014
Venue - Anfield
Scorer(s) – Kaboul O.G., Luis Suarez, Philippe Coutinho
Star Man – Raheem Sterling

Team: Mignolet; Johnson, Skrtel, Agger, Flanagan; Gerrard (Lucas), Henderson, Coutinho (Allen); Sterling (Moses), Sturridge, Suarez:

After the arse twitching win over Sunderland in midweek this was just what the doctor ordered. Thank God for Spurs and their lack of fight eh? The Londoners were beaten from the moment Kaboul put through his own net inside two minutes. They were never coming back from that, it was just a case of how many goals they'd ship and if they could avoid a repeat of the 5-0 whupping they suffered at our hands earlier in the season.

I'd liken that early goal to a surfer who strayed too far from shore and had his leg chomped on by a Great White. Spurs were a long way from the beach and there was blood in the water. Our players got a whiff of it and just never let them come back up for air. Poor old Tottenham 'needed a bigger boat', but all they had was a rubber dingy, sat up in the directors box looking thoroughly disgusted with the bunch of fucking losers he's been put in charge of. I hated Sherwood before he got that job; he was a dickhead as a pundit, an even bigger dickhead as a player and he's generally carried that on into management with his Captain Caveman approach to the job. And yet I can't lie, I find that there's something endearing about him. I'm not even sure what it is, the fact he's pretty useless and Spurs have been garbage since he took over is obviously part of it, but it's more than that, he's actually quite likeable. There's an honesty about him that you don't often see with top flight managers. That's not necessarily a good thing in terms of being able to do the job well of course, but it makes for great entertainment and it should probably be said that he was very complimentary about us both before and after this game. Then again, what's there to not be complimentary about, we're fucking ace aren't we?

Still, I kind of like Tim Sherwood, I hope they keep him a while longer. Sherwood took some stick from the Spurs fans during the game for not being on the touchline, but he basically said afterwards that he sat in the stands because he knew his team were completely overmatched and he wouldn't be able to effect the outcome by being on the touchline, so he figured he'd sit in the stands to see what he could learn. In other words, he just wanted the best possible view he could get of 'Rodgeball'.

As we've so often done at home this season, we blitzed the opposition from the opening whistle and never really let up until it was over. Even in the closing stages of the game we were still chasing and harrying when we didn't have the ball, and we were trying to score when we did have it. I fucking love this team; they're relentless and they keep going right until the final whistle, regardless of how many they lead by. This was typified by Flanagan's crunching challenge on Soldado as he ran into the box looking for a late consolation. Carragher-esque that was, and as Soldado lay broken on the floor Flanno was being high fived by team-mates who not only wanted the win, but also the clean sheet. This team is just so hungry and they're all in it together, there's a spirit there that neither Chelsea nor City can match.

This was an utterly dominant display from start to finish. Given what's at stake it was seriously impressive stuff. No nerves, no tension, just taking care of business. Of course, Tottenham didn't offer a great deal of resistance, they were pathetic and never really looked especially interested at any point. With no Adebayor they were never going to offer much threat, especially as Sherwood left out Dembele and Sandro to go with a midfield two of Bentoleb and Sigurdsson. Am I missing something here, have Sandro and Dembele been THAT bad? I know one thing, when I saw their midfield I knew it was going to be piss easy for us. I'm not sure Spurs had even touched the ball before we scored. In fact, I'm not sure if half of our own players had either. Coutinho found Sterling in acres of space, he played in the overlapping Johnson and his cross hit Vertonghen first, and then Kaboul bundled it into his own net, just past the despairing toe poke of Sturridge who tried to reach it before it crossed the line. He didn't get anything on it, but fuck it, they should give him the goal anyway as he was close enough.

Anfield had been rocking prior to kick off and that was just the start we needed. A great tackle by Flanno on Lennon early doors had the Kop roaring it's approval, as did the frequent attacks we were launching against a beleaguered Spurs rearguard. Sterling was terrorising Tottenham's left flank and Rose was struggling to cope with him. He was quick, direct, but even more impressive was the way he was able to collect the ball and wriggle away when under real pressure, he was just fantastic and on a day when everyone in Red performed to a high level, he stood out above all others. Spurs never got near him all day.

Vertonghen went off through injury and several of his team-mates were no doubt looking on enviously and wishing they could get the hell out of dodge too. Dawson came on to replace him and his first touch put Kaboul in trouble as Suarez swarmed all over him and robbed possession. The ball appeared to have got stuck under his feet and it looked like Luis would leave it behind as he'd already set off running. I doubt if anyone else on the field could have adjusted their feet to take the ball with them the way he did, it was absolutely brilliant. You'd think having seen Suarez do so many incredible things since he came here that I'd have a bit more confidence in him, but when he was running through I wasn't expecting him to score. I thought maybe Kaboul would catch him, but if not I still wouldn't have backed him to score with his left foot from that angle. Oh me of little faith. It was similar to his derby goal but maybe slightly better, in terms of the finish at least. Stunning. His celebration was even more intense than usual too, the players obviously knew how important this game was and their reaction to the goals - and at full time - showed that. During the game though they were strictly business, as they have been for months. Rodgers has to take great credit for that, as well as all the other things he gets great credit for, the smooth talking, shiny toothed little fucking genius.

Suarez almost added a third when Sterling pressured Kaboul into another error and then picked him out on the back post. His header was powerful and well directed but Lloris tipped it onto the bar and it somehow stayed out, even though most of the stadium were celebrating having thought it had gone in. Great save, he's top drawer is Lloris. We were playing some lovely stuff with Sterling involved in most of it. Henderson blasted one into the Kop after being teed up by the young winger. He really should have buried that (or at least hit the target) and he looked gutted that he hadn't. Suarez went over and gave him a quick word of encouragement and seconds later Hendo was haring off down the right hand side like a dog in a park, the missed chance completely forgotten. I love that lad.

After what happened against Sunderland, the third goal was always going to be crucial. As we've seen, no matter how dominant you are at 2-0 all it takes is for one flukey goal against the run of play and the game turns on it's head. If we got to 3-0 we could all relax, so it was a great moment when Coutinho's low shot found the bottom corner at the Kop end. If ever a goal summed up what Rodgers wants to do it was this one. We were moving the ball around at the back, trying to draw Spurs out, and when they forced us to go back to Mignolet it was looking like they had us in a bit of trouble. We didn't panic though, the ball was played out to Flanagan but Spurs had several players up the field looking to force a mistake. Lennon went to close Flanno down, but bought the little fake as the young scouser feigned to pass inside before 'Cruyff turning' his way down the touchline. Lennon didn't even bother to chase him as he advanced downfield before rolling it into space for Coutinho to collect. Usually I don't want to see Coutinho shooting from distance as he's woeful, but the sun even shines on a dog's arse somedays and it was a massive relief to everyone to see the ball hitting the net. Coutinho looked as relieved as anyone actually. Still don't want him taking many more shots though, quit while you're ahead Phil lad.

That goal killed the game and allowed everyone to relax and just enjoy the occasion. The atmosphere was brilliant all day but now it was party time. Chants new and old were given loud airings, and the players just kept on pouring forward looking for more goals. Allen came on to replace Coutinho and Rodgers was also able to get Gerrard off and protect him from a possible yellow card and suspension. In turn that meant Lucas was able to get some much needed minutes on the field and remind the Brazil coach that he's still alive. Poor Lucas, he looked a shoe in for the World Cup a few months ago but he might be in trouble now he's not getting any playing time. It would be devastating for him to miss on a World Cup in his home country, but if he has a Premier League winner's medal I'm sure that would soften the blow. He could just go on a summer long bender like the rest of us.

Sturridge almost scored a fantastic back heel but was denied by Lloris, but the fourth goal eventually came from a Henderson free-kick. I wondered if that was a training ground routine as Hendo and Suarez had a deep conversation about it beforehand. I'd love to know what was said between them as when Hendo whipped the ball in Suarez deliberately jumped up and opened his legs, allowing the ball to go through him and into the net.

At 4-0 it looked like Rodgers was going to really rub Sherwood's nose in it by giving him the 'Full Aspas', but instead we got Victor Moses. I don't even remember the last time Moses got on the field, it feels like months ago. Sturridge would have been the most obvious choice to go off but I love that Rodgers kept him on, presumably because he hadn't scored. Rodgers wants to keep both Suarez and Sturridge scoring, and it was a clever piece of man-management, I'm sure Sturridge appreciated it. It also ensured Sterling got the huge ovation his performance deserved too. He was brilliant at both ends of the field. Seeing him holding off man-mountain Dembele for around ten seconds down by his own goal-line was quite a sight, he's a strong, feisty little bugger is Raheem, that was a great moment in the game and the crowd loved it. He really needs a song, it was almost embarrassing that he left the field with no chant to accompany him.

The final whistle was greeted with huge cheers and chants of *"we're gonna win the league"*. The players and Rodgers gathered in the middle of the pitch to applaud the fans and there was a massive, spine chilling roar. We're getting stronger and stronger as the season goes on, our form is better than that of any of our rivals and there's just something special happening isn't there? I've been feeling it for weeks now, little things here and there that are putting me in mind of 2005. Even the *'We are Liverpool'* chant is giving me a good vibe, as in recent times our most successful seasons have had their own theme tune to accompany them. In 2001 it was *'Hou let the Reds out'*, in 2005 it was *'Ring of Fire'*. We had *'Campione'* and *'the Best midfield in the World'* in 2007 of course, but let's not focus too much on that! There'll be no negative thoughts from now until May thank you very much, only positive ones. We can definitely do this, and Chelsea and City should be more worried about us than the other way round, as *"we're the best football team in the land. Yes we are"*.

Premier League Round Up (30 March - 1 April 2014)

I almost felt sorry for David Moyes this week. That airplane bollocks was very nearly enough to make me sympathise with the fella, but then I read this: *"Really looking forward to coming up against him (Pep Guardiola). I've no doubt I'll be doing it plenty of times in the future"* and I remembered that this isn't some poor, sympathetic figure who's just doing his best in a job that's too big for him. No, he's actually a massively deluded fuckwit who doesn't even realise that the job is too big for him.

Their victory against Villa was a timely one, I certainly wouldn't say I wanted them to win but I could see some positives in it. The last thing we need is for those knobheads who hired the plane to build any kind of 'Moyes Out' momentum, and a 4-1 win made those knobheads who hired the plane look like... well, knobheads. If United had dropped points they'd have almost been vindicated. Of course nothing justifies hiring a plane for such a thing, but the message would have certainly carried more weight if the game had gone badly, and I bet they were genuinely gutted they won. No doubt they figured it was as good a time as any to do it, as after all, two weeks ago Villa had beaten Chelsea hadn't they. What those plane hiring morons failed to take into account was that YOU CAN NEVER RELY ON ASTON FUCKING VILLA.

Villa had only beaten United once in their previous 36 meetings. How is that even possible? Oh yeah, it's possible because they're Aston fucking Villa, that's why. They even managed to lose this despite taking the lead. The Mancs under Moyes never come back when they concede the first goal, but with Villa being Villa that was irrelevant and four goals later Moyes was looking all smug as he left the field with applause ringing in his ears. No-one loses at Old Trafford these days, least of all conceding four goals in the process. So yeah, nice one Villa. For a spell in the 2nd half they actually battered United but they were unable to make it count and grab an equaliser. Benteke missed two great chances, he's not all that him you know, I think last season was maybe a flash in the pan. Not an 'Andros Townsend' style flash in the pan, obviously, I mean Benteke is clearly a good player, I just don't think he's as good as last season suggested he might be. Unless of course he's just not that arsed because Villa are... well, Villa. United weathered that brief storm and Mata and Hernandez both then got on the scoresheet to give Moyes a rare good day. The fans even dusted off the *'Come on Davey Moyes'* song too. I thought that was as dead as Rio Ferdinand's career, but there's still life in the old dog yet it seems. The song I mean, not Rio, he's finished.

A United win is never especially palatable, but these days it's irrelevant to us as we've got bigger fish to fry. Such as Chelsea for example. Them losing at Palace was a nice little bonus wasn't it? I called it too, I'd been telling people all week Chelsea would drop points and that Palace might even win it. I'd been looking forward to this one and found myself a stream and watched the whole game on the laptop whilst putting together a chest of drawers from Ikea. I actually started it at 10am, figuring I'd have it finished in time to watch the Mancs in the lunchtime game. Bit ambitious that, I was still working on it whilst watching the Man City / Arsenal game that night. Dunno what happened there, I used to be ace at putting these things together, I even gave myself the nickname 'the Flatpack King'. I may have to abdicate my throne after this debacle though. *"You can hire someone to do these things you know"* said my Missus. *"It'll probably only cost about £30"*. *"I'm not paying anyone to do it"* I replied, indignantly. *"I'll do it myself, it'll only take me an hour or two"* Or nine, as it turned out. Seems like I'm the Fernando Torres of flat packs now, living off past glories. Still, I made a better fist of my job than Chelsea did of theirs. I could have put together three of those bad boys and they still wouldn't have scored at Palace, the fucking crabs.

Pulis had clearly done his homework on Chelsea as he shut them down completely and 1-0 didn't reflect the game at all; Palace should have had at least three. Their game plan was perfect, they made sure Hazard didn't get any room and once they'd nullified him Chelsea didn't have much else. Who knew? Well me, I've been saying for months that Hazard is more or less all they have. Me and Tony Pulis eh, great minds and all that. Chelsea had about three chances in the entire game, whilst Palace must have had seven or eight. My boy Jason Puncheon was brilliant, Messi-like in fact. I love Jason Puncheon, he's ace. He could have had a couple of goals and Cameron Jerome - who was also fantastic it should be said - hit the post and could have had a penalty. For all their chances though, it needed an oggy from 'Mr Chelsea' himself to break the deadlock. Have to say, the only thing better than Chelsea losing, is Chelsea losing thanks to a John Terry own goal. The cross looked like it was going to be met by Jerome, but the gravitational pull of Mongo's massive fod sucked it away from the striker and before Petr Cech could react it was in the back of his net, as I temporarily put down the screwdriver and bounced around the room belting out 'Glad All Over'.

For all the hype about Mourinho being some master tactician, he's pretty fucking clueless when they're losing, always has been. It was remarkable the amount of times Ivanovic just launched crosses into the box from about 40 yards out. They were so narrow and had no width at all, so they just got desperate and went full on alehouse. Where's Robert Huth when you need him, eh Jose? You know how people always say that Brendan learned his trade under 'the master', I reckon I've figured out just what happened there. He paid close attention to everything Mourinho did, studied him intently and made notes of everything from tactical approach, man-managing players and dealing with the media... and then he just went out and did the exact fucking opposite of everything. There are literally no similarities between Mourinho and Rodgers whatsoever, so this is the only plausible explanation.

Once again, Chelsea handled the defeat with typically bad grace. Actually that's unfair, the conduct of the players was fine, it was only soft shite who made a tit of himself, this time by threatening a ball boy after the kid took his time giving the ball back to Chelsea following instructions from Puncheon. Mourinho went running down the line to confront the kid (could you ever imagine Rodgers doing that?), but by the time he got there he obviously realised he needed to be careful, so calmly called the kid to him and then said something into his ear. When he was asked about it afterwards, this is what he said: *"It is not right to educate kids to do that. I went to stop Azpilicueta. I was afraid he would lose control of his emotions and push the kid or do something like Eden did last year at Swansea. I told the boy to not do that. I told him if he does this, 'one day somebody will punch you'."* Classy guy. And being lectured on time wasting by the guy who used to manage fucking Porto??? Really? He didn't share what the kid said back to him, but I imagine it was something like; *"I understand why you're upset Mr Special One, I really do, and you make a valid point. The only 'punch' that matters to me, however, is 'J-Punch'. When Jason Puncheon tells you to do something, you do it. I mean, that's Jason fucking Puncheon that is."*

Chelsea probably should have bought Puncheon instead of pissing £35m up the wall on that Willian jabroni, who's biggest attribute seems to be 'oh doesn't he work hard?' Here's a breakdown of the Brazilian in the form of a maths equation:

Willian = Dirk Kuyt + afro - goals.

Chelsea followed that loss at Selhurst with a 3-1 defeat in Paris. All the talk beforehand had been about the only man in world football with a bigger ego than Jose. #daretozlatan he likes to say, whatever the hell that means. Yet once again - as he's done every single frigging time - Zlatan came up against an English side in Europe and contributed the total sum of fuck all. I've got an equation for that one too:

English club + Champions League + Zlatan = dogshit

Is that what #daretozlatan means then, play crap against any English side? Coz it basically seems the same as #daretoaltidore and #daretojonwalters if you ask me. Fuckin' Zlatan, if youtube didn't exist no-one in this country would even know who he is, the flat track bullying show pony. *"ooooh did you see that back heel volley assist Zlatan did against Nimes last week?"* No I didn't, I don't watch French footy as it's shit, just like Zlatan. Even Bernard Diomede was ace over there remember. Let's see him do it in a big game against an English side, then we'll talk #daretozlatan Until then, he's a shit Andy Carroll with a Gary Neville tash.

Still, when Chelsea are repeatedly putting the ball in their own net and Mongo is laying on assists for opponents who needs Zlatan eh? I was actually trying to talk myself into hoping Chelsea would make the semis before getting stuffed as it would make our game with them easier. I found it impossible though, the overwhelming desire to see them lose stomped all over logic. I hope PSG bury them in the 2nd leg and then 'the scruffy one' won't have the Champions League excuse to fall back on when we bum his team senseless in a few weeks. Mourinho, of course, took no responsibility for the defeat, laying all the blame at the door of his players. What an absolute cock he is. He's happy to take the credit when his team gets a good result but when they don't it's the players' fault. He had another go at his strikers too, basically saying he once again went with no recognised centre forward because the ones he has are shite. Way to motivate your squad, helmet.

Whilst I'm on the subject of the Champions League, how funny was United's performance against Bayern by the way? I've never seen that before, a United side at Old Trafford playing like plucky underdogs, defending for their lives and being unable to put three passes together. Moyes was in his element, he'd love nothing more than to be in this situation every week, getting everyone behind the ball, punting it up to Fellaini's chest and hoping to nick something from a set-piece. This is who he is, no wonder he was made up with the performance. Their fans bought into it too, they created a great atmosphere and cheered every tackle and block like it was a goal. Reminded me of when we played at Mansfield in the cup last year.

Getting back to the domestic action now, and City dropped points too last weekend. Again I saw that one coming, if only because Arsenal would surely, finally, have to show some bottle after their recent embarrassments. When City went ahead early on through Silva I figured my faith in the Gunners had been gravely misplaced, they were shite in that first half but Wenger must have got into them at half time because they came out and had a right go. Flamini equalised (he played well, making a mockery of Wenger's decision to not play him at Chelsea last week) and Arsenal could even have won it as City retreated back and settled for a point. I thought that was quite interesting actually. It was almost as though City decided that a point was good due to Chelsea losing. Never mind the fact that we still had to play a home game the next day against a Spurs side who have more or less given up the ghost now. I don't think we're being that taken seriously you know. We're Butch from Pulp Fiction aren't we? That's how we'll beat em, they keep under-estimating us.

Elsewhere on Saturday, Cardiff and West Brom were involved in a crazy game at the Hawthorns. Amalfitano lobbed a stunning opener after just two minutes. If fat shite potato head Rooney had scored that we'd never hear the end of it. That goal pissed all over Rooney's at West Ham last week, but it probably won't even win April's goal of the month because 1) he's not a big enough name and 2) Suarez will probably score one that blows it out of the water anyway. Still, it was a fantastic goal that. Dorrans made it 2-0 and West Brom looked to be home and hosed, especially as Cardiff are shite. Tell you who's not shite though, Jordon Mutch. I like him (you can tell I like him as I'm even spelling his name correctly, with an 'o' instead of an 'a'), he's looked good all season and the goal he scored in this game was almost as good as Amalfitano's. Hell of an effort that. He's a 'Robert Snodgrass'; someone I watch and think *"he's boss him"* but I'd be horrified if he was ever linked with the Reds. Good, but not THAT good.

A player we most definitely have been linked with - Stephen Caulker - headed Cardiff level. I have absolutely no idea if he's any good or not, I'd lean towards 'Not' but I've not seen enough of him to have any real opinion, and it's a lot more difficult for the layman to judge defenders than attacking players I think. Rodgers has worked with him and apparently likes him a lot, but he likes Ashley Williams too so I'm not putting a great deal of stock in that. The fact he's scoring goals from set-pieces doesn't really come into it either, we score enough goals as it is so the main thing we need from a defender is for him to be able to, y'know, defend.

That loan signing with the terrible haircut looked to have won it for the Baggies with a goal deep into stoppage time, but incredibly Cardiff scored with the last kick of the game through that young Norwegian lad, Dahli or something. West Brom actually had a 4 v 1 counter attack seconds before the Cardiff goal, but young Berahino made a bad decision and gave the ball away. James Morrison lamped him in the dressing room afterwards, which is bang out of order, although I imagine Gerard Houllier would disagree. Ged's still not forgiven Daveeeed Ginola for doing the same thing for France all those years ago.

Meanwhile, Southampton's England contingent were ruling again as they demolished Newcastle at St Mary's. Rob Elliot made some stunning saves to keep them at bay in the first half but he was eventually beaten in stoppage time when Lambert sprung the offside trap and unselfishly teed up Rodriguez for a tap in. I say 'offside trap', it was basically just Newcastle's back four hanging around the halfway line not really paying much attention to anything. Alan Hansen described it as *'the worst bit of defending I've ever seen'*. I wouldn't go that far, not unless I'd never seen David Luiz in action anyway, but it was pretty bad like. Lambert added a second after brilliant play by Lallana, who then made it 3-0 with a piledriver with his left foot. I don't even know what Lallana's strongest foot is, he's brilliant with both. We should pay whatever it takes to get him this summer. If Rodgers got hold of him he'd turn him into a top five Premier League player, he's got so much ability he'd fit in perfectly with us and could play in three of four different positions.

I really like Rodriguez too, he made it 4-0 with a good finish late on. He's moved out of the 'Snodgrass' camp but he's not in the 'Lallana' one yet, but if we did make a move for him in the future I wouldn't object. We'd probably have to sell Borini first though, as there wouldn't be room for both. Obviously I'd take Luke Shaw as well if there was any chance (there isn't), but they can all leave those 1920s haircuts behind, we're not having any of that nonsense at Anfield. Even Raheem has sorted his barnet out now, all that's left is for someone to have a word with Coutinho and we're golden.

Elsewhere, Swansea took a big step towards survival by wiping the floor with Norwich at the Liberty Stadium. They played really well, you could even say that some of their football was almost 'Rodgers like'. 'The Gooseman' scored twice, the second one was a fabulous goal; that back heel from Bony was - I believe the term today's kids use is - 'sick'. If Zlatan had done that it would have been on a vine within seconds and would have gone viral. He wouldn't have done it though, not unless Norwich relocated to somewhere in mainland Europe. Routledge added a fine third after good work by Jonjo. Routledge is another in the 'Snodgrass/Mutch' camp. I've always liked him but he's just a good mid-lower table player at best. Probably could have been more than that if Brendan had got hold of him a few years earlier. He was the Raheem Sterling of his day, but spent about six or seven years in the wilderness until Rodgers arrived at Swansea. How great is Brendan, I reckon he could even make a player out of Zlatan you know, assuming Zlatan was willing to leave his ego at the door and submit fully to Brendan's teachings, no questions asked.

Difficult to see that ending well though. The likes of Hendo and Raheem have benefited because they're willing to listen and do whatever Brendan asks, regardless of whether it makes sense to them at the time or not. Brendan is Mr Miyagi, and Hendo is the Karate Kid. You tell Hendo to 'wax on, wax off', he does it with gusto and without question. Zlatan would throw down the sponge, take a shit on the bonnet and go and post some bollocks on twitter about how he #daredtozlatan He'd then piss off to some other Dojo down the street (probably run by some Mourinho-like wanker) where he'd be lauded as some kind of Billy Big Bollocks as he beats up on various neighbourhood chumps. Then before you know it, he's being 'Crane kicked' into the middle of next week by Hendo. That's a preview of next year's Champions League right there.

Aaaaanyway, the Norwich players decided after the game to reimburse the fans who made the long trip to South Wales, which was a nice touch. I can think of other sets of players who are far wealthier than the Norwich boys and who have given their travelling support far more reason to feel let down, but haven't made such a gesture. The same kind of players who take 'selfies' of themselves when they win.

At the Britannia, Stoke beat Hull 1-0 thanks to a Peter Odemwingie goal. I wonder who it was at Cardiff that thought it was a good idea to swap Odemwingie for Kenwynne frigging Jones? Mark Hughes must have thought he'd won the lottery that day. That's the worst swap since Barca decided to send an 'in his prime' Eto'o and £40m to Inter for that Zlatan turd. £40m plus Eto'o? For Zlatan? Hahahahaha! A year later he was loaned to Milan and eventually signed permanently for around £20m. Barca have just been given a transfer ban for the next two windows for some kind of rule breach. They should have had one after that ridiculous swap, the crazy fools.

Speaking of fools, what's Mr T's favourite month? April, fool! Haha class that.

Anyway, Stoke have won three in a row now. They won't make it four of course, as no-one wins at Stamford Bridge, but imagine if they got a draw? I need to find me a stream for that one, and another Ikea chest of drawers, obviously. I'm not superstitious, but no point taking any chances with so much at stake.

There were only two games on Sunday, one of which of course was our demolition job on Spurs. The talk afterwards was of Sherwood allegedly punching either Soldado or Dawson (the twitter bullshit merchants couldn't make their mind up on that one). I wasn't having that at all, but it says a lot about the perception of Sherwood that so many people were willing to believe it. There's no way Sherwood hit any of his players, but there's every chance he called a few of them *"facking slaaaaaags"*.

The other game of the day saw the Blues win 3-1 at Fulham, but it was closer than the scoreline suggests and they needed two late goals to win it. Fulham included Moussa Dembele up front. No, not that one, it was some kid they threw in at the deep end. Is that Fulham's new game plan then, throw in some random kid and give him the name of a former Fulham great? Who are they gonna send out next week, some 17 year old called George Best maybe?

Seriously though, what's with the teenage strikers, Fulham? Last week it was that Woodrow lad, and now this kid. It's almost as though they've given up already and are deliberately looking to go down. Why else would you throw in untested teenagers when you have Darren Bent and Hugo Rodallega available? Makes no sense.

Finally, I can't believe Sunderland got beat at home by West Ham on Monday. About a month ago they looked safe but they're right up shit creek now. My brother-in-law has been telling me for a few weeks now that they're going down and the players aren't showing any fight since they lost the cup final, but West Ham at home is a game they have to win if they're gonna stay up, surely? Their next four games are Tottenham (a), Everton (h), Man City (a), Chelsea (a). After that it gets much easier with a home game against Cardiff and a trip to Old Trafford, but by then how big is the gap going to be? That West Ham game was vital for the Mackems, and they picked the worst possible time to serve up such a steaming pile of Zlatan.

chapter twelve

April

WEST HAM UNITED 1 LIVERPOOL 2

Competition - Premier League
Date - Sun 6 Apr 2014
Venue - Upton Park
Scorer(s) – Gerrard (2 pens)
Star Man – Steven Gerrard

Team: Mignolet; Johnson, Skrtel, Sakho, Flanagan; Gerrard, Henderson, Coutinho (Lucas); Sterling, Suarez, Sturridge (Toure):

Any chance we could just play Tottenham every week? Or better yet, those Arsenal losers? I'm not sure how much more of these difficult ones I can take; this was absolutely torturous at times. Well it was for those of us watching, I don't think it was actually too bad for the players as once they'd re-established the lead they looked to be in complete control, but it only takes a second to score a goal and when the stakes are this high... well it's almost impossible to watch isn't it?

Much like the Sunderland game, the closing stages of this one were completely nerve shredding. Every time the ball was launched towards our box I could barely watch, but looking back on it now that it's over I'd have to say that it was as comfortable as you're ever going to get when protecting just a solitary goal lead. It didn't feel like it at the time obviously, but in the cold light of day - with the result in the bag - you have to say that West Ham didn't ever look like they would force an equaliser as we defended resolutely and showed great composure.

This was a great win, a real show of mental strength and bottle. I know it's a cliché but a year ago or two we wouldn't have got the result in a game like this; the unjust setback on the stroke of half time would have killed us and we wouldn't have recovered from it. That was our excuse for not winning it right there and previously we'd have clung to that excuse like some kind of comfort blanket, but we're made of much sterner stuff these days. Rodgers has done an incredible job on that side of things (as well as everything else of course) and the players simply put that awful decision behind them and just went out and completely bossed the second half and picked up the win they needed. It wasn't a day when our free flowing football ever really clicked and in a way it's encouraging that we were able to still win the game in spite of that.

Our much maligned defence stepped up when they were needed and it's good to see that we can win however necessary. We had our moments in attack of course, but for once it wasn't the flair players who caught the eye for us, it was the defenders and those charged with protecting them. Gerrard was simply imperious, an absolutely majestic performance from him. He was clearly the stand out performer, but both Skrtel and the recalled Sakho were fantastic too, and dealt with the threat of Carroll about as well as you can expect anyone to. Carroll was fired up for this one, he may have said plenty of kind things before and afterwards but there was no question he wanted to prove a point and he was all over the field putting himself about. He played quite well in terms of winning his flick ons and holding the ball up, yet he only had one real threatening moment all day, when for once he was allowed an unimpeded run at a cross and soared above Johnson at the back post to thump a header against the bar. That was the only time he was able to escape the shackles put on him by Skrtel and Sakho, and I think that only happened because the cross took them by surprise and Carroll was able to find space as a result.

If that had gone in then who knows what may have happened. It was 1-1 at that stage and we may have found it very difficult to win from there given how tough the Hammers were proving to break down. Any side that wins a trophy can point to pivotal moments along the way, the last time we were in a title race United had several of them - Howard Webb's assist against Spurs and that late goal by that fucking nomark Federico Macheda immediately spring to mind - and if we win the title this year there'll be several moments that I'll think back to. Mignolet's penalty save on opening day, O'Shea's late miss at Anfield, the stoppage time pen against Fulham etc

The Carroll one may not be as dramatic as those as there was still plenty of time to play, but it was a hugely significant moment in this game. We were well on top at the time and we were well on top afterwards, but if that goes an inch or two lower... well I don't even want to think about it. Thankfully I don't need to now because we got the three points and can move on to the next one. Besides, if Anthony Taylor had done his job properly just before half time then we'd have gone into the break with the lead and may well have steamrollered West Ham in the second half, we'll never know.

It was a real arm wrestle this one as West Ham are horrible to play against. They're like Stoke used to be under Tony Pulis, it's very difficult to look good against them because of how they set up and how they break the game up all the time with set-pieces. We found it tough in the first half, mainly because our front three weren't at it. Suarez was giving the ball away a lot and spent a lot of time berating himself or complaining to team-mates about various things. Even on those days though he still produces moments of breathtaking quality. Sturridge and Sterling, however, were not having the best of days at all. For the first time so far I thought I could detect traces of nerves and hesitancy in some of the players, notably those two. Sterling had been electric last week against Spurs, he was on the front foot from the opening whistle and was direct and positive. In the first half against the Hammers he looked more like the timid, safety first kid who had lost his way in the early part of this season. The tactical switch at half time changed that and I thought he was brilliant in the second half, but Sturridge continued to look a little out of sorts, especially in front of goal.

He was snatching at shots all day, a sure sign that he wasn't playing with the usual confidence we see from him. He blasted a couple over the bar, he sliced one wildly wide and even on the incident that led to the second pen he somehow managed to put the ball wide from a couple of yards out. Fortunately the ref bailed him out by awarding the spot kick for the challenge on Flanagan, but this was not a good day for Sturridge. He's earned the odd off day though and I expect him to be flying against City next week.

The first half performance was nowhere near as good as the second half one, and - for whatever reason - the diamond worked better than 4-3-3 in this game. It was also apparent that in the first half neither full back could get forward much, yet after the break they were more or less camped out in the West Ham half. Neil Lennon highlighted this on MOTD2 and pointed out the things that untrained eyes like mine could see but not explain. He explained in detail why it was happening and it was very interesting I thought. It just made me appreciate Rodgers even more, the fucking clever bastard. He knows his shit does Brendan.

It didn't really look like a Rodgers team out there in the first half though. It was a scrappy game but we did have several good opportunities to counter attack but unusually for us we didn't make them count. There were only two real moments of stand out quality in the half: the Suarez shot against the bar and the move that led to the penalty. Gerrard's pass for that was just incredible, and moving him back into that deep lying playmaker role allows him to do that more than he could when he was playing further forward. It's sometimes referred to as 'the quarterback role', and Gerrard has been playing it like Peyton fucking Manning this season. Lots of short and intermediate passes, then all of a sudden BOOM he's going deep to his wide receiv... erm I mean striker. Suarez got himself isolated on the centre back and poor old James Tomkins found himself instinctively handling the ball as it was dinked past him. Yellow card for the defender (you could possibly argue it should even have been a red) and another penalty for Stevie who buried it with customary aplomb.

That should have been the breakthrough that set us on the way to a comfortable win. If West Ham had to come out and chase the game that would play right into our hands. The only real concern was going to be set-pieces, and so it proved as they equalised from a corner kick. And even then we dealt with it perfectly, it's just a pity the officials can't say the same. Mignolet caught the ball and was then struck in the head by Carroll, who also managed to then drag the keeper's arm free of the ball which dropped at the feet of Demel who tapped it in. Our players immediately appealed for the foul, the linesman was flagging but the ref had given a goal. That's ok though, he wasn't in a position to see a foul and can only call what he sees. Not a problem as the liner had seen it and brought it to the ref's attention. Taylor did the right thing by going to consult his linesman, and whilst initially I was blaming him for over-ruling his assistant, the more I think about it the more I'm sure it was the assistant shitting out and saying he wasn't sure. I mean, if he says to the ref *"it was a clear foul, I had a better view of it than you and I'm telling you that goal shouldn't count"*, there's no way Taylor is going to over-rule him. So I'm willing to bet that the liner got cold feet and said *"I think I saw a foul but I'm not sure, he may have just dropped it"* so the ref went with his initial decision. What made it all the more farcical was that, bizarrely, the incident was being shown on the big screen behind the officials and all of our players were pointing to it and telling them to look. There's no way they could do that, imagine if they'd looked at the big screen and then disallowed the goal? There'd have been all kinds of repercussions there.

At half time I was feeling pretty damn sorry for myself. I was even wondering whether that decision would cost us the title, and when I saw the half time substitution by Rodgers I wasn't feeling too much better either. Coutinho had not gotten into the game (a recurring theme away from Anfield) but we needed goals and we were taking off one of our most creative players and replacing him with Lucas. How was that going help? Fair to say my arse had completely gone at that point. It proved to be an inspired change by Rodgers though as West Ham couldn't get the ball off us in that second half. We enjoyed so much possession and pinned them back that it allowed the full backs to get forward and we looked much more threatening, even if we were still lacking a cutting edge for once.

We did create chances but they weren't gilt edged ones until Taylor pointed to the penalty spot as Flanagan was brought down by Adrian. The keeper did get the ball but he didn't push it away from Flanagan. If he hadn't brought Flano down then he was going to reach that ball before it went out and may have scored. It was probably 60-40 against being a pen, but having made the earlier mistake Taylor was intent on evening things up. Two wrongs never make a right, but Taylor redeemed himself a little and by 'evening it up' he ensured that all the headlines were about Liverpool's continued title charge rather than the referee who screwed them out of it with his incompetence.

Fat Sam was obviously beside himself with rage afterwards, coming out with all kinds of bollocks about Flanagan looking for it and being on his way down before the keeper reached him. Not true at all, Flano's touch said it all for me, most players in that position don't care about where the ball goes, they just want to get there before the keeper and then wait for contact and even in that situation it's still a penalty. Usually the ball goes flying out of play but when you look at this one Flano's touch is perfect. He wasn't looking for a pen he was trying to knock it past the keeper and retrieve it himself, and he only went down when the keeper grabbed his ankle and hauled him over. You can argue it wasn't a pen, but don't be casting aspersions on Flanagan, you fat, mashed potato faced, long ball merchant twat.

There's a lot of bollocks written about things evening themselves out over a season - even Stevie was spinning that line afterwards - but it's horseshit. A steaming, rancid pile of Hibbert if you will. They don't even themselves out at all but they did in this particular game and for that I'm grateful. Gerrard once again buried the pen, shrugging off the attempted mind games of the keeper who pointed to the corner where he wanted Stevie to put it. The skipper just stepped up and duly obliged, he went where the keeper wanted him to but made sure it was out of his reach. Balls of steel that fella.

We should have killed West Ham off with a third goal as we were utterly dominant now but unfortunately it wouldn't come. Suarez hit the bar again with another ridiculous chip and also mis-kicked after a brilliant passing move ended with Lucas putting one on a plate for him. Sturridge was wasteful too and it eventually became clear that to see this one out was going to require defensive concentration and resilience as well as composure in possession, because we were not going to get the safety net of a third goal. With a few minutes to go I seriously considered the option of just going outside to get away from it all, such was the tension I was feeling. When I look back on it now it seems daft as we were under no pressure at all and defended everything they threw at us with ease, but when you're watching it live though you always feel that a goal for the opposition is just around the corner.

We've done brilliantly to get ourselves to where we are and nine wins on the bounce is a great achievement. It's all been building up to our next game though; all of these wins are just setting us up for this huge showdown with City. It's the biggest domestic game at Anfield I can remember, there's so much riding on this one that Anfield is going to be bouncing next week. If we lose, I doubt we'll be able to come back from that. If we win, we will have one hand on it and it will probably all come down to whether we can beat Chelsea or not. I'm not sure how much more of this I can take though. This game was nerve wracking enough but it's nothing compared to what we have in store over the next few weeks. Remember what we had to go through before winning number 5? Olympiacos, that Juventus away game, both legs against Chelsea, the first half in Istabul, extra time and finally the penalty shoot out. So far this has been a walk in the park compared to that. I don't know if my heart will be up to it, but it's great to be in a position to find out isn't it? Roll on next week.

Premier League Round Up (5-7 April 2014)

I guess it was too much to ask for 'same as last week' wasn't it? Both City and Chelsea had potentially tricky games, not as difficult as a week earlier (they were both at home) but strange things can happen at this stage of the season. Sadly both came through with ease. If we're gonna do this it's going to be the hard way, nothing is going to be handed to us unfortunately.

City were once again indebted to Dodgy Linesman, who provided yet another assist when he kept his flag down despite David Silva being four yards offside. Aside from Yaya Toure, Dodgy Linesman has been City's key man this season, I've lost count of the telling contributions they've had from him. He may even make the final six in the Player of the Year awards. That was the worst offside call since... well since Sterling got flagged off for being about the same distance ONSIDE that Silva was OFFSIDE. And let's not even start on the disallowed Tiote goal a few weeks before that. Refs haven't been bailing City out, but weirdly, the liners have helped them big time all season. Maybe they're cheaper to pay off than refs? FFP and all that.

Southampton were well on top at that stage too, they'd stormed back from conceding a second minute penalty and were all over City for the next 20 minutes or so before eventually levelling through a pen of their own, Mr Reliable Rickie Lambert burying it. They'd missed three great chances prior to that and were bossing it until that offside goal went in and affected their concentration just before half time. Dzeko added another about a minute later and that was game over. Gutted. I really had a strong feeling they'd give City all they could handle, and it was shaping up like that too until they let those two quick goals in. Jovetic then tapped in to make it 4-1 late on. City deserved the win but it would have been nice to see it not handed to them on a fucking plate.

What about that City penalty though, fucking hell. Jose Fonte, hang your head in shame. That was the worst piece of individual defending of the season so far. The way he lazily dangled out his back leg and caught Dzeko was unforgivable. The City striker made a complete meal of it in fairness and under normal circumstances I'd hammer him for that.

But Fonte's challenge was so unbelievably stupid I don't even blame Dzeko for going to ground, if ever a player deserved to concede a pen it was Fonte. That foul actually deserved two penalties, what a complete fucking dolt he is. This is why I'd never be able to be a manager as that kind of thing would make me sub a player immediately, call him a useless sack of shit in my post match press conference and then immediately stick him on the transfer list.

Pochettino was mighty pissed afterwards, but not with Fonte. No, he was kicking off about the linesman, which was understandable of course. His and Lallana's interviews afterwards spoke volumes I thought. Lallana looked like he was going to cry, and Pochettino actually spoke in English, that's how pissed off he was. Lallana was going on about how hard done by they were and how they could all see how far offside he was by watching it on the big screen. Thing is though, they lost 4-1!!! Yes, the second goal was a turning point, but only because they allowed it to be by letting it cabbage their heads. That's why they lost the game. They'd already come back from one goal down and played City off the park, they could have done it again but instead they felt sorry for themselves and paid the price. Contrast that with what we did at Upton Park in similar circumstances. We've got Brendan though haven't we, the massive leg.

Yaya was booked for an awful dive. I can only imagine what Kolo thought when he saw that, truly shocking stuff that. I'm not going to get too worked up about the lack of a media backlash as let's face it Sturridge pretty much got away scot free after his tumble at Old Trafford. Luis would have been deported had he pulled something like that though. What about poor old Jay Rodriguez eh? I feel terrible for the lad, he's been in great form lately and looked like a cert for the World Cup until he blew his knee out under no challenge from anybody. How come stuff like that always happens to the decent lads like him, and never to massive gobshites like Eden Hazard, Jonas Olson or that Fellaini arsewipe?

Chelsea had a much easier time of it than City. Stoke had won four or five on the spin going into this and I thought they might even be able to frustrate Chelsea but they were fucking woeful and could barely get out of their own half. Adam came on at half time and had committed a foul within four seconds. Impressive stuff, he was only just back from a ban but he didn't let that slow him down. He followed it up by stamping on Schurrle's foot and then raking his studs down the chest of Luiz, and spent the rest of his time on the pitch slipping over any time he tried to run. His performance was laughably bad, the only thing you can say in his defence is at least it wasn't 'Andy Wilkinson bad'. Yes, Andy Wilkinson, the hapless right back who was a regular under Tony Pulis is still alive and still stealing a Premier League wage it seems. Hughes brought him on at half time and you'd have to ask the question: What the fuck had Useless been smoking? I've said before that Wilkinson might be the worst player in the league. Jozy Altidore has made a good fist of taking up the mantle this year as Wilkinson (and that other turd Ryan Shotton) hasn't had much of a look in, but he showed within a few minutes he's not giving up his crown without a fight. The penalty he gave away for chopping down Salah was a joke. Absolutely terrible decision making. Not the decision to make the tackle, although that was bad enough, no, I mean the decision to ever lace up a pair of boots in the first place.

You know who I really fucking hate at Chelsea? Well all of them obviously, but in this instance I'm talking about Willian. After me ripping him last week he goes and scores a boss little goal against Stoke. I hate it when shit like that happens and makes me look bad, although I still stand by what I said; he's Dirk Kuyt without the goals. You know how I know that? Because it's impossible for anyone to talk about Willian with referencing *'how hard he works'*. Honestly, look out for it, every fucker who ever mentions him has to bring it up, like he's the only fella in the league who puts a shift in or something. Does my head in.

Moving swiftly along, and Palace had another great win, spanking Cardiff largely due to another great performance by my boy Jason Puncheon who scored two crackers. Have to feel a bit for Cardiff, in recent weeks they've had to deal with Suarez, Sturridge and Puncheon. Triple whammy. No wonder they look a little gun shy. Joe Ledley scored the other one and looked absolutely gutted about it. Not only did he used to play for them but he's actually from Cardiff and they're his team. J-Punch had no such concerns, after his stunning second he put his hands to his ears and then thumbed his nose at the Cardiff fans. That's ma boy!

The mancs beat Newcastle 4-0 at St James' Park, but does anyone actually give a shit what they do anymore? When they lose it's funny of course, but when they win it's all just very 'meh'. United are almost irrelevant these days and the Geordies are already on their summer hols. Their players don't even look arsed anymore, and this was a cake walk for the mancs. Fellaini was still pulling his blatant elbow shit and getting away with it too. He completely levelled Gosling with a forearm smash as the Newcastle man tried to make a challenge. Kevin 'Nobody's' Friend actually gave United a free-kick for that. What's it going to take until Fellaini is dealt with? Is it going to need someone to get their face shattered like Gary Mabbutt back in the day? If so, allow me to nominate Oscar for the job.

Mata scored twice, I haven't seen him that happy since that big party him and the rest of his little furry mates had on Endor when the Death Star was destroyed. Hernandez got one and Januzaj managed to stay on his feet long enough to grab a goal as well. Ten away wins that for United. Hopefully that's enough to keep Moyesy in a job, despite them being dumped out of Europe in hilarious circumstances. Plucky United had been giving a really good account of themselves in Germany and even had the temerity to take the lead through an Evra thunderbolt. I didn't watch it but I read that Moyesy actually started to set off down the touchline but for whatever reason didn't reach his players as Mourinho had done the night before. May have been the fact that Bayern had equalised before he could get there?

No doubt he did that run we've all done when trying to catch a bus, where it pulls away and you try to just casually slow down and make out you weren't actually running for the bus; you were just giving the old legs a bit of a stretch. And whatever you do, don't make eye contact with anyone on it as no-one wants to see those smug, self satisfied faces staring mockingly out of the window do they? Of course, it was boss when you were the one sat on the bus ripping the piss out of the loser who was too slow to catch it. Come on, it wasn't just me who did that was it?

I eventually learned that in that situation it was best to just carry on running right past the bus stop and make it look like I was in a hurry to get somewhere and wasn't interested in no stupid bus anyway. Thankfully I drive now, as those years of bus travel were pretty fucking traumatic. I'd live in constant fear that the drunken loon who seems to appear on every bus journey regardless of time of day or destination, would come and sit next to me. I'd see it every day, he'd get on and sit next to someone, and then start singing to them whilst everyone else on the bus pissed themselves, in some cases literally if the smell was anything to go by. Incredibly I managed to always dodge that particular bullet (the singing drunk I mean, I got stuck with more than my share of piss smelling old folk unfortunately, but that serves me right for travelling with my dad I guess. What? It's ok for him to call me Gerry fucking Francis but I can't have a go back?), but I'm still haunted by the day a white van pulled up next to the bus I was on, and I made the rookie mistake of making eye contact with the three workmen in it. There was this stunning looking bird in the seat in front of me, I didn't know her but we got the same bus home from work every day. Anyway, one of the lads in the van was trying to tell me something and eventually I realised he was trying to get her attention, as though he knew her. He was asking me to tap her on the shoulder to get her attention, so I did. *"Err...excuse me"* I stammered, nervously, and then pointed to the van slightly behind her right shoulder. She looks over, as did I, and to my horror the lad is now just casually sat reading the paper whilst his two mates are staring straight ahead, paying no attention whatsoever to the bus. Bastards, they've done me there haven't they. She just turned back to what she was doing, and I'm sat there feeling like a massive quim. I looked back to the van, and the three fellas are roaring with laughter now. I'm still mortified even thinking about it all these years later, but looking back it could have been a hell of a lot worse, they could have been showing their arses.... or worse, wearing Chelsea shirts. Anyway, the moral of that long winded story is that white van men can't be trusted, buses are bad, that stunning bird thought I was a crank and Moyesy must stay.

Moving on, and Villa were without Benteke and Delph against Fulham and it showed as they somehow managed to get beat by a team that hasn't been able to beat anyone for months. Only Villa could lose to Fulham couldn't they, the fucking losers. Speaking of which, Motson was commentating on this one. I say commentating, I'm not exactly sure what he was doing, but there were so many ooohs and aaaaahs I'm not sure I want to know. He needs fucking off after this season though, surely? I know I've been saying that for ten years but eventually they need to send him to the glue factory surely? Failing that, I'd settle for them forcing him to retire.

Richardson's stunner put Fulham ahead but Holt equalised soon after only for Rodallega to win it for the visitors with a few minutes remaining. See what happens when you play an experienced frontman instead of some untested kid, Fulham? Of course, that sentence could just as easily read: See what happens when you play Aston fucking Villa? Penfold was hilarious afterwards, saying *"this is a message to the rest of the Premier League... we are back!"* Hahaha yeah I bet everyone is shitting themselves now, after you've beaten the might of Aston Villa. Kinell.

Two more deadbeat teams met at Carrow Road as West Brom beat Norwich thanks to an early Amalfitano goal. Norwich were a bit unlucky and hit the woodwork twice as they pushed for an equaliser. Hughton was sacked afterwards and the youth team manager was appointed in his place. In a season of fucked up sackings this one may just be the worst. Don't get me wrong, I've been saying for weeks that Norwich would probably go down and they may still do so (the only thing preventing it is likely to be Sunderland ineptitude), but they've actually been doing ok and prior to that goal hadn't conceded at home since December, so what's the point in sacking him now just as they are about to head into a run of games where they are unlikely to even take a point, no matter who is in charge? They've got Fulham next but after that it's mission impossible for them, so why ditch Hughton now? Has Delia been at the cooking sherry again? Seems pretty stupid to me, but I won't be losing any sleep over it, especially as it probably made our game there in a couple of weeks considerably easier. Suarez might actually score six this time.

George Boyd was back from suspension after grebbing at Joe Hart the other week, and he scored the only goal of the game as Hull beat Swansea. Steve the Pirate reckons Routledge should be given an England call up. Who does he get in instead of then? Gaaarrrr, hadn't thought of that had you? Ain't gonna happen, Steve.

Sunday saw the latest leg of the *"Takin' it up the Arse"* comedy tour, as the Gunners arrived at Goodison Park. It wasn't quite as funny a gig as the ones they performed at Anfield, the Emirates and Stamford Bridge but Arsenal still managed to give everyone a good old belly laugh once again. We set the blueprint for how to ruin Arsenal and both Chelsea and Everton followed the same method; push up on them, force them to lose possession in their own half and then hit them quick. They're just so lightweight it's not even funny. Well ok, it is funny, but they are shockingly weak aren't they?

The win actually puts the Blues in pole position for 4th now, which has not exactly been met with universal approval inside Goodison according to defender Sylvain Distin: *"We've spoken about it with some of the staff and said: 'What if we have to beat City to be in the Champions League but by doing that Liverpool win the league?' The funny thing is, some people would rather we don't get Champions League as long as they don't win the league. It's mad."* No, it's not mad Sylvain, it's #evertonarentwe

Onto Monday night, and Sunderland are going down aren't they? I didn't expect them to get a result at Spurs but you can't be losing 5-1 either. They've got games in hand but it's not going to mean anything if they can't pick up any points. Gus Poyet seems to have given up already, *"We need a miracle to stay up. We need something unique, a shock. I know where I am. If you look at the table and the games we have got left to win. I cannot see it coming."* That was bad, but if you're a Sunderland fan surely this is the last thing you want to hear from your manager: *"As soon as we go forward we cannot defend. We cannot pass the ball, we cannot get a shot on target. There are so many things that we cannot do. I blame myself. I pick the players, I pick the shape, I make the changes."* Fucking hell! It's true what he's saying of course, but sometimes maybe honesty isn't always the best policy Gus?

And why all this Sherwood hatred? Come on people, the guy is facking hilarious, a pwoper geeza. The mutual salute between him and Adebayor after the striker's goal against the Mackems was just pure, unadulterated comedy gold. Arsenal should hire him as a warm up act for their *"Takin' it up the Arse"* tour actually.

There's only so much hate to go round and it seems daft wasting it on good old 'Timmy Tactics' when Mourinho and Chelsea are in existence. I don't even have enough hate in me to be bothered by people like Allardyce and Pardew anymore, it's all taken up by that fucking helmet and his cronies at Chelsea. It boiled over again this week with their win over PSG. As much as the head said that Chelsea going through to the semis was good for the Reds, and it provided at least some crumb of comfort when they did just that, I can't deny that I threw up in my mouth a little when Ba got that late goal and that attention seeking, limelight hogging floater went charging up the touchline. Always has to make it about himself doesn't he, the self absorbed arrogant fuckface. There he was, Champions League quarter final and he's stood on the touchline in a pair of sweaty jogging bottoms, the fucking meff. Put a suit on you scruffy, horrible, Russian sounding cuntbucket. And get a shave too.

I knew they'd go through as PSG are French and every French team that's ever come over here needing a result seems to have shit their pants and blown it. I think maybe Monaco beat the Mancs once, but pretty much every other memory I have of French teams playing in England is of them crumbling under pressure. You know how I'm not exactly a fan of Zlatan, well guess what, I'd take him over that other over-rated, over-priced skeletor looking show pony Cavani. If he was even remotely decent PSG would have gone through, but they got knocked out because he's more interested in showing people how hard he can hit a ball than in putting it in the back of the damn net. Get a big giant box, mark it 'over-priced, over-hyped shite' and stick him and Zlatan in it, along with Ribery, Dani Alves and that bellend with the stupid haircut at Napoli, Hamsik or whatever the fuck his name is. Shite, the lot of them. *"Oh you don't know what you're talking about, have you not seen what Zlatan can do with a tennis ball?"* Don't. Fucking. Care. I watched our lads doing keep ups with a tennis ball and guess what, Suarez was comfortably the worst at it, he barely managed double figures despite doing that thing that people who are shit at keep ups do. You know what I'm talking about, where they try and do as many as they can on their thigh because they know they can't use their feet. You know who the best in the LFC squad was with a tennis ball? Conor Coady, that's who. So no, I don't give a fuck what Zlatan can do with a tennis ball, he can shove it up his overrated arse. Or better yet, shove it up Cavani's. And then make Mourinho eat it.

LIVERPOOL 3 MANCHESTER CITY 2

Competition - Premier League
Date - Sun 13 Apr 2014
Venue - Anfield
Scorer(s) – Sterling, Skrtel,
Coutinho
Star Man – Steven Gerrard

Team: Mignolet; Johnson,
Skrtel, Sakho, Flanagan;
Gerrard, Coutinho (Moses),
Henderson, Sterling (Lucas);
Suarez, Sturridge (Allen):

What a game! It not only lived up to expectations, it exceeded them. Most of the great Anfield occasions seem to have come 'under the lights' but in terms of day games I'm struggling to think of one to compare with this. Absolutely spine tingling stuff from start to finish and if we manage to see this one out and go on to win the title then this is a game we'll be telling our grandkids about. It will be

there alongside all of the great Anfield occasions, as make no mistake about it, we beat a seriously good team here.

The players had been given an incredible welcome on Anfield Road as the coach made it's way to the stadium. A similar thing had taken place before Sunderland of course, but this time there were at least three times as many fans lining the streets. Expect even more for the final two home games. The place was completely buzzing in the build up, the streets were busier than I've seen all season and presumably the pubs will have been hit in the pocket as everyone seemed to be hanging around outside before this one. After one of the most incredibly silent of 'minutes silences' prior to kick off the noise was ear splitting once again. Credit to City for the respect they showed, even unfurling a banner showing unity with us in the campaign for justice, but I don't think that will have come as a surprise to anybody as they've always been a decent bunch. Equally it will have surprised no-one that the pond life following Chelsea failed to observe it during their game at Swansea, as they've always been... well.. a not so good bunch.

There's always a danger that sombre occasions such as this can have a negative effect on the team and put added pressure on them to get a favourable result (see United's loss to City on the 50th anniversary of Munich for example), but Rodgers had said before-hand that it would inspire his team and so it proved. The boss had spoken of 'unleashing the fans' on City and I think everyone knew it was going to be one of those Anfield occasions when the crowd would undoubtedly play a huge part, and more often than not when Anfield is like this the result tends to follow. It's remarkable really, down the years there have been so many of these massive games, but they've almost exclusively been in Europe and losses have been incredibly rare when crowd and team have been as one. This was the biggest domestic game we've had in well over 20 years though, probably since the ill fated Arsenal game that decided the title in 1989 in fact.

Whilst it wasn't exactly going to decide the title, it was certainly going to give us a much better idea of where we stood. Lose and we were pretty much out of it. Draw and *gulp* we'd be relying on Everton doing us a favour. Win, and it was still in our own hands. We won, but in typical Liverpool style it wasn't straightforward; it never is. But it wouldn't be the same without the odd heart stopping moment would it? For Eidur Gudjohnsen read David Silva being a stud's length away from converting Aguero's pass. For the 'Ghost Goal' see the late Skrtel handball that wasn't given. Things could so easily have gone against us but they didn't. I said weeks ago there is a '2005 feeling' about what's happening this year and I'm even more convinced of it now.

This was a pulsating game from start to finish, two great attacking teams going at it hammer and tong. It won't be like this in a fortnight, Chelsea could play like City if they were coached that way; they have bags of talent in their squad but Mourinho would rather bore his way to victory. I'm not sure Pellegrini is a particularly great coach but what he is is a man who recognises the attacking talent he has at his disposal and allows them to go out and play to their strengths and they've been hugely entertaining this season.

I'm assuming we must have lost the toss as we attacked the Kop in the first half. I know traditionally a lot of visiting sides like to stop us from kicking that way in the second half, but given how quickly we tend to start games and considering how whipped up the crowd were, I'd say City made a big mistake there in hindsight. They were probably caught a little off guard by Rodgers' team selection too. Not specifically the eleven players on duty, but the way in which they were deployed. Pellegrini would surely have expected the same kind of formation and tactics that we'd used in those other big games we've had at Anfield lately, with Coutinho operating in a midfield three, Sterling wide and Suarez and Sturridge taking turns working the other flank. Instead we saw a midfield diamond with Coutinho on one of the sides and Sterling at the point of it. It was an extremely attacking side Rodgers picked, but such was the phenomenal work rate of Coutinho in the opening half an hour or so that City were unable to take advantage of any possible defensive weakness in our midfield. The little magician probably made more tackles than anyone else on the pitch in that period, he was everywhere. Sterling too for that matter.

As expected, we flew at them from the off and it took just six minutes for us to go in front. Suarez - harshly booked a minute earlier for a nothing foul on Demichelis - was the creator as he showed great strength to initially withstand the challenge of the Argentine and then even greater strength to completely barge Clichy out of the way. He then slid a pass into Sterling but what happened next was quite remarkable. Sterling collected the ball and everyone thought he was going to shoot. Instead he stood Kompany up, moved the ball to his left and then once again looked like he was about to take the shot. The whole stadium was expecting the shot, including Kompany and Hart who were then both caught flatfooted when Sterling calmly shifted back onto his right and stroked it into the empty net. Raheem had the coolest head inside Anfield; incredible composure for a kid still in his teens. What a fucking player he's turned into over the last four or five months, in that period he's been as important as anyone I'd say, he's made so many telling contributions.

That goal was the last thing City needed, it was going to be tough enough for them anyway but the early goal just amped the crowd up even more and in turn inspired the players further. Brian Moore once famously observed on the Anfield Rap video that *"No-one knows quite what to expect when the red machine's in full effect"*. That's no longer true, everyone knows what to expect: absolute fucking carnage. They just can't stop it. Everton were blown away by it early doors, Arsenal even more so, Spurs went the same way and even Manchester City, a much superior side than any of the aforementioned, could do nothing to prevent Liverpool's early onslaught. I'd give anything to see Chelsea go the same way in a fortnight. Scumbags.

Sturridge should have doubled our advantage when more brilliant play from Sterling put a chance on a plate for him. It looked like he tried to be a little too precise in guiding his shot into the corner as the ball went across his body, and it drifted just past the far post. City's cause obviously wasn't helped by the early departure of Toure, warmly applauded off the field by the entire stadium after appearing to pull a muscle in the act of shooting. We were glad to see him go off as he obviously represented a huge threat to us, but the applause recognised that he's a great player. Besides, he's Kolo's brother and that has to count for something, right?

Generally though, we don't mind City too much do we? Relatively speaking at least.

Of course there's some resentment at how they suddenly got a brand new stadium and massive cash injection without doing anything to earn it, but from my point of view I'd say that if any side was going to 'win the lottery' like that, there are few I'd have begrudged less than City. They've always had good support despite having very little to cheer about and being run by complete buffoons, and even now they've had success I don't think they've become especially obnoxious, whereas most probably would have. It's a healthy rivalry and there's no real depth of bad feeling on either side. The common bond of hating United has always meant things were relatively cordial between the two sets of fans, and the applause for Toure was testament to that too. Put it this way, if ANY Chelsea player suffers a similar fate in a couple of weeks, he'll be leaving the field with deafening jeers in his ears, not warm applause. And I doubt we'll see Suggs in an exec box wearing an HJC scarf and sticker either, as Noel Gallagher was.

We were swarming at City from all angles in those early exchanges. When we had possession we were creative, when City had it we were even more dangerous because as soon as we won the ball we were tearing at them on lightning quick counters. It must be completely terrifying facing our front five at Anfield, the pace and incisiveness of the attacks are just a joy to behold. One such break was the catalyst that would eventually lead to the second goal.

Flanagan's long clearance was met with an immaculate touch from Suarez who put the ball into the path of Sterling. He carried it forward and then found Sturridge on the right, who cut inside and then tried to thread a ball through for Suarez. Kompany just about cut it out at full stretch and City scrambled the ball away for a corner. Exhilarating stuff again though, and look at the lung busting run Hendo made to get up there as well. Coutinho took the corner and Gerrard found himself unmarked in the middle of the goalmouth. His powerful header was brilliantly tipped over by Hart, but City's respite was only temporary as Gerrard decided to take this one himself and Skrtel glanced in the 7th goal of an incredible season for him.

We were in dreamland now and it was looking like the Arsenal game all over again, with Sterling and Skrtel both scoring and the Reds tearing the opposition to shreds with every attack. We almost added a third with another thrilling counter attack as Coutinho brilliantly released Suarez over the top and he was within a whisker of finding Sturridge. It was too far ahead of the striker but Sterling got onto it and he so nearly managed to cut it back to give Sturridge a tap in, but City just about got it away.

As the half wore on and the pace dropped just a fraction, City slowly managed to get a foothold in the game and went close on a few occasions. Dzeko had a decent penalty shout when Sakho lunged in wildly and missed both ball and man. Dzeko realised too late what had happened and by the time he initiated contact with the prone defender and fell over, Clattenberg wasn't buying it. Hugely risky challenge from Sakho though. It might have been the only thing he did wrong in an otherwise fine performance, but that could have proved very costly.

Sturridge then gave the ball away cheaply on the edge of the City box and they broke quickly down the right. It ended with Silva flashing a header wide from a Navas cross, but Clattenberg gave a corner much to the displeasure of the Liverpool defenders.

Mignolet came for the corner but didn't get there and it needed Sterling to head the ball off the line to deny Kompany. The ball looped into the air and Johnson then did incredibly well to head out from under his own bar under massive pressure from Fernandinho. Mignolet claimed it as the crowd roared their approval. That incident summed up Liverpool's approach to the first half, they simply wanted it more than City. Shortly after that Navas crossed again and this time Fernandinho met it on the half volley forcing a great save from Mignolet. We were living dangerously and half time couldn't come quickly enough as City had gotten over the initial blitz and looked to have regained their composure.

The second half started exactly as we wouldn't have wanted it to, with City pinning us back and dominating possession. We found it difficult to get hold of the ball but in fairness we still tried to play out from the back and to do what we'd done in the first half, it's just that the intensity of the game had slowed slightly and that allowed City to play their natural game. It's impossible to keep up the pace that we start these games off with and when the speed of the game inevitably drops that's when we need to be defensively resilient and clinical with our chances to break. The pace dropped in the games against Everton, Arsenal and Spurs too, but in those games we were either completely out of sight or they didn't really have the quality to hurt us once it became more of a level playing field. It's almost like we begin these games with an extra man, and we have to make it count before it becomes 11 v 11 again when the tempo slackens in the 2nd half.

City are much better than anyone else we've faced this season though and they were able to dominate once the early storm had subsided. It would be wrong to say they weathered the storm as they were 2-0 down after all and could easily have trailed by more, but they were just about still afloat. A third goal and they may have sunk without trace but at 2-0 they were still in the game and you have to give them credit for how well they played in that second half. And you have to give our lads even more credit for being able to overcome it.

City's first goal was brilliant football and they'd been threatening it for a while. Silva was running the show and even when we got players around him it didn't feel like we did; rarely do you see a player able to make it look like he has all the time in the world when he's surrounded by opponents. He was phenomenal at times in this game, just gliding around playing little inch perfect short passes and shifting the ball on before we could get near him. Still, it took the introduction of a far less glamorous player for City to get back into it. Be honest, how many of you thought *"we're in trouble now"* when James Milner came on? It's not that he's a bad player, far from it, but Navas would surely be regarded by most as a much bigger threat. As it was, Pellegrini had to ask Flanagan to take Navas out of his pocket so he could make the substitution and get Milner on.

Flanno completely bossed it against Navas but Milner brought a different set of problems for the young full back to deal with. Navas wanted to run at him but Milner wasn't really interested in doing that, instead he'd pop it off to Silva or Nasri and then run in behind for a return ball. That's much more difficult to defend against, especially when there's no natural wide player in front to help out and double up. City started to get in behind us a lot and both of their goals came from very similar moves. The first expertly slid in by Silva, the second unluckily diverted past Mignolet by Johnson. No blame attached to either player, it was just one of those unfortunate incidents but a real choker for us.

What made that second goal a real killer was that we'd had a great chance to go 3-1 up just before it. Sturridge had ran through and spurned the option to pass in favour of going on his own, and he was stopped by a good challenge by Zabaleta. Sturridge had been a little selfish on occasion and Suarez was completely losing his shit over it, and this one was the final straw as Suarez went nuts and was complaining to the bench about his partner's antics. Had he not been injured I'd say there's a good chance Sturridge would have been subbed anyway at that point, as we desperately needed to bolster the midfield and it clearly wasn't going to be his day.

I just felt he was trying too hard all afternoon, I don't think it was a case of deliberately being selfish or wanting the glory, not at all, it was just bad decision making, perhaps due to the pressure. Sometimes when a bit of nerves or doubt creeps in, you go yourself rather than try and play a pass and that's what I think happened. The occasion maybe affected him a little more than most. He's been a bit below par for a few weeks now and maybe his confidence isn't what it was, but hopefully the injury doesn't rule him out for long as we'll have a much better chance of winning the league with him than without him.

It's easy to analyse the City goals and point to where we could have done better, but the thing for me is that it was all happening so quickly it's difficult for players to react. Look at how quick and intricate the passing was inside the area from the likes of Milner, Nasri and especially Silva. It was like pinball in there at times, especially as they often managed to work overloads which gave them one more man than we could deal with. It's an area where we can certainly improve - and next year we'll need to when we come up against some of Europe's best - but it's not a test we'll face again this season as no-one else we have to play can do what City's players did in that mesmerising spell of pressure. The biggest danger against Chelsea is they may actually send us to sleep.

Allen belatedly came on for Sturridge but it seemed like a case of closing the stable door after the horse had done a runner. The fans and players were massively deflated but everyone sucked it up, dug deep and just got on with it. There's a title to be won after all, and no-one ever said it was going to be easy.

Silva should have given City the lead when Skrtel dived in on Aguero on the touchline and didn't get there, presenting City with a 2 v 1 break. Sakho couldn't close down Aguero too quickly as Silva was in the middle, and he couldn't just watch Silva either as Aguero would have a free run on goal. He did what he could to make the pass difficult, and fortunately Aguero put a little too much on and Silva's desperate sliding touch sent the ball just past the post. Massive, massive let off that. Aside from that one major scare, we did manage to slow City down after switching to 4-3-3 and the game became more of an even contest. Suarez wasn't having the best of days and was fortunate not to be given a second yellow when Clattenberg waved away his claim for a free-kick after a challenge by Dimichelis. If it wasn't a foul, then it had to be a dive, there was no in between on that. The correct decision would have actually been to award a free-kick as the defender did catch Suarez, but the theatrical way in which he hurled himself to the floor did him no favours. He was walking a tight rope all afternoon as having been booked so early on he kept running his mouth at Clattenberg and other refs would have sent him off.

Have to laugh at Demichelis complaining though considering the histrionics out of him to get Suarez booked early on. Luis barely touched him but he was rolling round like he had a broken leg. Suarez did the same back to him and he's acting all indignant, the cheeky bastard. Clattenberg may have let Suarez off the hook but he clearly decided he wasn't giving him anything from that point on, which was kind of fair enough in a way, morally at least. In this kind of mood Suarez would test the patience of any ref and does himself no favours.

He should have had a pen when Kompany grabbed at him twice as he went round the big defender in the box and there were numerous free-kicks that should have been given but all were waved away by the ref. On each of them Suarez was hurling himself around like a rag doll and that probably counted against him as much as the 'dive' he escaped punishment for. He needs to knock this shit off before we play Chelsea, as Mourinho gets his way with refs far more than Pellegrini is ever likely too. And we all remember what happened in that fixture last season when Luis lost the plot as he got so worked up. Send him to Steve Peters, Brendan!

The winning goal came out of nothing really. A long throw to no-one, a sliced clearance from Kompany and a thumping finish from Coutinho. Most of the time his shooting is pitiful (there was one pathetic effort in the first half when I wanted to strangle him!), but he couldn't have picked a better moment to strike one so cleanly. Anfield went mental and even though there was still 12 minutes or so left I felt that having somehow managed to recover from the huge momentum shift of them equalising there was no way we'd lose the lead again. It just felt like destiny, and even when Hendo was sent off for an overly enthusiastic lunge on Nasri, I wasn't too concerned that we'd concede. Of course there was the Skrtel handball incident, but I knew nothing about that until I got home. No-one appealed for it at the time and I imagine most of the crowd were as oblivious to it as I was. It could have gone against us but thankfully it didn't. After what happened at the Etihad then this makes us even I guess, and I look forward to things evening out against Chelsea after the way we got shafted at Stamford Bridge.

Really feel bad for Hendo though. He'll be missed, especially against Chelsea. It was his own fault but Moses also played a part as it was his poor touch that lost possession (had he been able to keep the ball and pick out Suarez we'd have been in on goal), and then Hendo followed it up with a heavy touch of his own before his adrenaline took over and he over stretched for a ball he should never have gone for. He got the ball first but he was a little bit high and definitely out of control and caught Nasri with his follow through. I think we all knew what was coming, as did the poor lad himself who despondently trudged off the field. Rodgers responded by withdrawing Sterling and sending on Lucas to shore up the middle, but not before telling Sterling to go and stand as far away from the touchline as possible to waste a few precious seconds when he was brought off. Gotta love Brendan, the canny bastard. He'd done the exact same thing with Coutinho too. Lucas did his job and we held on without any further incident as Anfield erupted at the final whistle. *"And now you're gonna believe us, we're gonna win the league"* echoed around the ground, and at this point few would argue.

I've just realised I haven't even mentioned Flanno's thunderous tackle on Milner. That got the crowd fired up again just when we all needed something to get us going. He had another great game, City threw everything they had at him and although Milner gave him some problems for a while, that was as much down to tactics as his own individual play and the arrival of Allen and a switch to 4-3-3 helped him shore things up again. After that thumping challenge on Milner, Gerrard rushed over and was telling the youngster *"Breathe, breathe!!"* Love that though, and fair dues to Milner for just getting on with it. Almost every one of his team-mates would have been writhing around looking for the ref to take action there. Milner is proper old school though, you'll get none of that shit from him. He probably even congratulated Flanagan on the challenge. Mans man.

Oh, and that Stevie Gerrard 'huddle speech' at the end is one of the greatest things I've ever seen. I've got chills now just thinking about it. If Stevie told me to go and run through a brick wall right now I reckon I would you know. What a fucking hero. Gerrard is so fucking awesome that even 'Ace Rimmer' looks at him and says *"what a guy!"*. I'll admit that I almost cried watching that clip of him at the end and if he gets to lift the Premier League trophy in a few weeks, there'll be no 'almost' about it, I doubt if there'll be a dry eye in the house in fact. As the great man himself said, *"this does not fucking slip now!!"* Just four more wins, come on Redmen!!!!

Premier League Round Up (12-16 April 2014)

Saturday was one of those nothing days when all the irrelevant sides faced off against each other. This is what happens when you're in a title race and are no longer one of those bums with nothing worthwhile to fight for, Saturday night's MOTD is pretty pointless. Saturday's games all involved no hopers at the bottom fighting to stay up or those also rans fighting it out for the spots between 4th and 8th. I almost feel sorry for them, the poor insignificant bastards. Almost. I mean no-one felt sorry for us, did they?

Managerless Norwich absolutely pummelled Fulham at Craven Cottage yet somehow lost 1-0 as Rodallega got the only goal of the game. Fulham have been the worst team in the league by a mile this season but they might somehow stay up and are now just two points behind Norwich. As a footnote to this, Wolf Van Winkel hasn't scored since opening day, which means he's nailed on to get one against us next Sunday. No-one comes to the rescue of strikers in need quite like we've done over the years.

West Brom had two big fuck off mascots lined up with their players during the minute's silence for the 96 at the Hawthorns. That's just wrong that is, I know there's no harm meant but it just looks terrible. It's meant to be a sombre, respectful moment and the players are all stood there, heads bowed, arm in arm, and you've got two dopes stood either end of the line in giant bird costumes. Come on West Brom, fucks sake. Still, at least they kept quiet and paid their respects, unlike some Spurs fans who chanted *'Always the victim'*. Cant get my head around that, since when did Spurs have that kind of beef with us? Obviously it was just a tiny minority and you can't judge a fan base on the antics of a handful of dickheads, but it still shocked me. I expected it from Chelsea, not from Spurs.

I didn't expect them to come from 3-0 down to get a draw either. The Baggies are experts at throwing away leads late on, but this one has to really sting. A win here would have gone a long way to ensuring safety and they couldn't have made a better start, going 2-0 up inside a couple of minutes. It got even better when Adebayor then missed a pen. Sherwood could have been forgiven for giving his striker a different kind of 'hand salute' than the one from a week ago, but he's a bigger facking man than that. Instead, he laughed casually, pointed to his watch and shouted in the direction of the West Brom bench *"still time, still time"*. He's the ultimate 'irrational confidence guy' isn't he? If Sherwood was as good as he thinks he is, we'd all be in trouble. Even when Sessegnon made it 3-0 after half an hour I bet Tim still thought they'd win. As it was, he had to settle for a draw.

You know what he said afterwards? *"This comeback was like Liverpool's comeback in Istanbul. Fantastic."* No, I'm not winding you up, he really said that, word for word. He really believes it too I bet. I'll ask again, how can anyone not like Tim Sherwood??? He also said *"We thought Chiriches was pulled back for their third goal, but I'm trying to think of as many excuses as I can for our defending which was HORRENDOUS"* Hahaha he's fucking boss, if Spurs sack him I'm gonna be devastated. There's been a Steve Kean sized hole in my affections that I haven't been able to fill. Until now that is.

As for West Brom, Pepe Mel is one of the most uninspiring fellas in the Premier League, he's like a Spanish Roy Hodgson. Having said that, they were a bit unlucky to catch Aaron Lennon on the one good day he has every season as you can't really game plan for that.

Moving on, and Sunderland's woes continued with a home loss to Everton. They played really well according to my brother in law (who told me afterwards if they keep playing like this they'll *"win us the title by taking points off City and Chelsea"*), but it wasn't enough as 'Captain Fuckup' himself Wes Brown put through his own net for the only goal of the game. If he's not getting sent off he's scoring own goals, the shit baked bean looking loser. If, nay, when, Sunderland go down I'm blaming him and that other manc bum O'Shea. Poor old Fabio has been like a thoroughbred racehorse this season, so good that the Premier League had to handicap him by having the likes of Brown, O'Shea and Altidore shoved in his saddlebags to slow him down.

Sunderland's situation got a whole lot worse with Cardiff surprisingly winning at St Mary's. Southampton dominated the game but couldn't make the breakthrough and Cardiff won it with a great 2nd half strike from Juan Cala. Little known factoid, 'Juan Cala' is actually Spanish for how scousers describe Ole Gunner Solskjaer. "Wanker, la".

The Saints piled on the pressure but Marshall had another great game in goal and Cardiff held on. Fonte did his best to give away another daft pen but unlike Dzeko last week, Zaha opted to stay on his feet and try to score. He failed, obviously. How much did Ferguson pay for him? About the same as we 'gambled' on Sturridge I believe. The worst thing about Cardiff winning a game is undoubtedly having to look at Solskjaer's stupid smiling face. Hate listening to him talking about *'de fansss'* and *'de ladsss'* too. Little fucking orc.

Arsenal and Hull didn't have a league game at the weekend as they were involved in the FA Cup semi finals. Hull won a thriller against plucky League One Sheffield United, whilst Arsenal needed a late equaliser and then penalties to see off Championship side Wigan. There was much piss taking at Arsenal's expense over their celebrations afterwards, but a lot of it was over the top for me. Ok, they got through by the skin of their teeth against a side a division below them, but the bottom line is they reached a cup final, they're entitled to celebrate. Should we not have celebrated when we needed pens to beat Birmingham in 2001 or Cardiff in 2012? What about when we needed a last gasp equaliser and penalties to beat Pompey in the FA Cup semis in 1992? So no, I'm not going to take the piss out of Arsenal fans, or indeed the players, for being happy about beating Wigan and reaching the FA Cup semi final.

I am, however, going to mock the shit out of them for the way they did it. All those years of listening to the smug, arrogant, *"Hoooooooofffff"* chants any time one of our defenders played any kind of pass that went more than six inches off the floor, and what did they do when they were trailing at Wembley to a fucking Championship side??? They went full on alehouse, that's what they did. Mertesacker camped out in the Wigan box and they launched cross after cross at him until eventually the big fucking lummox got on the end of one and equalised. Where's your pretty football now Arsenal, eh? Eh? Hoooooooooooooofffff!!!

Then of course you had the on pitch celebrations from the players. Be happy by all means, but at least act natural. In the NFL there's an expression used for whenever a wide receiver makes an arse of himself after getting in the end zone; *"act like you've been there before"*. Wenger should have that phrase pinned up on the dressing room wall to stop his players making themselves look like wankers any time they win the kind of game that Arsenal are expected to win. Taking fucking selfies on the pitch again? Really? Still, I guess that is 'natural' behaviour when you're a complete wanker, as most of the Arsenal squad seem to be.

Look, don't get me wrong here, I don't think there's any malice in those Arsenal lads, I mean look at Giroud's touching gesture to the families of the 96 after he scored against West Ham on Tuesday night, or Podolski putting out a tweet the other day about 'remembering Hillsborough' (he got caned by several Arsenal fans for that too, sadly). They aren't complete twats like, say, most of the Chelsea squad. They are wankers though, but I mean that in the nicest possible way. There's a huge distinction between a twat and a wanker. A twat is someone like Mourinho or Terry for example, who when you look at them you can feel your anger rising and can't help but spew out the words *"look at that fucking twat there"*. A wanker is someone like Scziezny or Podolski, who you look at, shake your head, smile and say *"look at that wanker!"*.

In addition to twats and wankers, you also have cunts of course. One man who unquestionably comes into that category is Howard Webb and he was involved in another contentious 'non penalty' decision as Palace entertained Villa at Selhurst. Bolasie had his heel clipped in the act of shooting and was sent sprawling right in front of the egghead official, who did what he always does and waved it away. John Motson - a rare hybrid of twat and wanker, let's call him a twanker - bizarrely stated in commentary: *"did he stumble over his own foot? I don't think it was a Villa contact that really made him go down"* Fucking hell beeb, you're still using our licence fee to keep this clueless old goat in sheepskin coats? Kill him. Kill him with fire!!

Webb would later give a penalty and then reverse his decision. Palace were furious but this time he was right for once. He only gave it because he thought the linesman had signalled for handball but it turned out the liner was pointing to his chest and when he told Webb it wasn't a pen he needed no second invitation to change his mind. Bet he was even more relieved than the Villa players.

Palace could have been forgiven for feeling sorry for themselves and allowing their heads to drop, but when you've got Jason Puncheon in your side though it's like having an extra man as he's just so fucking ace. My boy came up trumps once again with the only goal of the game. How many winning goals is that he's scored for Pulis now? There's a lot of talk of Pulis winning manager of the year. If that happened I'd hope he'd have the good grace to thank J-Punch in his acceptance speech as he's won at least five or six games for Palace single handedly, the fucking superstar. Only the post denied him a second goal in this one too. He's probably the only non-LFC player worthy of making the shortlist for Player of the Year. He's the single biggest threat remaining to our title hopes, I just hope he goes easy on us when we play them.

Paul Ince was on MOTD and was asked about what the secret of Palace's good results has been, as his lad is there now of course (not getting much playing time though). He said *"It's the togetherness, the spirit, there's no stars there"*. YOU WHAT??? Well it's easy to see why he's been such a failure in management. No stars he says!! Three words Incey: Jason. Fucking. Puncheon. What makes his oversight even worse is that Ince managed 'the Knockout Punch' when he was at MK Dons so should know as well as anyone that the guy is a phenom. If Ince hadn't sold him then he might still be there managing MK Dons, in the Premier League. 'No stars', he says. Kinell.

Finally on Saturday, Newcastle's piss poor run continued as they lost at Stoke. The only shock there is that it was just a one goal defeat. The goal was a complete fluke too; an over-hit cross by Pieters. At least he had the self awareness to not really celebrate it, I can only imagine what an Arsenal player would have done in the same situation. Probably had an oil painting commissioned to commemorate the occasion. Pieters just looked a bit sheepish, although it could have just been that he's forgotten what to do as he hadn't found the net since 2008. That's even longer than Shola Ameobi's goal drought. At least I think it is, I could be wrong. Newcastle's fans unveiled a 'Pardew Out' banner. Yeah, good luck with that boys, that fifteen year contract he signed has bought him a fair bit of job security I reckon. That and the incriminating photos he has of Ashley.

Hang on, did the Mancs play? I don't think they did, but with no-one even being arsed about them anymore it's possible they slipped under the radar. I assume they must have been due to play Hull.

Onto Sunday now, and it was certainly a case of the cart full of horse shit rolling up after the Lord Mayor's Show as Chelsea bored their way to a 1-0 win over ten man Swansea following our pulsating clash with City in the early game. It's almost unforgivable that a team with all their attacking talent plays the way they do, Mourinho should be getting hammered for it but instead he's lauded as some fucking genius. Swansea were all over them until Chico Flores got two bookings in a minute. In that situation the ref has to show a bit more common sense. The second one especially was just a foul, it didn't need a yellow. Mongo was in Dowd's ear and Dowd told him *"I'm thinking about it John"* before pulling out his card. *"I just said 'that's a second yellow'. Fair play to Phil. It was a big decision to make and he made the right one"* said the huge fodded goon. *"I'm speaking as a Chelsea player, but I think everyone would say it was a second yellow."* Well I'm speaking as a football fan, and I think everyone would say you're a massive fucking cunt.

Leaving aside the fact that Chico is a bad snide and probably deserved a red card if only for putting highlights in his newly cropped hair (which along with his facial hair makes him look like a member of a 'Village People' tribute act), it was just incredibly harsh from Dowd and made Swansea's task almost impossible. Yet even with ten men Swansea still created as many chances as Chelsea. In the end, Demba Ba was the hero for the second time in a week as his shot squirmed through Vorm to give Chelsea the points. Not bad for a Joe Average eh? I've said it before, but this narrative about Chelsea's strikers that has been spoon fed to people by Mourinho is just complete bollocks. 80% of the league would love to have any of Eto'o, Torres or Ba to call upon. Hell, even Matic said *"People who say Chelsea don't have any good strikers know nothing about football"*. I wouldn't go that far lad, Mourinho may be a knob but he obviously knows a lot about football. Matic probably should have said, *"People who say Chelsea don't have any good strikers are looking to blame others for their own shortcomings"*.

That Portuguese shit kicker refused to do any interviews afterwards and also fucked off down the tunnel without shaking the hand of Steve the Pirate. You stay classy, you scruffy prick. Pellegrini had said prior to those games on Sunday that *"it would be terrible for football if those bus parking cockney cunts won the title ahead of City or the Mighty Reds"*. Ok, I'm paraphrasing there, but only a little (he may have said 'awful' rather than 'terrible'). He's right though, I don't think I could cope if Chelsea somehow ended up winning the title you know. If City won it I'd obviously be gutted because it would mean we hadn't, but if Chelsea did it I honestly don't know how I'd be able to live with that.

Remember a few months back when I said that it gravely offended me how Spurs were within three points of us because they're not fit to breathe the same air as our team? Well I feel the same way about Chelsea, we're fucking miles better than them but it's all going to come down to that one game at Anfield. The idea that a mistake or a referee's decision may be the difference between us winning it and Mourinho spawning his way to another title is just too much to even contemplate. We need to win this thing, not just for ourselves but also for football. Fuck Chelsea, the lowlife twats.

Moving on to the midweek games, and as I mentioned earlier, Giroud scored as Arsenal came from behind to beat West Ham. I really don't care what happens with 4th place, I'll be more than happy to see either Arsenal or Everton miss out, I just hope it goes to the last day as that means the Blues may have taken points off City and helped us out. If they get fourth, good for them. I'm not rooting for it though, fuck that. What will be will be.

They've made it harder for themselves by losing at home to Palace. Prior to that shock loss the Blues had won seven on the bounce, but they hadn't come up against my boy J-Punch in any of those games. He made Everton his bitch, scoring one and making one as Palace won 3-2. We should buy him, imagine the carnage he'd wreak if he had Suarez, Sturridge, Sterling and Coutinho up there with him instead of Bolasie and Jerome.

Some Blues didn't handle their first loss in months particularly well and decided to vent their anger at Sylvain Distin on twitter. He wasn't having it though and fired back some barbs of his own, including this classic:

Random Angry Blue: *fuken leg it distin u give your all mate but your not good enough*
Distin: *maybe not mate but you can't afford better at the minute so stop moaning kid*

Hahahaha I like this new Distin far better than the fucking doormat who walked around Wembley with his *"my bad"* hands in the air apology. You tell em big fella!

Meanwhile, over at the Etihad!!! *deep breath* Wooooooooooo! *Ric Flair strut* How great was that? It would have been even better had Big Vito not thrown one in to allow City to equalise of course, but a draw was still a seriously unexpected bonus for us wasn't it? It wasn't a fluke either, they had so many chances they deserved at least a point. Poyet said afterwards *"I am sure Luis Suarez is happy tonight. One less team"*. Haha he loves Luis doesn't he, his team talk was probably *"come on lads, let's do Luis and his mates a favour tonight and take something from these feckers"*. Hendo was there in the crowd cheering them on too. the big leg.

Big Vito though, bloody hell that looked suspicious didn't it? Wonder if his bosses were running a book on the game? Made him an offer he couldn't refuse and that. If they did, I bet Vito got a nice little taste after that, y'know, wet his beak a little. He best not pull that shit at the Bridge this weekend or I'll make sure he sleeps with the fishes.

When we beat City at the weekend my brother-in-law text me and said: *"It's the Sunderland connection - Mig, Hendo and Pascoe. We'll take points off City and beat Chelsea for you next week and you'll be Champions"*. I won't even tell you what I replied, but if I could take it back I would. Sorry about that Sunderland. Haway the lads!!! Now go and beat those plastic flag waving, minutes silence ruining, helmet worshipping chav bell ends for us. Imagine if Borini got the winner. Kinell.

NORWICH CITY 2 LIVERPOOL 3

Competition - Premier League
Date - Sun 20 Apr 2014
Venue - Carrow Road
Scorer(s) – Raheem Sterling (2),
Luis Suarez,
Star Man – Raheem Sterling

Team: Mignolet; Johnson,
Skrtel, Sakho, Flanagan;
Gerrard, Lucas, Allen (Agger),
Coutinho (Moses), Sterling;
Suarez:

Only three more games to go now. Good job too, I'm not sure how much more of this my heart can take. It's not just our games either, I was a lot more nervous watching the closing stages of the Chelsea game the night before than I was the end of this one, but even so this was still pretty stressful. In fairness we closed it out quite well in the end but it shouldn't have come to that considering we were 2-0 up after ten minutes. It should have been a stroll but it ended up a dogfight.

This is the kind of thing that happens at the back end of the season when the pressure is on and teams are fighting for titles or to stay in the league. Strange things happen this time of year, and there'll probably be another twist or two before this thing is over. Thankfully we managed to ensure we weren't the victims of an upset at Carrow Road but we certainly made it harder than it needed to be. It was all going according to plan as we raced into an early lead thanks to the electrifying Sterling. In the absence of Sturridge there was extra responsibility on the teenager to help Suarez shoulder the goalscoring burden and he responded big time with a stunning goal and a brilliant assist inside the opening ten minutes. I'm not even sure what his exact position was; Rodgers said beforehand that he was playing a midfield diamond with an extra man in there to give us a numerical advantage over Norwich (who were playing a diamond of their own). Not really sure how that works (it's more of a Christmas tree than a diamond) but it did. At least it did until Norwich changed their system and suddenly we didn't look so good anymore.

In that first half though we were top class. The two goals were brilliant, but it was the way we passed the ball around and moved Norwich all over the pitch that really impressed. There was a real swagger and confidence in our play and if we'd made it 3-0 we might have gone on to get six or seven. Sterling's first was a beauty; there was a very slight deflection, but even so, I've never seen him hit a ball like that before. Shooting isn't his strong point, but this was a corker and gave us just the start we needed.

The impressive Allen then almost made it 2-0 with a goal that would have epitomised everything that is good about 'Rodgeball'. We didn't have to wait long for the second goal though and again it was just typical of how we were playing. The ball was shifted around the park, Sakho rolled one up the line to Flanagan who feigned to go inside before taking off down the touchline and knocking it into space for Sterling. What followed was a work of art. Suarez went to go near post then broke off behind Turner's back, and Sterling delivered an exquisite ball across with his left foot that Suarez expertly steered into the corner. Absolutely brilliant goal, and there were less than 11 minutes gone.

This was the start we'd dreamed of and everything was coming up Millhouse for us, but then Norwich started to get into it a bit as our intensity dropped off. Still, we defended superbly in that first half. Whenever it looked like there was danger one of our players would be on the scene to snuff it out before it reached Mignolet. I don't think he even had to make a save in the first half did he? Actually yeah he did, he kept out an effort by Redmond after Johnson had given it away. It wouldn't be the first time Johnson's sloppiness put us in trouble either. He had 'one of those days' of his.

Our defensive tenacity in that first half was typified by one almighty scramble following a free-kick that seemed certain to result in a Norwich goal. Hooper looked like he would get a shot away but Allen nipped in to block him not once, but twice. Gerrard then blocked the next follow up and when Norwich tried to work it back into the box Allen won a great tackle to snuff that out too. There were many similarities with last week's game against City as the same thing happened in that first half too. Fast start, a couple of goals, then the opposition have a little spell where it looked like they could score only to be denied by a 'thou shalt not pass' mentality from our players. *"We go Norwich. Exactly the same"* indeed, eh Stevie? Hopefully his post match rallying cry this time was more along the lines of, *"We go Chelsea. Exactly the same…. as we did to Arsenal"*

Sterling had an early chance to make it 3-0 just after the break when Suarez dribbled around an opponent inside his own half and pinged a glorious 60 yd ball to Coutinho, who held it up until support arrived and cut it back for Sterling who shot just over with his left foot. Good strike, he just couldn't keep it down. Would have been some goal, it might have even made our top ten for the season if it had gone in. A bold statement, I know.

That was as good as it got for a while as Norwich grew into the game the longer the second half went on. I was impressed with how well Skrtel was playing but at the same wasn't pleased with how much he was having to do, if that makes sense? I'd rather have not seen him at all, but it seemed as though the camera was on him more than anybody as he made clearance after clearance.

The goal that got Norwich back into the game was really cheap though, we do ourselves no favours letting goals like this in as they're just so unnecessary. It was little more than a hopeful cross floated in from our left and Skrtel would have dealt with it had Mignolet just left him to it. Instead he came out to try and punch the ball clear, so Skrtel ducked out of the way to make it easier for his keeper. Unfortunately Mignolet was beaten to it by Bradley Johnson and that left a tap in for Hooper. Skrtel was furious with the keeper and rightly so; that was a real howler. He didn't even need to come for it, but having decided to that's fine, just make sure you fucking get it.

The goal may have been just what we needed to wake us from our slumber, we'd been mostly crap in the second half but suddenly the urgency was back in our play at last. Suarez curled one inches wide before Sterling restored our two goal lead with a somewhat fortuitous goal. Still, I'd say Sterling earned that bit of luck due to how positive and direct he was. He intercepted a pass, ran 60 yards past two challenges and his shot deflected in off the unfortunate Johnson. He who dares, Rodders, he who dares.

Norwich wouldn't lie down though and, worryingly, they looked more likely to score the next goal than we did. Mignolet made a decent save from a Snodgrass 30 yarder, and then Martin headed over from a corner as the keeper hesitated as to whether to come for it or not. That earlier howler certainly affected how Mignolet approached the rest of the game, he was completely rooted to his line after that. Norwich eventually found the net again as once more we failed to deal with a bread and butter cross. It was a great leap and header by Snodgrass although Flanagan never really made a challenge for it and instead tried to lean on the Scot hoping to put him off. I'd also look at the keeper again though, it's the kind of cross he could have dealt with had he not been scared to come out.

We were looking extremely vulnerable now whenever the ball was slung into the box and we had a huge let off when Mignolet made a good save from Van Wolfswinkel's header. That was Norwich's moment, it was their big chance and when it didn't go in I was sure then we'd hold on for the win, and in fairness we did without any further incident. Brendan had to make some changes though to swing the balance back in our favour. First, Moses was introduced to replace the fading Coutinho, and then Agger came on for Allen to boost the defence against the aerial bombardment from the flanks. Both changes had the desired impact and we saw it out to record the win, our 11th on the spin. A remarkable achievement really.

That's the beauty of this run we've been on, we've won games by showing all kinds of different qualities, playing all kinds of different formations and utilising all kinds of different tactical ploys. The only constant has been goals, and tons of them. Rodgeball!

The funniest moment of the game was obviously Suarez getting clobbered and writhing around in pain, until Allen nicked the ball and he realised we had a counter attack and leapt to his feet before sprinting into space looking for a pass. The ball didn't come to him, and he immediately began grimacing and hobbling again. Of course it looked ridiculous and Suarez will be roundly mocked for it, but the replay showed what a bad challenge it was and I'd bet that must have hurt like hell. Leroy Fer can consider himself fortunate not have been red carded for that, as it was a naughty one. Luis though, 'kinell.

We can all pick holes in the performance and call out certain individuals *cough* Glen Johnson *cough* for being below par or whatever, but I just feel like it's well harsh to be criticising anybody. I mean, this team has exceeded all of our expectations and are on the brink of the title, are we really going to be concerning ourselves with talk like *"yeah but he's not good enough"* and *"so and so needs replacing"*? Bollocks to all that - there's plenty of time for that in the summer - right now let's just enjoy what's happening as we're on the verge of doing something that we'll cherish for the rest of our lives. This team is on the brink of making history, if they can see this through it will be seriously fucking monumental, way bigger even than Istanbul. These lads have won 11 Premier League games on the bounce and have only dropped four points in 2014. So what if individually they haven't always played 'lights out' every week, it's impossible to do that and despite whatever flaws we may have individually or even collectively, it's not caused us to lose a league game so far this calendar year, so clearly it can't be THAT big a flaw.

How good was Sterling again though? He was the one his team-mates looked for at every opportunity to relieve the pressure. He scored twice, he created the other, he did his job helping out defensively, he carried the fight to Norwich when we were under pressure and the maturity in his play was staggering. Late on it was just a case of 'give it to Raheem'. He'd either carry it forward and allow us to get up the field, or he'd put his foot on it and slow things down by winning a free-kick or just playing keep ball. Best player on the pitch by a mile, and not for the first time in this run in either.

We keep winning despite the incredible burden of pressure that has suddenly been heaped on the players when it became clear that the title was not a pipe dream, but an attainable goal if we kept our heads. They could have buckled under that pressure but so far they've handled it admirably. That's all that matters right now so well done to each and every one of them. Keep it going for three more games, lads, just three more games. That's all. And for God's sake, don't let those classless, snide, chav twats come into our house and win next week. Let's fucking bury them. Do that, and as the supremely talented, and somewhat unconventionally, strangely attractive songstress Lady Gaga famously crooned, we're 'on the Edge of Glory'.

Premier League Round Up (19-21 April 2014)

"Imagine if Borini got the winner? 'Kinell!" **That's how the last round up ended, and fittingly it's how this one starts, with Fabio Magnifico indeed** *"getting the winner. 'Kinell!!!"* **In a season where everything seems to be going right for us, this was perhaps one of the biggest signs yet that it's going to be our year. Mourinho losing his unbeaten home record, in a game they had to win, against the bottom side in the league? That was sweet enough, but to have a Liverpool player score the winner.... Carlsberg don't do 'rubbing a turd in Mourinho's stupid smug face' days, but if they did....**

That had to be the best non-LFC moment of the season (maybe even decade?). I celebrated Fabio's penalty winner with more gusto than I have a lot of our own victories this season. The significance of this result for us is potentially huge, but even putting that aside it was just so fucking funny wasn't it? Chelsea were actually leading and threw it away, and they even conceded a pen by fouling Jozy friggin' Altidore!!! Why on earth would you do that, Azpilecueta? You just step aside and say *"Go ed there Jozy, do your worst, big fella"* and then let your keeper take the inevitable goal kick that follows. Clearly he hasn't been watching Match of the Day this season or he'd know this.

I'm still basking in the warm glow of that Chelsea defeat as I write this days later, but it's nothing to how I felt at the time. I was like a kid on Christmas morning. I couldn't wipe the smile of my face all night, partly because of the result, partly because of the way Mourinho handled it, and also because I just knew we'd beat Norwich the next day and open up a five point gap over them. I might even start calling myself 'the Happy One' now, well it's not like Jose uses it anymore is it? Didn't last long that one. He's come out with some bollocks this season, but that *'I'm the Happy One'* at his first press conference was probably the biggest lie of all, as he's looked like a miserable, disinterested bastard for most of the season, even when they were winning. There's no joy with that prick at all is there, you have to wonder why he bothers anymore. Maybe he just gets off on the aggro?

And how about that brother in law of mine then eh? Did he call this one or what? No-one gave Sunderland a chance (not of winning anyway, some of us fancied they might sneak a draw) but he was adamant all week they'd win, and so they did. Had Big Vito not thrown one in at the Etihad the other night they'd have taken six points from City and Chelsea and more or less handed us the title. That said, four points will do us nicely and it might be enough to kick start their relegation fight. And I think I speak for all Liverpool fans now when I say that I really, really hope they manage to stay up after what they did to Chelsea (and City for that matter). Up the Mackems!

Of course, Chelsea handled the loss with the (lack of) dignity and class you'd expect. Mourinho's post match interviews were predictably cringeworthy. Usually I'd be spitting feathers about it, but then usually we'd be languishing around 20 points behind them and I'd be feeling pretty bitter about our lot in life. Now though, as we look down on him from our lofty perch, I'm not mad about what he said at all, why would I be? I just find it really funny seeing pressmen and pundits alike rounding on him for acting in such an embarrassing fashion. He couldn't have possibly done a better job of showing the world what an absolute helmet he is and the press who once ate out of the palm of his hand are now lining up to slam him for acting the twat. You're almost a decade late, but welcome to the party boys, good to have you on board at last.

"Who's the scouser in the black" chanted the Chelsea fans in the closing stages as their side looked to force an equaliser with all the effectiveness of Wayne Rooney doing the Times crossword. Get your facts right you ignorant chavs, Mike Dean's from the Wirral, he's a plazzy scouser. And come on, you really want to blame Dean for that pitiful display from a team that cost hundreds of millions to assemble? How about laying the blame where it should be, at the door of your beloved 'Jose'. Chelsea didn't deserve to beat Sunderland, just like they didn't deserve to beat Palace, West Ham or Villa either. It's ironic really, I mean considering he's the master of the 'parking the bus' approach, you'd think he might actually have some clue on how to break it down.

And who the fuck was that no-mark assistant coach who lost his shit with Dean after the pen? I've never seen him before, but it would appear that Mourinho's eye for staff isn't what it was either. From Brendan, AVB and Clarke to this gobshite. I saw him kicking off at Dean and my first thought was *"hahaha who's this mouthy gobshite??"* He put me in mind of one of those jobbers you'd see in the WWE, the random chump who's there to run his mouth and then get chokeslammed into the middle of next week by Kane or the Undertaker. That's Chelsea all over though isn't it? At least it was until they won the lottery. They were the 'Brooklyn Brawler' of football until Roman showed up with his billions.

There are a lot of theories being bandied about as to why Mourinho said what he did afterwards. One was that it was a smokescreen so he wouldn't be asked about the conduct of his assistant. Another was he was trying to deflect criticism from his players onto the officials to ensure their confidence wasn't dented ahead of the Atletico game. There were other explanations put forward too, but I just think people look far too deeply into all this *"Jose never does anything without a reason"* bullshit. Hell, I even read some people suggesting the whole 'old man Eto'o' faux pas was deliberately done to fire up the striker. Newsflash, there isn't always a plan, it's not always calculated and he's not always in control of what he's doing. You know why he said what he did about Eto'o and came out with that bollocks after West Ham, Villa and Sunderland? Because he's a cunt, and this is how cunts act when they aren't getting their own way. There's nothing clever about it, it isn't 'mind games' or psychology, it's just a cunt acting the cunt. It really is that simple.

You can set your watch by it, after any kind of setback he displays all the traits of a tantrum throwing kid. Whether it's laughably calling out his strikers, sobbing when he didn't get the United job, blaming Mike Dean, Chris Foy etc, Mike Riley or even the Premier League for changing their fixture list to suit him, the common denominator is blaming anyone and anything but himself. He's a fucking joke and people are finally beginning to see it.

The FA should nail him to the wall after that interview he did. I say interview in it's singular form, but he actually gave the same speech at least three different times. He spoke to Sky, then the BBC, and then he went into his press conference and gave the exact same quotes to all of them, whilst refusing to answer questions from anybody. Of course he didn't actually criticise Mike Dean or Mike Riley, in fact he did the opposite. He 'congratulated' them on their 'fantastic' performances before stomping off. I half expected him to then pop his head round the door, and say - Homer Simpson style - *"oh yeah, in case you didn't know, I was being sarcastic"*. Fucking helmet. If and when we eventually win it can we get medals made for Sweet Smelling Fabio and Connor Wickham? I'd also get one made for Mike Dean, just to piss soft shite off.

Remember this? *"It's phenomenal you have a player that, even when he is not playing for you, is scoring against your opponents"* Yes, Jose, isn't it just! The difference between us and Chelsea right now are the goals scored by Assaidi and Borini against them (and the point Moses earned us at Swansea). How d'ya like them apples, Maureen? Compare him with the other manager chasing us for the title. Manuel Pellegrini said this week: *"If Liverpool win 14 games in a row and take 53 points from a possible 57 in the second half of the season, they'll have deserved it"*. So not because of Mike Riley then? This is the same fella who refused to complain about decisions that went against him at Anfield last week and who waited patiently at pitchside for our players to stop celebrating so he could shake each and every one of their hands. Class act. No wonder Mourinho hates him.

City had slipped up against Sunderland last week so it was too much to expect West Brom to do us a favour as well on Monday night at the Etihad. They didn't even look arsed, I thought they were a disgrace actually and Sessegnon in particular was really doing my fucking head in. City took care of them without even breaking sweat, although they lost Silva in the process to what looked a bad injury.

What about Arsene Wenger though, the bitter arl bastard. *"Liverpool played very well in the second part of the season. You wouldn't want to take anything away from them, but they were able to focus only on the Premier League. If you look at the injuries, the players we have missed, plus the schedule we had, then of course it was much more heavy than Liverpool."* You wouldn't want to take anything away from us yet you still tried to do exactly that. You want to talk injuries, Arsene? Ok, let's talk injuries. We lost Enrique for almost the whole season. Johnson has missed a load of games, Sturridge has missed nine league games, Suarez was banned for five, Gerrard had an injury that put him out for a bit (including away games at City and Chelsea), we've never had a settled centre back pairing all season as Agger and Sakho have been playing musical chairs because neither can stay fit for more than five games. Lucas has been out for a lengthy spell, Allen missed games early on and Coutinho was out for a month or so when he did his shoulder at Swansea.

Everyone has injuries, and it's not as though Arsenal have ever looked like they were down to the bare bones. The only real issue they've had is Giroud playing too many games because the only alternatives were those deadbeats Bendtner and Sanogo. And who's fault is that, Arsene? Liverpool winning the league would be the worst possible outcome for Wenger as it blows away the myth that no-one can compete with the billionaires and puts his 'achievement' of clinging onto a top four spot into context. No wonder he's trying to downplay what we've done, Brendan has completely exposed him.

The Gunners are doing their usual trick again now. Every year it's the same, they have a run that has people thinking they may be title contenders. Then they shit the bed and Wenger comes in for heavy criticism only for them to rally when the pressure is off, sneak a top four spot and then party like it's 1999. They beat Hull at the weekend to stay in 4th and it wasn't long before twitter was awash with the 'Arsenal selfie' again. Our players do it too in fairness, in fact Lucas put one out immediately after the Norwich game, but there's a massive difference. Our lads are usually just smiling and posing for a normal photo, as you do. Arsenal's players always look like they've just won the fucking World Cup! As I said, wankers.

Which segues nicely into Tim Sherwood's latest comments. I'm a Sherwood guy now, but even I would admit he is a bit of wanker. *"If you add the points Gareth Bale's goals won us last year to what we've done this season, we'd be challenging for the title"*. I love this guy though, he's fucking ace. I'm not sure if anyone pointed out the flaw in his logic, they probably didn't have the heart to burst the bubble he lives in. He's right though of course, I mean I often find myself thinking *"If we could add the clean sheets that Clem kept for us back in '78 to what we're doing now, we'd already have the title wrapped up"*. He also said this about Bale: *"He certainly dealt with it and I think to be fair, he wanted to go. Once a player wants to go, it is very difficult to keep him. Unless you are Liverpool of course."* See that? Knows when to give credit where it's due does Tim. Good lad, ignore all those haters, I've got your back, son.

It was a good weekend for my man Tim, as his Spurs side edged out Fulham 3-1 at the Lane. It wasn't a great performance and Lloris was actually Spurs' best player, even saving a penalty from Sidwell. Nevertheless, they picked up the points and look like they've got a top six spot secured now. Sandro wasn't involved in the game and took to twitter to tell everyone he wasn't injured. Sherwood was asked about it and said *"He's right in what he's saying, he's not injured he's just not selected. He's not good enough to play in my team at the moment. When I think he's good enough he'll play."* Sandro then tweeted *"lol lol lol"* which in itself is enough reason to banish him to the fucking ressies. I mean text speak? FFS.

There's a youtube clip doing the rounds called *'You don't mess with Sandro'* where he's doing all kinds of martial arts shit and roundhouse kicks and stuff. I watched it and all I could think of was that scene from Indiana Jones when the fella is twirling his sword around showing how badass he is, only for Indy to just draw his pistol and shoot him like the dog that he is. I can just imagine Sandro doing all that bollocks in front of Sherwood, only for Tim to just casually lay him out with a baseball bat or a right hook and then continue his team-talk as though nothing had happened. You don't mess with Sandro? No, you don't mess with Tim facking Sherwood, you slaaaaag.

Cardiff v Stoke was a game completely rife with diving. Odemwingie won a pen against his former club when he took an exaggerated tumble and somehow managed to get Webb to make a decision for once. Fraizer Campbell was 'acting the Januzaj' all afternoon and he too convinced Webb to give a pen when he was caught by NZonzi. This one was a foul, unlike the half dozen or so other ones he went looking for. Really not sure what got into

Webb though, most unlike him this was.

Elsewhere, Newcastle lost to a stoppage time penalty at home to Swansea. Shola Ameobi's first goal in ten years or something put them ahead, but Bony levelled with a bullet header and then secured the win with a cool as you like pen at the very end. He's a cracking player him. Massive head though, it's almost Jon Obi Mikel-esque.

Moving on, and Palace won at West Ham. That was a mild surprise to me. My boy Jason Puncheon didn't score, which shocked me to my core. A penalty from skipper Jedinak gave them the points as West Ham's keeper Adrian tried to pull that psyche out shit he tried with Stevie, pointing to the corner he wanted Jedinak to put it. Like Stevie, Jedinak duly obliged and the keeper got nowhere near it. Might wanna pack that in lad, it's not working and it's making you look like a knob.

The Hammers crowd booed the hell out of Fat Sam once again at the final whistle. They also took the piss out of him following his substitutions too with the usual *"you don't know what you're doing"* taunts. The big fella probably throughout he was back at St James Park for a second. He'll be gone at the end of the season surely? If only there was an opening at a Premier League club close to his North West roots. Hmmm…. Might be time for Allardici to call in one of the dozens of favours Ferguson must owe him for 'services rendered'.

Steve the Pirate's interview afterwards made me chuckle. He's a right miserable bastard him, he didn't even smile when Bony scored that winning pen, and his interview with Lineker saw more of the same dourness. *"What a miserable fecker"* I was thinking, until Lineker asked him about ref Chris Foy getting hit in the face with the ball and he starting laughing his head off! Everyone loves a ref getting flattened don't they? Would love to see that happen to Webb, maybe with a steam roller instead of a football though.

How shit are Villa? I hadn't realised this but until last weekend they hadn't picked up a single point since they beat Chelsea a couple of months back. They have now, as they just about hung on for a fortunate 0-0 at home to Southampton. They've slowly been dragged into the relegation scrap now and seeing as how they must be wondering where their next win is coming from, they're far from safe.

Finally, I have to end on a very sad note. The bastards finally went and did it didn't they? They unchose 'the Chosen One'. Fuckin' arlarses, they could have at least let him stay til the end of the season. The 2020/21 season. The final straw was Everton handing them their arses at Goodison on Sunday. The score was 'only' 2-0, but this was probably as comfortable a win as Everton have had all season. They were in complete control of this from start to finish but the beauty of it was they allowed Moyes to think United were controlling it. Martinez just let them have as much of the ball as they wanted as all their possession was in front of Everton's back four and Tim Howard may as well have been sat in the Gwladys Street. At least there he can spit and swear without it being obvious he has Tourette's. Whilst Moyesy was thinking 'we're bossing this', Everton were happy to just pick them off on the counter and should really have scored more than the two goals they got. The fans made it an even more depressing day for Moyes by constantly mocking him, whilst United fans entertained themselves by taunting the Blues with chants of *'Murderers'* and *'Justice for the 39'*. They even had a banner about Heysel, which was roundly booed by the Evertonians. Ok, what kind of bizarro world is this? It's like us going to the Etihad and singing Munich songs to get a rise out of City. The difference being City would probably have joined in, whereas the Blues shouted the Mancs down. Fair play, it's nice to see Everton treating them with the contempt they deserve, both on and off the pitch.

Poor old Moyesy though. This hurts, but he'll be ok I guess. He's earned millions from this and for all the jokes everyone has had at his expense (including his own players based on the reports that have come out since he left), he's a good manager who will have no problems finding another job. He won't ever get a crack at one of the big boys again of course as he's just not a 'big club manager'. I don't even mean that as an insult and I'm not kicking him whilst he's down (I can't get near enough to kick him due to all the United players who are falling over themselves to do it by drip feeding little tales about him to the media now he's gone), Moyes is just suited to being an underdog, that's all. If he'd taken over from Holloway at Palace he'd probably have done a similar job to Pulis. And if Pulis had taken over from Ferguson he'd probably have done a similar job to Moyes. In fact, I propose United put that theory to the test. Pulis and Big Sam were probably two and three on *"Fergeh's"* list of replacements, United should just keep working their way through his mates I reckon until they either get it right or they disappear into oblivion.

It was pretty shitty how they handled his sacking though. It seems Giggs knew about it on Sunday night after they'd lost to Everton, although there was some initial confusion on the part of the Welsh walking carpet when he was told he'd be in charge of 'first team affairs'. *"Great, I've had my eye on Colleen for ages"* he declared, before someone clarified it for him. He got over his initial disappointment and agreed to take over from Moyes. Given how much time he's spent undermining Moyes all season he was hardly going to say no was he? As if that wasn't disrespectful enough to Moyes, it was then leaked on Monday that he was a gonner but officially United still said nothing (the suggestion being that was done to try and get Moyes to resign) until they eventually announced it on Tuesday morning. Mind you, their official twitter account first wished Dion Dublin a 'Happy Birthday', before then tweeting that Moyes had been sacked. You stay classy Manchester!

Of course we all knew this day would inevitably come, and although it's incredibly sad I think that rather than mourn his departure we should instead rejoice in the brief but glorious time he spent trying to fill Ferguson's shoes. I mean come on, it was fucking great while it lasted wasn't it?

Some highlights from the Moyes era:

* All the records he set.
* Buying Fellaini.
* Saying *"I could see why we are Champions"* after they'd stunk Anfield out in a 1-0 defeat to a Liverpool side that didn't even have Suarez or Sterling in it. I mean fucking hell, Aspas was playing that day!
* *"Come on Davey Moyes, play like Fergie's boys, we'll go WILD WILD WILD"*
* The run down the touchline. You know the one, the run that spawned a million hilarious photoshopped pictures and made twitter the best place in the world after any United loss.

* Buying Fellaini.
* Playing Mata on the wing
* 'The Chosen One' banner.
* Making Van Persie so miserable that he completely vanished from the face of the earth.
* Overseeing Rooney's 300k a week contract. *"He's not leaving. Not on my watch"* Hahaha
* The constant *"I thought we played well"* comments after every humiliating defeat.
* His happy little face after they went 2-1 ahead against bottom club Fulham.
* His sad little face after Fulham made it 2-2.
* Buying Fellaini.
* Trying to run up the line to celebrate with his players in Munich only for them to completely snub him. By the time he'd got back to his seat Bayern had scored.

There's probably loads more I've forgotten, it really was a laugh a minute and I feel like we've been a bit short changed as the best was surely yet to come. I haven't felt this way since 'Father Ted' was cut short due to the tragic passing of Dermot Morgan. I'm not sure as Liverpool fans if we'll ever experience a better 10 months than this. Not unless they let Fergie choose their next manager again. Maybe we should dust off the old "Thanks DM" mosaic and display it on the Kop this weekend? After all, he's more deserving of the honour than the fuckwit it was originally made for.

LIVERPOOL 0 CHELSEA 2

Competition - Premier League
Date - Sun 27 Apr 2014
Venue - Anfield
Scorer(s) –
Star Man – Martin Skrtel

Team: Mignolet; Johnson, Skrtel, Sakho, Flanagan (Aspas); Gerrard, Lucas (Sturridge), Allen; Coutinho, Suarez, Sterling:

It really is the hope that kills you, and boy were we full of hope. Some still are, while others are now resigned to the dream being over and have now gone into defiant mode; putting on a brave face, pointing to how proud they are of the team's progress and adopting a *"never mind, we'll get 'em next year"* attitude. Sorry, I can't do it, not right now anyway. I'm just too fucking gutted.

Maybe come the weekend when I've had time to lick my wounds and allow the pain of this to subside a little, I'll be able to rejoin the *"we go again"* bandwagon in time for Palace, but right now I'm just devastated. That was a truly horrible footballing experience, the worst I've had at Anfield since Arsenal nicked the title off us in '89. Of course it ain't over til it's over and all that, and it's true that we've come back from greater adversity than this to win trophies before, but I can't help but feel that we're probably done after this. Then again, I thought we'd smash Chelsea everywhere so what do I know? The door has been opened again for City now though and I'd be amazed if they let it get away from them again. It's been a hell of an effort and like everyone else I'm proud of what Brendan and the lads have done this season, but my gut feeling is we're going to miss out and as a result I'm just wallowing in my own misery here.

It's no consolation to me at this moment in time that we've played so well all season, in fact that just makes it even harder to take. Hopefully I'll snap out of this funk soon enough and in time will be able to look at the positives, as God knows there are plenty of them. They just mean very little right now as I feel completely numb. I've barely spoken to anyone since the game, it's like I can't really muster the energy to even bother talking. It's not so much that we lost, it's that we lost to THEM. And to HIM.

Often after a bad defeat I find it's cathartic to write about it and getting some things off my chest can sometimes make it easier. Not this time, it's soul destroying and this is incredibly difficult to write. When the team has had a stinker it's easier to write about it as often it helps to slaughter those who haven't been pulling their weight. I can't do that now, it would be unfair to single out any players after this as they gave their all and no-one expected us to be this close. I'm not disappointed with them, far from it. I'm gutted for them, for Brendan, for myself and for all of you reading this. And most of all for Steven Gerrard.

Did we play well enough against Chelsea? In most cases no (Skrtel was brilliant whilst Sakho, Sterling and Flanagan played well too I thought), but to be fair to the players it's nigh on impossible to look good in this kind of game, especially if you're an attacking player. I thought Atletico Madrid looked shite the other night too, yet they're top of the Spanish league so clearly they're no mugs. Even City were shite against Chelsea and we know from experience how good a side they are. When only one team wants to play, it's very, very difficult, especially when the side who comes to spoil are so well versed in the dark arts. It was like watching a WWE event. Good against bad, heel against babyface, Hulk Hogan against the Million Dollar Man. Chelsea being the complete shithouse who rolls out of the ring and won't fight, picking arguments with angry old ladies on the front row while we're stood in the middle of the ring, getting increasingly frustrated, arms outstretched in complaint. They get back in, we land a blow and they roll out the ring again complaining to the referee and threatening to walk back to the changing room whilst the crowd goes apeshit at them. It was almost surreal at times, like some sick, twisted, horrifying pantomime playing out before our eyes. No-one plays the villain quite like Mourinho and Chelsea of course, there's absolutely no redeeming qualities about them at all. They're absolute fucking vermin and if there was one club I could wipe off the face of the planet it would be them, without hesitation.

They were actually time wasting in the first fucking minute. I don't think I've ever seen that before. I say time wasting, but it was more about slowing the game down and not letting us get into any rhythm at that point. The real time wasting would come later on when they had a lead to cling onto. They saw what we did to Arsenal, Everton, City, Spurs etc and they were going to ensure it didn't happen to them, by hook or by crook. It's understandable, prudent even, but also more than a little unpalatable considering the money they've spent and the talent they have at their disposal.

Still, if they want to play like that it's up to them I guess, but it's also up to the referee to deal with it and I'd say Martin Atkinson failed miserably on that score. He knew what they were up to but he did nothing about it. He eventually booked Ashley Cole for time wasting in the 92nd minute for fucks sake. Good job ref, well done. Not that it was his fault we didn't win, in terms of decision making he was excellent and short of booking every one of their players there was probably little he could have done to completely stop the time wasting. I just would have liked to have seen him be a bit more pro-active to what they were doing and at least try and put a stop to it, but it's a minor quibble. On a list of grievances, Atkinson isn't even on the first page.

Chelsea had ten men behind the ball at all times, not just behind the ball, but usually camped on the edge of their own box. Their attacking ambition extended only to launching it up to Ba and letting him fight for it and hope to win throw ins or corners. Interestingly he always lined up to their right when they launched it to him. Why was that? Because Azpilicueta has a long throw, Ashley Cole doesn't. Tactical genius though, dontchya know.

It felt like we were playing a more negative, more expensive, more cunty version of Tony Pulis' Stoke. If they weren't feigning injury to stop the game, they were fucking about with throw ins or having Schwarzer take an age on his goal kicks. Hell, we even saw Mourinho doing his best impression of a Crystal Palace ball boy as he prevented Flanagan taking a quick throw in.

Let's just quickly put some context to that. A few weeks back he threatened an 11 year old kid who took his time giving the ball back by saying *"you shouldn't listen to people who tell you to do that, as one of my players might punch you"*. Tell you what, I'd give anything to see one of our players punch him in his stupid fucking unshaven face, the hypocritical snide cunt. At one point Suarez became so pissed off with Chelsea's gamesmanship he began sarcastically applauding the keeper for his antics. I agreed with him, but I didn't like to see it as it showed just how frustrated he was and we needed him focussed on his own game, not to be seeing his arse with what Chelsea were doing. Can't say I really blame him, he was a lot more restrained than I'd have been if I'd been in his shoes. Last year's bite would have seemed like child's play if I'd been out there.

The worst example of their piss taking for me though was when Coutinho threw the ball to Cole and he just deliberately allowed to it go past him and then looked as if to say, *"What do you expect, we're cunts, this is what we do"*. They wasted an eternity in both halves, and just to rub salt into the wounds they then managed to score in the added time that they had created in both halves. There really is no karma in this universe is there? And cheats prosper all the fucking time. This game could not have turned out any better for Mourinho, it went exactly according to his fucked up, warped, shithouse plan. Strangle the game, frustrate the opposition, wait for a mistake, defend for your lives. Classic Mourinho tactics, and sickeningly it worked for him again.

Life just isn't fair sometimes, and if this is to be the end of our title challenge then it's just about the worst possible ending. I'd rather have lost to City the other week, the only thing they have in common with Chelsea is money, in every other aspect they're poles apart, especially in terms of the manager and the supporters. If City win the title it will obviously be hard to stomach, but the worst part of it for me would not be that we came up just short, it would be that it was Mourinho and his bus parking that ended it for us. I'm really struggling here, it's seriously hard to accept what went down in this game. Losing to a better team is one thing, losing to a team who didn't even try to attack is another. And losing to a team managed by that cunt, and followed by those fans, well that's something else again. Fucking hell.

All that said, we were the architects of our own downfall. Gerrard's unfortunate slip proved to be decisive as once they had a lead to defend there was never any chance of dragging them out of their ratholes. We needed to score first and we couldn't do it. In fairness, at no point in the second half did I ever think we were going to draw level and the risk of a breakaway goal for them loomed large the longer this went. We were well and truly Mourinho'd in the end.

What could we have done differently? Not much for me. It's easy to say that we should have took the 0-0 as it would have kept our destiny in our hands, but how much of that would be hindsight talking? Who would have said before the game: *"if they want to sit back in their own box, let's just do the same and make sure we don't lose"*? Don't get me wrong, I wish it had ended 0-0, but I don't wish we'd gone out and tried to play for it. We've not played for a 0-0 all season, we've got where we are by going for it and imagine if we'd tried to be cautious and then conceded from a set-piece or something and lost 1-0? Or if we'd played for a draw, got it and then suffered some misfortune at Palace next week? Rodgers have been slaughtered for changing his approach to suit Chelsea and for abandoning what got us here in the first place.

So no, I have no problem with us going for it and losing the way we did, and if we had to play this game all over I'd want to see us go at them again rather than just sit back. They weren't coming out of their 'Testudo' formation no matter what we did. They'd have happily sat back in their own box and allowed Mignolet to play one bounce with his defenders. Maybe Ba would have closed them down, but he'd have been on his own.

I don't think there was much else Brendan could have done with his team selection either as clearly Sturridge wasn't deemed fit enough to start. Admittedly we didn't need Lucas as the way Chelsea set up they had conceded the midfield anyway, so we had no need for a third player in there. But it's not as though things got any better when he made way for Sturridge did they? Sturridge barely got a kick, but as with Sterling and to a lesser extent Suarez it was very difficult for him to do anything when there was no space to run in behind.

In that situation an Andy Carroll type helps, and before you all start harrumphing and calling me unpleasant names, I'm not saying we should have kept him or even that we should go and buy a player like him. That's not going to happen and nor should it, as you can't have a player like that and use him only in this kind of scenario as he'd hardly ever play. I'm fully aware of that, I'm just saying that in this particular, unique situation we were in, Carroll would be far more likely to be effective than some of the players we have. There were times in this game when we were putting the ball into the box and we had only one player in there, and occasionally that one player was Joe Allen!

You could say that tactically we played right into Chelsea's hands but what else could we have done? You can't get in behind a team that's playing so deep, and without an aerial presence there's little point sending crosses into a packed box as you're relying mostly on luck and hoping something falls kindly for one of your players. Passing your way through with intricate one twos around the box doesn't work either. Better teams than us have come unstuck against these tactics too let's not forget. Maybe we should have remained patient and tried to work an opening but that didn't work for the likes of Barca and Bayern when Chelsea parked the bus against them did it? Besides, we were losing, we couldn't be THAT patient. I don't think nerves played any real part either, we just understandably got desperate the longer it went on and that inevitably leads to mistakes.

We were so desperate we even sent on Iago fucking Aspas, a man who couldn't even get on the field in games we were running away with. That might actually have been the worst cameo of all time, it's certainly up there with Sean Dundee against Leicester. Seriously, just what the fuck was that corner all about? It may go against Brendan's ideology, but he'd have been better served sticking Agger up front than 'Kermit the Frog arms' Aspas. It was almost cruel to the lad to put him in that situation, but it was more cruel on those of us who had to watch him.

The way Chelsea set up we were never going to be able to create any really clear cut chances so it was vital that we were able to take one of the half chances we'd get. Failing that, perhaps we'd get a bit of luck with a shot from distance. Some were getting pissed off with Gerrard constantly looking to shoot from 25 yards but I was happy for him to keep trying his luck. Maybe he was trying to over-compensate to rectify his mistake, or it could just be that he figured he was as likely as anyone to score. And let's face it, he's come up trumps for us before in this situation so why shouldn't he chance his arm? We were never going to score any other way, and I was far more pissed off watching Suarez trying to dummy and flick his way through the middle of a packed defence, or Johnson constantly coming inside onto his left foot and then running into traffic and losing the ball. That was NEVER going to work in a million years, so no, I didn't have a problem with Gerrard taking potshots whenever he could. Next time we come up against this kind of shithousery, I'd have Gerrard, Suarez and Sturridge (definitely NOT Coutinho) take turns on picking the ball up 25 yards out and having a shot. I'd instruct all the other forwards to run in on the keeper for any rebounds too. That has to be better than all that tippy tappy shit in front of them. Chelsea can defend that all day without even breaking sweat.

We had a few decent openings in the first half but we really needed one of them to go in. The second half was similar, Gerrard had three or four efforts saved (comfortably) by Schwarzer, Allen also forced a couple of saves from him and Suarez was denied at the end of normal time with a dipping half volley that was a goal if it was a yard either side of the keeper. It wasn't meant to be though, Chelsea defended well, we didn't get the bit of luck that's needed in a game like this and the winning run comes to a heart breaking end at eleven games.

We'll no doubt be subjected the typical 'Mourinho tactical masterclass' bollocks now from the media, but honestly, just like Rodgers said afterwards there's nothing difficult about doing what he did. It would have been hard enough to break down a League One side playing that way, but when you're faced with world class defenders like Ivanovic, Cole and Azpilicueta, supplemented by wingers playing as extra full backs and three midfield destroyers camped in front, it becomes almost impossible. As I said, better teams than us have come unstuck against Chelsea when they play like this. The vast majority of Premier League managers could do this if they wanted to, maybe not quite as effectively with the players they have at their disposal, but with defenders and defensive midfielders like Chelsea have? It's a piece of piss. Roberto Di Matteo won a European Cup with Chelsea doing this exact same thing, is he a genius too then?

I'm certain that Roy Hodgson could go to the World Cup and have England play like this too, and I'd be willing to bet they wouldn't concede a goal if he did (they wouldn't score either of course). He'd get slaughtered for playing that way though, because he's Roy Hodgson, the uncool old fella with the slight speech impediment who looks like an owl. Maybe if he spoke like a Russian robot, gave himself a cool nickname and dressed like he'd slept in a fucking skip he'd be lauded too?

I'm not sure I can ever remember a side coming here and playing as negatively as this, even Moyes showed more ambition when he was at Everton. That's probably why he never won here actually, he never went full on shithouse, only three quarters of the way. That's the bottom line here though - winning. When you play such a horrible style of football you can get away with it if you get the result. For Mourinho, the end always, always, justifies the means. He won, that's all that matters. The record books will show that Chelsea won 2-0. It won't show that their hot little physio was on the field for longer than Fernando Torres, that Schwarzer wasted around 15 minutes on goal kicks, or any of the other shit they pulled for that matter.

The question is if it's so easy then why don't other teams play this way? Thankfully there are few managers who are as completely shameless about playing that way as the self proclaimed 'Special One'. Maybe Allardyce, but in fairness even he has never come to Anfield and been as mind numbingly negative as this. Neither has Pulis, or anyone else I can think of for that matter. Imagine if everyone played the Mourinho way. TV companies wouldn't be investing billions in the 'product', fans would desert the game in their droves and the arse would fall out of the whole thing. Maybe people should bear that in mind when lauding the 'genius' of that fucking arrogant ballbag. He's not special, he's just a sweaty skid mark on the underpants of football. And what the fuck did the scruffy twat come dressed as anyway?? He looked like a tramp who'd raided the lost property bin at Chelsea's training ground.

I hear that he went charging up the touchline when Willian scored that late break-away goal. I didn't see it as I just turned away as soon as Torres squared it, but I did see the cunt whipping up their fans like some kind of hobo cheerleader a couple of minutes before. All I can say is I'm glad I don't sit in the Paddock, as if I'd been close enough to get to him... well I'm not 100% sure I'd have been able to restrain myself. The hatred I've got for that man and his team really isn't healthy, I need to somehow take a step back from it as sometimes it's almost all consuming. Not easy though is it?

The only tiny crumb of comfort is that Torres didn't score, and in fairness to him he could have but chose not to and set up Willian instead. From what I've been told, he also chose to not over celebrate it whilst his team-mates were all giving it the beans. You know, I wouldn't have blamed if he had scored and rubbed our noses in it. We've (justifiably) given him plenty of shit, so if he wanted to enjoy his moment I would have understood that. I'd have still thought he was a twat, obviously, but no more so than I did before. As it is, fair play to him for not rubbing it in I guess. That might make him one of the least cuntish people at that club.

The Kop immediately belted out YNWA when that goal went in and there were certainly no recriminations towards the side, only gratitude and admiration. I feel the same, I'm not angry with anyone (other than Mourinho, obviously) and I don't blame any individual players. None of that changes the fact that I'm just completely fucking devastated right now though. The *"back in August we would have snatched your hand off to be in this position"* argument is valid of course, but it means nothing to me at all right now, we passed the point weeks ago where that would be of any comfort if it all went wrong for us.

I wish I could be positive and issue some kind of rallying call. I can't though, I'm just absolutely fucking gutted and almost out of hope. Whatsmore, I'm terrified that if we don't win it this year we never will. And if we do miss out, then what the hell kind of fucked up world do we live in that Steven Gerrard ends up having to be the one who makes the mistake that proves crucial? Not even a mistake, a slip. This coming two weeks after his *"this does not slip now"* speech? Just fuck off world, what kind of sick, twisted bullshit is that. That kind of shit should be happening to the Mourinhos and Terrys of this world, not a stand up guy like Stevie fucking Gerrard.

Their fans were chanting *'Murderers'* and *'Justice for the 39'*, which is par for the course for them these days. Maybe I'll feel differently in a few days, but the way I'm feeling right now if we were to miss out on the title after playing the way we have this year, and Chelsea go on to win the Champions League (or God forbid, the Premier League) having played the way they have, I might just be done with football altogether you know.

But after all we've been through this season, all the incredible performances, iconic moments and dramatic victories, this surely can't be how it ends for us? With Gerrard of all people slipping over against THEM and us missing out on the title, possibly on goal difference? No, it simply can't end this way. Life can be cruel, but not THIS fucking cruel, surely? There has to be another twist left in the tale yet. Doesn't there?

Premier League Round Up (26-28 April 2014)

Sunday was really hard to take and, like most of you I expect, I was still on a real downer days later. By Wednesday night it's fair to say my mood had lifted somewhat. Our title hopes hadn't improved any, but still, if you can't enjoy Mourinho losing in yet another semi final and Mongo blubbering like a teenage girl at a One Direction gig then you must be dead inside. Laugh? I nearly shat.

When they went ahead through Torres it didn't look good though, that was the last thing Atletico needed. That coward Mourinho had already named a team with six defenders in it, and with a lead to protect... well we know the script there don't we? Big Blue Bus time. Everything changed when Atletico equalised though, now Chelsea had to score or they were out, and as Eden Hazard later complained *"Chelsea is not built to play football"*. It's funny watching Chelsea try to chase a game, they just can't do it. Not because they don't have quality players, but because they aren't coached to play that way by their anti-football loving bell end manager. Hazard also said *"Often I'm asked to do it all by myself and it's not easy"*. Have I not been saying that for months? Their game plan is basically 'everybody defend and then give it Hazard and see if he can produce a bit of magic'. Attacking players should look at how they play and think *"bollocks to that, I ain't signing for them boring bastards"*. They won't because so many players are either stupid, greedy or both. The smart ones will steer well clear though.

Defenders will be lining up round the block to sign for them of course, those tactics can make a very good defender look like the world's greatest (not even 'parking the bus' can make David Luiz look like a servicable centre half though, he's beyond help that boy). If you're a centre forward who's name isn't Didier Drogba though, then stay the fuck away as that twat Mourinho will make you look like a pub player. And if you're an attacking midfielder with a bit of flair, he'll turn you into a Jon Walters type workhorse in no time. Instead of people talking about your skill, goals and talent, we'll be hearing about 'hard working' 'disciplined' and *gulp* 'honest' you are.

How sweet was it seeing him get his arse handed to him in another semi final though? He's lost more semis than Pele before he discovered viagra. When they were losing it was fantastic seeing the Atletico players wasting time and feigning injury. At one point Costa hit the deck and wanted the physio on, and two Chelsea players were trying to drag him to his feet and telling him to get on with the game. Shameless bastards. Next year they'll be loving him when he's doing that in a blue shirt.

Atletico's keeper looked good didn't he? Chelsea should probably throw a bid in for him... Seriously though, at least they can console themselves with the knowledge that one of their players will be representing them at the final. No, not Courtois, I mean Mongo, who when he eventually stopped crying not only swapped shirts with an Atleti player, he exchanged his whole kit and he's all set for some more 'trophy bombing' if they win it.

Bet Wenger was pissing himself watching this, especially if he wins the FA Cup this season. What was it soft shite said about him? 'Specialist in failure' I believe it was.

The scruffy fuck also said on more than one occasion if he didn't win trophies he'd quit. Yeah right, because Abramovich would let HIM make the decision. Wouldn't even surprise me if the dopey Russian has had enough of him already. Mourinho has helped to make Chelsea the most reviled team in the land. Abramovich's vision was for Chelsea to be like Barcelona. Instead they're known as the most boring, negative team in Europe. All that money and so little return. Sack his bitch ass, Roman lad.

When Atletico took the lead Raheem Sterling tweeted out a load of smiley faces. Jose Enrique went one better, saying *"That's what happens when you don't play football... ."* It's fine for us as fans to take the piss, but I'm not entirely comfortable with our players doing stuff like that. At least I wouldn't be if it was anyone other than Chelsea. Because it's them, it's ok. Besides, there's no way either of them would have that kind of attitude if it was any other side. It's just that Chelsea are impossible not to hate.

As for the weekend's action, Fat Sam must be on borrowed time now. West Ham's travelling support gave him dogs abuse as their side lost at the Hawthorns. *"Fuck off Sam Allardyce"* and *"You don't know what you're doing"* amongst other things were chanted. He's surely going to get canned, I just hope it's not until the season is finished as we might yet need him to 'out-tactic' Pellegrini on the last day.

Good weekend for Sunderland though who are now out of the bottom three. They strolled to a 4-0 win over Cardiff, helped significantly by the sending off of Juan Cala in the first half. Wickham had already put Sunderland in front at that point but Cardiff were incensed when Phil Dowd then gave a penalty and sent Cala off after the Spaniard has hauled back Wickham. The in form striker stayed on his feet and went round the keeper, who also impeded him, but again the striker didn't go down. He couldn't finish it off as he was forced too wide so Dowd pulled it back for the initial offence. It seemed a soft decision and you'd be pissed off if it went against your team, but really I think Dowd should be applauded for it. Had Wickham gone down after either challenge he'd have got a pen, so why should he be punished for being honest? We always complain you get nothing for staying on your feet so this was good to see.

Fabio buried the pen, obviously, then set one up for Giaccherini before Wickham bagged his second late on. Poyet described Dowd's call as *'the best decision I have seen in my whole life'*. Not sure I'd go that far like, and I doubt Gus would either if it had gone against his team, but Dowd was brave to make that call as the easy option would have been to do nothing. Well played Phil Dowd.

You know, in all my excitement about Sunderland's win at Chelsea last week I forgot to mention something that happened in the latter stages of that game. I can't believe I didn't mention this actually as it was pretty staggering, one of the most braindead things I've seen all season. Sunderland had a three v one counter attack right at the end as Chelsea had thrown everyone forward desperately looking for an equaliser. Giaccherini is leading the break and he has Fabio Magnifico to his right and Dozy Altidore to his left. He only went and played it left didn't he!!! I said last week that Azpilicueta must have not been watching MOTD this season because he fouled Altidore in the box rather than just letting him a free run. Well that's almost excusable, but Giaccherini trains with Dozy every single day, there's no way he can not know how shit he is, yet he still chose to pass to him? That's as dodgy as Big Vito throwing that one in at City.

For the record the pass reached Altidore in the penalty area with just the keeper to beat. He eventually controlled it, assessed the situation and correctly determined that he had as much chance of being named PFA Player of the Year as he had of beating Schwarzer with his left foot from that angle. So he passed the ball all the way back to Cattermole in the centre circle. I don't blame Altidore, he knows his massive limitations and did the right thing. Giaccherini should be fined two weeks wages for that act of stupidity though. Ignoring Fabio was bad enough, but passing to Altidore??? That's unforgivable.

Saying that, I'm writing this after coming home from my weekly game of footy and tonight I too was part of a three man break but with just the keeper to beat and not a defender in sight. It got played to me, back to goal, 10 yards out with team-mates either side in support and no defenders anywhere to be seen. I could have turned and gone myself, or drew the keeper and then rolled it either side to a team-mate for a tap in. But do you know what I did? To my shame I tried to back heel a bouncing ball past the keeper and it flew over the bar. To any of my team-mates reading this, I whole heartedly apologise. Worst football related decision since Fergie chose his replacement that was.

Speaking of the Chosen One, 'Moyeseh' may have gone, but 'Giggseh' is in charge now and he's got 'Scholeseh', 'Butteh' and erm... Phil Neville helping him out. 'Rooneh' put them ahead from the spot just before half time, they'd been shite prior to that but the goal set them on their way and they battered hapless Norwich after that. Interesting to see how the Manc players were all smiles all of a sudden, celebrating together and generally looking all pleased with themselves. Shower of bastards, they got poor old Davey the sack and I for one can never forgive that.

The best thing that happen now is that they win their next three games handsomely and the clamour for Giggs to get the job is such that the Glazers give in. Won't happen though, they'll probably lose to Sunderland. Van Gaal looks like he's nailed on for that. Ideally I'd want Mourinho to get it, that would end in tears for all of them. They deserve eachother.

Elsewhere, Fulham suffered late heartbreak at home to Hull. They were 2-0 up but Jelavic pulled one back and then the closing stages saw Hull pile on the pressure and hit the woodwork twice before Long eventually headed them level right at the death. Long is a real pain in the arse isn't he? I mean that as a compliment, he's the kind of player you'd hate to play against as he chases absolutely everything, puts himself about, dives all over the place and is generally just a massive fucking nuisance. Still can't get my head around West Brom selling him you know, the mad bastards. And who's that Diarra fella for Fulham? Is he the one who was at Lyon and then Madrid? Quite a comedown that if it is.

Spurs won 1-0 at Stoke thanks to an early header by Danny Rose. Shawcross was sent off for two yellows, the second was a bit harsh and the Stoke fans (wrongly) blamed Rose for it. Their players were looking to take retribution on the full back and Cameron clobbered him soon after. Rose flipped and went running to confront the American and shoved him in the chest with both hands. He got a yellow card when everyone connected to Stoke was howling for him to be sent off. Mark Hughes kicked off and was screaming *"he raised his hands, you've got to send him off"* Fuck off 'Useless' you big drama queen. Some of the snide crap he pulled down the years and he's losing his shit over a shove to the chest??? Anyone who uses that 'if you raise your hands you have to go' for anything other than a smack in the face can fuck off, it's one of the worst things about modern football that is.

Sherwood promptly subbed Rose to diffuse the situation and protect his player. Smart cookie is my guy Tim, always thinking on his feet. Seems as though Levy & co have been fooling around behind his back though. Frank De Boer claimed he'd been approached about the job, and Van Gaal has already made similar noises. Muthafuckers. Poor Tim, it must be getting to him as his eyes were all bloodshot and he looked like he hadn't slept for a week. Still immaculately dressed though, he's a dapper swine isn't he? The Jamie Redknapp of football managers. His record there is pretty good too, albeit he's been a real flat track bully.

Moving on, and what a goal that was from Jonjo. Can't believe there are people saying it wasn't as good as Rooney's at West Ham. Horseshit! You know how I know Shelvey's goal was miles better? Because I could never have scored that in a million years, but as I said previously I'm convinced I could do what Rooney did, given enough attempts. Superb Jonjo lad, take a bow. Swansea hammered Villa and look safe now. Pleased for them, the football they play means they bring a lot to the Premier League and you want sides like that to stay up. It's the West Hams and Chelseas of this world who need relegating. I like Steve the Pirate too, I hope he gets the job full time and I don't mean that in a Tim Sherwood/Ryan Giggs 'give it to him for a laugh' type way either. He may have the makings of a good manager and is a decent sort of chap by the looks of it.

Villa though, kinell. I often rather cruelly refer to them as Aston Vanilla, but there's good reason for it. Do you want to know how irrelevant Villa are? They were actually relegated in the 80s and I can't even remember it. A mate mentioned it before the Chelsea game, and the rest of us were like *"nah you're wrong, Villa never got relegated, we'd remember something like that"*. Turns out he was right, they did get relegated in 1987. That's how insignificant they are, that five years after they won the European Cup they got relegated and no bugger can even remember it. That should have been a huge story, I mean we all remember how shocking it was when Forest first went down, and then there's Leeds too. Who remembers Villa going down though? Or coming back up for that matter. I just thought they'd always been in the top flight, mostly being bang average but having a few glory years in the early 80s. And then I find out they were relegated. Who knew? Well my mate Julian, obviously, but apart from him I mean.

Tell you what though, if Villa manage to take points off City next week I swear I'll never say nasty things or take the piss out of them ever again. Scouts honour. Same goes for Fat Sam. Obviously I can't make the same promise about Everton, I'd be making it in good faith but there's no way I could ever stick to it. They make piss taking so damn easy.

I had hoped Palace might have been able to do us a favour too, but City rolled them over quite comfortably really. If we'd beaten Chelsea I'm convinced City would have dropped points, but we gave them the motivation they needed to go out and get the job done and they did it without any real issues. Toure was the difference, he was ridiculously good and his return from injury couldn't have come at a worse time for us.

We need to do a similar job on Palace this week and at least take this thing down to the last day. If I could have hand picked any opponent for that final day it would have been Newcastle, they're an absolute mess and look to have given up the ghost weeks ago. They went to Arsenal on Monday night and turned in a typically gutless performance, and the fans there are desperate to see Pardew go now. He certainly looks like he needs a 'new castle' to storm as things have gone seriously pear shaped for him up there now. What price him ending up back at West Ham? Shorter odds than Fat Sam making the opposite journey anyway.

I'll end with our friendly neighbourhood blue boys, who had a rather unfortunate mishap on the road at Southampton. Funny story, I was in the supermarket on Saturday lunchtime and caught a glimpse of the Echo. The headline read *"Alcarez: We can take on the world"*. I got back to the car, checked Livescore on my phone and what do I see? Southampton 1 Everton 0 (Alcaraz OG 1 min) Hahahahahaha brilliant. I remember a couple of years ago I called Alcaraz the worst player in the league. He improved a bit the season after that but he still stinks, even the Blues I've spoken to reckon he's terrible. *"Take on the world"* hahahaha. Seamus 'Owngoalman' then followed suit and the Blues' hopes of 4th took a huge knock. As amusing as it is, I'd have preferred them to have won and kept in the hunt for a top four spot. They're not out of it yet, but it's not looking good now that Arsenal have got their act together.

Martinez had a bit of a moan this week about the loan rules that state players can't play against their parent club. Well he would, wouldn't he? Everton have done more borrowing this season than a fucking Tory government. It's like turkey's voting against Christmas.

Like every other Red though, I'll be rooting for the Blues this weekend and I'm sure they'll give it a good go. I think they may have too many injuries to be able to pull it off, but it won't be for a lack of trying. Martinez will want to win the game and he won't be arsed about what it means in terms of our title challenge. He's not a bitter twat like Moyes, he just isn't wired that way. The players will want to win too, and although there'll be loads of fans hoping they lose that's neither here nor there. Besides, we've been in this position a couple of times, and when the game kicks off generally everybody tends to think *'fuck it, let's just win and worry about the consequences later'*.

Staying with Everton, I went past their club shop last weekend on the way to Anfield, and they've got this big ad campaign running that just says *"It's in our DNA"*. It doesn't say what is in their DNA unfortunately, which is not particularly helpful for most of the patrons of that shop, who come to think of it probably can't even spell DN.... actually no I'm not going to finish that gag. It's 'Hug an Evertonian' week after all. So yeah, I'll be cheering for them this Saturday, hell if they have any songs that aren't about us I'll even sing along with them. Come on you Blues!!!!

(Note: I reserve the right to absolutely fucking muller them next week if they lose)

chapter thirteen

May

CRYSTAL PALACE 3 LIVERPOOL 3

Competition - Premier League
Date - Mon 5 May 2014
Venue - Selhurst Park
Scorer(s) – Allen, Sturridge, Suarez
Star Man – Raheem Sterling

Team: Mignolet; Johnson, Skrtel, Sakho, Flanagan; Gerrard, Lucas, Allen, Sterling (Coutinho); Sturridge (Moses), Suarez:

Well that's that then, right? It was a fun ride but now it's over. At least that's what you'd think after watching the reaction of the players and fans at the end of this horrendous capitulation at Selhurst Park. Me? Honestly, I wouldn't be the least bit surprised now if City managed to lose one of their last two games, it's been that kind of a season. If they don't, then good luck to them they'll be worthy Champions and we can have no-one to blame but ourselves for coming up short.

That's if you want to 'blame' anyone, I mean if we finish second to a team that has spent hundreds of millions on their squad and who have the highest wage bill in world sports, I'm not sure 'blame' is really the right word. Whatever happens now, Brendan and the players deserve great credit for what they've given us this season, and not even this staggering show of late incompetence against Palace changes that. I'm nowhere near as devastated about this as I was after Chelsea. I'm annoyed, pissed off, frustrated, disgusted even. But devastated? No. After Chelsea it was the unfairness and injustice of it all that did me in. It was just a horrible, deflated feeling. Absolutely heartbreaking. The feeling that we deserved so much more and were going to miss out because of a cruel slip by the one man least deserving of befalling such a fate was almost too much to bear. This was different. If we can't hold onto a 3-0 lead with ten minutes left of a game we need to win, then we probably don't deserve to win the title. Honestly, it's a lot easier to accept that than it is to be blaming the 'Football Gods' for screwing us over like I was doing a week ago. If we fall short now, it's due to our own failings, pure and simple.

What makes this one hard to stomach is that for around 80 minutes this was one hell of a job we were doing. Palace parked the bus but we managed to create chances and led through Allen's header from a superbly worked training ground corner. The movement of Allen and the strategical blocking of Lucas and Suarez was brilliant. Palace hadn't conceded from a set-piece since Pulis took over, but Sakho should have buried a header from a corner even before Allen's goal.

Suarez wasn't looking himself at all though and Sturridge was hardly in the game either until he burst into life in the second half and hit the post with one effort before scoring a few minutes later. Suarez appeared to be feeling unwell before the game, and you could tell in the second half he wasn't right as at times he looked out on his feet. Didn't stop him getting on the scoresheet of course, but the sight of him sat on the advertising hoardings desperately gasping for breath on a couple of occasions showed that something was clearly amiss with him.

Having gotten to 3-0 everyone was now looking at boosting our goal difference. When we beat Palace 9-0 all those years ago six of those goals came in the last half an hour or something, so we were in the same position now. Obviously nine was overly ambitious, but maybe we could get five or six. We had chances to do it too but failed to take them and then what happened after that will be remembered for a long, long time. For all the wrong reasons from our perspective.

It's far from over though, not yet. Whatever happens it will go to the last day of the season and that in itself is remarkable given where we were a year ago and considering the two poor transfer windows we've had since. This game showed just how unpredictable football is and a lot of strange things have happened this season. If City do win both of their games then there can be no argument that they deserve to be Champions and we don't. It will hurt like hell and it will be massively disappointing, but I'll get over it. Had we beaten Palace and missed out on the title basically because of Gerrard's slip against Chelsea, however, I don't think I'd have ever recovered from that.

All season we've been letting in stupid goals but because we've been scoring so many some of us got swept along with it, and in a way even got a kick out of it. Those realists/pessimists (delete as appropriate) who pointed out how those defensive flaws were going to prove to be our undoing were dismissed as being miserable, negative bastards who needed to cast those worries aside and just enjoy the ride. I'm as guilty of that as anyone, I actually spent a good hour on Saturday night trying to talk a mate around who can't get fully on board with Rodgers because of how shite we are at the back. I think I was winning him over too, and then this happens. Well my friend is right, we can't go on like this and the manager is the one who needs to accept the responsibility for it and to fix it. There's nothing he can do about individual errors of course, but what happened against Palace was as much on Brendan as anybody.

At 3-0 there is absolutely nothing wrong with chasing more goals and trying to claw back some of the goal difference on City. When it went to 3-1 though, that's when you have to forget about the goal chase and take the sting out of it. You may still get a chance or two on the counter but you can't carry on chasing it at that stage, you just secure the three points and get the hell out of there. Instead, we send everyone up for a corner, have a shot blocked and within seconds the ball is in our net and it's 3-2. I think at that point we all knew what was going to happen, but it doesn't make it any less unforgivable. A team protecting a lead in a game they need to win cannot concede a goal from their own corner; it doesn't get any more stupid than that.

It's easy to blame the back four for our capitulation but for me it's far more complex.

I could point the finger at almost every one of them on that pitch for us drawing this game. We should have just kept possession and took the sting out of Palace, but we didn't. We kept losing the ball and inviting pressure and that's on the entire team. We also missed chances that would have made this a repeat of Stoke or Cardiff away or Swansea at home. We should have scored more than three, but obviously three SHOULD be enough and so that is not the main issue here.

We defended poorly as a team as well as a back four, we didn't show enough composure on the ball to kill the game and the manager didn't help matters either. The substitutions didn't benefit the team at all (unusual for Rodgers). Coutinho for Sterling shouldn't have really weakened us too much but it did and Sterling was probably the last player on the pitch who should have been taken off. Moses for Sturridge didn't help either for that matter. Brendan said he did that to try and stop them getting down the side (where Bulasie was having his way with Johnson), which makes sense to be fair, but we really needed Agger on to bolster the defence as he had done in a similar situation against Norwich two weeks ago.

Whatever reasons you want to look at though, the fact is that we let in too many goals and although we've managed to overcome it so many times due to how prolific we are at the other end, it was always going to end in tears at some point. And this one, literally, ended in tears. Suarez was sobbing his heart out at the final whistle as were some fans. Maybe I'm being a dick about this but that pissed me right off. Yeah, we all felt like crying, hell I wanted to cry after Chelsea but I didn't. Crying is understandable, but do it away from the cameras because all you're doing is providing great enjoyment to the millions of opposing fans who lap that shit up. If Suarez can't control his emotions, fine, run off the pitch as fast as you can and then cry as much as you want in the dressing room. Don't do it on the pitch though (or in the stands for that matter) as all you're doing is making a bad situation worse. I mean fucking hell, how are we supposed to laugh at John Terry when our own players and fans are doing it?

The weird thing is that although it felt like the dream was over when that whistle blew, when you take away the emotional devastation due to how it happened, we're actually not in THAT much of a worse spot than we were. We needed City to fail to win one of their games, now we need them to lose one. Still, if they draw against Villa then it's going to be pretty sickening no matter how I try and rationalise it. Unless Villa or West Ham do us a big favour this Palace game may haunt us for years.

And yet even when it went to 3-3 we still almost pulled off a remarkable victory. It would have been so typical of our season if we had done too, but unfortunately the one clear chance we had fell to Victor fucking Moses. I've had a feeling for weeks that Moses was going to have a say in the title race and the Palace game was the one I had in mind. I would have been right too if the useless turd hadn't mis-kicked in front of an open goal deep into stoppage time. No excuse whatsoever for a professional footballer showing that level of ineptitude. Should have left him there and not let him travel back up with the squad. End his loan there and then and for the weekend bring Teixera or Jack Dunn into the squad in his place. I don't want to even set eyes on him again after that.

Then there's Johnson. After the game he went on twitter to cryptically say *"absolute-*

ly clueless...." I thought he must have been referring to his own performance, turns out he was on about the *'sofa experts'* who *'know nothing about football'*. Don't know who he was referring to, probably some nuggets sending him abuse on twitter, but he needs to shut the fuck up really doesn't he? I'm not condoning people sending him abuse, but why is he even logging on to twitter after a game like that? What the fuck is he expecting? If he had any brains whatsoever he'd have given it a wide berth for the rest of the week.

As for lashing out at his critics, someone at the club needs to tell him to knock that shit off. In fact, Rodgers should tell him and he should also tell him that the criticism is valid as he was a fucking disgrace at Selhurst and he's been shite for most of the season. It may or may not have been due to his injury problems, but even since he came back he's been very up and down. He's had some good games and some bad ones. This one showed the best and worst of him in the same game. He was a real threat going forward in the first half, but when we came under pressure he folded like a fucking accordion. In fact, you could say he's the reason we initially came under pressure anyway, due to him half arsing an attempted block. It took him ages to even bother trying to close Delaney down, and when he finally did he then turned his back on the shot, which deflected off him and past Mignolet. He's being paid over 100k a week and he's scared of being hit by the fucking ball?

The second goal is partly on him too as he should have just rugby tackled Bolasie and stopped that counter attack on the half way line. It would have cost him a yellow card but would have been worth it. In fact, even if it had cost him a red it would have been worth it. Instead he just let him run past unopposed. Others were culpable for that goal too (Coutinho could also have fouled him before he even reached Johnson), it's not just on him by any means, but I'm just sick of Johnson now. Even the third goal is partly on him for not covering round the back of Skrtel when he (foolishly) tried to win the ball and left Gayle unmarked. You'd maybe accept the poor defending if he was delivering at the other end (and not being a bellend on twitter), but he's not doing that anymore either. He has a reputation for being good going forward but he hasn't scored a single goal this season and more often than not he just cuts inside and runs into trouble or hits a hopeful shot with his left foot. I don't think he'll ever get out of my doghouse after tonight.

We've been living a dream for months but it just feels like reality has finally caught up with us now. We've known all season that this was a flawed team; we just hoped that we could keep covering up those flaws long enough to finish in top spot. We may still do it of course, but regardless of that it's now up to Rodgers to address the defensive issues to ensure that next year they don't undermine all the brilliant attacking play we'll no doubt see again. We're still a work in progress, the difference is that whereas almost everyone else builds from the back when they take over, Rodgers has done it the other way. I have no doubt he'll get the defensive side of it right for next season though.

I tell you who can go and fuck themselves though; the rest of the country, that's who. All of them laughing their tits off at us, first after Gerrard's slip and now buzzing about 'Crystanbul'. We even had Tottenham Hotspur's official twitter account mocking us. That's right, the same Tottenham Hotspur who are perennial losers and who we beat 5-

0 and 4-0 this season, are laughing at us!!!! Really Spurs? How's that Gareth Bale money working out for you then?

I'm not even mad about it, you know why? Because we piss on Spurs and we piss on all the other fucking losers getting their kicks out of what is happening to us at the moment too. The only people who are in a position to laugh at us and take the piss are City fans, who ironically are probably the least likely to do so. The rest can all laugh as much as they like, I'm not arsed what any of them think as they're all going to finish below my team, and City might yet too for that matter. So laugh it up losers, but it ain't over yet. We are Liverpool, tra la la la....

Premier League Round Up (3-7 May 2014)

So that thing about Everton doing us a favour then, how'd that work out for us? Even worse than expected I'd say. Just enough effort to avoid suspicion, but not enough to threaten taking points off City. The 2-3 scoreline looks like they gave it a go, the performance itself tells a different story.

I didn't see the game live as I was at a mate's wedding and the wifi was shite (I've watched the highlights and spoken to plenty who did watch it), but a few of us did manage to sneak out and catch the last half hour on the radio. The weird thing was, for the final twenty minutes it was basically Collymore and Matterface chatting amongst themselves. *"What's happening, commentate on the fucking game, knob heads!!"* we cried. Turns out nothing was happening, when that big dope Dzeko wasn't wasting five minutes by playing dead when there was fuck all wrong with him, Everton were playing tiki-taka in their own fucking half. It was pathetic, the only one who was even trying was Barkley, who mustn't have read the same script his team-mates had. Actually that's a little harsh on Naismith who also gave it a go, but as one of my mates said he's a *"Poundland Dirk Kuyt"* who doesn't know how to give anything other than his all. *"Oh look at how we celebrated Barkley's goal"* cried Martinez and the fan. *"That shows how much we wanted to win"*. No, it doesn't, it's easy to get caught up in the moment when you're winning, the real test of Everton's resolve was how they reacted when things started slipping away. And they didn't react, at all. They rolled over and let City tickle their belly.

Did they go out wanting to lose? No, but when it looked they were going to lose they weren't really that arsed were they? Look at how they played the last twenty minutes, that shows how little they wanted to win or even draw. No urgency at all. Small time losers. Baines had his worst game of the season, Jagielka was either unfit or just not arsed, Howard gave it the full Hans Segers, Osman spent the entire time passing the ball backwards and just look at Alcarez on the third goal for God's sake. Then there's the fans. Look at what happened when Lukaku headed them back into it, he actually had to go and try to whip the crowd up as the goal was met by a half hearted cheer and polite applause. Laughable really.

City were reeling on the ropes when it went to 3-2, but instead of delivering the knock out blow Everton decided to shadow box in their own corner instead. Still, as long as Liverpool don't win anything it's all good, eh lads? They were gleefully singing about Steven Gerrard when their own team were 3-1 down at home. Think about that for a second. In a game they needed to win to stay in contention for a Champions League place, their fans didn't give a fuck that they were losing because hey, at least they can take the piss out of Gerrard and 'der redshite'. Well laugh it up losers, because a couple of weeks ago you had fourth place in your hands and then shit the bed by losing three of your next four games. Hell, even the one you won doesn't really count because United's players were trying (and succeeding) to get Moyes sacked. Everton spent 30 years blaming us for them not being able to play in the European Cup yet when they had a shot at getting in there themselves, they were far happier losing just to sabotage our title bid. #evertonarentwe

Elsewhere on Saturday Sunderland won again. I called that one last week to be fair, Moyes may be gone but United are still shite and that Norwich win wasn't fooling me. Larsson got the only goal of the game from a Wickham cross and United never really looked like getting back into it. It could have been worse too, Giaccherini hit the post in the second half and Fabio Magnifico hit the bar with a brilliant effort, although a number of United fans won't have seen that as according to the BBC loads of them got off at half time. So much for them getting back on side once Moyes had been canned.

Spurs had Kaboul sent off as they lost at West Ham. He's shite him isn't he? One of those players you always think has a red card in him. Big Andy caused havoc all day and West Ham's first came when his header deflected in off Harry Kane. Downing made it 2-0 with his first goal for the Hammers, a free-kick that went right through the middle of the Spurs wall. Hugo Lloris was understandably furious with Paulinho and Adebayor who pulled 'a Glen Johnson' and moved out of the way in case they got hurt. Absolutely shocking that, Adebayor was especially embarrassing. Big bastard like him scared of getting hit by the ball? Disgusting behaviour. Lloris was the only thing standing between Spurs and a cricket score on the day, he was ace. He's probably the best keeper in the league for me. Good to see Stewy on the scoresheet and the big fella on form though ahead of this weekend. Come on you Irons!!

Southampton beat Swansea with a freak goal right at the death from Lambert, Arsenal beat West Brom at a canter but seriously, who cares, and Chelsea produced another display of free flowing attacking football in a thrilling 0-0 draw at home to Norwich. Mourinho, of course, blamed his players. Well it can't be his fault can it, I mean he's 'special' isn't he? Newspaper reports claim he said to Matic that he was *"starting to regret signing him in January"*, and also told Salah at half time to *"come back next season ready to be a footballer"* before replacing him with Eden Hazard. Yes, the same Eden Hazard who he had lambasted publicly the day before for not being *"a team player"*. And yes the same Eden Hazard who a couple of months back he claimed was the best young player in the world and the heir to the throne of Messi and Ronaldo. Those Chelsea players must fucking hate him given the way he's carried on this season. It's all going a bit 'Real Madrid' isn't it?

Moving on, and Cardiff were relegated at the weekend, and so they should be after getting dicked by a Newcastle side who haven't been able to beat anyone lately. Loads of 'Toon' fans got off after 69 minutes in a pre-arranged protest. It's easy to laugh at Newcastle fans - and God knows I do - but you can't blame them for being pissed off with Ashley and how he's running things. The Kinnear fiasco alone was enough reason for a protest, I'm surprised it's taken them this long to be fair. The 69th minute was because 1969 was the last time they won a trophy. I'm still trying to work out what the significance of the 45th minute was for those Mancs who fucked off though. The amount of millions they wasted on Mata perhaps? Anyway, Shola Ameobi, and Remi had given the Geordies a 2-0 lead before Steven Taylor added a third in stoppage time and went fucking mental, like Marco Tardelli in the '82 World Cup. Thick as pigshit that lad isn't he?

Fulham are down too after losing at Stoke. Odemwingie got the first and Arnautovic hit a superb second following a counter attack led by the lively Assaidi, who then added a third himself after another swift counter attack. Richardson pulled one back but Walters then made it 4-1 after outpacing Riise (oh dear John, if that doesn't tell you to call time on it then nothing will), and that was all she wrote for Fulham who will be playing in the Championship next season and probably for the foreseeable future. Assaidi was quality, but then he was up against a 6ft 6 left footed centre back being asked to play right back for the first time in his life. Seriously Magath lad, what the fuck was that all about? Assaidi said afterwards that the beleaguered Dan Burn even asked him to switch wings because he didn't want to play against him anymore! Poor lad, you just know he goes to bed every night dreaming about that time he played against a David Moyes side and headed away cross after cross and being the hero.

Elsewhere Villa had a decent win against Hull, who clearly have one eye on the cup final now and aren't really at it anymore. Weimann bagged a brace as Villa ran out 3-1 winners. Nice to see him scoring against someone other than us for a fucking change anyway.

Onto the midweek games, and United got back to winning ways as James Wilson scored twice on his debut in a 3-1 win over Hull. He was a surprise inclusion, selected ahead of Van Persie and Hernandez. Hang on, wasn't Giggs known as Ryan Wilson before he changed his name after falling out with his arl fella? Pretty sure he was you know. Maybe this lad is some relation? Like a son or a nephew? Or a son AND a nephew.

All the talk is that Van Gaal will take over there soon and the question has been raised as to what will happen to 'the class of 92' if the Dutchman takes over. Will they want to stay together and if one goes will they all go, or will Giggs just negotiate on his own behalf if Van Gaal doesn't want Scholes, Butt and Phil Neville? Given that those lads are like brothers to him, I guess they're fucked really.

Sunderland won on Wednesday too, sweet smelling Fabio scored a cracker as they beat West Brom 2-0 to ensure safety and relegate Norwich. Poyet said a few weeks ago they needed a miracle and they got one. Good for them, I'm glad they saved themselves and I'm happy enough with the three who went down too.

Finally, there's a few rules I live my life by. One is never trust a man in white jeans (I'm not even sure why, I just remember a mate saying it to me once years ago and it's stuck) and another is never rely on Aston Villa for anything, ever. That one has stood me in good stead my entire adult life, so needless to say I didn't get my hopes up about them helping us out against City. One look at their team sheet beforehand was enough to know how that game was going to go. That starting eleven would struggle to beat most Championship sides, let alone a side chasing a Championship. The one hope would have been Agbonlahor, who - average as he is - tends to have five or six games a season where is completely unplayable (and at least one of those is usually against us, the dopey looking bastard). Villa without Agbonlahor is like the X Factor without Simon Cowell. It's complete dog shit anyway, but take away the main star and it becomes completely unwatchable. I didn't even consider tuning in for this, I mean why would I? It was never going to end well for us, the only surprise was Villa held out as long as they did. I occasionally checked twitter to see how it was going, but no way was I sitting through that torture. And empty seats in a game when they were going for the title?? Really City fans? Fucking hell. It was the same when they played Sunderland the other week too. Just highlights the unfairness about it all really. We're greeting the team coach in our thousands when it arrives at the stadium, they can't even fill their stadium. It's not like they have the excuse of being used to it either, if it was United it would almost be understandable, but City have won one Premier League title, this should all still be new and exciting to them, the ungrateful feckers. That song of theirs about *'We're not really here'* couldn't be any more apt really. Fuckin' part timers. And singing about Gerrard when your team is on the verge of winning the title? Congratulations City, you've become the thing you've always hated; you're Manchester United. I can say hand on heart that had the roles been reversed and - let's say - Yaya Toure had suffered the misfortune that Stevie did, there is not a chance in a million years we'd be singing about him whilst on the verge of a title. You stay classy, Manchester.

Interesting how smug they were in their celebrations too, as though the title is now in the bag. It probably is like, but still, tempting fate is never wise. For most of my lifetime City have been known for being complete fuck ups, for getting things wrong, for being losers. In fact, even on the one occasion they managed to avoid fucking it up they were actually so close to the biggest fuck up of all time, when they were 2-1 down to 10 man QPR and needed two stoppage time goals to win the title. Anyone who thinks they aren't capable of shitting the bed against West Ham hasn't been paying attention to City's history, or to how this season has gone for that matter. I'm not saying I expect it to happen (I don't), but it's far from being beyond the realms of possibility. We bought Andy Carroll and Stewart Downing with the aim of winning us the league, it's time for them to deliver.

sings *"Sweeeeeet Carroll nine, der der der, you and Stewy are so good (so good so good so good)..."* What? Ok look, I know it's a long shot, but it could be worse, we could be relying on Villa or the Blueshite.

LIVERPOOL 2 NEWCASTLE 1

Competition - Premier League
Date - Sun 11 May 2014
Venue - Anfield
Scorer(s) – Agger, Sturridge
Star Man – Raheem Sterling

Team: Mignolet; Johnson,
Skrtel, Agger, Flanagan
(Cissokho); Gerrard,
Henderson, Allen (Coutinho),
Sterling; Suarez, Sturridge
(Lucas):

And so it ends, in a mixture of disappointment and pride. It's easy to wonder 'what might have been' but I'm largely past that now I think. Falling so agonisingly short hurts of course, but we didn't 'lose' the title, Manchester City won it. In 2014 we've taken 48 points out of a possible 57. That's actually more than City managed but it just wasn't quite enough. Still, it was an incredible effort and any talk of 'choking' or 'bottling' from outsiders should be treated with the contempt it deserves.

Yes, some points were dropped along the way but unless you're expecting a team to play perfect, flawless football then that's always going to happen. We didn't lose the title, we just didn't quite have enough to win it. There's no shame in that, in fact pride should be taken in the fact we went as close as we did and topped the 100 goal mark in the process. And if we 'bottled it' then what the hell do you call what Chelsea did? They were seven points clear at one point. Or Arsenal for that matter, who were top for months until we bitch slapped them all over Anfield. So no, we didn't bottle it and Brendan and his players should be proud of what they've done, because the fans sure as hell are.

There is still an obvious sadness as well of course (summed up by Sturridge's post match interview in which he appeared completely gutted), especially as it turns out that Gerrard's slip against Chelsea was indeed the 'decisive moment' in the title race, the moment where the balance of power shifted for one final time. That defeat allowed City back in and there was to be no further twist in the tale because unfortunately this is a cruel, screwed up world that we live in. Not winning the title is one thing, having people (and by people I obviously mean gobshites) point the finger at Gerrard and say he fucked it up, that's another thing entirely. That just shouldn't be happening, not to Steven fucking Gerrard.

Despite not winning the title I'm feeling quite upbeat, probably because I made my peace with it well before this weekend's games. I'm excited about the direction we're going and the massive strides we took this year and I feel a closer bond to the team than I've felt in a long time. It feels like the club is back to what is used to be, we've got an inspirational manager who completely 'gets it' and who has us playing wonderful, free flowing football and we have a group of players who should only get better. They say what doesn't kill you makes you stronger, and this didn't kill us, far from it. We proved that by coming from a goal down to beat Newcastle when we could have just felt sorry for ourselves and accepted defeat. No, we're still fighting and we'll come back next year even better for the experience.

The truth is I'm far more upset for Gerrard than anything else because as much as he'll put a brave face on it, that moment against Chelsea will stay with him. Let's face it, there's not much chance of him being able to forget it when he's being reminded of it by every set of small time, knob head opposition fans we come across. Not that he needs me to tell him, but if I had the opportunity to speak with Stevie I'd just say: *"Fuck them all, they laugh because they're scared of you and this team. Take the pain of how this season ended and use it to go on and win it next year. Go into every game next year remembering how it felt to miss out by such a small margin. It wasn't the Chelsea game that cost us, it was Villa, Hull, Southampton, City, Palace and all the other games where we dropped points. Every game counts, remember that next year and just go out and win the fucking thing. We'll see who's laughing then"*. Actually, I'm kidding myself there, I'd probably just hug him and tell him I love him, so probably best that I don't get the opportunity to talk to him really, as it'd be a bit uncomfortable all round I imagine.

The captain has suffered disappointments before and he always bounces back. He's already bounced back from this one and he was the main reason we beat Newcastle as it was not going well at all until his dead ball expertise saved the day. He's going to need some help for next season though as he can't play every game like he basically has this season; we're going to need another option in there and I don't think that option is Lucas, but we'll see. That's a discussion for another day though.

If I had to pick two words to describe the mood at Anfield before and during this one, they'd be 'deflation' and 'defiance'. As much as deep down we all knew West Ham had no chance of winning at City, you still live in hope don't you, and once again the team were greeted by thousands as they arrived by coach on Anfield Road. Other fans would have turned on their players after dropping five points in their previous two games, but our support has been fantastic over this closing stretch of the season. Maybe we weren't going to win the title, but for the first time since we last won it we went into the last game of the season still in with a chance. A slim chance, but no other club aside from City could say that and the fans once again showed they were there for the team. It's a shame they couldn't be in two places at once, as maybe they could have inspired the West Ham players too. They were going to need all the help they could get if they were going to derail City. Anything can happen in football of course, a sending off here, a mistake there, a huge stroke of luck or a stray beach ball... you just never know. Prior to kick off though the main thing I was hoping for was just three points for us, anything else would have been a glorious, unexpected bonus, but I was just desperate for us to beat Newcastle. After all we've been through in 2014, we couldn't let the season end on a downer, it would have completely ruined the summer.

It was vital we ended the season on a winning note, but for a while it was looking like we were going to fall flat our faces. Imagine if West Ham had somehow upset City but we failed to beat Newcastle? Fucking Newcastle, who everyone has been beating in 2014. They're a mess, a laughing stock, and yet we found ourselves trailing to them at half time and as usual, the damage was self inflicted. There was an element of bad luck about Skrtel's own goal but this kind of thing is happening too often (not specifically own goals, just cheap goals conceded where teams don't have to do much to score). It could have been worse as Newcastle then had a great chance to make it 2-0 and it needed a good save from Mignolet to deny Gouffran.

It was interesting that Rodgers brought Agger back in for Sakho. I'd have done it too, but it is a little cruel on Sakho isn't it? None of the goals conceded against Palace were down to him in any way shape or form, but it is a fact that when he's played we've shipped goals at an alarming rate. The goals against record with Agger in the side isn't great either, but for whatever reason it's a damn sight better than it is when Sakho is in there. Agger and Skrtel have played together for years so it's naturally a better pairing and they have more of an understanding of one another's game, but they aren't the long term answer and if Sakho and Skrtel isn't going to work then Rodgers has some big decisions to make this summer.

The first half was pretty depressing really, the players seemed to be feeling sorry for themselves and it was all a bit flat. The fans did their best to create an atmosphere suitable for the occasion, but the disappointment the team seemed to be feeling eventually started to transfer to the stands as well. The mood wasn't helped by the first half display of Glen Johnson either, who single handedly almost managed to completely snap the crowd's patience. Horrendous.

The team performance was laboured, slow and tired looking. There was no sparkle, no zip and it was all too easy for Newcastle's packed defence to keep us at bay. The one time we breached it was when Suarez improvised with a quick free-kick out wide and chipped Krul brilliantly with the outside of his foot only for Phil Dowd to rule it out as he hadn't given the signal for it to be taken. It was just about the only time Newcastle were grateful to Dowd all afternoon, as he would later harshly send off two of their players.

The longer the first half went the more frustrating it got. As soon as news filtered through just before half time that City had gone in front any faint title hopes we had were well gone, but still, the most important thing at that point was just beating Newcastle. It wasn't about the league title anymore, it was just about finishing the season in a manner befitting of what had gone before. And also, it was about shutting up those fucking dickhead Geordies, who were a complete embarrassment, even by their own standards.

The repeated airings of the Gerrard song were both predictable and smalltime, but constantly chanting for Demba Ba - a player who dropped them like a stone to sit on Chelsea's bench - was cringeworthy beyond belief. There's no rivalry between us and Newcastle, no bad blood, and no reason for them to be taking such great pleasure in our missing out on a title. I don't expect them to be wanting us to win it or to be feeling sorry for us, hell the day we have Geordies pitying us is the day we're in serious fucking trouble, but something really doesn't sit right with me about all these twats up and down the country mocking Gerrard now when they'll be crawling up his arse in a few weeks when he's captaining THEIR country. Hypocritical cunts, the lot of them.

And what's with the deification of Ba just because he scored against us??? It's the equivalent of us chanting for Fernando Torres because he'd scored a goal that was going to deny, say, Tottenham the title. It's completely fucking ridiculous, but then as a rule Newcastle fans are fucking ridiculous, always have been, always will be. They were even chanting *"1-0 to the Man City"* until some of them then must have realised that their own team were actually winning too and belatedly followed it up with *"1-0 to the Geordie boys"*. Bunch of losers. You know something, they deserve Mike Ashley and they deserve Alan Pardew, I just wish they still had Joe Kinnear as well. Funny how the Mike Ashley chants didn't start until they found themselves losing too. (Disclaimer: some of the Geordies stayed behind and applauded Gerrard when he did his TV interview on the pitch. They were a minority and the above doesn't apply to them, the rest, however, are an embarrassment)

Being laughed at by Newcastle is just not acceptable, if I'd been in Rodgers' shoes that would probably have been my half time team talk actually. *"Lads, Newcastle are taking the piss out of you and our fans. Fucking Newcastle!!! The biggest joke in the Premier League are laughing at us. That's unacceptable, now go out there and fucking wipe the floor with the stupid stripy twats."* He may well have done that for all I know, but one thing that we know for certain he did at half time was make a substitution. When Aly Cissokho readied himself to come on for the start of the 2nd half, I think everyone in the ground assumed Johnson had been hooked. Instead it was Flanagan, who can consider himself a little unfortunate under the circumstances. He wasn't having a great game by any means, but stuck out on the left wing with no support what was he meant to do? Most of the time when the ball went to him he had no team-mate within 30 yards. He's not going to go taking on anybody down the outside, and he's not going to overlap and whip crosses in on his left foot either, so he was rendered largely ineffective against a side parking the bus like that.

Getting Cissokho on made sense as it gave us more natural width, but I expect most inside Anfield would have moved Flanno to right back and dragged Johnson out behind the Kop and put him out of his misery. To be fair to Rodgers, he didn't just make a switch in personnel, he switched the formation too and went with three at the back, with Johnson operating as the right sided centre back (and looking far more comfortable as a result of it in fairness). Sterling initially went to the right wing and we immediately began to look more threatening, especially when Coutinho then came on for Allen to give us a bit of extra zip.

Suarez was having a stinker though and Sturridge was largely anonymous, which is obviously going to have a pretty big impact on how threatening we are going to be. On days like this you need to get goals however you can, and set-pieces have been very productive for us this season. That's been one of many areas we've seen great improvement, although it should be said that many of our corners against Newcastle (especially the ones taken by Suarez) were terrible. We were deadly from free-kicks though. The outstanding Sterling kept winning them by running past two and three opponents until they eventually brought him down, and Gerrard kept pinging in great deliveries. Two of them ended with goals for Agger and Sturridge (the Dane's finish was especially impressive) and two more could easily have had the same outcome as Agger missed a great chance and another brilliant delivery was narrowly missed by Skrtel and Suarez.

Newcastle lost all composure at 2-1 and Ameobi was hilariously sent off for dissent. Obviously we couldn't tell exactly what was being said, but Dowd booked him and even pointed towards the dressing room as a warning as to what would happen if he didn't shut it. He also called over the captain, Colloccini, to tell him to calm Ameobi down. Before the Argentine could do anything though Ameobi had said something else and Dowd was reaching for his red card. Ameobi, by all accounts, doesn't swear, and he claims his second yellow was for saying *"are you going to send me off for trying to plead my case for my team?"* to which Dowd said *"yes"* and then pulled out the red card. All very bizarre, and the red card for the other kid was harsh too, although without the benefit of replays it's easy to see why Dowd sent him off, especially as the linesman was flagging to tell him it was a bad one. It was actually just clumsy and nowhere near as dirty as it first appeared, but I'll take it as it made the closing stages comfortable as we just passed the ball around on halfway to see the game out.

Some of the fans didn't like that and wanted us to go for more goals. Suarez didn't like it either, he was getting properly pissed off as no-one would pass him the ball, but after what happened at Palace this was the prudent thing to do, as was sending on Lucas for Sturridge. Another goal wasn't going to make any difference to our season, but imagine we got done on a counter through trying to score another?

The lap of appreciation at the end was not how we'd hoped it would be a few weeks ago. For a start there was no trophy there. There was a great show of support for Gerrard though and a deafening roar of 'BREN-DAN ROD-GERS' as the manager made his way around after everyone else. The rest of the country may be taking great pleasure in our so-called 'collapse', and the last few weeks have certainly been a painful experience, but bollocks to everyone else. I'm proud of this team, I'm proud of the support and I'm especially proud of our manager, who has been fucking incredible throughout all this. We'll take these blows and come back stronger, and then let's see who's laughing next year.

I think Rocky Balboa said it best. *"The world ain't all sunshine and rainbows. It's a very mean and nasty place. And I don't care how tough you are. It will beat you to your knees and keep you permanently there if you let it. You, me, or nobody is gonna hit as hard as life, but it ain't about how hard you hit, it's about how hard you can get hit and keep moving forward, how much you can take and keep moving forward. That's how winning is done."*

Typically wise words from the 'Italian Stallion' there. We've been hit hard by life in the last couple of weeks, but we're still moving forward and next year...

....we go again.

Premier League Round Up (11 May 2014)

I can't believe another season is behind us already. This one absolutely flew over, maybe because it was so much fun, at least up until the last couple of weeks anyway. When the dust settled on the 2013-14 campaign, there was no great surprise in how things turned out.

Back in August most were tipping City to win it and few would have been surprised with Cardiff and Norwich going down. Fulham finishing in the bottom three was perhaps slightly surprising, Everton finishing 5th definitely was and of course not many would have seen us coming 2nd and still being in with a chance of the title on the final day. I suppose you'd have to say United finishing 7th was the biggest 'shock', but they were always going to take a giant stride backwards after losing Ferguson, and a further one after appointing 'the Chosen One'. If only they could have let him see out the season we'd probably be Champions now, it's like the spell was broken they gave him the old heave ho. Selfish bastards.

United ended their season with 1-1 draw at Southampton, which in the context of where they are at right now was a good point for them. Lambert deservedly put the Saints in front with a class finish but United were much improved in the second half and equalised through a Mata free-kick. Funny the way no-one has given a shit about them for months though, long may that continue.

Moving on, and relegated Norwich were comfortably beaten by Arsenal at Carrow Road. Ramsay's brilliant volley put the Gunners ahead and that Jenkinson jabroni scored the other. Sacking Hughton worked out well for Norwich then eh?

Sunderland's amazing recent run came to an end when they lost at home to Swansea. Dyer got the first inside ten minutes with a typical Swansea goal, and Emnes made it 2-0 with a brilliant goal, his first in 28 games. Nothing 'typical' about that one. Sweet Smelling Fabio pulled one back on his final appearance before coming back here (he will won't he? I hope so, no point selling him as we'll have to buy a replacement) but yet another goal from Bony ensured Swansea ended on a high. It shows how good he's been that I've not been hammering him for having 'Wilfried' on the back of his shirt and wearing gloves in May. Steve the Pirate has got the Swansea job full time and it will be interesting to see how they do next year. I suspect he'll do ok, I mean he learned from the master didn't he?

As you know, I often find myself asking random, pointless questions, like does anyone under 60 eat kippers, and who would win a footrace between Per Mertesacker and Gunnersaurus Rex. The question I've been asking this week though, is what the hell is the Argentina coach smoking? Franco Di Santo made their initial 30 man World Cup squad!!! Yes, THAT Franco Di Santo, he was the original Jozy Altidore and was my favourite whipping boy in these round ups for two years, but he may actually be lining up with Messi, Aguero & co in Brazil this summer. My tiny mind simply can't get to grips with that. I hadn't given Di Santo a single thought since last season when I was ridiculing him on a weekly basis, but then there he is popping up on my twitter feed after being named ahead of Carlos Tevez in the Argie's squad. Apparently he's playing for Werder Bremen these days, and according to wikipedia has scored a whopping four goals for them this season. I'm not sure what's most surprising; him being named in the world cup squad or that Michael Laudrup didn't buy him in January. Actually I bet Ngog is cursing his luck this week that he wasn't born in Buenos Aires.

Moving on, and Palace ended the season in 11th place after a draw at Fulham. Dwight Gayle put the visitors in front but Woodrow levelled after the break. Gayle hit his second with a great free-kick but Chris David's last second screamer gave Fulham something to cling onto ahead of next season. They've got a great youth system there and maybe relegation will allow them to bring some players through. He's a good player that Gayle (seven goals in just eight starts this season) but just the mere mention of him will always bring back horrible memories from now on. I can't even look at him to be honest, hopefully he'll be sold to a Championship side or retire or something.

Staying with Palace, and I see Pulis won the LMA Premier League manager of the year award. He's done a great job, no question, but Brendan won the overall LMA award, which was voted by the managers throughout all the divisions. So the conclusion we can draw from that is that most Premier League managers are either stupid or just bitter bastards. I bet my boy Tim voted for Brendan though.

Speaking of whom, Sherwood ended the season with a win over Villa that secured a Europa League spot for Spurs, but it wasn't enough to save him from the bullet. *"If you have a supply teacher who comes in, sometimes they're not treated with the respect of a headmaster"* he said in the build up to the game. He knew it was coming, he's known it was coming for weeks, but he held his head up and he had a fucking blast didn't he? Even against Villa he was having fun, calling a fan out of the stands, handing him his body warmer and allowing him to sit on the bench and manage the team. *"That guy's an expert, seriously. Every week he tells me what to do. So I gave him the opportunity to do the job. He bottled it at first but then he swallowed it. It was just good banter. There were a couple I could have picked. We've got the police looking for him because he's nicked the gilet. But it's fine, he can have it."* That's boss that is, I love Tim Sherwood me.

He reckons if he'd started the season as manager they'd have made the Champions League. You may laugh, but only Pellegrini, Rodgers and Mourinho picked up more points than Sherwood after he took over so he might have a case. Looks like it was player power that did for him in the end though, with reports claiming that Sandro, Paulinho, Epoue, Vertonghen and Lloris all told Daniel Levy 'he goes or we do'.

Sandro: A man who's most notable contribution to the season was to make a video of himself doing round house kicks like some kind of jarg Chuck Norris.

Paulinho: One of the biggest flops of the season and a man who lost his place to that Bentoleb kid.

Epoue: A man who... actually I don't even know he is to be fair. I assume he is one

343

of the dozen slapdicks they wasted the Bale cash on.

Vertonghen: Ah yes, Vertonghen. Let me tell you something sunshine, it wasn't Tim Facking Sherwood that gave a goal away after falling on his arse whilst attempting a Cruyff turn at Stamford Bridge.

And finally **Lloris**: Yeah ok, fair enough.

The others though, bunch of under achieving bums who simply couldn't hack it under my main man Tim. Bet they wanted AVB gone too, he was my boy as well. Fuck you Spurs players, you don't deserve either of them, you deserve Christian Gross, you sorry gang of losers. Still, I heard on the radio this morning they were hoping to lure Ancelotti from Real Ma.... hahahahahaha sorry I can't even finish that sentence.

I feel like I'm the only one who gets Timmy though, he just doesn't get anything like the love he should do. It's like that song about Rosemary: *"Love grows where my Tim Sherwood goes and nobody knows but me"*. If I could be mates with any Premier League boss other than Brendan, it'd be this guy, hands down. He's a laugh a minute, I like to think we'd go on pub crawls and give random strangers the 'Adebayor salute' in the street and get up to all sorts of other crazy, madcap capers. Someone had better give him a job in time for next season or I'm gonna be one very sad panda.

West Brom ended their season with a home loss to Stoke as Adam bagged a late winner to secure a top half finish for the Potters. Pepe Mel was sacked, but they waited until the England squad was announced before sneaking that bit of news out. Obviously the Baggies thought they could slip that one under the radar without getting any stick for what was a completely ridiculous appointment that so nearly got them relegated. Hopefully they've learned their lesson and will appoint someone more suitable. I hear the coach with the fourth best winning record in the league is available... go on West Brom, you know it makes sense.

I don't like saying this, but Hughes has done a good job with Stoke hasn't he? They finished in the top half but he also transformed their style of play in the process. Aside from Hughes himself, there's not too much to dislike about Stoke these days. Thank God for Jon Walters.

Elsewhere, City obviously beat West Ham, but I've not watched any of that game and certainly didn't watch any of their title celebrations. Fuck that noise. I said earlier in the season that if we didn't win it then City were my 'Plan B' because it was more palatable than seeing a Chelsea or Arsenal win it, and although I stand by it, it still hurts because we went so damn close. We've lost out to the most expensively assembled team in world sport and there's no disgrace in that at all, but you know where there is disgrace? In City's blatant disregard for FFP and the ridiculous stunts they're pulling to try and get around it. 'Intellectual property' indeed.

West Ham will be the next ones going down that road too. According to reports Fat Sam won't be sacked even though most of the fans want him gone. Why would they keep him? Perhaps because Sullivan and Gold don't give a toss about the football, they just need to stay up by hook or by crook until they get their shiny new FREE stadium, at which point they'll sell to some arabs and the Premier League will have another Man City on it's hands. I can almost live with the financial doping and ludicrous spending, but the whole *"here you go, heres a brand spanking new, state of the art 60,000 seater stadium free of charge"* thing seriously grates. That's just not right that. The free stadium makes a club so much more attractive to potential buyers, there's no way Sheikh whatshisface would have gone near City if they were playing at Maine Road, but West Ham will be the next ones, you just watch.

What City have done in the last couple of years is basically cheating. Maybe not initially, but rules have since been put in place and they're flouting them. UEFA are at least trying to punish them (to a fashion) but the Premier League clearly couldn't care less. Rule breaking aside, there's not a great deal to dislike about City and that one bizarre rant after Barca apart, Pellegrini has handled himself with class and decorum. He's not a knob, which is a rare trait amongst Premier League managers.

Most of the players are ok but there's two I can't stand though; Dzeko and Nasri. I never used to mind Dzeko until recently, but him scoring all those crucial goals has made me suddenly realise what a fucking stupid, annoying, dopy face he's got. Can't believe I'd never got onto that before, but then his goals weren't denying us a title before. The other thing was him playing dead at Goodison. Wanker.

As for Nasri, he's just a snide and has the kind of face you'd never tire of slapping. It's funny that he's been left out of the French World Cup squad though, as clearly he should be in there if it's being picked on ability. Deschamps has his reasons though, *"Samir is an important player for Manchester City but he has not performed that well with France. He is a starter at City, which is not the case with France and he has made clear that he is not happy when he is not [a starter], and I can tell you it can be felt in the squad. I built the best squad, I did not pick the 23 best French players."* In other words, *"I'm not picking him, he's a snivelling little prick"*.

His girlfriend didn't take the news well, taking to twitter to say *"Fuck france and fuck deschamps! What a shit manager!"* She sounds like a real sweetheart, quite the catch there, Samir. She followed that up with: *"Lets just get this straight! Im not mad i get my bf for 2 months.... I just think theres a level of respect to be had!"* Ah right, now I get it, you just have to read between the lines a little. She's pissed off with France because instead of spending the summer going on wild shopping sprees with Nasri's credit card, she now has to look at his ridiculous, lesbian looking grid for the entire summer. No wonder she's angry. Imagine how much of a twat you'd need to be to be unable to get into a French squad because you were seen as being too much of a twat! Nasri must be some kind of supertwat, or thundertwat even.

Speaking of thundertwats, Mourinho showed himself up again this week. First he was talking bollocks about how Dzeko should have been player of the year and not Suarez, because he doesn't dive and plays the game fairly and blah blah blah zzzzzzzz ah shut up you boring fucking bastard. There was a whole lot of talking but it basically amounted to him jumping up and down, waving and yelling *"Hey everyone, don't forget about me. Look at the Special One, I'm still here, I'm still relevant. I'm still Special. Please, someone listen to me."* Helmet.

He also had this to say about the possibility of a Lampard statue being erected at Stamford Bridge: *"Not now, he's too young... maybe in a few years. He's one of the club's biggest players."* Ho! That's a bit uncalled for. He's called his strikers shite, Hazard selfish, told Matic he wished he hadn't signed him, told Salah he isn't a footballer and now he's saying Lampard's fat?

He's probably done the worst job of any manager in the Premier League this season with the obvious exception of Moyes and maybe Solskjaer. Not that the Chelsea fans can see it, they're too wrapped up in the 'cult of Jose'. My Chelsea counterpart at ESPN actually gave them a B+ for this season. Considering what he has at his disposal, to finish third and to play the kind of turgid, vile brand of football that Chelsea have played this season (including trying - and failing - to bore their way to another CL final) puts him right up there with any of the managers who got the sack for me.

Tell you what else I was thinking this week, remember how fired up he was about winning at Anfield even though he knew they had no chance of winning the title? Why did that game mean so much to him? Because his 'apprentice' has made him look like a complete dick this season by winning games AND playing great football, that's why. He was hell bent on not losing that game, and it was all about his own gigantic ego, the fucking whopper. Bet he didn't vote for Brendan in the LMA thing. I hope Abramovich gives him the old concrete overcoat treatment this summer. Actually wait, no I don't. They might get someone in who can maximise the huge talent of the players they have and play to win games instead of trying to bore everybody to death, in which case we'll all be in trouble. So er yeah, long live Jose I guess.

Staying with Chelsea, and Paolo Ferreira got a special award at their end of season awards bash. He was a player at Chelsea for 9 years apparently. 9 years!!! Damn. We only saw him for about three of them like, but I hear he did a sterling job as an interpreter for all the Brazilians they bought in over the last few years. Now that Jose is back they no longer needed a translator so Ferreira retired.

Chelsea though. 'Kinell. Their official facebook account sent out a pic with the caption *'great away following as usual'* after their game at Cardiff (they won 2-1 after trailing to a Bellamy goal). It certainly was some passionate support like, you could see that from the picture. You could also see that they were Cardiff fans. That's Everton behaviour that.

Speaking of our friendly neighbourhood bluenoses, I can't believe I forgot to include this in last week's rant about them lubing themselves up for City, but at half time in that game the Everton PA guy played 'Masterplan' by Oasis. Firstly, playing any Oasis song tells you all you need to know about those smalltime fuckers, but the song selection is interesting too, don't you think? Masterplan? How obvious do you want to make it you bitter blue fucks?

They ended the season with a win at pre-occupied Hull, thanks to goals by McCarthy and Lukaku. Their fans were singing Blue Moon and doing the Poznan. Hilarious. Even more hilarious was their official twitter account posting the picture of it. Completely smalltime, and absolutely shameless about it too. #evertonarentwe

It is kind of sweet though, I mean I think it's nice that they've got new a Mancunian lover after their accrimonious split from the last one. Nice to see them moving on and getting on with their lives, no doubt they'll be very happy with City. Until they come knocking for Barkley and Martinez in a year or two anyway.

Tim Howard said before the game that; *"Arsenal were the only one in our crosshairs - next season we're looking for even bigger and better things. I think fourth place would be a minimum requirement."* He failed to add *"Unless of course that in the process of trying to get fourth it may indirectly help Liverpool out, in which case all bets are off"* but I guess that goes without saying...

"Twats of the season XI"

GK: Wojciech Szcesny - Laughing at Spurs for conceding six to Man City and then doing the same himself, combined with his penchant for those stupid 'selfies' made the Arsenal keeper a shoe-in for this year's side. Regular incumbent - scruffy arse Jaaskelainen - will have to make do with a place on the bench. Shouldn't be a problem for him as he's done it the Hammers for most of the season.

RB: Willian - Not a natural right back but playing for Mourinho he may as well be. Flirted with us in the summer, started following Lucas and Coutinho on twitter then fucked us off when Spurs offered more money. Followed Sandro and Paulinho on twitter and jibbed Spurs off too when Chelsea stole in at the last minute (immediately following Luiz and Oscar on twitter of course). Then tweeted a picture of himself with his 'entourage' saying *"the best agent in the world"*. Wrong. That title surely has to be whoever is handling Adel Taraabt, but that's besides the point. Willian is indeed a twat. He works hard though.

CB: Rio Ferdinand - Undermined poor old Moyesy from day one because he didn't take kindly to coaching methods such as *"Jags would never do that"* and *"watch this DVD of Jagielka, you might learn something"*. You're never to old to learn Rio, maybe if you'd listened to 'the Chosen One' you'd have got a new contract?

CB: Jan Vertonghen - Wound me up with his ridiculous mistake when Spurs were comfortably holding Chelsea at bay at the Bridge and then made things worse by coming out with some crap about Suarez being the only reason we were doing so well. Good player, bit of a dickhead.

LB: Kieran Gibbs - Arsenal were leading against us and Gibbs ended up over the touchline after cutting the ball back. He then rolled himself back onto the pitch and stayed down injured, as Arsenal's players and fans demanded we put the ball out for him to get treatment. Or was that Oxlade-Chamberlain?

MR: Kevin Mirallas - The shocking lunge at an already limping Suarez at Goodison. Enough said.

CM: Michael Carrick - One incident alone is enough to get the usually inoffensive Carrick in here. Fouling Sturridge in the box and then standing over him accusing him of diving before chasing after the ref demanding he produce a yellow card.

CM: Oscar - I keep hearing how great he is but when I watch him he does nothing except dive, foul and look like a bad, chinless dweeb. One of the only people in the world to have ever made Lucas lose his temper, that in itself is enough to get him a place in this side.

LM: Adnan Januzaj - He's got more yellow cards for diving than anyone in Premier League history and he's not yet out of his teens. Also has a really annoying face and dates the kind of skanks who go running to the S*n for a quick buck.

CF: Robin Van Persie - Did as much as anyone to ensure Moyes got the sack. Selfish, egotistical prick.

CF: Edin Dzeko - His blatant cheating in the closing stages at Goodison was enough to get him in, but factor in the crucial goals he scored and his dopy face and he ended up the first name on the teamsheet this year. My missus thinks he's "attractive", so there's that too.

chapter fourteen

They made us dream

101 goals and 84 points. Three years ago that would have won us the title. Ending the season with 12 wins and just one loss from the final 14 games feels like it *should* have been enough to win it this year. Just one more poxy win (against Chelsea) would have been enough, but how many sides have ever won 13 of the last 14 games when involved in a title race? It was always going to be a tall order, but we went so, so close.

What we did was almost unbelievable but it kind of feels like it was all in vain now. Of course we got back in the Champions League which was the priority when the season began, but at some point we went beyond that and the title became the goal. I'm disappointed with finishing second; not because finishing second in itself is disappointing (not at this stage of our development anyway; in a year or two hopefully 'first is first, second is nothing' will be our mantra once again), but because we were so close to being first. So, so close. In fact it was so close we were beginning to taste it - even the most sceptical of souls began to believe after we beat City - so for it to then be taken away so cruelly... Well, how can we feel anything other than disappointed? Not disappointed with them; just disappointed for them. I can't say we deserved to win it because that would be doing Man City a disservice. Leaving the financial doping issue to one side, City were the best team because they scored more than us, conceded less than us and got more points than us. It could easily have been different but sadly it wasn't.

Taking 37 points out of the final 42 available really feels like it should have been enough. I mean it's not like we were way off the pace at that point - or indeed at ANY point. We were in or around top spot for most of the season and at no stage did we have any sort of bad run that would have seen us fall away. Those two defeats in the festive period really proved costly in the end and that's hard to take as neither were deserved. Things were so bunched up at the top at that time and those two defeats were huge. We went from top at Christmas to being one defeat away from 7th place at New Year. In 2014 though we only lost one game. ONE GAME!!! Not having a title to show for it seems pretty unfair, but then life is rarely fair is it? And football certainly isn't. The only consolation is that we didn't lose it on goal difference because if that Palace game had cost us the title I'm not sure how any of us would have ever got over it. Certainly, Glen Johnson would be shacked up somewhere with Salman Rushdie.

It was a hell of a ride though, wasn't it? So many moments stand out: Mignolet's penalty save on the opening day. Starting off with three consecutive clean sheets and thinking that we were going to be a 'grind out results' kind of team. Kolo starting the season like a Ferrari and ending it like a clapped out old banger. Suarez coming back from suspension and going on a massive goal spree. Hendo being ace all year. Gerrard's huddle. Skrtel's goals. Destroying Arsenal and Everton in the space of a few weeks. Getting three pens at Old Trafford. Sturridge dancing. Raheem. Fucking. Sterling. Flanno's goal and celebration. I could go on and on. As far as trophy-less seasons go, this was about as enjoyable as it gets. In fact, judging the season as a whole, I enjoyed it more than any I can remember since I was a kid.

The Spurs game was a huge turning point for us. Up until that day they were a side we thought we were competing with and hoping to overhaul. They had finished above us for a few years and our record at White Hart Lane of late has been abysmal. A draw would have been a decent result for us going into that fixture but we absolutely dismantled them in every facet of the game. That was as complete a performance as we'd seen in a long time - and we did it without Gerrard and Sturridge. It felt like a huge monkey was off our back after that win and suddenly the belief began to grow after that display. We'd lacked that 'signature win' under Rodgers but that was a real statement.

Brendan himself said it was a turning point as it was the day the players completely bought into what they were doing. The work they'd been putting in finally paid off, they had a new belief about them and what they were being asked to do. We battered a lot of teams after that and there was certainly a new found swagger about the side. Sterling in particular really elevated his game after that. He was brilliant against Spurs, not just with the ball but also in his pressing. That was the most impressive aspect of the performance for me: the way we completely harried the life out of Spurs and kept winning the ball back. That was supposed to be a staple of the Rodgers style of play but we didn't see it for a long time; it was very odd.

I remember speaking to a "sports science" fella about it. He works for another Premier League club but is a big Red and a regular at Anfield. I asked him why we couldn't play a high tempo pressing game when we only had one game a week, and I wondered if it was because of the presence of Gerrard in one of the 'box to box' roles. He said in theory they should be able to play that way with no midweek games but that in his opinion it was indeed Gerrard that prevented it. There's a lot of science goes into it all: measuring how many sprints players do in a game, the recovery time involved and a load of stuff I've got no clue about. The gist of it was that at 33 years of age Gerrard simply can't charge around like a dog in the park for 90 minutes anymore; it just isn't possible. Jordan Henderson can though. So can Joe Allen (and Sterling and Coutinho), but the thing about playing a pressing game is that everyone has to do it; you need to hunt in packs. If Gerrard isn't pressing but Henderson is, the opposition will simply pass around Hendo and gaps will appear all over the place. So what we saw was a lack of pressing and Gerrard and Lucas never really looking like a good combo.

That Spurs game set the blueprint for a lot of what followed, I'd say. Stevie's absence meant Allen and Henderson got a rare opportunity to play together in the middle with Lucas in the sitting role behind. Perhaps that was the day that Rodgers decided on using Gerrard in that deeper role permanently as it wasn't too long afterwards that the switch was made. When the skipper moved there full time he took it like a duck to water and the midfield balance looked so much better. The energy in our play was much higher and we blew a lot of teams away, often inside the first half an hour when our intensity was at its highest.

Suddenly opponents were running scared of us, especially at Anfield. Eleven straight wins left everyone choking on our dust as we hit the top of the table with three games to go. Arsenal, Spurs and Everton had long since been blown away but now, incredibly, Chelsea and City were behind us too and not even City's games in hand would have changed that if we could have kept winning. At the start of the season none of this seemed possible, yet there we were: top with our fate in our own hands at the end of April. I'm sure back in August none of us expected Chelsea to be trailing us with just three games left, especially with Mourinho having dragged his sorry, egotistical, preening arse back to the Stamford Bridge hot seat. They were trailing though, and not even their sickening win at Anfield was enough to overhaul us. It's only scant consolation of course - that result will haunt me forever I think - but if they'd finished above us it would have been even worse.

I didn't handle that defeat well at all. For a day or two I was in foul form and didn't even really want to speak. I just stewed over the injustice of it all and began to hatch an assassination plan for Mourinho. Ok that last bit isn't completely true. I wasn't planning on killing him; just roughing him up pretty bad. The last time I felt that bad about a loss was probably when Arsenal snatched the title off us in '89. It just seemed so fucking cruel. Liverpool did not deserve that. Steven Gerrard did not deserve that. Losing to THEM? Like THAT? It was like some sick joke. Two weeks earlier we'd had that amazing win over City: the Gerrard huddle and the *"This does not fucking slip now"* speech. Next thing he's literally slipping and our title hopes were suffering a fatal blow. That was hard to take. I mean we'd only just started to believe it could actually happen and then, just like that, it was taken away in the toughest of circumstances. Eventually after about 48 hours I snapped out of it and convinced myself that surely it couldn't end like that for us. After everything we'd been through, the amount of times that winning run could have come to an end but didn't, it wasn't going to be decided by 'the slip'. It couldn't be. There was surely going to be another twist. After all, it had been that kind of season. Yet there was no twist, unless you count the late collapse at Palace which - painful as it was - ultimately proved irrelevant due to City winning their last three games.

That didn't stop all the bullshit about how we "choked", "threw the title away", "couldn't handle the pressure", etc. We had to endure relentless piss-taking from the rest of the country, which was kind of ironic given how they'd all been kissing our arses before that Chelsea game. It's a ridiculous notion, though. We didn't blow it at all. We won 12 of our last 14 games and the only game we lost was to the side that finished immediately below us; a side who also happened to have done the double over City too. Losing to Chelsea isn't choking or throwing it away, in fact I'd suggest it's almost to be expected - especially when they adopt those kind of negative tactics. I mean, come on! They once won a European Cup like that, defeating better sides than us along the way. We didn't blow anything. We simply came up a little short after a wonderful effort. If we'd scored first against Chelsea then this book would probably be called *"Back on our Perch"*, but we didn't and it isn't. We have to learn from that and try and come back stronger to ram the taunts back down the throats of all the losers taking pleasure from what happened to us.

It never really sat well with me that whole *"all the neutrals want us to win it"* thing anyway. It certainly seemed like they wanted us to win it, until we 'lost' it and they then took perverse pleasure in our failure. Bollocks to all the neutrals anyway. I want us to be successful but I couldn't care less if 'neutrals' are happy about it or not. They may or may not have wanted us to win it, but they sure as hell tuned in to watch and the TV companies are milking that for all it's worth. We were on telly more than anyone and I expect it to be the same next year. You're guaranteed goals watching us: goals at both ends.

The mocking of Gerrard though, that really grates with me. If he was a figure of national-al loathing like John Terry then fair enough. But he's not, is he? He's generally regarded as one of the good guys. So many people were saying they wanted us to win the title because *"Gerrard deserves it"*. We don't win it and suddenly he's being mocked all around the country, even in stadiums we aren't even playing in? These fucking dickheads chanting about his slip, but how many of them will be cheering him on at the World Cup when he captains THEIR COUNTRY? I was more upset for Gerrard than I was for myself after that Chelsea game: he's waited his whole career for that chance and for it to go down the way it did? Well, that's the kind of thing that stays with you forever - unless of course he can win it in the next couple of years before retiring. He might never get another opportunity though and this may prove to be his best chance at winning a title, especially if the club continue their ineptitude in the transfer market.

It really was truly remarkable what Rodgers and his small squad did. It's not just about finishing second and almost going one better, though; it's the way they did it that was so impressive. Teams can often over achieve due to a combination of organisation, hard work and luck. Atletico Madrid this year for example. Their wage bill is less than Fulham's but they were brilliantly coached by Diego Simeone and not only won the Spanish title but were also within seconds of becoming European Champions too. They've got good players of course; it's not like Simeone has turned a bunch of deadbeats into La Liga champions. They don't have the superstars that their rivals do, however, and their success was based on organisation, incredibly hard work and being difficult to beat. They were never going to win La Liga by playing like Real or Barca but they found a way to get it done.

I'm a big believer in goal difference being a true indicator of a side's quality. Often you'll see a side finish 5th or 6th with a big goal difference and a side a place or two above them with a much smaller one. One is an under achieving, inconsistent side with a lot of quality, the other has punched above it's weight and is often managed by David Moyes. Everton actually finished 4th in 2005 with a goal difference of -1. Ironically this year Moyes found himself at the opposite end of the scale. United ended the season 5 points behind 6th placed Spurs but with a goal difference of +21 compared to the Londoners paltry +4.

What you rarely see is a so-called underdog - as we were this season - tearing shit up and hammering teams left right and centre, including sides who are in and around them in the table. That's what I found so amazing about what we did. By rights we should not have been battering Arsenal, Everton and Spurs the way we did. Those games weren't even competitive: they were absolute massacres. Those teams were supposed to be around our level or even better, but we destroyed them and, had Chelsea tried to take us on in a game of football instead of showing up with the sole intention of boring us into submission, they'd have gone the same way too. Mourinho is many things but stupid is not one of them. He knew what would happen if they tried to attack and the worry moving forward is that others will follow suit and simply try to frustrate us and slow down our free flowing attacking football. I'm sure Brendan has already come up with a way to counter that though as he's a real forward thinker on that kind of thing. Hopefully he's figured out a way of tightening us up that doesn't rely completely on us buying new players, as the transfer market is the one area in which we're a bit, for want of a better word, shit.

Scoring 101 league goals in a season is pretty incredible and has only been bettered a couple of times (and never by us). Of course City managed to score one more whilst conceding a lot less and that's the benchmark for us moving forward. We have to try and maintain our level of scoring whilst tightening up at the other end. Can we come close to 100 goals again? On the one hand you have to think not because we've never done it before (not in the post war years, anyway). On the other though, you'd have to say why not? If we get through another summer of Suarez speculation and keep him here, combined with Sturridge, Sterling, Coutinho and Henderson, who should all continue improving, and with Rickie Lambert, Adam Lallana and whoever else comes in (hopefully not another Aspas) then there's no reason why there should be any significant drop off.

To go from 7th place to just missing out on the title on the final day is almost unheard of in the modern game and usually the only way it can be done is by splashing the cash or - as mentioned above - by being organised and tough to beat. What makes our season so out of the ordinary is that not only did we do it by going all out attack, we did it largely with the same team that had finished 7th a year earlier. The huge improvement we saw was due to Rodgers' work on the coaching field and his in-game management, along with the players buying into it and individuals improving their games significantly (which again is credit to the work of the manager). The improvement in results was in spite of our transfer dealings, not because of them. That's very rare and it's definitely not sustainable as all of our rivals will strengthen significantly this summer. It's imperative that we do too and we cannot afford a repeat of the last two transfer windows or we will unquestionably be left behind.

I wrote a piece in the fanzine a few weeks before the January transfer window opened about the lack of trust I had in the team and also in the transfer committee. I didn't trust the team because every time they looked like they'd cracked it, they'd throw in a stinker like they did at Hull in December, or against Villa and West Brom at home the previous season. I also spoke about not trusting those in charge of transfers after the ineptitude shown last summer. Fast forward six months and the team have now shown they can most certainly be trusted. They didn't win every game but they certainly didn't produce another 'Hull' and their record in 2014 was better than anybody else's. The team and manager have more than earned our trust. The transfer committee? Not so much.

January was actually a complete disaster but the great run the players went on glossed over it and those responsible (not just the much maligned Ian Ayre) largely escaped the criticism they deserved. Without going into it too much, once again I was left wondering if they actually had any idea what they were trying to do as they spent weeks farting around before failing to meet the asking price for a player who had told friends, family and team-mates he was coming to Anfield only to end up at Chelsea (who did the deal in around 48 hours). After missing out on Mohamed Salah we ended up offering more money for the second choice, Yevhen Konoplyanka. At least I assume he was second choice, otherwise why didn't we move for him first? For whatever reason we failed to get that done either. Perhaps, as Ayre said, that deal was impossible due to the conduct of the Dnipro president, but when you leave it until so late in the window you're asking for trouble.

Brendan deserves much better than he's been getting from that committee. I know he's a part of it but as I said earlier in the book, when you take responsibility away from the manager you also take away culpability. We don't know how much responsibility Rodgers has with transfers (the rumour is he'll have a bigger say since he signed his new contract), but we do know he's responsible for coaching the players, selecting the team, implementing the system, making substitutions, dealing with the media, motivating his squad and getting the best out of what he has. On all of those I'd give him an A+. He got every last ounce out of the players he had. However, if the club had shown a bit more competence in either transfer window then the likelihood is that we would have won the title. That little bit of quality from the bench could have been the difference against Villa and Chelsea at home or away at West Brom. Even at Palace we sent on Moses who then missed a sitter to win it at the end.

Of course there are plenty of excuses about how difficult the transfer market is and how it's not easy finding the right players and getting deals done, blah blah blah. No-one said it was easy, though and that's why we have a massive team of scouts and statistical analysts (not to mention Ayre) who are all paid a small fortune to do a job they are failing miserably at. Don't tell me how choppy the water is; dock the fucking boat.

Last summer we sold Downing and replaced him with Moses. We loaned out Borini and replaced him with Aspas. We sold Shelvey and bought Alberto (for £1m more despite him being a Spanish 2nd division player and Shelvey a full England international) And yet we STILL took the title race down to the last day. Rodgers may actually be a bona fide genius because we really should not have been able to do what we did. What he's done is incredible considering it's not been off the back of multi million pound superstar signings, but I can't help but imagine what we could have done last season if we'd got the signings right. Instead of bringing on Aspas, Moses or Alberto when we were chasing a game, we might have been able to bring on someone who could have been of some use. Imagine that!

As great as this season was, we can't just sit back and expect it to happen again just because Rodgers is ace and we've got some fine players. Improvements are needed because those around us will get better. If the club delivers the players he needs, I have no doubt whatsoever that Rodgers can make us great again. We're so close to something very special and, while I'm not a subscriber to the *"You have to lose one before you can win one"* theory, it's certainly true that plenty of title winners have had to overcome heartbreak the previous year. This season was great: it was a lot of fun and we've put ourselves back in a position to contend. It's gone now though, so next year we go again.

Come on you Reds!

EPILOGUE

So Luis Suarez then eh? I could fill at least another chapter on what happened after the season finished. The knee injury, the comeback against England, the emotional response to it, the complaining about the English press going on about him biting, sinking his teeth into Chiellini 24 hours after those complaints, the denial, the massive ban, the belated apology to 'the football family' but not to LFC or the fans that had stood by him, the Barcelona bid...

Publishing deadlines mean that this book will be going to print before the latest 'Suarez saga' is resolved one way or the other, but it is looking increasingly likely that his turbulent but brilliant Liverpool career is now coming to an end. If I had to sum up Suarez's time at Anfield in one word, it would have to be "unforgettable". Good or bad, rough or smooth, one thing is for certain. There is never, ever, a dull moment with Luis Suarez.

His departure would provide Brendan Rodgers with massive funds to strengthen his side, but it would also leave an enormous void in his forward line and possibly damage the morale of the squad. Sturridge and Sterling proved their worth last season, but Suarez was still the catalyst for what we achieved and his goals, assists, unrelenting brilliance and unflinching determination to win every game and fight for every ball will be almost impossible to replace.

Liverpool have replaced the irreplaceable before, however, and hopefully they will be able to do so again. When Kevin Keegan moved on Kenny Dalglish was brought in and not only replaced Keegan, but bettered him. This is different as there simply isn't a player out there who can come in and replicate what Suarez did for us. Suarez is in the top three players in the world right now, and given that the other two members of that trio aren't available then replacing him with a player of similar quality is impossible. That doesn't mean all is lost though, as there's more than one way to skin a cat. When Ian Rush was sold to Juventus he wasn't replaced by one man. The money was used to sign three players to fill the void and they formed an integral part of what is regarded by many to be Liverpool's greatest ever side. Finding a Dalglish may be close to impossible but if Suarez departs then the funds will be there to bring in three top players to make the side stronger than it was before. Suarez was in many ways Barnes, Beardsley and Aldridge rolled into one, but if the money is invested in the right players his departure needn't slow down the momentum that has been built up over the past 18 months.

Of course the danger is that we could go the same way that Spurs did when they sold Gareth Bale and spent £100m on players who didn't fit in. That's a risk, a big risk given the recent track record of those charged with player recruitment, but with Champions League Football to offer and a huge pot of cash to attract top players, this summer there can be no excuses. Losing a star player always causes uncertainty, but it need not be the end of the world. Atletico Madrid sold Falcao a year ago and went on to win the Spanish title, so all is not lost. What happens next though is a story for another time, and another book.

So I guess I'll see you in 12 months then, for *"Back on our perch - the Story of the 2014/15 Season"*. What? Oh you don't believe in all that jinx stuff do you? Besides, this year I'll make sure that Paul wears those lucky red boxers every match day. Hell, I think he should wear them permanently just to be on the safe side. His wife and kids might not be impressed with the smell but we all have to make sacrifices if we want number 19, right?

Printed in Germany
by Amazon Distribution
GmbH, Leipzig